Core Concepts of
ACCOUNTING INFORMATION SYSTEMS

Eighth Edition

Stephen A. Moscove, Ph.D.

Professor
Department of Accounting
University of New Haven

Mark G. Simkin, Ph.D.

Professor
Department of Accounting and
Information Systems
University of Nevada

Nancy A. Bagranoff, DBA, CPA

Professor
Department of Accountancy
Miami University

JOHN WILEY & SONS, INC.

EXECUTIVE EDITOR	Jay O'Callaghan
MARKETING MANAGER	Keari Bedford
SENIOR PRODUCTION EDITOR	Patricia McFadden
SENIOR DESIGNER	Karin Kincheloe
PRODUCTION MANAGEMENT SERVICES	Hermitage Publishing Services

This book was set in Garamond Book by Hermitage Publishing Services and printed and bound by Hamilton Printing. The cover was printed by Lehigh Press.

This book is printed on acid-free paper. ∞

To order books or for customer service please, call 1(800)-CALL-WILEY (225-5945).

Materials from the Certificate in Management Accounting Examinations, by the Institute of Management Accountants, 10 Paragon Drive, Montvale, NJ 07645-1760 U.S.A., are reprinted and/or adapted with permission.

Materials from the uniform CPA Examination Questions, by the American Institute of Certified Public Accountants, Inc., Harborside Financial Center, 201 Plaza Three, Jersey City, NJ 07311-3881 U.S.A., are adapted with permission.

Materials from the Certified Internal Auditor Examinations, by the Institute of Internal Auditors, Inc., 249 Maitland Ave, Altamonte Springs, FL 32701 U.S.A., are adapted with permission.

ISBN 0-471-07290-7

Printed in the United States of America

10 9 8 7 6 5 4

To my wife Laura, and my children, Justin, Jodi, Sarah, and Stephanie. (Steve Moscove)

To my parents, Edward and Selma Simkin. (Mark Simkin)

This one's for my students. (Nancy Bagranoff)

ABOUT THE AUTHORS

Stephen A. Moscove earned his B.S. degree in accounting and his M.S. degree in accounting from the University of Illinois. Dr. Moscove received his Ph.D. degree in business administration (majoring in accounting) from Oklahoma State University (1971). Dr. Moscove worked as an auditor for Price Waterhouse & Company during 1966 and 1967. From 1970 to 1980 he was a member of the faculty of the Department of Accounting at the University of Hawaii. During this period, Dr. Moscove was a visiting professor at the University of Miami and a visiting professor at the University of New Orleans. Dr. Moscove subsequently joined the faculty at the University of Nevada, Reno and served as department chair of the Department of Accounting and Computer Information Systems for six years. He also served as Professor and Chair of the Department of Accounting at Central Connecticut State University. Currently Professor Moscove is a professor at the University of New Haven. Dr. Moscove has published numerous articles in professional journals and is the author of several textbooks in accounting. These professional journals include *Management Accounting, The National Public Accountant, Cost and Management, Managerial Planning, Journal of Systems Management,* and *Healthcare Financial Management.*

Mark G. Simkin received his A.B. degree from Brandeis University and his MBA and Ph.D. degrees from the Graduate School of Business at the University of California, Berkeley. Before assuming his present position of professor in the Department of Accounting and Information Systems, University of Nevada, Professor Simkin taught in the Department of Decision Sciences at the University of Hawaii. He has also taught at California State University, Hayward, and the Japan America Institute of Decision Sciences, Honolulu; worked as a research analyst at the Institute of Business and Economic Research at the University of California, Berkeley; programmed computers at IBM's Industrial Development—Finance Headquarters in White Plains, New York; and acted as a computer consultant to business companies in California, Hawaii, and Nevada. Dr. Simkin is the author of more than 100 articles that have been published in such journals as *Decision Sciences, JASA, The Journal of Accountancy, Communications of the ACM, Interfaces, The Review of Business and Economic Research,* and the *Journal of Bank Research.* He has also authored several textbooks in the information systems area, including *Applications Programming in Visual Basic 5* (Scott/Jones, 1998).

Nancy A. Bagranoff received her A.A. degree from Briarcliff College, B.S. degree from the Ohio State University, and M.S. degree in accounting from Syracuse University. Her DBA degree was conferred by The George Washington University in 1986 (accounting major and information systems minor). From 1973 to 1976, she was employed by General Electric in Syracuse, New York, where she completed the company's Financial Management Training Program. Dr. Bagranoff is a Certified Public Accountant, licensed in the District of Columbia, since 1982. She spent Fall 1995 as Faculty in Residence at Arthur Andersen where she worked for the Business Systems Consulting and Computer Risk Management groups. Professor Bagranoff has published several articles in such journals as *Journal of Information Systems, Journal of Accounting Literature, Computers and Accounting, The Journal of Accounting Education, Behavioral Research in Accounting, Journal of Accountancy,* and *The Journal of Accounting and EDP.* Dr. Bagranoff is also co-author of *Core Concepts of Consulting for Accountants.* She is currently Professor of Accountancy at Miami University.

ACKNOWLEDGMENTS

We wish to thank the many people who helped us during the writing, editing, and production of our textbook. First on our list of acknowledgments are our families and friends. We thank them for their patience and understanding as we were writing this book. We also wish to thank those instructors who read earlier drafts of this edition of our textbook, and provided many useful suggestions for improving the final product. These people include Ed Scribner, New Mexico State University, Jane E. Campbell, Kennesaw State University, and Rubik Atamian, University of Texas—Pan American.

Many of our colleagues and professional acquaintances were also extremely helpful. We thank our editor at John Wiley and Sons, Jay O'Callaghan. We'd also like to thank Susan Elbe and Keari Bedford. This will be the third time that Larry Meyer and the staff at Hermitage Publishing Services has been responsible for the editing and production of our book, and we are grateful for their efficiency and professionalism. For providing a student perspective, we thank the many undergraduate and graduate students who provided us with feedback on our chapters. In particular we thank Methuselah Nyang'oro for his editing work. We also extend our thanks to Paula Funkhouser who has helped us with our supplementary materials on this and several previous editions.

Special thanks go to Julie David, Arizona State University, for her ERP figure. We'd also like to thank Guido Geerts for his help in linking us to Stevie. Thanks to Jane Fedorowicz for looking over the materials on XBRL and to Skip White for providing us with XBRL code. We thank Jan Eighme for previewing our materials on data modeling using REA and, of course, we are grateful to Bill McCarthy, Michigan State, for his development of the REA approach to data modeling. We are also appreciative of the comments of the many individuals who teach AIS whom we have spoken with and listened to at various professional meetings. Their comments about AIS courses and textbooks have been helpful. Finally, we wish to thank Brian Ferrell and Larry Bagranoff, both of whom worked very hard helping us correct the page proofs of our manuscript as well as assisting us with the instructor's manual.

June 2002
Stephen A. Moscove
Mark G. Simkin
Nancy A. Bagranoff

PREFACE

Every aspect of accounting has been fundamentally changed by information technology and the Internet, including financial reporting, managerial accounting, auditing, and tax. Thus, the accounting profession is in a state of flux as the information age forces accountants to redefine the work they do and recent business and auditing failures force the profession to rethink the state of assurance services. No matter how it all settles, the subject of accounting information systems (AIS) will continue to be an important part of the new vision of the accounting profession.

The purpose of this book is to help students understand basic AIS concepts. Exactly what comprises these AIS concepts is subject to some interpretation, and is certainly changing over time, but most accounting professionals believe that it is the knowledge that accountants will need for understanding and using information technologies and for knowing how an AIS gathers and transforms data into useful decision-making information.

In developing the content of this textbook, we have considered both the 1987 American Accounting Association *Report of the AAA Committee on Contemporary Approaches to Teaching Accounting Information Systems* and the recommendations made by the International Federation of Accountants (IFAC) in Guideline No. 11. The AAA report identified nine content areas for AIS and prerequisite courses. In this textbook, we have addressed all of these content areas. The table below identifies the chapters that provide the major coverage of each topic.

ACCOUNTING INFORMATION SYSTEMS
COURSE CONTENT AREA COVERAGE

Content Area	Chapter(s)
Database Concepts	7, 8
Internal Control	9, 10, 11
Technology of Information Systems	All
Use of Systems Technology	All
AIS Applications	4, 5, 6
Management Use of Information	1, 4, 5, 6, 13
Management of Information Systems	1, 13
Systems Development Work	13, 14, 15
Auditing	12

The IFAC Education Committee's guideline, *IEG-11: Information Technology for Professional Accountants,* describes the general IT knowledge requirements and competencies needed relative to IT controls. The framework describes several different roles accountants may take with respect to IT and then describes IT competencies and skills needed relative to each role. While our book discusses many of the topics described in this report, it does not cover everything. For instance, we assume that most students will already have a basic understanding of computer hardware and software concepts. Nevertheless, this book does cover many of the knowledge areas covered in the IFAC report, particularly those related to accounting information systems. For an in-depth description of the IFAC's recommendations, we suggest you view the report at the web site, www.ifac.org.

About This Book

Despite the commonality of subjects in the AAA study, the content of AIS courses continues to vary widely from school to school. Some schools, for example, use their AIS courses to teach accounting students how to use computers. In other colleges and universities, the course focuses on business processes and data modeling. Yet other courses emphasize transaction processing and accounting as a communication system, and have little to do with the technical aspects of how underlying accounting data are processed or stored.

Given the variety of objectives for this AIS course and the different ways that instructors teach it, we have developed a textbook that attempts to cover only the core concepts of AIS. In writing the text, we have only assumed that students will have completed basic courses in financial and managerial accounting as well as a basic knowledge of computer hardware and software concepts. The text is designed for a one-semester course in AIS and may be used at the community college, baccalaureate, or graduate level.

Our hope is that individual instructors will use this book as a foundation for an AIS course, building around it to meet their individual course objectives. Thus we fully expect that many instructors will supplement this textbook with other books, cases, software, or readings. The arrangement of the chapters permits *flexibility* in the instructor's subject matter coverage. Certain chapters may be omitted if students have covered specific topics in prior courses.

Part One introduces students to the subject of AIS. In the first chapter, we lay the basic foundation for the remainder of the text and set the stage for students to think about accounting in the information age. This chapter also includes a section on careers in AIS so that students can understand career paths that combine accounting with the study of information systems. Although we have integrated Internet technology throughout this book, its influence on accounting information systems is so great that we have devoted a special chapter to it. Thus, Chapter 2 discusses Internet technology and the World Wide Web, and also discusses special technology issues for accountants such as XBRL. Finally, Chapter 3 is about systems documentation, a matter of critical importance to the success of an AIS and also to one's understanding of an information system. This chapter describes the various tools that accountants can use to document AIS for their own and others' understanding of information flows.

Part Two explains how AISs collect, record, and store business data. Chapters 4 and 5 cover business processes. Instructors who focus on transaction cycles in their AIS courses may choose to use supplemental pedagogical tools, such as software and practice sets, to cover this material in more depth. In addition to providing an overview of the basic transaction processing cycles in Chapters 4 and 5, Chapter 5 explains to students that many organizations have unique AIS needs. This is, we believe, an important idea, as accounting students frequently think of an organization's AIS needs as generic and are unfamiliar with the special information requirements of a vertical market organizations. Chapter 6 is new to this edition of the book. In it, we discuss accounting and enterprise software. Finally, in this edition of our textbook, we have expanded our coverage of databases and data modeling to two chapters—an enhancement that responds to increasing instructor interest in teaching the REA approach to data modeling.

An important function of accountants working with AISs is to develop effective internal control systems. Although the subject of internal control appears repeatedly throughout the book, Part Three examines this subject in depth. A unique chapter here is Chapter 11, which focuses on computer crime, security, and ethics in the information age. Chapter 12 covers the important topic of information systems auditing. We have tried to present the material in Part Three so that it will be useful to students who study AIS prior to taking an auditing course, as well as to students who study auditing before AIS.

Part Four of this book examines systems studies through an in-depth coverage of performing one for an organization. Recognizing that some students in current AIS courses may have taken a prior course in management information systems (MIS) and thus are already familiar with systems development topics, the emphasis in Chapters 13,14, and 15 is on the accountant's role in designing, developing, implementing, and maintaining a system. Thus, these chapters integrate many of the computer and accounting concepts of previous chapters in Part Four's discussion of systems study.

Special Features

This edition of our book uses a large number of special features to enhance the coverage of chapter material as well as help students understand chapter concepts. Thus, each chapter begins with an outline and a list of learning objectives that emphasize the important subject matter of the chapter. This edition of the book also includes many real world Cases-in-Point, which are woven into the text material. Each chapter also includes a more-detailed real-world case or concept in an end-of-chapter *AIS-at-Work* feature.

Each chapter ends with a summary and a list of key terms, and also includes four types of end-of-chapter exercises to help students understand the material and test this understanding: discussion questions, problems, Internet exercises, and cases. This wide variety of questions, problems, Internet exercises, and cases enables students to examine many different aspects of each chapter's subject matter and also enables instructors to vary the exercises they use each semester. The end-of-chapter materials also include a list of references, recommended readings, and web sites that allow interested students to explore the chapter material in greater depth.

There are two major supplements to this textbook. One is an instructor's manual containing suggested answers to the end-of-chapter discussion questions, problems, and cases. There is also a test bank of true-false and multiple-choice questions.

What's New in the Eighth Edition

This edition of our book includes significant changes from prior editions. These include:

- Expanded and earlier coverage of electronic commerce and the Internet. We've moved our Internet chapter to Section One and expanded our coverage of the topic throughout the book.
- Detailed explanation of XBRL. XBRL promises to be a significant area of importance to financial reporting. As a result, we've included several pages describing it in Chapter 2.

- New chapter on accounting and enterprise software. There are many issues associated with accounting and enterprise software of concern to accountants, and some schools even devote a separate course to enterprise systems. For this reason, we have added a chapter on this topic in the current edition which should be of interest to AIS instructors who currently use ERP software in their AIS class or wish to teach students how to select such software.

- Expanded coverage of data modeling and databases. This edition dedicates two chapters to these topics. The new material includes detailed discussions and illustrations of the REA approach to data modeling, as well as expanded coverage of data warehouses and data mining.

- Updated materials on computer crime. This edition's chapter incorporates the latest developments to discuss this fascinating, fast-moving topic. Like the other chapters in this book, the emphasis is on those issues most directly impacting accounting systems.

CONTENTS

PART ONE   AN INTRODUCTION TO ACCOUNTING INFORMATION SYSTEMS/   1

Chapter 1   Accounting Information Systems and the Accountant/   3

Introduction/   4
What Are Accounting Information Systems?/   4
Accounting in the Information Age/   9
Careers in Accounting Information Systems/   17

Chapter 2   Electronic Commerce and the Internet/   29

Introduction/   30
The Internet and World Wide Web/   31
Electronic Commerce/   38
Privacy and Security on the Internet/   44

Chapter 3   Documenting Accounting Information Systems/   56

Introduction/   57
Why Documentation Is Important/   57
Document and System Flowcharts/   59
Data Flow Diagrams/   67
Other Documentation Tools/   73
End-User Computing and Documentation/   78

PART TWO   COLLECTING, STORING, AND USING ACCOUNTING INFORMATION/   95

Chapter 4   Accounting Information Systems and Business Processes: Part I/   97

Introduction/   98
Business Process Fundamentals/   98
Collecting and Reporting Accounting Information/   104
Core Business Processes/   109

Chapter 5/   Accounting Information Systems and Business Processes: Part II/   132

Introduction/   133
Additional Business Processes/   133
Business Processes in Special Industries/   148
Business Process Reengineering/   154

Chapter 6   Accounting and Enterprise Software/   165

Introduction/   166
Integrated Accounting Software Programs/   166
Enterprise-Wide Accounting Software Solutions/   170

Chapter 7   Data Modeling/   193

Introduction/   194
An Overview of Databases/   194
How to Create Databases with REA/   198
Additional Database Design Concerns for AISS/   206

Chapter 8   Organizing and Manipulating the Data in Databases/   219

Introduction/   220
Normalization/   220
Defining and Validating the Data in Databases: Data Definition Languages (DDLS)/   223
Extracting Data from Databases: Data Manipulation Languages (DMLS)/   230
Object-Oriented Databases, Multimedia Databases, and Data Warehouses/   235

PART THREE   CONTROLS AND SECURITY IN ACCOUNTING INFORMATION SYSTEMS/   247

Chapter 9   Introduction to Internal Control Systems/   249

Introduction/   250
Internal Control Systems: Definition and Components/   250
Control Procedures Analyzed/   255
Control Activities Within an Internal Control System/   258
Cost-Benefit Concept for Developing Controls/   268

Chapter 10   Computer Controls for Accounting Information Systems/   281

Introduction/   282
General Controls within IT Environments/   282
Application Controls within IT Environments/   294
Database Controls/   303
Controls in the Information Age/   303

Chapter 11   Computer Crime and Ethics/   319

Introduction/   320
Computer Crime: An Overview/   320
Examples of Computer-Crime Cases/   326
Thwarting Computer Abuse/   332
Computers and Ethical Behavior/   337

Chapter 12   Auditing Computerized Accounting Information Systems/   351

Introduction/   352
The Audit Function/   352
Auditing Through the Computer/   360
Auditing with the Computer/   367
Auditing in the Information Age/   370

PART FOUR   DEVELOPING EFFECTIVE ACCOUNTING INFORMATION SYSTEMS/   387

Chapter 13   Systems Study: Planning and Analysis/   389

Introduction/   390
The System Development Life Cycle: An Introduction/   390
Systems Planning and the Initial Investigation/   393
Systems Analysis/   396

Chapter 14   Systems Study: System Design and Selection/   417

Introduction/   418
The Feasibility Evaluation/   418
Detailed Systems Design/   425
Selecting a Final System/   433

Chapter 15   Systems Study: Implementation, Follow-up, and Maintenance/   447

Introduction/   448
Systems Implementation/   448
Systems Follow-Up and Maintenance/   459
Outsourcing/   461

Glossary/   479

Index/   497

PART ONE

AN INTRODUCTION TO ACCOUNTING INFORMATION SYSTEMS

CHAPTER 1
Accounting Information Systems and the Accountant

CHAPTER 2
Electronic Commerce and The Internet

CHAPTER 3
Documenting Accounting Information Systems

Part One introduces the subject of accounting information systems (AISs). It defines accounting's principal goal, which is to communicate relevant information to individuals and organizations. Part One further describes the strong influence of information technology on this communication process.

Chapter 1 defines information systems and then introduces the subject of AIS in the information age. This chapter examines the impact of information technology on financial accounting, managerial accounting, auditing, and taxation. Information technology's impact on electronic commerce within the environment of the Internet is also briefly discussed. Finally, Chapter 1 describes a number of career opportunities in AISs.

The Internet and electronic commerce impact AISs in many ways. As an increasing number of business organizations engage in electronic commerce, it becomes important for accountants to understand the fundamentals of doing business electronically. Chapter 2 describes the hardware and software technology that underlies the Internet and electronic commerce, including a special language for financial reporting. The chapter also discusses intranets and extranets as well as general categories of electronic commerce, such as retail sales. Finally, the chapter describes the special privacy and security issues for business enterprises engaged in electronic commerce.

The documentation of an AIS is critical. It allows management, auditors, systems analysts, and other users to understand the basic processes and functions of the system. Chapter 3 describes various techniques for documenting AISs. These techniques include document and system flowcharts, data flow diagrams, and computer-assisted software engineering (CASE) tools.

Chapter 1

Accounting Information Systems and the Accountant

INTRODUCTION

WHAT ARE ACCOUNTING INFORMATION SYSTEMS?

The Information Age

An Information System

Accounting Information Systems and Their Role in Organizations

ACCOUNTING IN THE INFORMATION AGE

Financial Accounting

Managerial Accounting

Auditing

Taxation

CAREERS IN ACCOUNTING INFORMATION SYSTEMS

Systems Consulting

Information Systems Auditing and Security

AIS AT WORK—THE CPA VISION PROJECT

SUMMARY

KEY TERMS YOU SHOULD KNOW

DISCUSSION QUESTIONS

PROBLEMS

INTERNET EXERCISES

CASE ANALYSES

The Annual Report

Hoden's Hamburger Corporation

Universal Concrete Products

Ross, Sells, and Young, LLP

REFERENCES, RECOMMENDED READINGS, AND WEB SITES

After reading this chapter, you will:

1. *Know* how our economy has changed through the agricultural age, the industrial age, and the information age.

2. *Be able to define* systems, information systems, and accounting information systems.

3. *Have learned* how information technology influences all aspects of accounting.

4. *Understand* how financial reporting is changing in the information age.

5. *Appreciate* how information technology is allowing management accountants to adopt new costing systems and performance measures.

6. *Know* about the expanded role of auditing into a variety of assurance services.

7. *Understand* the impact of the Internet and electronic commerce on accounting information systems.

8. *Be aware of* career opportunities for those who study and work with accounting information systems.

The American Institute of Certified Public Accountants (AICPA) has projected that two of the top technology issues facing the accounting profession during the first several years of the 21st century are (1) Information security and controls within information systems, and (2) Electronic commerce.

> Issie Rabinovitch, "The Top Ten Tech Issues
> for 2001," *CPA Magazine,* January-February
> 2001, p. 2.

INTRODUCTION

The accounting function is critical in the successful operation of today's businesses. This function provides individuals and groups both inside and outside a company with relevant information for planning, decision making, and control. We will begin this chapter by discussing the information age. We will then define information systems and describe the role of AISs in organizations. In our book, we take the view that an AIS is the dominant organizational information subsystem. This approach considers AISs to be much more than bookkeeping or transaction processing systems. We hope to help you understand that AISs provide opportunities for accountants to build systems that can provide a variety of decision makers with the information they need for optimal planning, decision making, and control.

As you probably know, information technology is changing the way we do just about everything. Just a few years ago, the authors never imagined that people could someday purchase a copy of our book from a giant "virtual" bookstore on the Internet. The explosion in electronic commerce is just one example of the many ways information technology is influencing how people do business and how we account for business events. In fact, going back to the quote at the beginning of this chapter, electronic commerce as well as information security and controls within information systems are two of the top technology issues that the accounting profession must address in the current century. Both of these technology issues are addressed in this book. The present chapter describes the ways that information technology is affecting financial accounting, managerial accounting, auditing, and taxation. In addition, Chapter 1 briefly looks at the impact of electronic commerce and the environment on AISs.

Students taking courses in AISs often wonder if there are special career opportunities combining the study of accounting with computer science and information systems. The answer is that almost endless employment opportunities await such graduates. Accounting employers are very interested in hiring students who have emphasized information systems in their study of accounting. This means that the traditional jobs in accounting are available to those who study AISs in addition to other career opportunities that you may never have considered. The last part of this chapter describes a number of special job opportunities for those with an interest in AISs.

WHAT ARE ACCOUNTING INFORMATION SYSTEMS?

Information technology is the hardware and software used in computerized information systems and has had as much impact on our society as the industrial revolution. In the **information age,** fewer workers are making products, and a large segment of the employee population is involved in producing, analyzing, and distributing information. Information systems play a vital role in our economy and our everyday lives. An accounting information system is a special type of information system that provides information about business processes and events affecting an organization.

The Information Age

In the information age, companies are finding that success or failure is increasingly dependent on their management and use of information. A characteristic of the information age is the employment of much of the labor force as **knowledge workers.** These workers are producing and using information and knowledge. Accountants are knowledge workers, as are information systems employees and consultants.

The information age has implications for accounting. Accountants have always been in the information business, for their role is to communicate accurate and relevant information to parties interested in knowing how organizations are performing. Information technology has influenced the accounting profession, and how and what we communicate, in many ways. The impact of information technology as it relates to financial accounting, managerial accounting, auditing, and taxation will be discussed in detail later in this chapter.

An important contributor to the information age is the **Internet.** It is a global collection of tens of thousands of interconnected business, government, military, and education networks that communicate with each other. The number of Internet users is increasing daily. The wide variety of computers employed on the Internet is able to send, receive, and view information. Among the many services available on the Internet are electronic mail, entertainment, discussion forums, education, access to a wide variety of databases, news, software downloads, stock quotes, and electronic commerce (which refers to conducting business with computers and data communications). A unique aspect of this book is that each chapter contains Internet exercises that expose students to the important role of the Internet in our current information age. Many of the chapters talk about different aspects of the Internet that apply to accounting information systems. In fact, Chapter 2 focuses entirely on the subject of electronic commerce and the Internet.

An Information System

People typically think of computers when they hear the term *information system,* but an information system need not be a computerized system. Many times each day we see examples of information systems that do not rely on computers. For example, you witness an information system at work when you go to a movie, purchase a ticket, and then present the ticket to an usher who tears off a stub. Of course, a computer may issue the ticket and scan the stubs to update the information system. But an information system exists, with or without a computer.

An information system is part of an overall system. A **system** is an entity consisting of interacting parts or components that attempt to achieve one or more goals. An entity is a separate unit of accountability. This book emphasizes the **business entity,** such as partnerships and corporations. *Subsystems* are system components. For

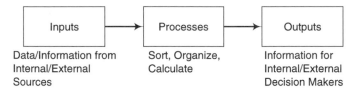

FIGURE 1-1 An information system's components. Data or information is input, processed, and output as information for planning, decision making, and control purposes.

example, political parties are a component or subsystem of our political system. Systems generally have an imposed organization that requires relationships among the systems' components.

An **information system** is a set of interrelated subsystems that work together to collect, process, store, transform, and distribute information for planning, decision making, and control. An illustration of an information system appears in Figure 1-1. Every information system consists of three major components: inputs, processes, and outputs. The input to an information system may be **data** or **information.** Data are raw facts about events that have no organization or meaning. Data may, however, be organized in such a way that they are useful or meaningful to people. When data exhibit these characteristics, they are information. Information systems process data or information by sorting, organizing, or calculating them in such a way that they are output as information. Managers and others use information to plan, make decisions, and control organizational activities. For example, deciding to buy equipment may require information about alternatives, the cost of alternatives, and an organization's equipment needs. Information frequently is used for control purposes. Accountants prepare budgets (a planning function) so that managers can compare their actual performance with targets and control their activities to avoid variations.

As we noted, an information system does not need to be computer-based. For example, your personal checkbook that you maintain manually is an example of a noncomputerized information system. However, in this book we emphasize formal, **computer-based information systems.** These systems may simply use computers to process paper-based information, or data may be captured and input electronically, processed by computer, and output to a computer screen.

Accounting Information Systems and Their Role in Organizations

In many ways, accounting itself is an information system. It is a communicative process that collects, stores, processes, and distributes information to those in need of it. For instance, accountants in corporations gather data about their organization's performance, process them, and output and distribute these data as information in financial statements and other reports (e.g., an *accounts receivable aging analysis*). Accountants are in the information producing and analyzing business. They are not line workers, involved directly with the production of goods and services. Instead, accountants occupy *staff positions* in an organization, supporting the organization in its objectives. An **accounting information system (AIS)** is the information subsystem within an organization that accumulates information from the entity's various subsystems and communicates it to the organization's **information processing subsystem** (Figure 1-2.) The information processing subsystem is

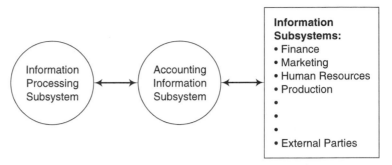

FIGURE 1-2 The accounting information system's relationship to the organization's various information subsystems.

likely to be a separate department in the organizational entity that is responsible for computer hardware and software.

Figure 1-2 brings out the importance of interaction between the accounting information subsystem and the other subsystems in an organization. For this interaction to be effective, individuals working in subsystems such as finance, marketing, etc., must have an understanding of the types of information that an AIS can generate to aid their planning, decision making, and control functions. Presented below are examples of information that an AIS can provide to the information subsystems listed in Figure 1-2.

Finance—cash forecasts and actual payment and receipt information

Marketing—sales summary analyses, cost information, and sales forecasts

Human Resources—payroll analyses (including employee benefit information) and projections of future personnel costs

Production—inventory summaries and product cost analyses. The preceding examples illustrate why an AIS course is useful not only for accounting majors at a college or university, but also for nonaccounting majors (e.g., students majoring in finance or marketing).

The AIS has traditionally focused on collecting, processing, and communicating financial-oriented information to a company's external parties (such as investors, creditors, and tax agencies) and internal parties (principally management). Today, however, the AIS is concerned with nonfinancial as well as financial data and information. Under the traditional view of an AIS, each organization's functional areas, such as finance, marketing, human resources (or personnel), and production maintain a separate information subsystem. All of this information is channeled through the entity's information processing function. One problem with this view is that it requires separate storage of data (with the possibility of duplication) and separate information gathering and reporting responsibilities within each subsystem.

Organizations today are finding that there is a need to integrate their functions into one large, seamless database or **data warehouse.** This integration allows managers and, to some extent, external parties to obtain the information needed for planning, decision making, and control, whether or not that information is for marketing, accounting, or another functional area in the organization. Software vendors are developing *software programs* that link all of an organization's information subsystems into one application. An example of such a software product is SAP R/3, which includes accounting, manufacturing, and human resource subsystems combined as an **enterprise-wide information system.** (Software products for AISs are discussed later in the text.)

The AIS of today should be an enterprise-wide information system, focused on *business processes.* The view of AIS as an enterprise-wide information system considers the linkages between management information systems and accounting. In the 1960s, computerized information systems were developed to automate such accounting applications as payroll. During the next few decades, **management information systems (MIS)** developed into a separate functional area of an organization. Management charged the MIS department with processing and distributing all the information in the organization used for planning, decision making, and control purposes. The AIS was considered one of many subsystems within MIS. The accounting subsystem was concerned only with an organizational entity's financial or economic information. How the MIS and AIS fit together today is a matter of some debate. As Peter Drucker notes:

> *The two systems increasingly overlap. They also increasingly come up with what look like conflicting—or at least incompatible—data about the same event, for the two look at the same event quite differently. Till now this has created little confusion. Companies tended to pay attention to what their accountants told them and to disregard the data of their information system, at least for top-management decisions. But this is changing, as computer-literate executives are moving into decision-making positions.[1]*

Users of accounting information sometimes criticize the AIS for capturing and reporting only financial transactions. The account structure in financial statements and the limitations it imposes often ignore some of the more important activities that influence business entities. For example, within a company's traditional AIS, activities such as hiring key personnel and obtaining a large sales order from a new customer would not result in journal entries being recorded under the company's double-entry system. We define AISs as information systems that capture, record, and communicate all relevant financial and nonfinancial information about important business activities. This perspective leads to the AIS's creation of more useful and timely information for planning, decision making, and control purposes.

Our definition of an AIS, as an enterprise-wide system, views accounting as an organization's primary producer and distributor of information. The definition also considers the AIS as *process focused.* This matches the contemporary perspective that accounting systems are not primarily financial systems. Again, according to Peter Drucker:

> *People usually consider accounting to be "financial." But that is valid only for the part, going back 700 years, that deals with assets, liabilities, and cash flows; it is only a small part of modern accounting. Indeed, accounting deals with operations rather than with finance, and for operational accounting, money is simply a notation and the language in which to express nonmonetary events. Indeed, accounting is being shaken to its very roots by reform movements aimed at moving it away from being financial and toward being operational.[2]*

---

[1] Peter Drucker, "Be Data Literate—Know What to Know," *Wall Street Journal* (December 1, 1992), p. C1.
[2] Ibid.

Operational accounting focuses on **business processes,** which are a collection of activities or flow of work in an organization that creates value. Examples of business processes are the revenue process and the expenditure process. Most business organizations are involved in the production or creation of goods and services that they in turn sell to customers. These processes characterize an organization's operations. Knowledge of business processes allows managers to streamline those processes and thus produce and sell goods or services more efficiently.

ACCOUNTING IN THE INFORMATION AGE

The information age and the information technology that created it are influencing all areas of accounting. This section of the chapter considers the impact of information technology on financial accounting, managerial accounting, auditing, and taxation.

Financial Accounting

An AIS has two primary informational components: financial accounting and managerial accounting (see Figure 1-3). The major objective of **financial accounting** is to provide relevant information to individuals and groups *outside* an organization's boundaries. Financial accounting information users include current and potential investors, federal and state tax agencies, and creditors. Accountants achieve financial accounting's objectives principally by preparing periodic financial statements, such as the income statement, the balance sheet, and the cash flow statement. Of course, many individuals within a company, such as managers, also use financial accounting information for planning, decision making, and control. For example, a manager in charge of a particular division would be interested in the profitability of that segment of the organization. Managers could use knowledge of profitability in making decisions about future investments, and an understanding of the organization's current profitability as compared to the past could also help control expenses.

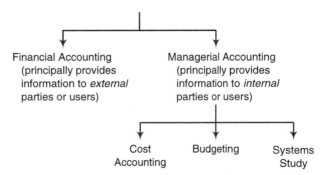

FIGURE 1-3 An accounting information system. (The financial and managerial accounting components are not mutually exclusive; that is, information from the financial accounting component is used within the managerial accounting component, and vice versa.)

The Financial Accounting Information System   The basic inputs to the traditional financial accounting structure are transactions measured in monetary units. An **audit trail** of accounting transactions maintained within a company's system enables information users to follow the flow of data through the system. Figure 1-4 is an example of a financial accounting audit trail. The audit trail example in Figure 1-4 parallels an organization's **accounting cycle,** which begins with transaction data being reflected on source documents and ends with producing financial statements as output. Accounting clerks input relevant data from source documents into the financial accounting system and file the documents for possible later use (e.g., to verify the dollar amount recorded in a particular journal entry). The transaction processing function encompasses *recording* journal entries from the source documents, *posting* these entries to general and subsidiary ledger accounts, and *preparing* a trial balance from the general ledger account balances. In most companies today, a central computerized information system handles the processing function. Thus, information about the journal entries and the ledger account balances is maintained on computer storage devices (magnetic tape, magnetic disk, floppy disk, or another medium). With the use of computer programs, accountants are able to obtain printouts of a company's financial statements (based on account balances) periodically, along with any other desired output reports.

A good audit trail within the financial AIS permits a manager, for example, to follow any source document data from input through processing to the data's location on an output report. It should also allow an accountant to trace financial statement account balances back to the original source documents that caused transactions affecting these balances. To illustrate, a sales invoice should be traceable through the audit trail to the appropriate customer accounts receivable account and revenue account. Similarly, an accountant can verify the balances in accounts receivable and revenue accounts by examining originating transactions and source documents. In an effectively developed audit trail, an accountant can follow data through a system. This is possible because people within the system thoroughly understand the methods and procedures for accumulating and processing the data. As a result, accountants can reconstruct how the system handled data. Information technology can sometimes make the audit trail more difficult to

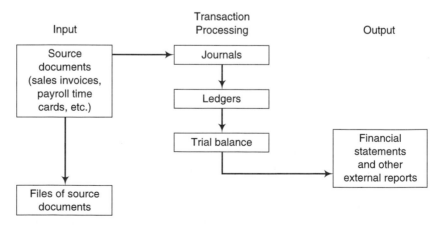

FIGURE 1-4   A financial accounting audit trail.

follow because computer systems often leave no paper trail. In other cases, however, a well-designed computerized system might improve the audit trail by providing listings of transaction sets and account balances both before and after transactions update the accounts. A major focus of this book is on developing effective internal control systems for companies, of which audit trails are important elements of these systems.

Criticisms of the Financial Accounting Information System   AISs have been criticized for failing to produce accounting information that is timely and useful. Many of these criticisms have been directed at financial accounting. Recognizing this problem, the American Institute of Certified Public Accountants (AICPA) assembled a committee to investigate financial reporting, the AICPA Special Committee on Financial Reporting. In 1994, the special committee issued its report. The report included recommendations about how to improve the types of information included in business reporting. Some types of information that the committee recommended for reporting were financial and nonfinancial data, management's analysis of data, forward-looking information such as opportunities and risks, information about management and shareholders, and background information about the reporting entity. The committee also recommended **segment reporting.** This type of reporting concerns the reporting of disaggregated information. A criticism of current financial reports is that accountants accumulate or aggregate the information too much. This aggregation fails to show how different components of an organization contribute to the entity's total financial picture.

Computerized accounting systems are blurring the lines between financial and managerial accounting systems. Many accounting software programs today can capture both financial and nonfinancial data and organize these data in ways that are meaningful to both external and internal information users. These programs can also provide information in real time, or almost instantaneously as activities occur, and, while a company's investors may not be interested, for example, in a minute-by-minute update of product sales, information technology today makes it possible for a company to report this type of information. In fact, the company can even report the information on its web page or Internet site so that anyone interested can look it up.

The capability of information technology to produce vast amounts of information quickly can create a problem known as **information overload.** Too much information, and especially too much trivial information, can overwhelm information users, possibly causing the relevant information needed by users for business decisions to be lost. It is up to the accounting profession to decide the nature and timing of information created and distributed by the AIS. Currently, technology's influence on financial reporting primarily concerns the delivery of financial accounting information. You might note that the recommendations made by the AICPA's Special Committee on Financial Reporting were not driven by technology. As we become more experienced with technologies, such as the Internet, more changes may take place in the content of financial reports or the availability of information related to the basic financial statements.

Although information technology may in the future impact the nature and content of financial accounting, to date the influence has been primarily in the area of *delivery* of the information, as mentioned previously. Internet technology allows financial report users to access data and information in a variety of ways, as we will discuss in Chapter 2.

Managerial Accounting

The principal objective of the **managerial accounting** component of an AIS is to provide relevant information to a company's managers, who are *internal* parties (or users). Cost accounting, budgeting, and systems study are three typical parts of a company's managerial accounting system (refer again to Figure 1-3). Several important features of managerial accounting are summarized in Figure 1-5.

Cost Accounting   The managerial accountant makes an important contribution to the planning, controlling, and decision-making functions associated with a company's cost accounting system. The **cost accounting** part of managerial accounting specifically assists management in these functions, which are associated with an organization's various acquisition, processing, distribution, and selling activities. In the broadest sense, the focus is on the *value added* by an organization to its goods or services. This focus remains the same whether the organization is a manufacturing firm, a bank, a hospital, or a police department. For example, a bank performs a value-added function by providing checks and credit cards, thus easing a customer's ability to pay for goods and services.

Information technology helps cost accountants by allowing them to track costs more carefully and by enabling them to trace specific costs to specific activities. An example of information technology's impact on cost accounting is the emergence of **activity-based costing systems.** Traditionally, most manufacturing firms identified manufacturing costs as "raw materials," "direct labor," and "production overhead." Cost accountants frequently assigned overhead (i.e., indirect production costs) to products as a function of direct labor. If, for example, production overhead was assigned at 200 percent of direct labor cost and direct labor cost during a particular period was $100,000, then production overhead costs assigned to products manufactured during that period would be $200,000. The problem is that with increased use of automation techniques in production plants, we are using less and less direct labor in manufacturing processes.

Activity-based costing systems are more than just a costing technique. These systems are evolving today into management systems that can move an organization in a new strategic direction, as illustrated by Case-in-Point 1.1:

- Managerial accounting focuses on providing accounting information for internal parties, such as management, rather than for external investors and creditors.
- Managerial accounting information is mostly forward-looking.
- Managerial accounting information is not regulated by generally accepted accounting principles, nor is it mandatory to prepare it.
- Managerial accounting reports include both nonmonetary and financial data.
- Managerial accounting is influenced by many business and nonbusiness disciplines, such as economics, behavioral science, and quantitative methods.
- Managerial accounting information is flexible and frequently involves nonroutine reporting.

FIGURE 1-5   A summary of features characterizing managerial accounting.

Case-in-Point 1.1 The United States Postal Service (USPS) recently hired Pricewater-houseCoopers to conduct activity-based costing studies. This was done in conjunction with a planned strategy to move from a cash-only revenue collection system to a credit and debit card system. PricewaterhouseCoopers developed activity cost models for cash and check activities and similar models for projected debit and credit card activities. Based on their findings and recommendations, considering competition and other factors, the USPS plans to move to national acceptance of credit and debit cards at its retail sales points.[3]

Many organizations use a **responsibility accounting system** to help managers trace unfavorable performance to the department or individual that caused the inefficiencies. Under a responsibility accounting structure, each subsystem within an organization is accountable only for those items over which its employees have control (i.e., items they can increase or decrease). Thus, when a particular cost expenditure exceeds its standard cost, managers can take immediate corrective action (i.e., execute their decision-making function).

Responsibility accounting systems are part of an organization's total performance measurement system. **Performance measurement** is yet another area of accounting impacted by information technology. There is growing dissatisfaction with current measures of performance—many information users believe that some of the more traditional accounting performance measures are shortsighted and may even create undesirable behavior. Consider, for example, a division of an organization evaluated only on the basis of its profitability. It would be to this division's advantage to cut costs to boost profits. Cutting costs, however, may affect quality, and this could lead to long-term problems for the organization.

Decision makers are beginning to use new types of performance measures to accompany such traditional financial measures as net income, return on investment, and earnings per share. These additional measures include customer satisfaction, quality, innovation, and effectiveness. The **balanced scorecard** approach uses performance measurements in four categories to evaluate and promote certain activities and behaviors. Financial performance is just one category evaluated by management. The other categories are customer knowledge, internal business processes, and learning and growth. A company may choose to rank these categories to align with their strategic value. For example, one company may stress customer knowledge due to the importance of customer satisfaction to its market position and planned sales growth. Note that measuring a company's success on both financial and nonfinancial attributes presents both a dilemma and an opportunity for traditional accounting.

Budgeting A **budget** is a financial projection for the future and thus is a valuable managerial *planning* aid. Companies develop both short- and long-range budget projections. The short-range budget projections disclose detailed financial plans for the coming 12-month period, whereas the long-range budget projections, to illustrate, reflect less detailed financial projections for 5, 10, or more years into the future.

A good budgetary system is also a useful *managerial control* mechanism. Because budgets indicate future financial expectations, a company's management is concerned about the causes of significant variations between *actual* and *budgeted*

---

[3] T. L. Carter, A. M. Sedaghat, and T. D. Williams, "How ABC Changed the Post Office," *Management Accounting,* (February 1998), pp. 28–36.

results during the budget year. Through timely performance reports comparing actual operating results with preestablished budgets, a company's management can investigate the reasons for significant budget variations. Management should then initiate corrective action on unfavorable variations and reward favorable variations. A favorable budget variation may direct management to decisions on specific activities that can benefit the company's future operating performance.

The budgetary function within an AIS affects all the subsystems within an organization. Budget preparation therefore requires good communication among them. Because of the strong financial emphasis in budgets, the managerial accounting component of an organization's AIS normally has major responsibility for the organization's budget system. This component coordinates the preparation of the other subsystems' budgets and then monitors each subsystem's actual performance. Computerized processing of budget data contributes to the output of timely reports showing significant discrepancies between actual and projected performance. Information technology allows decision makers to organize and compare data in an almost endless number of ways to facilitate the budget process. Information technology also allows accountants and managers to prepare budgets under a variety of assumptions and to evaluate the impact on performance when assumptions change.

Systems Study   A company having a problem with its current information system (e.g., reports are not timely) may hire outside consultants to recommend changes. Or, it may use company employees to help solve the problem. The managerial accountants' ability to understand internal financial systems has qualified them to perform **systems studies** for organizations (Figure 1-6). Of course, accountants are not the only professional group that does systems study work, since expertise beyond accounting is often needed. For this reason, many business-consulting firms use a team approach when performing a systems study. This team of consultants might include, in addition to accountants, marketing specialists, computer experts, production managers, engineers, and industrial psychologists. Because of the importance of the systems study area to AISs, later chapters explore this topic in detail.

Auditing

Auditing is arguably the area of accounting most affected by information technology. The traditional financial statement audit has become a mature industry. The Securities and Exchange Commission's requirement that publicly traded companies undergo an external financial statement audit supports the audit industry. How-

---

Planning
  Develop strategic plans.

Analysis
  Review current system.

Design
  Design new system.

Implementation, Followup and Maintenance
  Put the new system in place and continue to monitor it.

FIGURE 1-6   Steps in systems study.

ever, the investors and creditors who make use of financial statements are increasingly turning to sources other than auditing for information to aid their decision making. In part, this is due to audited financial statements often not being available on a timely basis.

Information technology has fueled many new areas in which auditors are seeking to do business. In 1993, the AICPA arranged a conference to discuss the future of auditing. The conference focused on auditing and **assurance.** Auditing and assurance are closely related. Auditors study and evaluate financial statements in conducting corporate audits. The audit report provides some *assurance* to the public regarding the fairness of an organization's financial reports. Assurance as to fairness is also a valuable commodity in arenas other than financial reporting. The 1993 AICPA conference created a Special Committee on Assurance Services (which started functioning in 1994) to study other areas in which accountants could provide services, thereby expanding their expertise and business base into additional markets. The committee developed business plans for six new assurance services, as described in Figure 1-7. It also identified hundreds of other possible assurance services that Certified Public Accountants (CPAs) could offer to their clients.

Many new assurance services proposed by the AICPA Special Committee concern information technology. An example is *CPA WebTrust,* a service that provides assurance that a company engaged in **electronic commerce** (i.e., selling products or services over the Internet) can provide the goods or services purchased as promised. The AICPA is providing training to public accounting firms interested in engaging in this new business. (Chapter 2 extensively discusses electronic commerce.)

Regarding the information technology area, a 1999 study by the AICPA and the Canadian Institute of Chartered Accountants (CICA) focused on the "information systems reliability" assurance service area (mentioned in Figure 1-7). As stressed by the AICPA and the CICA:

Risk Assessment
   Provide assurance that an organization's set of business risks is comprehensive and manageable.

Business Performance Measurement
   Provide assurance that an organization's performance measures beyond the traditional measures in financial statements are relevant and reasonable for helping the organization to achieve its goals and objectives.

Information Systems Reliability
   Provide assurance that an organization's information system has been designed to provide reliable information for decision making.

Electronic Commerce
   Provide assurance that organizations doing business on the Internet can be trusted to provide the goods and services they promise, and that there is a measure of security provided to customers.

Health Care Performance Measurement
   Provide assurance to health care recipients about the effectiveness of health care offered by a variety of health care providers.

Eldercare Plus
   Provide assurance that various caregivers offering services to the elderly are offering appropriate and high-quality services.

FIGURE 1-7 Assurance services identified by the American Institute of Certified Pubic Accountants Special Committee on Assurance Services.

Developments in information technology are making far greater power available to entities at far lower costs. The systems supported by this technology are not just doing bookkeeping—they are running businesses, producing products and services, and dealing with customers and business partners. As a result, information technology permeates all areas of a company, differentiates companies in the marketplace, and requires increasing amounts of capital. As business dependence on information technology increases, tolerance decreases for systems that are unsecured, unavailable when needed, and unable to produce accurate information on a consistent basis. Like the weak link in fence, an unreliable system can cause a chain of events that negatively affect a company and its customers, suppliers, and business partners.[4]

Based on the above observation by the AICPA and the CICA, these two professional groups have introduced a service that provides assurance by public accountants on the reliability of systems. This assurance service is called **SysTrust** and it is designed to increase the comfort of customers, managers, and business partners with the systems supporting a business or a specific activity. SysTrust involves public accountants performing an assurance service whereby they evaluate and test whether a system is reliable when it is measured against four relevant principles: availability, security, integrity, and maintainability.

During the past few decades, public accounting firms have increasingly engaged in consulting services. Some of the impetus for the expansion of consulting services came from opportunities related to consulting about information technology; for example, helping a company to implement a new AIS. Another factor was the slow growth of audit and tax services. The Securities and Exchange Commission and others, such as members of the US Congress, have been concerned about the possible impairment of audit independence that could result when public accounting firms perform consulting services for their clients. The collapse of Enron and other corporate bankruptcies in 2002 increased these concerns. As a result, the largest public accounting firms have divested themselves of all or parts of their consulting practices. Nonetheless, there are still many areas in which these firms provide consulting services or advice to clients. Consulting services encompass a wide range of activities, such as business valuations, litigation support, systems implementation, estate planning, strategic planning, health care, financing arrangements, and forensics (fraud) investigations. There are many areas of consulting related to audit or assurance services for which accountants are particularly qualified. Two of these areas are *CPA WebTrust* and *SysTrust,* which we mentioned earlier.

Information technology has the potential to reduce the value of financial audits because many more sources of information are available, often on a timelier basis, in addition to the information contained in audited financial statements. On the other hand, we have seen how information technology creates new business opportunities and also influences the delivery of audit services. Auditors today use information technology to perform many tasks that once required manual labor. Furthermore, audit evidence changes as companies move away from keeping all of their data and

---

[4] American Institute of Certified Public Accountants and Canadian Institute of Chartered Accountants, "SysTrust Principles and Criteria for Systems Reliability," July 15, 1999, p. 5.

information in a paper format to electronic images stored on computer disks. The risks associated with producing information with computers also create a need for auditors to study the risks associated with computer systems. Chapter 12 focuses on the audit of computerized accounting information systems and the ways in which auditors use information technology to do their jobs.

Taxation

Although some individuals may still complete their income tax returns using pencil and paper, many others are turning to computer programs such as *TurboTax* for help. Information technology has automated income tax return preparation for individuals and CPAs alike. Using a tax software program, a preparer can enter data such as income and deductions and have a tax return printed for the Internal Revenue Service (IRS). The preparer could alternatively choose to file the tax return electronically by saving it on a disk or by using hardware and software to transmit the return information directly to an electronic filing service center, which forwards the information to the IRS.

Information technology not only affects the way we prepare tax returns, but it can also be very helpful to tax professionals in researching tax questions. Tax researchers may use an electronic tax library at less cost and with greater efficiency than traditional paper book libraries. These electronic tax libraries are available either as online services or on CD-ROM. A tax professional may subscribe to an online tax service by paying a fee for the right to access databases of tax information stored at centralized computer locations. Online services or CD-ROMs can provide tax researchers with databases of federal and state tax laws, tax court rulings, court decisions, and technical advice. A tax professional can search the databases of information by using key words. For example, a CPA may want to advise a client about whether the IRS is likely to allow an income tax deduction for maintaining a home office. The CPA can perform a computer search of other cases by asking the software to look for the key words "home" and "office" and "deduction" in a database of tax cases.

CAREERS IN ACCOUNTING INFORMATION SYSTEMS

Career opportunities abound for those with a solid foundation in accounting information systems. These opportunities include traditional accounting vocations in financial and managerial accounting, and careers in consulting and information systems auditing. An accountant who understands the information needs of a variety of organizational entities and has knowledge about information technology and accounting software can help businesses solve both information technology and accounting problems.

Recognizing the importance to accountants of knowledge about information systems, the AICPA recently developed a new designation to accompany the CPA. CPAs may now become **Certified Information Technology Professionals (CITP)** through business experience, lifelong experience, and examination. The

CITP designation has several objectives, including increasing recognition of the CPA as an information technology professional.

Systems Consulting

While concerns over independence and conflict of interest have prompted many public accounting firms to divest themselves of their consulting practices, accountants remain in the consulting business in several areas. For example, accounting firms provide clients with assurance services that provide value-added to clients. Many professional accountants today consider themselves consultants or business advisors. A consultant is someone outside an organization who helps in problem solving or provides technical expertise on an issue. **Systems consultants** provide help with issues concerning information systems. They may assist an organization in designing an information system, selecting computer hardware or software, or **reengineering** business processes so that they operate more effectively. Simply put, reengineering means starting over from scratch. For businesses, this may entail taking an objective view of the total organization and its processes and goals, and mapping out ways to redesign them. You can reengineer accounting processes and other business processes. For instance, the sales order process might be a good candidate for change. Some companies are finding that it takes too long to fill an order for a customer. A consultant taking a fresh look at the entire sales order process can find ways to reduce the order time. Later chapters discuss reengineering in more detail.

Individuals who are skilled in both accounting and information systems are highly desirable as systems consultants. Accounting education provides these individuals with an understanding of information flows in an organization as well as knowledge of business processes. As an example, consider a business investigating a redesign of its information system. Many employees will possess knowledge about how the current system works. However, these employees are not likely to know much about ways in which other organizations design their information systems. They are also unlikely to have knowledge about available hardware and software options.

A systems consultant has the opportunity to work with a variety of organizations such as professional service organizations, private corporations, and government. This broad work experience, combined with technical knowledge about hardware and software, can be a valuable asset to clients. Since it is likely that a newly designed system will include accounting-related information, a consultant who understands accounting is particularly helpful.

Consulting careers for students of accounting information systems can take several different forms. Many systems consultants work for large professional service organizations, such as Accenture or Cap Gemini Ernst & Young. Others may work for specialized organizations that focus on the custom design of accounting information systems. **Value-added resellers (VARs)** are a special type of systems consultant. Software vendors license VARs to sell a particular software program and provide consulting services to companies, such as help with their software installation, training, and customization. A VAR may set up a small one-person consulting business or may work with other VARs and consultants to provide alternative software solutions to clients. Case-in-Point 1.2 describes a VAR.

Case-in-Point 1.2   Matrix Integrated Solutions is a US national consulting firm started by Kevin Martin in 1983. Kevin, a CPA, left a job with a large professional service firm to open an accounting business that would help companies implement AISs. Today the company describes itself as follows:

Matrix Integrated Solutions is a Microcomputer Consulting/CPA firm, specializing in helping businesses install and use their accounting and management information systems. (www.matrixintegrated.com)

Information Systems Auditing and Security

An earlier section of this chapter discussed the impact of information technology on auditing. The complexity of computerized information systems creates new risks for business organizations, risks that must be considered by auditors when performing their work. These risks can affect an organization's financial reports and even, in extreme cases, a company's viability.

Auditors who concern themselves with analyzing the risks associated with computerized information systems are **information systems auditors.** An information systems auditor may work closely with financial auditors to provide an assessment of the risks associated with processing financial information through a computer. Since it is likely that computers now produce virtually all the information considered by financial auditors in determining the reliability of financial reports, it is important to audit the computerized information itself. Financial auditors may make use of an information systems risk assessment in deciding how much time to devote to their review of a company's transactions. This assessment may lead to a determination that the controls within the company's information system are so reliable that less time need be spent on the audit. (The subjects of controls and information systems auditing are emphasized in Part Three of our book.)

Information systems auditors and financial auditors may be separate individuals. The former may also be financial auditors with the technical information systems understanding needed to assess both an organization's financial and information systems risks. In either case, auditors who possess knowledge about accounting information systems are better equipped to understand any risks associated with both the information system and the financial transactions of an organization.

Information systems auditors are involved in a number of activities apart from assessing risk for financial audit purposes. Many of these auditors work for professional service organizations, such as Ernst and Young, PricewaterhouseCoopers, or KPMG Peat Marwick. (See Figure 1-8 for a partial listing of the types of services offered by Ernst and Young.) Security issues associated with advanced information technologies, such as the Internet, are of great concern to many business entities. Information systems auditors with an understanding of both internal controls and security are in high demand.

Sometimes the best way to assess the risks associated with a computerized system is to try to penetrate the system. Many organizations today, concerned with protecting their information resources, contract with professional **hackers,** who will use specialized techniques to see if they can obtain protected information. As an example, a consultant can use special tools to try to guess the passwords needed to access a company's information system.

Information systems auditors might be CPAs or be licensed as **Certified Information Systems Auditors (CISAs).** The CISA is a certification given to professional information systems auditors by the **Information Systems Audit and Control Association (ISACA).** To become a CISA, you must take an examination and obtain

---

Accounting and Advisory Services
- Business Risk Services
- Enterprise Risk Management
- Fraud Investigation Group
- Transaction Support
- Technology and Security Risk Services

Corporate Finance

Entrepreneurial

Online Services

Tax

FIGURE 1-8 A sample of the many types of services offered by Ernst and Young LLP, one of the largest international professional service organizations.

specialized work experience. Many CISAs have accounting and information systems backgrounds, although accounting education is not required for certification.

AIS AT WORK
The CPA Vision Project

The accounting profession conducted a visioning project to define the CPA of the future. The CPA Vision Project was prompted by the profession's recognition that CPAs are facing increasing competition from other professionals, fewer individuals are entering the profession, and the traditional financial audit is a mature product. Information technology is another factor behind this project. The increased use of information technology not only affects *how* CPAs work, but it also offers opportunities for them to expand their services.

The visioning process requires accounting professionals to think about their future and to envision what they would like that future to be. Accountants from all segments of the profession, together with professional organizations such as the AICPA, have identified the values, services, competencies, and issues most important for the CPA profession in the 21st century. The top five values identified by the process are continuing education and lifelong learning, competence, integrity, attunement with broad business issues, and objectivity. The top five services that CPAs believe they are likely to offer in the coming years are assurance, technology, management consulting, financial planning, and international services. Five critical competencies CPAs will need to master are communications skills, strategic and critical thinking skills, a focus on the client and market, interpretation of converging information, and technological adeptness. In addition, the visioning project identified the five issues CPAs must contend with in the near future. They are as follows:

- The future success of the profession relies on public perceptions of the CPA's abilities and roles.
- CPAs must become market driven and must not be dependent on regulations to keep them in business.

- The market demands less auditing and accounting and more value-adding consulting services.
- Specialization is critical for the future survival of the CPA profession.
- The marketplace demands that CPAs be conversant in global business practices and strategies.

By embarking on a visioning process, more than 300,000 CPAs demonstrated their commitment to moving the accounting profession forward. For those who welcome the changes, the future looks especially bright.

SUMMARY

We are living in an age in which information plays a large part in our daily lives. Information systems are important in this age for their role in collecting, processing, storing, transforming, and distributing information for planning, decision-making, and control purposes. AISs are a special type of information system that are important to business entities for these purposes. AISs, which have traditionally focused on reporting financial information, may be defined as process-focused, enterprise-wide information systems.

Information technology affects virtually every aspect of accounting, including financial and managerial accounting, auditing, and taxation. With respect to financial accounting, critics contend that periodic, audited financial statements are less relevant in the information age. The accounting profession has responded by studying the needs of financial accounting information users and taking measures to improve the relevance of accounting information. Managerial accounting is changing as new costing approaches, such as activity-based costing systems, and new performance measurement approaches, such as the balanced scorecard, become possible with new information technologies. Auditing practice is expanding to include a variety of new assurance services, and the nature of the audit has shifted as well. The availability of tax software and extensive tax databases influences both tax preparation and tax planning.

Students who study AISs will find many career opportunities open to them. These include traditional accounting careers as well as jobs in consulting and information systems auditing and security. Finding a specialized niche, a student of AISs has opportunities to start his or her own consulting business.

KEY TERMS YOU SHOULD KNOW

accounting cycle
accounting information system (AIS)
activity-based costing systems
assurance
audit trail
balanced scorecard
budget
business entity
business processes
Certified Information Systems Auditors
   (CISAs)
Certified Information Technology
   Professionals (CITP)

computer-based information systems
cost accounting
CPA WebTrust
data
data warehouse
electronic commerce
enterprise-wide information system
financial accounting
hackers
information
information age
information overload
information processing subsystem

information system	performance measurement
Information Systems Audit and Control Association (ISACA)	reengineering
	responsibility accounting system
information systems auditors	segment reporting
information technology	system
Internet	systems consultants
knowledge workers	systems studies
management information systems (MIS)	SysTrust
managerial accounting	value-added resellers (VARs)

DISCUSSION QUESTIONS

1-1. Take a survey of the students in your class to find out what jobs their parents hold. How many are employed in manufacturing? How many are employed in service industries? How many could be classified as knowledge workers?

1-2. According to Peter Drucker, computer-based data processing and accounting functions operate separately from each other in most organizations. Discuss some ideas about how these two functions might be merged.

1-3. Hiring an employee and taking a sales order are business activities but are not accounting transactions requiring journal entries. Make a list of some other business activities that would not be captured as journal entries in a traditional AIS. Do you think managers or investors would be interested in knowing about these activities? Why or why not?

1-4. The information age is likely to have a continuing impact on financial accounting. What are some changes you think will occur in the way financial information is gathered, processed, and communicated as a result of increasingly sophisticated information technology?

1-5. Managerial accounting is impacted by the information age in many ways. One important impact is that computerization makes it possible for companies to estimate costs more precisely by using multiple cost drivers to allocate indirect costs. Drawing on your understanding of managerial accounting, discuss some other ways the information age influences managerial accounting.

1-6. Look at the list of assurance services shown in Figure 1-7. Can you think of other assurance services that CPAs could offer which would take advantage of their auditing expertise?

1-7. Interview a sample of auditors from professional service firms in your area. Ask them whether or not they plan to offer any of the assurance services suggested by the AICPA. Also, find out if they offer services other than financial auditing and taxation. Discuss your findings in class.

1-8. Many people have a stereotyped image of accountants as persons with ice water in their veins. Accountants are seen as individuals who sit at a desk all day recording debits and credits, and who consider balancing the books to the penny their number-one priority. If a high school senior (trying to decide what major to study in college) asked you what accounting is and what types of functions the accountant performs in an organization, what would you tell this student?

1-9. This chapter described several career opportunities available to students who combine a study of accounting with course work in accounting information systems, information systems, and/or computer science. Can you think of other jobs where these skill sets would be desirable?

PROBLEMS

1-10. The accounting profession publishes many journals such as the *Journal of Accountancy, Internal Auditor,* and *Management Accounting.* Choose, at random, three or four issues of each of these journals and count the number of articles that are related to information technology. In addition, make a list of the specific technology discussed in each article (where possible). When you are finished, decide whether you believe information technology is influencing all aspects of accounting.

1-11. Nehru Gupta is the controller at the Acme Shoe Company, a large manufacturing company located in Franklin, Pennsylvania. Acme has many divisions, and the performance of each division has typically been evaluated using a return on investment (ROI) formula. The return on investment is calculated by dividing profit by the book value of total assets. In a meeting yesterday with Bob Burn, the company president, Nehru warned that this return on investment measure might not be accurately reflecting how well the divisions are doing. Nehru is concerned that by using profits and the book value of assets, division managers might be engaging in some short-term finagling to show the highest possible return. Bob concurred and asked what other numbers they could use to evaluate division performance. Nehru said, "I'm not sure, Bob. Net income isn't a good number for evaluation purposes. Since we allocate a lot of overhead costs to the divisions on what some managers consider an arbitrary basis, net income won't work as a performance evaluation measure in place of return on investment." Bob told Nehru to give some thought to this problem and report back to him.

Requirement
Explain what managers can do in the short run to maximize return on investment as calculated at Acme. What other accounting measures could Acme use to evaluate the performance of its divisional managers? Describe other instances in which accounting numbers might lead to dysfunctional behavior in an organization.

INTERNET EXERCISES

1-12. Search the Internet to find the home pages for several of the largest public accounting firms. What key services or lines of business do each offer?

1-13. Find a web site for accounting students. What information does it provide you about careers in accounting?

1-14. Visit an Internet bookstore (e.g., Amazon or Barnes and Noble). Print out a list of all the books about accounting information systems offered for sale.

CASE ANALYSES

1-15. The Annual Report (Communicating Accounting Information)

The annual report is considered by some to be the single most important printed document that companies produce. In recent years, annual reports have become large documents. They now include such sections as letters to the stockholders, descriptions of the business, operating highlights, financial review, management discussion and analysis, segment reporting, and inflation data as well as the basic financial statements. The expansion has been due in part to a general increase in the degree of sophistication and complexity in accounting standards and disclosure requirements for financial reporting.

The expansion also reflects the change in the composition and level of sophistication of users. Current users include not only stockholders, but financial and securities analysts, potential investors, lending institutions, stockbrokers, customers, employees, and, whether the reporting company likes it or not, competitors. Thus, a report that was originally designed as a device for communicating basic financial information now attempts to meet the diverse needs of an ever-expanding audience.

Users hold conflicting views on the value of annual reports. Some argue that annual reports fail to provide enough information, whereas others believe that disclosures in annual reports have expanded to the point where they create information overload. The future of most companies depends on acceptance by the investing public and by their customers; therefore, companies should take this opportunity to communicate well-defined corporate strategies.

Requirements

1. The goal of preparing an annual report is to communicate information from a company to its targeted users.
   a. Identify and discuss the basic factors of communication that must be considered in the presentation of this information.
   b. Discuss the communication problems a company faces in preparing the annual report that result from the diversity of the users being addressed.
2. Select two types of information found in an annual report, other than the financial statements and accompanying footnotes, and describe how they are useful to the users of annual reports.
3. Discuss at least two advantages and two disadvantages of stating well-defined corporate strategies in the annual report.
4. Evaluate the effectiveness of annual reports in fulfilling the information needs of the following current and potential users:
   a. Shareholders
   b. Creditors
   c. Employees
   d. Customers
   e. Financial analysts
5. Annual reports are public and accessible to anyone, including competitors. Discuss how this affects decisions about what information should be provided in annual reports.

1-16. Hoden's Hamburger Corporation (Performance Reporting)

Hoden's Hamburger Corporation operates a chain of restaurants throughout the United States. The top management at corporate headquarters exercises control over the functions of each restaurant: the construction of each restaurant's building facility and the depreciation method selected for the building, the number of managers hired at each restaurant as well as their annual salaries, and all expenditures associated with promotional efforts and advertising at each restaurant.

The managers of the individual restaurants have decision-making authority and responsibility for all the many other operating activities associated with their specific restaurant. Presented in the following table is the monthly budget performance cost report for the Hoden's Hamburger Corporation's restaurant (located in Springfield, Illinois) for June 2003.

Cost Item	Budget	Actual
Salaries of clerical workers at the Springfield restaurant	$5,000	$5,200
Salaries of cooks, waitresses, and dishwashers at the Springfield restaurant	7,000	7,400
Salaries of supervisory managers at the Springfield restaurant	12,000	12,500
Depreciation of Springfield restaurant's cooking equipment, dishes and silverware, tables and chairs, and cash registers	4,500	4,300
Depreciation of Springfield restaurant's building	3,000	3,400
Electricity, water, and telephone expense	300	375
Cost of food used in cooking meals	25,000	24,500
Cost of cooks' and waitresses' uniforms	400	
Cost of napkins, dish towels, and cleaning soap	175	190
Advertising and promotional expense	1,000	1,400
Totals	$58,375	$59,685

Requirement

Hoden's Hamburger Corporation's top management has decided that a responsibility accounting system would be an effective means of evaluating each restaurant's monthly operating cost performance. Prepare the June 2003 performance report for the Springfield, Illinois, restaurant under the corporation's responsibility accounting system.

1-17. Universal Concrete Products (Information for Performance Evaluation)

Jack Merritt is the controller for Universal Concrete Products (UCP), a manufacturing company with headquarters in Columbus, Ohio. UCP has seven concrete product plants located throughout the Midwest region of the United States. The company has recently switched to a decentralized organizational structure. In the past, the company did not try to measure profitability at each plant. Rather, all revenues and expenses were consolidated to produce just one income statement. Under the new organizational structure, each concrete manufacturing plant is headed by a general manager, who has responsibility for operating the plant like a separate company.

Jack has asked one of his accountants, Scott McDermott, to organize a small group to be in charge of performance analysis. This group is to prepare monthly reports on performance for each of the seven plants. These reports consist of budgeted and actual income statements. Written explanations and appraisals are to accompany variances. Each member of Scott's group has been assigned to one specific plant and is encouraged to interact with management and staff in that plant in order to become familiar with operations.

After a few months, the controller began receiving complaints from the general managers at several of the plants. Common to many of these complaints is the observation that Scott's staff members are interfering with operations and, in general, are "getting in the way." In addition, the managers worry that someone is constantly "looking over their shoulders" to see if they are operating in line with budget. Two plant managers have pointed out that the work the performance analysis staff is trying to do should be done by them (i.e., explanation of variances). As Andrew Boord, one of the most vocal plant managers, stated, "How can these accountants explain the variances when they don't know anything about the industry? They don't know what's happening with our suppliers or our labor unions, and they haven't got a clue about our relationships with our customers."

The president of Universal Concrete Products, Hector Eschenbrenner, has also complained about the new system for performance evaluation reporting. He claims that he is unable to wade through the seven detailed income statements, variances, and narrative explanations of all variances each month. As he put it, "I don't have time for this and I think much of the information I am receiving is irrelevant!"

Requirements

1. Do you think it is a good idea to have a special staff in charge of performance evaluation and analysis?
2. In a decentralized organization such as this one, what would seem to be the best approach to performance evaluation?
3. What information would you include in a performance evaluation report for Mr. Eschenbrenner?

1-18. Ross, Sells, and Young, LLP (Information Technology and Auditing)

Carrie Ross, the Managing Partner of Ross, Sells, and Young, LLP, has just finished reviewing the firm's detailed income statement for the previous quarter. The statement showed that auditing revenues were about 4 percent below last year's value and tax revenues were about the same. Carrie also noted that the income from financial auditing was 10 percent less than that of the same quarter for the previous year. She is dismayed, but not surprised, by the figures. During the past few years, competition for new audit clients has been intense and Ross, Sells, and Young has cut its hourly billing rates. The client base of the organization consists mostly of small- and medium-sized retailers and wholesalers besides several midsize property management companies.

Carrie and the other partners have been discussing ways to expand the revenue base of the organization. Knowing that information technology is a tool that the firm can use to develop new lines of business, Ross, Sells, and Young hired several college graduates during the past few years with dual majors in accounting and information systems or computer science. Given the recent financial results, Carrie thinks now is the time to begin offering other professional services.

Requirements

1. Would it make the most sense for Carrie to consider developing new types of clients or to consider offering different types of services to the types of clients typically served by Ross, Sells, and Young?

2. Carrie knows that the AICPA has developed a list of various types of assurance services that auditing firms might consider offering. Describe three of these assurance services that might be a good fit for this organization. (*Hint:* Visit the AICPA's web page for a listing of assurance services.)

3. How can Ross, Sells, and Young capitalize on its new hires' combined strengths in accounting and information systems/computer science?

REFERENCES, RECOMMENDED READINGS, AND WEB SITES

References and Recommended Readings

Alles, Michael, Alexander Kogan, and Miklos Vasarhelyi, "Accounting in 2015," *The CPA Journal* vol. LXX, no. 11 (2000), pp. 15-16, 18, 20, 70-72.

American Institute of Certified Public Accountants, "Improving Business Reporting—A Customer Focus," AICPA Special Committee on Financial Reporting, Supplement to *Journal of Accountancy* (October 1994).

American Institute of Certified Public Accountants and Canadian Institute of Chartered Accountants, "SysTrust Principles and Criteria for Systems Reliability," AICPA/CICA Systems Reliability Task Force (July 15, 1999).

Anand, Vikas, et al., "An Organizational Memory Approach to Information Management," *Academy of Management Review* (October 1998), p. 796.

Banham, Russell, "Better Budgets," *Journal of Accountancy,* vol. 189, no. 2 (2000), pp. 37-40.

Beets, S. Douglas, and Christopher C. Souther, "Corporate Environmental Reports: The Need for Standards and an Environmental Assurance Service," *Accounting Horizons* (June 1999), pp. 129-145.

Boggs, Scott M., "Accounting—The Digital Way," *Journal of Accountancy,* vol. 187, no. 5 (1999), pp. 99-108.

Bremner, Brian, and Moon Ihlwan, "Edging Toward the Information Age," *Business Week* (January 31, 2000), pp. 90-91.

Cashell, June, James D. and George R. Aldhizer III, "Web Trust: A Seal of Approval," *Internal Auditor,* vol. LVI, no. 3 (1999), pp. 50-33.

Cohn, Laura, "The Wild New Workforce," *Business Week* (December 6, 1999), pp. 38-44.

Elliott, R. K., and D. M. Pallais, "Are You Ready for the New Assurance Services?" *Journal of Accountancy* (June 1997), pp. 47-51.

Elliott, Robert K., "A Perspective on the Proposed Global Professional Credential," *Accounting Horizons* (December 2001), pp. 359-372.

Figg, Jonathan, "Partnering with IT," *Internal Auditor,* vol. LVII, no. 4 (2000), pp. 73-75.

Kaplan, R. S., and D. P. Norton, *The Balanced Scorecard* (Boston: Harvard Business School Press, 1996).

Kaplan, Robert S., and David P. Norton, "Transforming the Balanced Scorecard from Performance Measurement to Strategic Management: Part II," *Accounting Horizons* (June 2001), pp. 147-160.

Keen, P.G.W., and E. M. Knapp, *Every Manager's Guide to Business Processes* (Boston: Harvard Business School Press, 1996).

Koch, Christopher, "The Middle Ground," *CIO* (January 15, 1999), pp. 48–54.

Laudon, K. C., and J. P. Laudon, *Management Information Systems* (Upper Saddle River, NJ: Prentice Hall, 1998).

Leahy, Tad, "Building a Unified Reporting System," *Business Finance,* vol. 6, no. 12, (2000), pp.57–160.

Noll, D. J., and J. J. Weygandt, "Business Reporting: What Comes Next?" *Journal of Accountancy* (February 1997), pp. 59–62.

Pugliese, Anthony, and Ronald Halse, "SysTrust and WebTrust: Technology Assurance Opportunities," *The CPA Journal,* vol. LXX no. 11 (2000), pp. 29–30, 32, 34.

Richards, Dave, "Envisioning Our Future," *Internal Auditor* (August 2001), pp. 60–67.

Taylor, Alex, "How Toyota Defies Gravity," *Fortune* (December 8, 1997), pp. 100–108.

Teach, E., "Look Who's Hacking Now," *CFO* (February 1998), pp. 38–50.

Wallman, S., "The Future of Accounting and Reporting, Part IV: 'Access' Accounting," *Accounting Horizons* (June 1997), pp. 103–116.

Web Sites

Information about a variety of professional accounting organizations may be found at the following World Wide Web sites: www.aaa-edu.org (American Accounting Association), www.aicpa.org (American Institute of Certified Public Accountants), and www.isaca.org (Information Systems Audit and Control Association). A web page with links to many accounting sites can be found at www.rutgers.edu/Accounting/ (Rutgers Accounting Web). The Institute of Management Accountants may be accessed at www.rutgers.edu/Accounting/raw/ima/. The Institute of Internal Auditors is also accessible at www.rutgers.edu/Accounting/raw/iia.

For information about financial reporting, see the home page of the Financial Accounting Standards Board at www.fasb.org.

For more information about the CPA Vision Project, visit its web site at www.cpavision.org.

To access professional articles on topics related to accounting information systems, go to the web site of *The CPA Journal* at www.cpaj.com.

Chapter 2

Electronic Commerce and the Internet

INTRODUCTION

THE INTERNET AND WORLD WIDE WEB

Internet Addresses and Software

Intranets and Extranets

The World Wide Web

E-mail, Groupware, and Electronic Conferencing

XBRL–Financial Reporting on the Internet

ELECTRONIC COMMERCE

Retail Sales

E-Payments and E-Wallets

Business to Business E-Commerce

Electronic Data Interchange

PRIVACY AND SECURITY ON THE INTERNET

Privacy

Security

Firewalls and Proxy Servers

Data Encryption

Digital Signatures

Digital Time Stamping

AIS AT WORK—THE SEC HOSTS FAKE COMPANY WEB SITES

SUMMARY

KEY TERMS YOU SHOULD KNOW

DISCUSSION QUESTIONS

PROBLEMS

INTERNET EXERCISES

CASE ANALYSIS

DeGraaf Office Supplies

Small Business Computers, Inc.

REFERENCES, RECOMMENDED READINGS, AND WEB SITES

After reading this chapter, you will:

1. *Understand* IP, URL, and web page addresses on the Internet.

2. *Appreciate* why electronic communication is useful to accountants.

3. *Know* why XBRL is important to the future of financial reporting.

4. *Understand* electronic data interchange (EDI), and why it is important to AISs.

5. *Know* the differences between business-to-consumer and business-to-business electronic commerce.

6. *Appreciate* the privacy and security issues associated with electronic commerce.

7. *Know* why businesses use firewalls, proxy servers, and encryption techniques.

8. *Understand* digital signatures and digital time-stamping techniques.

The days when the Internet was primarily a research tool are long gone. Today, it is positioned as the engine that will drive the future of business.

G. Norris, J.R. Hurley, K.M. Hartley,
J.R. Dunleavy, and J.D. Balls, *E-business
and ERP: Transforming the Enterprise*
(New York: John Wiley and Sons, Inc., 2000).

INTRODUCTION

It is difficult to discuss accounting information systems without also discussing the Internet and electronic commerce. Reasons for this are abundant. For many accountants, for example, electronic communication has become as natural a form of communication as speaking over a telephone system. Similarly, most accountants now use the World Wide Web—the graphic component of the Internet—as a valued research and learning tool. Then, too, auditors now regularly recommend and evaluate those Internet controls and procedures that ensure complete, accurate, and authentic transmissions over Internet transmission channels. The Internet is both a disruptive technology (because it changes so much) and an enabling technology (because it makes the economy more efficient). The Internet may be even more influential than previous technologies because of the speed of adoption and impact. Consider that in 1993 only 90,000 Americans were online versus in 143 million in September 2001.[1] It took twenty years for the television to reach 50 million people and only four years for the Internet to do the same.

This chapter describes the Internet and some of its accounting uses in detail. The first section describes Internet components such as Internet addresses and software. This section also discusses some Internet concepts of special importance to accountants (i.e., intranets, extranets, the World Wide Web, and e-mail). We next discuss XBRL, a financial reporting language that will improve access to and analysis of corporate financial data.

One of the most important uses of the Internet is for electronic commerce (e-commerce)—the topic of the second section of this chapter. While the terms e-commerce and e-business are often used interchangeably; there *is* actually a difference. E-commerce involves buying and selling electronically, whereas e-business entails automating business processes in general via the Internet. Here, we discuss such vital concepts as retail sales, E-cash, business-to-business e-commerce, and electronic data interchange.

As more organizations conduct at least some business on the Internet, it is only natural that managers increasingly recognize the importance of Internet privacy and security. This includes protecting consumers' personal privacy, protecting data from external hackers, and safeguarding information that businesses send to one another over the Internet. The final section of this chapter discusses these topics in detail.

---

[1] Source: *A Nation Online: How Americans Are Expanding Their Use of the Internet,* published by the National Telecommunications and Information Administration and the Economics and Statistics Administration, www.ntia.doc.gov.

THE INTERNET AND WORLD WIDE WEB

The **Internet** is a collection of hundreds of thousands of local and wide area networks that are now connected together via the Internet backbone (i.e., the main electronic connections of the system). Describing the Internet as an "information superhighway" makes sense because it now connects almost 200 million people in more than 200 countries electronically just as a set of state, interstate, and international highways connect people physically. Experts estimate that the Internet is growing at the rate of 40 percent per year. Almost all universities are connected to the Internet, as are most commercial information services, businesses, government agencies, and not-for-profit organizations.

If you are taking classes at a college or university, there is a good chance that your school has a direct ("hard-wired") link to the Internet. This link is usually a high-capacity, dedicated phone line that connects your school's computer(s) to at least one other Internet computer. Alternatively, you may have an account with an **Internet service provider (ISP)** such as America Online, Bellsouth, Ameritech, Netcom, AT&T, or Sprint, each of which maintains its own Internet computers.

Internet Addresses and Software

To transmit data over the Internet, a computer uses an Internet address and a forwarding system that works much the same way as the post office system. On the Internet, the initial computer transmits a message to other computers along the Internet's backbone, which then relay the message from site to site until it reaches its final destination. If the message is long, the original data packet may be divided into pieces and even routed along separate routes. The receiving computer then reassembles the packets into a complete message at the final destination.

Message-routing is important to accountants because the security of a data transmission rests on the safety of all the intermediate computers along a given communications pathway. Thus, the further the distance between the sending station and the destination computer, the more intermediary routing computers are involved in the transmission and the more vulnerable a message becomes to interception and abuse. This is why businesses often use their own (proprietary) networks or encrypted (coded) messages when transmitting data electronically. We shall return to this point shortly.

An Internet address begins as a **domain address,** which is also called a **universal resource locator (URL).** This is text—for example, AccountName@computerX. siteY.com. As suggested by this generic example, the lead item is an account name, the first element following the @ symbol is a particular computer, and the second element following the @ symbol is a site locator. The last entry (com or commercial user) is the organization code. Other organization codes are edu (education), gov (government), mil (military), net (network service organization), org (miscellaneous organization), and int (international treaty organization).

For transmission purposes, Internet computers translate text-based domain addresses into a pure numeric **Internet protocol (IP)** address such as "198.105.232.4." The elements in this address contain a geographic region ("198"), an organization number ("105"), a computer group ("232"), and a specific computer ("4"). The IP address enables Internet computers to deliver a specific file to a specific computer at a specific computer site—for example, an e-mail message to a friend at another university—using the standard Transmission Control Protocol (TCP)/IP Internet protocol. (TCP/IP lets computers communicate with each other across networks.) IP addresses are important to auditors because they help identify the sender, an important control in electronic commerce applications.

Intranets and Extranets

Because Internet software is so convenient to use, many companies also create their own **intranets** for internal communications purposes. These are networks that use the same software as the Internet (discussed later), but are internal to the organization that created them. Thus, outsiders cannot access the information on intranet networks (unless special provision is made for this)—a convenient and often-desirable security feature.

Companies are finding many uses for their intranets. These systems allow more users to access and interact with a range of internal and external databases. Advanced search engine technology coupled with an intranet can deliver user-defined information when needed. For example, a manager can request notification from the intranet when departmental expenses exceed a prespecified dollar amount. Employee information sharing is another value-added use of an intranet. Employees can collaborate with each other by posting messages and data on the internal network. Another valuable use of the intranet concerns the human resource process. Employees can update records, check out job postings, fill out forms to request goods and services, and enter expenses (e.g., travel expenses) through their organization's intranet. Case-in-Point 2.1 describes how James River Corporation uses an intranet for employee services.

> **Case-in-Point 2.1** James River Corporation, a leading maker of consumer products, used *Lawson Insight's* human resources system to develop an intranet for employees to retrieve and update their personal information. The Lawson system lets employees go to the intranet to change W-4 forms, check on their vacation time, and make changes to personal information such as address and phone number. For many personnel functions, employees can now serve themselves.[2]

Some businesses are creating **extranets** that enable selected outside users to access their intranets. Connections are either through the Internet itself or through a separate data communications channel. An example is a large manufacturer that wants to communicate electronically with its vendors. Thus, extranets are networks that organizations establish between themselves and their trading partners. An example is the extranet created by General Electric (Case-in-Point 2.2).

> **Case-in-Point 2.2** GE, which spends about $30 billion on supplies, now uses its proprietary "Trading Process Network" (TPN) to communicate with more than 1,400 suppliers online. TPN enables GE to distribute requests for bids to both large and small vendors, provide information about how to bid, and obtain bids electronically in a fraction of the time it takes to exchange manual documents. In 1997, GE purchased nearly $1 billion worth of supplies in this manner. It expects to save $500 million over the next three years using this extranet.

---

[2] "Lawson Insight – A World of Difference for James River Corporation," *Management Accounting Internet/Intranet Supplement,* January 1997, p. 22.

The World Wide Web

The software that we use to send and receive messages on the Internet includes general types of e-mail software, and also specialized search software such as *Gopher* and *Veronica*. All these items are text-based software that limits viewable outputs to words and phrases—not figures, graphics, or animated outputs.

The graphics portion of the Internet is commonly called the **World Wide Web,** or just "the web." As you probably already know, you view the graphics files available through this portion of the Internet using a software package called a **web browser.** The two most popular web browsers today are Microsoft's Internet Explorer and Netscape's Navigator, but there are many other, less-popular software packages as well.

A typical output on the web is called a web page (Figure 2-1) (i.e., a collection of text, graphics, and links to other web pages that are stored in one or more files on Internet-connected computers). Many web pages, in fact, are collections of files drawn from both local and distant sources. This is one reason why some web pages take so long to appear onscreen after the initial host is contacted; you may be waiting for your system to assemble text and graphics images from distant sources.

Developers create web pages in an editing language such as **hypertext markup language (html)** or a programming language such as *Java*. Figure 2-2 shows a portion of the html code for the web page of Figure 2-1. The Internet transfers these web pages from one computer to another using a communications proto-

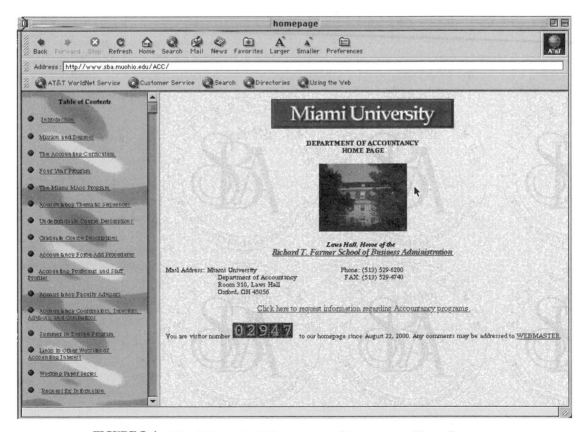

FIGURE 2-1   Miami University's Department of Accountancy Home Page.

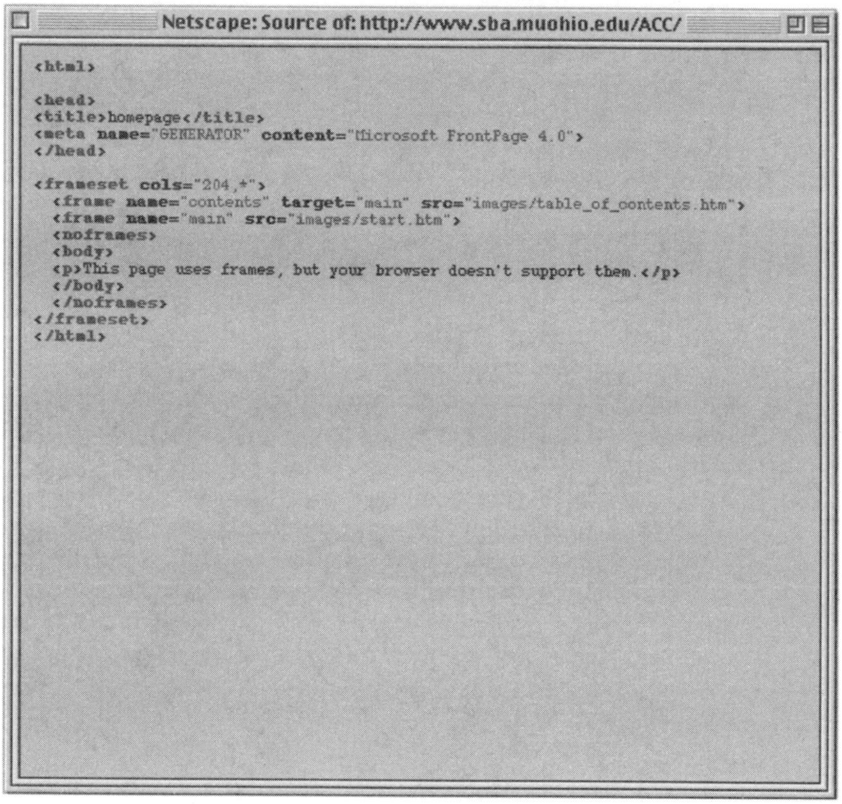

```
Netscape: Source of: http://www.sba.muohio.edu/ACC/

<html>

<head>
<title>homepage</title>
<meta name="GENERATOR" content="Microsoft FrontPage 4.0">
</head>

<frameset cols="204,*">
  <frame name="contents" target="main" src="images/table_of_contents.htm">
  <frame name="main" src="images/start.htm">
  <noframes>
  <body>
  <p>This page uses frames, but your browser doesn't support them.</p>
  </body>
  </noframes>
</frameset>
</html>
```

FIGURE 2-2 This example of hypertext markup language (html) created a portion of the web page in Figure 2-1.

col such as **hypertext transfer protocol (http).** Your web browser then deciphers the editing language and displays the text, graphics, and other items of the web page on your display screen.

The first web page that a user sees when he or she supplies a web browser with a domain address is called the web site's home page. Typically, this **home page** acts as a table of contents with **hyperlinks** to other web pages that contain more specific information. These links are the icons, colored text, or graphic images on which you click, for example, when your mouse pointer turns into a hand icon onscreen. Typically, these other web pages are stored on distant computers, making access speeds slow during times of peak Internet usage.

E-mail, Groupware, and Electronic Conferencing

E-mail is short for **electronic mail.** In a typical e-mail application, you create a message on your microcomputer, and then send it to someone else using the recipient's e-mail address. On local area networks, a person's e-mail address is usually the same as the person's account number or name, for example, "AnnBorland." If you send e-mail over the Internet, you must also include the full domain address, for example, AnnBorland@ computerX.siteY.edu.

When a computer system receives an e-mail message, it stores it in the user's mail box (on disk) as a text file. The recipient then uses e-mail software to read the message and respond as necessary. This person can also forward the message to others, print a hard copy, or delete it. E-mail attachments allow users to append separate files to e-mail messages, for example, graphics files or text files in non-ASCII formats. Figure 2-3 lists some additional advantages of e-mail.

E-mail enables individuals or companies to communicate with other Internet users around the corner or around the world. This allows accountants, for example, to gather information from remote or distant sources, consult with experts outside their organization on complex technical issues, and forward accounting documents such as a set of financial statements for review by corporate headquarters. A problem with e-mail is that hackers can use it to spread computer viruses, as described in the following case.

Case-in-Point 2.3 In May, 2000, companies and individuals were hit with the worst computer virus to date, the LoveLetter worm. A hacker sent a message worldwide with the subject line "I Love You." Opening the attachment caused the virus to replace or hide numerous picture, music, and video files. It also quickly replicated itself and spread. The "I Love You" virus may have attacked more than 40 million people's computers and damages were in the billions of dollars. This type of virus illustrates the vulnerability of information systems to widespread attacks.

Newer work group software called **groupware** allows users to send and receive e-mail, plus perform a wide range of other tasks. Examples include *Exchange* (Microsoft), *Groupwise* (Novell), *Lotus Notes* (Lotus Development Corporation) and *Outlook* (Microsoft). In addition to e-mail support, these network packages allow users to collaborate on work tasks, make revisions to the same document, schedule appointments on each other's calendars, share files and databases, conduct electronic meetings, and develop custom applications.

At the high end of groupware communications packages are **electronic conferencing** tools that enable users to teleconference with one another. These packages, for example, enable accountants to use computers and phone lines to interview re-

---

(1) *Eliminates "telephone tag."* Your message goes directly to your recipient.
(2) *Eliminates inaccurate or misleading messages.* Your message will be delivered in exactly the same way as you send it. Some e-mail software includes spell checkers to eliminate spelling errors.
(3) *No interruptions.* E-mail is delivered silently and users do not have to be physically present to receive messages.
(4) *Time shifting.* Messages can be sent to people in different time zones.
(5) *Message distribution.* You can send the same message to many different individuals without composing a separate message to each one.
(6) *Facilitates replies.* You can enclose a copy of the message you receive as part of the message you send. This makes it easy to ask specific questions, or to reply to specific parts of an earlier message.
(7) *Maintaining information.* E-mail software enables you to maintain messages in an orderly, paperless fashion. Some e-mail software enables you to archive your messages, sort them by date of receipt or sender, or search them for key words.
(8) *Attaching files.* You can attach files in different formats to your e-mail message, including text and graphics files.

FIGURE 2-3 Some advantages of e-mail.

mote clients, consult with one another about tax or audit problems, or plan corporate budgets.

Groupware has been the technology behind the **knowledge sharing** that many professional service firms (such as accounting and consulting firms) use as a competitive advantage. Knowledge sharing allows an organization to distribute expertise within the organization. Large consulting and accounting firms, for example, have access to a wealth of information within their organizations. This information includes descriptions of clients' best practices, research, links to business web sites, and customized news. An employee with a client issue can access the knowledge database to find out how other clients handle that issue. For example, what is the best practice for processing accounts payable transactions? Case-in-Point 2.4 describes one such system.

Case-in-Point 2.4   In 1997, Arthur Andersen, a large professional service firm, launched *KnowledgeSpace,* a web-based repository of knowledge for employees and business subscribers. The knowledge database included global best practices, links to over 400 business resources, stock quotes and portfolios, book recommendations, and online conferences on hot issues. A basic subscription to the service cost less than $400 per year and allowed employees and subscribers to receive custom information that fit their user profile.

XBRL—Financial Reporting on the Internet

More and more companies are reporting financial information on the Internet. While it's easy enough to view one company's financial reports and other disclosures, it is not so easy to access financial information about multiple enterprises for comparison purposes. If you were to try to compare several companies within one industry in terms of a specific financial statement element, such as current assets, you could not do so. The primary repository of financial information on the Internet is the Security and Exchange Commission's **Electronic Data Gathering and Retrieval (EDGAR)** database. This database contains the financial report filings of U.S. publicly held companies. The reports, however, are in a plain text format. You can search for information for one company, for example, Company ABC's 10-Q filing for the third quarter of 2001. However, you cannot access account information from one company and compare it to that of another. To overcome the search limitations in the EDGAR database, PricewaterhouseCoopers developed **EdgarScan**™. EdgarScan takes the information in the database and changes it to a common format, which allows users to extract data from multiple companies and compare it. EdgarScan even includes graphical capabilities that allow you to show bar charts comparing, for example, the sales revenues of two or more companies for the same period. Figure 2-4 shows a bar chart in *Microsoft Excel* format produced by EdgarScan's Benchmarking Assistant feature.

While the EDGAR database and EdgarScan are valuable resources for obtaining financial information about publicly traded companies, they are limited to formal financial report filings for a limited set of enterprises. The information they include is historical and concerns past performance. Many financial managers, investors, and other information users are interested in obtaining financial information that is reported on a more timely basis. While the Internet allows for this type of reporting, retrieving the information requires a common specification for reporting and analyzing financial data. **eXtensible Business Reporting Language (XBRL)** is a specialized software language for the financial reporting industry.

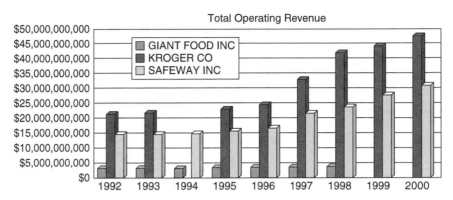

FIGURE 2-4 Sample report produced by EdgarScan™. Used with permission of Pricewater-houseCoopers.

XBRL is a subset of **eXtensible Markup Language (XML).** Most Internet users are somewhat familiar with Hypertext Markup Language (HTML). HTML is the source code for web pages. If you wanted to format your own web page, you would do so using the **tags** defined in HTML. These tags are specifications in brackets surrounding the text that describe how to display the data. For example, <TITLE>XYZ Corporation Financial Statements<TITLE> indicates that "XYZ Corporation Financial Statements" should appear in a web browser's title bar or at the top of the web page. HTML has a limited set of predefined tags; users cannot create new ones.

XML is similar to HTML in that it also uses tags to describe data. There are two important differences, however. XML's tags are "extensible," which means users can create new tags. Another difference is that the tags in XML actually describe the data rather than indicating how to display it. Suppose a business wants to report Sales Revenue of $1,000,000. HTML tags may specify how to display the dollar amount (e.g., in the title or in a table), but they will not convey meaning about what it represents. You could use XML tags to mark the data as: <Sales Revenue> $1,000,000<Sales Revenue>. Now the data has meaning. One problem remains, however. Perhaps you mark your financial statements with a tag for sales revenue but another company chooses to use a different marker for sales revenue, for instance, Revenues. Without a predefined standard set of markers, users still are not able to extract data for comparison purposes, nor can they exchange financial information. To enable information preparation, publication, exchange and analysis, industries are creating their own dialects of the XML language. XBRL is the XML-based language specification for the accounting industry. Figure 2-5 shows XML-tagged data describing income statement information.

XBRL is a global effort of groups with a stake in financial reporting, such as the American Institute of Certified Public Accountants. Software vendors are involved too and they're building XBRL into their software applications. XBRL-compliant software will insert the appropriate tags automatically. The XBRL Steering Committee (see www.xbrl.org) is working to spread the development and usage of XBRL standards. Developing XBRL is not easy. The language requires classification systems for different reporting segments and standards such as US generally accepted accounting standards (GAAP). The various classification systems define the tags and describe the relationships among the data items. To understand the need for multiple

```
<ci:salesRevenueNet numericContext="NC1">123456</ci:salesRevenueNet>
<ci:operatingExpenses numericContext="NC1">5438</ci:operatingExpenses>
<ci:operatingProfit numericContext="NC1">118018</ci:operatingProfit>
<ci:investmentIncome numericContext="NC1">897</ci:investmentIncome>
<ci:incomeBeforeTaxesAcctingChangesExtraordinaryItems
numericContext="NC1">117121</ci:incomeBeforeTaxesAcctingChangesExtraordinaryItems>
<ci:incomeTaxes numericContext="NC1">29250</ci:incomeTaxes>
<ci.netIncome numericContext="NC1">87871</ci.netIncome>
```

FIGURE 2-5   Income statement data written in XBRL v.2 specification. (Source: Clinton E. White, Jr., University of Delaware)

sets of tags, think about the charts of accounts in different industries. The oil and gas industry has accounts regarding reserves, for instance. Sets of tags need to be created for each industry's financial reports, each set of accounting standards, and also for information that doesn't appear on formal financial statements. For instance, for businesses to exchange financial information, they need to agree on the markers in source documents, such as purchase orders.

XBRL has many potential benefits. A company that needs to file its financial information can do so in just one format, avoiding the errors that may come from re-entering data multiple times. They can save financial data in their software in the XBRL format. The Securities and Exchange Commission (SEC) will accept this format for electronic filing of financial statement reports. Creditors can accept the filing and convert it to complete forms for loans. The company can directly upload their business information in this format onto their web site. Anyone interested in comparing the cash and cash equivalents of several companies can search for the data and export it to a spreadsheet for analysis purposes. The hope is that XBRL will make financial information available on the Internet more accessible and of greater use. It should do this, too, for less cost since the business had to key-in the data only once.

Despite the benefits, XBRL may take a while to catch on. While the SEC supports the idea of a financial reporting standard, it does not yet endorse XBRL. Few companies to date have chosen to file their SEC reports in XBRL format either. Finally, XBRL does not resolve the issues of standardized financial reporting. The primary motivator for using XBRL is likely to be a reduction in cost that comes from single data entry. Until the standard becomes more widely accepted, however, users will not be able to easily access the wealth of financial information that's available on the web.

ELECTRONIC COMMERCE

The term **electronic commerce (EC)** refers to conducting business with computers and data communications. Often, EC is done over the Internet, but businesses also conduct a great deal of electronic commerce over proprietary transmission lines, for example, over extranets set up between suppliers and their manufacturers. The FBI estimates that the banking industry transfers over $1 trillion each week by electronic means. The impact of business-to-business e-commerce is likely to have a major impact on accountants. As a result, the American Institute of Public Accountants (AICPA) ranked business-to-business e-commerce as the most important technology application and technology issue for the year 2000. Some general categories of electronic commerce and usage are retail sales, e-payments and e-wallets, and electronic data interchange, each of which we examine briefly in the paragraphs that follow.

Retail Sales

The World Wide Web has enabled businesses to open virtual stores that sell merchandise directly to customers. Some obvious advantages of such virtual stores are (1) creating web pages is usually much cheaper than creating and mailing catalogs; (2) distribution is worldwide; (3) selling takes place around the clock with no additional staffing requirements; (4) product descriptions, sales prices, and information on merchandise availability can be updated immediately as they become known or change; (5) customers create their own sales orders online; and (6) the sales personnel required for these virtual stores is minimal, thus reducing labor costs per dollar of sales.

Testimony to the success of retail electronic commerce abounds. The number of online shoppers has increased steadily during the past few years. More than half the US population is online, and about 39 percent of Internet users have bought something. Online retail sales increased so much during the 1999 holiday season that some Internet companies couldn't keep up with sales.

Case-in-Point 2.5 Wal-Mart Stores, Inc. posted a note on its web site in early December 1999 that it couldn't guarantee on-time Christmas deliveries. When toysrus.com let customers know they might not be able to make deliveries, customers were particularly upset. Telling kids the toys weren't under the tree because of online shopping problems wasn't a pleasant task. One of the authors of this book ordered a book for her son for Christmas. When the book hadn't arrived by December 20, she checked her order at Amazon.com online to find that the book was back-ordered but would be shipped soon. Two days after Christmas the book arrived—or at least the packing slip for the correct book came, accompanied by a different book. A call to Amazon (getting through took about two minutes) resulted in instruction to return the book. The author had to go to the post office to mail the book back in order to receive a refund. To their credit, Amazon tried to make up for their error with a gift certificate. Since the book originally ordered appeared to be on back-order for weeks, the author finally cancelled the order for it.

Many traditional brick-and-mortar companies were at first slow to get online. This phenomenon allowed some previously unknown businesses to grab market share of online sales first. It appears though that brand names are important to customers, whether they are *in* line or *on* line. Media Metrix, a company that tracks web site traffic, reported that almost half of the 50 most visited web sites during the 1999 holiday season were associated with older, established businesses. These companies included Toys "R" Us, J.C. Penney Co., Sears, Roebuck & Co., and Wal-Mart Stores Inc. As the dot com "bubble" burst at the onset of the new millennium, it became increasingly clear that many of the new Internet retailers would lose out to the "click and mortars." Features that make online retailers successful include the web site's appearance, the ease with which customers can search the site for desired products, customer service, product availability, pricing, and ability to deliver as promised.

While many of these features are common to brick and mortar stores too, the Internet introduces special issues. Customers have to rely on e-mail to handle customer service complaints, and do not have the satisfaction of speaking with someone in person. Online stores frequently rely on suppliers rather than their own shelves for merchandise to satisfy orders and this can create stock out and backorder problems.

There are also security and privacy issues. The online communication in an electronic purchase transaction provides retailers with a wealth of data about customers. They can use this data to better serve customers, but there are also privacy and security concerns. For example, suppose you buy mysteries from an online bookseller. The bookseller's information system, tracking your purchase history, could offer to e-mail you as books you might be interested in reading become available. This is a benefit to you as a consumer, but you might be concerned about the retailer maintaining rich data about your purchase patterns. A later section of this chapter addresses privacy and security issues in depth.

E-Payments and E-Wallets

How do customers pay for the merchandise they order over the Internet? You are probably already familiar with the most common method—supplying a credit card number. But this method presents a problem to vendors because acceptable credit card numbers only indicate that a card is valid. They do not indicate that an online customer is authorized to use it. This is also a problem for the customer because **identity fraud,** in which individuals discover that their identities have been stolen and their good credit used by others to buy merchandise, is on the rise. A related problem with online payments is that, while an online customer might not mind sending their credit card number to a trusted merchant, they do not wish to share the number with lesser known businesses or individuals. Finally, another issue is that not everyone has a credit card, or one with available credit.

Some merchants and auction sites solve these problems with **electronic payment (e-payments),** which proponents claim is a faster, easier, and safer way for both customers and sellers to handle online transactions. The following Case-in-Point describes how one such system works.

> *Case-In-Point 2.6*   Users who have bought and sold on E-bay or other online auction sites may be familiar with Paypal (www.paypal.com), an online payment system that operates via e-mail. Customers who successfully bid for an item in an online auction, but who don't wish to share their credit card number with sellers, may open an account with Paypal. Account-holders can put cash in their Paypal account through their credit or debit card, or via their checking account. Paypal sends an e-mail to the sellers, notifying them that the payment has been put in their Paypal account. Upon request, Paypal will transfer the money to the sellers' bank accounts or send them checks.

Another payment option is the **e-wallet.** Despite the fact that many potential customers lack available credit, it's still likely that most online consumers will use credit cards directly to make their purchases for some time to come. E-wallets are software applications that store consumers' personal information, including credit card numbers and shipping addresses. To use an e-wallet, a shopper can reference it when completing an online retailer's checkout payment form and charge a purchase easily, as described in Case-in-Point 2.7.

> *Case-In-Point 2.7*   Quick Checkout is America Online's e-wallet application. AOL partners with a number of online retail merchants such as Macy's and Eddie Bauer, and shoppers can

use Quick Checkout at all of them. When you visit an affiliated retailer, the Quick Checkout software enters your name, address, phone, credit card number, and other relevant information automatically in the payment form.

The advantages of an e-wallet are that you have access to passwords and credit card numbers as you visit various retail web sites and you do not have to enter all your information each time you make an online purchase. Also, because the information is usually stored on the hard drive of a shopper's own computer, it is controlled by the user. E-wallets may be as important for retailers as they are for consumers because many consumers cancel e-commerce transactions before they are complete, for example, due to frustrations in filling out online forms. Case-in-Point 2.8 describes another e-wallet application.

Case-In-Point 2.8   An online vendor may maintain an e-wallet for its customers. Amazon.com's 1-Click technology is an example of this approach. Amazon lets shoppers choose its 1-Click option where the retailer automatically inserts all the personal shipping and billing information from the last purchase. The downside of the 1-Click approach is that it only works at one online store. To counter this problem, Amazon and others are seeking ways for shoppers to use similar technology at multiple vendors.

Business-to-Business E-Commerce

In 1999, online retail sales were approximately $16 billion. While there has been tremendous growth in retail e-commerce during the past few years, it is dwarfed by the actual and potential growth in the business-to-business (or b2b) e-commerce segment (i.e., one business firm selling goods or services to another business firm). According to Forrester Research, e-commerce revenues should grow to $2.7 trillion by 2004. Businesses are increasingly buying and selling from each other over the Internet.

A big part of b2b e-commerce concerns purchases of supplies and equipment electronically or **electronic procurement.** Buying goods online shortens the time from purchase to delivery, and also allows purchasing departments to choose from vendors all over the world. Employees in an organization can select their items for purchase themselves, from online catalogues. A company's e-commerce software sends the employee order to the appropriate sites for approvals. Electronic procurement systems benefit an organization by reducing prices paid for goods and services and also by reducing the cost of processing purchase requisitions, as described in Case-in-Point 2.9.

Case-In-Point 2.9   Owens Corning, a global glass maker, was able to use e-procurement to cut costs of several of its products, including water jugs, stretch wrap, and rock salt. In total, the firm was able to cut its annual purchases spending of more than $3 billion, by 10 percent! Some businesses use e-procurement for just some of their purchases. Lucent Technologies, for example, uses e-procurement to buy about 15 percent of their indirect materials and Hewlett-Packard Co. saved money by buying electrical power online.[3]

Another feature of b2b e-commerce is real-time business views that allow you to access up-to-date information at any time. By having real-time information about

---

[3] Source: "Industry Week," *Supply Chain Management Review,* March 1, 2002 (www.manufacturing. net/scm).

operations (such as various expense items) available, managers can act instantly to adjust spending. There are many other uses of this "instant" information availability. For example, customers of delivery services such as Federal Express or UPS can track their packages online, truckers can check cargo status online to make carry loads more efficient, and workers in a manufacturing plant can have up-to-the-minute information about product and parts status on the assembly line.

As far as AISs are concerned, the Internet has had a large impact on the accounting and enterprise software world. Even vendors of very inexpensive software now include an e-commerce interface with their products. (A good example is *Peachtree* software's *Peachlink* feature that provides users with tools to create and use a web site and accept Internet orders.) Enterprise resource planning (ERP) vendors (see Chapter 6) were not as quick as the marketplace would have liked in developing their e-commerce products. In the recent past, businesses made big investments in ERP systems both to avoid the y2k problem and to integrate their internal business processes. Once they realized the benefits from improving their internal functions, their interest shifted to external relations, notably the **supply chain** between a company and its customers and suppliers. E-commerce links to internal ERP systems provide advantages to companies in terms of better supplier and customer relationships. Suppliers and customers have better access to company information through a web site. For example, customers can check on the progress of their orders. Suppliers can look ahead to see when their product might be needed. ERP vendors can offer web site add-ons to their software that provide these capabilities.

While the Internet is speeding up the supply chain in terms of procurement and inventory tracking, it has been slow to impact the accounts payable and accounts receivable aspects of an AIS. In part, this is because companies like to hold onto their money as long as possible, making use of the float that comes from paying bills in less than real time. Prompt bill payment, however, works two ways. While a business may enjoy float on the accounts payable side, a lack of speed in collecting accounts receivable works to the company's disadvantage. Software such as that produced by Time Capital allows vendors and customers to view purchase and shipping documents so that they can resolve discrepancies quickly and cut checks or make electronic payments faster. Companies engaged in electronic commerce are likely to realize more benefits as new software and services become available to speed up the payment process along with the shipping process.

Electronic Data Interchange

Electronic Data Interchange (EDI) allows organizations to transmit standard business documents over high-speed data communications channels. Examples of EDI business documents include requests for quotes (RFQs), purchase orders, bills of lading, freight bills, sales invoices, customs documents, payment remittance forms, and credit memos, all of which are relayed electronically—and therefore almost instantaneously—to their recipients. Thus, EDI automates the exchange of business information and permits organizations to conduct many forms of commerce electronically, as shown in Case-in-Point 2.9.

Case-in-Point 2.9   Pratt and Whitney is a large-engine manufacturer that buys over 26,000 parts from more than 700 suppliers. This company now transmits over 50,000 EDI documents per month, including purchase orders, procurement schedules, and sales invoices.

The company estimates savings between $10 and $20 on every purchase order—over $6 million per year.

For many firms, EDI is a superior way of doing business. Perhaps the most important advantage is that EDI users no longer are required to manually transcribe the data from a trading partner's hard-copy forms (such as purchase order information) into their own systems—the data are already in computer-readable formats. This saves businesses time and labor, and significantly reduces the number of errors typically introduced into job streams when manual data transcription is required. EDI also streamlines processing tasks because (1) business partners exchange documents quickly and easily, (2) there are no postal delays, and (3) EDI eliminates most of the paperwork.

Although most EDI applications are found in private businesses, EDI can also be used effectively by government agencies. One example is the U.S. Customs Service:

Case-in-Point 2.10 Before EDI, imported goods could wait on docks for weeks while officials processed the paperwork. But information about some imports can be sent weeks before the merchandise itself arrives. The U.S. Customs Service now uses EDI to process almost 95 percent of all customs declarations. This usage has lowered error rates from 17 percent before EDI, to about 1.7 percent now. This improvement translates into annual savings of $500 million in processing costs, and also into productivity gains of about 10 percent.

Some firms find the advantages of EDI so compelling that they refuse to do business with those companies that do not use EDI. This helps explain why EDI has been the fastest-growing segment of electronic commerce, with an annual growth rate of greater than 20 percent. But EDI also places a greater burden on auditors because electronic transactions are more difficult to verify, authenticate, and therefore audit. We shall return to this point shortly.

To implement EDI applications, most businesses currently use private, point-to-point communication channels called **value-added networks (VANs).** These VANs are proprietary networks that large IT organizations design and maintain for their customers. When it first implements an EDI system, the user, for example, a large retailer, assigns each vendor a unique account code that simultaneously identifies the supplier and authenticates the supplier's subsequent electronic transactions. Figure 2-6 depicts a VAN-based EDI system.

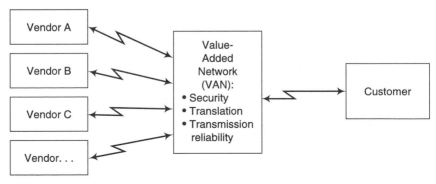

FIGURE 2-6 A VAN-based EDI system.

An alternative to VAN-based EDI is to use the Internet, which is also growing rapidly. One advantage of Internet-based EDI over VAN-based EDI is the ability to use well-understood Internet technology and a preexisting, costless network to transmit business data. This allows a company to avoid acquiring or building a private VAN. Another advantage is convenience. For example, several familiar accounting packages now support Internet modules that enable users to transmit basic accounting data electronically. (Again, as with *PeachLink* in *Peachtree Accounting*.)

PRIVACY AND SECURITY ON THE INTERNET

The most important advantage of the Internet and World Wide Web—accessibility—is also its greatest weakness—vulnerability. This means that someone who *poses* as an authorized user may be able to access any e-mail, web page, or computer file that an authorized user can access through the Internet. This section of the chapter discusses privacy and security on the Internet in detail. Chapter 10 discusses internal control and third-party assurance associated with the Internet.

Privacy

An Internet presence for companies introduces unique privacy and security concerns. Customers who shop on the web want to know that their privacy is protected. But companies doing business on the web are sometimes hard pressed not to use the wealth of data that online shoppers provide them, as illustrated by Case-in-Point 2.11.

> *Case-In-Point 2.11* Amazon.com's use of "purchase circles" upset privacy advocates. The "circles" are lists of best selling products based on the most frequent purchases of specific customer sectors such as corporations and universities. The targeted best-seller lists are sales tools for potential customers as they tell them what others in their sector are buying. After privacy advocates protested the practice, Amazon gave customers the option of declining to participate.

Most web sites accessed by online users collect personal information. What they collect and how they use it are dictated by their privacy policy. An example is the one issued by www.jcrew.com (February 13, 2001). J Crew's privacy policy states that the company may make their customer list available to a limited number of parties, but they will not share e-mail addresses with anyone who would use the addresses to send unsolicited e-mail. Shoppers are given the option of choosing or declining to receive promotional e-mails from J Crew. Finally, the policy promises that the company will not use your phone number for promotional purposes. Because businesses vary widely in the amount of privacy protection for customers, it is important to read a company's privacy policy carefully. State governments, prompted by concerns over consumer privacy rights, particularly in the financial and health care industries, are introducing a variety of privacy legislation. Groups such as The Electronic Frontier Foundation and the Online Privacy Alliance are also working to protect the privacy of data transmitted over the Internet.

Security

Security includes the policies and procedures that ensure authorized access to data and information transmitted electronically. When ordering from J Crew, shoppers interact with the company's computers in a *secure* mode as evidenced by the use of "https" as the web address versus "http." Sometimes security and privacy issues are at odds with one another as demonstrated by the "too" smart card in Case-in-Point 2.12.

> **Case-In-Point 2.12** Five years from now each US citizen may have a taxpayer's digital certificate (discussed later in the chapter) within a smart card. Citizens could use the smart card for all their transactions with the federal government. The government program responsible for developing this card is called Access Certificates for Electronics Services project, or ACES. While ACES is meant to ensure secure communications, privacy advocates are afraid that maybe the cards are *too* smart, since they contain *all* your personal information in one place. ACES does include safeguards to ensure that the data on the cards can't be used in the private sector and is available only to a federal or authorized agency but those concerned with privacy worry that the existence of the card will prove tempting for unintended uses.

Privacy and security concerns associated with the Internet and electronic commerce call for specialized controls that limit data and information access to authorized users. Firewalls, proxy servers, and data encryption (discussed in the next sections) are effective controls over access. They use filtering and authentication techniques to limit access to authorized users. **Authentication** involves verifying that users are, indeed, who they say they are.

There are three levels of authentication: (1) what you *have,* (2) what you *know,* and (3) who you *are.* What you *have* may be a plastic card that provides you physical access. Examples of these cards are your ATM debit card or a key card that provides you access to certain premises. What you *know* refers to unique information you possess, such as a password. You can authenticate who you *are* with a unique physical characteristic such as your fingerprint or the pattern of the retina in your eye. As you might guess, using security that forces a user to display a unique physical characteristic (i.e., who they are) is the highest level of authentication. Some security systems require users to make use of a combination of authentication techniques. For example, you use both your debit card and your password to withdraw cash from an ATM.

Firewalls and Proxy Servers

To gain access to a company's files, a computer hacker (an unauthorized user) must obtain access to that company's computers. Firewalls and proxy servers are designed to protect against unwarranted intrusions from external parties.

Firewalls   One way to guard against unauthorized access to sensitive file information from external Internet users is to create a **firewall** (Figure 2-7). This is security software that a company installs on Internet computers and that limits file accesses to authorized users.

Firewall software examines packets of incoming messages and ensures that they are from authorized users. To do this, the software maintains an **access control list** of bonafide IP addresses that company network administrators create for this purpose. If the software does not recognize the IP address of an external user, it refuses

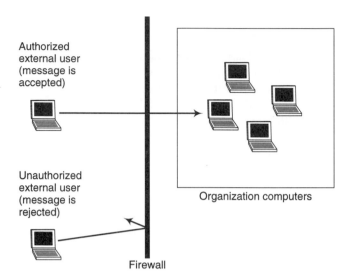

FIGURE 2-7 A firewall acts as a barrier between unauthorized external users and an organization's computers.

that user access to the files he or she requested. Although firewalls are an obvious control for commercial applications, universities commonly use the same technique to limit access to their library and research resources to authorized parties.

A firewall is a useful Internet security control but (like most security features) is not foolproof. One obvious problem is **spoofing** (i.e., masquerading as an authorized user with a recognizable IP address). A less obvious, but potentially more serious, problem is the ability of a determined hacker to copy the contents of the access control list itself. If a hacker obtains the information in this file, he or she has the ability to pose as one of many authorized users—a security breach that is especially difficult to overcome.

Proxy Servers Given the large amount of information now available on the web, some organizations seek to limit the number of sites that employees can access, for example, to ensure that employees do not use web-access privileges for frivolous or counterproductive purposes. A **proxy server** is a computer and related software that creates a transparent gateway to and from the Internet, and that can be used to control web accesses. In a typical application, the user logs onto his or her familiar file server as before. But when this user attempts to access a page on the World Wide Web, the initial network server contacts the proxy server to perform the requested Internet access.

One advantage of using a proxy server is the ability to funnel all incoming and outgoing Internet requests through a single server. This can make web access more efficient because the proxy server is specifically designed to handle requests for Internet information. A second advantage is the proxy server's ability to examine all incoming requests for information and test them for authenticity (i.e., the ability to act as a firewall). Yet a third advantage is the proxy server's ability to limit employee Internet access to approved web sites (i.e., to only those IP addresses contained in an access control list). This enables an organization to deny employees access to pornographic or game-playing web sites that are unlikely to have any productive benefits.

A fourth advantage is the ability to limit the information that is stored on the proxy server to Internet-related materials—information that the company can afford to lose. If this server fails or is compromised by hackers, the organization is only marginally inconvenienced because its main servers remain functional. To recover, the company can simply restart the system and reinitialize the server with backup data.

A final advantage of proxy servers is the ability to store frequently accessed web pages on the server's own hard disk. This enables the server to respond quickly to user requests for information because the data are already available locally. The savings in time can be considerable, for example, Netscape Communications estimates that between 30 and 60 percent of Internet requests are redundant. This feature also enables managers to obtain some idea of what information employees most need and perhaps to take steps to provide it internally (rather than through web sources).

Firewalls and proxy servers give online companies some protection from hackers, but they cannot protect against **denial of service attacks.** These attacks occur when hackers "flood" a web site with bogus traffic. Case-in-Point 2.13 describes a denial of service attack on popular web sites.

Case-in-Point 2.13   In February, 2000, hackers launched a series of denial of service attacks against several popular online companies, including Amazon, eBay, E-Trade, Buy.com, and ZDNet. In some cases, the attacks blocked access to the web sites for several hours. The attacks differed from previous denial of service attacks because they used many layers of computers to "launder" their location and they harnessed hundreds of computers in the attack. The problem with this type of security violation is that it is difficult to prevent. This particular coordinated attack highlighted the vulnerability of companies doing business online.

Data Encryption

Because so much of the information transmitted over the Internet is private or sensitive, businesses often use **data encryption** techniques to transform plaintext messages into unintelligible cyphertext ones. The transformed messages are then decoded at the receiving station back into plaintext for use. The advantage of this system is that the encrypted message cannot be understood during data transmission, even if unauthorized users intercept it.

There are many encryption techniques and standards. The simple method shown in Figure 2-8 uses a cyclic substitution of the alphabet with a displacement value of "5" to transform the letters of a plaintext message into alternate letters of the alphabet. To decode the message, the recipient's computer performs the encryption process in reverse, decrypting the coded message back into readable text. To make things more secure, the sender can use a different displacement value for each coded message.

The method that computers use to transform plaintext into cyphertext is called the **encryption key.** This is typically a mathematical function that depends on a large prime number. The **data encryption standard (DES)** system used by the U.S. government to encode documents employs such a system. DES uses a number with 56 binary digits to encode information, a value equal to approximately 72 quadrillion. Thus, to crack the code, a hacker must guess which of 72 quadrillion values was used to encrypt the message.

```
Encryption Scheme:
Letters of the alphabet:     A  B  C  D  E   F   G   H  I  J ...
Numerical equivalent:        1  2  3  4  5   6   7   8  9 10...
Plus displacement key:       5  5  5  5  5   5   5   5  5  5
New values:                  6  7  8  9 10 11 12 13 14 15
Letters to use in code:      F  G  H  I  J  K   L  M N O ...

Example:

Plaintext Message:           HI, ABE!
Cyphertext Message:          MN, FGJ!
```

FIGURE 2–8   A simple data encryption method.

The data encryption method illustrated in Figure 2-8 uses a single cryptographic key that is shared by the two communicating parties and is called **secret key cryptography.** This system derives its name from the fact that the key must be kept secret and controlled only by the parties with access to it. The most common encryption methods today use **public key encryption,** a technique that requires each party to use a pair of public/private encryption keys. Two examples are SSL (Secure Socket Layer) and S-HTTP (Secure Hypertext Transport Protocol).

To employ public key encryption, the party sending information uses his or her private key to encode the message and the receiving party uses a second private key to decode it. A major advantage of public key encryption is that the same private key cannot be used to both encode and decode a message. The sending party retains one key as a private key and uses the receiving party's public key to encode the message. The recipient uses the public key as well as a second private key to decode the message and translate it into plaintext. Data transmissions using public key encryption are likely to be secure because the transmitted message itself is scrambled and because neither of the parties knows the other's private key. This is the main reason why most web applications use the public key encryption system.

Digital Signatures

Many businesses require proof that the accounting documents they transmit or receive over the Internet are authentic. Examples include purchase orders, bids for contracts, and acceptance letters. To authenticate such documents, a company can transmit a complete document in plaintext, and then also include a portion of that same message or some other standard text in an encrypted format, that is, can include a **digital signature.**

In 1994, the National Institute of Standards and Technology adopted Federal Information Processing Standard 186—the **digital signature standard (DSS).** The presence of the digital signature authenticates a document. The reasoning is straightforward: if a company's public key decodes a message, then that company must also have created the message. Thus, some experts consider digital signatures even more secure than written signatures (which can be forged). Further, if the sender includes a complete message in both plaintext and cyphertext, the encrypted message provides assurance that no one has altered the readable copy. (If someone has altered the plaintext, the two copies will not match.)

Another authentication technique is the **digital certificate.** Digital certificates are verification of identity provided by an independent third party called a **certificate**

authority. Certificate authorities, such as Thawte and VeriSign, issue certificates to individuals and organizations. These certificates are signed documents with sender names and public key information. Certificates are generally encoded, possibly in a certificate standard such as the X.509 certificate format. Digital certificates can also be used to assure customers that a web site is real.

Digital Time Stamping

Many important business documents are time sensitive. Examples include bidding documents that must be submitted by preestablished deadlines, deposit slips that must be presented to banks before the close of business, buy orders for stock purchases that depend on the date and time of issue, and legal documents that must be filed in a timely fashion. Then, too, most businesses also want to know when particular purchases were ordered, when funds were disbursed for required expenditures, or when specific data items were entered or modified in important databases. What these items have in common is the need for a time stamp that unambiguously indicates the time of transmission, filing, or data entry.

The PGP **Digital Time Stamping Service** is one of several digital time-stamping services (DTSSs) that attaches digital time stamps to documents either for a small fee or for free. In a typical application, the user sends the document to the service's e-mail address along with the Internet address of the final recipient. When the service receives the document, it performs its time-stamping task and then forwards the document as required.

Digital time stamping performs the same task electronically that official seals and other time stamps perform manually. It authenticates the time and perhaps the place of a business transaction. This can be important over the Internet. Although most documents are transmitted almost instantaneously, time delays can occur, for example, when file servers temporarily falter or power failures disrupt wide area networks. Time stamps enable businesses to overcome these problems.

AIS AT WORK
The SEC Hosts Fake Company Web Sites

The Securities and Exchange Commission (SEC) has become concerned about investors being "scammed" by investing in companies that aren't real. The ability for anyone to develop and host a web site means that some unscrupulous parties have developed sites with fictitious information. These sites masquerade as legitimate corporate sites and include information about a fictitious company that is designed to lure site visitors to investing in the business.

To show how easy it is to fall prey to such a hoax, the SEC developed several "fake" company sites of its own. An example is the McWhortle Enterprises site at www.mcwhortle.com. McWhortle's home page describes the company as a manufacturer of biological defense mechanisms that it sells to Fortune 500 companies. As you read the page, it becomes clear that the Bio-Hazard Alert Detector is a pretty exciting and timely product. McWhortle's homepage includes links to more information, including testimonials, press releases, and an opportunity to invest. When you click on the "About Us" link, you will see a very nice picture of McWhortle's headquarters offices and you'll also learn about the company's founder, James McWhortle, III. Clicking on the "Invest Now" link takes users to a web page that explains that the Pre-IPO investment has been oversubscribed, but there are still investment opportunities remaining. A link on that page states that you should click on it when you're ready to invest in the company. Click on that link, and you pull up a web page that begins with the phrase, "If you responded to an investment idea like this ... You could get scammed!" It is only there that an unsuspecting Internet investor-wannabe will learn that the entire McWhortle site is a fraud!

The SEC hopes that its fake company examples will help to educate Internet users about the potential for fraud on the Internet. The McWhortle site contains many helpful links where users can learn more about investment scams and ways to protect themselves (e.g., a link to the SEC's brochure, "Internet Fraud: How to Avoid Investment Scams"). The site further reminds users that they should do their own research before making investments and identifies some of the giveaways that should have alerted a user that the McWhortle site promises were unlikely to be real. The use of sites, such as McWhortle by the SEC, is an interesting approach to combating some of the new risks introduced in an E-business environment.

SUMMARY

The Internet is a collection of local, wide-area, and international networks that accountants can use for communication, research, and business purposes. Most accountants also use the World Wide Web—the graphics portion of the Internet—for similar purposes. Intranets are private networks that enable employees to use web browser software and that businesses create for such internal purposes as distributing e-mail. Extranets are similar to intranets, except that they allow external parties to access internal network files and databases.

One use of the Internet is for electronic communication (i.e., transmitting text messages and perhaps graphics attachments over the Internet). Groupware is software that supports e-mail on business networks, plus allows users to share computer files, schedule appointments, and develop custom applications. Knowledge sharing enables accountants to share research and information about the best practices of their clients throughout their businesses.

To make all the financial information available on the Internet accessible, users will need a new reporting language such as XBRL. XBRL is a form of XML and provides a common format for financial data that allows searches of the data and extraction for comparison purposes.

Another important application of the Internet is electronic commerce (EC). Retail sales are booming on the Internet, as are applications of electronic data interchange (EDI). For a variety of reasons, most businesses prefer to use private value-added networks (VANs) rather than the Internet to support EDI applications. This may change, however. Business-to-business electronic commerce will be the biggest Internet application yet.

Privacy and security concerns associated with the Internet prompt many businesses to construct firewalls, use proxy servers, and employ data encryption techniques, digital signatures, and digital time stamping to achieve control objectives. One issue that is of concern over the Internet is authentication—the ability for users to prove they are who they say they are. Privacy is also an important issue. This concerns users' ability to protect data about themselves and the transactions in which they engage while buying and selling online.

KEY TERMS YOU SHOULD KNOW

access control list

authentication

certificate authority

data encryption

data encryption standard (DES)

denial of service attacks

digital certificate

digital signature

digital signature standard (DSS)

digital time stamping service

domain address

EdgarScan™

electronic commerce (EC)

electronic conferencing

Electronic Data Gathering and Retrieval
(EDGAR)

Electronic Data Interchange (EDI)

electronic mail

electronic payments (E-payments)

electronic procurement

encryption key

e-wallet

Extensible Business Reporting Language
(XBRL)

Extensible Markup Language (XML)

extranets

firewall

groupware

home page

hyperlinks

hypertext markup language (HTML)

hypertext transfer protocol (HTTP)

identify fraud

Internet

Internet protocol (IP)

Internet service provider (ISP)

intranets

knowledge sharing

proxy server

pubic key encryption

secret key cryptography

spoofing

supply chain

tags

universal resource locator (URL)

value-added networks (VSNs)

web browser

World Wide Web

DISCUSSION QUESTIONS

2-1. What is the Internet? What is an Internet domain address? What is an IP address?

2-2. What are intranets? What are extranets? Why are intranets and extranets important to accountants?

2-3. What is hypertext markup language? How does it differ from XML and XBRL?

2-4. How does e-mail work? What are some advantages of e-mail? How might the employees of a public accounting firm use e-mail?

2-5. Describe some important uses of electronic commerce. Why is EC important to accountants?

2-6. What are electronic payments? How are they different from credit card payments?

2-7. What is electronic data interchange? Why do companies use EDI?

2-8. Most retail-sales web sites require customers to use their credit cards to make purchases online. How comfortable are you in providing your credit card number in such applications? Why do you feel this way?

2-9. What are Internet firewalls and proxy servers? How are they created? How do businesses use them for Internet security?

2-10. What is data encryption? What techniques are used for data encryption?

2-11. Describe and contrast the three levels of authentication. Can you think of a business situation where someone would need to use a combination of all three levels to gain access to information?

2-12. What are digital signatures? Why do businesses use them? How can businesses use a digital certificate for Internet security?

2-13. Analysts claim that businesses can increase sales on the Internet, but not profits. What evidence does this chapter provide to support or refute this claim? Discuss.

PROBLEMS

2-14. The Internet uses many acronyms. Within the context of the present chapter, what words were used to form each of the following?

a. ISP b. URL c. IP address
d. WWW e. http f. e-mail
g. EC h. VANs i. IETF
j. EDI k. XML

2-15. Examine the data encryption technique illustrated in Figure 2-8. Use a displacement value of "8" to encrypt the following message:

"Those who ignore history are forced to repeat it."

2-16. The message below was encrypted using the technique illustrated in Figure 2-8 (using a displacement key other than 5). Using trial and error, decode it:

OZ OY TUZ CNGZ CK JUTZ QTUC ZNGZ NAXZY AY

OZ OY CNGZ CK JU QTUC ZNGZ PAYZ GOTZ YU

INTERNET EXERCISES

2-17. Visit the e-Bay (www.ebay.com) web site. How can buyers and sellers in an auction exchange their goods and money?

2-18. A number of accounting journals now publish portions of their journals or even complete issues online. Access the *Journal of Accountancy* web site at www.aicpa.org (or another web site selected by your instructor). Select an article of interest and write a one-page report on it. What are some of the advantages of publishing journal articles online?

2-19. Using your Internet browser and a search engine such as Yahoo, find a separate web site that sells each of the following products: (a) books, (b) CDs, (c) cars, (d) stocks, (e) clothing, (f) tools, and (g) airline tickets. Which product(s) would you be willing to purchase on the Internet? Which products would you prefer to purchase in a store? Provide reasons for your answers.

CASE ANALYSES

2-20. DeGraaf Office Supplies (Business Web Sites and Security)

DeGraaf Office Supplies is a national retailer of office supplies, equipment, and furnishings. The company opened its first store in 1932, in Columbus, Ohio. Currently, DeGraaf has 300 stores nationwide. Owner-managers purchase and run franchised stores. Kim DeGraaf, the founder's daughter, currently is President and CEO of the corporation.

Sales revenues grew steadily during the past decade, but 2002 sales were quite disappointing, down 8 percent from 1998. The company's stock price has also taken a big hit during the past few months. Kim resisted developing an Internet presence for the company, and it appears now that this was a mistake. Online sales of office supplies are growing rapidly, particularly in the business-to-business sector as business organizations are finding it faster and more efficient to enter their office supply orders electronically. The following is a conversation between Kim and Peter Brewer, Vice President of Marketing.

Peter: "Kim, I warned you that we were going to see sales decline if we didn't hurry up and get on the Internet. The established brick-and-mortar businesses in many industries are suffering."

Kim: "You were right, Peter. I think I've been overly concerned about security and privacy issues. I also didn't really believe that online sales in our industry would take off the way they have. I hope we're not too late, because I want to move ahead immediately in developing a web site. I know other companies have a jump start but hopefully our brand name recognition and reputation for quality will help us. I have contracted with a consulting firm to start the web site development and am going to give a press release this afternoon about our plans. Fortunately, our current enterprise software has electronic commerce features and the consultants tell me that our Internet site should be ready for business in about six months. I need you to have your staff prepare an analysis of our competitor web sites. I would also like as much information as possible related to providing retail and business customers with security and privacy over online transactions with us."

Peter: "This is great news! I will get my staff busy at once providing you and the consulting team with the information they need. There will be a lot of decisions to make. I've studied all the office supply web sites and they are organized in a variety of ways. For instance, some sites provide customers with the option to select a type of product such as ballpoint pens and then show the vendor options in that category, while other sites are organized around the vendors. This type of site allows customers to select a vendor name, such as PaperMate, and then lists all the product offerings from that vendor. Hopefully, the consultants have a lot of experience with business web sites and they can help us with many of these issues."

Requirements

1. Visit the web sites of two office supply stores on the Internet. Develop a set of four to five criteria for evaluating their web site.
2. Evaluate DeGraaf's chances for catching up to competitors in the online marketplace.
3. Discuss the privacy and security concerns for companies doing business electronically. Make recommendations to DeGraaf Office Supplies for addressing these concerns.

2-21. Small Computers, Inc. (Security on the Internet)

The following stated policies pertain to the e-commerce web site for Small Computers, Inc., a personal and handheld computer manufacturer and seller.

Privacy Statement

- We will only use information collected on this web for legitimate business purposes. We do not give away or rent any information to third parties.
- We will only contact you for legitimate business purposes, possibly from time to time, as needed. Please be 100 percent assured that we hold all transactions between you and our company in the strictest confidence.

Disclosure of Business Practices, Shipping, and Billing

- We will ship all items at the earliest possible date.
- We will not require you to accept items that you did not order.
- We will accept any returns from you of damaged or defective merchandise.
- In the event that we should accidentally bill you more than once for the same item, we will immediately issue you a refund.

Requirement

Evaluate these stated policies in terms of how well they promote customer trust and confidence in Small Computers, Inc.'s electronic business operations.

REFERENCES, RECOMMENDED READINGS, AND WEB SITES

References and Recommended Readings

Adam, N.R., O. Dogramaci, A. Gangopadhyay, and Y. Yesha, *Electronic Commerce* (Upper Saddle River, NJ: Prentice-Hall, Inc., 1999).

Anders, George, "Amazon.com's Shares Illustrate How Wild Internet Stocks Can Be," *Wall Street Journal,* vol. 139, no. 16 (July 23, 1998), pp. A1, A8.

Coffin, Zachary, "The Top 10 Effects of XBRL," *Strategic Finance,* June 2001, pp. 64–67.

Fry, J., "A Too-Smart Card?" *The Wall Street Journal Interactive Edition,* December 13, 1999.

Gillmore, Dan, "The Art of Internet Commerce: Dell Computer Corporation," *Hemispheres* (June 1998), pp. 36–41.

Glover, S.M., S.W. Liddle, and D.F. Prawitt, *E-Business Principles & Strategies for Accountants* (Upper Saddle River, NJ: Prentice-Hall, Inc., 2001).

Greenstein, M., and M. Vaserhelyi, *Electronic Commerce: Security, Risk Management and Control,* 2nd ed. (Boston: Irwin McGraw-Hill, 2001).

Helms, Glenn L., and Jane Mancino, "Electronic Auditor," *Journal of Accountancy,* vol. 185, no. 4 (April 1998), pp. 45–49.

Hof, Robert D., Gary McWilliams, and Gabrielle Saveri, "The 'Click Here' Economy," *Business Week* (June 22, 1998), pp. 122–128.

Hoffman, Charles, and Carolyn Strand, *XBRL Essentials* (New York: American Institute of Certified Public Accountants, 2001.)

Jeffery, S., "The Power of B2B E-Commerce," *Strategic Finance* (September 1999), pp. 22–26.

Judge, Paul C., "How Safe Is the Net?" *Business Week* (June 22, 1998), pp. 132–138.

Kiesnoski, K., and B. Curley, "Digital Wallets: Card Issuers Seek to Ease Web Shopping," *Bank Systems and Technology* (October 1999), pp. 26–34.

King, J., "Business-to-Business E-commerce Projections Soar," www.computerworld.com (December 21, 1999).

Kogan, Alexander, Ephraim F. Sudit, and Miklos A. Vasarhelyi, "In the Era of Electronic Commerce," *Management Accounting* (September 1997), pp. 26–30.

Koreto, Richard J., "In CPAs We Trust," *Journal of Accountancy* (December 1997), pp. 62–64.

Lawson, Richard, "Achieving 'Net' Results," *Management Accounting* (January 1998), pp. 51–54.

Lownie, Ken, and Neal Granoff, "The Pandora's Box of Groupware Costs," *Business Communications Review,* vol. 26, no. 2 (February 1996), pp. 48–52.

McConnell, Christopher P., "Lotus Notes Allows Many Practitioners to Share Documents," *Taxation for Accountants,* vol. 50, no. 5 (May 1993), pp. 314–332.

Norris, G., J.R. Hurley, K.M. Hartley, J.R. Dunleavy, and J.D. Balls, *E-business and ERP: Transforming the Enterprise* (New York: John Wiley and Sons, Inc., 2000).

Reinnhardt, Andy, "Extranets: Log On, Link Up, Save Big," *Business Week* (June 22, 1998), pp. 132–138.

Sliwa, Carol, "Net Is Not Always Best: Users Keep Value-Added Nets to Exchange Data," *Computerworld* vol. 32, no. 23 (June 8, 1998), pp. 49–50.

Sokol, Phyllis K., *From EDI to Electronic Commerce* (New York: McGraw Hill, 1995). See especially Chapter 4 ("The Biggest Payoff Applications of EDI") and Chapter 5 ("Business Issues of EDI").

Stone, William A., "Electronic Commerce: Can Internal Auditors Help to Mitigate the Risks?" *Internal Auditor* (December 1997), pp. 27–34.

Strand, C.A., B.L. McGuire, L.A. Watson, and C. Hoffman, "The XBRL Potential," *Strategic Finance,* June 2001, pp. 58–63.

Tauhert, Christy, "Process-Centric Financials (Workflow and Groupware Technologies Change Insurers' Financial Processes)," *Insurance & Technology,* vol. 22, no. 7 (July 1997), pp. 36–40.

Watson, L.A., B.L. McGuire, and E.E. Cohen, "Looking at Business Reports Through XBRL-Tinted Glasses," *Strategic Finance* (September 2000), pp. 41–45.

Wilson, T., "Accounting On E-Time—Service Synchronizes Financial, Supply Chain Data to Speed Payments," *Internetweek* (November 22, 1999), pp. PG1–PG3.

Zarowin, S., and W.E. Harding, "Finally, Business Talks the Same Language," *Journal of Accountancy* (August 2000), pp. 24–30.

Web Sites

To access EdgarScan, visit http://edgarscan.pwcglobal.com.

You can access the EDGAR database through the website of the Securities and Exchange Commission at www.sec.gov.

Two sites with resources, references, and examples for XBRL are: www.xbrl.org and www.xbrlsolutions.com

There are several web sites associated with online payment systems. Check out www.paypal.com., www.billpoint.com., and www.checkfree.com.

There are several research firms that collect and distribute data about e-commerce. Two of these are Forrester Research at www.forrester.com and Gartner Group, www.gartner.com. These companies charge for some of their research but they also publish many reports for free.

Two sites with general information about e-commerce are http://ecommerce.internet.com and http://ecommercetimes.com.

Chapter 3

Documenting Accounting Information Systems

INTRODUCTION

WHY DOCUMENTATION IS IMPORTANT

DOCUMENT AND SYSTEM FLOWCHARTS

Document Flowcharts

Guidelines for Drawing Document Flowcharts

System Flowcharts

Guidelines for Drawing System Flowcharts

DATA FLOW DIAGRAMS

Data Flow Diagram Symbols

Context Diagrams

Physical Data Flow Diagrams

Logical Data Flow Diagrams

Guidelines for Drawing Data Flow Diagrams

OTHER DOCUMENTATION TOOLS

Process Maps

Program Flowcharts

Decision Tables

Software Tools for Graphical Documentation

END-USER COMPUTING AND DOCUMENTATION

The Importance of End-User Documentation

Controls for End-User Computing and Documentation

AIS AT WORK: DOCUMENTING SYSTEMS AT HUGHES SUPPLY

SUMMARY

KEY TERMS YOU SHOULD KNOW

DISCUSSION QUESTIONS

PROBLEMS

INTERNET EXERCISES

CASE ANALYSES

Excelling at Documentation

The Berridge Company

FreezeTime, Inc.

The Dinteman Company

The Jack Edmonds Company

REFERENCES, RECOMMENDED READINGS, AND WEB SITES

After reading this chapter, you will:

1. *Understand* why documenting an AIS is important.

2. *Be able to draw* simple document flowcharts and explain how they describe the flow of data in AISs.

3. *Be able to draw* simple system flowcharts and data flow diagrams.

4. *Know* how process maps, program flowcharts, and decision tables help document AISs.

5. *Be able to explain* the importance of end-user documentation.

6. *Know* software available for documenting AISs.

A flowchart will provide a quick overview and enable you to get your arms around the whole system.

Claudia L. Campbell, "The Hired Problem Solver: Your Mission: Clean Up the Accounting Mess," *Management Accounting,* vol. 74, no. 2 (August 1992), pp. 25–29

INTRODUCTION

Documentation explains how AISs operate and is therefore a vital part of any accounting system. For example, documentation describes the tasks for recording accounting data, the procedures that users must perform to operate computer applications, the processing steps that computer systems follow, and the logical and physical flows of accounting data through the system. This chapter explains in greater detail why accountants need to understand documentation and describes some tools for creating it.

Accountants can use many different types of diagrams to trace the flow of accounting data through an AIS. For example, document flowcharts describe the physical flow of order forms, requisition slips, and similar hard-copy documents through an AIS. These flowcharts pictorially represent data paths in compact formats and therefore save pages of narrative description. System flowcharts are similar to document flowcharts, except that system flowcharts usually focus on the electronic flows of data in computerized AISs. Yet further examples of documentation aids include data flow diagrams, process maps, program flowcharts, and decision tables. This chapter describes all of these documentation aids, as well as some computerized tools for creating them.

Today, many end users develop computer applications for themselves. This end-user programming has been a boon to many companies, who consequently do not require IT professionals to develop simple word processing, spreadsheet, or database applications. But end-user programming can also be a problem because many employees do not know how to document their work properly, or are simply not required to do so. The final section of this chapter examines the topic of end-user programming and documentation in greater detail.

WHY DOCUMENTATION IS IMPORTANT

Accountants do not need to understand exactly how computers process the data of a particular accounting application, but it is important for them to understand the documentation that describes how this processing takes place. Documentation includes all the flowcharts, narratives, and other written communications that describe the inputs, processing, and outputs of an AIS. Documentation also describes the logical flow of data within a computer system and the procedures that employees must follow to accomplish application tasks. Here are seven reasons why documentation is important to AISs.

1. Depicting how the system works. Just observing large AISs in action is an impractical way to learn about them, even if they are completely manual. In computerized systems, this task is impossible because the processing is electronic and therefore invisible. On the other hand, studying written descriptions of the inputs, processing steps, and outputs of the system make the job easier, and a few graphs or diagrams of these processing functions makes things easier still. This is one purpose of documentation—to help explain how an AIS operates. Documentation helps employees understand how a system works, assists accountants in designing controls for it, and gives managers confidence that it will meet their information needs.

Case-in-Point 3.1 In August of 2001, a forensic team of two CPAs and an IT professional were sent to the government offices of a Persian Gulf sovereignty to investigate the suspected siphoning of large sums of money into foreign currencies and personal accounts. But tracing the flow of assets became a difficult task because the number of transactions was large and the flow of monies both inside and outside the country was complicated. To help, the team created a flowchart for these fund flows that enabled its members to better understand the entire process, identify existing controls that could be thwarted, and suggest how the investigation should proceed. In the end, the team found hundreds of suspect transactions that led to an out-of-court settlement.

2. Training users. Documentation also includes the user guides, procedure manuals, and similar operating instructions that help people learn how an AIS operates. Employees usually do not like to read the user manuals that typically accompany application software, but these instructional materials are invaluable reference aids when they are needed. Whether distributed manually in hard-copy format or electronically in the familiar Help files or "tours" of microcomputer applications, these documentation aids help train users to operate AIS hardware and software, solve operational problems, and perform their jobs better.

3. Designing new systems. Documentation helps system designers develop new systems in much the same way that blueprints help architects design buildings. For example, professional IT personnel commonly hold structured walkthroughs in which they review system documentation in order to ensure the integrity and completeness of their designs, and to identify design flaws. Well-written documentation, along with other systems-design methodologies, often plays a key role in reducing systems failures and decreasing the time spent correcting "emergency errors" in computer systems. Conversely, as suggested by Case-in-Point 3.2, poorly designed systems usually lead to critical mistakes and expensive writeoffs.

Case-in-Point 3.2 When it decided to spend $56 million to modernize its computer systems in 1995, FoxMeyer Drug Company was the fourth-largest pharmaceutical distributor in the country, with annual sales exceeding $5 billion. Failure to adequately plan for the new system, lack of good end-user documentation, and poor systems integration were among the many reasons why the system failed—and the company's stock plummeted from $26 per share in 1994 to $3 the next year. The company filed for bankruptcy in 1996, largely because of this system failure.

4. Controlling system development and maintenance costs. Microcomputer applications typically employ prewritten, off-the-shelf software that has been designed and developed for mass markets. For this reason, the software itself is relatively reliable and inexpensive. In contrast, custom-developed business systems often cost millions of dollars. Good documentation helps system designers develop

object-oriented software, that is, programs that contain modular, reusable code. This object-orientation helps programmers avoid writing duplicate programs and facilitates changes when programs must be modified later. If you have ever replaced a specialized part in your car, you have some idea of how frustrating, time-consuming, and expensive "nonstandardization" can be, and therefore how useful object-oriented programming might be to business organizations.

5. Standardizing communications with others. Narrative descriptions can vary significantly, depending on who writes them. Similarly, the individual reading a narrative may interpret it differently from the way it was intended. Documentation aids such as system flowcharts or data flow diagrams are standard industry tools, and they are more likely to be interpreted the same way by all parties viewing them. Thus, documentation tools are important because they help describe an existing or proposed system in a "common language" and help users communicate with one another about these systems.

> ***Case-in-Point 3.3*** KPMG Peat Markwick uses process mapping software to assist clients in evaluating and redesigning their business processes. For example, the firm's business reengineering practice recently helped a financial services company cut its costs and become more efficient. The company was able to cut in half the time it took to approve a loan—and it needed 40 percent fewer staff to do it.

6. Auditing AISs. Documentation helps depict audit trails. When investigating an AIS, for example, the auditors typically focus on internal controls. In such circumstances, documentation helps auditors determine the strengths and weaknesses of a system's controls, and therefore the scope and complexity of the audit. Similarly, the auditors will want to trace sample outputs to the original transactions that created them (e.g., tracing inventory assets back to original purchases). System documentation helps auditors perform these tasks.

7. Documenting business processes. Accounting systems automatically create a record of some business's processes because they record selected financial events as they occur. A study of these processes can lead to better systems. Thus, by mapping these processes, documentation can help managers better understand the ways in which their businesses operate.

> ***Case-in-Point 3.4*** In a parallel universe, the master accountant for the great warlord took on an apprentice. One day, the apprentice approached his mentor and asked "Master, is it always necessary to document accounting systems?"
>
> The master accountant answered "No. Such documentation is not needed by those who can feel the complete tao and beauty of such systems."
>
> The apprentice continued "Who are such people?"
>
> The master accountant responded "I do not know anyone with such abilities."

DOCUMENT AND SYSTEM FLOWCHARTS

Despite all the reasons why documentation is important, most organizations find that they document less than they should. One explanation for this deficiency is that organizations often create large computer systems under tight deadlines. In such cases, the urgency to develop "a system that works" overrides the need for "a system that is well-documented." Another reason is that most IT professionals much prefer creating systems to documenting them. Thus, many developers actively resist it, arguing that they will "get around to it later" or that documenting is a job for nonexistent assistants.

The record suggests that insufficient or deficient documentation costs organizations time and money and that good documentation is as important as the good software it describes. What tools are available to document AISs? Two examples are document flowcharts and system flowcharts.

Document Flowcharts

A **document flowchart** traces the physical flow of documents through an organization, that is, from the departments, groups, or individuals who first create them to their final dispositions. Figure 3-1 illustrates common document flowcharting symbols, and the examples below illustrate how to use them to create simple document flowcharts.

Constructing a document flowchart begins by identifying the different departments or groups that handle the documents of a particular system. The flowcharter then uses the symbols in Figure 3-1 to illustrate the document flows. Let us first examine two simple cases and then discuss some general flowcharting guidelines.

Example 1 Your boss asks you to document the paperwork involved in acquiring office supplies from your company's Central Supplies Department. Your administrative assistant explains the process as follows:

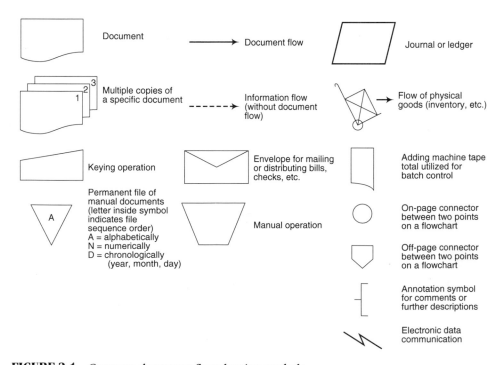

FIGURE 3-1 Common document flowcharting symbols.

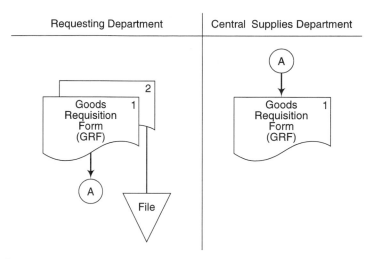

FIGURE 3-2 A simple document flowchart.

Reordering supplies requires a requisition request. When I need more sta-tionery, for example, I fill out two copies of a goods requisition form (GRF). I send the first copy to central supplies and file the second copy here in the office.

There are two departments involved in this example—your department (which we shall call the Requesting Department) and the Central Supplies Department. Thus, you should begin by naming these departments in headings on your document flowchart (Figure 3-2). Next, you draw two copies of the GRF under the heading for the Requesting Department because this is the department that creates this form. You number these copies 1 and 2 to indicate two copies.

Finally, you indicate where each document goes: copy 1 to the Central Supplies Department and copy 2 to a file in the Requesting Department. A document's first appearance should be in the department that creates it. A solid line or the on-page connectors shown here indicates its physical transmittal from one place to another. The transmitted document should then be redrawn to indicate its arrival at the de-partment that receives it. These are drawn as shown in Figure 3-2, completing your flowchart for this narrative.

Example 2 Let us now consider a slightly more complex example—the task of hir-ing a new employee at Hanley-Mott and Associates, an industrial goods supplier. The process begins when a department develops a vacancy. The Human Resources (HR) director explains the process as follows:

The department that develops a vacancy must first complete a job vacancy form, which it forwards to my department. We then advertise for the posi-tion and, with the help of the requesting department, interview applicants. When the vacancy is filled, the HR Department prepares a position hiring form (PHF) in triplicate. We file the first copy in a manual file, which is or-ganized by employee Social Security number. We staple the third copy to the job vacancy form and return it to the Requesting Department, where clerks file it alphabetically by employee last name.

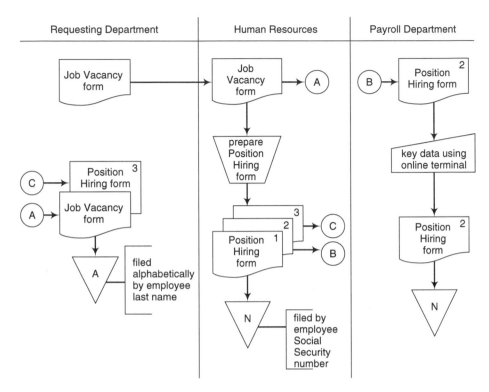

FIGURE 3-3 A document flowchart illustrating the flow of documents involved in the hiring of a new employee.

> *The HR Department forwards the second copy of the PHF to the Payroll Department. The Payroll Department uses the form as an authorization document to create a payroll record for the new employee. Thus, the information on the form is keyed directly into the company's computer system using an online terminal located in the payroll office. This copy of the PHF is then filed numerically for reference and also as evidence that the form has been processed.*

Figure 3-3 is a document flowchart for this example. To draw it, your first step is the same as before—to identify the participants. In this case there are three of them: (1) the department with the job vacancy (i.e., the Requesting Department in Figure 3-3), (2) the Human Resources Department, and (3) the Payroll Department. You thus identify each of these departments in separate columns at the top of the document flowchart.

Your next step is to identify the documents involved. There are two major ones: (1) the Job Vacancy form, which we presume is prepared as a single copy, and (2) the Position Hiring form, which we are told is prepared in triplicate. In practice, multiple-copy forms are usually color-coded. However, in document flowcharts, usually these are simply numbered and a separate page is attached to explain the color-number equivalencies.

Your third step is to indicate where the documents are created, processed, and used. This is probably the most difficult task, and a document flowchart designer must often use considerable ingenuity to represent data flows and processing activities accurately. Figure 3-3 illustrates these flows for the hiring procedures just described. Where there are a large number of document transmittals, you can use on-page connectors (circles) to connect document flows from one place on a page to another and avoid complicated flow lines. Thus, Figure 3-3 uses several on-page connectors (with letters A, B, and C) to avoid cluttering the drawing and shows the completed document flowchart. You should use a unique identifier in each connector (such as a letter) for identification purposes. You can also use off-page connectors (to connect data flows to other pages) if necessary.

Guidelines for Drawing Document Flowcharts

Document flowcharts concentrate on the physical flow of reports and similar documents. When constructing them, some analysts also include any movement of physical goods in their document flowcharts—e.g., moving inventory from a receiving department to an inventory storeroom. (Document flowcharts typically use hand-truck symbols for this task.) Some document flowcharts also illustrate information flows that do not involve documents (for example, a sales clerk telephoning to check a customer's account balance before approving a credit sale). Thus, the term "document" broadly includes all types of organizational communications and data flows.

Unlike other types of symbols—for example, the system and program flowcharting symbols discussed later in this chapter—document flowcharting symbols are not standardized. But even though creating document flowcharts is more an art than a science, you can follow certain guidelines to make these flowcharts clearer. Among them are the following:

1. Identify all the departments that create or receive the documents involved in the system.
2. Carefully classify the documents and activities of each department, and draw them under their corresponding department headings.
3. Identify each copy of an accounting document with a number. If multiple-copy documents are color-coded, use a table to identify the number-color associations.
4. Account for the distribution of each copy of a document. In general, it is better to overdocument a complicated process than to underdocument it.
5. Use on-page and off-page connectors to avoid diagrams with lines that cross one another.
6. Each pair of connectors (a "from" and a "to" connector in each pair) should use the same letter or number.
7. Use annotations if necessary to explain activities or symbols that may be unclear. These are little notes to the reader that help clarify your documentation.
8. If the sequence of records in a file is important, include the letter "A" for alphabetical, "N" for numeric, or "C" for chronological in the file symbol. As indicated in guideline 7, you can also include a note in the flowchart to make things clearer.
9. Most employees reference forms with acronyms (e.g., GRF or PHF in the preceding examples). To avoid confusion, use full names (possibly with acronyms in parentheses) or create a table of equivalents to ensure accuracy in identifying such forms.
10. Consider using automated flowcharting tools. See the section of this chapter on CASE tools and also the chapter's AIS-At-Work feature for examples.

Case-in-Point 3.5 Accountants disagree about the usefulness of document flowcharts relative to other documenting tools, but one manuscript reviewer of this book wrote: "Flowcharting is one of the most essential skills, in my opinion, for a student to learn in a systems course. During my tenure at a CPA firm, I had the opportunity to document several accounting information systems and document flowcharting was the key skill. When word got around the office that I was a good flowcharter, I got placed on more important clients, furthering my career."

System Flowcharts

Whereas document flowcharts focus on tangible documents, **system flowcharts** concentrate on the computerized data flows of AISs. Thus, a system flowchart typically depicts the electronic flow of data and processing steps in an AIS. Figure 3-4 illustrates some common system flowcharting symbols. Most of these symbols are industry conventions that have been standardized by the National Bureau of Standards (Standard ×3.5), although additional symbols are now necessary to represent newer data transmission technologies—for example, fax and Internet data flows.

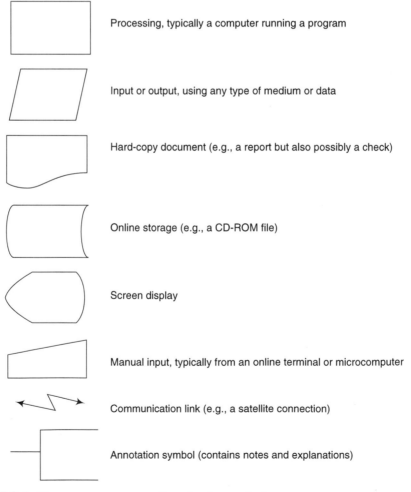

FIGURE 3-4 Some common system flowcharting symbols.

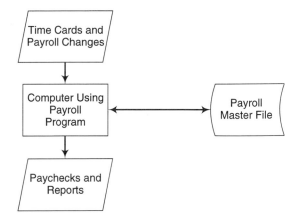

FIGURE 3-5 A high-level system flowchart for payroll processing.

Some system flowcharts are general in nature and merely provide an overview of the system. These are high-level system flowcharts. Figure 3-5 is an example. The inputs and outputs of the system are specified by the general input and output symbol, a parallelogram. In more detailed system flowcharts, the specific form of these inputs and outputs would be indicated—for example, by magnetic disk symbols.

Figure 3-5 refers to only one process—preparing a payroll. A more detailed system flowchart would describe all the processes performed by the payroll program and the specific inputs and outputs of each process. At the lowest, most-detailed level of such documentation are program flowcharts that describe the processing logic of each application program. Program flowcharts are described in the next section.

Like document flowcharts, the process of drawing system flowcharts is probably best understood by studying an illustration. Figure 3-6 is a system flowchart for the following example.

The Sarah Stanton Company is a magazine distributor that maintains a file of magazine subscribers for creating monthly mailing labels. Magazine subscribers mail change-of-address forms or new-subscription forms directly to the company, where input personnel key the information into the system through online terminals. The computer system temporarily stores this information as a file of address-change or new-subscription requests. Clerical staff keys this data into computer files continuously, so we may characterize it as "daily processing."

Once a week, the system uses the information in the daily processing file to update the subscriber master file. At this time, new subscriber names and addresses are added to the file, and the addresses of existing subscribers who have moved are changed. The system also prepares a Master File Maintenance Processing Report to indicate what additions and modifications were made to the file. Once a month, the company prepares postal labels for the magazine's mailing. The subscriber master file serves as the chief input for this computer program. The two major outputs are the labels themselves and a Mailing Labels Processing Report that documents this run and indicates any problems.

The system flowchart in Figure 3-6 documents the flow of data through the company's computerized system. Thus, it identifies sources of data, the places where

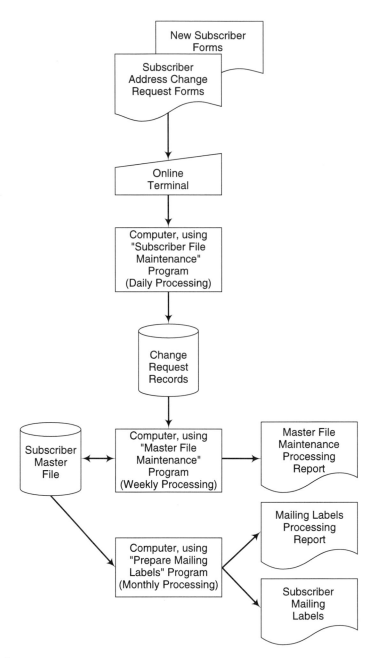

FIGURE 3-6 A system flowchart illustrating the computer steps involved in maintaining a subscriber master file and creating monthly mailing labels.

data are temporarily stored, and the outputs on which processed data appear. In Figure 3-6, for example, the system flowchart begins with the subscriber request forms and documents the flow of data on these forms through the keying phase, master-file-maintenance phase, and finally, the monthly mailing phase.

Indirectly, system flowcharts also indicate processing cycles (daily, weekly, or monthly), hardware needs (e.g., disk drives and printers), and potential bottlenecks in processing (e.g., manual keying). In Figure 3-6, we can also identify the major files of the system (a temporary log file of change-request records and a subscriber master file) and the major reports of the system. Finally, note that each processing phase of a system flowchart usually involves preparing one or more control reports. These reports provide processing-control information (e.g., counts of transactions processed) for control purposes and exceptions information (e.g., the identity of unprocessed transactions) that helps employees correct the errors detected by the system.

Guidelines for Drawing System Flowcharts

System flowcharts depict an electronic **job stream** of data through the various processing phases of an AIS and therefore also illustrate audit trails. Each time the records of a file are sorted or updated, for example, a system flowchart should show this in a separate processing step. Generally speaking, this is the way processing proceeds in almost all AISs, one step at a time, and is therefore the way system flowcharts must portray processing phases. In recognizing the usefulness of system flowcharts, both the American Institute of Certified Public Accountants (AICPA) and the Institute of Management Accountants (IMA) consistently include test questions in their professional examinations that require a working knowledge of system flowcharts.

Although no strict rules govern exactly how to construct a system flowchart, the following list provides some guidelines.

1. System flowcharts should read from top to bottom and from left to right. In drawing or reading such flowcharts, you should begin in the upper-left corner.
2. Because system flowcharting symbols are standardized, you should use these symbols when drawing your flowcharts—do not make up your own.
3. A processing symbol should always be found between an input symbol and an output symbol. This is called the **sandwich rule.**
4. Use on-page and off-page connectors to avoid crossed lines and cluttered flowcharts.
5. Sketch a flowchart before designing the final draft. Graphical documentation software tools (discussed shortly) make this job easier.
6. Add descriptions and comments in flowcharts to clarify processing elements. You can place these inside the processing symbols themselves, include them in annotation symbols attached to process or file symbols, or add them as separate notes on your systems documentation.

DATA FLOW DIAGRAMS

Like system flowcharts, **data flow diagrams (DFDs)** document the flow of data through an AIS. They are used primarily in the systems development process—for example, as a tool for analyzing an existing system or as a planning aid for creating a new system. Because documented data flows are important for understanding an AIS, many of the remaining chapters of this book use DFDs to illustrate the flow of data in the AISs under discussion.

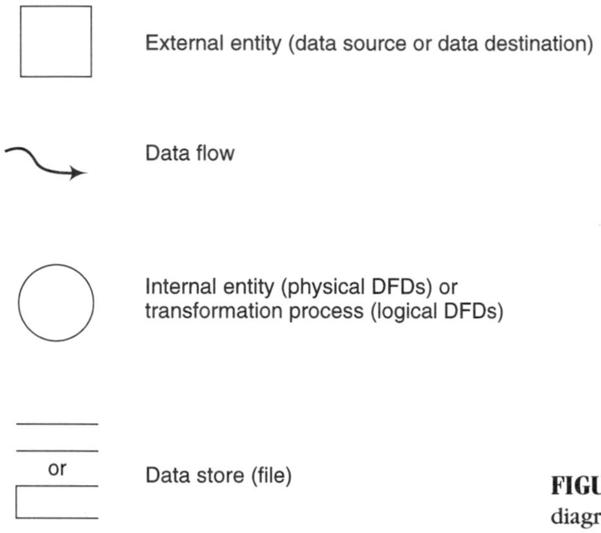

External entity (data source or data destination)

Data flow

Internal entity (physical DFDs) or
transformation process (logical DFDs)

or   Data store (file)

FIGURE 3-7   Symbols for data flow diagrams.

Data Flow Diagram Symbols

Figure 3-7 illustrates the four basic symbols used in DFDs. A rectangle or square represents an external data source or data destination—for example, a customer. To show this, a DFD would include the word "customer" inside a data source or destination symbol. In Figure 3-7, the term "external entity" means "an entity outside the system under study," not necessarily an entity that is external to the company. Thus, for example, a "customer" might be another division of the same company under study.

Data flow lines are lines with arrows that indicate the direction of data flow. Thus, data flow lines indicate the paths that data follow into, out of, or through the system under study. For this reason, every data source symbol will have one or more data flow lines leading away from it, and every data destination symbol will have one or more data flow lines leading into it. For clarity, each data flow line should be labeled to indicate exactly what data are flowing along it.

A circle or "bubble" in a DFD indicates a system entity or process that changes or transforms data. (Some authors prefer to use squares with rounded corners for this symbol.) In physical DFDs (discussed shortly), the label inside a bubble typically contains the title of the person performing a task—for example, "cashier." In logical DFDs (also discussed shortly), the label inside the bubble describes a transformation process—for example, "process cash receipts."

Finally, DFDs use a set of parallel lines or an open rectangle to represent a store or repository of data. This is usually a file of some sort. If data are permanently stored, a data store symbol is mandatory. If data are collected over time and stored in some temporary place, you are not required to use a file symbol for this (although experts recommend including one for clarity).

Context Diagrams

As with system flowcharts, DFDs are typically drawn in levels that show increasing amounts of detail. Designers typically first prepare a high-level DFD called a **context**

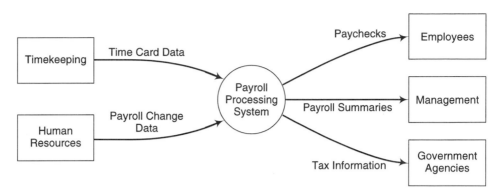

FIGURE 3-8   A context diagram for a payroll processing system.

diagram to provide an overall picture of an application or system. Figure 3-8 is an example of a context diagram for the payroll processing of Figure 3-5.

The DFD in Figure 3-8 shows the inputs and outputs of the application (payroll processing) as well as the data sources and destinations external to the application. Thus, this context diagram uses rectangles to identify "Timekeeping" and "Human Resources" as external entities, despite the fact that these departments are internal to the company. This is because these entities are external to the payroll processing system under study. The data flow lines connecting these entities to and from the system (e.g., time card data) are called system interfaces.

Physical Data Flow Diagrams

A context diagram shows very little detail. For this reason, system designers usually elaborate on the elements in context DFDs by exploding or **decomposing** them into successively more detailed levels. These subsequent DFDs show more particulars, such as the detailed processes of the application and the inputs and outputs associated with each processing step.

The first level of detail is commonly called a **physical data flow diagram.** Figure 3-9 is an example for our payroll illustration. A physical DFD closely resembles the document flowcharts discussed earlier in this chapter; that is, it focuses on physical entities such as the employees involved in the system under study, as well as the tangible documents, reports, and similar hard-copy inputs and outputs that flow through the system. Thus, for example, the bubbles in the physical DFD of Figure 3-9 identify the data-entry clerk who enters payroll information into the computer, the payroll cashier who distributes paychecks to employees, and the tax accountant who sends tax information to the Internal Revenue Service of the federal government.

Figure 3-9 illustrates several important characteristics of physical DFDs. First, we observe that each bubble contains a number as well as a title. Including a number in each bubble makes it easier to reference it later. This also assists designers in the decomposition tasks discussed shortly. Second, we notice that a physical DFD includes the same inputs and outputs as its predecessor context diagram in Figure 3-8—that is, the context DFD and the physical DFD are balanced. This **balancing** is important because unbalanced DFDs are inconsistent and therefore probably contain errors. Third, we find that all the bubbles in the physical DFD contain the

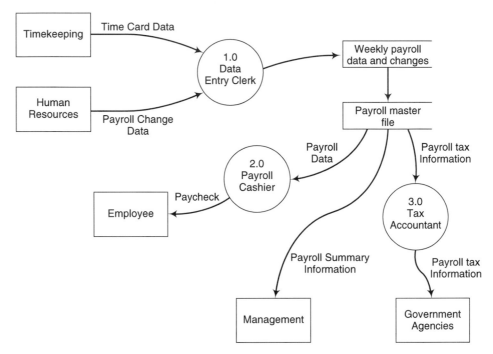

FIGURE 3-9 A physical data flow diagram.

names of system entities (i.e., the titles of employees). These titles should correspond to the titles in an official organization chart.

Finally, we see that a physical DFD lists the job title of only one typical employee in an entity symbol, despite the fact that several employees may perform the same task—for example, several data-entry clerks or payroll cashiers. This last characteristic also applies when several employees perform the same task at different locations—for example, a company has several payroll cashiers who distribute paychecks at each of its manufacturing facilities. This keeps the DFD simple, more readable, and therefore more easily understood.

Logical Data Flow Diagrams

A physical DFD illustrates which internal and external entities participate in a given system but does not give the reader a good idea of what these participants do. For this task, we need one or more **logical data flow diagrams** that address this requirement.

An Example Figure 3-10 provides an example of a logical DFD for the payroll illustration in Figure 3-9. In our new, logical DFD, note that each bubble no longer contains the name of a system entity, but rather, contains a verb that indicates a task the system performs. For example, instead of a single bubble with the title "data-entry clerk," as shown in Figure 3-9, the logical DFD in Figure 3-10 shows two bubbles with the titles "process employee hours worked" and "process payroll change data"—because these are separate data processing tasks such clerks perform.

From the standpoint of good system design and control, describing system processes is important because how a system performs its tasks is often more

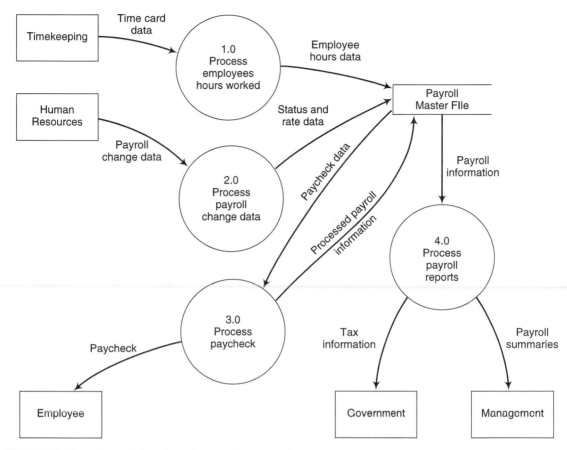

FIGURE 3-10 A logical data flow diagram for a payroll processing system.

important than what tasks it performs. For example, all payroll systems prepare paychecks, but not all payroll systems do this exactly the same way. The differences may require different hardware, software, procedures, or controls. Logical DFDs help designers decide what system resources to acquire, what activities employees must perform to run these systems, and how to protect and control these systems after they are installed.

Decomposition Figure 3-10 is often described as a **level 0 data flow diagram** because it shows only in broad terms what tasks a system performs. Most systems are more complex than this and therefore require more detail to describe them completely. The task of creating such detail is called **decomposition,** which becomes necessary because DFD designers try to limit each level diagram to between five and seven processing symbols (bubbles).

Figure 3-11 shows an example of a **level 1 data flow diagram**—an "explosion" of symbol 3.0 (in Figure 3-10) with caption "process paycheck." Here, we see that "processing paychecks" entails computing gross pay, determining payroll deductions, and calculating net pay. If necessary, you can also show ancillary computer files at this level.

To fully document the system, you would continue to perform these decomposition tasks in still further DFDs. For example, you might decompose the procedure

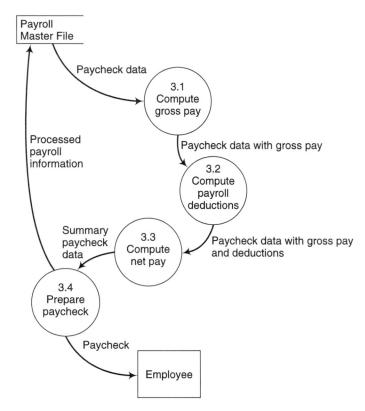

FIGURE 3-11   An exploded view of the "process paycheck" bubble of Figure 3-10.

"compute payroll deductions" in bubble 3.2 of Figure 3-11 into several additional processes in lower-level DFDs—for example, separate DFDs for "compute medical deductions," "compute savings plan deductions," "compute tax deductions," and so forth. In this way, a set of DFDs become linked together in a hierarchy.

Guidelines for Drawing Data Flow Diagrams

Data flow diagrams use fewer symbols than system flowcharts and to some people are therefore easier to prepare and understand. Many companies use both types of documentation, with the choice often hinging on the preference of the designer. But like creating other types of system documentation, creating DFDs is as much art as science. The following rules can help you design them better, make them clearer, and assist you in avoiding simple errors.

1. Avoid detail in high-level DFDs (i.e., in levels 0 and 1). Where appropriate, combine activities that are performed at the same place or same time or that are logically related.

2. As a general rule, each logical DFD should contain between five and seven processing bubbles. This guideline helps keep things simple and, again, helps you avoid showing too much detail in high-level DFDs.

3. Different data flows should have different names. This avoids confusion about what data are flowing where.

4. Unless they are outside the system or used for archiving, all data stores should have data flows both into them and out of them. Thus, an internal file symbol that lacks both of these data flow lines is usually in error.

5. Even if a file is temporary, it is usually desirable to include it in a DFD.

6. Classify most of the final recipients of system information as external entities.

7. Classify all personnel or departments that process the data of the current system as internal entities.

8. Display only normal processing routines in high-level DFDs. Avoid showing error routines or similar exception tasks in them.

9. Where several system entities perform the same task, show only one to represent them all. This rule also applies when system personnel perform the same task at different locations of the organization—for example, at different plants.

OTHER DOCUMENTATION TOOLS

There are many other tools for documenting AISs besides document flowcharts, system flowcharts, and data flow diagrams. Three of them are (1) process maps, (2) program flowcharts, and (3) decision tables. Because these tools are used mostly by consultants and computer professionals rather than accountants, we will describe them only briefly. Accountants should have some familiarity with these tools, however, because they may see them—for example, when reviewing the design for a revised accounting system.

Process Maps

A *business process* is a natural grouping of business activities that create value for an organization. A **process map** documents such a process, and uses rectangles and arrows as its primary symbols (Figure 3-12). Each rectangle represents either a process or an activity, depending on the map level. For example, a major process in most business organizations is the sales or order fulfillment process. A process map for the entire business would show this process in a rectangle, along with other processes.

Within the sales process, there may be various activities, such as the customer placing an order, warehouse personnel picking goods, or clerks shipping goods. A more detailed process map can indicate each of these activities with a rectangle, using arrows to indicate relationships among the activities. Successively more detailed process maps can show each step within activities. Figure 3-12 shows a process map for an order fulfillment operation.

Internal and external auditors can use process maps to help them learn how a department or division operates, to assist them in documenting what they have learned, and to help them identify internal control weaknesses or problems in existing operations. An additional benefit is to use such maps as training aids.

Case-in-Point 3.6 At Farmer's Insurance, internal auditors are now using process maps to help them audit approximately 80 percent of the company's branches each year. The auditors

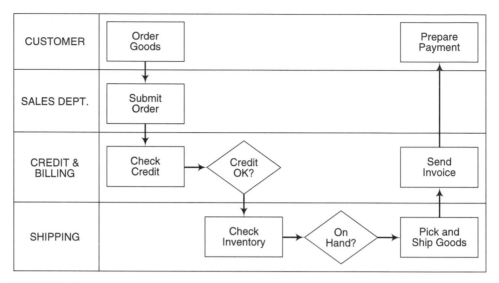

FIGURE 3-12 A process map for the order fulfillment process (created with *Microsoft Word*).

report that the maps not only help them define the scope and intensity of each audit engagement, but also facilitate discussions about their work with the branch managers. One such manager was so enthusiastic about process maps that he described them as the most useful documents he had ever received from the auditing department. He is now also using them as training tools to help new employees learn about branch operations.

Consultants frequently use process maps to help them study business processes and redesign them for greater productivity. Accountants and managers can also use this tool to help them describe current processes to others, as the following Case-in-Point demonstrates.

Case-in-Point 3.7 A system analyst at Mobil Oil Corporation found that he could make good use of process maps he had constructed with Visio software to explain his projects to top management. He condensed 30 pages of text into process maps and graphs to describe the complex processes in the projects. Mobil Oil adopted Visio because employees can easily learn and use it.

Program Flowcharts

Because large computer programs today involve millions of instructions, they require careful planning and the coordinated work of hundreds of systems analysts and programmers. Typically, organizations use **structured programming** techniques to create these large programs in a hierarchical fashion, that is, from the top down. This means that the developers design the main routines first and then design subroutines for subsidiary processing as major processing tasks become clear.

To help them plan the logic for each processing routine, IT professionals often create one or more **program flowcharts** (Figure 3-13). Program flowcharts outline the processing logic for each part of a computer program and indicate the order in which processing steps take place. After designing such program flowcharts, the developer typically presents them to colleagues in a **structured walkthrough** or formal review

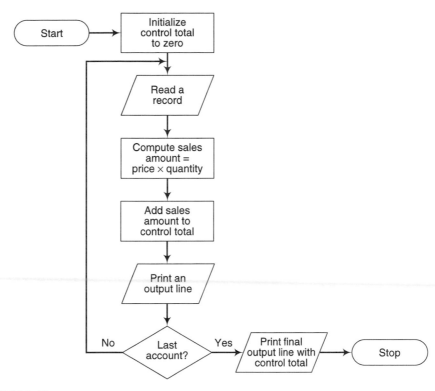

FIGURE 3-13 A program flowchart for a sales application.

of the logic. This process helps the reviewers assess the soundness of the logic, detect and correct design flaws, and make improvements. Upon approval, the program flowchart then becomes a "blueprint" for writing the instructions of the computer program itself and of course serves to document the program as well.

Program flowcharts use many of the same symbols as system flowcharts (refer back to Figure 3-4). A few specialized symbols for program flowcharts are the diamond symbol (which indicates a decision point in the processing logic) and the oval symbol (which indicates a starting or stopping point).

Like system flowcharts and data flow diagrams, program flowcharts can be designed at different levels of detail. The highest-level program flowchart is sometimes called a **macro program flowchart** and provides an overview of the data processing logic. A lower-level program flowchart would indicate the detailed programming logic necessary to carry out a processing task. Figure 3-13 is a detailed (lower-level) program flowchart for a sales report application.

Decision Tables

When a computer program involves a large number of conditions and subsequent courses of action, its program flowchart tends to be large and complex. A **decision table** (Figure 3-14) is a table of conditions and processing tasks that indicates what action to take for each possibility. Sometimes, decision tables are used as an alternative to program flowcharts. More commonly, they are used in addition to these flowcharts. To illustrate decision tables, consider the following scenario:

		Rules			
		1	2	3	4
	Conditions				
Condition stub	Account balance less than $5	Y	N	N	N	Condition entries
	Account balance less than $1,000	*	Y	*	N	
	Account 1 year old or less	*	*	Y	N	
	Actions				
Action stub	Pay no interest	X				Action entries
	Pay 5 percent interest		X	X		
	Pay 5.5 percent interest				X	

FIGURE 3-14   This is a decision table to help a credit union decide how much interest to pay each account. An asterisk (*) means that the condition does not affect the course of action.

A credit union pays interest to its depositors at the rate of 5 percent per year. Accounts of less than $5 are not paid interest. Accounts of $1,000 or more that have been with the union for more than one year get paid the normal 5 percent, plus a bonus of .5 percent.

Figure 3-14 illustrates a decision table to help the credit union decide how much interest to pay each account. Note that the decision table consists of four parts: (1) the condition stub outlines the potential conditions of the application, (2) the action stub outlines the available actions that can be taken, (3) the condition entries depict the possible combinations of conditions likely to occur, and (4) the action entries outline the action to be taken for each combination of conditions.

The rules at the top of the decision table set forth the combination of conditions that may occur and the action entries show what to do for each of them. For the illustration at hand, three conditions affect the data processing of each account: (1) an account balance less than $5, (2) an account balance less than $1,000, and (3) an account one year old or less. As defined, each of these conditions can now be answered "yes" or "no." Figure 3-14 is a decision table for the illustration at hand, in which Y stands for "yes" and N stands for "no." The combination of Ys and Ns in each column of the table illustrates each possible condition the system might encounter. Using Xs, the decision table also shows what course of action should be taken for each condition (i.e., how much interest should be paid to each account).

The major advantage of decision tables is that they summarize the processing tasks for a large number of conditions in a compact, easily understood format. This increases program understanding, resulting in fewer omissions of important processing possibilities. Decision tables also serve as useful documentation aids when new data processing conditions arise or when changes in organizational policy result in new actions for existing conditions. This advantage is particularly important to AISs because of organizational concern for accuracy and completeness in processing financial data.

One drawback of decision tables is that they do not show the order in which a program tests data conditions or takes processing actions, as do program flowcharts. This is a major deficiency because the order in which accounting data are tested or processed is often as important as the tests or processing themselves. A second drawback is that decision tables require an understanding of documentation techniques beyond flowcharting. Finally, decision tables require extra work to prepare, and this work may not be cost effective if program flowcharts must be prepared anyway.

Software Tools for Graphical Documentation

Accountants, consultants, and system developers can use a variety of software tools to create **graphical documentation** of existing or proposed AISs. The simplest tools include presentation software, such as Microsoft PowerPoint, as well as word processing and spreadsheet software such as Microsoft Word and Excel. The advantages of using such tools closely parallel those of using word processing software instead of typewriters (e.g., easily revised documents, advanced formatting capabilities and coloring options, and a variety of reproduction capabilities). For example, the authors used Microsoft Word to create the process map shown in Figure 3-12.

Microsoft Word and Excel   Using the "AutoShapes" option in the Drawing Toolbar of Microsoft Excel or Word, you can reproduce most of the flowcharting and graphics symbols presented in this chapter, as well as create connector symbols with which to connect symbols to each other. (The connectors in Excel are different from, as well as better than, simple lines because they adjust automatically when you reposition symbols in your charts.) Two additional advantages of using Excel over Word to create graphical documentation are the ability to create large drawings (that exceed the margins of word-processing documents) and the option to embed computed values in flowcharting symbols. Case 3-24 at the end of the chapter describes how to use Excel to create such graphical documentation.

CASE Tools   The capabilities of specialized graphical documentation software exceed those of word-processing or spreadsheet packages. These **CASE tools** (an acronym for computer-assisted software engineering) automate such documentation tasks as drawing or modifying flowcharts, drawing graphics and screen designs, developing reports, and even generating code from documentation. Thus, CASE tools are to flowcharts what word processors are to text documents. Figure 3-15 is an example of a CASE package in use—drawing a data flow diagram.

Most CASE products run on personal computers. Examples include iGrafx (Micrografx, Inc.), allCLEAR (SPSS, Inc.), SmartDraw (SmartDraw Software, Inc.), and Visio (Microsoft Corp.). These products are especially popular with auditors and consultants, who use them to document AISs using the techniques discussed above, as well as to analyze the results (see the AIS At Work feature at the end of this chapter). Graphical documentation software enables its users to create a wide array of outputs, including data flow diagrams, entity-relationship diagrams (described in Chapter 7), system flowcharts, program flowcharts, process maps, and even computer network designs.

More complex CASE products enable their users to do even more. Examples include Application Factory (Cortex Corporation), Excelerator II (Intersolv), and Pacbase (CGI Systems, Inc.). These CASE tools enable system designers to create process models, data-entry screens, report formats, menu screens, structure charts, and customized user interfaces. Most CASE packages also include modules for creating data dictionaries and word processors for creating written documentation. Top-end packages include project management modules, support client/server applications, encourage object-oriented programming, and provide visual tools for workflow analyses and process redesigns.

Front-end CASE tools focus on the early ("front end") tasks of systems design— for example, requirements-design activities. *Backend CASE tools* automate the detailed design tasks required in the later stages of a project—for example, developing

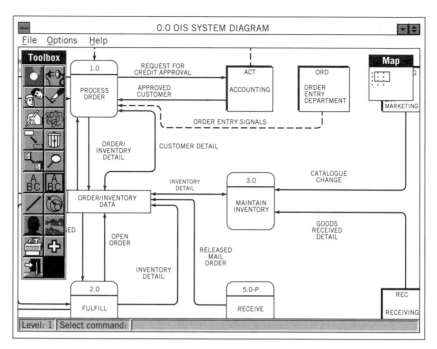

FIGURE 3-15   This CASE tool is a software program called *Excelerator*™ which is used here to create a data flow diagram. The toolbox on the left contains symbols that the user can select for his or her diagram.

detailed program flowcharts. Integrated CASE (I-CASE) packages enable users to perform both types of tasks and perhaps even generate computer code directly from logic diagrams. As a result, these tools help support **rapid application development (RAD)** and help organizations save money, as illustrated in Case-in-Point 3.8:

> ***Case-in-Point 3.8***   The Du Pont Corporation decided to use Application Factory to help it design some of its computer systems. The company was able to design a computer system for nylon stretch-wrap production at a cost of $30,000, instead of its original estimate of $268,000.

Graphical documentation software tools enable their users to generate documentation quickly and consistently, as well as to automate modifications to this documentation later as changes are required. They include templates and models that allow users to document almost any business and system environment. But these packages only create what they are told to create. Like word processors, they lack imagination and creativity, and they also require training to use them efficiently.

END-USER COMPUTING AND DOCUMENTATION

End-user computing refers to the ability of non-IT employees to create computer applications of their own. Today, we naturally take much of this "computing" for granted—for example, when employees manipulate data with word processing, spreadsheet, database management systems, or tax packages—because all of these programs were developed expressly so that end users can develop software applications for themselves.

The Importance of End-User Documentation

End-user applications often require substantial resources or perform mission-critical functions for busy organizations. Thus, end-user applications must be documented for many of the same reasons that professional applications must be documented. One rationale for this is that end users require complete, easy-to-follow training manuals, tutorials, and reference guides to help them use computer software and perform application tasks. New software always seems to place us at the "low end of the curve" (i.e., in unfamiliar territory), thus making documentation important for learning how to accomplish things or undo mistakes.

Documentation is also important when end users develop their own applications (for example, spreadsheet models or database applications). This self-development places the responsibility for documenting these applications on the same employees who created them. Unfortunately, this documentation task is often overlooked or is performed so poorly that it might as well be overlooked. Such oversight can be costly. For example, time is wasted when other employees must alter the system but lack the basic documentation to accomplish this task. Thus, even if the developer is the only one in the office who uses a particular application, managers should insist that he or she document it—for example, in case of sickness or dismissal.

The specific items that should be used to document any particular end-user application will, of course, vary with the application. For example, businesses often find it convenient to use systematic file names to identify word processing documents and to embed these file names within the reports to help others find them later. Figure 3-16 provides a few basic ideas for documenting spreadsheet applications.

---

1. Name of the developer.
2. Name of the file where the application is stored.
3. Name of the directories and subdirectories where the application is stored.
4. Date the application was first developed.
5. Date the application was last modified, and the name of the person who modified it.
6. Date the application was last run.
7. Name and phone number of person to call in case of problems.
8. Sources of external data used by the system.
9. Important assumptions made in the application.
10. Important parameters that must be modified in order to change assumptions or answer "What-if" questions.
11. Range names used in the application and their locations in the spreadsheet.

FIGURE 3-16 Examples of information to include when documenting spreadsheets.

Controls for End-User Computing and Documentation

Besides finding that some applications are poorly documented, organizations sometimes also discover that the end-user applications of one department duplicate those of another. Then, too, a lack of corporate-wide documentation standards can penalize both the developer and the organization in the long run. Finally, many firms find that end-user applications are not well-tested and that internal controls are either weak or nonexistent. To avoid such problems, businesses should establish and follow the guidelines outlined here to control end-user applications development:

1. *Formally evaluate large projects.* Employees should be allowed to create a large application only after it has withstood the scrutiny of a formal review of its costs and benefits. The larger the project, the higher the level of management that should be involved in the go-ahead decision.

2. *Adopt formal end-user development policies.* Employees usually do not develop poor applications because they wish to do so but because no organizational policies exist that restrict them from doing so. Policy guidelines should include procedures for testing software, examining internal controls, and periodically auditing systems.

3. *Formalize documentation standards.* At this point in the chapter, the importance of formal documentation should be self-evident. What may be less obvious is the need to create procedures for ensuring that these documentation standards are met.

4. *Limit the number of employees authorized to create end-user applications.* This restricts applications development to those employees in whom management has confidence, or perhaps who have taken formal development classes.

5. *Audit new and existing systems.* The more critical an end-user system is to the functioning of a department or division, the more important it is for organizations to require formal audits of such systems for compliance with the guidelines outlined previously.

Case-in-Point 3.9 In a parallel universe, the apprentice had yet another question for the master accountant. "Master," he said, "I now understand why documenting end-user applications is so important. Is it not correct, therefore, that all companies require such documentation?"

The master accountant shifted his weight a little and cleared his throat. "The lesson is over for today," he said.

 ### AIS AT WORK
Documenting Systems at Hughes Supply

Hughes Supply is a $1.5 billion wholesaler of industrial items, including plumbing, electrical, building materials, pipes, valve fittings, and heating and air-conditioning units. The entire internal audit department at Hughes uses allCLEAR, a flowcharting program, to display processes, identify control points, and analyze organizational efficiency. "We use allCLEAR to help determine department procedures and operations. After that, we use it to verify control points and to recommend improvements in a process," says Cowell, a senior internal auditor. The auditing department uses the following five-step process to help it perform more efficient audits:

1. The auditor interviews colleagues about the processes they follow.
2. The auditor details the process in a flowchart.
3. Staff personnel review the flowchart to ensure it correctly reflects their processes.
4. The auditor reviews redundancies, control points, and approval points to determine internal audit issues to address, review work to do, source documents to examine, and what sample sizes to collect.
5. The auditor presents his or her findings and recommendations, including the flowcharts, to management.

Auditors find allCLEAR easy to use. "It's packed full of user-friendly information like templates, shapes, sizes and colors, and it walks you through the process. I like the ease of writing it out in script and having allCLEAR draw the chart for me. With allCLEAR, I can make adjustments to the flowchart and it's done, letting me quickly do a flowchart and move on to my job duties," says Cowell.

Depending on the auditor's style, the auditors either type the information into a flowchart as they conduct an interview, or they just take notes and type it into the flowchart later. They can also choose between the outlining or drag-and-drop features. Cowell says they take advantage of the many shapes in allCLEAR to help colleagues identify processes easier. For example, they use a computer monitor shape to symbolize where someone enters data or a document shape to indicate documents. They also use clip art to make the chart look less intimidating and give it more variety. Cowell notes the average flowchart takes only 15 to 20 minutes to create from start to finish. During audit reviews, allCLEAR also enables its users to make changes in just a couple of minutes. The internal auditing department has been so pleased with allCLEAR's ease of use and completeness that they have begun sharing allCLEAR with other departments, beginning with the information systems department.

Source: SPSS Corporation. Used with permission.

SUMMARY

Seven reasons to document an AIS are: (1) to explain how the system works, (2) to train others, (3) to help developers design new systems, (4) to control system development and maintenance costs, (5) to standardize communications among system designers, (6) to provide information to auditors, and (7) to document a business's processes. Although written narratives can be used to document an AIS, several graphical tools are available that are usually more efficient. A document flowchart describes the physical flow of documents through an AIS, for example, by providing an overview of where documents are created, what departments receive and review them, what activities they trigger, and where these documents are stored.

Two other types of documentation tools are system flowcharts and data flow diagrams. A system flowchart describes the electronic flow of data through an AIS, indicates what processing steps and files are used and when, and provides an overview of the entire system. Data flow diagrams provide both a physical and a logical view of a system, but concentrate more on the flow and transformation of data than on the physical devices or timing of inputs, processing, or outputs.

Three other documentation tools discussed in this chapter are process maps, program flowcharts, and decision tables. Accountants do not need to be programmers to evaluate or design an accounting information system, but they should understand in general terms how these tools work. A variety of software tools exist for documenting AISs. These include standard personal productivity tools such as word processing and spreadsheet software as well as specialized CASE tools.

End-user computing refers to the ability of noncomputer employees to create their own computer applications, especially spreadsheet and database applications. In recent years, end-user computing has become important because more employees do it and because the resultant applications often contribute significantly to the efficiency of specific departments or divisions. But organizations also find that many employees do not document these applications very well and that this lack of documentation costs firms time and money. Organizations are wise to control end-user programming efforts and to install policies to help overcome this problem.

KEY TERMS YOU SHOULD KNOW

balancing (data flow diagrams)	level 1 data flow diagram
CASE (computer-assisted software engineering) tools	logical data flow diagram
	macro program flowchart
context diagram	object-oriented software
data flow diagrams (DFDs)	physical data flow diagram
decision table	process map
decomposition	program flowcharts
document flowchart	rapid application development (RAD)
end-user computing	sandwich rule (system flowcharts)
graphical documentation software	structured programming
job stream	structured walkthrough
level 0 data flow diagram	system flowchart

DISCUSSION QUESTIONS

3-1. Why is documentation important to accounting information systems? Why should accountants be interested in AIS documentation?

3-2. Distinguish between document flowcharts, system flowcharts, data flow diagrams, and program flowcharts. How are they similar? How are they different?

3-3. What are document flowcharts? How does a document flowchart assist each of the following individuals: (1) a systems analyst, (2) a systems designer, (3) a computer programmer, (4) an auditor, and (5) a data security expert?

3-4. Although flowcharting is an art rather than a science, some guidelines can be used to make better flowcharts. What are these guidelines for document, system, and data flow diagram flowcharts?

3-5. What are the four symbols used in data flow diagrams? What does each mean?

3-6. Why are data flow diagrams developed in a hierarchy? What are the names of some levels in the hierarchy?

3-7. Look at the process map shown in Figure 3-12. Trace the steps in the order fulfillment process. Do you think this figure is more helpful than a narrative would be in understanding the flow of events in the process?

3-8. What is the purpose of a decision table? How might decision tables be useful to accountants?

3-9. What are CASE tools? How are they used? How do CASE tools create documentation for AISs? If you were a systems analyst, would you use a CASE tool?

3-10. What is end-user computing? Why is documentation important to end-user computing? What guidelines should companies develop to control end-user computing?

PROBLEMS

3-11. To view the Drawing ToolBar of Microsoft Excel, select the following options from the main menu: View\Toolbars\Drawing. (You can also click directly on the Drawing icon in the Standard Toolbar.) After the Drawing Toolbar appears, select Autoshapes\Flowchart and observe the symbols that appear in the selection list. There should be approximately 28 of them (using Office 2000). If you allow your mouse to hover over a specific symbol, its title and meaning will appear in a tool-tip box. Finally, if you click on a specific symbol, your mouse icon will change to a cross-hair and you will be able to draw this symbol on your spreadsheet. Create a list with items similar to the one below that contains all the symbols in your version of Excel.

 Predefined Process

3-12. Draw a document flowchart to depict each of the following situations.

a. An individual from the marketing department of a wholesale company prepares five copies of a sales invoice, and each copy is sent to a different department.

b. The individual invoices from credit sales must temporarily be stored until they can be matched against customer payments at a later date.

c. A batch control tape is prepared along with a set of transactions to ensure completeness of the data.

d. The source document data found on employee application forms are used as input to create new employee records on a computer master file.

e. Delinquent credit customers are sent as many as four different inquiry letters before their accounts are turned over to a collection agency.

f. Physical goods are shipped back to the supplier if they are found to be damaged upon arrival at the receiving warehouse.

g. The data found on employee time cards are keyed onto a hard disk before they are processed by a computer.

h. The data found on employee time cards are first keyed onto a floppy diskette before they are entered into a computer job stream for processing.

i. A document flowchart is becoming difficult to understand because too many lines cross one another. (Describe a solution.)

j. Three people, all in different departments, look at the same document before it is eventually filed in a fourth department.

k. Certain data from a source document are copied into a ledger before the document itself is filed in another department.

3-13. Develop a document flowchart for the following information flow. The individual stores in the Mark Goodwin convenience chain prepare two copies of a goods requisition form (GRF) when they need to order merchandise from the central warehouse. After these forms are completed, one copy is filed in the store's records and the other copy is sent to the central warehouse. The warehouse staff gets the order and files its copy of the GRF form in its records. When the warehouse needs to restock an item, three copies of a purchase order form (POF) are filled out. One copy is stored in the warehouse files, one copy goes to the vendor, and the third copy goes to the accounts payable department.

3-14. The Garcia-Lanoue Company produces industrial goods. The company receives purchase orders from its customers and ships goods accordingly. Assuming that the following conditions apply, develop a document flowchart for this company:

a. The company receives two copies of every purchase order from its customers.

b. Upon receipt of the purchase orders, the company ships the goods ordered. One copy of the purchase order is returned to the customer with the order, and the other copy goes into the company's purchase order file.

c. The company prepares three copies of a shipping bill. One copy stays in the company's shipping file, and the other two are sent to the customer.

3-15. The data-entry department of the Ron Mitchell Manufacturing Company is responsible for converting all of the company's shipping and receiving information to computer records. Because accuracy in this conversion is essential, the firm employs a strict verification process.

Prepare a document flowchart for the following information flow:

a. The shipping department sends a copy of all shipping orders to the data-entry department.

b. A data-entry operator keys the information from a shipping order onto a diskette.

c. A supervisor checks every record with the original shipping order. If no errors are detected, the diskette is sent to the computer operations staff and the original shipping order is filed.

3-16. Amanda M is a regional manufacturer and wholesaler of high-quality chocolate candies. The company's sales and collection process is as follows. Amanda M makes use of an enterprise-wide information system with electronic data interchange (EDI) capability. No paper documents are exchanged in the sales and collection process. The company receives sales orders from customers electronically. Upon receipt of a sales order, shipping department personnel prepare goods for shipment and input shipping data into the information system. The system sends an electronic shipping notice and invoice to the customer at the time of shipment. Terms are net 30. When payment is due, the customer makes an electronic funds transfer for the amount owed. The customer's information system sends remittance (payment) data to Amanda M. Amanda M's information system updates accounts receivable information at that time.

Draw a context diagram and a level zero logical data flow diagram for Amanda M's sales and collection process.

3-17. The order-writing department at the Winston Beauchamp Company is managed by Alan Most. The department keeps two types of computer files: (1) a customer file of authorized credit customers and (2) a product file of items currently sold by the company. Both of these files are direct-access files stored on magnetic disks. Customer orders are handwritten on order forms with the Winston Beauchamp name at the top of the form, and item lines for quantity, item number, and total amount desired for each product ordered by the customer.

When customer orders are received, Alan Most directs someone to input the information at one of the department's computer terminals. After the information has been input, the computer program immediately adds the information to a computerized "order" file and prepares five copies of the customer order. The first copy is sent back to Alan's department; the others are sent elsewhere. Design a system flowchart that documents the accounting data processing described here. Also, draw a data flow diagram showing a logical view of the system.

3-18. The LeVitre and Swezey Credit Union maintains separate bank accounts for each of its 20,000 customers. Three major files are the customer master file, the transaction file of deposits and withdrawal information, and a monthly statement file that shows a customer's transaction history for the previous month. The following lists the bank's most important activities during a representative month:

a. Customers make deposits and withdrawals.

b. Employers make automatic deposits on behalf of selected employees.

c. The bank updates its master file daily using the transaction file.

d. The bank creates monthly statements for its customers, using both the customer master file and the transactions file.

e. Bank personnel answer customer questions concerning their deposits, withdrawals, or account balances.

f. The bank issues checks to pay its rent, utility bills, payroll, and phone bills.

Draw a data flow diagram that graphically describes these activities.

3-19. The Mark Berrafato Publishing Company maintains an online database of subscriber records, which it uses for preparing magazine labels, billing renewals, and so forth. New-subscription orders and subscription renewals are keyed into a computer file from terminals. The entry data are checked for accuracy and written on a master file. A similar process is performed for change-of-address requests. Processing summaries from both runs provide listings of master file changes.

Once a month, just prior to mailing, the company prepares mailing labels for its production department to affix to magazines. At the same time, notices to new and renewal subscribers are prepared. These notices acknowledge receipt of payment and are mailed to the subscribers. The company systems analyst, Bob McQuivey, prepared the system flowchart in Figure 3-17 shortly before he left the company. As you can see, the flowchart is incomplete. Finish the flowchart by labeling each flowcharting symbol. Don't forget to label the processing runs marked computer.

3-20. The Bridget Joyce Company is an office products distributor that must decide what to do with delinquent credit-sales accounts. Mr. Bob Smith, the credit manager, divides accounts into the following categories: (1) accounts not past due, (2) accounts 30 days or less past due, (3) accounts 31 to 60 days past due, (4) accounts 61 to 90 days past due, and (5) accounts more than 90 days past due. For simplicity, assume that all transactions for each account fall neatly into the same category.

Mr. Smith decides what to do about these customer accounts based on the history of the account in general and also the activity during the account's delinquency period. Sometimes, for example, the customer will not communicate at all. At other times, however, the customer will either write to state that a check is forthcoming or make a partial payment. Mr. Smith tends to be most understanding of customers who make partial payments because he considers such payments acts of good faith. Mr. Smith is less understanding of those customers who only promise to pay or who simply ignore followup bills from the company.

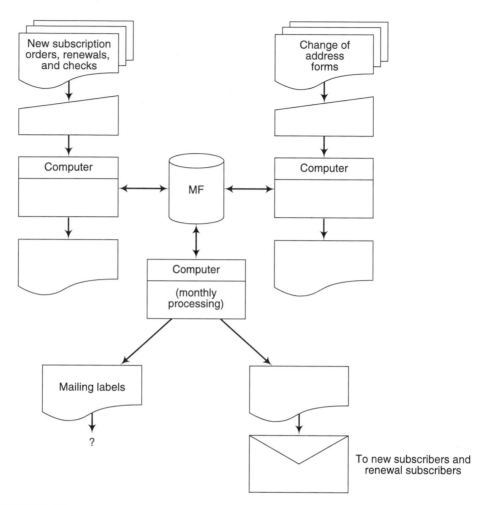

FIGURE 3-17   System flowchart for processing the subscription orders and changes for the Mark Berrafato Publishing Company.

Mr. Smith has four potential actions to take in cases of credit delinquency. First, he can simply wait (i.e., do nothing). Second, he can send an initial letter to the customer, inquiring about the problem in bill payment and requesting written notification of a payment schedule if payment has not already been made. Third, he can send a followup letter indicating that a collection agency will be given the account if immediate payment is not forthcoming. Fourth, he can turn the account over to a collection agency. Of course, Mr. Smith prefers to use one of the first three actions rather than turn the account over to a collection agency because his company only receives half of any future payments when the collection agency becomes involved.

a. Create a decision table for the Bridget Joyce Company and provide a set of reasonable decision rules for Mr. Smith to follow. For now, ignore the influence of a customer's credit history.

b. Expand the decision table analysis you have prepared in question "a" to include the credit history of the customer accounts. You are free to make any assumptions you wish about how this history might be evaluated by Mr. Smith.

INTERNET EXERCISES

3-21. Many professors teaching systems analysis or database courses post more complex data flow diagrams on their class web pages than were shown in this chapter. An example that was available at the time of this writing may be found at www.umsl.edu/~sauter/analysis/dfd/dfd.htm (University of Missouri, St. Louis). Use an Internet search engine such as Infoseek or Yahoo to find the addresses of one or more additional examples of these data flow diagrams. View the examples stored in one of these web pages, and print the DFDs in it on paper. On a separate piece of paper, write down each of the guidelines for drawing DFDs listed in this chapter, and for each guideline, indicate whether or not your web example(s) conform to it.

3-22. Visit the list of graphical documentation software tool vendors at the vendor-list address found in the web site references at the end of this chapter. Visit the web site of at least two vendors and describe in greater detail some of the features their software provides. Which particular product would you acquire for yourself, assuming that money is no object? Why did you choose this particular product?

3-23. Find a flowcharting software package on the World Wide Web that is available to download for a free trial or as free software. Does the trial or free version of the software differ from a full version? Do you think offering software in this fashion is a good marketing strategy for a graphical documentation software vendor?

CASE ANALYSES

3-24. Excelling at Documentation (Drawing Documentation Materials with Microsoft Excel)

Follow the directions in Exercise 3-11 to access Excel's drawing tools and then recreate the two program flowcharts shown in Figure 3-18. Draw each flowchart on a separate work sheet. Rename the first sheet "Main" and the second sheet "Sub." To embed text inside a symbol, right-click on that symbol with your mouse and then choose "Add Text" from the dropdown menu that appears. To center text inside a symbol, highlight the text and then click on the centering icon in the main toolbar.

Create the words "Yes" and "No" that appear in this flowchart using Text Box symbols from the drawing toolbar. To eliminate the black (default) borders around these words, right-click on a Text Box *border* (*not* the text inside the symbol). When the context menu appears, select the "Colors and Lines" tab, and then "No Line" from the "Line\Color" section of that tab. Finally, you can fine-tune the position of any object by clicking on its border and then using the Ctrl key plus an arrow key to reposition it as desired.

Linking Flowcharts   After drawing these two flowcharts, we want to link them together. In this case, we want the user to click on the "Process Record" symbol in the main flowchart and then be able to view the second spreadsheet you've created on the alternate sheet. To create this link, click on the border of the "Process Record" symbol, and then select Insert\Hyperlink from the main menu. Again, be sure to click on a symbol border—not the text inside the border.

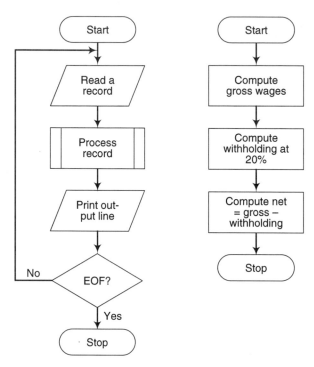

FIGURE 3-18 Draw the flowchart on the left on one Excel sheet and the flowchart on the right on a second sheet.

When the Insert Hyperlink dialog box appears, first select "Place in this Document" from the choices on the left side of the box, and then click on the name of the sheet in which you've drawn the second flowchart ("Sub") in the lower box on the right. If you wish, you can also select a particular cell for linking in the top box—a handy feature if you've drawn your flowchart in a lower portion of the Sub sheet. That's it! Now, when you move your mouse over the "Process Record" symbol in the "Main" sheet, your mouse icon should turn into a hand, indicating that clicking on this symbol links you to the supporting document's sheet.

Requirements

Using Excel software and the skills described above, create the documents from the list below or the ones required by your instructor:

- **a.** The document flowchart shown in Figure 3-2.
- **b.** The system flowchart shown in Figure 3-5.
- **c.** The context diagram shown in Figure 3-8.
- **d.** The physical data flow diagram in Figure 3-9.
- **e.** The logical data flow diagram shown in Figure 3-10.
- **f.** Link the DFD in part e to a new DFD similar to Figure 3-11.
- **g.** The process map shown in Figure 3-12.
- **h.** The program flowchart shown in Figure 3-13.

3-25. The Berridge Company (Drawing Document Flowcharts)

The Berridge Company is a discount tire dealer that operates 25 retail stores in a metropolitan area. The company maintains a centralized purchasing and warehousing facility and employs a perpetual inventory system. All purchases of tires and related supplies are placed through the company's central purchasing department to take advantage of the quantity discounts offered by its suppliers.

The tires and supplies are received at the central warehouse and distributed to the retail stores as needed. The perpetual inventory system at the central facility maintains current inventory records, which include designated reorder points, optimum order quantities, and balance-on-hand information for each type of tire or related supply.

The participants involved in Berridge's inventory system include (1) retail stores, (2) the inventory control department, (3) the warehouse, (4) the purchasing department, (5) accounts payable, and (6) outside vendors. The inventory control department is responsible for maintenance of the perpetual inventory records for each item carried in inventory. The warehouse department maintains the physical inventory of all items carried by the company's retail stores.

All deliveries of tires and related supplies from vendors are received by receiving clerks in the warehouse department, and all distributions to retail stores are filled by shipping clerks in this department. The purchasing department places every order for items needed by the company. The accounts payable department maintains the subsidiary ledger with vendors and other creditors. All payments are processed by this department. The documents used by these various departments are as follows:

Retail Store Requisition (Form RSR)   The retail stores submit this document to the central warehouse whenever tires or supplies are needed at the stores. The shipping clerks in the warehouse department fill the orders from inventory and have them delivered to the stores. Three copies of the document are prepared, two of which are sent to the warehouse, and the third copy is filed for reference.

Purchase Requisition (Form PR)   An inventory control clerk in the inventory control department prepares this document when the quantity on hand for an item falls below the designated reorder point. Two copies of the document are prepared. One copy is forwarded to the purchasing department, and the other is filed.

Purchase Order (Form PO)   The purchasing department prepares this document based on information found in the purchase requisition. Five copies of the purchase order are prepared. The disposition of these copies is as follows: copy 1 to vendor, copy 2 to accounts payable department, copy 3 to inventory control department, copy 4 to warehouse, and copy 5 filed for reference.

Receiving Report (Form RR)   The warehouse department prepares this document when ordered items are received from vendors. A receiving clerk completes the document by indicating the vendor's name, the date the shipment is received, and the quantity of each item received. Four copies of the report are prepared. Copy 1 is sent to the accounts payable department; copy 2 to the purchasing department, and copy 3 to the inventory control department, Copy 4 is retained by the warehouse department, compared with the purchase order form in its files, and filed together with this purchase order form for future reference.

Invoices   Invoices received from vendors are bills for payment. The vendor prepares several copies of each invoice, but only two copies are of concern to the Berridge Company: the copy that is received by the company's accounts payable department and the copy that is retained by the vendor for reference. The accounts payable department compares the vendor invoice with its file copy of the original purchase order and its file copy of the warehouse receiving report. Based on this information, adjustments to the bill amount on the invoice are made (e.g., for damaged goods, for trade discounts, or for cash discounts), a check is prepared, and the payment is mailed to the vendor.

Requirements

1. Draw a document flowchart for the Berridge Company using the symbols in Figure 3-1.
2. Could the company eliminate one or more copies of its RSR form? Why or why not? Explain.
3. Do you think that the company creates too many copies of its purchase orders? Why or why not?

3-26. FreezeTime, Inc. (Drawing Systems Flowcharts)

Carly Riccardi and her mother Nancy own and operate FreezeTime, Inc., a company specializing in freeze-drying flowers from clients' memorable events, such as proms and weddings. The company not only freezes the flowers, but also presents them in a variety of display packages. Each of these packages includes materials such as glass and frames that FreezeTime purchases from local suppliers. In addition to supplies for display, the company purchases office supplies and packaging materials from several vendors.

FreezeTime uses a low-end accounting software package to prepare documents and reports. As employees note a need for supplies and materials, they inform Carly or Nancy, who act as office manager and company accountant. Either Carly or Nancy enters order information into the accounting system and creates a purchase order that they fax to the supplier. Occasionally, Carly or Nancy will also call the supplier if there is something special about the product ordered. When ordered materials and supplies arrive at FreezeTime's small factory, either Carly or Nancy checks the goods received against a copy of the purchase order and enters the new inventory into the computer system.

Nancy pays bills twice each month, on the first and the fifteenth. She checks the computer system for invoices outstanding, and verifies that the goods have been received. She then enters any information needed to produce printed checks from the accounting system. FreezeTime mails checks and printed remittance advices (portions of the vendor bill to be returned) to suppliers.

Requirements

1. Use a software package to create a systems flowchart for FreezeTime's purchase and payment process.
2. Comment on the value, if any, that having a systems flowchart describing this process would have to Carly or Nancy.

3-27. The Dinteman Company (Document Analysis)

The Dinteman Company is an industrial machinery and equipment manufacturer with several production departments. The company employs automated and heavy equipment in its production departments. Consequently, Dinteman has a large repair and maintenance department (R&M department) for servicing this equipment.

The operating efficiency of the R&M department has deteriorated over the past two years. For example, repair and maintenance costs seem to be climbing more rapidly than other department costs. The assistant controller has reviewed the operations of the R&M department and has concluded that the administrative procedures used since the early days of the department are outmoded due in part to the growth of the company. In the opinion of the assistant controller, the two major causes for the deterioration are an antiquated scheduling system for repair and maintenance work, and the actual cost to distribute the R&M department's costs to the production departments. The actual costs of the R&M department are allocated monthly to the production departments on the basis of the number of service calls made during each month.

The assistant controller has proposed that a formal work order system be implemented for the R&M department. With the new system, the production departments will submit a service request to the R&M department for the repairs and/or maintenance to be completed, including a suggested time for having the work done. The supervisor of the R&M department will prepare a cost estimate on the service request for the work required (labor and materials) and estimate the amount of time for completing the work on the service request. The R&M supervisor will return the request to the production department that initiated the request. Once the production department approves the work by returning a copy of the service request, the R&M supervisor will prepare a repair and maintenance work order and schedule the job. This work order provides the repair worker with the details of the work to be done and is used to record the actual repair and maintenance hours worked and the materials and supplies used.

Production departments will be charged for actual labor hours worked at a predetermined standard rate for the type of work required. The parts and supplies used will be charged to the production departments at cost. The assistant controller believes that only two documents will be required in this new system—a Repair/Maintenance Service Request initiated by the production departments and a Repair/Maintenance Work Order initiated by the R&M department.

Requirements

1. For the Repair/Maintenance Work Order document:
   a. Identify the data items of importance to the repair and maintenance department and the production department that should be incorporated into the work order.
   b. Indicate how many copies of the work order would be required and explain how each copy would be distributed.
2. Prepare a document flowchart to show how the Repair/Maintenance Service Request and the Repair/Maintenance Work Order should be coordinated and used among the departments of Dinteman Company to request and complete the repair and maintenance work, to provide the basis for charging the production departments for the cost of the completed work, and to evaluate the performance of the repair and maintenance department. Provide explanations in the flowchart as appropriate.

(CMA Adapted)

3-28. The Jack Edmonds Company (Drawing Data Flow Diagrams)

The Jack Edmonds Company is a medium-size manufacturer of musical equipment. The accounts payable department is located at company headquarters in Asbury Park, New Jersey, and it consists of two full-time clerks and one supervisor. They are responsible for processing and paying approximately 800 checks each month. The accounts payable process generally begins with receipt of a purchase order from the purchasing department. The purchase order is held until a receiving report and the vendor's invoice have been forwarded to accounts payable.

At that time, the purchase order, receiving report, and invoice are matched together by an accounts payable clerk, and payment and journal entry information are input to the computer. Payment dates are designated in the input, and these are based on vendor payment terms. Company policy is to take advantage of any cash discounts offered. If there are any discrepancies among the purchase order, receiving report, and invoice, they are given to the supervisor for resolution. After resolving the discrepancies, the supervisor returns the documents to the appropriate clerk for processing. Once documents are matched and payment information is input, the documents are stapled together and filed in a tickler file by payment date until checks are issued.

When checks are issued, a copy of the check is used as a voucher cover and is affixed to the supporting documentation from the tickler file. The entire voucher is then defaced to avoid duplicate payments. In addition to the check and check copy, other outputs of the computerized accounts payable system are a check register, vendor master list, accrual of open invoices, and a weekly cash requirements forecast.

Requirements

Draw a context diagram and data flow diagram similar to those in Figures 3-8 and 3-9 for the Jack Edmonds Company's accounts payable process. Use the symbols shown in Figure 3-7.

REFERENCES, RECOMMENDED READINGS, AND WEB SITES

References and Recommended Readings

Bagranoff, N. A., and M. G. Simkin, "Picture That," *Journal of Accountancy* (February 2000), pp. 43–46.

Brockmann, John, "Illustrating Computer Documentation: The Art of Presenting Information Graphically on Paper and Online," *IEEE Transactions on Professional Communication,* vol. 35, no. 2 (June 1992), pp. 123–125.

Bulkeley William M., "When Things Go Wrong: Fox Meyer Drug Took a Huge High Tech Gamble; It Didn't Work" *Wall Street Journal* (November 18, 1996), p. R25.

Campbell, Claudia L., "The Hired Problem Solver: Your Mission: Clean Up the Accounting Mess," *Management Accounting,* vol. 74, no. 2 (August 1992), pp. 25–29.

Chapman, Christy, "Just Wired About Software," *Internal Auditor*, vol. 52, no. 4 (August 1995), pp. 24–36.

Coderre, David G., "Seven Easy CAATTs (Computer- Assisted Audit Tools and Techniques)," *Internal Auditor,* vol. 51 , no. 4 (August 1994), pp. 28–33.

Damelio, Robert, *The Basics of Process Mapping* (New York: Quality Resources, 1996).

Hagerty, M. R., "A Powerful Tool for Diagnosis and Strategy," *Journal of Management Consulting.* (November 1997), pp. 16-5.

Howard, Alan, "Why Accurate Records Must Not Be Neglected," *Computer Weekly* (January 18, 1996), p. 24.

Huberty, Peter J. "Worldwide Audit Automation" *The Internal Auditor,* vol. 57, no. 6 (December 2000), pp. 25-27.

Hunt, V. Daniel, *Process Mapping* (New York: John Wiley and Sons, 1996).

Jesitus, John, "Broken Promises? (Managing the Internetworked Corporation)," *Industry Week,* vol. 246, no. 20 (November 3, 1997), pp. 31-35.

Keller, Paulette, and J. Mike Jacka, "Process Mapping" *The Internal Auditor,* vol. 56, no. 5 (October 1999), pp. 60-64.

Kring, Richard, "Systems Control Strategies," *Internal Auditor,* vol. 55, no. 2 (April 1998), pp. 60-64.

Kuehn, Ralph E., "Data Flow Diagrams for Managerial Problem Analysis," *Information Executive,* vol. 3, no. 1 (Winter 1990), pp. 11-15.

Laudon, Kenneth C., and Jane P. Laudon, "Ensuring Quality with Information Systems," Chapter 13 in *Management Information Systems* (Upper Saddle River, NJ: Prentice Hall, 1998), pp. 464-505.

Lehman, Mark W. "Flowcharting Made Simple" *Journal of Accountancy,* vol. 190, no. 4 (October 2000), pp. 77-88.

Pallatto, John, "KnowledgeWare CASE Tools Speed Program Development," *PC Week,* vol. 8, no. 27 (July 8, 1991), pp. 51-52.

Selander, J. P., and K. F., Cross, "Process Redesign: Is It Worth It?" *Strategic Finance* (January 1999), pp. 40-44.

Senn, James A., "Developing Shared IT Applications," Chapter 12 in *Information Technology in Business* (Upper Saddle River, NJ: Prentice Hall, 1998), pp. 542-607.

Senn, James A., and Judy L. Wynekoop, "The Other Side of CASE Implementation," *Information Systems Management,* vol. 12, no. 4 (Fall 1995), pp. 7-15.

Siegel, Marc A. "Recovery of Embezzled Assets Half a World Away" *Journal of Accountancy,* vol. 192, no. 2, (August 2001), pp. 45-51.

Spencer, Cathy J., and Diana Kilbourn Yates, "A Good User's Guide Means Fewer Support Calls and Lower Support Costs," *Technical Communication,* vol. 42, no. 1 (February 1995), pp. 52-56.

Web Sites

The web sites for some flowcharting software developers are www.spss.com/software/allclear/(allClear), www.smartdraw.com (SmartDraw), www.microsoft.com/office/visio (Microsoft), and www.micrografx.com (iGrafx).

The Society for Technical Communication (STC) is a professional society for both technical writing teachers and professionals. Its quarterly, *Technical Communication,* contains articles about technical communication. More information about STC and its publications may be found at www.stc-va.org.

An excellent set of communications resources has been collected by John December. Visit his web site at www.december.com/john/study/comm/info.html.

Information systems journals frequently publish articles describing graphical documentation tools. Many of these periodicals publish articles online such as *PC Magazine* at www.zdnet.com/pcmag.

PART TWO

COLLECTING, STORING, AND USING ACCOUNTING INFORMATION

CHAPTER 4
Accounting Information System and Business Processes: Part I

CHAPTERS 5
Accounting Information System and Business Processes: Part II

CHAPTER 6
Accounting and Enterprise Software

CHAPTER 7
Data Modeling

CHAPTER 8
Organizing and Manipulating Data in Databases

A major role for an AIS is to help collect, record, and store financially oriented data and to convert these data into meaningful information for management decision making. The five chapters in Part Two discuss various data processing and data management approaches that provide relevant information to management in computerized AIS environments.

Chapter 4 discusses the inputs and outputs associated with the sales and purchases processes. The discussion includes an overview of the financial accounting cycle and its use of journals, ledgers, and coding. The chapter also describes the reports and source documents associated with AISs. Chapter 4 concludes with a discussion of common business processes: groups of activities or business events with similar characteristics. We describe in detail the sales and purchases processes found in most business organizations.

Chapter 5 continues our discussion of business processes. The chapter details additional processes found in many businesses, emphasizing events associated with resource management, production, and financing. Chapter 5 also considers the particular accounting information needs of specialized industries.

In Chapter 6 we discuss accounting and enterprise software options. These software programs process the transactions associated with the business processes discussed earlier. As business entities move to integrate their information processing systems, they are increasingly adopting an enterprise-wide systems approach. Our discussion of accounting software includes a description of enterprise-wide software, known as enterprise resource planning (ERP) systems. There are many issues associated with implementing accounting and ERP software that contribute to the success of an AIS. Chapter 6 discusses these issues in some depth.

Organizations collect, store, manipulate, and report data about business processes. Chapter 7 begins by explaining the data hierarchy and the function of a database in an AIS. The chapter then proceeds through the steps required to create a database to support an organization's business processes. This discussion is based on the REA approach to data modeling. The final section of the chapter explains the concept of normalization in creating efficient database models.

Chapter 8 addresses storage and manipulation of data in databases. The first section describes hierarchical, network, and relational database structures. The chapter then discusses object-oriented and multimedia databases, and data warehouses. Database users access, manipulate, and extract data from databases. Chapter 8 describes approaches to each of these, including queries, online analytical processing, and data mining. The chapter concludes with a discussion of other relevant database topics, including data integrity and security.

Chapter 4

Accounting Information Systems and Business Processes: Part I

INTRODUCTION

BUSINESS PROCESS FUNDAMENTALS

An Overview of the Financial Accounting Cycle

Coding Systems

COLLECTING AND REPORTING ACCOUNTING INFORMATION

Considerations in Report Design

Source Documents: Collecting the Data for Output Reports

CORE BUSINESS PROCESSES

The Sales Process

The Purchasing Process

AIS AT WORK—USING SALES DATA AT BOISE CASCADE OFFICE PRODUCTS

KEY TERMS YOU SHOULD KNOW

DISCUSSION QUESTIONS

PROBLEMS

INTERNET EXERCISES

CASE ANALYSES

McMart

Best Sellers Book Company

Universal Floor Covering

Larkin State University

Sales Processing at Uptown Bucks

REFERENCES, RECOMMENDED READINGS, AND WEB SITES

After reading this chapter, you will:

1. *Know* the steps in the financial accounting process.
2. *Understand* the use of journals and ledgers in processing accounting transactions.
3. *Recognize* different types of coding systems used by AISs.
4. *Understand* why planning an AIS begins with the design of outputs.
5. *Know* the elements of good forms design and how source documents collect data.
6. *Be able to explain* why organizations group business activities into business processes.
7. *Be familiar* with the objectives, inputs, and outputs of the sales and purchasing processes.

The importance of owners' attention to sales is critical to company success because so many elements of the sales process in today's marketplace differ from traditional practices of the past.

D.D. Buss, "Sell Your Way to Success," *Nation's Business,* February 1999, p. 15.

INTRODUCTION

AISs depend heavily on the flow of data through various organizational subsystems. It is important to manage, control, and speed this movement of data. As accounting data flow through organizational channels, the data might be lost, inaccurately copied, delayed, or misinterpreted. Effective processing systems ensure the capture of appropriate data and accurate information reporting.

This chapter begins by reviewing the financial accounting cycle. You have probably covered this material in an introductory accounting course. However, we review it here because it is the heart of an AIS. The financial accounting cycle may also be thought of as the "bookkeeping" process in accounting. Although AISs incorporate much more than this bookkeeping aspect of financial accounting, this cycle is important because it underlies a company's formal financial statements.

The financial accounting cycle contains several elements associated with processing accounting transactions. These elements include journals, ledgers, accounts, trial balances, and financial statements. Coding is another important element in processing accounting transactions. This chapter describes how AISs code accounting data to assist in their collection and processing.

The financial accounting cycle organizes transactions by an entity's business processes. The nature and types of business processes vary, depending on the information needs of a specific organization. Nevertheless, most business organizations have in common groups of transactions related to sales (sales and cash collection) and purchasing (expenditures for materials and supplies, and cash payment). This chapter describes the objectives, inputs, and outputs of these major business processes.

BUSINESS PPROCESS FUNDAMENTALS

The accounting cycle begins when accounting personnel analyze a transaction from a source document and ends with the issuance of financial reports and closing of temporary accounts in preparation for a new cycle. A **source document** is a piece of paper or an electronic form that records a business activity such as the purchase or sale of goods.

An Overview of the Financial Accounting Cycle

Based on the preparation of source documents, an AIS records each transaction or business event affecting an organization's financial condition.

Journals   Accounting personnel record transactions in a **journal.** The journal is a chronological record of business events by account. The account structure for an organization is its chart of accounts. A chart of accounts includes the asset, liability, revenue, and expense accounts that appear in an entity's financial reports.

A journal may be a special journal or a general journal. **Special journals** capture a specific type of transaction. They are usually reserved for transactions occurring frequently within an organization. For example, most organizations make sales on credit. A company making many credit sales might decide to set up a special sales journal for these transactions. Rather than debiting accounts receivable and crediting sales for each transaction, the accounting clerk records the debit to the particular customer's account within the **subsidiary ledger** for receivables. The transactions in the sales journal are totaled daily. Within the general ledger, an accountant debits the accounts receivable account and credits the sales account. In a computerized system, special journals may take the form of special modules with their own files. An accounting clerk would likely record a credit sale in an accounts receivable module.

Companies can set up a special journal for virtually any type of transaction. Commonly used ones are sales journals, purchase journals, cash receipts journals, and cash disbursements journals. Figure 4-1 shows these special journals and the types of entries recorded in them. If you think about it, almost all accounting transactions a business organization records fall into one of these categories. Special journals include entries for all but a few types of transactions and adjusting journal entries, such as for depreciation. The **general journal** records these entries.

Ledgers   Journal entries show all aspects of a particular transaction. Each entry shows debit and credit amounts, the transaction date, the affected accounts, and a brief description of the event. Once an AIS records a journal entry, it next posts the entry in the general ledger. Within an AIS, a **general ledger** is a collection of detailed monetary information about an organization's various assets, liabilities, owners' equity, revenues, and expenses. The general ledger includes a separate account (often called a "T account" because of its shape) for each type of monetary item in an organization. While journal entries record all aspects of business transactions, an AIS separately posts the monetary amounts in each account to the various accounts in the general ledger.

A company's **chart of accounts** provides the organizational structure for the general ledger. The chart of accounts makes use of a block coding structure (discussed in the next section of this chapter). Accounting clerks gather transaction information from various source documents and code the information with the ac-

---

Sales Journal
   Record of credit sales transactions.

Purchases Journal
   Record of credit purchase transactions.

Cash Receipts Journal
   Record of transactions involving receipts of cash.

Cash Disbursements Journal
   Record of transactions involving disbursements of cash.

FIGURE 4–1   Special journals for AISs.

counts to be debited and credited. Almost any type of source document may provide data affecting accounts in the general ledger. For example, a *remittance advice* is a source document that accompanies a customer's payment on account. The remittance advice signals an accounting clerk to make a journal entry to debit the cash account and credit accounts receivable. Note that this journal entry affects accounts receivable processing. Since the general ledger contains all accounts, transactions affecting other AIS applications will also impact the general ledger subsystem. For this reason, we say that an AIS is integrated, with relationships existing among various applications. An example of this integration is the relationship between the accounts receivable application and the general ledger. The general ledger contains a control account for accounts receivable, and the accounts receivable module (or a subsidiary ledger) maintains data about each individual customer's accounts receivable balance.

Trial Balances and Financial Statements   Once an AIS records journal entries and posts them to the general ledger, it can create a **trial balance.** The trial balance is a listing of all accounts and their debit and credit balances. A mismatch in dollar amounts for debits and credits indicates a recording error. Usually, the accountant or the computerized AIS prepares three trial balances, each at a different point in the accounting cycle. The first trial balance is called the unadjusted trial balance. Once debit and credit dollar amounts in this trial balance are equal, the accountant will record any necessary adjusting journal entries. A business event does not trigger these journal entries. Adjusting entries include journal entries for depreciation and other unrecorded expenses, prepaid expenses, unearned revenues, and unrecorded revenue. An AIS develops an adjusted trial balance after posting adjusting entries to the general ledger. Once debit and credit amounts in this trial balance are equal, an AIS is ready to produce financial statements.

   Financial statements are the primary output of a financial accounting system. These financial statements include an income statement, balance sheet, statement of owners' equity, and cash flow statement. Of course, an AIS can produce other reports as well. The variety and complexity of these reports depend on the underlying structure of an AIS. Chapter 6 discusses the flexibility of accounting and enterprise software in producing a broad variety of reports.

   The accounting cycle does not end when an AIS generates financial statements. The computerized system must close temporary accounts, such as revenue and expense accounts, so that a new cycle can begin. An AIS makes closing journal entries to erase the balances in these temporary accounts. This is necessary because users are interested in income information for a period of time. When a period ends, the balances in an AIS must start at zero before accumulating new account information for the next period. Since balance sheet accounts show financial performance at a point in time, they are permanent and need not be closed. Once an AIS posts closing entries to the appropriate ledger accounts, the computerized system can produce a final post-closing trial balance. This trial balance will show only the debit and credit amounts for permanent accounts. An AIS will carry these amounts forward to the next accounting cycle. Figure 4-2 summarizes the steps in the accounting cycle.

Coding Systems

AISs depend heavily on the use of codes to record, classify, store, and retrieve financial data. For example, it is possible in a manual system to use simple alphabetic

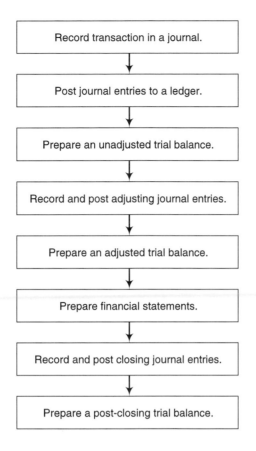

FIGURE 4-2 A summary of the steps in the accounting cycle.

descriptions when preparing journal entries. In contrast, computerized systems more often use **numeric codes** (codes that use numbers only) or **alphanumeric codes** (codes that use numbers and letters) to record accounting transactions. For example, a manual journal entry might include a debit to the "Direct Materials Inventory" account. In a computerized system, the debit might be to account "12345." Alphanumeric codes are important in computerized systems, as they help to ensure uniformity and consistency. Suppose that a clerk entered a debit to "Direct Materials Inventory" one time and another time entered the debit to "Dir. Materials Inventory." A computer would set up a new account the second time, rather than recognizing the intended account.

Purposes of Codes Codes serve many purposes in AISs. One is to uniquely identify such things as individual accounts or specific transactions. For example, more than one person may have the same name. Thus, payroll files or bank account files use a Social Security number or a bank account number, rather than an individual's name, to identify each account uniquely. Similarly, to guard against mix-ups in recording sales transactions, the typical firm will use a unique invoice number to distinguish among its many different credit sales.

Another purpose of codes is to compress data. In general, written descriptions waste space. For example, airlines use the code "F" to designate "first class" and "Y" to designate "coach" because these codes are simpler to use and do not require as much space. Similarly, most AISs will code a date such as March 24, 2003 as 03/24/03 (or 03/24/2003) because this code says the same thing in less space.

Usually, it is important for AISs to classify accounts by type (e.g., bank checking account) or to classify transactions by type (e.g., "cash" versus "credit" sale), by date, or perhaps by geographic location. A third purpose of codes, then, is to facilitate the classification of accounts and transactions. For instance, suppose we are interested in knowing what portion of a company's sales was for cash versus credit. By adding a one-digit code on sales invoices to show the payment type for each sales transaction, this type of analysis is possible.

A final purpose of codes is to communicate special meanings. It is sometimes necessary to convey data so that they are meaningless to most, but convey information to those "in the know." A department store, for example, might announce "Code 9" over the loudspeaker, which may be a call to a security officer. Passwords, credit ratings, and catalog numbers that include the item's price are examples of computer codes that communicate special meanings.

Types of Codes   There are several types of codes typically used in AISs. Among these are (1) mnemonic codes, (2) sequence codes, (3) block codes, and (4) group codes. **Mnemonic codes** help the user remember what they represent. Product codes often make use of mnemonic codes to denote colors and sizes. S, M, L, and XL are examples of mnemonic codes describing apparel sizes.

As the name implies, a **sequence code** is simply a sequential set of numbers used to identify customer accounts, employee payroll checks, customer sales invoices, and so forth. When a sequence code is also used for accountability, as in the coding of movie ticket numbers or the numbering of payroll checks, the sequence counts by units of one for control purposes.

Block codes are sequential codes in which specific blocks of numbers are reserved for particular uses. In a typical application, the lead digit, or two lead digits, in the sequence code acts as the block designator and subsequent digits are identifiers. A frequent use of block codes in AISs is in creating a chart of accounts. A chart of accounts is a list that describes all the accounts used by a business for its income statement and balance sheet. Figure 4-3 illustrates the use of a block code to create a chart of accounts. Notice that current assets occupy the block of numbers from 100 to 199, noncurrent assets occupy the block of numbers from 200 to 299, and so forth.

Combining two or more subcodes creates a **group code.** Since each subcode is a field of the group code, it is accurate to consider a group code as a set of fields, each of which describes separate accounting data. Figure 4-4 illustrates the use of group codes.

Examples of group codes abound. They are often used as product codes in sales catalogs. Fields in a product code designate such features as the item, the particular catalog in which the item appears, the department (such as clothing or housewares), stock number, and perhaps a code for color and/or size. Some companies choose to use a group code to organize their chart of accounts. Besides the block code for account number, this group code might include fields describing the financial statement on which the account appears, the order in which it appears (a sequence number), and whether the account normally has a debit or credit balance.

Design Considerations in Coding   The most important requirement of an accounting code is that it serve some useful purpose. For example, if a product code in a manufacturing firm is part of a responsibility accounting system, at least one portion of the code must contain a production department code. This allows a manager to identify the product with the department that produces it.

Major Accounts

100-199	Current assets
200-299	Noncurrent assets
300-399	Current liabilities
400-499	Long-term liabilities
500-599	Owners' equity
600-699	Revenue
700-799	Cost of goods sold
800-899	Operating expenses
900-999	Nonoperating income and expenses

Current Assets Detail

100	Current assets control
110	Cash
120	Marketable securities
121	Common stock
122	Preferred stock
123	Bonds
124	Money market certificates
125	Bank certificates
130	Accounts receivable
140	Prepaid expenses
150	Inventory
160	Notes receivable

FIGURE 4-3   A block code used for a company's chart of accounts.

Another important design requirement is consistency. This means that, wherever possible, accounting codes should be consistent with those codes already in use. Using Social Security numbers as employee identifiers is a good example of this design consideration. Beyond consistency, codes should be standardized throughout an organization. When two organizations merge, they generally decide to adopt one standard coding system. Imagine the difficulty in producing financial

Type of Code:	Example:	Where:
Telephone Number	(AAA) PPP-XXXX	AAA = area code PPP = prefix XXXX = local number
Bank Account Number	BB XXXXX	BB = branch number XXXXX = account number
Product Code	LL VVV XXXX	LL = location code VVV = vendor number XXXX = product number
Computer Access Code	NN XXXX T	NN = user initials XXXX = access number T = type of access
Universal Resource Locator (URL)	WWW.AAAAAAA.BBB	WWW = World Wide Web AAAAAAA = domain name BBB = organization code

FIGURE 4-4   Examples of group codes.

statements for the newly merged entity with two different code structures for the chart of accounts.

A tradeoff in designing account codes exists between obtaining efficiency and allowing for growth. Fewer digits in the code means less space needed to enumerate the code and less chance for data transcription errors, so the code becomes more useful. This is the "KIS" approach—keep it simple! On the other hand, managers must plan for future expansion. For example, the codes in a company's chart of accounts should allow for the creation of extra accounts. The Year 2000 problem described in Case-in-Point 4.1 is a worst case scenario showing what can happen when a code size is too small.

Case-in-Point 4.1   In the 1960s and 1970s, when programmers developed many of the first software programs, they used a two-digit code to represent a specific calendar year (e.g., "61" for 1961). They did so because computer storage was expensive at the time. As the year 2000 approached, systems developers realized the problems this created for many computer systems. A payroll system, for example, calculating an employee's pay for the period December 28, 1999 through January 11, 2000, would be confused because the year "00" has a lower value than the year "99." Although AISs were not the only information systems affected by the Year 2000 problem, the date dependence of these systems made them particularly vulnerable. Some problems were difficult to anticipate. A British retail giant scrapped all of its corned beef because the computer, in 1998, recognized a sell date of "02" as an indication that the meat was 96 years old. A major credit card company had to repair a program that showed credit cards with expiration dates of "00" as no longer valid. One utility company sent bills to customers with due dates of January 1, 1900. The Year 2000 problem represents an extreme example of the downside of poor coding systems.

COLLECTING AND REPORTING ACCOUNTING INFORMATION

The design of an effective AIS usually begins by considering the outputs from the system. These outputs are informational objectives for an AIS and are therefore goals toward which the system should strive. Thus, systems designers create outputs first. So that output reports serve managerial needs, it is necessary to first begin with informational requirements.

Among the outputs of an AIS are (1) reports to management, (2) reports to investors and creditors, (3) files that retain transaction data, and (4) files that retain current data about accounts (e.g., inventory records). From the perspective of managerial decision making, perhaps the most important of these outputs are the reports to management. These reports are the tools managers use to aid their decision-making activities. Furthermore, most accounting data collected by an organization ultimately appear on some type of internal and/or external report.

Report formats vary. There are hard-copy (paper) reports, soft copy (screen) reports, and audio outputs. If, for example, a manager queries a database system, the monitor screen shows the requested data and the system produces a hard-copy report only upon demand. Graphics enhance reports in any form. Many reports today appear on company web sites. While web page design is beyond the scope of this book, it is important to recognize that the rules for preparing good reports apply to web page reports as well as hard copy and other multimedia reports.

Considerations in Report Design

There are many different types of accounting reports. Some reports, such as financial statement reports, are prepared periodically. An AIS might issue other reports only when a particular event occurs. For example, the AIS may issue an inventory reorder report only when the inventory for a certain product drops below a specified level. Reports such as this that only list exceptional conditions are known as **exception reports.** An AIS produces some reports only on request from management. For instance, the sales manager concerned about sales performance might request a special report on product sales by territory. Good output reports share similar characteristics regardless of their type. Among these characteristics are (1) usefulness, (2) convenience of format, (3) ease of identification, and (4) consistency.

For a report to be useful, it must serve some managerial purpose. For example, the statement of cash flows provides information regarding changes in a company's cash balance and expresses these changes in a convenient format. Often, a convenient format not only serves internal managerial purposes but also helps stockholders, creditors, and potential investors.

Wherever possible, managerial reports should contain useful information, be concise and efficient, and, most important, be action oriented. Computerized AISs are often guilty of generating too many reports. These systems frequently include more data in reports than managers can use effectively. The term **information overload** describes this problem, although the term is a misnomer. By definition, information is useful and therefore should not overload an individual. (A better term would be *data overload.*) In any event, management reports should be prepared only if they will be useful, not because someone thinks they might be a good idea. Convenient formats vary on a case-by-case basis. For example, summary reports should contain financial totals, comparative reports should list like numbers (e.g., budget versus actual figures) in adjacent columns, and descriptive reports (e.g., marketing reports) should present results systematically. Finally, numbers should be expressed in the units (dollars, dozens, and so forth) most useful to the recipients.

Sometimes the most convenient format is graphical. A pie chart is an example. The pie chart in Figure 4-5 clearly shows a company's relative product sales. Other graphical formats include bar charts and trend lines.

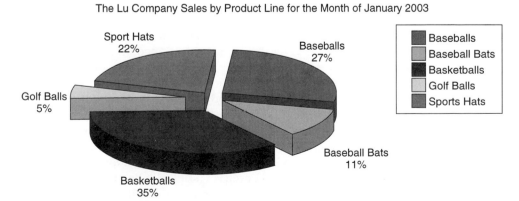

The Lu Company Sales by Product Line for the Month of January 2003

FIGURE 4–5 A pie chart showing the percentage of sales from various product lines.

Good managerial reports always contain fundamental identification, including headings (company name, organizational division or department, etc.) and page numbers. The reports of AISs are usually time-oriented and therefore should also include dates. Imagine that you are a manager who receives a sales analysis report that is undated. The report loses all its information value if you do not know the time period it covers. Balance sheets and similar reports should show the date as of a specific point in time. Reports such as lists of current employees, customers, and vendors should also indicate a specific date. Income statements and similar reports should show a span of dates for the reporting period (e.g., for the month ended June 30, 2003). The sales analysis report described here would indicate a time period rather than a fixed date unless it was just an analysis of sales for one day. Also, as a general rule, it is helpful to include the frequency of the report in the heading (e.g., "Quarterly Marketing Summary").

AIS reports should be consistent in at least three ways: (1) over time, (2) across departmental or divisional levels, and (3) with general accounting practice. Accounting reports should be consistent over time so that the information will be easy to understand. Consistency over time also allows managers to compare information from one period with that of another. This point reinforces the need for accurate report dating. Management will want to compare a sales analysis report for June with a similar report for the month of May of the same year, and perhaps June of prior years, to evaluate whether performance is improving or deteriorating. Reports should be consistent across departmental levels so that supervisors may compare departmental performance and create standards for the company. Sometimes the need for reporting consistency conflicts with the informational needs of individual departmental managers. In that event, system designers can either create several types of reports or reach a compromise in the format of specific reports. Finally, report formats should be consistent with general accounting practice. This makes a report intelligible to external readers and more understandable to internal managers.

Source Documents: Collecting the Data for Output Reports

In an AIS, the chief concerns in the data collection process are accuracy, timeliness, and cost-effectiveness. (From an accounting viewpoint, an activity or process is cost effective if its benefits exceed its costs.) The *purchase order* in Figure 4-6 is a case in point. This source document represents a computer-generated purchase order by Sneaks and Cleats, a retail sporting goods shop, to purchase goods from the Lu Company, a sporting goods distributor. Several copies of the purchase order may be prepared for internal use (these may be hard copies or computer images). For example, the purchasing department would retain one copy to document the order and to serve as a reference for future inquiries. Accounting and receiving departments would also receive copies. Note that the purchase order bears a serial number, 36551. Sequentially numbered purchase orders provide unique identification. This both enhances later referencing and serves as an important means of control.

To accommodate the purchase order of Sneaks and Cleats, the Lu Company will ship the desired merchandise and send a sales invoice under separate cover. Figure 4-7 illustrates the *sales invoice* document. The sales invoice duplicates much of the information on the original purchase order. New information includes the shipping address, a reference to the purchase order number, the shipping date, due date, the sales invoice number, and the customer identification number. The Lu Company might produce as many as six copies of the sales invoice. Two (or more) copies

ORDERED BY
Sneaks and Cleats
1 Sports Lane
Sports Shop, XX 12345

Purchase
Purchase Order No:
36551

To:

Lu Company
222 Main Street
Pleasantville, XX 23456

Date	Good Through	Account No.	Terms
9/1/03	9/30/03		2/10, n/30

Item	Description	Quantity	Unit Price	Total
G001	Golf Clubs	15.00	150.00	2,250.00
B001	Basketballs	20.00	30.00	600.00
			Total	$2,850.00

Authorized Signature _____

FIGURE 4-6   A sample purchase order.

would serve as a bill for the customer. The shipping department would retain a third copy to record that it filled the order. A fourth copy goes to the accounting department for processing accounts receivable. The sales department retains a fifth copy for future reference. Finally, the inventory department receives a sixth copy to update its records on the specific inventory items sold.

Source documents of the types illustrated here help manage the flow of accounting data in several ways. First, they dictate the kinds of data to be collected and help ensure legibility, consistency, and accuracy in the recording of the data. Second, they encourage the completeness of accounting data because these source documents clearly enumerate the information required. Third, they serve as distributors of information because individuals or departments needing the information receive copies of the same form. Finally, source documents help to establish the authenticity of accounting data. This is useful for such purposes as establishing an audit trail, testing for authorization of cash disbursement checks or inventory disbursements, and establishing accountability for the collection or distribution of money.

Both manual and computerized AISs use source documents extensively. In many AISs today, source documents are still written or printed on paper. However, large companies are increasingly moving to paperless offices via the Internet or electronic data interchange (see Chapter 2). Improving the design of source documents prepared online can save a business money as in the following case.

Invoice
Invoice Number:
15563
Invoice Date:
Sept. 3, 2003
Page:
1

Voice:
Fax:

Duplicate

Sold To:
Sneaks and Cleats
1 Sports Lane
Sports Shop, XX 12345

Ship To:
Sneaks and Cleats
1 Sports Lane
Sports Shop, XX 12345

Customer ID		Customer PO			Payment Terms	
C001		36551			2/10, n/30	
Sales Rep		**Shipping Method**		**Ship Date**	**Due Date**	
W. Loman		Rail		9/30/03	10/3/03	
Quantity	**Item**	**Description**			**Unit Price**	**Total**
15.00	G001	Golf Clubs			150.00	2,250.00
20.00	H001	Basketballs			30.00	600.00

Subtotal   2,850
Sales Tax
Total Invoice Amount   2,850
Check No.   Payment Received   0.00
TOTAL $2,850

FIGURE 4–7   A sample sales invoice.

Case-in-Point 4.2   Woerner Turf is a company that produces turf grass and sod for land-scaping. The company recently implemented a new software solution by *Microsoft Great Plains Business Solutions* that consolidated their sales order screen. It eliminated or condensed data entry fields to create a single screen. A sales person will enter orders through the screen approximately 50 to 100 times each day. The new design, which is similar to the paper form used previously, reduces order entry time from three minutes to one. This increased efficiency allows sales staff to spend more time selling and less time on accounting.[1]

The general ledger module of an AIS generates trial balance and financial statement reports as outputs of the financial accounting cycle. Transactions processed through the general ledger also produce other output reports. These include reports

---

[1] Adapted from www.greatplains.com/solutions.

on actual performance against budget projections, lists of transactions for each account, and a list of journal entries that are out of balance (i.e., debits do not equal credits). Performance reports can show variances from budget, or they may be exception reports, showing only those variances that exceed predefined parameters. For example, a report could list only expense accounts that are more than 20 percent over budgeted amounts. Transaction listings are useful in analyzing the activity for a specific account. Remember, however, that journal entries are chronological listings of transactions and they do not easily reveal all activity related to a particular account.

CORE BUSINESS PROCESSES

An AIS collects and reports data related to an organization's **business processes.** The nature and type of business processes vary with the characteristics of a specific entity, although most business entities have the same *core* processes. The AIS will collect data associated with economic and business events within these processes. An **economic event** is an activity that involves an increase and/or decrease in dollar amounts on the financial statements. An example would be collecting cash from a customer on account. Since economic events impact financial statements, they are often called **accounting transactions.** Accountants record these events or transactions in the journal. A **business event** is an activity that does not impact the financial statements, but is nevertheless important to the business. A sales order from a customer is an example of a business event. While accountants do not record business events in journals, they are likely to record data about them within the AIS. Two core business processes that are common to almost every business are *sales* and *purchases.*

The objective of grouping similar activities is to cluster these events together in a way that simplifies information processing. Information processing requires recording, maintaining, and reporting on the business and economic activities that make up a business process. For example, the sales process includes such activities as managing customer inquiries, taking sales orders, filling orders, and receiving payment. The AIS collects and stores data for each of these activities as part of the sales process.

This section of the chapter continues our discussion of reports and source documents by describing the particular reports and source documents associated with the sales and purchasing processes. Chapter 5 describes the AISs associated with more specialized business processes.

The Sales Process

The **sales process** begins with a customer order for goods or services and ends with the collection of cash from the customer. Figure 4-8 summarizes the AIS objectives, inputs, and outputs related to the sales process, assuming that sales are on credit and for merchandise rather than services.

Objectives of the AIS for the Sales Process   Revenues result from an organization's sale of goods or services. They may also result from donations or gifts, as in the case of many not-for-profit organizations. An organization that generates

---

THE SALES PROCESS

Objectives:
- Tracking sales of goods and/or services to customers
- Filling customer orders
- Billing for goods and services
- Collecting payment for goods and services
- Forecasting sales and cash receipts

Inputs (Source Documents):
- Sales Order
- Sales Invoice
- Remittance Advice
- Shipping Notice
- Debit/Credit Memoranda

Outputs (Reports):
- Financial Statement Information
- Customer Billing Statement
- Aging Report
- Bad Debt Report
- Cash Receipts Forecast
- Customer Listing
- Sales Analysis Reports

FIGURE 4-8   Objectives, inputs, and outputs associated with processing revenue transactions.

revenues, but fails to collect these revenues regularly, may find itself in a position where it cannot pay its bills. Many people unfamiliar with accounting make the incorrect assumption that companies with positive incomes cannot go out of business. The reality is that bankruptcy results from inadequate cash flow, not from insufficient income. The primary objective in processing revenues is to achieve timely and efficient cash collection.

To process sales in a timely and efficient manner, an organization must be able to track all revenues owed by customers. Once the AIS recognizes these revenues, the revenue portion of the system needs to monitor the resulting cash inflows. A good AIS matches each revenue with a customer. Maintaining customer records is an important function of the AIS for the revenue process. This includes validating customers' bill-paying ability and payment history, assigning credit limits and ratings to customers, and tracking all customers' outstanding invoices. Processing revenues includes filling customers' orders. This requires an interface with the inventory control function. The AIS should bill customers only for products shipped. The sales process must also allow for certain exception transactions, for example, sales returns.

Forecasting is another objective of the AIS for the revenue process. For an AIS to help management in its planning function, the system should include the ability to forecast revenues and cash receipts. The ability of an AIS to analyze sales orders, sales terms, payment histories, and other data accomplishes this objective. For example, sales orders are a good indicator of future revenues and the terms of sale provide information about likely dates of collection on accounts.

Events in the Sales Process   Figure 4-9 provides an overview of the AIS for the sales process in a high-level systems flowchart. This view assumes an online sales order. Notice the lack of paper documents—e-mail and electronic images replace writ-

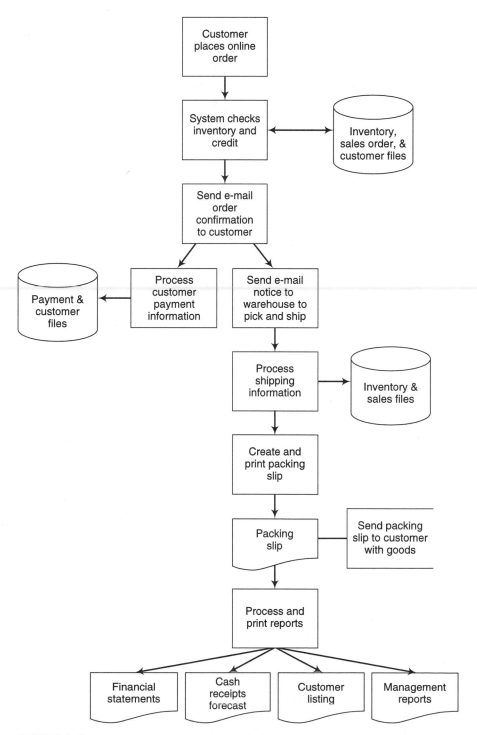

FIGURE 4–9   High-Level Systems Flowchart of the Sales Process in an online environment.

ten documents. The flowchart also assumes that the AIS uses a centralized database that integrates all the data files (discussed in Chapters 6, 7, and 8). The following fictitious example describes the sales process shown in Figure 4-9.

Example: Methuselah Nyang'oro needs to purchase a book for a class. He decides to buy the book online from Fast Text. At Fast Text's website, Methuselah enters information about his order. Fast Text's AIS, on receipt of the order, verifies Methuselah's credit card and checks its inventory to make sure the book is available. The company then sends Methuselah an e-mail confirmation, verifying the transaction. Fast Text's AIS next notifies its warehouse via e-mail to pack and ship the book. The warehouse processes the shipment information and creates a packing slip. Warehouse personnel then package the packing slip with the book and send it to Methuselah.

The major events in Fast Text's sales process are the sales order, the shipment of goods, and the customer payment. Fast Text will record information about each of these events. This information allows them to produce a variety of reports such as book sales by regions of the country. The next sections of this chapter describe the information inputs and outputs of the sales process.

Inputs to the Sales Process Figure 4-10 shows a data flow diagram of the sales process. The diagram includes identification of the data inputs and information outputs to the process. As mentioned, the inputs (and outputs) to an AIS need not be paper documents. Today, with the increasing popularity of EDI systems and electronic commerce, much of the input and output related to business processes is electronic.

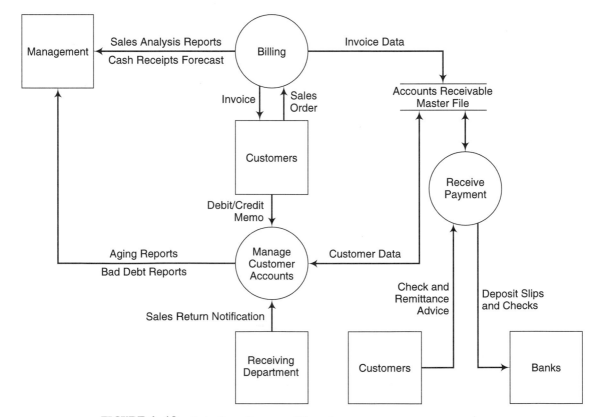

FIGURE 4-10 Data flow diagram of the sales process.

Inputs can also be voice inputs, touch-tone telephone signals, video signals, magnetic ink characters (as on checks), or scanned images.

The information processing system issues a *sales order* at the time a customer contracts for goods or services. For example, an accounts receivable clerk uses this sales order to prepare a sales invoice or the customer might generate one himself using the web page of an online retailer. The *sales invoice* reflects the product or products purchased, price, and the terms of payment. When the customer makes a payment, a *remittance advice* may accompany the payment. You have probably seen a remittance advice before. When you pay your Visa or MasterCard bill, for example, the portion of the bill you return with your check is a remittance advice. In processing sales revenues within an AIS, the accounts receivable clerk uses both the customer's check and the remittance advice to make a journal entry recording the payment on account.

In addition to sales orders, sales invoices, checks, and remittance advices, *shipping notices* are another input to sales processing. When the warehouse releases goods for shipment, the warehouse clerk prepares a shipping notice. A copy of this notice may serve as a *packing slip*. This document accompanies the goods and prompts the accounts receivable department to bill the customer.

Debit/credit memoranda are source documents affecting both the sales and purchasing process. An organization issues these memoranda to denote the return of damaged goods or discrepancies about the amount owed. For example, Customer A may have returned $500 in damaged merchandise to Company B. Since Customer A has not yet paid the bill for the goods, Company B issues a credit memorandum to reduce the customer's accounts receivable balance. In another case, if Company B finds that it has charged Customer A too little for goods sold, Company B would issue a debit memorandum. This debit memorandum signifies a debit to Customer A's account receivable with Company B to reflect the amount not charged originally. Customer A now owes more to Company B.

Business organizations are beginning to recognize the value of the data they collect about their customers and sales transactions in terms of improving customer satisfaction and profitability. As a result, they are purchasing or developing **customer relationship management (CRM)** systems to gather, maintain, and use these data. For example, a retail store may collect data about its customers' buying habits. The store can then use that information to target customers with specialized discounts and services. The following case describes an example of CRM, which we discuss again in Chapter 6.

Case-in-Point 4.3   Kroger, the nation's largest grocery chain, signs its frequent customers up for a Shopper's Kroger Plus card. Customers apply for the card by completing a form that provides the store with their names, addresses, and other personal data. The store offers special discounts to cardholders, based on the number of dollars they spend, as a way of rewarding customer loyalty. Each time a Kroger Plus card-carrying customer makes a purchase, the grocery clerk swipes the card to record the customer's purchases. Knowledge of customer buying habits allows the store to tailor special promotions to specific customers.

Outputs of the Sales Process   Processing sales transactions creates several outputs. An AIS uses some of these outputs to produce external accounting reports, such as financial statements, as well as internal reports, such as *management reports*. Management reports can be in any format. The information these reports contain is a function only of the information needs of managers to aid their decision-making activities. In this and the following sections of the chapter, we discuss only a few of the unlimited number of reports that may be output from business processes.

One output of the sales process is the *customer billing statement*. This statement summarizes outstanding sales invoices for a particular customer and shows the amount currently owed. Other reports generated by the sales revenue process include aging reports, bad debt reports, cash receipts forecasts, approved customer listings, and various sales analysis reports. The *aging report* shows the accounts receivable balance broken down into categories based on time outstanding. For instance, if terms of sale are Net 30, the aging report might show current accounts receivable, those accounts that are 1 to 30 days overdue, accounts receivable 31 to 60 days overdue, 61 to 90 days overdue accounts, and balances that are more than 90 days past due.

It is important to consider what information is most important for a particular organization when designing report formats. Reports are usually custom-designed; for example, categories for overdue accounts in an aging report will reflect a particular company's billing and collection patterns. The *bad debt report* contains information about collection follow-up procedures for overdue customer accounts. This allows management to track the effectiveness of collection efforts. In the event that a customer's account is uncollectible, the account will be written off to an allowance account for bad debts. A detailed listing of the allowance account may be another output of the sales process.

All of the data gathered from source documents in processing sales transactions serve as input to a *cash receipts forecast*. Data such as sales amounts, terms of sale, prior payment experience for selected customers, and information from aging analysis reports and cash collection reports are all inputs to this forecast.

We previously indicated that maintaining customer records is an important function of the AIS in the sales process. The billing or accounts receivable function should approve new customers, both to ensure that the customers exist and to assess their bill-paying ability. This may require obtaining a credit report from a reputable credit agency such as Dun and Bradstreet. The billing function assigns each new customer a credit limit based on credit history. From time to time, the AIS produces an *approved customer listing* report. This report is likely to show customer ID numbers (for uniquely identifying each customer), contact name(s), shipping and billing addresses, credit limits, and billing terms.

As AISs become increasingly sophisticated, their outputs become more useful to management. One valuable output of sales processing is various *sales analysis reports*. By capturing detailed data about each sale, the AIS produces reports to help management monitor sales activities and plan production and marketing effort. However, the sales process can only produce effective sales analysis reports if the AIS captures appropriate sales data. For instance, for an AIS to produce a management report showing sales made by each salesperson, it must record the name of the salesperson with every sales transaction. Similarly, sales analysis reports showing sales by customer, product line, and geographic region require that appropriate data be captured at the time the customer places a sales order. As information systems become increasingly sophisticated, businesses are "mining" their sales data for information to help them better target their customers (see Chapter 8).

The Purchasing Process

The **purchasing process** begins with a request for goods or services and ends with the payment of cash to the vendor. Figure 4-11 shows the objectives, inputs,

---

THE PURCHASING PROCESS

Objectives:
- Tracking purchases of goods and/or services from vendors
- Tracking amounts owed
- Maintaining vendor records
- Controlling inventory
- Making timely and acccurate vendor payments
- Forecasting purchases and cash outflows

Inputs (Source Documents):
- Purchase Requisition
- Purchase Order
- Vendor Listing
- Receiving Report
- Bill of Lading
- Packing Slip
- Debit/Credit Memoranda

Outputs (Reports):
- Financial Statement Information
- Vendor Checks
- Check Register
- Discrepancy Reports
- Cash Requirements Forecast
- Sales Analysis Reports

FIGURE 4-11 Objectives, inputs, and outputs associated with the purchasing process.

and outputs associated with purchasing events. Our discussion assumes that credit purchases are for goods (i.e., manufacturing inventory) rather than for services. In reality, purchases may be for either goods or services and for cash or on credit.

Objectives of the Purchasing Process   The purchasing process encompasses activities or events related to the purchase of both goods and services, payment for the items purchased, and inventory control. Credit transactions create accounts payable. Accounts payable processing closely resembles accounts receivable processing; it is the flip side of the picture. With accounts receivable, companies keep track of amounts owed *to* them from their customers. An accounts payable application tracks the amounts owed *by* the company to vendors. The major objective of accounts payable processing is to pay vendors at the optimal time. As a result, a company can take advantage of cash discounts offered and avoid finance charges for late payments.

Maintaining vendor records is as important to the purchasing process as maintaining customer records is for the sales process. The purchasing department is responsible for maintaining a *list of authorized vendors.* This entails ensuring the authenticity of vendors. The purchasing department is also responsible for finding reputable vendors who offer quality goods and services at reasonable prices. Vendor shipping policies, billing policies, and reliability are also important variables in the approval process. Businesses today are strengthening their relationships with their vendors or suppliers, recognizing that they are partners in a **supply chain.** Case-in-Point 4.4 illustrates this point. We discuss supply chains in more detail in Chapter 6.

Case-in-Point 4.4   Harley-Davidson's supply chain is key to its success and its ability to get high demand products into consumers' hands as quickly as possible. One initiative in the company's recent supply chain overhaul was to cut the supplier base from 4,000 to 800. The company realized the importance of decreasing the number of vendors and strengthening their relationships with them *before* investing in technology. Harley-Davidson is now integrating its smaller supply base into its purchasing, product design, and manufacturing operations. Resident suppliers even have access to Harley's intranet.[2]

The purchase of goods affects *inventory control*. The objective of inventory control is to ensure that an AIS records all goods purchased. The inventory control component of the purchasing process interfaces with production departments, the purchasing function, the vendor, and the receiving department. Chapter 5 describes coverage of the production process inventory control and specialized inventory systems in depth.

A final objective of the purchasing process is forecasting cash outflows. The addition of outstanding purchase requisitions, purchase invoices, and receiving reports provides an estimate of future cash requirements. With the forecast of cash receipts produced by the sales process, this estimate allows an organization to prepare a cash budget

Events in the Purchasing Process Figure 4-12 shows a high-level systems flowchart that describes the purchasing process. As with the sales process, the flowchart assumes a centralized database and a mix of paper documents and electronic images. The following fictitious example describes the purchasing process shown in Figure 4-12.

Example: Anita Joarder, an employee at Fast Text, needs to purchase a new computer. She pulls up the purchase requisition form from the company's intranet and fills in the appropriate information. By clicking her mouse on the "Submit" button, she forwards her request electronically to the purchasing department. A purchasing agent creates an electronic purchase order based on the information Anita provided. The agent consults the vendor file to locate an authorized vendor for the requested computer. The AIS then sends an electronic version of the order to the receiving department and another copy to the vendor. When the computer arrives from the vendor, a receiving clerk consults the AIS to make sure that a purchase order exists for the goods received. The clerk then enters information about the receipt (e.g., date, time, count, and condition of merchandise) to create an electronic receiving report. Upon receipt of an electronic vendor invoice and the receiving report, the accounts payable system remits payment to the vendor.

The economic and business events in Fast Text's purchasing process are the purchase request, purchase order, receipt of goods, and payment to the vendor. The company's AIS records information about each of these events and produces a variety of reports. The next two sections describe the information inputs and some of the reports associated with the purchasing process.

Inputs to the Purchasing Process Figure 4-13 is a data flow diagram for the purchasing process. The figure identifies many of the inputs and outputs associated with the purchase of goods and services.

As explained earlier, the purchasing process often begins with a requisition from a production department for goods or services. (Sometimes, the AIS triggers

---

[2] Adapted from: Sullivan, Missy, "High-Octane Hog," *www.forbes.com, Best of the Web Feature,* September 10, 2001.

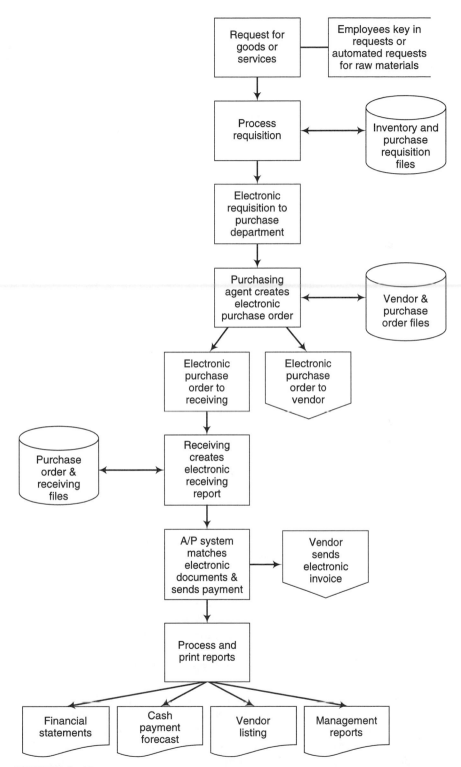

FIGURE 4-12 High-level systems flowchart of the purchasing process in an online environment.

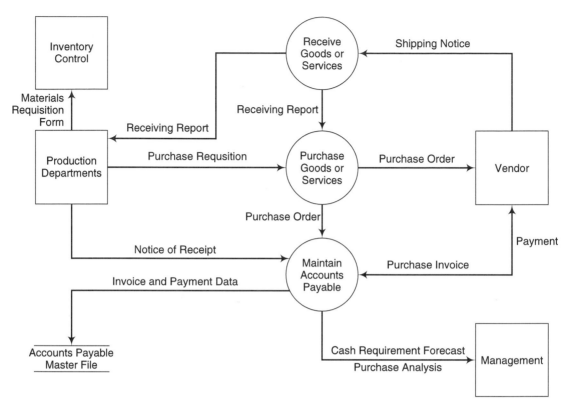

FIGURE 4–13   Data flow diagram of the purchasing process.

the purchase order automatically, for instance, when inventories fall below prespeci-fied levels.) The *purchase requisition* shows the item requested and may show the name of the vendor who supplies it. As previously mentioned, an important part of the AIS for the purchasing process is a list of authorized vendors to avoid payments to unauthorized or nonexistent vendors.

In Figure 4-13, the accounts payable system matched three source documents before remitting payment to the vendor. These documents are the purchase order, the receiving report, and the purchase invoice. A *purchase invoice* is a copy of the vendor's sales invoice. The purchasing organization receives this copy as a bill for the goods or services purchased. The purpose of matching the purchase order, receiving report, and purchase invoice is to maintain the best possible control over cash pay-ments to vendors. For example, the absence of one of these documents could signify a duplicate payment. Computerized AISs call this a *three-way match*. It is relatively easy for an automated system to identify discrepancies between quantitative data such as quantities ordered and dollar amounts. A computerized AIS can search more efficiently for duplicate payments than a manual system. For example, auditors can instruct an AIS to print a list of duplicate invoice numbers, vendor checks for like dollar amounts, and similar control information. While manual or computerized matching of purchase orders, receiving reports, and purchase invoices is a good con-trol over accounts payable, it does slow down the payment process. Some compa-nies may not wish to pay their bills faster, as they count on the "float" they get from delaying payments. This has actually been a problem for business-to-business electronic commerce (discussed in Chapter 2). While the Internet speeds sales and purchases, companies still wait for a match among source documents before making electronic payments. Of course, the same companies want to collect their accounts receivable as quickly as possible.

The purchase requisition precipitates the purchase order. Besides the information on the requisition, the purchase order includes vendor information and payment terms. (See Figure 4-6.) The purchasing department prepares several copies (or images) of the purchase order. In a paper-based system, the purchasing clerk should send one copy of the purchase order to the receiving department to serve as a receiving report or, preferably, to prompt the receiving department to issue a separate receiving report. This copy of the purchase order is specially coded (or color-coded) to distinguish it from other copies of the purchase order if there is no separate receiving report. The receiving department copy might leave out the quantities ordered that are identified in the purchase order. This is done for control purposes, so that workers receiving the goods must do their own counts, rather than simply approving the amounts shown on the purchase order.

Another source document, a *bill of lading,* accompanies the goods sent. The bill of lading is a receipt provided by the freight carrier to the supplier when the carrier assumes responsibility for the goods. It may contain information about the date shipped, the point of delivery for freight payment (either shipping point or destination), the carrier, the route, and the mode of shipment (e.g., rail). The customer may receive a copy of the *shipping notice* with the purchase invoice. This is important to the accounts payable subsystem, since accounts payable accruals include a liability for goods shipped free on board (FOB) from the shipping point. Goods shipped this way have left the vendor, but the customer has not yet received them. Another source document, the *packing slip,* is sometimes included in the merchandise package. This document indicates the specific quantities and items in the shipment and any goods that are on back order. The next time you order goods through a catalogue or over the Internet, look for a *packing slip,* such as the one shown in Figure 4-14, in the container with your merchandise.

Outputs of the Purchasing Process   Typical outputs of the expenditure portion of the purchasing process are the vendor checks and accompanying check register, discrepancy reports, and a cash requirements forecast. The check register lists all checks issued for a particular period. Accounts payable typically processes *checks* in batches and produces the *check register* as a byproduct of this processing step. *Discrepancy reports* are necessary to note any differences between quantities or amounts on the purchase order, the receiving report, and the purchase invoice. The purpose of the discrepancy report is to ensure that no one authorizes a vendor check until the AIS properly explains any differences. For example, assume that a receiving report indicates the receipt of twelve units of product, whereas the purchase order shows that a company ordered twenty units and the purchase invoice bills the company for these twenty units. The accounts payable function records the liability for twenty units and notes the situation on a discrepancy report for management. This report would trigger an investigation. It is likely in our example that the vendor made two shipments of merchandise, and one shipment has yet to be received. If this is the case, receipt of the second shipment will clear this discrepancy from the next report.

The purchasing process produces a *cash requirements forecast* in the same manner as revenue processing produces the cash receipts forecast. By looking at

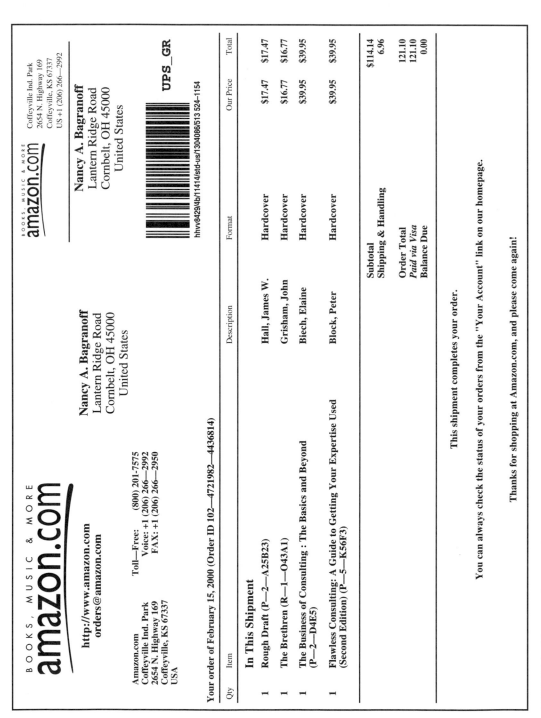

FIGURE 4-14 A packing slip from amazon.com.

source documents such as outstanding purchase orders, unbilled receiving reports, and vendor invoices, an AIS can predict future cash payments and their dates. Naturally, this forecast is easier to make with a computerized system than with a manual system. In either processing environment, however, accounts payable clerks must be careful to include all amounts for which the company is liable. These include charges for goods shipped FOB shipping point by the vendor, since these goods belong to the purchasing company (customer) at the time they leave the vendor.

AIS AT WORK
Using Sales Data at Boise Cascade Office Products[3]

Businesses today often collect large quantities of data about their customers. The trouble is, they don't always use it! Boise Cascade Office Products (BCOP), a division of Boise Cascade, is one company that *has* put their customer and sales data to work. BCOP sells its office products to corporations, the government, and offices of all sizes. Increasingly customers are ordering their office supplies from BCOP's online catalogue of more than 12,000 items.

BCOP collects customer data from phone and online orders. A few years ago the company decided to put to use the huge volumes of data they had stored in a variety of databases to improve customer service. It wasn't all that easy. The databases could not communicate with each other. The company also wanted to make sure that they did not disturb normal operations while implementing a customer relationship management (CRM) system. Another problem was that the new system would require considerable retraining. For instance, sales representatives would have to share their data with reps in other territories.

With the new CRM system, a customer calling in will enter a unique ID. The phone call is routed to a sales representative who can bring up a customer transaction history. Special routing is available too. Based on prior transactions, the call might be routed to a specialized salesperson. Customers ordering online need an ID assigned by a sales representative. Otherwise customers may shop as a guest at the web site but they lose out on special features such as free shipping. A customer lost on the web site can click on a "Need Assistance" icon to get help by phone or through instant messaging. A guest can click on an icon to have a sales representative contact him or her. Of course, this requires completing a form that asks for, among other information, where you currently buy your office supplies! The web site has some helpful service features, including a Boise Webzine where office workers can ask questions and get answers concerning issues they face in the workplace.

Phase One of the CRM project went online in April 2001. The project was implemented on time and at very close to the $20 million budgeted cost. It's hard to say yet to what extent the improved customer service stemming from BCOP's new CRM system is benefiting the bottom line. What the company does know is that customers shopping with the new system are likely to leave impressed with the "slickness" of their experience.

---

[3] Adapted from Selden, Larry and Geoffrey Colvin, "A Measure of Success," *Business 2.0* (November 2001), p. 68.

SUMMARY

Elements of transaction processing include the accounting cycle, ledgers, journals, trial balances, coding, reports, and source documents. This chapter provided an overview of the financial accounting cycle. This cycle begins with the journal, a chronological record of accounting transactions. Accounting clerks must analyze transactions from source documents or other sources and enter them in a general or special journal. The ledger differs from a journal since it does not show all accounting aspects of a transaction. Instead, a ledger focuses on all activities associated with a particular account.

Transaction processing requires the management of accounting data as they flow through an AIS. When planning a new system, the developers usually start by designing the outputs from the system. These outputs, and especially managerial reports, then become the goals of the AIS and therefore provide a focus for the prerequisite tasks of data collection and data processing. Poorly designed reports can harm the value of an AIS. Sometimes reports include too much data. To avoid overloading managers with data, an AIS should incorporate elements of good report design.

Outputs, then, drive the inputs to an AIS. The fundamental instrument for collecting data in a typical AIS is the source document. Source documents should be easy to read, easy to understand, and serve to collect and distribute information as well as establish authenticity or authorization.

For a transaction processing system to gather and process data efficiently, accounting data are often coded. AISs can use codes to identify accounting information uniquely, to compress data, to classify transactions in accounts, and to convey special meanings. This chapter discussed four types of codes: (1) mnemonic codes, (2) sequence codes, (3) block codes, and (4) group codes. The choices among these codes and the way these codes are constructed are determined by (1) the code's use, (2) the need for consistency, (3) considerations of design efficiency, (4) an allowance for growth, and (5) the desire to use standard codes throughout a company.

AISs process transactions associated with business processes. These processes are groups of business and economic events that add value in an organization. Two core processes found in almost every type of organizational entity are the sales and purchasing processes. The sales process begins with a customer order and ends with the collection of cash from the customer. Important source documents associated with the sales process are sales orders, sales invoices, remittance advices, shipping notices, and customer checks. The AIS for the sales process outputs many reports. These include customer billing statements and reports concerned with analyzing outstanding debts and sales transactions. For the purchasing process, the AIS is concerned with timely payment for purchased goods and services. Many source documents initiate accounting entries in the purchasing process. These include purchase requisitions, purchase orders, receiving reports, purchase invoices, and bills of lading. The primary output of the purchasing process is the checks for vendors. However, there are many other outputs, some of which relate to inventory control.

KEY TERMS YOU SHOULD KNOW

accounting transactions	economic event
alphanumeric codes	exception reports
block codes	financial statements
business event	general journal
business processes	general ledger
chart of accounts	group code
customer relationship management (CRM)	information overload

journal	sequence code
ledgers	source document
mnemonic codes	special journals
numeric codes	subsidiary ledger
purchasing process	supply chain
sales process	trial balance

DISCUSSION QUESTIONS

4-1. How are journals and ledgers used in processing transactions? If a manufacturing company were to maintain special journals for purchases, sales, cash receipts, and cash disbursements, describe five journal entries that an AIS might make directly to the general journal.

4-2. AISs produce at least three trial balances within the financial accounting cycle. Explain the importance of each.

4-3. What are the purposes of accounting codes? How are they used? Bring to class some examples of codes used by manufacturing firms, accounting firms, and merchandising firms.

4-4. Describe some considerations useful in the design of accounting codes. For each consideration you name, provide an example, other than those presented in the textbook, to illustrate your point.

4-5. What are some typical outputs of an AIS? Why do system analysts concentrate on managerial reports when they start to design an effective AIS? Why not start with the inputs to the system instead?

4-6. What are some criteria that systems designers should consider when developing managerial reports for an AIS? Can you think of any others beyond those described in the chapter? If so, what are they?

4-7. Visit a local business and collect some examples of source documents used in an AIS. For each source document example you collect, discuss its purpose(s). Are different source documents required for manufacturing firms versus merchandising organizations? Are all the business' source documents paper based?

4-8. This chapter discussed many inputs to an organization's sales process. What are the specific data items to input to this process when adding a new customer and recording a sales order?

4-9. How does a data flow diagram for the sales process differ from a system flowchart describing that process?

4-10. How are the inputs and outputs of the purchasing process likely to be different for a restaurant versus an automobile manufacturer?

PROBLEMS

4-11. Listed below are several types of accounting data that might be coded. For each data item, recommend a type of code (mnemonic, sequence, block, or group) and give reasons for your choice.

a. Employee identification number on a computer file.

b. Product number for a sales catalog.

c. Inventory number for the products of a wholesale drug company.

d. Inventory part number for a bicycle manufacturing company.

    e. Identification numbers on the forms waiters and waitresses use to take orders.

    f. Identification numbers on airline ticket stubs.

    g. Automobile registration numbers.

    h. Automobile engine block numbers.

    i. Shirt sizes for men's shirts.

    j. Color codes for house paint.

    k. Identification numbers on payroll check forms.

    l. Listener identification for a radio station.

    m. Numbers on lottery tickets.

    n. Identification numbers on a credit card.

    o. Identification numbers on dollar bills.

    p. Passwords used to gain access to a computer.

    q. Zip codes.

    r. A chart of accounts for a department store.

    s. A chart of accounts for a flooring subcontractor.

    t. Shoe sizes.

    u. Identification number on a student examination.

    v. Identification number on an insurance policy.

4-12. Ghymn Gadgets is a marketer of inexpensive toys and novelties that it sells to retail stores, specialty stores, and catalog companies. As an accountant working for the company, you have been asked to design a product code for the company. In analyzing this problem, you have discovered the following:

    a. The company has three major product lines: (1) toys and games, (2) party and magic tricks, and (3) inexpensive gifts. There are major subproducts within each of these product lines, and the number of these categories is 25, 18, and 113, respectively.

    b. The company has divided its selling efforts into five geographic areas: (1) the United States, (2) the Far East, (3) Europe and Africa, (4) South America, and (5) International (a catchall area). Each major geographic area has several sales districts (never more than 99 per area). Between 1 and 20 salespeople are assigned to each district.

    c. As noted earlier, there are three major categories of customers, and certain customers can also purchase goods on credit. There are five different classes of credit customers and each rating indicates the maximum amount of credit the customer can have.

Design a group code that Ghymn Gadgets could use to prepare sales analysis reports. Be sure to identify each digit or position in your code in terms of both use and meaning.

4-13. Figure 4-15 is a system flowchart for P. Miesing and Company's purchase order event.

Requirement

Prepare a narrative to accompany the flowchart describing this purchase order event. Include in your narrative the source documents involved, the computerized data processing that takes place, data inputs used to prepare purchase orders, and the outputs prepared from the processing function.

INTERNET EXERCISES

4-14. Businesses today are enhancing their sales process through customer relationship management (CRM). Search the Internet for a vendor web site for CRM software. Identify two advantages that this software provides to a business that uses it.

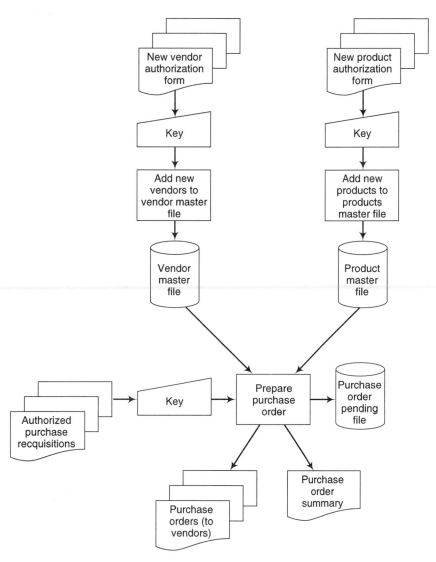

FIGURE 4–15   System flowchart illustrating the preparation of purchase orders for P. Miesing and Company.

4-15. Electronic commerce may impact a company's business processes. Visit www.amazon.com. What are the source documents (they may be screen images) associated with the company's sales process? How are these different from the ones described in this chapter?

CASE ANALYSES

4-16. McMart (Sales Process)

McMart is a national discount retail store chain with annual revenues of more than $1 billion. The stores sell primarily clothing and housewares. The stores are self-service.

Customers select merchandise and take it to the sales counter. A sales clerk scans the bar code on the merchandise to record the sale. Customers may pay with cash or debit or credit card. McMart's accounting software records sales transactions in real time and tracks inventories on a perpetual basis.

Top management is considering establishing an online store. They are interested in collecting as much information about customers on the site as they possibly can. The web site will sell the same products as are available in the stores. Customers will be able to use credit cards only for online payments.

The CEO believes that the company needs to be careful to make sure that an online store will complement their brick and mortar retail operations. The marketing manager is excited about the possibility of learning about McMart's customers and using the information to improve both in-store and online sales.

Requirements

1. Contrast the sales process of McMart's retail store operation with the sales process in an online store environment. Would any of the events in the process change?

2. At what points do you collect data about customers and sales transactions in the retail store? In the online environment?

3. What data might you collect about retail store and online customers to improve your profitability? What data might you collect to improve customer satisfaction?

4. How is the sales process different for a public accounting firm? What data can they collect to improve customer relationships and grow revenues?

4-17. Best Sellers Book Company (Report Design)

The Best Sellers Book Company is a college textbook publisher. The company's operating data are centrally processed by its information processing department. Each company subsystem (production, marketing, accounting, finance, and personnel) receives computerized performance reports and has decision-making authority delegated from top management.

In the past few months, the managers of most subsystems have been complaining about the criteria used by top management for evaluating their operating performances. The major complaint has been the number of noncontrollable items included within an individual subsystem's performance report.

You are one of the accountants working with the company's AIS and have been asked by top management to design and implement a responsibility accounting system for evaluating each subsystem's monthly operating performance. You suggest to top management that a further improvement could be made in the company's performance reporting system if a management-by-exception structure were also incorporated into the new system. The top management executives agree with the suggestion, and you are given the approval to design and implement the new reporting system.

You are currently analyzing the marketing subsystem's March 2003 budget projection data compared with its actual cost performance during March under the company's old reporting system. The March 2003 performance report computer printout appeared as shown on the opposite page.

Cost Item	Budget	Actual	Variation Favorable (Unfavorable)
Allocated Building Depreciation	$ 1,000	$1,100	($ 100)
Sales Personnel Salaries	8,000	9,000	(1,000)
Promotional Textbook Materials	2,000	2,600	(600)
Allocated Administrative Expenses	1,000	1,600	(600)
Textbook Advertising in Journals	800	825	(25)
Utilities Expense	300	375	(75)
Marketing Clerical Salaries	5,000	4,900	100
Totals	$18,100	$20,400	($2,300)

After familiarizing yourself with the delegated authority given the marketing subsystem managers by top management, you accumulate the following information.

1. The marketing subsystem managers make their own decisions regarding the number of salespeople and clerical people to hire and how much to pay these employees.
2. The marketing subsystem occupies the entire second floor of the company's building and has a separate electric utilities meter on this floor.
3. The marketing subsystem managers have complete decision-making authority for all advertising expenditures associated with promoting textbook sales.

Your next major task is to determine the variations from budget that should be considered significant. Through discussions with marketing subsystem personnel and top management, the following budget variability schedule is developed.

Budgeted Dollar Cost Range	Acceptable Budget Variation
$ 1–$ 500	+ or – $ 50
$ 501–$1,000	+ or – $100
$1,001–$3,000	+ or – $300
$3,001–$5,000	+ or – $500
$5,001–$7,000	+ or – $700
$7,001–$9,000	+ or – $900
Over $9,000	+ or – $1,200

You then talk to computer specialists within the company's IT department about the required revisions in marketing's monthly performance report. Based on the information you provide these computer specialists, they make the necessary computer program changes to accomplish your new responsibility accounting system with a management-by-exception reporting structure.

Requirements

1. What elements of good report design should be incorporated in the new monthly performance report?
2. Prepare a new report for the marketing subsystem, incorporating a management-by-exception reporting structure.

4-18. Universal Floor Covering (Coding System)

Universal Floor Covering is a manufacturer and distributor of carpet and vinyl floor coverings. The home office is located in Charlotte, North Carolina. Carpet mills are located in Dalton, Georgia, and Greenville, South Carolina; a floor-covering manufacturing plant is in High Point, North Carolina. Total sales last year were just over $250 million.

The company manufactures more than 200 different varieties of carpet. The carpet is classified as being for commercial or residential purposes and is sold under five brand names with up to five lines under each brand. The lines indicate the different grades of quality; grades are measured by type of tuft and number of tufts per square inch. Each line of carpet can have up to fifteen different color styles.

Just under 200 varieties of vinyl floor covering are manufactured. The floor covering is also classified as being for commercial or residential use. There are four separate brand names (largely distinguished by the type of finish), up to eight different patterns for each brand, and up to eight color styles for each pattern.

Ten different grades of padding are manufactured. The padding is usually differentiated by intended use (commercial or residential) in addition to thickness and composition of materials.

Universal serves over 2,000 regular wholesale customers. Retail showrooms are the primary customers. Many major corporations are direct buyers of Universal's products. Large construction companies have contracts with Universal to purchase carpet and floor covering at reduced rates for use in newly constructed homes and commercial buildings. In addition, Universal produces a line of residential carpet for a large national retail chain. Sales to these customers range from $10,000 to $1,000,000 annually.

There is a company-owned retail outlet at each plant. The outlets carry overruns, seconds, and discontinued items. This is Universal's only retail sales function.

The company has divided the sales market into seven territories, with the majority of concentration on the East Coast. The market segments are New England, New York, Mid-Atlantic, Carolinas, South, Midwest, and West. Each sales territory is divided into five to ten districts with a salesperson assigned to each district.

The current accounting system has been adequate for monitoring the sales by product. However, there are limitations to the system because specific information is sometimes not available. A detailed analysis of operations is necessary for planning and control purposes and would be valuable for decision-making purposes. The accounting systems department has been asked to design a sales analysis code. The code should permit Universal to prepare a sales analysis that would reflect the characteristics of the company's business.

Requirements

1. Account coding systems are based on various coding concepts. Briefly define and give an example of the following coding concepts:
   a. Sequence coding
   b. Block coding
   c. Group coding

2. Identify and describe factors that must be considered before a coding system can be designed and implemented for an organization.

3. Develop a coding system for Universal Floor Covering that would assign sales analysis codes to sales transactions. For each portion of the code:
   a. Explain the meaning and purpose of the code.
   b. Identity and justify the number of digits required.

(CMA Adapted)

4-19. Larkin State University (Purchasing Process)

Larkin State University is a medium-sized academic institution located in the Southeastern United States. The university employs about 250 full-time faculty and 300 staff personnel. There are 12,000 students enrolled among the university's four colleges.

The Purchase Process

The university's budget for purchases of equipment and supplies is about $25,000,000 annually. Peter Reese is in charge of the Purchasing Department. He reports directly to the Vice President of Finance for the university. Pete supervises four purchasing clerks and three receiving personnel. The office is responsible for purchases of all equipment and supplies except for computer equipment and software, and plant purchases or additions.

The Payment Process

The various departments across campus manually fill out hard copy purchase requisition forms when there is a need for equipment/supplies. Each department forwards these forms to the Purchasing Department. If the request is for computer equipment or software, the requisition is forwarded to the Department of Information Technology for action.

Purchase requisitions are assigned to one of the three purchasing clerks by department. For instance, one purchasing clerk makes purchases for all university departments beginning with the letters A through G (Accounting – Geology). Purchasing clerks check the requisition to make sure it is authorized and then consult the Approved Vendor Listing to find a supplier. The clerk may contact a supplier for pricing and product specification. Once this task is complete, the purchasing clerk enters the purchase requisition, and vendor and price information into the computer system, which prints out a multiple part purchase order. Clerks send copies of the purchase order to Central Receiving, to the vendor, and to the Accounts Payable Department. (The university considered using EDI for its purchases, but chose not to adopt it due to the large number of vendors used.)

When Central Receiving receives an order, a receiving clerk consults the Purchase Order file to make sure the correct product and quantity have been delivered. The clerk also checks the product for damage. Central receiving does not accept any over-shipments. Receiving clerks forward accepted shipments to the adjacent warehouse for distribution to the appropriate department. Clerks file one copy of the Receiving Report, send one copy to the Purchasing Department, and forward a third copy to Accounts Payable.

George Vaughn is the Supervisor of Accounts Payable. Two accounting clerks report to him. He assigns invoices to them for payment based on vendor name. One clerk processes payments for vendors A - M and the other clerk handles payments to all vendors with names beginning with letters N - Z. The clerks match each vendor invoice with a copy of the receiving report and purchase order before entering it into the computer for payment by due date. There are often discrepancies among the three documents. This requires frequent phone calls to the vendor, the Receiving Department, or Purchasing for resolution. As a result, the company frequently makes payments late and loses out on cash discounts.

Requirements

1. Identify the important business events that occur within Larkin's purchase/payment process.

2. What changes would you suggest to the current process that IT might enable?

4-20. Sales Processing at Uptown Bucks (Sales Process)

Uptown Bucks (UB) is an off-campus meal plan business in Oxford, Ohio. Students, or their families, buy debit cards with fixed amounts that they can use to purchase food only at more than 18 local restaurants. Customers can buy the cards at UB's office in the center of town, or they may purchase the cards online. The following paragraph describes the online card sale process.

A customer enters their credit card information online, and the amount of purchase. UB's software automatically checks the card number to determine that it is a valid credit card number; for instance, there are certain digits that indicate Visa cards. The software displays an error message if the number is not valid. The usual cause of these errors is typographical. Once the customer completes the card order screen, the software sends the data in an encrypted form to UB's host computer. Periodically, the UB accountant retrieves transactions from the server. This is done by clicking on the "Get Transactions" screen button. For each online transaction, the accountant then manually copies down the credit card number on a scrap of paper, walks across the office to the credit card machine, and keys in the credit card number, the amount, and the numerical portion of the address. The credit card software checks to see if the card is valid and charges it for the amount. The accountant next writes down the validation number, returns to the host computer, and enters it. She prints a receipt for the transaction and puts it in a file. The customer database now reflects the new customer. When a customer purchases a card off-line with a credit card, the accountant swipes the card directly, checks its validity, charges the card, and then writes down the validation number and enters it in the host computer.

UB is considering the purchase of credit card software that can reside on the host computer and interact with their accounting software. The credit card software costs about $400. The credit card company rates are likely to increase by about .5% because cards could no longer be swiped directly — all credit card purchases would need to go through the online software. The rate UB has to pay the credit card company is based on this mix. Credit card companies typically charge more if card numbers are punched rather than swiped because they have more chance of invalid transactions due to theft. It's easier to steal a number than a card. Currently about half of UB's sales transactions arise from online sales; the other half result from sales through the office.

Requirements

1. Should UB buy the credit card software?

2. Develop a flowchart for UB's online sales process. What are the business risks associated with this process?

REFERENCES, RECOMMENDED READINGS, AND WEB SITES

References and Recommended Readings

Anonymous, "Accounts Payable Can Save Company Dollars," *The CPA Journal* (May 1999), p. 11.

Bartholomew, Doug, "First, Analyze the Processes," *Industry Week* (November 1, 1999), p. 37.

Courtney, H. M., and D. Benco, "Can Your Software Make It Into Year 2000?" *Journal of Accountancy* (December 1997), pp. 36–40.

Keen, P. G. W., and E. M. Knapp, *Every Manager's Guide to Business Processes* (Boston: Harvard Business Press, 1996).

Kumar, V., "Current Trends in Transaction Processing Systems," *Journal of Systems Management* (January 1990), pp. 33–37.

Palmer, R. J., "Reengineering Payables at ITT Automotive." *Management Accounting* (July 1994), pp. 38–42.

Pavlinko, J. L., "Paperless Payables at Lord," *Management Accounting* (July 1993), pp. 32–34.

Selden, Larry, and Geoffrey Colvin, "A Measure of Success," *Business 2.0* (November 2001), pp. 59–68.

Whitney, S., "One Size Does Not Fit All," *Best 's Review* (October 1999), pp. 123–127.

Wilson, Tim, "Accounting on E-Time–Service Synchronizes Financial, Supply Chain Data to Speed Payments," *Internetweek* (November 22, 1999), p. PG1.

Web sites

There are several software vendors that specialize in CRM software. Visit www.siebel.com and www.peoplesoft.com. to learn more about these systems.

Many companies use specialized software to design reports. Visit the web site for Crystal Reports at www.seagatesoftware.com.

Chapter 5

Accounting Information Systems and Business Processes: Part II

INTRODUCTION

ADDITIONAL BUSINESS PROCESSES

The Resource Management Process

The Production Process

The Financing Process

BUSINESS PROCESSES IN SPECIAL INDUSTRIES

Specialized Accounting Information Needs

Examples of Industries with Specialized AISs

BUSINESS PROCESS REENGINEERING

Principles for Successful Reengineering

Why Reengineering Sometimes Fails

AIS AT WORK—RETAIL INFORMATION SYSTEMS OPEN UP

SUMMARY

KEY TERMS YOU SHOULD KNOW

DISCUSSION QUESTIONS

PROBLEMS

INTERNET EXERCISES

CASE ANALYSES

Grace Ho And Associates

Graduate Programs at Riley University

Wilshire Credit

Nyang'oro Manufacturing

REFERENCES, RECOMMENDED READINGS, AND WEB SITES

After reading this chapter, you will:

1. *Know* the objectives, inputs, and outputs of the resource management, production, and financing processes.

2. *Be able to explain* why some organizations have special accounting information needs.

3. *Recognize* the special information needs of several different types of organizations.

4. *Understand* how companies use business process reengineering (BPR) to cut costs and improve their operational efficiency.

Aetna Life & Casualty Company may have deserved an award for simpleminded tasks and complicated processes with an approach to applications handling that took an average of twenty-eight days to do twenty-six minutes of work.

Michael Hammer, *Beyond Reengineering* (New York: HarperBusiness, 1997), p.28.

INTRODUCTION

The previous chapter discussed the elements of business processes and two processes common to almost every organizational entity. This chapter continues the discussion of business processes with descriptions of three additional processes: the resource management, production, and financing processes. Businesses use many different resources. The resource management process is concerned with two of those resources: human resources and fixed assets. The production manufacturing cycle concerns the conversion of raw materials (another resource) into finished goods available for sale. The production process includes **inventory control.** It interfaces with both the purchasing process (which accounts for inventory acquisitions) and the sales process (which accounts for inventory sales). Most organizations must obtain financing for their assets either through borrowing or by selling shares of ownership. The financing process concerns the information inputs and outputs associated with these activities.

Many organizations have specialized information needs, apart from the typical AIS requirements for information about revenues, purchases, and resources. The second section of this chapter considers the unique aspects of various organizational entities that need other accounting information.

The focus of AISs is moving from transaction processing to capturing data associated with the events that make up business processes. Maximizing the efficiency of these processes is important to business success. The final section of this chapter discusses the concept of reengineering business processes.

ADDITIONAL BUSINESS PROCESSES

Three important business processes common to many organizational entities are the resource management, production, and financing processes. Most organizations need fixed assets such as office buildings and equipment in order to conduct their activities. It is hard to imagine an organization that does not need human resources as well. The resource management process includes activities related to both fixed and human assets. Manufacturing organizations buy raw materials and convert them into finished goods through a production process. The production processing in an AIS concerns the capture of data and the reporting of information associated with producing goods in manufacturing organizations. Another important business process common to almost all organizations is the acquisition of capital (or funds) needed to do business (i.e., the financing process). The financing process concerns the inputs, processing, and outputs associated with financing an organization's resources.

The Resource Management Process

Organizations use resources to produce goods or services sold to generate revenues. Managers must monitor and control these resources. We have already discussed one such resource in Chapter 4: inventory and its management. Two other resources requiring attention by an AIS are an organization's human resources and its fixed assets. The resource management process consists of events related to these resources. Because the inputs, processing, and outputs for human resources and fixed assets are quite different, we shall examine them separately.

Human Resource Management An organization's **human resource management** activity includes the personnel function, which is responsible for hiring employees and maintaining personnel records, and the payroll function, which is responsible for maintaining accounting records related to employee remuneration. The primary objective of the **personnel function** is to hire, train, and employ appropriately qualified people to do an organization's work. The main purpose of **payroll processing** is to pay employees for work performed. Payroll processing also involves maintaining employee earnings records (a payroll history), complying with various government tax and reporting requirements, reporting on various deduction categories (e.g., pension funds and group insurance), and interacting with the personnel function.

A data flow diagram for the human resource management process appears in Figure 5-1. Figure 5-2 shows the objectives, inputs, and outputs associated with this process. Figure 5-3 is a high-level system flowchart for the personnel function and Figure 5-4 depicts the payroll function.

Inputs to Human Resource Management Processing The source documents used in payroll processing are personnel action forms, time sheets, payroll deduction authorizations, and tax withholding forms. The personnel department sends *personnel action forms* to payroll that document the hiring of new employees or changes in employee status. For example, payroll receives a personnel action form when an employee receives a salary increase. This document is very important for control purposes. For example, auditors will detect an employee who increases his or her own salary within the computerized AIS when they fail to find a personnel action form authorizing the increase.

Many companies use *time sheets* to track the hours employees work. Other companies use a time clock instead, and employees must "punch in" when they arrive for work. Still others equip employees with access cards that record the time and verify employees when they enter and leave the workplace. However an AIS records time, an employee's supervisor should authorize hours worked, and a payroll clerk should look for appropriate authorization before processing these hours. If a company uses a job cost system, time sheets for employees can be cross-referenced with time recorded on individual jobs.

Employees fill out *payroll deduction authorizations* to authorize the payroll system to deduct amounts from gross pay for items such as parking, health and life insurance, retirement, and union dues. An authorization form should document each deduction. Every employee must also complete tax-withholding forms, which authorize the payroll system to reduce gross pay by the appropriate withholding tax. The system uses each employee's W-4 withholding form to calculate the correct withholding for federal income taxes.

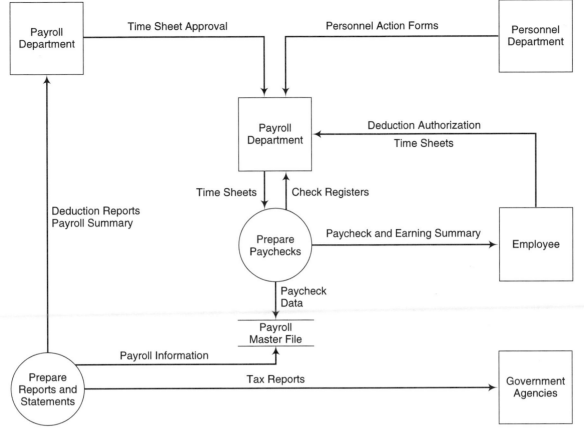

FIGURE 5-1   Data flow diagram of the human resource management process.

THE HUMAN RESOURCE MANAGEMENT PROCESS

Objectives:
- Hiring, training, and employing workers
- Maintaining employee earnings records
- Complying with regulatory reporting requirements
- Reporting on payroll deductions
- Making timely and accurate payments to employees
- Providing an interface for personnel and payroll activities

Inputs (Source Documents):
- Personnel Action Forms
- Time Sheets
- Payroll Deduction Authorizations
- Tax Withholding Forms

Outputs (Reports):
- Financial Statement Information
- Employee Listings
- Paychecks
- Check Registers
- Deduction Reports
- Tax (Regulatory) Reports
- Payroll Summaries

FIGURE 5-2   Objectives, inputs, and outputs for the human resource management process.

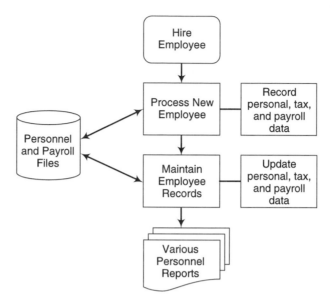

FIGURE 5–3   High-level systems flowchart of the AIS for the personnel function.

Outputs of Human Resource Management Processing   The outputs of human resource management processing include employee listings, check registers, paychecks, deduction reports, tax reports, and payroll summaries. As you can imagine, the processing of paychecks should include very strict internal control procedures. (See Chapters 9 and 10.) *Employee listings* show current employees and may contain addresses and other demographic information. *Check registers* accompany each printing

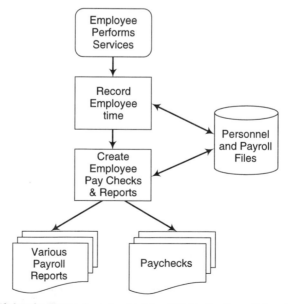

FIGURE 5–4   High-level systems flowchart of the AIS for the Payroll function.

of paychecks and list gross pay, deductions, and net pay. Payroll clerks use the check register information to make journal entries for salary and payroll-tax expenses. *Deduction reports* contain summaries of deductions for employees as a group.

The government requires various *tax reports* for income tax, Social Security tax, and unemployment tax information. The employees pay some taxes in their entirety, but employers share others. For instance, both the employee and employer pay equal amounts of Social Security taxes. The payroll system allocates shared taxes to the appropriate accounts. Taxes paid by employees are allocated to payroll expense, but employer taxes are part of the employer's tax expense.

Besides paychecks, check registers, deduction reports, and tax reports, the payroll function issues various *payroll summaries*. These summaries are important to management in analyzing expenses. A typical payroll summary report might distribute payroll expenses by department or job. Another payroll summary report could show overtime hours worked in each department.

Manual payroll processing can be both tedious and repetitive. Consequently, the payroll function was the first computerized accounting activity in many organizations. Today, some companies find it easier and more cost-effective to use outsourcing companies for processing paychecks and payroll reports. Case-in-Point 5.1 describes one such organization.

> ***Case-in-Point 5.1***   Automatic Data Processing, Inc., or ADP, is the world's largest payroll service provider. Almost a half-million companies in fifteen countries outsource their payroll processing and, in some cases, their human resource administration to ADP. The company has been in business for more than 50 years and is responsible for paying more than 33 million employees.

Fixed Asset Management   Fixed assets are assets with usable lives of more than one year. The objective of the **fixed asset management function** is to manage the purchase, maintenance, valuation, and disposal of an organization's fixed assets (also called long-term assets). Figure 5-5 shows a data flow diagram for the fixed asset management activity and Figure 5-6 summarizes the function's objectives, inputs, and outputs. Figure 5-7 is a high-level systems flowchart showing fixed asset acquisition, maintenance, and disposition.

Even small organizations generally own many fixed assets, which management must track as they are purchased and used. In thinking about how complex it might be to track fixed assets, consider all the fixed assets found in a typical college classroom. There are desks, chairs, blackboards, computers, overhead projectors, podiums, and so on. A university must record each of these fixed assets on its books when it purchases the asset. In addition, the university must maintain depreciation schedules for its fixed assets. Not only does an AIS calculate the depreciation for a company's financial statements, but it also prepares separate depreciation schedules for income tax reporting purposes. Employees often move fixed assets around within an organization, and although an AIS should keep track of all asset locations, this can be quite difficult in practice. Again, using the college classroom example, imagine keeping track of overhead projectors that professors might switch from one classroom to another! The following Case-in-Point illustrates the complexity of managing IT assets in particular.

> ***Case-in-Point 5.2***   Sears, Roebuck and Co. implemented an asset management system in 1997 to prepare for Y2K and account for its more than 300,000 pieces of hardware and the software that goes with it. The move away from centralized mainframe computers to desktop

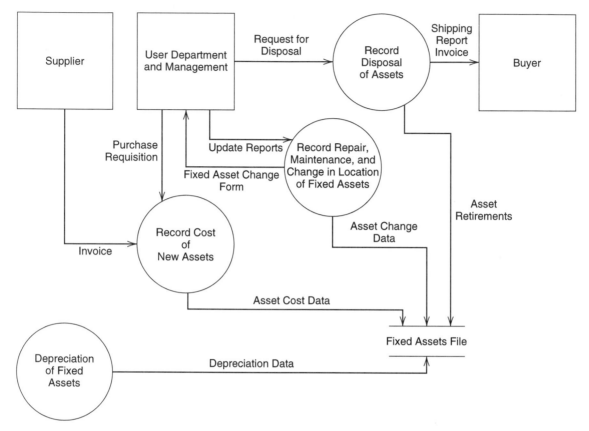

FIGURE 5–5 Data flow diagram of the fixed asset management function.

THE FIXED ASSET MANAGEMENT PROCESS

Objectives:
- Tracking purchases of fixed assets
- Recording fixed asset maintenance
- Valuing fixed assets
- Allocating fixed asset costs (recording depreciation)
- Tracking disposal of fixed assets

Inputs (Source Documents):
- Purchase Requisition
- Receiving Reports
- Supplier Invoices
- Construction Work Orders
- Repair and Maintenance Records
- Fixed Asset Change Forms

Outputs (Reports):
- Financial Statement Information
- Fixed Asset Register
- Depreciation Register
- Repair and Maintenance Reports
- Retired Assets Report

FIGURE 5–6 Objectives. inputs. and outputs for the fixed asset management function.

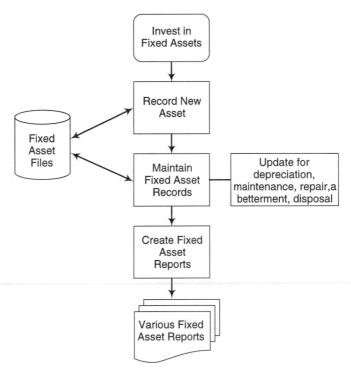

FIGURE 5-7 High-level systems flowchart of the AIS for the fixed asset management function.

PCs also contributed to American Home Products' decision to adapt a fixed asset strategy and management system. IT management requires accounting for initial hardware and software costs, maintenance costs, upgrade costs, and so on. Software licenses and contracts further complicate matters.[1]

Since fixed assets often require repair, an AIS should keep track of repair costs, distinguishing between **revenue expenditures** and **capital expenditures.** (Revenue expenditures are ordinary repair expenses, whereas capital expenditures add to the value of assets.) Finally, the AIS calculates the amount of gain or loss upon disposal of individual fixed assets. By comparing the amount received for the asset with the asset's book value, the AIS can compute a gain or loss. Accountants cannot calculate gains or losses accurately without a good recordkeeping system that tracks all costs associated with fixed asset accounts and their related depreciation amounts.

Inputs to Fixed Asset Management Processing Fixed asset transaction processing begins with a request for a fixed asset purchase. The individual making the request enters it on a purchase requisition form. *Fixed asset requests* usually require approval by one or more managers, especially where purchases call for substantial investments. Other documents associated with fixed asset purchases are receiving reports, supplier invoices, and repair and maintenance records. The receiving department fills out a *receiving report* upon receipt of a fixed asset. The asset's supplier

---

[1] Adapted from "Controlled Substances," *CIO Magazine,* June 1, 2000.

sends an *invoice* when it ships the asset. Sometimes a company builds a fixed asset, for example, a warehouse, rather than acquiring it from an outside vendor. Here, processing fixed assets requires a *work order* detailing the costs of construction.

There is no type of source document that prompts depreciation expense. There may, however, be some documentation dictating the appropriate depreciation method or methods for this allocation. AISs often allocate fixed asset costs using multiple depreciation methods. Not only is a separate depreciation method commonly used for tax versus financial reporting purposes, but government or industry regulations may require the use of still other depreciation methods for special reports.

Those responsible for a particular fixed asset should complete a *fixed asset change form* when transferring fixed assets from one location to another. The fixed asset change form also records the sale, trade, or retirement of fixed assets. Fixed asset management requires maintaining repair and maintenance records for each asset individually or for categories of fixed assets. The department performing this service should record these activities on a *repair and maintenance form*. This form notifies the AIS to update expense or asset accounts.

Outputs of Fixed Asset Management Processing   One output of the fixed asset processing system is a report listing all fixed assets acquired during a particular period. A *fixed asset register* lists the identification number of all fixed assets held by a company and each asset's location. Bar codes can facilitate fixed asset tracking. If each asset is bar-coded with an identification number, auditors can verify locations by automatically scanning the codes.

The *depreciation register* shows depreciation expense and accumulated depreciation for each fixed asset. Repair and maintenance reports show the current period's repair and maintenance expenses, as well as each fixed asset's repair and maintenance history. Finally, a *report on assets retired* reflects the disposition of fixed assets during the current period.

The Production Process

The **production process** (sometimes called the conversion process) begins with a request for raw materials and ends with the transfer of finished goods to warehouses. Figure 5-8 is a data flow diagram of the production process and Figure 5-9 shows the objectives, inputs, and outputs associated with the production of goods and services. The high-level systems flowchart in Figure 5-10 shows the information flow for a manufacturer.

Objectives of the Production Process   The primary objective of a manufacturing organization's production process is to convert raw materials into finished goods as efficiently as possible. Chapter 4 discussed transaction processing for the purchase of raw materials and an AIS's inputs and outputs associated with the sale of finished goods. Producing goods and services often requires expensive factory machinery. Accounting for the acquisition and use of this machinery is part of the fixed asset management process described in the previous section of this chapter. Another important part of an AIS's production process is the cost accounting subsystem.

Cost Accounting Subsystem   Since the cost of goods sold is likely to be the largest expense on a manufacturing firm's income statement, an important part of

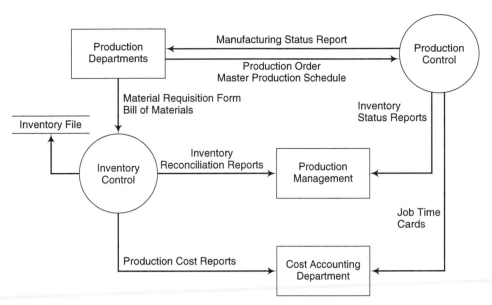

FIGUER 5-8 A data flow diagram of the production process.

the production process is an AIS's **cost accounting subsystem.** The cost accounting subsystem provides important control information (e.g., variance reports reflecting differences between actual and standard production costs) and varies with the size of the company and the types of product being produced. As you might guess, a bakery producing baked goods would have an AIS quite different from that of an

---

THE PRODUCTION PROCESS

Objectives:
- Track purchases and sales of inventories
- Monitor and control manufacturing costs
- Control inventory
- Control and coordinate the production process
- Provide input for budgets

Inputs (Source Documents):
- Materials Requisition Form
- Bill of Materials
- Master Production Schedule
- Production Order
- Job Time Card

Outputs (Reports):
- Financial Statement Information
- Materials Price Lists
- Periodic Usage Reports
- Inventory Reconciliation Reports
- Inventory Status Reports
- Production Cost Reports
- Manufacturing Status Reports

FIGURE 5-9 Objectives. inputs. and outputs associated with the production of goods and services.

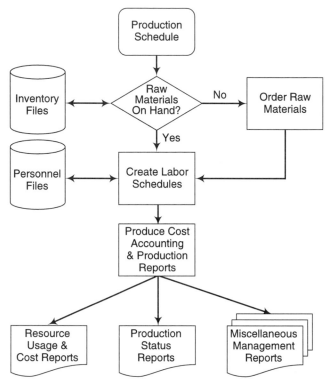

FIGURE 5–10.   High-level systems flowchart of the AIS for the production process in a manufacturing organization.

automobile manufacturer. Cost accounting subsystems for most manufacturing organizations, however, may generally be characterized as either job costing or process costing systems.

A **job costing** information system keeps track of the specific costs for raw materials, labor, and overhead associated with each product or group of products, called a "job." This type of costing system is most appropriate for manufacturers of large-scale or custom products, such as home-builders or book publishers. Manufacturers of homogeneous products (such as oil or soft drinks) that are produced on a regular and constant basis use a **process costing system.** In this system, it is not feasible or practical to keep track of costs for each item or group of items produced. Instead, process costing systems use averages to calculate the costs associated with goods in process and finished goods produced.

Just-in-Time (JIT) Inventory Systems   Inventory control ensures that the production process handles inventory transactions appropriately so that the financial statements correctly state the value of the inventory and cost of goods sold accounts. Carrying inventory has costs associated with it. These costs include warehousing costs and the costs related to obsolescence or reduction in sales value. To minimize inventory costs, many manufacturing organizations use a **just-in-time (JIT)** inventory system. Some managers refer to a JIT system as a **make-to-order** inventory system. This phrase notes that the organization is producing goods to fill an order rather than **make-to-stock,** which infers that production is for inventory purposes.

The objective of a JIT system is to minimize inventories at all levels. Each stage in the production operation manufactures (or acquires) a part just in time for the next process to use it. While the best possible JIT system would maintain zero inventory balances, this is often not practical in real-world applications. Manufacturing organizations need some inventories to protect against interruptions in supply from manufacturers and fluctuations in demand for their finished goods. Case-in-Point 5.3 illustrates this point.

> **Case in Point 5.3** In 1992, a strike against a General Motors parts plant in Ohio required the auto maker to halt production of minivans because there were no side panels in stock. GM's use of a JIT inventory approach meant that the assembly plant kept only one day's supply of affected parts on hand. In 1998, a General Motors truck assembly plant also had to shut down due to lack of parts. General Motors makes most of its own parts, which, where a just-in-time inventory approach is used, gives its workers a great deal of leverage when they strike.

A JIT system is highly dependent on an AIS. The production process must operate at the highest level of efficiency for a JIT system to be successful. If the AIS does not process transactions on a timely and accurate basis, manufacturing processes may lack the raw materials inventory necessary to maintain a constant work flow. Inefficient processing of transactions can also lead to shortages of finished goods that in turn translate into lost sales.

Inputs to the Production Process   When the production area needs raw materials, it issues a materials requisition form to acquire more material from stores (a storeroom or warehouse), where the raw materials are kept. If the level of inventory in stores falls below a certain predetermined level, the inventory control clerk issues a purchase requisition to the purchasing department. Finished goods consist of a complex array of parts or subassemblies. For example, an armchair consists of four legs, a seat, two arms, and a back. The *bill of materials* shows the types and quantities of parts needed to make a single unit of product.

A very important input to the production process is the *master production schedule.* This schedule shows the quantities of goods needed to meet manufacturing quantities required for anticipated sales. It also coordinates the various manufacturing operations so that they produce goods in timely fashion. The *production order* authorizes the manufacture of goods and "drives" the production schedule. The marketing function's sales projections and desired inventory levels form the basis for the production order.

Tracking labor time is important to a job costing system because one employee may work on many jobs and one job might require the work of many employees. An input to a job costing system is the *job time card.* This card shows the distribution of labor costs to specific jobs or production orders. Each worker completes a job time card (usually daily or weekly), detailing the hours worked on specific operations and jobs.

The inventory control system monitors the raw materials needed by production processes. This is a complex process because each finished product is likely to include a variety of parts or subassemblies. A **material requirements planning (MRP I)** system monitors the acquisition and use of these parts. This AIS subsystem integrates the production schedule with the bill of materials to ensure that parts are available as needed. A more complex version of the material requirements planning system is a **manufacturing resource planning (MRP II)** system. An MRP II system also uses the information from the bill of materials and production schedule to coordinate the purchase and use of raw material inventories. But an MRP II system takes this further and integrates with the purchasing and revenue processes to provide information associated with purchasing, sales, and cash forecasting. MRP II systems improve decision making because managers use them to plan and control the manufacturing process.

MRP II systems facilitate planning in a production environment. Executing the plan is the role of **lean manufacturing** system tools. The lean manufacturing concept focuses on improving the ability to meet real-time customer demand by aligning an organization's sales, engineering, distribution, and production processes. A key aspect of lean manufacturing is production flexibility — the ability to respond quickly to customer demands when they vary from demand forecasts.

Outputs of the Production Process   Examples of output reports for the production process include materials price lists, periodic usage reports, an inventory reconciliation report, a detailed inventory status report, production cost reports, and manufacturing status reports. The *materials price list* shows prices charged for raw materials. The purchasing department updates this list. Cost accountants use price lists to determine the standard costs needed to budget production costs. *Periodic usage reports* show how various production departments are using raw materials. Managers can use these reports to detect waste by comparing raw material usage to output, the latter reflecting the units of finished goods produced.

A company using a perpetual inventory system issues an inventory reconciliation report. When auditors take a physical inventory, the accounting subsystem compares the physical inventory results with book balances, and notes discrepancies on this *inventory reconciliation report.* Another report important for inventory control purposes is the periodic detailed *inventory status report.* This report allows purchasing and production managers to monitor inventory levels.

Cost accountants use *production cost reports* to calculate budget variances. Some manufacturing organizations use standard costing systems that allow them to compare standard costs with actual costs and compute variances for materials, labor, and overhead. The production cost report details the actual costs for each production operation, each cost element, and/or each separate job. *Manufacturing status reports* provide managers with information about the status of various jobs. Because the manufacture of a single product unit may require coordination of many operations, it is important to report on production status regularly.

The Financing Process

The financing process is the process by which a company gets and uses financial resources, such as cash, other liquid assets, and investments. Cash and liquid assets are an organization's working capital. The financing process interfaces with the revenue, purchasing, fixed asset, and human resource processes. Much of the capital available in an organization comes from sales revenue, and an entity uses its financial resources to pay for its expenses, personnel, and fixed assets.

Besides obtaining financial resources through the sales of goods and services, most organizations also get funds by borrowing cash or selling ownership shares.

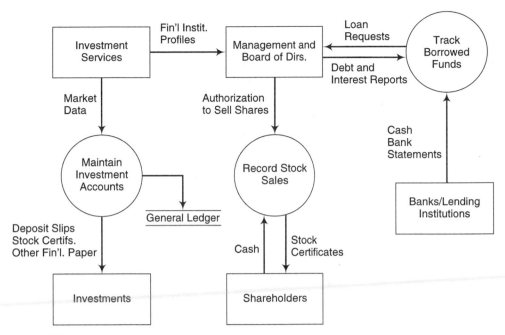

FIGURE 5-11 A data flow diagram of the financing process. This data flow diagram does not include cash management related to sales revenue, purchases, payroll, and fixed assets.

The **financing process** includes the management of these activities. Figure 5-11 is a data flow representation of the financing process and Figure 5-12 summarizes the objectives, inputs, and outputs of this process. Figure 5-13 is a high-level systems flowchart of the AIS for the financing process.

Objectives of the Financing Process The financing process has multiple objectives. These include managing cash effectively, minimizing the cost of capital, investing for maximum returns, and projecting cash flows.

Effective cash management requires collecting cash as soon as possible and spending it carefully. To collect cash quickly, an organization's AIS can provide useful information about how quickly customers pay their bills. An AIS can also show trends in cash collections. Organizations may make use of tools such as **lock-box systems** to reduce the float period during which checks clear the bank. A lock-box system is an effective cash management tool because banks typically require several days, and sometimes a full week, to provide an organization with credit for out-of-state checks. With a lock-box system, a company directs its customers to mail their checks on account to a lock-box in their home state. A local bank will provide the service of collecting checks in the lock-box, clearing them, sending the customer payment data in an electronic format, and depositing the cash into the company's account. In this way, cash is available for use more quickly.

Electronic funds transfer (EFT), or electronic payment, is another cash management technique. Using EFT, business organizations do not need to exchange paper documents. The transfer of funds is electronic or computer-to-computer. Many companies today pay their employees electronically, increasing each employee's bank account directly rather than issuing a paycheck.

THE FINANCING PROCESS

Objectives:
- Effective cash management
- Cost of capital optimization
- Earn maximum return on investments
- Project cash flows

Inputs (Source Documents):
- Remittance Advices
- Deposit Slips
- Checks
- Bank Statements
- Stock Market Data
- Interest Data
- Financial Institution Profiles

Outputs (Reports):
- Financial Statement Information
- Cash Budget
- Investment Reports
- Debt and Interest Reports
- Financial Ratios
- Financial Planning Model Reports

FIGURE 5-12   Objectives, inputs, and outputs associated with the financing process.

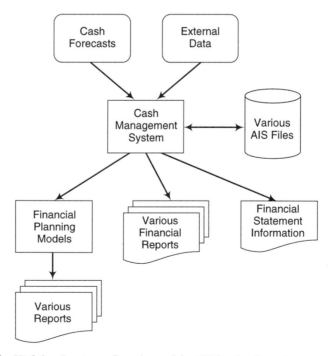

FIGURE 5-13   High-level systems flowchart of the AIS for the financing process.

Managing cash on the expenditure side requires ensuring the availability of cash to pay bills as they come due and to take advantage of favorable cash discounts. While an organization wants to make sure there is cash available for timely payments to vendors and employees, it is also possible to have too much cash on hand. Idle cash is an unproductive asset and short-term investments typically earn less of a return than long-term investments. Effective cash management includes ensuring that cash balances are not unreasonably high and managers invest excess cash optimally. Managers in large companies will monitor excess cash and invest it for very short times, sometimes less than a day.

Minimizing the **cost of capital** (i.e., the cost of obtaining financial resources) requires management to make decisions about how much cash to borrow versus obtain through selling shares of ownership (stock). Borrowed funds require interest payments. While there are no interest payments required for sales of stock, a company typically pays dividends to shareholders. Financial managers frequently use **financial planning models** to help them select an optimum strategy for acquiring and investing financial resources. These models are often information systems that make complex calculations and consider alternative investment, borrowing, and equity (sales of stock) strategies.

A final objective of the financing process is to project cash flows. An output of the revenue process is a cash receipts forecast, and the purchasing and human resource processes contribute to a forecast of cash disbursements. The financing process makes use of these forecasts to invest excess funds and decide debt and equity strategies. The AIS for the financing process contributes to cash flow predictions through estimates of interest and dividend payments and receipts.

Inputs to the Financing Process   Many inputs to the financing process originate outside an organization. Externally generated data or source documents might include remittance advices, deposit slips, checks, bank statements, stock market data, interest data, and data about financial institutions. Chapter 4 explained that a *remittance advice* accompanies a customer's payment on account. Banks provide *deposit slips* to document account deposits. (You receive a deposit slip when you make a cash deposit to your account through an automated teller machine [ATM].) Companies both receive and issue *checks.* Some banks return canceled checks with bank statements, which accountants use to reconcile any account discrepancies or as proof of payment. Accountants use *bank statements* to reconcile the cash account balance in the company's ledger against the cash balance in the bank account. Discrepancies between these two accounts arise from outstanding checks, deposits in transit, and various other transactions. Sometimes, of course, discrepancies are due to errors, or even fraud. Because cash is a company's most liquid asset, an AIS should incorporate control procedures (see Chapters 9 and 10) to ensure against misappropriations.

Outputs of the Financing Process   Like all other business processes, the financing process provides general ledger information that contributes to an AIS producing periodic financial statements. Examples include interest revenue and expense amounts, dividend revenue and expense amounts, and summaries of cash collections and disbursements. It also provides information about balances in debt, equity, and investment accounts. Besides providing general ledger information, the financing process of an AIS produces a *cash budget* showing projected cash flows.

The AIS for the financing process can produce a variety of reports relative to investments and borrowings. Investment reports may show changes in investments for a period, dividends paid, and interest earned. Reports on borrowings could show new debt and retired debt for a period. These reports should list the lending institutions, interest rates charged, and payments of principal and/or interest for the period.

To manage an organization's capital effectively, an AIS's financing subsystem should perform *ratio analyses.* Significant ratios, such as return on investment (net income divided by total assets) and debt to equity (total liabilities divided by total stockholders' equity), help management decision making regarding investment and borrowing strategies. A company's financial planning model may output these ratios. The planning model will also output recommendations regarding the appropriate mix of debt versus equity financing, and short- versus long-range investments. Case-in-Point 5.4 shows the importance of this type of analysis.

> ***Case-in-Point 5.4*** When Bill Harrah, the founder of Harrah's hotels and casinos, died, his heirs sold the majority of his estate to the Holiday Inn Corporation. Among the assets was Harrah's fabled automobile collection, which was then appreciating by approximately $2 million per year. But when Holiday's accountants estimated that the market value of the entire collection was currently worth $50 million, the company decided to liquidate most of the collection because management felt the return of only 4 percent was below market rates.

BUSINESS PROCESSES IN SPECIAL INDUSTRIES

The term **vertical market** refers to markets or industries that are distinct in terms of the services they provide or the goods they produce. When you think about it, most organizations fit into a vertical market category. For example, an accounting firm is a professional service organization; a grocery store is in the retail industry. Large conglomerates may operate in several different vertical markets. For instance, many large manufacturers have branched out to provide professional services such as financial services. The same is true of retail firms. Consider, for example, Sears and Roebuck. While still known primarily as a retailer, a large share of the company's profit comes from providing consumer credit.

Specialized Accounting Information Needs

Vertical market organizations need much of the same accounting information about revenues, purchases, and resources described in Chapter 4 and so far in this chapter. Manufacturing organizations need the information generated by the production process. Organizations in other specific industry segments may need information structured in a distinctive way. The nature of an organization's activities dictates the kinds of information needed to operate efficiently and effectively. AISs are becoming increasingly specialized. They can fit not only special industry needs, but also the needs of organizations occupying a very specialized niche within an industry. For instance, within the retail industry, computerized accounting software is available specifically for video rentals, pet stores, and florists.

Some organizations may require more information than is typically output by a traditional AIS. As technology becomes more sophisticated, AISs can capture and process information in new ways. Businesses may be able to use this information to compete against others. Consider, for example, cost accounting systems. In the last few years, many organizations have learned to use computers to track costs better. This allows them to associate more costs directly with a product, or as in **activity based costing systems,** with a cost driver, rather than *allocating* costs to a product. If management can trace costs directly to the underlying source of those costs, the cost driver, they can keep costs and the resultant prices charged to customers at a lower level than the competition. Besides reducing costs, tracing rather than allocating costs pleases customers. For example, customers are likely to be more comfortable paying an invoice that shows a detailed breakdown of costs, rather than paying a lump sum billing. Many accounting firms use this approach for this reason. These firms use accounting information accumulated in-house through special **time and billing** AISs to maintain precise records for costs incurred on behalf of each client. This ensures that an AIS bills clients fairly and does not charge them for overhead items associated with another client.

AISs provide financial and economic information to both managers and external parties. In general, an AIS uniformly structures the information provided to external parties, such as investors and creditors, to produce standard financial statements. However, with vertical market companies, the ways an AIS gathers the information may vary. For instance, the most significant difference in the AISs of retail organizations versus other vertical market organizations is the **point-of-sale** data capture. The system uses the information captured at this point (perhaps by bar code scanners like you see in grocery stores) in the transaction (i.e., the "point-of-sale") to update inventory, record revenue and cost of goods sold, identify customers who might like coupons for specific products, and predict future sales or learn which products are selling well and which are not.

The accounting information provided to managers is often less structured than information for external parties because there are no generally accepted accounting principles to dictate the type and form of internal managerial reports. Managers' information needs determine the type of information the AIS collects and reports to them. These needs are tied to the types of decisions managers make. In retail organizations, sales and cost information might tie into decisions about which products to purchase from wholesalers. In the construction industry, organizations need to capture cost information and use it to bid on projects. They also need to compare the actual cost of projects in progress to cost and profit targets.

Examples of Industries with Specialized AISs

Vertical markets with specialized AISs include organizations in the following industries: professional services, not-for-profit, health care, retail, construction, government, banking and financial services, and hospitality. This section describes a few of these organizations in terms of their unique characteristics and AIS needs.

Professional Service Organizations   **Professional service organizations** are business establishments providing a special service to customers. The special type of service is a *professional* service because a rigorously trained staff provides it. Examples are accounting, law, engineering, consulting, and architectural firms.

Compared with organizations that provide tangible goods (such as automobile manufacturers), professional service organizations have several unique operating characteristics: (1) an absence of an inventory of saleable merchandise, (2) the importance of professional employees, (3) difficulty in measuring the quantity and quality of output, and (4) small size. These are common characteristics, although not every organization in this industry segment has all of them. For instance, some accounting and consulting firms have hundreds of partners and international offices in dozens of cities around the world.

Because professional service organizations do not maintain a product inventory, they do not need an AIS that tracks the level of tangible goods held for sale. Sophisticated manufacturing resource planning systems and JIT systems have little meaning for an organization that does not produce or buy tangible products. Instead, the primary accounting information needed by professional service organizations relates to time and billing for their professional staff.

Time and billing AISs are similar to job order costing systems. The time and billing system tracks hours and costs associated with each job (i.e., each client) and each employee (i.e., professional staff). There are two major outputs of the time and billing system: (1) the client bill and (2) the professional staff member's record of **billable hours.** (See an example of a software consulting firm's client bill in Figure 5-14.) The client bill may show in detail the number of hours worked by every professional staff

---

MARTIN & ASSOC.

10385 Spartan Dr.
Cincinnati, OH 45215
Office 513/772-7284
Fax 513/772-4529

Invoice #	7031
Invoice Date	2/29/2002
Terms	Net 15 Days
Due Date	3/15/2002
Customer Number	WMI

Mr. Richard Wilson
WMI. Inc.
5917 Hamilton Ave.
Cincinnati, OH 45224

FOR SERVICES RENDERED

Work Type	Date	Comments/Description	Staff	Hours
Chargeable	2/04/02	Connectivity Planning	ADB	0.50
No Charge	2/07/02	F9 issues/set-up	KMM	0.25
Chargeable	2/08/02	AP processing Error	KMM	0.25
Chargeable	2/17/02	AP and ODBC errors	KMM	0.50
Chargeable	2/18/02	Bank lock/GL detail/plan	KMM	3.00
Chargeable	2/19/02	Drive to and from WMI	KMM	1.00
Chargeable	2/19/02	Hard drive reformat	KMM	0.50
Chargeable	2/21/02	Training on GL and AP	ADB	1.25
No Charge	2/21/02	Shipping	CLP	0.25
Chargeable	2/23/02	GL recap file/Adrian	KMM	0.25
			WMI Total Hours:	**7.75**
			Not Charged Hours:	**0.50**
			Chargeable Hours:	**7.25**
			Invoice Dollar Total:	**725.00**

FIGURE 5-14 A sample client bill for a software consulting firm. (Printed with permission from Kevin Martin and Associates.)

member and the rate charged by each. For example, an audit client might incur charges for audit staff, supervisors or seniors, managers, and partners. An AIS multiplies the hours worked by each staff member by his or her respective billing rate to compute the total charge. Time and billing systems can also show other charges on the bill or client invoice. These expense items would include charges for overhead and detailed charges for phone, fax, mail, support staff, and copy charges.

Billable hours are important in a professional service organization. Law firms, for example, stress to new lawyers the importance of accumulating an accurate accounting of the number of billable hours. These are the hours actually spent working on client business. Nonbillable hours are hours spent in training, marketing, and general research. While these latter activities are important and, of course, necessary, they do not directly generate revenue for a law firm. Therefore, to produce profits, professional staff members need to spend most of their time on client work.

A time and billing system can track each staff member's hours in many ways. Accounting personnel show lawyers, accountants, engineers, and other professional staff how to record their hours on a time sheet. The increments of time recorded vary by firm. Some professional service firms record every fifteen minutes spent working on a client job. Some law firms may record time in six-minute increments. Since time is literally money, it is important to keep records as detailed and accurate as possible.

Manually recording every six minutes spent on client work is a time-consuming task. It is also one that professional staff members (including accountants) often see as annoying busywork. Some professional service organizations ensure that staff members keep these records by withholding pay from those who fail to turn in detailed time records. A less-punitive way to ease capturing billable hours data for input to time and billing systems is through the use of technology. For example, phone systems that record the time of calls to client numbers can feed into the time and billing system. A copy machine in which users enter client numbers for each job is another technological tool that helps track input for professional service firms' AISs. Finally, as professional staff members rely increasingly on their computers to do their work, special computer programs can record the time spent on each job automatically as the staff member logs on to different programs identified with a specific client number.

The special nature of each type of business decides other unique information needs. For instance, law firms may require their accounting systems to maintain client databases to help them avoid taking cases resulting in a conflict of interest. Architectural and engineering firms need accounting systems that can assimilate costs to provide bids for jobs. The type of firm within a particular vertical market thus has special information needs all its own.

Not-for-Profit Organizations **Not-for-profit organizations** lack a profit goal as they exist primarily to provide services for the protection and betterment of society. Examples include public schools, museums, churches, and public governmental agencies. Apart from their lack of a profit motive, other distinguishing characteristics of most not-for-profit organizations may include (1) a service organization usually staffed by professional employees, (2) a smaller role of the market mechanism, and (3) a political emphasis.

As with other vertical markets, not-for-profit organizations have special accounting information needs that reflect their unique characteristics. For example, the need for public schools (such as a university) to keep records of students' schedules, grades, health records, and so on is a special information need unique to educational institutions. Religious organizations, on the other hand, must track members and maintain an accounting system for donations. The federal government (certainly the largest not-for-profit organization) must value various unique assets that are not traded in a market. How much, for instance, is the Lincoln Memorial worth, and how would you go about depreciating it?

In general, it is the lack of a profit goal that most influences the special AIS needs of not-for-profit organizations. Accounting standards, such as the Financial Accounting Standards Board's Statement No. 117, Financial Statements of Not-for-Profit Organizations, have changed the financial reporting requirement of these organizations so that their external financial statements more closely resemble those of profit-seeking entities. However, the internal reporting systems for not-for-profit organizations focus on funds, rather than income. Fund accounting systems show the resources available for carrying out an organization's objectives. Funds may be restricted for special purposes (e.g., funds donated to a university for student scholarships) or available for general use. To reconcile the internal and external accounting systems, an AIS for not-for-profit institutions must be able to cross-walk or reconcile between these two different reporting structures.

Although not-for-profit organizations cannot be evaluated using profit measures, and these institutions typically operate in a less competitive environment than profit-oriented entities, some mechanism for performance evaluation is still desirable. A frequently used mechanism is a budgetary AIS. By evaluating actual performance against planned activity, the managers in not-for-profit entities can determine how well they meet their goals. Many not-for-profit organizations (especially governmental organizations) employ formal long-range budgetary techniques. These budgets include projections of future activity that may serve as performance measures when compared with actual data. One difficulty often encountered in not-for-profit budgetary systems is the lack of a monetary measure of performance output. Consequently, managers must often use *process measures* (i.e., nonmonetary measures) to measure performance output. In a police department, for example, the process measures might be number of arrests, number of tickets issued, or reduction in crime rate. As another example, a process measure used by a public university could be the number of students graduating each academic year.

A good short-range budgetary planning and controlling system is typically more important to a not-for-profit organization than to a profit-oriented institution. The reason is the result of the fixed, rather than flexible, nature of these organizations' annual budgets. In a not-for-profit organization, budgetary revisions are difficult, if not impossible, to carry out once the budget year begins. For example, in a governmental institution such as a publicly financed state university, the state legislators and the governor approve the educational institution's annual operating budget. If subsequent operations under the approved budget reveal that actual costs are higher than anticipated costs in specific areas of the university, additional budgetary appropriations may be impossible to obtain. If these additional appropriations required legislative action at a time when the state legislators were not in session, the university has to live with its original budget. Thus, in those not-for-profit organizations subject to fixed or static budgets, good short-range planning is necessary to obtain accurate budget projections for the coming year.

Health Care Organizations The dollars spent for the **health care industry** have made this vertical market segment the target of much controversy and concern as the United States struggles to contain health care costs. Health care reform is a

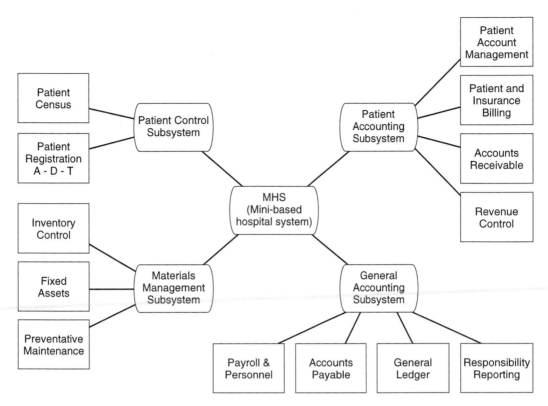

FIGURE 5–15 Mini-based hospital system (used with the permission of McDonnell Douglas Corporation. Hazelwood, Missouri).

very important political issue. Interestingly, the AISs associated with health care are a large part of the controversy. Paperwork has been a major bottleneck in delivering efficient health care, and it is also a major cost. Figure 5-15, which shows the many subsystems in a health care organization's AIS, demonstrates part of the problem.

Health care entities share many characteristics with professional service organizations and not-for-profit institutions. Like these entities, health care organizations do not provide tangible goods to their customers (except for drugs). In addition, health care organizations also count professional staff as their most important asset resource. Some health care organizations are public and operate on a not-for-profit basis. Finally, output is exceptionally difficult to measure for this industry. For example, a patient may get well due to the quality of health care received, or the patient may simply get well due to his or her body's ability to overcome an illness. On the other hand, patients sometimes die despite excellent health care and heroic measures.

The special accounting information needs of health care organizations primarily relate to **third-party billing.** Health care organizations usually do not directly bill their customers for services received. Rather, they bill insurance companies or government agencies. Bills to third-party payers (insurance companies) are prepared using standardized codes for both the medical diagnosis and the procedures performed by medical personnel. Although standardized codes promote efficiency in processing information, coding can still be difficult. For example, sometimes a diagnosis is hard to pinpoint, and medical personnel often do procedures for multiple purposes. Reimbursement from an insurance company depends on the codes used. Insurance companies vary in their coverage. Thus, one plan may cover a particular procedure, and another may not. Because doctors often have discretion in making a diagnosis or prescribing a procedure, the accounting staff needs to understand the nuances of the codes and general classifications. Errors in coding can be costly, and not just in terms of the processing costs associated with them; errors can also lead to fraud charges by insurance carriers.

Payment policies and filing forms may vary among third-party insurers. Government insurance (Medicare and Medicaid) presents another problem in terms of claim forms. These health care programs are state administered and each state has special filing requirements. The several hundred medical insurance carriers in the United States all use the same coding base. However, clerical personnel and AISs do not uniformly apply these codes. As previously mentioned, special AIS needs for the health care industry relate mostly to third-party billing, but other features of the industry also require special processing. Health care AISs generally need to maintain patient information. Hospitals, doctors' offices, and nursing homes all need systems to efficiently schedule patients. Home health care services need to keep track of travel costs for employees. Information needs may be unique to very specific industry segments. For instance, physical therapy offices, chiropractic practices, ophthalmologists, optometrists, and dental offices each have some very special information needs. For example, physical therapy offices are different from other medical offices in that a patient may spend an hour in therapy on many different kinds of equipment. An AIS might charge differently for ten minutes spent in the whirlpool versus ten minutes on exercise equipment. The following Case-in-Point describes one specialized health care software program.

Case-in-Point 5.5   The *Chiropractors Assistant* is a specialized software program for professional chiropractors. It includes an accounting system through its general ledger section as well as a billing and clinic management system. The software tracks patient histories, treatments, payments, appointments, and claims. The *Chiropractors Assistant* is configured to handle a variety of insurance policy claims including those related to worker's compensation.

BUSINESS PROCESS REENGINEERING

As explained in Chapter 4, AISs in the Information Age are less concerned with accounting transactions and more concerned with **business events.** Information systems developers build AISs that capture financial and nonfinancial data about these events, which comprise an organization's business processes.

The focus of AISs on business processes allows organizations to fundamentally rethink those processes. **Buiness process reengineering (BPR)** concerns redesigning business processes from scratch. As an example, consider the order process that begins with inquiries from a customer about the products available for sale and ends when the customer's cash is collected from a completed sale. In many organizations, several individuals handle the order process. Each person has responsibility for a particular function: a receptionist or secretary may handle inquiries, a salesperson follows up on product inquiries, warehouse personnel assume responsibility for filling the order, an accounts receivable clerk bills the customer, and so on. This division of responsibility makes it difficult for some organizations to fill customer orders quickly. The result: dissatisfied customers. Reengineering the order process may result in an integration of functional activities so that one specified individual handles customers from start to finish. This redesign means a customer knows who to talk to when an order is late and the customer is not passed around from one person to another when problems occur.

Principles for Successful Reengineering

The techniques used to redesign business information systems are perhaps best understood by example. Here are three principles for successfully reengineering business systems, and for each principle, a case that illustrates how a specific company implemented that principle.

Case-in-Point 5.6 *Organize Around Outcomes, Not Tasks* Approving an insurance application at Mutual Benefit Life previously included 30 steps performed by 19 people in five departments. Because paperwork moved among so many workers, an approval took from 5 to 25 days. When the insurance company reengineered its system, it abolished existing job descriptions and departmental boundaries. In their place, the company created the position of "case manager" and provided each manager with the authority to perform all application approval tasks. Because every case manager is in charge of the entire process associated with approving applications, files are not passed around. The results have been fewer errors, decreased costs, and a significantly improved turnaround time for approval. A new application can now be processed in approximately four hours, with an average approval turnaround time of two to five days.

Case-in-Point 5.7 *Centralize and Disperse Data* Before reorganizing, Hewlett-Packard had a decentralized purchasing system for its 50 manufacturing plants that made it difficult for the company to exploit its extensive buying power and negotiate quantity discounts on purchases. By reengineering its purchasing system, Hewlett-Packard introduced a corporate-wide purchasing department that developed and maintained a shared database of approved vendors. Now, each plant continues to make its own purchases, but from the centralized database of approved vendors. The corporate office tracks the purchases of all 50 plants, negotiates quantity discounts, and handles disputes with vendors. The reengineered system has resulted in a significantly lower cost of inventory purchased, a 50 percent reduction in lead times, and a 150 percent improvement in on-time deliveries.

Case-in-Point 5.8 *Capture Data Once—At Their Source* The management of Sun Microsystems noted that many of its information systems were not able to communicate with one another. As a result, employees had to reenter the same information into each separate system requiring it, as many as ten times into incompatible systems. Through BPR, the company integrated its systems. Now, the inputs required by any of the company's information systems are entered only once and made available to all users through its integrated modules.

Why Reengineering Sometimes Fails

Despite the success of many organizations with BPR projects, a number of BPR efforts fail. There are several reasons for these failures, including unrealistic expectations, employee resistance, and lack of management support. Some organizations that contract with consultants for BPR services hold overly optimistic expectations of improvements in their products and services as well as dramatically lower costs. Successful BPR projects can result in larger profits and more satisfied customers, but often not to the extent envisioned. Employees frequently dread hearing the term BPR because it has become synonymous for many with "downsizing." It is often a challenge to get employees to embrace change, especially change that may make what they do unnecessary or possibly more difficult.

While employee resistance is often fatal to BPR efforts, management support can help to overcome the obstacles. BPR needs champions in top management who are willing to push projects forward despite some employee resistance. Without champions, BPR projects may end when obstacles appear. Successful BPR efforts also need top managers who are good communicators. Management must relay to employees both good and bad news. Managers who try to mask the downside of change are likely to run into difficulty.

AIS AT WORK
Retail Information Systems Open Up

The retail industry today is fiercely competitive. This competition is driving retailers to innovate and to use IT to improve how they manage their businesses. One way to better manage with IT is through the use of automated receiving and point-of-sale systems. These systems capture data about purchases and sales (often with bar coding) so that managers can determine inventory levels without relying on estimates. Accurate, real-time information about inventory quantities allows managers to learn which items are selling fast and which are not. It also lets managers look at the mix of items they are selling so that they can promote items with higher profit margins, and quickly determine the effects of the promotions.

Another way retailers are using IT is to integrate their information systems. AISs can be integrated at two levels: internally and externally. Wal-Mart's information system has mastered total integration. Not only are its stores and distribution centers linked, but the company has also hooked up its suppliers and customers. A 7.5-terabyte data warehouse combined with satellite links allows for information sharing internally as well as with outside parties. Buyers and suppliers can query the data warehouse to find out what products are available at each store, what products are selling well, which stores need certain inventory items, and so on. The benefits of such integration are fewer out-of-stock situations, and lower inventory costs. This is a tricky combination, but sharing information with suppliers helps managers to pull it off. When retailers keep their marketing plans secret from their suppliers, they take the risk that the suppliers will not be able to provide them with the merchandise they want—when they want it.

Direct, online customer product ordering (electronic commerce) is another aspect of integration. Retailers, including Wal-Mart, are making their products available to customers over the Internet. Products sold through retailer web sites may be delivered by the retailer or directly by the retailer's supplier. This use of IT by retailers demonstrates the importance of innovating quickly, ahead of the competition. The book retail industry segment is a prime example. Amazon quickly became the third-largest bookseller, without owning a single fixed asset! Retailers who lag behind in their use of IT may find themselves losing out on market share, and bearing higher inventory costs to boot.

SUMMARY

Three business processes that are important in many organizations are the resource management, production, and financing processes. The resource management process includes two subprocesses: human resource management and fixed asset management. Human resource management encompasses both the personnel activities in an organization and the payroll events.

The production process includes the events related to converting raw materials into finished goods inventories. Controlling inventory and costs are important objectives of the production process. One approach to inventory control is the use of a just-in-time (JIT) system. JIT systems seek to reduce all inventories to minimum levels.

The financing process overlaps all the other processes in a sense, since it is concerned with the acquisition and use of funds needed for operations. However, the financing process also includes investing, borrowing, and stock-selling activities. In addition, cash management is an important part of the financing process. Sound cash management requires companies to constantly monitor cash balances, investing any excess and covering temporary shortfalls with bank loans.

There are many other business processes unique to specific industries. Each industry, or vertical market segment with specialized processes, has associated custom AIS needs. This chapter described some of these AISs for professional service, not-for-profit, and health care organizations. Of course, there are many other vertical market organizations with special accounting information needs apart from the ones described here.

Knowledge of business processes provides opportunities to reengineer them in ways that help organizations achieve their objectives. Business process reengineering (BPR) is the practice of examining business processes and redesigning them from scratch. Many companies today are engaged in BPR as a way to improve customer service and satisfaction, increase profitability, and decrease costs. Accounting processes and procedures are also being reengineered to make them more efficient and cost-effective.

KEY TERMS YOU SHOULD KNOW

activity based costing systems	human resource management
billable hours	inventory control
business events	job costing
business process reengineering (BPR)	just-in-time (JIT)
capital expenditures	lean manufacturing
cost accounting subsystem	lock-box system
cost of capital	make-to-order
electronic funds transfer (EFT)	make-to-stock
financial planning models	manufacturing resource planning (MRP II)
financing process	material requirements planning (MRP I)
fixed asset management function	not-for-profit organizations
health care industry	payroll processing

personnel function
point-of-sale
process costing system
production process
professional service organizations

revenue expenditures
third-party billing
time and billing
vertical market

DISCUSSION QUESTIONS

5-1. The resource management process includes events associated with both personnel and payroll functions. Describe four data items that could be used by both functions. Describe two data items for each function that would not necessarily be needed by the other (e.g., spouse name for personnel but not payroll).

5-2. Why are accounting transactions associated with payroll processing so repetitive in nature? Why do some companies choose to have payroll processed by external service bureaus rather than in-house?

5-3. In this chapter, we discussed many data inputs to an organization's production process. What are the specific data items to input to a system when adding a new raw materials inventory item? What specific data items need to be input when a worker records time spent on the production line?

5-4. What nonfinancial information would be important for an AIS to capture about a manufacturing firm's production process?

5-5. Are the inputs and outputs of a production process likely to be different for a home builder than for a cement company? How?

5-6. The financing process uses data from a variety of external sources to provide management with the information needed to make optimal investment decisions. What are some specific data items that would be important in deciding whether to invest in a company's stock?

5-7. What would you want to know about a business if you were a bank manager considering making a million-dollar loan?

5-8. This chapter discussed four unique characteristics of professional service organizations. Of these four characteristics, which one do you feel causes the greatest problem for a professional service organization's AIS? Explain.

5-9. There are many vertical market industries with special accounting information needs apart from the industries discussed in this chapter. What are some additional vertical market industries you can think of? What are the unique characteristics of these industries that affect their AISs?

5-10. How is the accounting information system for a retail store that sells merchandise different from the accounting information system for a retail store that rents merchandise?

5-11. Discuss specific steps you would take as a manager to ensure that a business process reengineering effort is successful.

PROBLEM

5-12. Choose an industry described in this chapter and find out what vertical market accounting software is available for that industry. You may use resources such as the library, trade associations, interviews with organizations within the industry, and interviews with software consultants.

INTERNET EXERCISES

5.13. Go on the Internet and look up the industry code for the construction industry in the North American Industry Classification System. What types of organizations does that industry classification include? Do they all have the same accounting information needs?

5.14. Use an Internet search engine to find two accounting software packages for each of the following industries: construction, health care, and retail.

5.15. Visit the web site for Automated Data Processing. What services do they offer besides payroll? What are some security concerns you might have in outsourcing your payroll processing? Does the company's web site address any of these concerns?

CASE ANALYSES

5-16. Grace Ho and Associates (Time and Billing System)

Grace Ho started her own law practice ten years ago. Her firm, Grace Ho and Associates, specializes in estate planning and currently employs five attorneys, two legal assistants, one legal secretary, and a bookkeeper/receptionist. The firm has always used a manual accounting system, which includes procedures for time and billing. Each attorney fills out time sheets in 15-minute increments. These time sheets are turned over to Susan Burgess, the bookkeeper, each week. Susan uses the time sheets to prepare client bills. Once a month, Susan delivers the time sheets and other accounting data to the outside accountant who uses the information to prepare financial reports and tax returns.

There are several problems with the current system. Recently, a few clients have complained about the lack of detail on their bills. A customer invoice simply shows a total dollar amount due, which is calculated by multiplying the billing rate for each attorney times the number of hours spent on a client's work. The system adds an overhead figure of 70 percent to the bill to cover the costs of the legal assistant's time, secretarial work, phone and office expense, copy charges, postage expense, and so on. Besides client complaints, Susan is upset because she has a very difficult time getting the attorneys to fill out their time sheets properly and turn them in on time. She is not confident that the bills she sends to clients are accurate. She suspects that an attorney often has to go back and reconstruct his or her time sheet from memory rather than recording time as it is spent on a client task. Finally, attorneys are unhappy because they do not like to be bothered with "all that accounting detail" when they feel their time is better spent on client matters.

Grace's practice is expanding. She is now doing bankruptcy work plus estate planning. As a result, she intends to hire two more attorneys and another legal assistant next year. She is concerned that she needs to automate her accounting system to solve its current problems and to help the expansion of her practice.

Requirements

1. How can an automated time and billing system help Grace Ho and Associates?
2. What technology is available to automatically capture a professional employee's time spent on a particular client engagement?

3. Design a new client bill for Grace Ho and Associates. Rather than using a 70 percent overhead charge, show a breakdown of cost in detail and explain how you would gather the data to calculate each cost.

5-17. Graduate Programs at Riley University (Business Process Reengineering)

Riley University is located in a large mid-western metropolitan area. The School of Business offers two graduate degree programs, the Master of Business Administration (MBA) and the Master of Science in Information Systems (MSIS). During AY 2000/03, there were 350 students enrolled in the part-time MBA program, 120 students in the full-time MBA, and 52 students who were pursuing the MSIS. The programs are administered as follows:

The Associate Dean for Academic Affairs has authority over both programs. However, Keith Houghton, Director of the MBA program and Gail Wright, Director of the MSIS have primary direct responsibility for the programs. Details of the administration and activities related to each degree program are as follows.

The MBA Program

Keith Houghton runs the MBA office and supervises a seven person staff. He sets the budget and makes pricing, hiring, and curriculum recommendations. Applications to the MBA program are sent, to the admissions department of the university. They are screened for completeness, entered into a database, and then forwarded to Dahli Gray, the MBA Admissions and Recruitment Director. Dahli's assistant, Stephanie Bryant, maintains a database of all inquiries and applications. The MBA program office runs several information sessions and other promotions throughout the year. The Inquiry database includes a field for tracking where the prospective students first heard about the program. Dahli admits students, helps students to find financial aid, and assigns graduate assistants to faculty.

Once students are admitted to the MBA program, they are assigned to an adviser. There are two MBA advisers, Mark Simkin and Steve Moscove. Mark handles all full-time graduate business students and Steve is charged with advising all part-time MBA students. Steve and Mark have other duties as well, assisting in program administration and recruitment efforts as needed. From time to time, they assist Pete Brewer, who is in charge of graduate student placement. Pete works with students on their career development. He also liaisons with employers.

Two other administrative staff in the MBA program office are Joe Cheung and Jane Hronsky. Joe takes care of coordinating special program events, such as the MBA orientation, skill workshops, and a speaker series. Jane is Keith Houghton's direct assistant, and she covers the office, directing students and other visitors to an appropriate person for help. She also serves other staff and students as needed.

The MSIS Program

Gail Wright is a full-time faculty member in the Department of Information Systems within the School of Business. She also directs the MSIS. Applications to the MSIS are sent to the university's admissions department and recorded in the same fashion as the MBA applications. They then go to Dahli Gray, who immediately forwards them to Gail. Gail, with the help of her graduate assistant, maintains a database of inquiries and applications to the MSIS. She often runs promotions and develops her own program brochures and advertising. Gail has admissions authority over all MSIS applicants and she also assigns graduate assistants. She advises each student in the MSIS and generally handles any problems the students have. She also helps with placement, working in conjunction with the university's Career Center. Occasionally, she receives assistance on a particular task from the MBA office.

Issues

The MBA program office is very busy. Everyone works at least a nine-hour day. Keith has asked the dean for more help. Students in the MBA program are often dissatisfied with the service they receive from the office. They are also not always sure who they should talk to about issues they have with courses, faculty, and other concerns. Students are frustrated too because they sometimes receive different answers to the same question from different staff members. The dean is resisting providing more resources for the program. He has noticed that there seem to be communication problems within the MBA office and feels that adding another person would just complicate things further. The dean points out that although Gail is overworked, providing all services to the MSIS students, there is a high level of satisfaction among the students in that program.

Requirements

1. Identify the business events for both graduate programs.
2. How would you reengineer the graduate program process? Be specific about the duties that would be performed by specific individuals.

5-18. Wilshire Credit (Business Process Reengineering)

Wilshire Credit is a wholly owned subsidiary of Putnam Technologies. Wilshire is in the business of financing the medical equipment and services sold by its parent, a business that is extremely profitable. In the past, Wilshire's procedure for credit involved several steps that can be summarized as follows.

- The salesperson negotiating the lease agreement would call the receptionist in the Credit Department who would log the request on a paper form.
- The form was sent to a credit specialist in the Credit Department who checked the potential borrower's creditworthiness. The specialist entered certain information into a computer program and recorded the results on the form which was then sent to a business practices specialist.
- Using a separate computer program, the business practices specialist would modify the standard lease agreement terms to fit the customer's request. These special terms were then printed and attached to the original request form which was forwarded to a pricing specialist.
- The pricing specialist was responsible for determining the appropriate interest rate to charge the customer using a spreadsheet program designed for this purpose. The selected interest rate was then written on the request form.

- The completed request form was finally delivered to the clerical group that was responsible for entering all the appropriate information in a quote letter to be delivered back to the salesperson.

This process could take from six to fourteen days, during which time the customer could find another source of financing, another vendor, or cancel the deal entirely. When the salesperson called to follow up on a request, no one knew exactly where it was in the process. Wilshire attempted temporary procedural changes such as establishing a control desk to which documents were returned and logged in between each step. The salesperson could then find out where the request was, but this procedural change added additional time to the process.

One day, the vice president of sales walked a credit request through the process. He asked personnel in each department to put aside their current task and process the request as they normally would. He learned that the actual work took only two hours, and the remainder of the time was consumed by passing the request form from department to department.

As a result of this discovery, Wilshire has reengineered its credit process by replacing its specialists with generalists who are able to handle 90 percent of all requests. A new computer system supports this process change by providing a credit-rating database, a standard model for pricing, and generic clauses for quotations. A small pool of highly specialized technicians exists to handle the complex situations.

Requirements

1. The reengineering of business processes causes changes to be made throughout an organization. Describe how reengineering changes:
   a. Functional departments
   b. Jobs and job preparation
   c. Roles of process team members
   d. Organizational structure
2. Identify and describe at least three possible outcomes that Wilshire Credit can expect from a successful reengineering effort.

(CMA Adapted)

5-19. Nyang'oro Manufacturing (AIS for Production Process)

Nyang'oro Manufacturing, located in Detroit, Michigan, manufactures automotive parts for the Big Three U.S. automobile corporations. The company is currently implementing a new AIS. Metty Nyang'oro, the CEO, has asked Amy Alba to work with Ray March, from the consulting firm that is implementing the new system, to determine the inputs and outputs needed for the new AIS. Of particular concern is the data the system will need to collect about inventories.

Metty is hoping that better information about inventory levels will help the company to minimize inventory investments. Their customers, the automobile manufacturers, are increasingly putting pressure on their suppliers to provide them with parts not only as needed, but exactly when needed. This is costly down the supply chain for Nyang'oro, as the company has needed to stockpile more of their parts inventories to be able to quickly meet customer orders. The costs of holding inventories are rising rapidly. A lot of cash is tied up in inventory that Nyang'oro could put to better use elsewhere. There are also warehousing, obsolescence, and insurance costs to consider. Metty feels that his company is being "squeezed" in the supply chain. He has to buy from his raw materials suppliers, hold raw materials inventories plus make-to-stock parts, or his customers will find another supplier!

Amy and Ray meet to discuss the issues. They decide that they need to do two things. First, they need to determine whether it is feasible for the AIS to solve the inventory problem. Second, they need to decide what data elements they need to capture about each inventory item to improve inventory management and control. Amy notes that while some inventory descriptors are easy to determine, such as item number, description, and cost, others are more difficult. For instance, inventory on hand and inventory available for sale could be two different data items since some of the inventory on hand might be committed but not yet shipped.

Requirements

1. Explain how an AIS can help a manufacturing company improve inventory management and control.
2. What data elements would you include in the new AIS to describe each inventory item?

REFERENCES, RECOMMENDED READINGS, AND WEB SITES

References and Recommended Readings

Boyle, R.D., "Avoiding Common Pitfalls of Reengineering," *Management Accounting* (October 1995), pp. 24–33.

Bradford, Marianne, Tony Mayfield, and Chad Toney, "Does ERP Fit in a LEAN World?," *Strategic Finance* (May 2001), pp. 29–34.

Carr, L.P., "Unbundling the Costs of Hospitalization," *Management Accounting* (November 1993), pp. 43–48.

Cole-Gomolski, B., "Hospitals Face Information Overhauls," *Computerworld* (May 25, 1998), pp. 39, 42.

Hammer, M., and J. Champy, *Reengineering the Corporation* (New York: HarperBusiness, 1993).

Hammer, M. *Beyond Reengineering* (New York: HarperBusiness, 1996).

Hoffman, T., "Logging Vendor Cuts Production Time," *Computerworld* (May 18, 1998), pp. 37–38.

Katros, V., "Coming of Age," *Computerworld* (May 25, 1998), p. S24.

Kettlehut, M.C., "Strategic Requirements for IS in the Turbulent Healthcare Environment," *Journal of Systems Management* (June 1992). pp. 6–9.

Moynihan, J.J., "Improving the Claims Process with EDI," *Healthcare Financial Management* (January 1993), pp. 48–52.

Piturro, M., "How Midsize Companies Are Buying ERP," *Journal of Accountancy* (September 1999), pp. 41–48.

Romney, M., "Business Process Reengineering," *Internal Auditor* (June 1995), pp. 24–29.

Shapiro, B.P., V.K. Rangan, and J.J. Sviokla, "Staple Yourself to an Order," *Harvard Business Review* (July/August 1992), pp. 113–122.

Singhvi. V., "Reengineering the Payables Process," *Management Accounting* (March 1995), pp. 46-49.

Sterling, R.B., "Vertical Market Software Offers Your Clients a Better Fit, and More Profits for Your Firm," *Computers in Accounting* (June 1991). pp. 36-44.

Switzer, G. J., "A Modern Approach to Retail Accounting," *Management Accounting* (February 1994), pp. 55-58.

Web Sites

The web site for Automated Data Processing (ADP) is www.adp.com.

Many software vendors offer AIS for specialized industries; MAPICS is a software vendor specializing in softwate for manufacturing companies. Their website is at http://mapics.com. SoftAid at www.soft-aid.com offers practice management and medical billing software for the health care industry. A-Systems Corporation offers a construction accounting program. Their URL is www.a-systems.net.

At www.findaccountingsoftware.com you can search for software by industry. The site lists software packages for all special industries discussed in the chapter.

Chapter 6

Accounting and Enterprise Software

INTRODUCTION

INTEGRATED ACCOUNTING SOFTWARE PROGRAMS

Selecting Accounting Software

Specialized Accounting Software

ENTERPRISE-WIDE ACCOUNTING SOFTWARE SOLUTIONS

Enterprise System Functionality

The Architecture of Enterprise Systems

Business Processes and Enterprise Systems

Implementing an Enterprise System

Risks and Benefits of Enterprise Systems

AIS AT WORK: MOTORCYCLES RIDE THE ERP WAVE

SUMMARY

KEY TERMS YOU SHOULD KNOW

DISCUSSION QUESTIONS

INTERNET EXERCISES

CASE ANALYSES

Swami Consulting

Springsteen, Inc.

B and R, Inc.

REFERENCES, RECOMMENDED READINGS, AND WEB SITES

After reading this chapter, you will:

1. *Know* the evolution of accounting and enterprise software.

2. *Understand* the differences among various types of accounting and enterprise software.

3. *Be able to explain* how various functions in enterprise software work together.

4. *Understand* the architecture of enterprise systems, including its use of a centralized database.

5. *Be able to describe* the relationship between business process engineering and enterprise system implementation.

6. *Know* the steps in an enterprise software implementation.

7. *Be able to assess* the costs and benefits associated with enterprise systems.

Enterprise systems offer the first great opportunity to achieve true connectivity, a state in which everyone knows what everyone else is doing in the business all over the world at the same time.

Thomas H. Davenport, *Mission Critical* (Boston: Harvard Business School Press, 2000), p. 5.

INTRODUCTION

A computerized AIS makes use of accounting software. Sometimes, the AIS uses personal productivity software, such as spreadsheet or database programs, to process accounting transactions. Usually, however, the AIS uses an accounting or enterprise software system. This chapter describes various types of accounting and enterprise software.

In its early days, accounting software primarily processed bookkeeping transactions for businesses. Today's software incorporates features such as the ability to process transactions for multiple departments and in foreign currencies. It also provides for customized financial reports with sophisticated ratio analyses and forecasting functions. The end of the last decade saw accounting software evolve into yet another phase as it became a part of integrated enterprise software, called *enterprise resource planning (ERP) systems.* These software solutions include financial functions interfaced with manufacturing, sales and distribution, and human resources applications. The largest enterprises today, realizing the benefits of integrating their information systems, extend their ERP systems up and down their supply chains. This chapter discusses various aspects of integrated accounting software and enterprise systems in some detail, including their functionality, architecture, impact on business processes, implementation issues, and associated costs and benefits.

INTEGRATED ACCOUNTING SOFTWARE PROGRAMS

Integrated accounting software programs process all types of accounting transactions. These include transactions affecting accounts in both general and special journals. Integrated accounting software programs organize transaction processing in modules and provide links among these modules. The general ledger module, which includes the chart of accounts, is the foundation for the system. Personnel using the accounting software record the general journal transactions in this module. Other modules typically found in integrated accounting software programs include accounts receivable, accounts payable, inventory, and payroll. These modules correspond to the business processes we discussed in the previous two chapters. Journal entries recorded in accounting software modules update the general ledger module on a periodic or real-time basis. Depending on an accounting program's level of sophistication, it may include additional modules such as job costing, purchasing, billing, invoicing, and fixed assets. Figure 6-1 lists some features commonly found in integrated accounting software programs. Note that one of the features listed is Year

Cash-based versus accrual accounting
Ability to handle multiple companies
Sample chart of accounts
Recurring journal entries
Variance analysis (budget to actual)
User-defined financial statements
Product and service data
Check printing
Graphic reports
Financial analysis tools
Inventory management
Audit trails
Budgeting capability
Year 2000 compliance
Multi-user network capabilities
Internet connectivity

FIGURE 6-1   A sample of features commonly found in integrated accounting software programs.

2000 compliance. Since many companies chose to solve the Year 2000 problem by purchasing and implementing new software, the ability for accounting software vendors to promote their programs' capability to handle this problem was often a key selling point. In fact, the Year 2000 problem provided impetus for many companies to acquire new accounting and enterprise software systems at the end of the twentieth century.

Selecting Accounting Software

Accounting software programs vary from very simple, inexpensive bookkeeping packages to complex **enterprise resource planning (ERP) systems.** (Figure 6-2 summarizes accounting and enterprise software options.) At the low end, commercial programs are available for less than $50. An example is *Quicken,* which primarily helps individuals organize their personal finances. However, its bill-paying capabilities make it a popular software tool for small businesses as well. A program with more features for business use is *Quickbooks.* This is an example of an integrated accounting software package, since it includes a chart of accounts and processes general ledger transactions, accounts receivable transactions, and accounts payable transactions. This program produces many kinds of accounting reports, including basic financial statements and budget reports, as well as bar graphs and pie charts.

Another example of a low-end integrated accounting software program is *Peachtree Accounting.* This program includes separate modules for processing general ledger, accounts receivable/invoicing, accounts payable, job cost, and payroll transactions. Even low-end accounting software is quite sophisticated and generally includes several sample charts of accounts for different types of organizations. Users can select one of these charts of accounts and then customize the selection to match their organizations' account structures.

The variety of features offered in packages such as *Peachtree Accounting* continues to grow. One feature that even low-end packages include today is **Internet**

Software Type	Business Characteristics	Cost Range	Examples
Low-End General Ledger (Entry Level)	Small transaction set and no special information needs; $100,000–$5,000,000 revenue	Less than $2,000	Peachtree, QuickBooks, Oracle Small Business Suite
Middle to High-End Modular	Moderate to large transaction set with some special information needs; $1,000,000–$20,000,000 revenue	$2,000 – $30,000	Accpac, Macola Progression, Platinum, MAS90, Icode ACCWARE, Solomon, Dynamics, Macola Progression
Middle to High-End Expanding (Small) Enterprise	Large transaction set, custom needs, desire to integrate systems; $20,000,000–$249,000,000 revenue	$30,000 – $150,000	E by Epicor, Sage Enterprise Suite, IMPACT Encore, eEnterprise, Navision, Lawson
Large Enterprise Resource Planning	Large transaction set, custom needs, desire to integrate systems and reengineer processes; >$250,000,000 revenue	Several hundred thousand– hundreds of millions of dollars	SAP, BAAN, JD Edwards, PeopleSoft, Oracle
Special Industry (Vertical Accounting Software)	Large transaction set, custom needs, specialized industry information needs; >$10,000,000 revenue	$10,000 – $100,000	Construction, retail, healthcare, manufacturing, government, not-for-profit, banking, insurance, and other industry packages
Custom-Built	Moderate to large transaction set with very specific information needs; >$20,000,000 revenue	$100,000 – hundreds of millions of dollars	Available from software developers/ consultants

FIGURE 6–2.   A summary of types of accounting and enterprise software.

connectivity, which permits small businesses to create web sites and engage in *electronic commerce.* For example, *Peachtree Accounting* has a special link that allows companies to take orders and receive payments over the Internet.

Low-end accounting software is a good AIS solution for businesses with less than $5 million in revenue and few employees. The number of transactions processed monthly impacts the choice between low-end software and more sophisticated programs. For example, if a company processes only a few accounts receivable transactions daily, an inexpensive package should be able to handle this processing satisfactorily.

When transaction processing needs grow in number and complexity, a middle-range software program may be a better solution. Some examples of accounting software programs of this type are *Solomon, Dynamics, Macola, Icode ACCWARE, ACCPAC,* and *MAS 90.* With these programs, modules costing several hundred dollars or more individually are often sold separately. These software programs offer many features needed by mid-size or large companies. For example, many large companies do business internationally and need software to handle transactions in multiple currencies. Some mid-range software can convert transactions from one currency to another and can even write checks in foreign currencies. An example of a feature included in higher-end accounting software is the ability to split commissions among multiple salespersons.

Shopping mall software retailers typically do not sell middle-range or high-end accounting software packages. Instead, customers are most likely to purchase them from a **value-added reseller (VAR)** or a qualified installer. VARs and qualified installers make special arrangements with the software's vendor to sell the programs. They also provide buyers with services such as installation, customization, and training. These services are necessary due to the complexity of the middle-range accounting programs. A VAR offers a broader array of services for more software programs than a qualified installer.

Accounting software can be expensive. Even low-end packages require significant investment to install the software, convert old data for the new system, customize features, train users, and so on. While the software itself is not the major cost component, today some companies are choosing to "rent" the software rather than buy it. This arrangement is available through an **application service provider (ASP).** Many accounting software vendors offer this option, in addition to firms that specialize in this solution. An ASP hosts the software and processes your data on its own computer. You access the software and your data across the Internet. An example of this arrangement is *ePeachtree,* a version of *Peachtree* software. One of the biggest advantages of using an ASP (such as *ePeachtree*) is that you do not need to install upgrades—they are automatic. In addition, there is actually greater security than when you host your own systems because an ASP must offer high levels of security to survive.

Large organizations with quite specialized accounting information needs may decide to build a custom AIS from scratch. While custom systems are difficult and expensive to develop, they are becoming less so with advances in object-oriented programming, client/server computing, and database technology. Still, a custom system is likely to be costly and take longer to develop than management anticipates. Custom-designed accounting systems may be a good choice only when there is no other. Consultants usually find that packaged software can handle about 80 percent of a client's processing needs. Rather than develop a custom-designed accounting system, a company can either ignore the other 20 percent, meet it with other software, such as a spreadsheet or database program, or develop its own modules.

Specialized Accounting Software

The development of accounting software began with programs written to automate common, repetitive transactions. With advances in hardware and software technology, accounting software has become increasingly sophisticated and customized for specific industry needs.

Many integrated accounting software package developers offer add-on modules that firms can use to process special information. These extra modules might be job-cost modules that are useful to manufacturers and construction companies or point-of-sale features that are tailored to retailers. For instance, the hotel industry needs software that includes many specialized functions. *Hotel™,* by Execu/Tech, integrates property management functions, reservations systems, housekeeping management, phone call and in-room movie accounting, with a back office accounting system that processes general ledger, payroll, and accounts payable transactions.

Some vendors of general integrated accounting packages offer programs written by independent developers to interface with their packages and provide features needed by customers in specialized industries. Other software vendors sell *source code* with their programs so that the businesses can customize the software to fit their specialized information needs. (Source code is program instructions written in a high-level computer language.) Customizing software is a good business for value-added resellers or consultants who have programming ability and an understanding of the needs of special businesses.

There are literally thousands of software vendors who sell vertical market accounting software specially designed to fit a particular specialized industry or even a very small niche within an industry. Some examples of these packages are accounting software programs for dental offices, pet retailers, video stores, and schools.

ENTERPRISE-WIDE ACCOUNTING SOFTWARE SOLUTIONS

An organization's information system must do much more than process strictly financial data. The capabilities of accounting software programs to process enterprise-wide data expand with the price and complexity of the software. Examples of software in this category, known as **enterprise resource planning (ERP) systems,** include *J. D. Edwards One World Xe, Oracle, PeopleSoft,* and *SAP.* Two important features of this software are its integration and a central database. Typically, the software integrates the financial or accounting subsystem with human resources, manufacturing, and distribution or sales subsystems. Figure 6-3 illustrates this point in the main menu categories of *JD Edwards One World* software.

SAP R/3, sold by SAP AG, is the largest-selling software program that is truly an enterprise-wide software solution. Since SAP can cost millions of dollars to implement, it is mostly used by the world's largest business organizations. Despite its high cost, however, many organizations find that the savings it brings make it a good investment. *SAP* forces companies to reengineer or redesign their business processes for maximum efficiency. Such multinational corporations as Eastman Kodak Company, Owens-Corning Fiberglass Corporation, and Procter and Gamble have spent millions of dollars implementing *SAP R/3* for its potential cost savings. Cost savings (discussed in detail later in the chapter) often can come from streamlining and speeding up processes, as demonstrated in Case-in-Point 6.1.

Case-in-Point 6.1 When Belvedere Co's order fulfillment process experienced problems, the company implemented an ERP. Once the new system was in place, the company could process 15 percent more orders daily with no additional staff. They also reduced inventory by 30 percent, began filling and shipping customer orders within 48 hours (versus 5 days in the old system).[1]

---

[1] M. Piturro, "How Midsize Companies Are Buying ERP," *Journal of Accountancy,* September 1999, p. 41.

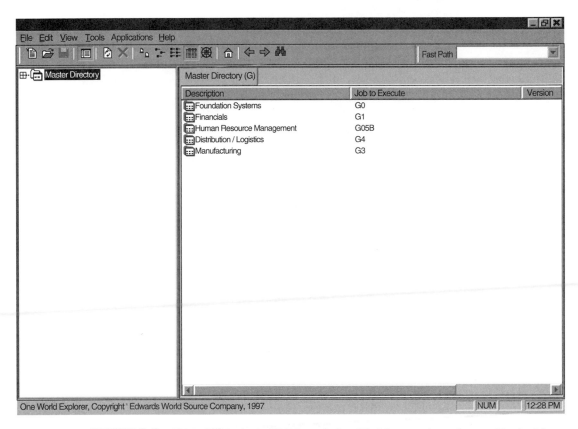

FIGURE 6-3 The main menu in *JD Edwards One World* enterprise software. Used with permission, JD Edwards & Company.

Enterprise System Functionality

ERP systems get their name from their early origins as manufacturing systems. Early business information systems served individual application areas such as accounting, marketing, and personnel. As information needs grew and technology improved, integrated systems evolved, beginning with **material requirements planning (MRP I) systems.** These information systems used marketing sales projections, combined with production schedules, to plan for raw materials purchases. **Manufacturing resource planning (MRP II) systems,** as their name implies, expanded these capabilities and included forecasting and planning for all manufacturing resources, including labor and overhead. These systems were integrated with the accounting and finance functions to produce cash forecasts and other budget information.

Traditional ERP Functions Today's ERP systems provide integration among all of an organization's major business processes, as shown in Figure 6-4. As you can see from the ERP system drawing, order processing and fulfillment, manufacturing, purchasing, and human resources functions all provide data to each other and to the financial system. This integration means, for example, that a salesperson taking an order in a manufacturing company is able to check inventory availability immediately. If inventory exists, the information system will notify shipping to pick the goods and

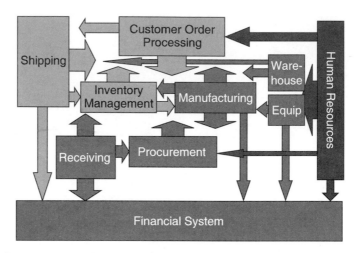

FIGURE 6–4 The integration within ERP systems. (Used with permission from Julie Smith David, Associate Professor of Accounting, Arizona State University.)

fill the order. If no inventory is on hand, the ERP system can trigger the manufacturing subsystem to make more of the product. The integration between the customer order and manufacturing subsystems can result in a revision to production schedules to accommodate the needs of the new order. If there are no raw materials available to start the manufacturing process, the procurement function can order the raw materials needed. Human resources may be involved too, if the new order requires extra workers or workers to be reassigned. In short, all functional areas of the organization can use the same information to perform their tasks in an efficient fashion, thereby acting in a coordinated effort to meet customer needs.

Extended ERP Systems The business processes integrated by ERP systems are known as **back-office** functions because they primarily concern an enterprise's internal systems. Traditional ERP systems focus on internal data, generated for use primarily by internal processes (e.g., human resources and manufacturing) and an enterprise's own decision makers. Today's ERP systems, or **ERP II** systems, are extended with e-business and other **front-office** capabilities. Extended enterprise systems or ERP II bring customers, suppliers, and other business partners, such as investors and strategic business relations, into the picture.

Figure 6-5 shows a model of an extended enterprise information system. The ERP system, or an extension of the system, interfaces with suppliers and customers through **supply chain management (SCM)** applications. Supply chains have been around since the first merchandise transaction took place. The supply chain for a single enterprise extends from the suppliers, from whom it purchases raw materials, to its end customers. However, the supply chain of one company is but part of a *linked* supply chain. Figure 6-6 demonstrates this concept by showing the supply chain for a segment of the automotive industry. Note that goods and money are not the only commodities exchanged by partners along the chain. Information is fed backward from customers to suppliers. The SCM provides suppliers with access to the buyer's internal data, including inventory levels and sales orders. These data allow a business to reduce the cycle time for procuring goods for manufacture and sale. At the same time, the customer is able to view the supplier's information related to his order.

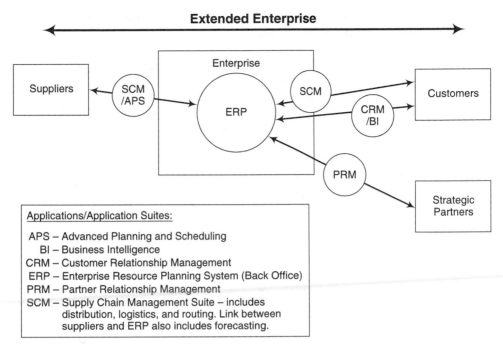

FIGURE 6–5 The extended enterprise information system.

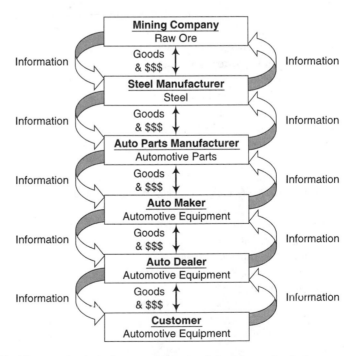

FIGURE 6–6 The supply chain for a component of the automotive industry.

Case-in-Point 6.2 shows how ERPs can increase profitability in the supply chain through information sharing.

> ***Case-in-Point 6.2*** Timberjack, a logging vendor, recently invested in an enterprise resource planning (ERP) system that allows its customers to monitor their equipment orders. The software, IPS Applications '98, provides interfaces for customers so that they can check the status of their custom orders, a feature known as supply-chain automation. Timberjack expects this feature and others, such as faster machinery design time and elimination of redundancy in data entry, to contribute to an 18-month payback on its $2.5 million software investment.

SCM applications in a manufacturing environment may include **advanced planning and scheduling systems (APS).** These systems work to synchronize the flow of materials within the supply chain. The planning features help an organization to determine whether its capacity is adequate to meet expected orders. It incorporates estimates of inventory levels, lead times, and costs to develop optimal manufacturing schedules. APS are important in **lean manufacturing** environments, which we discussed in Chapter 5.

Another tool that helps companies optimize their supply chain is **customer relationship management (CRM).** CRM is not an application per se, but rather a collection of applications including databases, sales order and customer service systems, and financial packages. The integrated CRM collects the data from these disparate applications and integrates them for use in decision making. Businesses use CRM to analyze customer data, for example, looking for trends and buying patterns. This analysis can improve customer relations when the business uses the information to better meet customer needs. For example, have you ever been asked for your Zip code when you make a purchase at a store? The retail clerk will enter your Zip code into a customer database. The CRM can use that data to find the location of frequent shoppers at the store. Perhaps the store management will decide to relocate its business based on the information the system gathers. Analysis of the data can even show what products customers in certain locations purchase most frequently. **Business intelligence (BI)** tools are data analysis software that helps managers get the most information from their CRM. CRM combined with BI analysis enables businesses to serve their customers better, and these tools also impact the bottom line. Analysis of buying trends can improve sales forecasting and also optimize inventory levels, as demonstrated in the following Case-in-Point.

> ***Case-in-Point 6.3*** Nordstrom department stores operate a web site, nordstrom.com, where customers can shop online. Not all of the brick and mortar stores' products were always available through their online site. For instance, you used to have to visit a particular store if you wanted a Kate Spade handbag. However, searching for Kate Spade products at the web site would redirect you to the stores and sales personnel who could help you purchase those items. Management added this feature after their business intelligence tools revealed that Kate Spade was one of the top search phrases entered by customers at the nordstrom.com site. Now, they sell the bags through the online site.[2]

Figure 6-5 also shows an application linking business partners to the enterprise. Of course, many of these partners are suppliers and customers, but there are

---

[2] Maselli, Jennifer, "Business-Intelligence Service Pays Off for Nordstrom," *Informationweek,* February 19, 2001, p.91.

others as well. These include investors, creditors, and strategic partners, with whom the enterprise might team up to offer special services. **Collaborative business partnerships** are springing up today as organizations find that there is often an advantage to working with other businesses, even their competitors, to increase their power to meet customer demands, or for other reasons. For instance, General Motors has a partnership with the Nature Conservancy to sponsor an initiative to protect and restore a portion of the Brazilian rainforest. **Partner Relationship Management (PRM)** software enhances the working relationship of partners, particularly when they use the Internet.

> ***Case-in-Point 6.4*** Siebel offers PRM software that automates business processes among partners and allows them to work collaboratively. The software includes a partner portal, and a methodology that provides a collaborative environment for partners to work together in defining their strategies and performance measures.

The Architecture of Enterprise Systems

Four components of an ERP's architecture or technical structure are the systems configuration, centralized database, application interfaces, and Internet portals. Let us examine each of these in greater detail.

ERP Configurations   ERP systems originated on mainframe computers. The mainframe computer stored and ran the ERP software application. Users interacted with the software from terminals or personal computers (PC) with little or no computing capability. Today, ERP systems are client-server based. Both computing and storage are shared between the server(s) or host computer(s) and a user or client machine. ERP systems may require more than one server, for example, one to store the ERP application and another that holds the databases. In an ERP system, there may be hundreds of clients or user PCs. Sometimes we describe a client as being "thin" or "fat." These terms refer to the computing power of the client. The thin client has little processing capability, while a fat client has more. Clients and servers are networked, typically via a local area network (LAN) or wide area network (WAN). Today, clients and servers may also interact via the Internet.

   ERP systems can typically run on many operating system platforms, such as UNIX, Windows NT, or Windows 2000. Individual ERP packages like *PeopleSoft* and *SAP* also support multiple database management systems, including *Oracle, Microsoft SQL Server,* and *Sybase.*

A Centralized Database   To accomplish integration, ERP systems architecture is built around a **central database.** The database stores information about each data item just once (thus avoiding data redundancy) and makes it immediately available to all the various functions in an organization. This central database means that the data in an ERP system have data integrity; they can be relied on in terms of their accuracy. To appreciate the value of a central database, consider the following example.

> ***Example***   Most businesses maintain price lists of product selling prices. The marketing department, which sets the prices, creates and maintains a price list. Accounts receivable also has a price list to reference in invoicing. The production department will have a price list for reference purposes. Finally, the web master has a price list and uses it to update the selling

prices displayed at the company's online store site. Suppose the marketing department makes a price change. The production and accounts receivable price lists may or may not be updated. If the marketing department does not notify the web master, the company web site will state the online prices incorrectly. The point is that in an information system where various departments keep their own files or databases, a change by one requires a change by all.

Data integrity is an important issue for many kinds of businesses. Imagine a manufacturing organization where several functional units each maintain information about inventory levels. One company reported that before adapting an ERP system, it frequently had to send employees to the shop floor to make sure there was actually inventory available to ship to customers!

Application Interfaces   Although an ERP system has the capacity to integrate data from many business units within one organization, not everyone wants or needs an ERP system, or at least not an extended ERP system. While purchasing one software package that has everything (e.g., *SAP*, which incorporates e-business, supply chain, and CRM functionality in its software) offers maximum integration, the flexibility of choosing the best software in different categories may argue for a *best-of-breed (BOB)* approach. For instance, a company may implement an ERP system from SAP and then choose to interface it with an e-procurement system by Ariba. There are other reasons an organization might forego the "one-integrated-system" approach. One company, for example, ran out of money as it added ERP modules and had to complete its system with a piecemeal approach.

Businesses that purchase extended functions from specialized vendors, and interface them with their ERP systems or other applications, can do so via middleware called **extended application interfaces (EAI).** These application interfaces allow different software applications to share information among them. They do so without requiring companies to build their own custom interfaces to tie multiple applications together. The next Case-in-Point is an example of a company's use of EAI.

Case-in-Point 6.5   Home Depot will spend the next year or so on an EAI project that will link its mainframes, databases, sales terminals, and other applications. The EAI project's goals are to enable real-time (versus batch) data transfer of customer store transactions to a central database and to relieve network clogs that result from the huge volume of data Home Depot transmits.[3]

Internet Portals   Extended ERP systems interface with customers, suppliers and partners through e-business **portals.** A portal is a gateway to other web sites or services. It's a web site that allows outsiders with authorized access to see into a company's internal information systems (i.e., its ERP). For example, a company can allow its suppliers to see its price lists and also to learn the payment status of their invoices on a real-time basis. Early portals simply acted as a starting point for users to access multiple associated web sites. Today, ERP portals are providing not only communication links, but also personalized services, such as e-mail and custom newsletters. These portals may even involve a trading aspect, allowing vendors of related products to sell services to customers through their sites.

---

[3] Kemp, T., "Home Depot's Net Improvement—Massive EAI Project Will Enable Real-time Data Transfers and Ease Network Congestion," *Internetweek* (July 9, 2001), p. 10.

Business Processes and Enterprise Systems

As we mentioned earlier in the chapter, an ERP system typically integrates financial, human resource, manufacturing, and sales and distribution functions within an organization (Figure 6-4). To a great extent, these functions mirror the business processes we described in Chapters 4 and 5. However, integration means that the processes interact seamlessly.

Integrated Business Processes Accountants and other financial personnel record an organization's accounting transactions in the finance module of an ERP system. These transactions include purchases and sales, and payments and receipts. In traditional accounting software applications, the financial accounting system doesn't exchange data directly with other functions, meaning that data sometimes must be entered and stored multiple times. In an ERP system, however the financial module can interact with the human resource, manufacturing, and distribution subsystems. For example, the finance module can exchange payroll and tax data with the human resources subsystem. When a customer places an order, the distribution subsystem can check the customer's credit limit and accounts receivable balance in the finance module. A salesperson can also check inventory levels. In a manufacturing environment, if the order requires additional inventory to be made, the customer order can impact the production schedule. The following fictitious example describes how the integration of business processes might work in an extended ERP system.

> *Example* A retail toy store chain sold out of a new toy after a popular television series showed a child actor playing with the toy, a talking bear. The retailer, Toys and Games, had recently installed an ERP system with e-commerce capabilities. A store buyer logged onto a web site that hosted a **trading community** for the toy industry. The trading community linked buyers and sellers, and also provided information relevant to the industry. At the site, the Toys and Games buyer placed an order to buy 10,000 of the talking bears from the bears' supplier. The supplier, Bear It!, has the same ERP system as Toys and Games. It receives the order immediately and begins steps to fulfill it. This included modifying the production schedule to accommodate the new order and checking inventories of the raw materials needed to manufacture the 10,000 talking bears. Because the bears require some specific labor skills in their manufacture, the ERP system also checks with personnel to see if enough workers with the required skills are available to work on the order. The electronic order interfaces with accounts receivable, and the ERP system determines that the new order will cause Toys and Games to exceed its credit limit. The information system of Bear It! sends an e-mail to the credit manager to get approval to proceed with the order. Toys and Games receives notification of the acceptance of the order and a tracking number so that the retailer can keep tabs on the order's progress.

The preceding example demonstrates how the sales order of one company triggers a number of activities in another company—almost instantly! Because the ERP system has a centralized database, everyone who logs onto the system will see the same customer order and can follow it as it moves through the system.

ERP Systems and Business Process Reengineering Buying an ERP system is akin to buying a new way of doing business. It entails reengineering an organization, hopefully to conform to the **best practices** of the industry. For example, *PeopleSoft* is well-known for incorporating the best practices for the human resources process in its software. In Chapter 5 we explained that reengineering means that you are fundamentally redesigning or changing your processes. Case-in-Point 6.6 demonstrates the benefits that can come from these redesigned processes in an ERP environment.

> ***Case-in-Point 6.6*** Vail Resorts implemented *PeopleSoft*'s human resource and financial management software modules to integrate the two systems. Each September the company hires about 7,000 employees. The season after implementing the new software was an especially busy one. One benefit of the newly automated hiring process was that it freed up staff who used to be busy processing paper transactions to help with interviewing job applicants.[4]

Sometimes multiple business units within one company do the same thing in many different ways. For instance, their accounts payable processes may differ. Another advantage of implementing an ERP system is that it encourages, if not demands, that the separate units conform. If all units standardize to adopt the best practice, the company should be more productive overall.

A company considering an ERP system may choose to conduct a BPR initiative before implementing the software, or they may undertake BPR concurrent with the implementation. The choice depends on how unique the business may be. For enterprises operating in a fairly straightforward industry, it's likely that the ERP software incorporates the best ways of doing business. This means that the organization can change its own processes to conform to those incorporated in the software and there may be no need for up-front BPR work. However, many companies may choose to conduct BPR first to figure out what processes they already have that incorporate best practices. Doing the BPR work at this time will help management to understand what kinds of process changes it needs, and this can also dictate which ERP software is best.

When an organization's practices and the processes dictated by the ERP system don't agree, a business must either change its processes or change its software. Usually, you want to change the process. Customizing ERP software should be done as a last resort because it can introduce bugs into the system and it also creates problems with software upgrades. Each time the software vendor issues an upgrade, you'll have to recreate the customized features. Of course, sometimes an organization *must* customize as described in the following case.

> ***Case-in-Point 6.7*** When American University was implementing an ERP system, the payroll office sent out memos advising faculty that due to the constraints of the new information system, it could no longer pay them on a ten-month basis. University faculty with a ten-month contract usually have the choice to receive their annual salary over either ten months or spread over twelve months. The ten-month arrangement is more beneficial since the faculty member can bank the excess and earn interest on it. Needless to say, the faculty were very upset that the school's new ERP system would force them to, in effect, take a pay cut. The system implementers got the message and changed the software to accommodate the ten-month pay period.

Sometimes changing processes is desirable, but not feasible or at least problematic, for political or behavioral reasons. An enterprise that has had a nonintegrated legacy system for some time may struggle quite a bit during the ERP implementation. People who are used to doing their job in a certain way might resist the changes brought

---

[4] Adapted from www.peopletalkonline.com/en/new/peopletalk/jul2001/solutions_vail.html.

about by redesigned processes. This is sometimes true even when everyone knows the change is for the better. For instance, employees may be used to filling out travel request forms in a certain way. It may be a great improvement for them to be able to complete these forms online and in a new improved format that speeds up their reimbursement. However, if they're used to doing it the old way, they must learn how to do it the new way. This learning takes time and almost always meets some resistance. To obtain the most benefits from the new ERP system, the employees will have to learn to accept changes. This is why **change management** activities (discussed in the next session) are such an important aspect of an ERP implementation.

Implementing an Enterprise System

Implementing an enterprise system is a major effort, requiring high levels of planning and coordination. Many ERP projects are not successful, not because the software doesn't work, but because of weaknesses in the implementation process. In this section, we discuss some special issues surrounding ERP implementation. Chapters 13 to 15 provide a general and thorough discussion of systems analysis, design, and implementation issues.

Figure 6-7 shows the steps involved in implementing an ERP system. Traditionally, ERP implementations have been lengthy, perhaps lasting several years. However, not all ERP implementations take years and cost millions of dollars. A "fast track" implementation can be had for much less. Companies with revenues of less than $500 million may choose this path, which requires adapting a plain vanilla ERP system, that is, one with little or no customization.

> ***Case-in-Point 6.8*** CompanyStore, a company that builds online stores, wanted an ERP system but couldn't afford a big price tag or the time for a long implementation. The company implemented materials management and function planning and finance modules of *SAP R/3* in less than two months.[5]

Templates incorporating preconfigured system settings allow these faster and cheaper implementations. Major ERP vendors now have enough experience with a variety of industries to be able to preconfigure the software with an industry's best practices for a quick start.

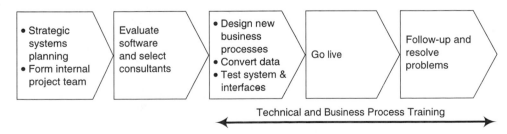

FIGURE 6-7 The ERP implementation process.

---

[5] Pender, Lee, "Faster, Cheaper ERP," *CIO Magazine,* May 15, 2001.

Systems Planning and Forming the Project Team   During the first stage of an ERP implementation, an organization undertakes strategic systems planning and forms an internal **project team.** Management and employee buy-in is vital to the success of an ERP system; for this reason it's important to get broad representation on the initial project team.

Software and Consultant Selection   The next set of steps in the ERP implementation process is software evaluation and consultant selection. These steps may be done sequentially, but there is a question about which to do first! The software selected can impact the consulting firm choice. On the other hand, it may be a good idea to engage a consulting firm first to assist the organization in choosing the best ERP software. One solution to this dilemma is to conduct the ERP software selection in-house and then the in-house project team can ask the chosen consulting team to verify the appropriateness of the software selection. Another option is to engage a consulting organization for software selection only and then put the implementation out for open bid to additional consulting firms.

Preimplementation Work   The next phase of the implementation includes three steps: (1) design new business processes, (2) convert data, and (3) test system and system interfaces. This phase is the longest. The time required to design the new business processes depends on the amount of reengineering to be done and the amount of software customization required. **Data conversion** can be a very time-consuming process in an ERP implementation. Before actually entering converted data into the new database, the project team will have to agree on the parameters for each data field. This agreement is not always easy to accomplish. For instance, suppose one organizational unit feels very strongly that the product code should be "intelligent," or have meaning (e.g., lge means large), while another unit thinks that this will limit growth and is not necessary because the new system will use bar codes anyhow. Sometimes political issues take as much or more time to resolve in an ERP implementation as do the technical issues. The final step in the preimplementation phase is to perform readiness tests of the ERP system and the interfaces among the system and any other information systems with which it will interface.

Go Live and Follow-Up   Finally it's time to **"go live."** Actually installing the software and switching over is momentous, but it's not the end of the process. Since a new ERP system requires many people in the organization to change their behavior to adapt to new business processes, there may be some back-sliding that occurs postimplementation. For example, suppose that under the old legacy system, a manager was used to getting a sales report in a certain format. The new ERP system doesn't provide a report set up in the same way and so the manager develops a spreadsheet that will provide him with the same information he used to get, even though information from the new ERP may actually be superior. As another example, imagine that a salesperson is used to entering sales orders without carefully scrutinizing them. In a legacy environment, where the system wasn't integrated, an error didn't create a very large problem. The sales order did not interface with the other systems the way it does in an ERP environment. With the new system, however, the sales order may immediately trigger a change to the production schedule, an instantaneous credit check, and perhaps even a raw materials order. Follow-up work is required to make sure users of the new system use it the right way and do not revert to old behaviors.

Training and Change Management   The preceding examples point to another need in an ERP implementation. This is the need for training throughout the implementation process. Most people who think about ERP training consider the technical training only. Just as important, however, is training in concepts and the new business processes. The salesperson described in the previous paragraph has to learn to understand the impact of a sales order in an integrated system. A worker on the shop floor who, under a legacy system, needed to physically check inventory levels because the system lacked data integrity will need to learn not to do so and to trust the information provided by the ERP system. Employees will have to be trained to use new interfaces, processes, controls, and reports.

In addition to training, other types of **change management** activities are important in an ERP implementation. These include designing user interfaces and documentation so that they are easy and friendly to use, and constant communication. Many employees are fearful about major change and implementing an ERP system, especially when it entails major process redesign, is likely to cause significant disruption in an organization. Case-in-Point 6.6 described how the new ERP system at Vail Resorts freed up human resources personnel from completing paperwork so that they could help interview potential hires. This is great except that maybe the employees liked filling out paperwork better, or at least they're concerned they may not be as good at interviewing as they were at doing what they used to do. These fears are real and not recognizing them can result in the implementation failures we discuss next.

Risks and Benefits of Enterprise Systems

ERP systems carry big risks and big rewards. One risk is that the system won't work, and because of the power of integration, a failed implementation can do a lot of harm. This was the case for Hershey, as illustrated in Case-in-Point 6.9.

Case-in-Point 6.9   Hershey, the candy maker, is a poster child for the downside of a failed ERP implementation. The company implemented *SAP R/3* right before Halloween, a time when the company typically had its largest candy shipments. The candy didn't arrive at the stores in time for the holiday and the new ERP system got the blame. Profits for the third quarter of 1999 dropped almost 20 percent below those of the previous year. Management attributed at least some of this decline to lost sales and inventory problems resulting from the new business processes incorporated in the ERP system.

Besides the risks from failed implementations, ERP systems have many costs associated with them. (Figure 6-8 summarizes the costs and benefits associated with ERP systems.) Implementation costs requiring cash outlays are for hardware, software, and professional services. There are also costs for training, data conversion, and reengineering. Training costs include technical training and training in the new business processes. Data conversion can be very expensive. Imagine a multinational corporation that is exchanging more than 100 legacy systems for an ERP system. It's possible, for example, that each of the 100 systems represented an employee number in a different format. The new system will have just one uniform employee number. Management must agree on the format of the new employee number, and staff working on the implementation will have to convert all employee data to the new standard. Use of a software conversion program may facilitate the process.

Costs	Benefits
• Hardware	• Reduced inventory investment
• Software	• Improved asset management
• Training:	(e.g., cash and receivables)
– technical	• Improved decision-making
– business processes	• Resolved data redundancy and
• Data conversion	integrity problems
• Interfaces and customization	• Increased flexibility and
• Professional services	responsiveness
• Reassigned employees	• Improved customer service and
• Software maintenance	satisfaction
• Software upgrades	• Global and supply chain integration

FIGURE 6–8   A summary of costs and benefits typically associated with ERP systems.

In addition to the costs identified previously, there are also many costs that don't always make it into the cost/benefit equation. These include internal staff costs. The implementation will need some inside help, even if an organization hires consultants. Staff dedicated to the project cannot do their other jobs. If they are assigned to the implementation, their salaries should be too. There are also many costs that will continue, even after implementation. These include software maintenance and upgrade costs. One company noted that it hadn't realized how much it would cost for the highest level of vendor support and also to constantly send their IT staff to training on the software and its upgrades. ERP costs can vary from a hundred thousand to hundreds of millions of dollars.

Despite the high costs, there are many compelling reasons to implement an ERP system. These benefits can be difficult to quantify. Sometimes the specific benefits aren't as important as is the business imperative to integrate an organization's IT systems because the competition is doing it. Most often, however, organizations make an attempt to identify the benefits they expect from the new ERP system. Many of the benefits are from cost reductions, such as reductions in inventory and employees. Other benefits are those that accrue from not having to solve an organization's IT problems another way, for instance, the Y2k problem, or replacing legacy systems with separate applications to accommodate growth expectations.

Perhaps the most difficult benefits to quantify are those that stem from organizational change and enhanced revenues. It is hard to assign a dollar value to benefits that are expected to stem from increased customer satisfaction, for example, through improvements in on-time delivery and better customer service. Nonetheless, organizations need these types of improvements to make a **business case** for the ERP system. The business case describes how the organization will look after the implementation, for instance, its competitive position, the new supply chain, and its processes. The business case includes the improvements expected from the ERP system in areas that are difficult to quantify, such as better decision making and increases in sales. It is the business case, rather than the cost reductions, that really justifies an ERP investment.

AIS AT WORK
Motorcycles Ride the ERP Wave[6]

Indian Motorcycle Company hopes to come back from the dead and inject some competition into the U.S. motorcycle industry, which Harley-Davidson currently dominates. The company plans to use an ERP system to help them do it. Indian is a new company that's not so new. The company was successful years ago but "went under" in 1953. Indian has pretty much been out of business ever since, but a few years ago, a Canadian and California company got together to form the new Indian Motorcycle Company of America.

The new Indian took a very unusual step. Management spent over $1 million on a complete *Oracle* ERP system—right off the bat. Usually companies buying an ERP system have established business processes in place. Indian had no processes; they let the software define how they should structure the company from the beginning. However the software defined a process—that's how Indian organized theirs. One advantage in getting the ERP system first is that you don't have to change the processes—nothing existed to be changed! You can build all your processes around the best practices incorporated in the ERP software.

Indian's new ERP system provided them with a centralized database that management felt would help them react quickly to demand and sales orders. Motorcycle inventory is expensive to carry; these machines can cost more than $20,000. As a result, a success factor for the new company would likely be keeping inventories low. The ERP system also should help them to manufacture bikes according to best practices, with tight controls over the process. In addition to the integrated ERP, Indian also created a B2B extranet. The extranet allows Indian's more than 200 dealers to manage their accounts and orders and monitor product availability.

Two thousand and one was Indian's centennial year and they released several new designs to commemorate it. They aren't shipping in the hundreds of thousands yet, but they did get a boost last June when they received $45 million in investment. Many are banking on the company's comeback and riding on their ERP.

SUMMARY

This chapter described various types of accounting and enterprise software. Categories of integrated accounting software include low-end, middle to high-end modular and expanding enterprise, ERP, special industry, and custom-built software. We discussed each of these types briefly, along with the common features found in accounting software packages.

The chapter discussion emphasized the issues surrounding enterprise-wide software. We did so to demonstrate the integration that is occurring in modern information systems. The financial accounting system is but part of an entity's information system and to add value, it is vital to integrate both financial and nonfinancial information associated with business processes. Traditional ERP systems are back-office information systems, integrating financial, manufacturing, sales and distribution, and human resource systems. Extended ERP systems

---

[6] This AIS at Work is adapted in part from S. Deck, "How Indian Got Its Vroom Back," *CIO Magazine,* June 15, 2001.

add front-office features to the traditional systems, helping an organization to integrate its supply chain.

ERP architecture is built on a central database. This database helps organizations to reduce data redundancy and to enhance data integrity. Integrated business processes use the data and information in the central database. Enterprises invest in ERP systems in part because these information systems incorporate best practices for many business processes. An organization may choose to configure its business processes around those represented in the software (e.g., sales order processing), or the ERP project team may customize the software to fit existing processes. Implementing an ERP system is a costly and time-consuming undertaking. The process includes systems planning and forming the project team, software and consultant selection, preimplementation work, go live and follow-up, and training and change management. There are many risks and benefits of an ERP system. Costs include hardware and software costs, expenditures for professional services, training, data conversion, and reengineering costs. The benefits result both from cost reductions and revenue enhancements.

KEY TERMS YOU SHOULD KNOW

advanced planning and scheduling systems (APS)	go live
	integrated accounting software programs
application service provider (ASP)	Internet connectivity
back-office	lean manufacturing
best practices	manufacturing resource planning (MRPII) systems
business case	
business intelligence (BI) tools	material requirements planning (MRPI) systems
central database	
change management	partner relationship management (PRM)
collaborative business partnerships	portals
customer relationship management (CRM)	project team
data conversion	reengineering
enterprise resource planning (ERP) systems	source code
ERP II	supply chain management (SCM)
extended application interfaces (EAI)	trading community
front-office	value-added reseller (VAR)

DISCUSSION QUESTIONS

6-1. Which accounting software features are likely to be most important for a new retail business?

6-2. While you are likely to purchase a middle-end accounting software package from a value-added reseller (VAR), why should you be cautious about hiring one to recommend a software package for your business?

6-3. The difference between the price tag for low-end accounting software versus an ERP system can be millions of dollars. What can these high-end systems do that the less expensive integrated accounting packages cannot?

6-4. How is the accounting information system for a retail store that sells merchandise different from the accounting information system for a retail store that rents merchandise?

6-5. Discuss the differences between traditional ERP and ERP II systems.

6-6. What are some of the benefits of a centralized database architecture? What are some of the difficulties in moving from multiple databases or files to a centralized database structure?

6-7. A new company will have no business processes in place. Explain the advantages for such a company in acquiring an ERP package immediately.

6-8. Which activity in an ERP implementation do you think would be most time-consuming? Which do you think would pose the most challenges?

6-9. Why are change management activities so critical in an ERP implementation?

6-10. Find an article about a company that has adopted an enterprise-wide AIS such as *SAP*. What are some cost savings realized by the company? Were there any problems implementing the system? What were the costs and the length of time it took to implement the new information system?

6-11. Do you think it is easier or more difficult to select a low-end accounting software program or an ERP vendor? Why?

INTERNET EXERCISES

6-12. Use an Internet search engine to find two accounting software packages for each of the following industries: construction, health care, and retail.

6-13. Visit the software web sites of the two low-end accounting software package vendors and two ERP vendors. Do you see a relationship between the complexity of the web site and the price of the software?

6-14. Visit the web site of one of the ERP vendors discussed in this chapter. What differentiates the ERP package from an accounting software program? In answering this question, identify the software's specific functions (e.g., manufacturing).

6-15. Visit www.mysap.com/ides. This is the Internet Demonstration and Evaluation Site for *SAP* software. A number of demos are available at the site, including examples of *SAP* solutions for various industries. You can complete various exercises at this site. You may summarize the steps for a particular process for a specific industry. You can view the ways that e-business can enhance business partnerships and describe any additional risks you see from such relationships. Another option would be for you to summarize the features *SAP* offers for specific processes, such as e-procurement.

CASE ANALYSES

6-16. Swami Consulting (General Ledger Application)

Rajeev Swami left his job as a management consultant with a national consulting firm in December 2000 to start his own business, Swami Consulting, a sole proprietorship. The firm offers both systems and general management consulting services to medium-sized retail chains. Fees charged to clients fall into one of two categories: (1) management consulting revenue or (2) systems consulting revenue.

Swami Consulting employs three consultants (Boris Baker, Lin Fang DeGraaf, Patsy Souder) and one administrative assistant (Nancy Hoffman). Accounting at Swami Consulting has always been done manually by an outside accountant. Last year Rajeev decided that in view of the firm's growth, he would like to have accounting done in-house with the help of an integrated accounting software package.

The outside accountant, Anne Riley, gives you the balance sheet as of December 31, 2002. She also gives you subsidiary ledgers for accounts receivable, accounts payable, and all other necessary supplementary information.

Several of Swami Consulting's accounting policies are as follows. Customers send checks only; cash is not accepted and checks are deposited in the bank daily. Salaries are paid every other week, on Friday. Clients are billed each month for consulting work done during the period. Revenues are recorded in separate revenue accounts, depending on whether the work involved management consulting or systems consulting.

The new accounting system will be implemented for January 2003. Swami Consulting uses the accrual basis of accounting. The first business day (Monday) in January is 1/1/03. Employees will be paid on 1/14/03 and 1/28/03. To ensure success, Anne Riley will account for the first month's operations both manually and using the new software. Documents to be sent to Anne include a manually prepared check register and duplicate deposit slips documenting amounts received from clients. Anne will also receive summaries of client billings and summaries of vendor billings to Swami Consulting.

Figures 6-9 through 6-15 show the documents pertaining to Swami Consulting's operations for January 2003. In addition to these documents, the following supplementary information is available:

- All furniture and fixtures and office equipment have an estimated five-year life with no salvage value. Depreciation is amortized monthly.

- The prepaid insurance is a general insurance policy and expires in one year.

SWAMI CONSULTING	
STATEMENT OF FINANCIAL POSITION	
DECEMBER 31, 2002	
ASSETS	
Cash in Bank - Checking	$ 9,700
Marketable Securities - Certificates of Deposit	15,000
Accounts Receivable	53,700
Office Supplies	1,875
Prepaid Insurance	2,400
Rent Deposit	1,500
Furniture and Fixtures	22,000
Accumulated Depreciation - Furniture & Fixtures	(8,800)
Office Equipment	8,000
Accumulated Depreciation - Office Equipment	(2,200)
Total	$103,175
LIABILITIES AND OWNER'S EQUITY	
Accounts Payable	$ 12,300
Payroll Taxes Payable (Employer FICA)	1,650
Interest Payable	4,800
Notes Payable	20,000
Rajeev Swami, Capital	64,425
Total	$103,175

FIGURE 6-9 Statement of financial position for Swami Consulting.

SWAMI CONSULTING
SUBSIDIARY ACCOUNTS RECEIVABLE LEDGER
AS OF DECEMBER 31, 2002

Customer Code	Name	Address	City	State	Zip Code	Phone	Cust Type	Balance
A001	Ann's Candy	1018 Westminster Dr.	Vienna	VA	22030	284-9292	02	$ 6,500
A005	Art's Art	1287 E. Main St.	McLean	VA	22081	273-4060	01	11,200
B002	Bits and Bytes	386 Tech Plaza	Reston	VA	22042	284-6555	01	8,000
G001	Greg's Gadgets	1200 Hampton Ct.	Vienna	VA	22030	284-9878	01	3,900
M002	Mike's Menswear	221 Primrose Lane	McLean	VA	22082	273-7111	02	14,100
S003	Sewing Oats	3030 Sonoma Way	Fairfax	VA	22032	676-8000	01	1,000
T006	Tommy Tunes	8888 E. Main St.	McLean	VA	22081	273-2364	01	9,000
								$53,700

FIGURE 6-10   Subsidiary accounts receivable ledger for Swami Consulting.

SWAMI CONSULTING
ACCOUNTS PAYABLE SUBSIDIARY LEDGER
AS OF DECEMBER 31, 2002

Vendor Code	Name	Address	City	State	Zip Code	Amount Owed
F001	1st National Bank	2100 W. Broad St.	Richmond	VA	23235	$ 3,700
G001	General Office Supply	9872 Oakcrest Dr.	Fairfax	VA	23032	1,050
B003	Bell Telephone	2321 Winding Way	Vienna	VA	23030	219
V002	Virginia Power	6980 Electric Ave.	Vienna	VA	23030	192
C003	Computer World	2370 Lee Highway	McLean	VA	23082	5,173
G002	Gray's Advertising Ag.	620 Parkview Dr.	Reston	VA	23042	1,566
S004	Anne Riley, CPA	10810 Fieldwood Dr.	Fairfax	VA	23031	400
						$12,300

FIGURE 6-11   Subsidiary accounts payable ledger for Swami Consulting.

SWAMI CONSULTING
SUMMARY CLIENT BILLINGS
FOR JANUARY 2003

Date	Customer Code	Name	Amount	Reason
1/3	U001	Unlimited Sizes	$ 2,400	Management Consulting
1/3	S005	Shirley's Secret	6,300	Management Consulting
1/17	B003	Betty's Baked Goods	3,700	Systems Consulting
1/31	B002	Bits and Bytes	2,800	Management Consulting
1/31	W003	Wanda's Wonders	1,200	Systems Consulting
1/31	A001	Ann's Candy	600	Systems Consulting
1/31	M001	Moore's Mowers	9,100	Management Consulting
1/31	K002	Kits and Kaboodles	1,700	Systems Consulting
			$27,800	

FIGURE 6-12   Summary client billings for Swami Consulting.

SWAMI CONSULTING
DEPOSITS
JANUARY 2003

Date	Check	Customer Code	Name	Customer Amount
1/3	7116	B002	Bits and Bytes	$ 8,000
1/6	3045	W003	Wanda's Wonders	1,200
1/7	223	A001	Ann's Candy	6,500
1/7	1013	A005	Art's Art	11,200
1/10	7232	M002	Mike's Menswear	14,100
1/13	3545	G001	Greg's Gadgets	3,900
1/24	2401	U001	Unlimited Sizes	2,400
1/25	892	S003	Sewing Oats	1,000
1/31	3789	T006	Tommy Tunes	4,400
				$52,700

FIGURE 6–13   January deposits for Swami Consulting.

SWAMI CONSULTING
VENDOR INVOICES
JANUARY 2003

Date	Vendor Code	Vendor Name	Invoice #	Amount	Expense
1/7	G002	Gray's Advertising Ag.	120	$ 800	Advertising
1/10	B003	Bell Telephone	3204	184	Telephone
1/12	S005	Staple's Office Supplies	62	39	Supplies
1/17	C003	Computer World	781	276	Software
1/17	V002	Virginia Power	934	237	Utilities
1/24	G001	General Office Supply	1260	703	Supplies
1/25	S004	Anne Riley, CPA	379	400	Accounting
1/31	F001	1st National Bank	28463	460	Miscellaneous
				$3,099	

FIGURE 6–14   Vendor invoices for Swami Consulting.

- The rent deposit represents the last month's rent on a three-year lease. The lease runs one more year.
- Notes payable are due to Keating Savings and Loan. Interest is accrued each month and the annual interest rate is 12 percent. The note and interest are due 12/31/07.
- Payroll taxes payable are for the employer's last quarters' FICA withholding tax.
- All clients have a $20,000 credit limit. Billing terms are net 30 and no cash discounts are offered. The same terms hold for all vendors.
- Assume that Swami Consulting operates in a perfect world where there are no sales taxes. Since the organization is a sole proprietorship, no income tax is charged against the company.
- Office supplies are counted at the end of each month. Supplies on hand at 1/31/03 are $1,750.

Date	Check#	Payee	Amount	Explanation
		SWAMI CONSULTING		
		CHECK REGISTER		
		JANUARY 2003		
1/3	765	IRS	$1,650	Employer's FICA payment
1/5	766	Gray Adv.	1,566	Payment on account
1/5	767	Bell Telephone	219	Payment on account
1/7	768	Info Systems Assoc.	495	Seminar fee
1/10	769	Rajeev Swami	2,100	Personal Withdrawal
1/12	770	Computer World	5,173	Payment on account
1/12	771	Virginia Power	192	Payment on account
1/14	772	Boris Baker	1,050	Salary (1500 gross, 330 income tax withheld, 8% FICA)
1/14	773	Henry Henderson	620	Salary (900 gross, 208 income tax withheld, 8% FICA)
1/14	774	Patsy Pride	1,300	Salary (1800 gross, 356 income tax withheld, 8% FICA)
1/14	775	Nancy Nelson	460	Salary (600 gross, 92 income tax withheld, 8% FICA)
1/14	776	IRS	1,370	Payment of income tax withheld and employee FICA
1/19	777	General Office S.	1,050	Payment on Account
1/19	778	Anne Riley	400	Payment on Account
1/20	779	Rajeev Swami	2,100	Personal Withdrawal
1/26	780	1st National Bank	3,700	Payment on Account
1/26	781	Properties, Inc.	1,500	Rent for month
1/28	782	Boris Baker	1,050	Salary (1500 gross, 330 income tax withheld, 8% FICA)
1/28	783	Henry Henderson	620	Salary (900 gross, 208 income tax withheld, 8% FICA)
1/28	784	Patsy Pride	1,300	Salary (1800 gross, 356 income tax withheld, 8% FICA)
1/28	785	Nancy Nelson	460	Salary (600 gross, 92 income tax withheld, 8% FICA)
1/28	786	IRS	1,370	Payment of income tax withheld and employee FICA

FIGURE 6–15   Check Register for Swami Consulting.

Requirements

This case requires use of an accounting software package. You have been given all documents and information necessary to automate Swami Consulting. You will need to take the company through the accounting cycle for January 2003. This involves entering accounts with their beginning balances, entering all transactions for the month, making adjusting entries, and producing financial statements. Use the appropriate software module to enter your data. For example, it is *not* appropriate to enter a sale on account through the general ledger accounts receivable account and payroll entries should be made through the software's payroll modules. Produce the following:

1. An unadjusted trial balance
2. A listing of all adjusting entries
3. An adjusted trial balance
4. A balance sheet and income statement (use software customizing options to make these reports look professional). Do not print zero balances.

6-17. Springsteen, Inc. (Enterprise Resource Planning System)

Springsteen, Inc. is a large furniture manufacturer, located in Asbury Park, New Jersey. They sell to furniture wholesalers across the United States and internationally. Revenues last year exceeded $500,000,000. Currently, the company has over 100 legacy information systems. Recently Wendy Stewart, the Chief Information Officer (CIO), met with Bruce Preston, Chief Financial Officer (CFO), and CEO Patty Fisher, to discuss some technical problems occurring in these systems. Patty noted that several competitors have implemented ERP systems and she wondered if maybe it wasn't time for Springsteen to do the same. Wendy and Bruce agreed, with some reservations. Each had heard that Hershey couldn't ship its candy bars one Halloween because of problems with an SAP implementation. They'd heard other horror stories as well. Bruce thought maybe a Best of Breed solution would be less costly. Patty suggested that they all meet with a consulting team from their accounting firm, Big Five Accounting and Consulting, to explore the issue.

The meeting takes place the next week. Present are:

Wendy Stewart—CIO

Bruce Preston—CFO

Patty Fisher—CEO

Clarence Martin—Partner, Big Five Accounting and Consulting

Rosalita Jones—Senior Manager, Big Five Accounting and Consulting

Steve Johnson—Senior Manager, Big Five Accounting and Consulting

Patty opens the meeting. Her role is to manage the discussion and look for a decision. She talks about what she thinks an ERP might be able to do in terms of providing competitive advantages, particularly with respect to business processes.

Bruce discusses what the dollar costs and benefits of an ERP are and the expected effect on the bottom line.

Wendy explains the architecture of an ERP and explains the technical issues associated with implementing these systems.

Clarence tries to sell the project any way he can. He also tells the company representatives what it is his firm will do for them, the expected cost of the system, and the implementation schedule to be expected.

Rosalita explains why projects sometimes fail and how Springsteen can have a successful implementation. She argues for 15 percent of the budget to be spent on change management.

Steve describes the functionality in an ERP—what the various modules are, etc. He also talks about options for extending the ERP through the Internet to integrate the supply chain.

Requirements

This case is designed for in-class role play. Each actor and assigned support staff have 20 minutes to prepare for the meeting. The support staff are the other class members. During the meeting one support staff member for each role will capture the main points brought out during the meeting, relative to that role. There should be six columns across the board. For example, a scribe for Wendy Stewart would make a list of every technical issue brought out in the meeting. The meeting is scheduled to last approximately one-half hour.

6-18. B and R, Inc. (Enterprise Resource Planning System)

B and R, Inc. is one of the world's largest manufacturers and distributors of consumer products, including household cleaning supplies and health and beauty products. Last year, the company's worldwide net sales revenues exceeded $5 billion. The company has multiple information systems, including an integrated accounting system, a computerized manufacturing information system, and a supply chain management software system. B and R has required suppliers to use electronic data interchange (EDI) for several years.

Beth Baker is CEO of the company. She was pleased that the company survived the calendar change to the year 2000 with few information systems problems. Both she and Kristy Ramey, worldwide company president, had considered adopting an ERP system toward the end of the last decade, but postponed the decision since the information systems steering committee felt that it was not needed with respect to the Year 2000 problem. Now, though, the company wants to conduct more of its business over the Internet. B and R hired a Big Five professional service firm to advise them as to whether an ERP system would be worthwhile at this time. The professional service firm's consulting team assigned to the project is recommending the move to the ERP system. They report that these programs have electronic commerce interfaces that will allow B and R to sell its products to its business customers through its web site. They also recommend that the company move to a web-enabled EDI system, which would be facilitated by ERP software. The cost/benefit justification for the new software, which comes with an estimated price tag of $100 million (including consultant fees, all implementation and training costs) shows that B and R can expect great cost savings from improved business processes that the ERP system will help the company to adopt. The consulting firm implements these systems adopting the industry's *best practices* for many of the business processes.

Beth and Kristy have met several times with the consulting team and the steering committee. They are convinced that now is the time to adopt an ERP system and have advised the outside consultants to begin to identify the best package for them.

Requirements

1. What are the likely advantages of an ERP system for B and R?
2. Visit the web sites of the major ERP vendors. What are some of the characteristics you notice about their customers?
3. Beth has heard some horror stories from other CEOs about ERP implementations. What are some of the concerns B and R should address as they move forward with this project?

REFERENCES, RECOMMENDED READINGS, AND WEB SITES

References and Recommended Readings

Brady, Joseph A., Ellen F. Monk, and Bret J. Wagner, *Concepts in Enterprise Resource Planning* (Toronto: Course Technology, 2001).

Collins, C., "How to Select the Right Accounting Software," *Journal of Accountancy* (September 1999), pp. 31–38.

Davenport, T. H., *Mission Critical* (Boston: Harvard Business School Press, 2000).

Davenport, T.H., "Putting the Enterprise into the Enterprise System," *Harvard Business Review* (July/August 1998), pp. 121–131.

Geishecker, L., "ERP vs. Best of Breed," *Strategic Finance* (March 1999), pp. 63–67.

Goldratt, Eliyahu M., *Necessary But Not Sufficient* (Great Barrington, Mass: The North River Press, 2000).

Hall, J. A., *Accounting Information Systems* 3rd ed, (Cincinnati: Southwestern Publishing, 2001).

Jeffery, Bill, and Jim Morrison, "ERP, One Letter at a Time," *CIO Magazine* (September 1, 2000).

Lebow, M.I., and A. Adhikari, "Software that Speaks your Language," *Journal of Accountancy* (July 1995), pp. 65–72.

Leibs, Scott, "Core Values," *CFO* (February 2002), pp. 53–58.

Norris, Grant, James R. Hurley, Kenneth M. Hartley, John R. Dunleavy, and John D. Balls, *E-Business and ERP* (New York: John Wiley and Sons, Inc., 2000).

O'Leary, D.E. *Enterprise Resource Planning Systems* (New York: Cambridge University Press, 2000).

Pender, L., "Enterprise Application Integration," *CIO Magazine* (September 15, 2001).

Pender, L., "Faster, Cheaper, ERP," *CIO Magazine* (May 15, 2001).

Piturro, M., "How Midsize Companies Are Buying ERP," *Journal of Accountancy* (September 1999), pp. 41–48.

Zarowin, S., "Accounting Software: The Road Ahead," *Journal of Accountancy* (January 1998), pp. 67–69.

Web Sites

Two sites with news, articles, and many other resources concerning ERP are: www.erpfans.com and www.erpcentral.com

A site with many articles related to accounting and ERP software systems is www.cio.com

Web sites with reviews of accounting and enterprise software solutions are: www.cpaonline.com, www.ctsguides.com, www.fsforum.com, www.accountingsoftwareworld.com, and www.softwarenews.net.

Chapter 7

Data Modeling

INTRODUCTION

AN OVERVIEW OF DATABASES

What Is a Database?

The Importance of Databases to AISs

Storing Data in Databases

HOW TO CREATE DATABASES WITH REA

Identify Business and Economic Events

Identify Entities

Identify Relationships Among Entities

Create Entity-Relationship Diagrams

Identify Attributes of Entities

Create Database Records

ADDITIONAL DATABASE DESIGN CONCERNS FOR AISs

Administration

Documentation

Data Integrity

Processing Accuracy and Completeness

Concurrency

Backup and Security

AIS AT WORK: RETAILERS NOW SAVE QUESTIONS AS WELL AS ANSWERS TO IMPROVE CUSTOMER SERVICE

KEY TERMS YOU SHOULD KNOW

DISCUSSION QUESTIONS

PROBLEMS

INTERNET EXERCISES

CASE ANALYSES

Carl Beers Enterprises

Martin Shoes, Inc.

Souder, Oles, and Franek LLP

REFERENCES, RECOMMENDED READINGS, AND WEB SITES

After reading this chapter, you will:

1. *Appreciate* the importance of databases to AISs.

2. *Be able* to describe the concepts of the data hierarchy, record structures, and keys.

3. *Know* how to create a database model with REA.

4. *Be able to name* three database structures comonly used to create databases.

5. *Understand* the uses of data dictionaries.

6. *Be able to explain* why such design concerns as processing accuracy, concurrency, and security are so important to multiuser databases.

7. *Be able to explain* the differences among the first, second, and third normal forms.

...I need to know the margin of profit over gross expenditure of every book we publish.... How can we cut out the unproductive authors if we don't know who they are? We need someone who will make money for us, not just tell us each year how we spent it.

P. D. James, *Original Sin,* Alfred A. Knopf, 1994,
p. 86.

INTRODUCTION

Civilizations have stored accounting data in systematic fashion for at least 6,000 years. The ancient Babylonians, for example, used clay tablets for recording such information as inventory receipts and disbursements, payroll information, and real estate transactions in their temples. Modern AISs use computers rather than clay tablets, but much of the same organizing requirements remain—that is, systematic recording of data, convenient and useful formats, and easy access to required information. In this chapter, we examine how to *design* a database. In the next chapter, we look at how to *use* a database effectively. We begin by examining some database concepts, and then describe database design and data modeling techniques in depth.

AN OVERVIEW OF DATABASES

In some ways, not much has changed since ancient Babylonian days. For example, even the most basic AIS needs to record accounting data in systematic fashion and to organize accounting records in logical ways. Usually, this is done in a database.

What is a Database?

A **database** is a large collection of related data that are typically stored in computerized, linked files and manipulated by specialized software packages called *database management systems.* Examples of databases include the repositories of information and related files for inventory systems, general ledger systems, and production-scheduling systems. In most applications, these systems are complex combinations of data, processing software, and perhaps separate hardware that interact with one another to support the specific storage and retrieval tasks required of them.

Technically, not every collection of data is a database. For example, the time-card data from a weekly payroll system might be stored in a computer, but a single file containing such data *alone* is generally too simplistic to be called a "database." Similarly, the budget or other financial information typically created in computer spreadsheets is often stored in linked files, but of course is typically manipulated by spreadsheet programs such as Excel, not a database management system such as Access. Most commercial databases are very large, invaluable collections of proprietary data that developers carefully design and protect, and that often form the core of efficient accounting information systems.

The Importance of Databases to AISs

It is difficult to overstate the importance of computerized databases to AISs. For example, accounts receivable applications must store information about customers, accounts payable applications must store information about suppliers, and payroll applications must store information about employees. What AIS does not require stored information of some sort? Here are several other reasons why databases are important.

- **Valuable information.** The information stored in an organization's databases is sometimes its most important asset. TRW, for example, is one of the nation's largest credit bureaus, maintaining credit information about millions of Americans. Its credit files *are* its business.

- **Volume.** Some of the nation's largest databases are truly spectacular. Ford Motor Company, for example, currently maintains a customer database of 50 million records. Citicorp uses a database of 30 million records. For General Foods, the number is 25 million. Organizing and managing databases of such great size are enormous and often daunting tasks.

- **Complexity.** The databases of some organizations are centralized (i.e., stored in a single location at corporate headquarters or maintained on a single file server in a local area network). Many other databases, however, are distributed (i.e., duplicated in local or regional computers as processing needs dictate). But distributing information makes it harder to (1) ensure data accuracy, consistency, and completeness, (2) secure information from unauthorized access, and (3) recreate files with backups in the event of system failures.

> *Case-in-Point 7.1* Walgreen's is a $13 billion drugstore chain that maintains a centralized Oracle database on 40 million patient-customers. Each time its Intercom Plus system receives a prescription order from one of its 2,446 pharmacies, it performs as many as eight checks for such potential problems as drug allergies or payment difficulties with the patient's HMO plan. When the system was first tested, these processing requests overwhelmed the company's hardware capabilities and led the company to acquire two new processors. Although the cost of the final system was more than $150 million, it reduces the time it takes professional pharmacists to fill orders by 30 percent.

- **Privacy.** Databases often contain sensitive information—for example, employee pay rates or customer credit card numbers. This information must be protected from those unauthorized to have it. Some of the most important control procedures for an AIS are those that protect databases from unwarranted access. (Some of these are discussed in Part Three of this textbook.)

- **Irreplaceable data.** The information of most AISs is necessarily unique to the organization that created it and, therefore, often priceless. Thus, a special dimension of database management is file security.

- **Internet uses.** As you might imagine, databases are critical components for both internal and external corporate web systems. These databases store such things as product information for online catalog sales, e-mail, product registration data, and dynamic corporate data about employment opportunities, stock prices, and executive officers. Internet applications often also store customer-entered data such as online product orders, credit card numbers, subscription information, airline reservations, and university-student registration data.

Storing Data in Databases

To be useful, the data in an organization's databases must be stored and organized efficiently. Three important ideas along these lines are the concepts of (1) the data hierarchy, (2) record structures, and (3) record keys.

The Data Hierarchy   Storing accounting data in computer files means organizing the data into a logical stucture. In ascending order, this **data hierarchy** is:

$$\text{bit} \rightarrow \text{character} \rightarrow \text{data field} \rightarrow \text{record} \rightarrow \text{file (table)} \rightarrow \text{database}$$

To illustrate, imagine a payroll file. The lowest level of information in this file is a binary digit or bit. At the second level, a computer combines eight of these bits to create a byte of data that can represent a single character—for example, a letter of the alphabet or a special symbol such as a plus sign. The third level combines several characters to form a **data field**—for example, an account balance. Other names for a data field are "attribute," "column," or simply "field."

At the fourth level, data fields combine to form a complete computer record. A computer **record** stores all the information about one file entity—for example, one inventory part in an inventory file, one employee in a payroll file, or one customer in a customer file. At this level, it may be helpful to liken the structure of a database to the data in a spreadsheet. Each column defines an individual data field, and each row defines a separate record or *tuple*.

At the fifth level of the data hierarchy, a set of common records forms a file, or in Access parlance, a *table*. Thus, a file or table contains a set of related records—for example, a set of inventory records or customer records. Master files typically store permanent information—for example, part number, part description, and location code for the individual records in an inventory parts master file. Transaction files typically store transient information—for example, inventory disbursements and replenishments for a specific time period.

Finally, at the highest level, several related tables create a complete database (i.e., a collection of files that contain all the information for an accounting application). In an inventory application, for example, this database might contain a part-number master table, a supplier table, a price table, an order transaction table, and so forth, as well as several other files (that we shall identify shortly) that might help end users organize, access, or output inventory information efficiently.

Record Structures   The specific data fields in each record of a database table are part of what is called the **record structure.** In many accounting applications, this structure is fixed, meaning that each record contains the same number, same type, and same-sized data fields as every other record on the file. This would probably be the case for the payroll record illustrated in Figure 7-1. In other applications, either the number of data fields in each record might vary, or the size of a given data field in

Last name	First name	Social Security number	Dept. code	Pay rate	Date of hire	Over-time OK?	Other info.
Smith	Mary	575-64-5589	A	7.75	10-15-95	yes	. . . . .

FIGURE 7-1   Some of the data fields in a computerized payroll record.

each record might vary. For example, in a file of customer complaints, the memo field in each record might vary in length to accommodate different-sized descriptions of customer problems.

Record Keys   The data field in each record that enables a database system to uniquely distinguish one record from another in a database table is called the **primary record key,** or "primary key" for short. For the payroll record in Figure 7-1, for example, the primary record key would be the employee's Social Security number. End users and computer programs use primary record keys to find a specific record—for example, the record for a particular employee, inventory item, or customer account. Businesses sometimes combine two or more data fields to serve as the record key for a computer record. For example, a bank might combine its branch code with a customer's account number to serve as the record key. Another example would be a ten-digit phone number for a customer, separated into an area code and a local phone number.

It is also possible for a computer record to have more than one record key. For the payroll file of Figure 7-1, some examples are the employee's last-name field or the department-code field. These data fields, which are typically not unique across records but which can also be used to search records for specific information, are examples of **secondary record keys.**

Finally, some accounting records contain data fields called **foreign keys** that enable them to reference one or more records in other tables. For example, in addition to the payroll table in Figure 7-1, a firm might have a department table with the data fields shown in Figure 7-2. The primary key for the department table is the department code (e.g., "A," "B," and so forth). With this arrangement, the department code field in the payroll record of Figure 7-1 would be a foreign key that the database system could use to reference the appropriate department record from the department table. These foreign keys enable a database system to combine the information from both tables to produce a report with the format:

Last Name	First Name	Dept. Code	Manager	Location	Secretary Phone
Smith	Mary	A	B. Wright	Bldg. 23	x8734
Coles	Harper	B	S. Garadis	Bldg. 23	x9330
etc.					

Department code (primary key)	Manager	Number of employees	Location	Secretary phone	Other info.
A	B. Wright	23	Bldg. 23	x8734	...

FIGURE 7-2   A sample record from a department file.

Note that each line of this report contains information from two tables: the employee table shown in Figure 7-1 and the department table in Figure 7-2. To accomplish this feat, the designers for the entire application must examine the data carefully and organize them efficiently. The following sections of the chapter explain this analysis in detail.

HOW TO CREATE DATABASES WITH REA

At a state department of social services, the director wants to know how many inquiries were made for a certain type of medical assistance last month. At the headquarters of a department store chain, a vice president wants to know how many credit customers made partial payments to their accounts last month. At a local university bookstore, a manager wants to know how many book orders went unfilled last month.

What all these data requirements have in common is a need for information that most AISs either do not collect, or do not collect in formats that easily provide managers answers to logical inquiries. The challenge of creating large, useful databases is to determine how to collect, organize, and store the data in such a way that they satisfy several diverse objectives. One obvious goal is to identify what informational outputs are required of the system. A second task is to find hardware and software platforms that can adequately perform the data-gathering, storage, and reporting tasks involved. Yet a third goal is to keep the databases manageable—for example, keep them from becoming too large, complex, and unwieldy. A fourth goal is to protect the privacy of sensitive information. A final goal is to reduce data redundancy, that is, storing the same data repeatedly in different tables. These goals make clear that databases must be carefully designed to serve their intended uses. The question is "how do we do this?"

The term **data modeling** describes the process of designing databases—a process that is best accomplished with an established methodology. One approach is to use the **REA model,** an acronym for resources (R), events (E), and agents (A). The REA model requires the following steps: (1) identify business and economic events, (2) identify entities, (3) identify relationships among entities, (4) create Entity-Relationship diagrams, (5) identify the attributes of data entities, and (6) create database tables and validate the database. The following discussions describe each of these steps in detail, using the sales process as an example.

Identify Business and Economic Events

Chapters 4 and 5 discussed business processes and explained that these processes involve a series of events or identifiable activities. There are primarily two types of events: economic events and business events. **Economic events** impact an organization's financial statements and are captured in accounting transactions. An example would be a sale on account. This economic event increases an entity's accounts receivable and revenue accounts on its financial statements.

As noted previously, critics of the accounting discipline sometimes charge that financial accounting systems often ignore organizational activities that are nonetheless important to investors and creditors. Such **business events** do not affect financial statements but can impact an organization in a value-added way. One example of such an event is a *sales order* from a customer. Because sales orders do not require journal entries, they do not appear anywhere in a company's financial statements. However, suppose that a company received a sales order from a customer that was equal to all its revenues for the previous quarter. This would certainly be important information that investors and creditors would want to know. Another example is when a firm hires a new CEO. Again, this event does not require a journal entry, but is nonetheless important information for stakeholders.

When creating a database using an REA approach, a systems designer will try to record all events in the database, whether they are business or economic ones. By including both types of events in the database, users can access and obtain important information about both business and economic activities.

Identify Entities

Databases contain data about objects of interest called **entities.** Database entities include business and economic events plus information about who and what was involved in those activities. The REA model is conveniently named to identify entities as resources (R), events (E), and agents (A).

We've already discussed events. Events both use and generate **resources.** For example, a sale may require an inventory resource and generate a cash resource. Resources are very similar to accounting assets, but they are more all-inclusive. For instance, a contract might be considered a resource, but it would not appear as an asset on a financial statement. To determine whether or not something constitutes a resource associated with an event, the resource should pass two tests. First, it must be an object of value associated with an event. Second, it should be an object of sufficient interest that you would want to collect information about it.

Agents are the "who" associated with events. For example, both a salesperson and a customer are likely to be involved in a customer order event. They are both agents. The REA model helps in identifying database entities because each resource, event, and agent is an entity in a relational database. Figure 7-3 provides several additional examples of each type of entity.

You may notice that Figure 7-3 does not list accounts receivable as a resource. This is because the REA model does not recognize "receivables" or "payables" as resources. Rather, receivables and payables are by-products of an information event and only represent *claims* on resources rather than resources themselves. Similarly, the REA model does not treat "billing" as a business or economic event. Billing is really just a notification that conveys information about an economic event such as a sale or purchase.

Resources:	Events:	Agents:
Cash	Sales Order	Employee
Contracts	Sales	Customer
Inventory	Purchase Order	Vendor
Equipment	Purchase	Manager
Plant Facilities	Receive Goods	Stockholder
	Hire an Employee	Creditor

FIGURE 7-3   Examples of resource, event, and agent entities.

Customer Order Table (Event)

Order #	Employee #	Customer #	Date	Comments
1003	M24SP	B104	01/03/02	
1004	R63SP	P202	01/03/02	Ship ASAP.
1005	M24SP	S200	01/03/02	
1006	W11SP	C100	01/03/02	

Inventory Table (Resource)

Item #	Description	Unit Cost	Sales Price	Beg QOH
1400	Goodie Bar	$0.20	$0.40	13025
1500	Almond Delight	$0.25	$0.45	5010
1600	Gummy Lions	$0.60	$0.95	20109
1700	Pecan Bar	$0.70	$1.09	4508
1800	Milky Bars	$0.18	$0.30	2207

Customer Table (Agent)

Customer #	Name	Address	City	State	Zip Code	Credit Limit
A101	Amanda Wills	22 Yellow Ln.	Charlotte	NC	79803	$20,000.00
B104	Boris Bailey	321 Church St.	Oxford	OH	45056	5,000.00
C100	Carly Riccardi	1899 Green St.	Dayton	OH	43299	10,000.00
P202	Peggy Martin	1260 Main St.	Columbus	OH	43320	10,000.00
S200	Bill Safer	860 Broad St.	Fairfax	VA	22030	5,000.00

Salesperson Table (Agent)

Employee #	Name	Address	City	State	Zip Code	Dept ID	Date Hired
A06SP	Sally Anderson	3026 Skye Ln.	Columbus	OH	43213	247	1/31/1989
M24SP	Randy Merit	262 Main St.	Bexley	OH	43209	182	7/2/1999
R63SP	Barry Rogers	80 N. Long St.	Gahanna	OH	43215	247	1/16/2001
R73SP	Jim Rudolph	64 Lantern Ave.	Columbus	OH	43213	76	8/15/2000
W11SP	John Walker	1028 Fields Ln.	Lancaster	OH	43307	182	9/1/1992

FIGURE 7–4 Four sample tables in a relational database.

Identify Relationships Among Entities

A database should contain a table for each entity. The table, consisting of rows and columns, contains data describing the entity's attributes. (We'll discuss these attributes later in this section.) Figure 7-4 shows four database tables: (1) an event table (Customer Order), (2) a resource table (Inventory), (3) an agent table (Customer), and (4) another agent table (Salesperson).

Entities are often related, either directly or indirectly. For instance, a sale may be *of* merchandise inventory and made *to* a customer. The relationship between a sale and inventory or between a sale and a customer is a *direct relationship*. Inventory and customer also share a relationship, but it is an *indirect relationship*. Typically, events have direct relationships with resources and agents, and also with other events. The links between resources and agents are *through* events.

Data modelers need to know about entity relationships so that they can create links between database tables. Without these links, database users could not access data from more than one table at a time. Referring again to the tables in Figure 7-4, in the absence of any database links, users could only obtain reports about order data, inventory data, or customer data. The database system would not be able to produce a report that showed the customer name on a customer order report because it would require information from more than one table to do so.

Before we can decide on the best way to link database tables, we must first understand the nature of the relationships among entities. We describe these relationships in terms of **cardinalities.** Cardinalities are a notation showing the nature of relationships among entities as *one-to-one, one-to-many, none-to-one, none-to-many,* or *many-to-many.* A one-to-one relationship between two entities, shown as (1,1), means that the entities relate to each other a minimum of one time and a maximum of one time. An example of a one-to-one relationship is the relationship between sales and customers. In a particular organization, the relationship might be that a sale is to a minimum of one customer (a sale cannot exist without a customer) and a maximum of one customer (an individual sale can be to only one customer).

Entity relationships are two-way. Not only does a sale relate to a customer, but customers also have relationships to sales. The relationship between a customer and a sale may be none-to-many (0,N). This would be the case if a customer could exist without a sale (you research credit ratings of potential customers and maintain them before selling goods to the customers), and there could be many sales to each customer (the usual case). The two-way relationship between a sale and a customer, then, can be shown as:

(Sale 1,1; Customer 0,N)

We would read this cardinality as: each sale is to a minimum of one customer and a maximum of one customer and each customer has a minimum of zero sales and a maximum of many sales.

Cardinalities are sometimes difficult to grasp at first but they become easier to develop and understand with practice, so let's try another one. What does the following cardinality tell us?

(Inventory 0,N; Sale 1,N)

Part of the answer is that inventory relates to a sale a minimum of zero times and a maximum of many times. This makes sense in a business organization that keeps inventory on hand to meet future sales. It is also likely that in most businesses, each inventory item can be involved in more than one sale. (Think about, for instance, a retail clothing store that stocks several white shirts in a specific size and style.) The rest of the answer is that a sale relates to inventory a minimum of one time and a maximum of many times, or each sale must be for at least one inventory item and may be for many inventory items. (So you would have to buy something in order to have a sale and you could be buying a white shirt plus some jeans and a jacket.)

Cardinal relationships are not fixed across organizations, but vary according to the rules or controls of the specific enterprise. To illustrate using our sales example, recall that a company could have a customer with no sales or a customer with many sales (0, N). This is probably true for some businesses, but not for others. For example, a video rental store will usually collect information about customers before renting movies to them. In contrast, a retail clothing shop may not consider someone a customer until it sells something to this person. Thus, cardinalities can be helpful in describing an organization's rules and thus can also tell us something about the controls for a given business process.

There is just one more point to make about cardinalities. In the case of a sequence of events, you will nearly always have a situation where subsequent events require a minimum cardinality of 1, and earlier events have a minimum of 0. This would be the case between Customer Order (O,N) and Sale (1,N). What these cardinalities mean is that each order relates to a sale (signified by a shipment of goods) a minimum of zero times and a maximum of many times. In plain English, this says that an order may result in no sales or many sales. This makes sense because a customer may place an order that is never shipped or, perhaps due to backorders, requires several shipments. The other side says that each sale relates to an order a minimum of one time and a maximum of many. Again, plainly stated, this means that you cannot have a sale without an order and you could ship several orders at once. Do you see why you could have an earlier event that might not result in a later event but, as a rule, would require an earlier event to take place before a later one was possible? It would be bad business to ship goods without an order.

Create Entity-Relationship Diagrams

Database designers use a graphical documentation technique called the **entity-relationship (E-R) diagram** to depict the entities and their direct relationships. The model consists of four symbols: rectangles, diamonds, ovals, and connecting lines. Rectangles represent entities, diamonds describe the nature of relationships, ovals denote an entity's attributes, and connecting lines depict relationships. Figure 7-5 provides examples of these symbols. For the sake of convenience, we may drop the diamonds and ovals, thus showing only entities and relationships.

Figure 7-6 is an E-R diagram that includes cardinalities for a sample business enterprise. Remember that these cardinalities could change, depending on an organization's rules or policies. For example, suppose a business starts selling services in addition to products. The cardinality between sale and inventory could change from (Inventory 0,N; Sale 1,N) to (Inventory 0,N; Sale 0,N). Do you see the difference? The

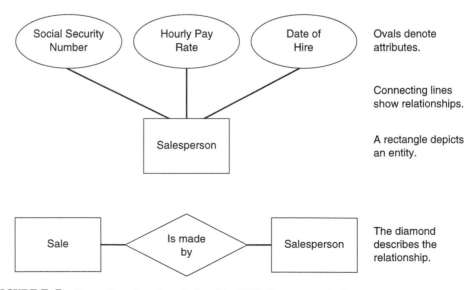

FIGURE 7-5 Examples of entity-relationship (E-R) diagram symbols.

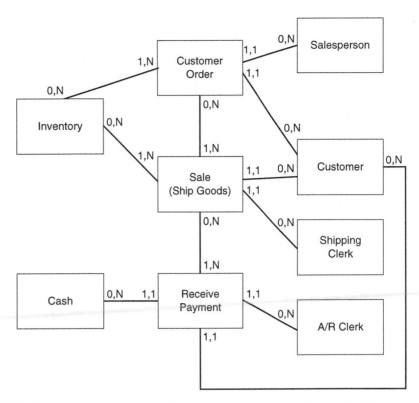

FIGURE 7-6 A sample E-R diagram for the sales process, including cardinalities.

cardinality now specifies that each sale can be for no inventory items, in the case of selling a service, or for many inventory items.

Identify Attributes of Entities

Entities have characteristics or **attributes** that describe them. We know that in a database model, a database table represents each entity. But what data appears in the table? The data within a table will be based on the attributes. For example, a salesperson, an agent, is an entity. The attributes are the data fields *describing* each salesperson. What data should you collect about a salesperson? Since each salesperson within the Salesperson database table is a unique record, one attribute should be unique to that record. This is the database primary key that we discussed earlier. The salesperson's identification number, which could be the employee's social security number, would be a likely attribute of a salesperson entity. Other attributes might be last name, middle name, first name, phone, address, e-mail, date of birth, date hired, department assignment, salary, and so on.

It is not always easy to decide what to include as attributes of an entity. There are, however, two guidelines you can use. First, the attributes should describe one entity and that entity only. For example, if you have an inventory table, you would not include in it information about the vendor. You can reference the vendor, but the name, address, and other information about the vendor belongs in a separate Vendor table. A second guideline for determining entity attributes is to keep in mind that the attributes included in the tables will *drive* the outputs of the database system. What you fail to include as an attribute is data that you will not collect and cannot report. For instance, have you ever been asked for your Zip code while shopping in a retail store? If so, the store is collecting an attribute of a sales transaction that can also be of value—for example, data that can help the store determine where to advertise or perhaps where to build another store.

Create Database Records

There are several ways to organize the individual records in a database. The particular method used is called the **database structure.** As with other design elements, the objective is to develop an efficient structure that enables users to access data quickly and store data efficiently. Three types of database structures are (1) hierarchical, (2) network, and (3) relational.

Hierarchical Structures   Accounting data are often organized in a hierarchy. For example, a sales office will have several salespersons, each salesperson will have several customers, each customer can make several purchases, and each customer invoice can have several line items. The data generated by the sales office have a natural **hierarchical structure,** with successive levels of data in an inverted, tree-like pattern. For this reason, hierarchical database structures are also known as **tree structures.**

> **Case-in-Point 7.2**   Hierarchical databases are often large. The Mervyn's Department Store chain uses a hierarchical data structure to store over 1 trillion bytes of information in its production and product-line databases.

Typically, hierarchical data structures have a genealogy that naturally organizes the data into a series of one-to-many relationships. For any two adjacent records, the "elder" or higher-level record is called the **parent record,** while the "younger" or lower-level record is called the **child record.** Two records on the same level (e.g., two line items on the same purchase invoice) are called **sibling records.**

Network Structures   Often, the data stored in an AIS are interrelated in several ways (i.e., in many-to-many relationships), and thus a single hierarchical structure cannot capture their relationships adequately. In such instances, AIS databases can use a **network structure** to link related records together and capture these relationships. This linking is usually accomplished with pointer fields embedded in each record that contain the disk addresses of related records. For example, the payroll record of Figure 7-1 could contain a pointer field for another employee working in Department A. The pointers maintain the data relationships, thereby enabling an AIS to prepare familiar reports—for example, a list of all employees working in Department A.

Relational Structures   Hierarchical and network database structures require advanced planning. This means that, if accounting data of one type (e.g., customer information) must be used with accounting data of another type (e.g., inventory information), the database must be planned to create these linkages. But many relationships can exist among data items, and it is difficult to anticipate all of them at the time a database is first constructed. Thus, hierarchical and network data structures afford little additional flexibility once further data processing needs are discovered.

This problem is overcome with a **relational database structure,** which enables users to identify relationships at the time the database is first created, or later, as accountants discover new informational requirements in the future. Each entity in the E-R diagram will be a table in the database. However, a database is likely to contain more tables than those representing entities. This is because we must provide links among the database tables to represent relationships among tables. As noted earlier, without these links a user would be unable to produce any database outputs that use information contained in more than one table.

The rows are database records and the columns consist of database attributes. Two important features of rows are that (1) within a row, there should be no attributes that are a result of a mathematical computation, and (2) there should be no repeating attributes. There is no reason to include attributes that the system can calculate by manipulating other data. For instance, inventory balances are constantly changing with purchases and sales. Rather than try to store that figure, including a formula to calculate it in a field will allow the data to change in real time as inventory levels fluctuate. As for repeating attributes, these indicate that you need a relationship table in the database. We discuss these next.

There are two ways to represent links within a relational database. The first uses foreign keys as described earlier. For example, in Figure 7-4, the Customer Number in the Customer Order table is a foreign key that references the primary key of a particular customer in the Customer table. As noted earlier, therefore, this value enables database software to link the two tables together—for example, to create a customer-orders report that shows the *name of the customer* associated with each order.

Linking tables with foreign keys is only appropriate in the absence of a many-to-many relationship between two entities. Looking at the sample E-R diagram for a sales process in Figure 7-6, for example, we see that the cardinality between Customer Order and Salesperson is (Customer Order 1,1; Salesperson 0,N). This is not a many-to-many relationship, so we can use a foreign key to link the tables to one another. In deciding which key to use as a foreign key, the general rule is to use the primary key from the table closest to a relationship (nearest the cardinality in the E-R diagram) containing a "many" or N, as the foreign key in the other table. In our example, this means that we would use the primary key from the Salesperson table as the foreign key in the customer order table. Looking at Figure 7-4, this is the case. The primary key for the Salesperson table, Employee #, appears in the Customer Order table.

A second way to represent relationships between two database tables is by creating a separate **relationship table.** Relationship tables are necessary when you have many-to-many relationships between database entities. The reason for this is that, without them, you would need to have repeating fields in a database table. For example, there is a many-to-many relationship between Sale and Inventory in Figure 7-6: (Inventory 0,N; Sale 1,N). Since a sale can be for multiple inventory items, if we posted inventory items in the Sale table, we would have to leave many fields available for the primary key for inventory. Alternatively, since a company can sell each inventory item many times, there would have to be repeating fields for the sales number field in the Inventory table to allow for this. To avoid these repeat fields, data modelers use relationship tables. A simple relationship table just lists the primary keys of the two tables that it joins. More complex relationship tables may include other data, such as quantity. Figure 7-7 shows a relationship table joining the Sale and Inventory tables. Notice that some of the sales are for more than one type of inventory item.

Sale #	Item #	Quantity
1004	1400	230
1003	1400	430
1005	1600	180
1005	1800	200
1005	1900	360
1006	1400	80
1006	1800	100

FIGURE 7-7   A relationship table joining the Sale and Inventory tables.

How many tables will a complete database have for the Sales process described in Figure 7-6? Looking at the diagram, we see that there are nine entities. If we have a table for each entity, the database would require nine tables. There are also three many-to-many relationships: (1) Inventory and Customer Orders, (2) Inventory and Sales, and (3) Sales and Receive Payment. Therefore, we might have as many as twelve tables in the finished database: nine tables for entities and three additional "joining" tables. There is another possibility, though: three of the entities are employees. It might be possible therefore to use just one database table for employees if we include a field or identifier that specifies the employee type. For instance, we could have a column or attribute for Employee Classification and within that you would specify Salesperson, Cashier, and so on. This reduces the table count to ten.

Figure 7-8 shows a complete listing of database tables and their attributes for our Sales Process example. Since data modeling is a creative process, there are many other possible sets of database tables and other attributes that you might include in a database for a sales process. Figure 7-8 is only an example.

ADDITIONAL DATABASE DESIGN CONCERNS FOR AISs

Small database systems such as the kind used by very small businesses or sole proprietorships tend to be fairly straightforward and manageable. However, large, multiuser databases pose special challenges for their designers because of their size and complexity. This final section of the chapter describes some database design concerns that are of special importance to accounting applications.

Administration

Without an overall supervisor, a large commercial database is somewhat akin to a rudderless ship (i.e., an entity without cohesion or direction). Similarly, it does not make sense to permit database designers to work unsupervised, or to develop large databases of critically important information without also creating accountability for subsequent changes. A **database administrator** is the individual charged with supervising the design, development, and installation of a large database system, and is also the person responsible for maintaining, securing, and revising the system's data. Although "technical competence" is an important asset for such a job, the ability to communicate effectively with users and reach compromises are often even more important skills.

INVENTORY TABLE
Item#, Description, Unit Cost, Sales Price, Beginning Quantity on Hand, Beginning Quantity on Hand Date

Cash Table
Account#, Account Type, Bank, Beginning Balance, Beginning Balance Date

Customer Order Table
Order#, [Employee#], [Customer#], Date, Comments

Sales Table
Sale#, [Employee#], [Customer#], Ship Date, [Order#]

Receive Payment Table
Cash Receipt#, Amount Received, Date, [Employee#], [Account#]

Employee Table
Employee#, First Name, Middle Name, Last Name, Address, City, State, Zip Code, [Department#], [Job Classification Code], Date of Birth, Date Hired, Last Date of Review

Customer Table
Customer#, Company Name, Address[1], City, State, Zip Code, Contact Person, Credit Limit

Inventory/Order Relationship Table
Order#, Item#[2], Quantity

Inventory/Sale Relationship Table
Sale#, Item#, Quantity

Sale/Receive Payment Relationship Table
Sale#, Cash Receipt#

[1] May use multiple addresses for different departments or for shipping versus billing.
[2] Relationship tables require two fields together to represent a primary key. Either field alone would not be unique to a record.

FIGURE 7-8   A schematic of database tables for the Sales Process. (Note: Underlining signifies a primary key and brackets denote foreign keys.)

Documentation

Especially during the design phase of a large database, database elements can change drastically. But even after it has "completed" database designs, the typical organization will find it necessary to make yet further modifications. This makes documentation critical. We have already discussed one important documentation tool: E-R diagrams. Descriptions of database structures, contents, security features (discussed later in this chapter), and password policies are other examples of important documentation materials.

In addition to all these items, it is usually vital to document "what stores what." The **data dictionary** of a database describes the data fields in each database record. In other words, a data dictionary is a data file about data. Although a data dictionary can be manual, it is usually a separate computer file that is created and maintained by the administrators of a database management system.

Figure 7-9 identifies some generic information that a data dictionary might contain (listed under the "Entry" column) and an example of such information for a Social Security number (listed under the "Example" column). In this figure, the data dictionary indicates that the Social Security number data field must be nine

Item	Entry	Example
1	Field name	Social Security number
2	Field size	9 characters
3	Type of data field	text
4	Default value	none
5	Required?	yes
6	Validation rule(s)	all digits must be numeric characters
7	Range	none
8	Source document	employee application form
9	Programs used to modify it	payroll X2.1
10	Individuals allowed access	payroll personnel
11	Individuals not allowed access	nonpayroll personnel

FIGURE 7-9 Examples of information that might be stored in a data dictionary for the Social Security number data field of a payroll database.

characters in length, is defined as a "text" data field (rather than a "number" data field because it is not manipulated mathematically), has no default value, and so forth. From this illustration, it should be clear that the entries in the data dictionary describe each data field in each record of each table (file) of an AIS database. When a new data field is added to the record structure of an existing table, the developer (or the system) also adds the appropriate information about it to the data dictionary. Similarly, when new computer programs are added to an AIS, the data dictionary is updated to reflect this change.

Data dictionaries have a variety of uses. One is as a documentation aid for those who develop, correct, or enhance either the database or the computer programs that access it. As suggested in items 10 and 11 of Figure 7-9, an organization can also use a data dictionary for security purposes—for example, to indicate which users can or cannot access sensitive data fields in a database.

Case-in-Point 7.3 When the IT professionals at Morton Salt of Chicago transferred its order entry, maintenance management, production scheduling, inventory management, and truck loading applications from a centralized IBM mainframe system to a distributed system of 25 AS/400 minicomputers, they used Lansa, a case tool, to assist them in the conversion process. A key element in that product was Lansa's Object Repository module–the equivalent of a data dictionary–that enabled the project team to define the record structures in database tables and other business rules. Morton completed its migration project in less than two years, thanks in large part to that case tool.

Accountants can also make good use of a data dictionary. For example, a data dictionary can help establish an audit trail because it identifies the input sources of data items, the potential computer programs that use or modify particular data items, and the managerial reports on which the data items are output. When accountants help design a new computer system, a data dictionary can help them trace data paths in the new system. Finally, a data dictionary can serve as a useful aid when investigating or documenting internal control procedures because the basis for data-entry tests, methods of data security, and so forth, can be stored as part of the data dictionary's file information.

Data Integrity

IT professionals estimate that it costs about ten times as much to correct information that is already in a database as it does to enter it correctly initially. Then, too, even simple errors in databases can lead to costly mistakes, bad decisions, or confusion. (Think about air traffic controllers as an example!) For these reasons, the software used to create databases should also include edit tests that guard databases from erroneous data at the time the data are entered. These **data integrity controls** are designed by the database developers and are customized for the application at hand. Examples include tests for data completeness, conformance to the data type specified for the data field, valid code tests (e.g., a state code such as "CA"), and reasonableness tests (e.g., regular payroll hours worked must be between "0" and "40"). We shall return to this point in Chapter 8.

Processing Accuracy and Completeness

Within the context of database systems, a **database transaction** refers to the sequence of steps that a database system uses to accomplish a specific processing task. AISs need **transaction controls** to ensure that the database system performs each transaction accurately and completely. To illustrate, imagine an inventory application with two types of inventory records: raw materials records and work-in-process records. An inventory manager wishes to decrease 200 units from a particular raw materials record and add the same number of units to a corresponding work-in-process record.

Now suppose that the database system executes the first part of this transaction (i.e., subtracts 200 units from the raw materials record) and then stops operating for some reason. This is a problem because the transaction has not been executed completely and the balance-on-hand field in the current work-in-process record is wrong. To overcome this problem, databases should either process a transaction entirely or not at all. To achieve this goal, database systems maintain an auditable log of transactions. When a specific transaction only partially executes, the system is now able to recover by verifying that a problem has happened, reversing whatever entries were made, and starting anew. In accounting applications, therefore, the ability to audit any particular transaction to ensure processing accuracy and completeness is critical.

Concurrency

In multiuser systems, it is possible for more than one user to access the same database at the same time. Without **concurrency controls,** it is also possible for two or more users to access the same *record* from the same table at the same time. This creates problems. To illustrate, imagine the same inventory file as the one discussed previously and suppose that two users—user A and user B—access the same inventory record at the same time. The initial balance-on-hand field for this record is 500 units. When User A accesses this record, the system transfers the entire record to A's work area. User A wants to add 100 units to the balance-on-hand field. The result is a new balance of 600 units. User A completes this transaction, the system writes the new record back on disk, and the new balance on hand in this record is now "600 units."

When User B accesses this same record, the system also transfers the same initial record to B's work area. User B wants to decrease the balance on hand by 200 units.

This results in a balance of 300 units because this user also starts with an initial balance on hand of 500 units. Because B completes this transaction after A is done, the system replaces the current record in the database with the new one. The end result is an inventory record with a balance on hand of 300 units, not the correct value of 400 (= 500 + 100 – 200). To guard against this problem, database systems must be able to prevent multiple-user access to the same file record. Rather, these systems must execute transactions serially (i.e., sequentially).

Backup and Security

As noted in an early portion of this chapter, the information in many accounting databases is both invaluable to the day-to-day operations of a company and, because it is unique, irreplaceable. It therefore must be protected. A key security feature of any database, therefore, is backup procedures that enable an organization to recreate its data if the original copies are lost or damaged.

> *Case-in-Point 7.4*   Several companies found out just how complete their disaster recovery and backup procedures were when terrorists attacked the World Trade Center on September 11, 2001. For many, the damage included (1) a loss of data, (2) the personnel most knowledgeable about that data, and (3) the building in which the data were stored. Dean Witter and Company is a large brokerage house that had prepared for such a contingency and was therefore able to resume business within two days in makeshift quarters across the Hudson River from the WTC towers in New Jersey. For 25 other companies such as Visa that conduct most of their businesses electronically and had subscribed to an elite, EDS "hot-site service," the delay was much shorter. In the case of Visa, it was three minutes!

In addition to backup security, an organization must also protect databases that contain sensitive information from unauthorized access. Another security feature, therefore, is a system's ability to assign, maintain, and require employees to use passwords and guard against unwarranted intrusions. Similarly, database systems can use encryption techniques to scramble data into unintelligible formats, thereby protecting file data even if an unauthorized user manages to obtain database access.

A final database security feature is to use **view controls** that limit each user's access to information on a need-to-know basis. In an inventory application, for example, a defense contractor might limit employee access to its supplier files, inasmuch as information about supplier identities and perhaps part prices might be sensitive information.

AIS AT WORK
Retailers Now Save Questions as Well as Answers to Improve Customer Service

---

Retailers throughout the world know that fast responses to customer questions helps them provide better customer service—a hallmark of profitable retailing. For some time, therefore, large organizations such as department stores and airlines have maintained large banks of computer-enabled agents and more recently, sophisticated web sites, to answer customer questions quickly, and, one hopes, sell these same customers goods and services on the spot.

These retailers are now also learning that saving the *questions* such customers ask—for example, using the search engines these organizations provide on their web sites—can also help sell merchandise. Thus, several companies such as Ask Jeeves, Vality Technology, and SAS are developing "natural language software tools" that can detect patterns in customer inquiries and alert such users as Dell, E-Trade, Nike, and Williams Sonoma to customer search patterns or difficulties using web sites. "If lots of people are asking questions on something and they're not finding information, the search engine will tell us" says Joan Broughton, director of Web publishing at Office Depot.

One retailer that is benefiting from such analyses is Amazon.com. By examining what products a web-site user requests, the e-commerce retailer's web site can match that user to a specific "customer profile" and therefore suggest similar products that "others like you have bought." Similarly, Nordstroms (a department store chain) now uses web-site monitoring software from DigiMine to analyze customer "clickstream data" and detect patterns. The company was surprised to learn that one of the top-ten search phrases entered by customers was "Kate Spade," a shoe and handbag maker. The company responded to this discovery by redirecting these customers to offline, phone personnel to provide more personal service and sell these products.

Etown.com sells electronic products on the web. The company's Ask Ida software asks consumers questions to determine desired features and price-feature tradeoffs. In one analysis, the company learned that that buyers of upgraded, feature-rich HD-TVs preferred smaller TV screens to save money. Finally, when Office Depot web designers examined web customer inquiries, they found that many asked about "next-day delivery"—information that was already on their web site, but not easily found. The discovery helped this company redesign its web site.

"You get in one question an entire snapshot of what's going on in that person's mind" says Michael Callahan, director of advance development at Ask Jeeves. And the better a retailer understands its customers, the better it can make a sale.

From: L. Scott Tillett, "A 24-Hour Focus Group—Sites Dig Into Search Queries to Learn Customer Preferences" *Internetweek* (April 10, 2000).

SUMMARY

Almost every AIS uses databases to store accounting data. The hierarchy of data in such databases is "bit, character, data field, record, file, and database." Other important database concepts are the uses of primary, secondary, and foreign record keys, which enable database systems to identify database records uniquely as well as link records to one another.

Databases must be designed carefully. The REA model is a methodology that encourages designers to think of database components in terms of resources, events, and agents. Using E-R diagrams, the REA model graphically depicts the entities involved in a database application and the types of relationships between them. The ultimate goal is to determine what to store in sets of records, and how to organize these records efficiently. Three database structures are hierarchical, network, and relational, of which the relational model is most commonly used today.

Large, multiuser accounting databases pose yet additional design concerns for designers. These include the administration and supervision of database development and maintenance, the need for documentation, the importance of data integrity, processing accuracy and completeness, and database security and backup. Finally, concurrency controls safeguard data when multiple users wish to make conflicting changes to the same record.

KEY TERMS YOU SHOULD KNOW

agent (REA model)	entity-relationship (E-R) diagram
business events (REA model)	foreign key
cardinalities	hierarchical data structure
child record	network data structure
concurrency controls	parent record
data dictionary	primary record key
data field	REA model
data hierarchy	record
data integrity controls	record structure
data modeling	relational data structure
data redundancy	relationship table
database	resources (REA model)
database administrator	secondary record key
database transaction	sibling record
economic events (REA model)	transaction controls
entity (REA model)	view controls

DISCUSSION QUESTIONS

7-1. Why is the storage of accounting data important to an accounting information system? Describe some important concerns, and explain why each one is important.

7-2. What is the hierarchy of data in databases? Provide an example for a particular accounting application.

7-3. Describe some generic types of record keys in typical accounting databases. Are such keys simple or complicated?

7-4. Name some specific accounting files and a potential primary key for each one.

7-5. What is the REA model of database design? How does REA differ from more traditional accounting views of data collection and storage? Hint: would a traditional accounting database store data about personnel matters?

7-6. What are database cardinalities? Give some examples of such cardinalities for an accounting application other than sales.

7-7. What is an entity-relationship diagram? Describe some symbols used in ER modeling, and explain the function of each one.

7-8. Suppose that a data modeler creates a database that includes a Sales table and a Salesperson table. Would you be likely to need a relationship table to link these two entities? Why or why not?

7-9. Why is it important to store primary key values consistently within different tables of the same database?

7-10. Describe each of the following database concerns, and give an example of each: (1) data integrity, (2) transaction accuracy and completeness, (3) concurrency processing, and (4) security.

PROBLEMS

7-11. An internal auditor should have a sound understanding of basic data processing concepts such as data organization and storage in order to adequately evaluate systems and make use of retrieval software.

   a. Define the following terms as used in a data processing environment (all are nouns): (1) field, (2) record, (3) file.

   b. (1) Define a database. (2) List two advantages and two disadvantages of a database system.

(CIA adapted)

7-12. What attributes (database table columns) would you be likely to include in a Cash table? In a Cash Receipts table?

7-13. Describe the meaning of each of the entity-relationship diagrams shown in Figure 7-10.

7-14. Draw entity-relationship diagrams for each of the following:

   a. The attributes of a customer in an accounts receivable database include name, address, and charge card number.

   b. The attributes of a student in a student database include student number (primary key), name, and class rank.

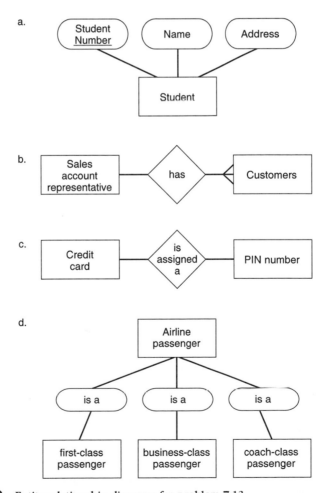

FIGURE 7–10   Entity-relationship diagrams for problem 7-13.

    c. The attributes of an asset in a general ledger database include inventory number (primary key), description, and date of purchase.

    d. The relationship between an employee and "is assigned parking" is one-to-many.

    e. The relationship between an employee and "completes training program" is many-to-many.

    f. The relationship between "employee" and "health plan" is many-to-one.

    g. A customer can be a cash customer or a credit customer. If the customer is a credit customer, an attribute is his or her credit card number.

    h. A patient is either an outpatient or an inpatient. If the patient is an inpatient, he or she is assigned a bed (one-to-one).

    i. An investment asset could be cash, a stock, a bond, or a certificate of deposit (CD).

    j. An account at a bank could be a checking account, a savings account, or a loan account. Each type of account requires an account or loan number. If it is a loan account, another attribute is the monthly payment amount.

INTERNET EXERCISES

7-15. Reread the AIS at Work Feature and then log onto a retail web site such as Amazon.com. What questions does the site ask you? Did you find evidence that the retailer collects information about you? (Hint: did you have to "register" or provide your e-mail address?)

7-16. Guido Geerts at the University of Delaware has created a tool for practicing your knowledge about cardinalities. You may access the site, Stevie, at www.aisvillage.com/stevie. Use basicpatterns/public as username/password if you would like to practice the 16 basic cardinality patterns. Use intro/public as username/password to practice your cardinality skills with some examples[1].

7-17. Access the Data Warehouse Information Center at www.dwinfocenter.org. Examine some of the issues posted on this web site. What is the definition of a data warehouse posted there? How is data warehousing related to the issue of decision support? What are some arguments *against* data warehousing?

CASE ANALYSES

7-18. Carl Beers Enterprises (Using a Relational Database)

Carl Beers Enterprises manufactures and sells specialized electronic components to customers across the country. The accompanying tables illustrate some of the records in its accounting databases. Thus, for example, the "Sales by Inventory Number" records show detailed sales data for each of the company's inventory items, and the "Customer Payments" records indicate customer cash payments, listed by invoice number. Use the information in these tables to answer the following questions.

---

[1] Instructors who are interested in creating their own problems and customized assignments can send an e-mail to Professor Geerts to obtain a User ID and Password to enter the system.

Sales by Inventory Number

Item Number	Invoice Number	Quantity	Price Each
I-1	V-1	1	2,000
	V-3	1	2,000
	V-6	3	1,575
I-2	V-5	2	3,000
	V-6	10	3,500
I-3	V-3	6	1,000
I-4	V-1	2	600
	V-5	2	300
I-5	V-3	2	4,000
	V-7	3	3,000
I-6	V-2	2	5,000
	V-4	2	5,000
	V-5	2	5,000
	V-7	2	7,000

Sales by Invoice Number

Invoice Number	Amount	Customer Number	Date	Salesperson Number
V-1	7,200	C-1	July 1	S-12
V-2	10,000	C-2	July 12	S-10
V-3	16,000	C-5	July 22	S-10
V-4	10,000	C-2	July 26	S-10
V-5	16,600	C-5	July 31	S-10
V-6	35,000	C-3	Aug 1	S-10
V-7	23,000	C-4	Aug 2	S-11

Sales by Salesperson

Salesperson Number	Quarterly Sales	Commission Rate
S-10	?	.10
S-11	?	.10
S-12	?	.12
S-78	0	.08

Customer Payments

Invoice Number	Remittance Advice Number	Amount
V-1	R-3	7,200
V-2	R-1	1,666
V-2	R-5	1,666
V-3	R-4	16,000
V-4	R-2	10,000
V-5	R-4	16,600

Customer Data

Customer Number	Customer Name	Accounts Receivable Amount	Salesperson
C-1	Dunn, Inc.	?	S-12
C-2	J. P. Carpenter	?	S-10
C-3	Mabadera Corp.	?	S-10
C-4	Ghymn and Sons	?	S-99
C-5	D. Lund, Inc.	?	S-10

Requirements

1. The "Sales by Inventory Number" records are listed by inventory item number. How is this useful? Why might this information also be useful if it were listed by invoice number instead of inventory number?

2. In the "Sales by Invoice Number," invoice V-3 shows a sales amount of $16,000. What was the name of the customer that made this purchase? What specific inventory items did this customer purchase? How much did this customer pay for each item?

3. Customers can choose among one of three payment options: (1) 5 percent discount if immediate cash payment, (2) 2 percent discount off list amount if total invoice paid by the fifteenth day of the month following purchase, or (3) deferred payment plan, using six monthly payments. Which option does J. P. Carpenter appear to be using for invoice V-2?

4. Using just the information provided, what are the quarterly sales amounts for salespeople S-10, S-11, and S-12?

5. Assume that customers C-1 through C-5 began this quarter with net accounts receivable balances of zero. What are their balances now?

7-19. Martin Shoes, Inc. (Planning a Database Using REA and E-R Methodology)

Martin Shoes, Inc. manufactures and distributes orthopedic footwear. To sell its products, the marketing department requires sales personnel to call on the shoe retailers within their assigned geographic territories. Each salesperson has a laptop computer, which he or she uses to record sales orders during the day and to send these sales orders to Martin's network nightly for updating the company's sales order file.

Each day, warehouse personnel review the current sales orders in its file, and where possible, pick the goods and ready them for shipment. (Martin ships goods via common carrier, and shipping terms are generally FOB from the shipping point.) When the shipping department completes a shipment, it also notifies the billing department, which then prepares an invoice for the customer. Payment terms vary by customer, but most are "net 30." When the billing department receives a payment, the billing clerk credits the customer's account and records the cash received.

Requirements

1. Identify the resources, events, and agents within Martin's revenue process.
2. Develop an E-R diagram for this process.
3. With a particular DBMS in mind, design the tables for this revenue process. Note that you will need tables for each resource, event, and agent, as well as tables for each many-to-many relationship.

7-20. Souder, Oles, and Franek LLP (Data Modeling with REA)

Souder, Oles, and Franek is an international consulting firm headquartered in Chicago, Illinois. The Entity-Relationship diagram in Figure 7-11 on the facing page shows a simplified version of the company's process for purchasing and paying for equipment and supplies.

Requirements

1. Insert appropriate pairs of cardinalities for the relationships in the Entity-Relationship model developed with the REA data modeling approach.
2. Describe the database table attributes for this model. You will need a table for each entity, as well as one or more relationship tables. Identify first the table name, then indicate the primary key by underlining it. Show any foreign keys by framing them in brackets (e.g., [Vendor#]). Include at least three fields in each table. Below is an example for the Vendor table and the Order Goods table:

   Vendor#, Name, Street Address 1, Street Address 2, City, State, Zip Code, Phone, E-mail, Fax, Contact, Comments.

   Order#, Date, [Vendor#], [Employee#], Shipping Instructions, Comments.

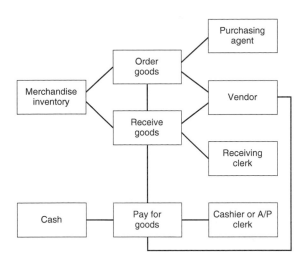

FIGURE 7–11   An E-R diagram for the purchasing system of Souder, Oles, and Franek LLP.

REFERENCES, RECOMMENDED READINGS, AND WEB SITES

References and Recommended Readings

Andros, David P., J. Owen Cherrington, and Eric L. Denna, "Reengineering Your Accounting the IBM Way," *Financial Executive* (July/August 1992), pp. 28–31.

Baxendale, Sidney J., "Activity-Based Costing for the Small Business: A Primer" *Business Horizons,* vol. 44, no. 1 (Jan/Feb 2001), pp. 61–68.

Codd, E. F., *The Relational Model for Database Management Version 2* (Reading, MA: Addison-Wesley, 1990).

Courtney, James F., Jr., and David B. Paradice, "Logical Database Design," Part II in *Database Systems for Management* (Homewood, IL: Irwin, 1992), pp. 73–174.

Fleischman, Gary M., C. Michele Matherly, and Karen B. Lanese, "Client/Server Financial Reporting: A Primer For Accounting Professionals" *The CPA Journal,* vol. 70, no. 3 (March 2000), pp. 67–69.

Flemming, C. C., and B. von Halle, "An Overview of Logical Data Modeling," *Data Resource Management* (Winter 1990), pp. 5–15.

Hayes, David C., and James E. Hunton, "Building a Database from Scratch," *Journal of Accountancy* (November 1999), pp. 63–73.

Hoffman, Thomas, "Walgreen Heals Prescription Net," *Computerworld,* vol. 32, no. 16 (April 20, 1998), pp. 43–46.

Hoffman, Thomas, "Tool Boosts Bank's Cross-Selling Abilities," *Computerworld,* vol. 32, no. 26 (June 29, 1998), pp. 71–72.

Hooper, Paul, and John Page, "Relational Databases: An Accountant's Primer," *Management Accounting* (October 1996), pp. 48–53.

Hunton, James E., and M.K. Raja, "When Is a Database Not a Database? (When It's a Spreadsheet)," *Journal of Accountancy* (June 1995), pp. 89–93.

McCarthy, William E., "An Entity-Relationship View of Accounting Models," *The Accounting Review* (October 1979), pp. 667–686.

McCarthy, William E., "The REAL Accounting Model: A Generalized Framework for Accounting Systems in a Shared Data Environment," *Accounting Review* (July 1982), pp. 554–578.

McFadden, Fred R., and Jeffrey A. Hoffer, "The Entity-Relationship Model," Chapter 4 of *Modern Database Management* (Redwood City, CA: Benjamin/Cummings, 1994), pp. 123–166.

Plattini, Mario, and Oscar Diaz (Eds.), *Advanced Database Technology and Design* (Artech House, 2000).

Sanders, G. Lawrence, *Data Modeling* (Danvers, MA: Boyd and Fraser, 1995).

Silberschatz, Avi, Michael Stonebraker, and Jeff Ullam, "Database Systems: Achievements and Opportunities," *Communications of the ACM,* vol. 34, no. 10 (October 1991), pp. 110–120.

Storey, Veda C, "Relational Database Design Based on the Entity-Relationship Model," *Data and Knowledge Engineering,* vol. 7 (1991), pp. 47–83.

The, Lee, "Distribute Data Without Choking the Net," *Datamation* (January 7, 1994), pp. 35–38.

Venkata, Ramana "The Importance of Hierarchy Building in Managing Unstructured Data" *KM World,* vol. 11, no. 3 (March 2002), pp. S4–S5.

Walker, Kenton B., and Eric L. Denna, "A New Accounting System is Emerging," *Management Accounting* (July 1997), pp. 22–30.

Web Sites

General information on data modeling can be found at the following web sites: www.microlib.cc.utexas.edu/cc/dbms/datamodel/, www.latnet.lv/LU/MII/Grade/newtcd.htm, and www.magicnet.net/~jbryson/DB.HTML#RA.

Most DBMS developers maintain their own web sites. Some examples are: www.oracle.com (Oracle), www.sybase.com (Sybase), www.microsoft.com (Microsoft), www.borland.com (Paradox and dBase).

There are many sources of information about data warehousing. One particularly rich one is the Data Warehousing Information Center at www.dwinfocenter.org. Another good source of information is the Data Warehousing and OLAP bibliography maintained by Professor Alberto Mendelzon at the University of Toronto at www.cs.toronto.edu/~mendel/dwbib.html.

Chapter 8

Organizing and Manipulating the Data in Databases

INTRODUCTION

NORMALIZATION

First Normal Form

Second Normal Form

Third Normal Form

DEFINING AND VALIDATING THE DATA IN DATABASES: DATA DEFINITION LANGUAGES (DDLS)

Database Management Systems

Using Data Definition Languages to Define Record Structures

Linking Tables

Data Validation

EXTRACTING DATA FROM DATABASES: DATA MANIPULATION LANGUAGES (DMLS)

Queries

Structured Query Language (SQL)

Online Analytical Processing (OLAP)

Hypertext

Sorting, Indexing, and Database Programming

Data Mining

OBJECT-ORIENTED DATABASES, MULTIMEDIA DATABASES, AND DATA WAREHOUSES

Object-Oriented and Multimedia Databases

Data Warehouses

AIS AT WORK: DATA WAREHOUSING AT DOW CHEMICAL COMPANY

KEY TERMS YOU SHOULD KNOW

DISCUSSION QUESTIONS

PROBLEMS

INTERNET EXERCISES

CASE ANALYSES

The Marcia Felix Corporation

Benson's Sports Supplies

Mason Manufacturing Company

Bonadio Electrical Supplies

REFERENCES, RECOMMENDED READINGS, AND WEB SITES

After reading this chapter, you will:

1. *Understand* the process of normalization.

2. *Be familiar with* techniques for defining record structures and tables, and validating data inputs.

3. *Understand* the importance of extracting data from databases, and AIS uses of such extractions.

4. *Understand* object-oriented and multimedia databases.

5. *Be familiar with* data warehouses and their uses in accounting applications.

Marketers are thirsting for knowledge about their customers. And in most cases they have it ... somewhere in their database. Companies harnessing the power of data warehousing and data mining will learn how to maximize their current customer bases and forge relationships with new customers in this dynamic market economy.

Kurtis M. Ruf, "Drowning in Data"
Target Marketing (July 1996), p. 26.

INTRODUCTION

In theory, system developers should design databases first, using the techniques described in Chapter 7, and then construct them later. In practice, organizations create many commercial databases from collections of preexisting manual files, computerized (but flat) files, personal or informal files, or the databases of acquired or merged companies. Thus, the key databases of a company are typically in a state of continuous evolution, reevaluation, and revision.

The previous chapter introduced the concept of databases and discussed data modeling—the process of designing a database. This chapter focuses on ways to structure and use databases in AISs. We begin with a discussion of normalization and then look at several methods of defining and using database tables in practice. Finally, we examine a few special types of databases: object-oriented databases, multimedia databases, and data warehouses.

NORMALIZATION

Chapter 7 made clear that, without advanced planning, accounting data are likely to wind up in flat files, that is, files with no sequence or order to them, except perhaps a chronological sequence. An example would be a file in which a professor enters the student grades of an examination in random order. Flat files make it almost impossible to find a particular record easily (because the records are not stored systematically), link files to one another to provide information from related records, or to store file data efficiently. The databases of most AISs require more discipline than this.

Normalization is the process of examining and arranging file data in a way that helps avoid problems when these files are used or modified later. One example of such a problem is the long waiting period that a university student may encounter when applying for financial aid. If student records are not integrated in a complete database, the scholarship director will have to request a copy of the student's transcript from one source, financial records from other sources, and perhaps library-fine information from other sources—a time-consuming process.

In commercial applications, an organization generally knows what data are involved in a specific application. The challenge is to organize the data intelligently. Thus, as an alternate to using some of the modeling techniques discussed in the last chapter, an organization might chose to use normalization techniques for this task.

Social Security Number	Last Name	First Name	Phone Number	License Plate		Ticket Number	Date	Code	Fine
				State	Number				
123-45-6789	Curry	Dorothy	(916)358-4448	CA	123 MCD	10151	10/15/03	A	$10
						10152	10/16/03	B	$20
						10121	11/12/03	B	$20
134-56-7783	Fong	May	(916)563-7865	CA	253 DAL	10231	10/23/03	C	$50
						12051	12/5/03	A	$10

FIGURE 8–1 A set of unnormalized parking ticket data.

There are several levels of normalization, but we shall only examine the first three of them: first normal form, second normal form, and third normal form.

First Normal Form

A database is in **first normal form (1NF)** if all the record's attributes (data fields) are well defined, and the information can thus be stored as a flat file. Interestingly enough, not every set of data automatically satisfies this requirement. For example, Figure 8-1 shows a set of university parking ticket data with repeating groups in its rightmost four columns. (An operative parking-ticket database will contain many more data fields than this one, but we will keep things simple here to focus on normalization tasks.) Databases cannot store more than one value in the same data field (i.e., column) of the same record, so we must do something to overcome this limitation.

One soluation to this problem is to use a separate record to store the information for each parking ticket a student has received. Figure 8-2 illustrates the results. For this file, the ticket number serves as the primary key. There are no repeating groups for any one column, so these records can now be stored in a conventional file.

Although we now have a well-defined file of student data, several problems remain. One difficulty is the large amount of *data redundancy* that results (i.e., the fact that much of the information in this file is repetitive). Another problem is that we have created an *insertion anomaly*—the fact that this database only recognizes students with parking tickets. Students with registered cars but without parking tickets will not be included in this file—a difficulty if school administrators want to use this file for car-registration purposes. A third problem is a *deletion*

Social Security Number	Last Name	First Name	Phone Number	License Plate		Ticket Number	Date	Code	Fine
				State	Number				
123-45-6789	Curry	Dorothy	(916)358-4448	CA	123 MCD	10151	10/15/03	A	$10
123-45-6789	Curry	Dorothy	(916)358-4448	CA	123 MCD	10152	10/16/03	B	$20
123-45-6789	Curry	Dorothy	(916)358-4448	CA	123 MCD	10121	11/12/03	B	$20
134-56-7783	Fong	May	(916)563-7865	CA	253 DAL	10231	10/23/03	C	$50
134-56-7783	Fong	May	(916)563-7865	CA	253 DAL	12051	12/5/03	A	$10

FIGURE 8–2 The data of Figure 8-1 in first normal form.

anomaly—the fact that those students who pay their ticket fines will no longer have a car registration record on file.

Second Normal Form

To solve these problems, let us redesign our database into **second normal form (2NF).** A database is in second normal form if it is in first normal form and all the data items in each record depend on the record's primary record key. To satisfy this requirement for our student-grade example, let us split our student database into two files—a "Car Registration File" and a "Ticket File"—as shown in Figure 8-3. This approach not only results in a more efficient design but also eliminates much of the first file's data redundancy.

In our new Car Registration File (or table), what should serve as the primary key? At first glance, you might guess "social security number." If students are only able to register one car, then this choice might be ok. If students can register more than one car, then it makes more sense to use the license plate number as the primary key. Remember: the primary key must uniquely identify a record, and this would not be possible if one person (with the same Social Security number) had two records in this table. Finally, we note that in an actual application, it is more likely that the license's "State" and "Number" data fields together would serve as the primary record key, but we shall keep things simple here.

What about the keys for our new Ticket file? In this table, the "ticket number" serves as the primary key, while the student's license plate number serves as the foreign key. Again, recall from Chapter 7 that a foreign key enables a database to link appropriate records together—for example, to trace a particular parking ticket to the

Car Registration File

Social Security Number	Last Name	First Name	Phone Number	(primary key) License Plate	
				State	Number
123-45-6789	Curry	Dorothy	(916)358-4448	CA	123 MCD
134-56-7783	Fong	May	(916)563-7865	CA	253 DAL
.	.	.	.	.	.
.	.	.	.	.	.

Ticket File

(primary key) Ticket Number	(foreign key) License Plate		Date	Code	Fine
	State	Number			
10151	CA	123 MCD	10/15/03	A	$10
10152	CA	123 MCD	10/16/03	B	$20
10231	CA	253 DAL	10/23/03	C	$50
10121	CA	123 MCD	11/12/03	B	$20
12051	CA	253 DAL	12/5/03	A	$10
.	.	.	.	.	.
.	.	.	.	.	.

FIGURE 8-3   The data of Figure 8-2 in second normal form.

car's registered owner. It also enables database users to answer such questions as "Does a particular student have any outstanding parking tickets?"

Third Normal Form

Although we are making headway in our database design, our goal is to create a database that is minimally in **third normal form (3NF).** A database is in third normal form if it is in second normal form and contains no transitive dependencies (i.e., no relationships in which data field A determines data field B). The Ticket file of Figure 8-3 suffers from this problem because the ticket code data field (e.g., a code of "A") determines the amount of the fine (e.g., "$10"). In other words, we have the following transitive relationship:

$$\text{Ticket Code} \rightarrow \text{Fine}$$

One way to solve this problem is to store the data for parking fines in a new "Parking Violations Code File," as shown in Figure 8-4. This enables us to eliminate the redundant information (the Fine data field) in the Ticket file of Figure 8-3 and streamline our data. Figure 8-4 illustrates the results. The ticket codes (A, B, and so forth) in the Ticket file serve as a foreign key that links the information in the Ticket file to an entry in the Parking Violations Code file. We now have a database in third normal form.

Chapter 7 noted that databases tend to become complicated, with multiple files that are linked together with foreign keys. The database in Figure 8-4, for example, is more complex than our original flat file in Figure 8-1, but it is also more efficient. For example, this database design will allow its users to store the car registration information of all students, even if they do not have any parking tickets. It also allows users to alter a student's name, phone number, or license plate by altering only one record in the Car Registration file—not several of them, as would be required using the flat file of Figure 8-1. Finally, this database design has allowed us to eliminate a lot of redundant information and therefore has made our file storage more efficient.

DEFINING AND VALIDATING THE DATA IN DATABASES: DATA DEFINITION LANGUAGES (DDLs)

After data have been normalized, it remains to actually create database tables and records. Typically, this is done with a database management system.

Database Management Systems

A **database management system (DBMS)** is a separate software system that enables users to create database records, delete records, access specific information, query (select subsets of) records for viewing or analysis, alter database information, and reorganize records as needed. This section of the chapter explains how to perform some of these tasks in greater detail.

A DBMS is not a database. Rather, a DBMS is a set of separate computer programs that enable users to create, modify, and utilize database information efficiently, thus

Car Registration File

Social Security Number	Last Name	First Name	Phone Number	License Plate (primary key)	
				State	Number
123-45-6789	Curry	Dorothy	(916)358-4448	CA	123 MCD
134-56-7783	Fong	May	(916)563-7865	CA	253 DAL
.	.	.	.	.	.
.	.	.	.	.	.

Ticket File

(primary key) Ticket Number	License Plate (foreign key)		Date	(foreign key) Code
	State	Number		
10151	CA	123 MCD	10/15/03	A
10152	CA	123 MCD	10/16/03	B
10231	CA	253 DAL	10/23/03	C
10121	CA	123 MCD	11/12/03	B
12051	CA	253 DAL	12/5/03	A
.	.	.	.	.
.	.	.	.	.

Parking Violations Code File

(primary key) Code	Fine	Explanation
A	$10	meter expired
B	$20	parking in no-parking zone
C	$50	no parking sticker
.	.	.
.	.	.

FIGURE 8-4 The data of Figure 8-3 in third normal form.

allowing businesses to separate their database system operations from their accounting system applications. This enables organizations to change record structures, query and report formats, video displays, and similar items without also having to reprogram the accounting software that accesses these database items. It also enables businesses to upgrade either system independently of the other one.

Examples of microcomputer DBMS packages include Access, dBASE, Paradox, FoxPro, Q and A, and rBASE. Examples of DBMSs that run on client/server systems include ADABAS, Oracle, Sybase, Ingrus, SQL Server, and Supra. Some microcomputer DBMSs are single-user systems, whereas others (especially those for larger applications) are designed for multiuser operation or network usage. The table in Figure 8-5 shows the operating characteristics of selected multiuser databases. Note that some of these systems are limited in how many concurrent users they support, the maximum number of transactions per day they can process, and so forth. Although it is not clear from the table, not every accounting package can access every database, so businesses are wise to make sure that any new accounting software they acquire can also read their existing databases, and vice versa.

Database Product	Maximum Company Sales (millions)	Maximum Transactions (per day/per year)	Maximum Concurrent Users
Peachtree Complete	$5	100/25,000	6
Microsoft Access	10	200/50,000	10
FoxPro	15	500/125,000	15
Microsoft Back Office Small Business Server (SQL Server)	15	2,000/500,000	50
Btrieve	25	5,000/1,250,000	25
Pervasive.SQL	100	20,000/5,000,000	250
IBM DB2	no limit	no limit	no limit
Microsoft SQL Server Enterprise 7.0	no limit	no limit	no limit
Oracle 8	no limit	no limit	no limit
Sybase SQL Server	no limit	no limit	no limit

FIGURE 8–5   The operating characteristics of selected multiuser database software. Source: J. Carlton Collins "How to Select the Right Accounting Software," *Journal of Accountancy*, vol. 188, no. 3 (September 1999), p. 4.

Using Data Definition Languages to Define Record Structures

The data definition language (DDL) of a DBMS enables its users to define the record structure of any particular database table (i.e., the individual fields that each record will contain). For example, to create the record structure for the car registration file shown in the top portion of Figure 8-4, you might define the following data fields and characteristics:

Data Field	Date Type	Size	Required?
Social Security number	text	9	yes
Last name	text	50	yes
First name	text	30	yes
Home phone number	text	14	no
License plate state	text	2	yes
License plate number	text	10	yes

Figure 8-6 illustrates how you would define this record structure using Microsoft Access. The user interfaces that enable you to define record structures in other DBMSs will, of course, differ. The top portion of the user interface in Figure 8-6 identifies the field names, data types, and optional descriptions for each data field in the record. When using this interface, you define your own field names— for example, "Phone Number." (Newer versions of Microsoft Access allow you to embed spaces in data field names.)

In most DBMSs, you must also specify the data type for each field you define for your record. Examples are text, number, memo, date/time, currency, and yes/no data types. Numbers that you do not plan to manipulate arithmetically such as Social Security numbers are usually defined as text data types, as illustrated in the example above. Numbers that you will manipulate such as pay rates are usually defined as "number" data types.

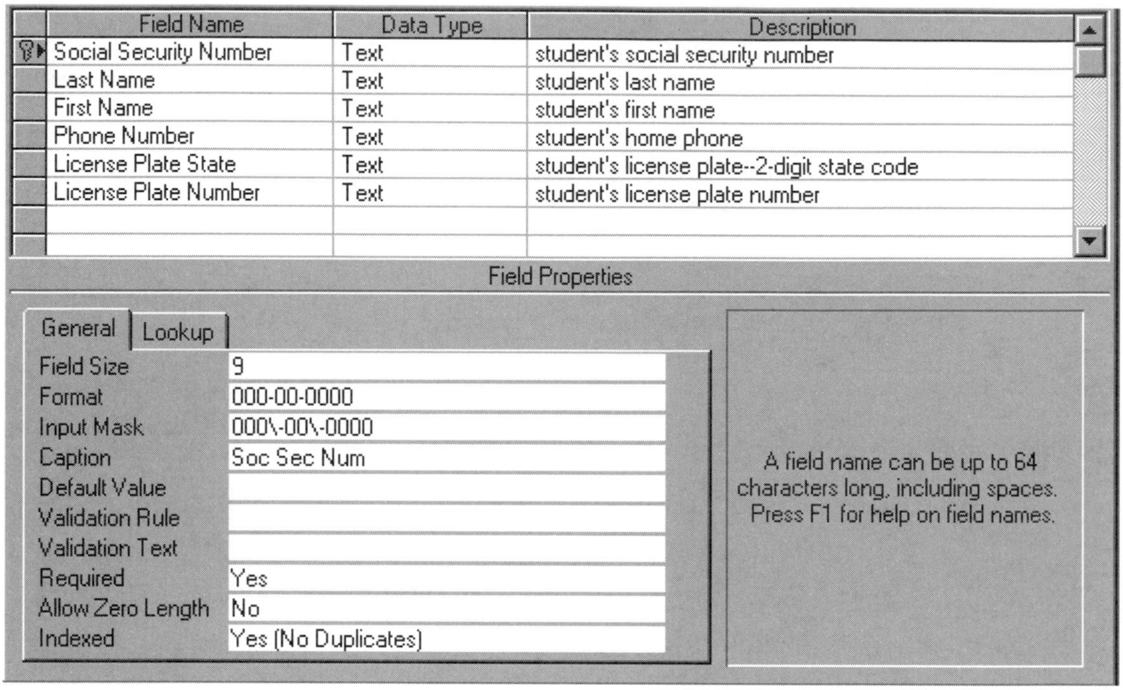

Field Name	Data Type	Description
Social Security Number	Text	student's social security number
Last Name	Text	student's last name
First Name	Text	student's first name
Phone Number	Text	student's home phone
License Plate State	Text	student's license plate--2-digit state code
License Plate Number	Text	student's license plate number

Field Properties

General | Lookup

Field Size	9
Format	000-00-0000
Input Mask	000\-00\-0000
Caption	Soc Sec Num
Default Value	
Validation Rule	
Validation Text	
Required	Yes
Allow Zero Length	No
Indexed	Yes (No Duplicates)

A field name can be up to 64 characters long, including spaces. Press F1 for help on field names.

FIGURE 8–6 Defining the structure of a table (file) in Microsoft Access. The "Field Properties" in the lower portion of the figure is for the Social Security number data field. You must define a separate set of properties for each data field in the table.

The bottom portion of Figure 8-6 shows the field properties for the Social Security number data field. The Format property enables you to format the output (i.e., so that the Social Security number appears in a desirable form such as "123-45-6789" instead of a long text string such as "123456789"). Similarly, the Caption property enables you to define a title for the column heading of subsequent forms and reports (instead of the default data field name)—a useful feature that enables you to substitute better titles for abbreviated field names such as "SSN" or long, cumbersome titles.

Finally, the "indexed property" in Figure 8-6 tells the DBMS how you want to organize records—for example, by Social Security number. Indexing is almost always performed for the primary key of a database table. (Microsoft Access uses the key symbol in the first column of the Social Security number row at the top of Figure 8-6 to indicate a primary key.)

Once you have created the record structure of a database table, you can begin to create records. Figure 8-7 shows some example records, again using Microsoft Access. This template is similar to a fill-in-the-blanks manual form but is better because you can erase a mistake simply by backspacing. Like other DBMSs, Microsoft Access will check for simple errors—for example, will reject the input of letters when you try to enter them for a numeric field.

Linking Tables

Let us return to the parking ticket example of Figure 8-4. Imagine that you have created the record structures for all three tables in this figure and created some records

CarRegistrationFile : Table

Soc Sec Num	Last Name	First Name	Phone Number	License	License Plate Number
102-67-9877	Hazen	Jerry	(916) 626-9821	NV	766 DUN
123-45-6789	Curry	Dorothy	(916)358-4448	CA	123 MCD
124-34-7854	Clevenger	Dottie	(510) 933-0742	CA	FUNSKI
134-56-7783	Fong	May	(916) 563-7865	CA	253 DAL
154-45-7869	Cook	Rebecca	(510) 785-5858	NV	546 ABC
___-__-____					

Record: 6 of 6

FIGURE 8–7 Some representative records for the car registration file of Figure 8-4 using the record structure of Figure 8-6. Note the input mask for the Social Security number that was created for this field and that helps ensure input accuracy.

for each of them. You now wish to create the weekly parking ticket report illustrated in Figure 8-8. The format for this report is fairly straightforward, but the data it contains are now scattered among three separate tables. For example, the "ticket number" comes from the Parking Ticket table, the "last name" field comes from the Car Registration table, and the "fine amount" comes from the Parking Violations Code table. The problem is how to tell a DBMS to link the information in the various tables and select the appropriate information from each for this weekly report.

To solve this problem, recall from Chapter 7 that the way to link information in relational databases is by using foreign keys. In Microsoft Access, you would use the Relationships Window illustrated in Figure 8-9 to perform this task. If no prior relationships exist, this window will first appear blank. To display the table list boxes shown in Figure 8-9, you must use the Add Table dialog box (not shown) to add the three list boxes that appear in this figure. However, adding these tables will only show the list boxes—not the connecting lines that also appear in the figure.

Weekly Parking Ticket Report

Uptown University, Anytown, USA
Week of: 10/12/03

Ticket	*State*	*License Plate*	*Date*	*Parking Code*	*Last Name*	*First Name*	*Fine Amount*	*Explanation*
10151	CA	123 MCD	10/15/03	A	Curry	Dorothy	$10.00	meter expired
10152	CA	123 MCD	10/16/03	B	Curry	Dorothy	$20.00	parking in no parking zone
10153	CA	253 DAL	10/16/03	A	Fong	May	$10.00	meter expired
10154	CA	123 MCD	10/17/03	A	Curry	Dorothy	$10.00	meter expired
10155	NV	253 DAL	10/18/03	C	Fong	May	$50.00	no parking sticker

FIGURE 8–8 A weekly parking ticket report generated from the data in Figure 8-4.

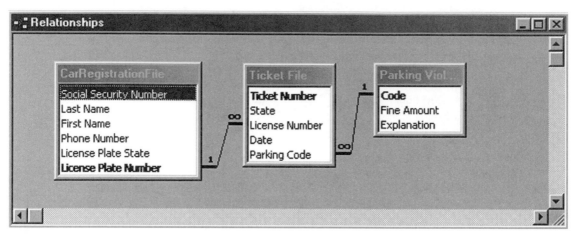

FIGURE 8–9 Access' Relationships Window for the three tables in Figure 8-4.

To link tables, you must use your mouse to drag field names from one box to the other. Thus, you would drag the field name "License Number" from the Ticket File to the License Plate Number field name in the Car Registration table. Similarly, you would drag the Code field in the Parking Violations table to the Parking Code data field in the Ticket File. The results are as shown in Figure 8-9. Access will draw the connecting lines displayed in the figure. The symbols "1" and "∞" mean that there is a "one to many" relationship between the records in the two tables.

Finally, note that the field names in the different list boxes are not identical. In Access, this is not necessary. As long as the information stored *in* these fields match, the field names are not important for linking purposes.

Data Validation

Mistakes in the important data fields of AIS databases are costly to a company in terms of the time and trouble required to correct them as well as the potential inconvenience and confusion caused by such errors *until* they are corrected. Simple examples include typing "4)" instead of "40" for hours worked, "NU" instead of "NY" for the state code in a mailing address, or "UPC" instead of "UPS" for the shipper code. Although it is impossible to guard against every possible type of error, database designers can use some of the tools that come with a typical DBMS to catch some of them.

Using Microsoft Access, one input control is inherent in the data type that you assign to a particular data field. For example, if you create a data field as a "number" data type, Access will reject all character inputs that are not numbers. Similarly, if you declare a data field as a "date" data type, Access will reject all input values (including alphabetic letters or punctuation marks) that cannot be part of a date. This is why it is often better to use data types *other than* "text" for data fields that can be declared with them.

A second input control is to use **input masks** that encourage users to enter proper data. The input mask property of a data field enables the user to create an input format such as "123-45-6789" for a Social Security number, "(123) 458-7890" for a telephone number, or "12/13/03" for a date. Although the system designer uses only special symbols for the mask, the DBMS is able to interpret these symbols as input requirements and act accordingly. At data-entry time, the user will see just the formatted part of the mask—for example, "___-___-___" (see the "Input Mask" row in Figure 8-6). Input masks help users input data correctly in databases by indicating a general input format, thereby reducing data-entry errors. Such masks also enable the system to reject incompatible data—for example, a letter character mistakenly input in a numeric field.

A third input control is to specify a **default value** for the data fields of new records. Examples include the number "40" for an hours-worked data field, a department code field of "123" when creating records for all the employees in the same department, or a default date of "12/10/03" when entering the date for all the sales transactions on a given day. Again, such default values help guard against input errors as well as speed data entry.

Finally, in many DBMSs, perhaps the most versatile data entry control is the ability to create your own validation tests using a **validation rule.** Using Microsoft Access, you create such rules as a record structure property of a data field. Figure 8-10 illustrates an example for the "Fine Amount" data field of the Parking Violations Code File (refer back to Figure 8-4). This (numeric) data field shows the amount of money that a person must pay for a particular parking violation. In Figure 8-10, the expression "Between 1 And 100" that appears in the properties window on the left side specifies the acceptable range of values. The error message on the right displays the "Validation Text" that you specify in this field's properties window. This is what will appear in the message box on the right when the user attempts to enter a value (such as "200") that falls outside the allowable range.

Validation rules can be simple, such as the one illustrated in Figure 8-10, or much more complex. For example, Access also enables you to use mathematical computations, predefined functions, and logical operators to create more complex validation rules. An example is *Between 1 And 100 AND Not 77*, which means that the entry value must fall in the specified range and not be "77". Another example is *<[fldStartDate] – [fldEndDate]*, which means that the entry value must be less than the difference between an employee's hire date and termination date.

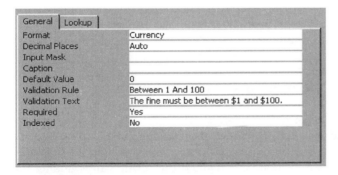
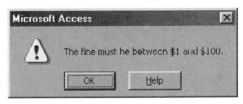

FIGURE 8–10   Left: the properties window for the Fine Amount data field of the Parking Violations Code table. Right: the error message that a user would see if he or she attempts to enter a value for this field that falls outside the specified range.

EXTRACTING DATA FROM DATABASES: DATA MANIPULATION LANGUAGES (DMLS)

The totality of the information in a database and the relationships of its tables (records) is called the database **schema.** Thus, the schema is a map or plan of the entire database. Using the previous student-parking example, the schema would be all the information that a university might store about car registrations and parking tickets.

Any particular user or application program will normally be interested in (or might be limited to) only a subset of the information in the database. We describe this limited access as a **subschema,** which is often called a "view" in database parlance. For example, one subschema for our parking database might be the information required by the registrar—for example, the student's name, Social Security number, and outstanding parking tickets. (Many universities do not allow students to graduate with outstanding parking tickets.) Subschemas are important design elements of a database because they dictate what data each user needs, and also because they protect sensitive data from unauthorized access. This is one reason why a university might design several subschemas for its parking database that purposely exclude student Social Security numbers.

The terms *schema* and *subschema* describe a simple idea—the distinction between the design of a database on one hand and the uses of a database on the other. The goal is to design a database schema that is flexible enough to satisfy the subschema uses required of it. This design can make the difference between an AIS that barely works and an AIS that provides a very real competitive edge to a profit-seeking business. Here are some ways of creating subschemas.

Queries

Queries allow database users to create subschemas of interest to them. For example, using the student car registration database, you might want to (1) look up something about a specific student (e.g., his or her license plate number), (2) change the information in a specific record (e.g., update a student's phone number), (3) delete a record (e.g., because the person sells his or her car), or (4) list file information selectively (e.g., prepare a list of all students with California license plates). The purpose of a **data manipulation language** (DML) is to help you perform such tasks.

Figure 8-11 illustrates a simple query example: how to display selected information from only one table using Microsoft Access. This example asks the system to display the last name, first name, phone number, license plate state, and license plate number for all cars registered in California. Note that the search criterion specified in the last line of Figure 8-11 is "CA." Figure 8-12 shows what the system displays in response (refer back to Figure 8-7 to see the entire set of records). Most DBMSs enable you to store the criteria for data queries in separate files, thus both eliminating the need to rewrite them every time one is needed and sparing novices the work of creating such queries in the first place.

Let us now return to the task of creating the report shown in Figure 8-8. We have already noted that this is a more complex task because the data come from three separate tables. But because we have already defined the relationships linking the three tables in Figure 8-9, this job is relatively straightforward. All we must do is select the data fields we need, and the Access query illustrated in Figure 8-13 will accomplish this task for us.

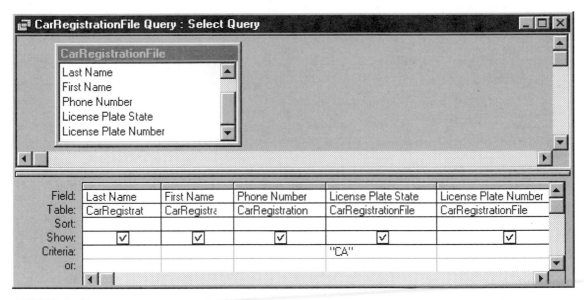

FIGURE 8–11   This Access data query enables a user to list all car registrations with state code "CA."

The tasks performed by the query shown in Figure 8-13 are nontrivial. To appreciate this, imagine that you had to create the report shown in Figure 8-8 manually, using the information shown in Figure 8-4. If there were hundreds of parking tickets in a given week and thousands of car registration records, the "lookup work" required for this job would be enormous. But a computerized DBMS using a DML such as Access can do this quickly and automatically in just a few seconds—an amazing feat if you think about it!

Structured Query Language (SQL)

In addition to using a DML in a DBMS, you can also access selected information from a database using a *data query language*. The American National Standards Institute (ANSI) has adopted standards for one such query language: **structured query language (SQL).** This language is important because many relational databases such as

	Last Name	First Name	Phone Number	Lic Plate State	Lic. Plate No.
▶	Curry	Dorothy	(916)358-4448	CA	123 MCD
	Fong	May	(916) 563-7865	CA	253 DAL
	Clevenger	Dottie	(510) 933-0742	CA	FUNSKI
✱					

Record: ◄◄ ◄ [1] ► ►I ►✱ of 3

FIGURE 8–12   The results of the query shown in Figure 8-11.

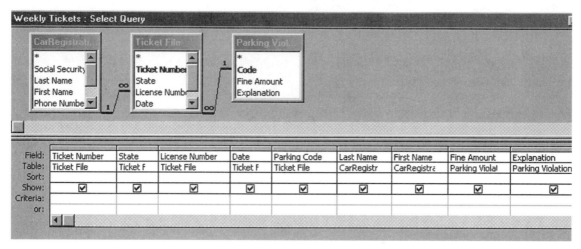

FIGURE 8–13 An Access query linking the information in three tables: Ticket File, Car Registration File, and Parking Violations File.

Access or *dBASE* support it. Figure 8-14 shows how you might construct the request for records with California license plates using SQL.

Knowledge of SQL is a useful tool for auditors. In *Microsoft Access,* the user points to a database table to include in a query. Using SQL, the user specifies a table and fields, using commands such as FROM, SELECT, and WHERE. FROM identifies the table source, and SELECT chooses the data fields to include in the query. The WHERE command can specify criteria, such as State = CA. An auditor could select files for review using these commands. For example, the WHERE command could refer to Sales Orders in excess of a specified dollar amount.

Online Analytical Processing (OLAP)

While SQL enables users to extract data from one or more database tables, **online analytical processing (OLAP)** allows users to extract complex information that not only describes "what" has happened, but also "why" it happened. Several software developers now market OLAP packages. Examples include *Integration Server* (Arbor Software), *Holos* (Seagate Technology), *PowerDimensions* (SyBase), *Plato* (Microsoft), and *WhiteLight* (WhiteLight Systems). These tools allow end users to perform their own database analyses, including data mining (discussed shortly).

```
SELECT (LastName, FirstName, PhoneNumber, LicPlateState, LicPlateNo)
FROM CarRegistrationFile
WHERE LicPlateState = CA;
```

FIGURE 8–14 An example of SQL instructions for the example of Figure 8-13. These instructions will list the last name, first name, phone number, license plate state, and license plate number of all cars with license plate state code "CA."

An important feature of OLAP is its ability to conduct multidimensional analysis. One dimension may be "time." Other dimensions might be "customer," "product," or "geography." For example, OLAP can help you examine sales over time, for a particular product, in a specific geographical region. Another feature of OLAP is its "drill-down" capability. This capability allows you to examine data at increasing levels of detail. As an example, you can take sales for one quarter shown by geographical region and drill down to see sales for each state, and then for each major city, within that region. Similarly, you can drill down sales from a product line to a specific product, and then to a specific product size or color. This type of analysis can provide the "why" behind what has happened.

An advantage of OLAP over queries and SQL for drill-down purposes is that it can drill through several layers instantly. SQL and DBMS query tools typically require you to construct a separate query for each drill layer. This means, for example, that to find sales by city for a region, you would first have to obtain results for sales by state, and then query again for city sales. With OLAP, you can click on the items you want to expand to see the layers beneath them. Figure 8-15 shows what you might see when drilling down through a data set selectively with OLAP.

OLAP has a variety of other helpful features. One is the ability to create **pivot tables,** which are two-dimensional statistical summaries of database information (and similar to the pivot tables of *Microsoft Excel*). The example in Figure 8-15 is a two-dimensional analysis of sales by product (on the vertical axis) and region (along the horizontal axis). Pivot tables enable users to choose what type of summary information to display (e.g., total sales, average sales, or maximum sales), as well as to change an overall selection category (e.g., change the period in which to view sales data).

Sales Report – Best Multimedia
2nd Quarter 2003

	Northeast	Northwest	Southeast	Southwest	Midwest	TOTAL
Total Sales						
CD's	**$50,000**	**$45,000**	**$37,000**	**$34,100**	**$34,000**	**$200,100**
Pop Rock	$30,500	$20,000	$22,000	$17,000	$19,000	$108,500
Jazz	$4,200	$7,500	$5,000	$4,100	$2,200	$23,000
Show Tunes	$8,200	$10,000	$4,800	$6,000	$4,700	$33,700
Rap	$7,100	$7,500	$5,200	$7,000	$8,100	$34,900
DVD's	**$80,800**	**$92,000**	**$78,000**	**$56,000**	**$60,200**	**$367,000**
Action	$12,000	$13,000	$11,000	$9,700	$9,000	$54,700
Classics	$14,000	$18,000	$25,000	$11,000	$7,000	$75,000
Comedy	$16,000	$17,000	$16,200	$13,400	$17,600	$80,200
Drama	$15,900	$17,100	$16,100	$13,400	$17,600	$80,100
Horror	$14,900	$17,900	$1,700	$1,500	$1,000	$37,000
Mystery	**$8,000**	**$9,000**	**$8,000**	**$7,000**	**$8,000**	**$40,000**
Suspense	$2,000	$3,800	$1,800	$3,000	$2,000	$12,600
Thrillers	$4,000	$4,000	$5,000	$3,000	$5,000	$21,000
True Crime	$2,000	$1,200	$1,200	$1,000	$1,000	$6,400
Software	**$22,000**	**$20,800**	**$19,700**	**$20,000**	**$25,000**	**$107,500**
TOTAL	**$152,800**	**$157,800**	**$134,700**	**$110,100**	**$119,200**	**$674,600**

FIGURE 8−15   A pivot table showing a drill-down of sales totals by product type and region.

Hypertext

Yet another way of finding information in a database is with **hypertext.** DBMSs that use hypertext highlight key words or display text in different-colored characters. Clicking on a keyword with your mouse directs the DBMS to move directly to that entry. One hypertext example is Apple's Hypercard for Macintosh microcomputers. Another example is Hypertext Markup Language (HTML), the hypertext language used by World Wide Web pages on the Internet. Hypertext systems are especially useful for researching technical materials in which you find it convenient to jump from subject to subject.

Sorting, Indexing, and Database Programming

In addition to accessing or listing records selectively, a DBMS also enables you to reorganize an entire table. One way to do this is by sorting records, which means physically rewriting records on a disk in the desired order. This is both time consuming and usually unneccessary. It is faster and easier to index your records (refer back to the last row of Figure 8-6), which merely creates a table of record keys and disk addresses that accomplishes the same purpose as sorting. Thus, when users specify "sort" in queries such as the one in Figure 8-11 (the third row in the lower portion of the figure), Access does not physically reorder records but instead merely temporarily reorders them for display purposes.

Even the best DBMS software cannot anticipate every user's processing needs. As a result, the software sometimes lacks the commands needed to perform specific tasks. For this reason, advanced DBMSs include screen-design and programming tools that enable users to develop their own processing applications. One common requirement is for customized data-entry screens, which enable users to include better data descriptions and more detailed instructions on input screens. Similarly, programming languages (such as VBA for Microsoft Access) enable users to create custom processing routines—for example, to create their own form letters and memos. This end-user programming is important because it enables users to perform their own data processing without the technical assistance of IT professionals.

Data Mining

Data mining means using a set of data analysis and statistical tools, such as regression analysis, to detect relationships, patterns, or trends among stored data. For example, data mining might reveal a preference by customers in older age groups for products like teeth whiteners. Detecting such direct relationships helps marketers in cross-selling activities or in offering tie-in promotions. For example, such information can help retailers in designing product placement in their stores (e.g., placing snacks near the frozen pizza section). Similarly, knowledge about trends enables managers to target their products and services more effectively, and to increase customer satisfaction.

Case-in-Point 8.1 Managers at Eddie Bauer had a "data headache" from the massive amount of data they had collected about their customers. They built a data warehouse that consolidated the disparate data in the organization and used data mining to extract useful data about direct-mail and online sales. They now use statistical mining techniques to determine who should receive special mailings and catalogues. For example, when it runs its annual outerwear specials, the company now knows which customers to target with information.

Many of the benefits of data mining are related to sales and marketing. However, there are other benefits as well. Because data-mining tools can search through massive amounts of data to detect patterns, auditors can use data mining to detect fraud. For example, fraudulent credit card transactions may follow a pattern, such as an increase in the total amount of purchases immediately following a credit card theft or products with special characteristics (such as ones that can easily be sold). If the auditors detect a pattern in the data they have, they can design preventive controls that will flag transactions exhibiting these characteristics. In this way, auditors can use data mining tools to make predictions based on the relationships they observe among data.

OBJECT-ORIENTED DATABASES, MULTIMEDIA DATABASES, AND DATA WAREHOUSES

The databases that we have discussed so far are traditional ones that mostly handle text data (i.e., data that can be neatly organized and categorized according to the values stored in text data fields). Not all databases are this simple.

Object-Oriented and Multimedia Databases

An **object-oriented database (OODB)** is a database that contains both the text data of traditional databases and information about the set of actions that can be taken on these data fields. For example, a payroll file might contain not only traditional information about an employee, but also instructions that indicate how to compute an employee's net pay.

Case-in-Point 8.2 The managers at Polo Ralph Lauren Corporation in Lindhurst, New Jersey, know that success in the fashion industry means getting a new product through the analysis, planning, and distribution steps as quickly as possible. Until recently, managers requiring a report from more than one of the company's seven business units would see multiple printouts and nonintegrated data. Officials at the company note that such projects can easily take years to create and run into the millions of dollars. Company officials are willing to endure these costs because the benefits of integrated data can justify them. Using an object-oriented modeling tool called "Rational Rose" from Rational Software Corp., the company's developers were able to create an integrated data warehouse or "operational data store (ODS)" inexpensively in about six months.

Many OODBs are **multimedia databases** that include graphics, audio information, and animation. These databases also typically store information about how to display their graphics, how to play their audio clips, and so forth. Multimedia databases are used by real estate brokers to store pictures and perhaps narrated tours of listed properties, by training companies to educate employees interactively, by police departments to store "mug shots" and voice prints of prisoners, and by publishing

FIGURE 8-16 The employee records of this security database contain both text data and the picture of each employee.

houses to enhance the descriptions of everything from cookbooks to encyclopedias. Even your own employer might use such a database to store your picture in one of its employee files (Figure 8-16).

Specialized accounting applications of multimedia databases include those that store the audio portions of audit interviews, pictures of important assets, or images of critical financial contracts. These "unstructured objects" require a new definition of what we mean by "data" and how we organize them. But OODB records can still be manipulated. For example, a speech still has such characteristics as "speaker," "subject," and "length," and these characteristics can be used to search the database and retrieve the desired object, whatever that might be.

Data Warehouses

Where feasible, it often makes sense to pool the data from separate applications into a large, common body of information called a **data warehouse.** The data in a data warehouse are rarely current. Rather, they are typically "older information" that were initially collected for other reasons during the conduct of normal operations and daily activities of an organization. For example, a sales transaction creates data that help management make decisions about production, cash availability, and so on. The sales transaction data also impact financial statements. Managers are learning, though, that much of the data gathered about sales and other operational activities can also be useful strategically. For example, in recording a sale, an AIS collects data about the customer, the product, the timing of the sale, and so on. This information can be helpful in predicting future sales of specific products or by a certain category of customers. To obtain these benefits from the data collected, the data need to be amassed in a central location. This location is the data warehouse.

To be useful, the data in data warehouses should have the following characteristics: (1) the data are "clean" of errors, (2) they are defined uniformly, (3) they are stored in several databases, not just one, (4) they span a longer time horizon than the company's transaction systems, and (5) the data relations are optimized for answering complex questions—for example, queries requiring information from several diverse sources.

Case-in-Point 8.3 Amazon.com, the web-based bookseller, is constructing a large, Oracle data warehouse to store and analyze information about its online customers, inventory carrying costs, and customer sales activities, especially sales during holiday seasons. The company expects the initial size of the data warehouse to be three terabytes—a large database by any standard—but this may grow to one thousand times this size, or three petabytes in the future.

One advantage of a data warehouse is to make organizational information available on a corporate-wide basis. For example, with such an approach, the marketing representatives of a company might then gain access to the company's production data and thereby be better able to inform customers about the future availability of desired, but as yet unmanufactured, products. This idea is also central to the concept of an **enterprise-wide database** (i.e., a large repository of organizational data that comes from, and is available to, a wide range of employees). Another advantage is to facilitate data mining.

Case-in-Point 8.4 With more than 9 million customers, KeyBank is the thirteenth largest bank in the United States. To help it market financial products, the bank created a million-dollor DB2 data warehouse that allows its managers to determine what investments its customers prefer (e.g., CDs or mutual funds), and how best to sell products (e.g., direct mail or Internet). Bank officials credit the data warehouse, the decision tools that mine it, and the ability of different departments to share data, for increasing customer contacts by 200 percent and the project's 100 percent return on investment in 14 months.

Building a data warehouse is a difficult job. The developers must first decide what data to collect, how to standardize and **scrub** (clean) the data to ensure uniform accuracy and consistency, and how to deal with computer records that typically begin in non-normalized form. One reason for these difficulties is that the data in data warehouses may come from several sources—for example, an AIS in one case and a production application in another case. As a result, the same data element could have two different representations or values—for example, an eight-digit numeric product code in the AIS and a six-digit alphabetic character code in the production application. Similarly, one corporate division might capture sales daily while another collects the same data weekly. The developers must determine data standards in both cases, reconcile any discrepancies, and account for missing fields and misspellings. Another challenge is to build the data warehouse in such a way that users can access it easily and find answers to complex questions.

If data warehouses are so costly, difficult, and time consuming to develop, why do companies bother with them? The answer is that they generate many benefits in return, including increased employee access to valuable information, the ability to answer complex questions, and a potential return on investment that can exceed 400 percent.[1]

Case-in-Point 8.5 Provident Central Credit Union is one of the largest credit unions in the United States. Recently, it created a data warehouse to make use of the rich transaction and customer data it gathers. The company plans to use the data in the warehouse to conduct one-to-one marketing campaigns for custom products and to improve its pricing and responsive-

---

[1] David, Julie Smith, and Paul John Steinbart, "Drowning in Data," *Strategic Finance*, December 1999, pp. 30–34.

ness to its membership of almost 90,000 customers. The data warehouse holds the answers to many complex questions such as, "Who are the most profitable customers?" and "How can we improve our customer relationships through product and service offerings?"

Where corporate executives believe the rewards for building a data warehouse are not high, they can opt instead to build a **data mart.** Data marts are smaller than data warehouses in storage size and typically focus on just one application area—for example, marketing data. However, in most other ways, they are similar to data warehouses.

AIS AT WORK
Data Warehousing at Dow Chemical Company

At the beginning of 1996, the major source of financial information at Dow Chemical Company was an inflexible management AIS that used a DB2 database and ran on an IBM mainframe. Two problems were that the reports it produced were difficult for nonaccountants to understand and often took several days to generate. Another problem was that its primary use was for reporting historical data, rather than helping managers make better decisions about current problems.

Things changed in 1996 when Mike Costa, the global process controller at Dow, supervised the installation of the company's new data warehouse—an Oracle relational database running on two Alpha 8400 servers under a DEC Open VMS operating system. This warehouse now enables 2,500 users—from corporate executives to shopfloor supervisors—to access corporate data and create reports usable by managers in finance, marketing, and logistics as well as in accounting.

One advantage of the new system is the ability to provide a variety of users with different views of the same data. For example, the new system allows managers in accounting, marketing, and production to examine sales data in many layers, starting at the global level and ending with the local level of a shipping address. Similarly, using PowerPlan, an online analytical processing tool, managers can also perform their own data inquiries, reducing data access times from "two days" to "five minutes."

Perhaps the biggest advantage of the new system is improved accountability. For example, Costa notes that the warehouse provides the information needed to track the daily activities and operational decisions of shop-floor supervisors, or the geographic sales data that upper-level managers require to make tactical or strategic decisions. It is for this reason that the company will develop a new planning and budgeting system as its first system enhancement.

How much does such a system cost? The company isn't telling, but Costa says that the system will pay for itself in less than a year. The fact that the company is already planning extensions to its system also says a great deal about investing in a corporate-wide data warehouse.

SUMMARY

Accountants interact with databases in a variety of ways. They may be involved in database design, particularly with respect to defining data elements. They are certainly likely to need to extract data from a database or data warehouse at one time or another, using data manipulation languages such as queries, online analytical processing tools (OLAP), and/or data mining tools.

Databases must be designed carefully. The process of normalization enables designers to minimize data redundancy, insertion and deletion anomalies, and transitive dependencies. The goal is to develop a database that is at least in third normal form.

Database management systems (DBMSs) enable users to create their own databases using data definition languages (DDLs) and to manipulate file data using data manipulation languages (DMLs). Some DBMSs support structured query language (SQL), hypertext, or end-user programming languages.

Object-oriented databases (OODBs) enable users to store both data and instructions on how the data should be displayed or computed. Multimedia databases are OODBs that enable users to store graphics, pictures, sound clips, and animation clips in addition to text data. Data warehouses typically combine the information from separate databases into large sets of cross-functional data repositories that can help businesses increase data-retrieval efficiency, output productivity, and long-term profitability.

KEY TERMS YOU SHOULD KNOW

data definition language (DDL)	normalization
data manipulation language (DML)	object-oriented database (OODB)
data mart	online analytical processing (OLAP)
data mining	pivot table
data warehouse	query
database management system (DBMS)	schema
default value	scrubbing data
enterprise-wide database	second normal form (2NF)
first normal form (1NF)	structured query language (SQL)
hypertext	subschema
input mask	third normal form (3NF)
multimedia database	validation rule

DISCUSSION QUESTIONS

8-1. What is the process of normalization? What levels are there, and why do database developers seek to normalize data?

8-2. What are database management systems? Are they the same as databases? Why are DBMSs classified as software and not hardware?

8-3. What are data definition languages (DDLs)? How are they related to DBMSs?

8-4. What is a record structure? When defining a record's structure, what is meant by the term "data type?" Give some examples of data types.

8-5. Why do database developers link tables together? How is this done using Access?

8-6. What is data validation? Why is it important? Give some examples of how to validate data inputs using Access.

8-7. What is a database schema? What is a database subschema? Give some examples of database schemas and subschemas for the payroll file of Figure 7-1.

8-8. What are data manipulation languages? How are these languages related to database management systems? How are these languages related to databases?

8-9. What is SQL? How is SQL like an Access query? How is it different?

8-10. What is online analytical processing? How is OLAP related to databases? What is a pivot table, and how are pivot tables and OLAP related?

8-11. What is the difference between "sorting records" and "indexing records" in a database?

8-12. What is "data mining?" How is data mining useful to profit-seeking companies?

8-13. What are object-oriented databases? What are multimedia databases? How are these two types of databases alike? How are they different?

8-14. What are data warehouses? How are they like databases? How do they differ from databases?

8-15. Why would a company be interested in creating a data warehouse? Why would a company *not* be interested in creating a data warehouse?

PROBLEMS

8-16. Discuss both the advantages and disadvantages of using a computerized database system rather than a manual system for storing and processing accounting data. In your discussion, provide some specific accounting examples that illustrate your advantages and disadvantages.

8-17. Professor Errorprone had read just enough about databases to be dangerous. During the course of one of his lectures, the professor stated, "Databases are a wonderful invention, but are only cost-effective for large computerized accounting applications. They are ill-advised for small accounting systems and, of course, cannot be implemented in manual systems." Comment.

8-18. What words were used to form each of the following acronyms?

(a) DBMS   (b) DDL   (c) DML   (d) SQL   (e) OLAP   (f) OODB

8-19. The Vreeland Manufacturing Company is nationally known for its fine golfing products, including clubs, bags, and related equipment. The company's payroll department is redesigning its computer records so that they can also serve the personnel department in a consolidated database. The following table lists several data items required by each department. Note that these items are not in any consistent order. Recommend a database record format for these records and, for each data item, recommend a field length (i.e., a maximal number of characters).

Item	Payroll File	Personnel File
1	Employee name	Social Security number
2	Employee 1st line of address	Employee number
3	City	Employee name
4	State	Employee 1st line of address
5	Zip code	City and state
6	Home telephone area code	Zip code
7	Home telephone number	Date of hire
8	Department code	Department code
9	Pay rate (regular)	In-house phone extension
10	Pay rate (overtime)	Home telephone area code
11	Social Security number	Home telephone number
12	Number of federal tax deductions	Date of last raise

8-20. The Wilmer Ruiz Corporation employs the individuals listed in the data shown in the accompanying table. Use a DBMS to create a database of this information.

Record number	Last name	First name	Social Security number	Dept	Pay rate	Over-time
1	ADCOX	NORMAN	901795336	1	6.50	Yes
2	KOZAR	LINDA	412935350	1	6.50	Yes
3	MCLEAN	KAY	405751308	1	7.50	No
4	CUNNINGHAM	TOM	919782417	3	7.50	Yes
5	DANIELS	PATRICIA	517351609	3	5.50	Yes
6	MCGUIRE	ANNE	201891647	3	5.50	Yes
7	REEDER	BRENDA	619294493	3	5.50	Yes
8	BLOOM	BRENDA	513321592	4	6.25	Yes
9	DAVIS	DENISE	517351608	4	5.50	Yes
10	DUFFY	LESLIE	314532409	4	8.50	No
11	HARPER	LINDA	615824130	4	5.75	Yes
12	MORGAN	MEREDITH	704563903	4	6.25	Yes
13	WELSH	KAREN	216253428	4	8.25	No
14	CHAPIN	GEORGE	203767263	5	7.50	Yes
15	FINN	JOHN	715386721	5	6.25	Yes
16	HALPIN	MARSHA	913541871	5	6.50	Yes
17	LAURIN	PHILIP	514484631	5	6.50	Yes
18	MIAGLIO	PEGGY	414224972	5	6.25	Yes
19	TURNER	BRENDA	713589164	5	8.50	No
20	ZORICH	MILDRED	504455827	5	6.50	Yes

a. What record structure did you use for this database? Identify the names, widths, and other characteristics of each field you created.

b. List all employees in Department 5. Print this list.

c. List all employees with first name "Brenda." Print this list.

d. List all those employees with pay rates over $6.50. Print this list.

e. List all those employees eligible for overtime (T = yes; F = no). Print this list.

INTERNET EXERCISES

8-21. Many professors post their data lectures on "database normalization" on the web. Find one or two of these and print a copy for yourself. Are the concepts discussed in these lectures consistent with the chapter's examples? Why or why not?

8-22. Use the web to find business applications of data warehousing. Why do companies create data warehouses, and what are some accounting uses of such warehouses?

8-23. Use the web to find business applications of online analytical processing (OLAP). Why do companies use OLAP? What is the connection between OLAP and databases?

CASE ANALYSES

8-24. The Marcia Felix Corporation (Using a DBMS)

The information in the accompanying table is for the employees of the Marcia Felix Corporation. Use a DBMS software package to create a database for it.

Personnel File
Date: October 10, 20xx

	Employee Number	Score on Aptitude Test	Department ID	Current Pay Rate	Sex
BAKER, JEFFREY L	1692	73	A	$7.50	M
BARRETT, RAYMOND G	3444	53	B	7.45	M
BLISS, DONALD W	6713	55	D	6.80	M
BOWERS, PAUL D	2084	42	B	5.90	M
BUCHANAN, CINDY	3735	41	E	7.80	F
CHEUNG, WAI KONG	8183	55	C	7.80	F
CONRAD, MARK E	8317	58	D	9.60	M
DAILY, REBECCA E	2336	45	D	8.90	F
DRISCOLL, DAVID M	5210	47	D	7.70	M
ERICKSON, KURT N	2217	53	B	8.50	M
FRANTZ, HEIDI L	6390	55	A	6.90	F
GARROW, SCOTT D	8753	61	A	7.40	M
HARDENBROOK, LISA A	7427	40	C	6.70	F
JACKSON, GREG W	4091	67	D	8.90	M
LANGLEY, JERRY W	3262	86	E	9.40	M
LUBINSKI, TRAVIS M	3865	37	D	7.50	M
LYNCH, SHERENE D	7857	66	D	8.90	F
MARKHAM, KYLE R	6766	62	A	7.90	M
MCGUIRE, TANA B	4052	55	A	9.20	F
MONACH, SHERI L	8082	48	B	9.10	F
MOORE, MICHAEL S	2431	67	E	8.50	M
NELSON, JOHN R	5873	46	B	7.40	M
PAPEZ, PETER M	7799	41	E	8.30	M
PETTINARI, DARIN M	1222	56	B	8.40	M

Requirements

1. What record structure did you design? Identify the names, widths, and other characteristics of each field in a typical record.
2. Sort these employees by department. Print this list.
3. Sort these employees by pay rate. Print this list.
4. Sort these employees by test score. Print this list.
5. Sort these employees by department and alphabetically by last name within department.
6. What is the average test score for these employees?
7. What is the average score for females? What is the average score for males?
8. What is the average pay rate for these employees?
9. What is the average pay rate for females? What is the average for males?
10. What females scored over 70 on their examinations? What males scored over 50?

8-25. Benson's Sports Supplies (Normalizing Data)

Benson's Sports Supplies is a wholesaler of sporting goods equipment for retailers in a local metropolitan area. The company buys sporting goods equipment direct from manufacturers and then resells them to individual retail stores in its area. The raw data in the accompanying table illustrate some of the information required for the company's purchase order system. As you can see, this information is characteristic of accounting purchase order systems but is not well organized. In fact, because of the repeating groups in the right-most columns, it cannot even be stored in a computer system.

Purchase Order Number	Date	Customer Number	Customer Name	Customer Phone Number	Item Number	Item Description	Unit Cost	Unit	Quantity Ordered
12345	8/19/03	123-8209	Charles Dresser, Inc.	(752) 433-8733	X32655	Baseballs	$33.69	dozen	20
					X34598	Footballs	53.45	dozen	10
					Z34523	Bball Hoops	34.95	each	20
12346	8/19/03	123-6733	Patrice Schmidt's Sports	(673) 784-4451	X98673	Softballs	35.89	dozen	10
					X34598	Footballs	53.45	dozen	5
					X67453	Soccer balls	45.36	dozen	10

Requirements

Store this data in a spreadsheet to make it easy to manipulate. Then perform each of the following tasks in turn:

1. Reorganize the data in first normal form and print your spreadsheet. Why is your data in first normal form?
2. Reorganize the data from part 1 into second normal form and print your spreadsheet. Why is your data in second normal form?
3. Reorganize the data from part 2 into third normal form and print your spreadsheet. Why is your data in third normal form?

8-26. Mason Manufacturing Company (Data Validation Using a DBMS)

The payroll department at the Mason Manufacturing Company has defined the following record structure for employee records.

Date field	Data type	Example
Last Name	Text	Kerr
First Name	Text	Stephen
Social Security number	Text	123-45-6789
Home phone number	Text	(987) 456-4321
Work phone extension	Number	123
Payrate	Currency	$12.34
Number of tax exemptions	Number	3
Department	Text	A

All fields are required. The employee's Social Security number serves as the record key. Work phone extensions are always greater than "100" and less than "999." Payrates are always at least $7.75 and no more than $29.85. The maximum number of tax exemptions allowed is "10." Finally, there are only three departments: A, B, and C.

Requirements

1. Using a DBMS such as Access, create a record structure for the Mason Manufacturing Company, using the data types identified earlier.
2. Create data validation rules for as many data fields as you can. For each data validation rule, also create validation text that the system can use to display an appropriate error message. Create a list of such rules on a separate piece of paper.
3. Create employee records for yourself, and employees with the last names Anderson, Baker, and Chapman using data that you make up. Print this information.
4. Attempt to create one more record that violates a data validation rule. Create a screen capture of one or more violations, as dictated by your instructor.

8-27. Bonadio Electrical Supplies (Advantages and Disadvantages of DBMSs)

Bonadio Electrical Supplies distributes electrical components to the construction industry. The company began as a local supplier 15 years ago and has grown rapidly to become a major competitor in the northcentral United States. As the business grew and the variety of components to be stocked expanded, Bonadio acquired a computer and implemented an inventory control system. Other applications such as accounts receivable, accounts payable, payroll, and sales analysis were gradually computerized as each function expanded. Because of its operational importance, the inventory system has been upgraded to an online system, while all the other applications are operating in batch mode. Over the years, the company has developed or acquired more than 100 application programs and maintains hundreds of files.

Bonadio faces stiff competition from local suppliers throughout its marketing area. At a management meeting, the sales manager complained about the difficulty in obtaining immediate, current information to respond to customer inquiries. Other managers stated that they also had difficulty obtaining timely data from the system. As a result, the controller engaged a consulting firm to explore the situation. The consultant recommended installing a database management system (DBMS), and the company complied, employing Jack Gibbons as the database administrator.

At a recent management meeting, Gibbons presented an overview of the DBMS. Gibbons explained that the database approach assumes an organizational, data-oriented viewpoint as it recognizes that a centralized database represents a vital resource. Instead of being assigned to applications, information is more appropriately used and managed for the entire organization. The operating system physically moves data to and from disk storage, while the DBMS is the software program that controls the data definition library that specifies the data structures and characteristics. As a result, both the roles of the application programs and query software, and the tasks of the application programmers and users are simplified. Under the database approach, the data are available to all users within security guidelines.

Requirements

1. Explain the basic difference between a file-oriented system and a database management system.
2. Describe at least three advantages and at least three disadvantages of the database management system.
3. Describe the duties and responsibilities of Jack Gibbons, the database administrator. (CMA Adapted)

REFERENCES, RECOMMENDED READINGS, AND WEB SITES

References and Recommended Readings

Casarin, P., "Using Data Mining Techniques in Auditing," *IS Audit and Control Journal,* vol. V, (1997), pp. 43–46.

Castelluccio, Michael, "Why All the Noise Over OOP (Object-Oriented Programming)?" *Management Accounting,* September 1997, pp. 53–55.

Classe, Alison, "Which Database and Why?" *Accountancy* (June 1991), pp. 109–111.

Codd, E. F., *The Relational Model for Database Management Version 2* (Reading, MA: Addison-Wesley, 1990).

David, Julie Smith, and Paul John Steinbart, "Drowning in Data," *Strategic Finance,* vol. 81, no. 6 (December 1999), pp. 30–34.

Dearing, George, "Accounting Systems That Stand the Test of Time" *Management Accounting,* vol. 79, no. 6 (December, 1997), pp. 32–37.

Giladi, Kreindy, and Hershey H. Friedman, "Direct Marketing, Database Marketing and Relationship Marketing for the Accounting Practitioner," *The National Public Accountant,* vol. 45, no. 3 (May, 2000), pp. 36–38.

Higgins, H. Ngo, "SQL Language for Accounting Auditors," *IS Audit and Control Journal,* vol. V (1997), pp. 22–24.

Hoffman, Thomas, "Walgreen Heals Prescription Net," *Computerworld,* vol. 32, no. 16 (April 20, 1998), pp. 43–46.

Hoffman, Thomas, "Tool Boosts Bank's Cross-Selling Abilities," *Computerworld,* vol. 32, no. 26 (June 29, 1998), pp. 71–72.

Kent, William, "A Simple Guide to Five Normal Forms in Relational Database Theory," *Communications of the ACM,* vol. 26, no. 2 (February 1983), pp. 120–125.

Korzeniowski, Paul, "Desperately Seeking Storage Solutions," *Datamation,* vol. 40, no. 16 (August 15, 1994), pp. 62–64.

Marks, Gene, "Technology: Why Isn't Microsoft Access Your Accounting Database?" *Pennsylvania CPA Journal,* vol. 71, no. 4 (Winter, 2001), p. 10.

McFadden, Patrick James, "Guarding Computer Data," *Journal of Accountancy,* vol. 84, no. 1 (July 1997), pp. 77–80.

Morris, Linda, and Steven Phaar, "Invasion of Privacy: A Dilemma for Marketing Research and Database Technology," *Journal of Systems Management,* vol. 43, no. 10 (October 1992), p. 10ff.

Olsen, David H., and Vance Cooney, "The Strategic Benefits of Data Warehousing: An Accounting Perspective," *Information Strategy* (Winter 2000).

Orenstein, David, "Objects Help Polo Speed Data Warehouse," *Computerworld,* vol. 33, no. 46 (November 15, 1999), p. 96.

Radding, Alan, "Support Decision Makers with a Data Warehouse," *Datamation,* vol. 41, no. 5 (March 15, 1995), pp. 53–58.

Ruf, Kurtis M., "Drowning in Data," *Target Marketing,* vol. 19, no. 7 (July 1996), pp. 2–29.

Sammon, David, and Pat Finnegan, "The Ten Commandments of Data Warehousing," *Database for Advances in Information System* (Fall 2000) pp. 82–91.

Sauls, Walter, "Leveraging the Data Warehouse," *Management Accounting,* vol. 78, no. 4 (October 1997), pp. 39–43.

Simon, Alan R., *Data Warehousing for Dummies* (Foster City, CA: IDG Books Worldwide, Inc., 1997).

Web Sites

Most DBMS developers maintain their own web sites. Some examples are: www.oracle.com (Oracle), www.sybase.com (Sybase), www.microsoft.com (Microsoft), www.borland.com (Paradox and dBase).

There are many sources of information about data warehousing. www.datawarehouse.com is a data warehouse community site that includes a chat room, forum messages, presentations, and other resources. Web sites for two well-known statistical software companies that contain a wealth of information about data mining are www.spss.com and www.sas.com.

PART THREE

CONTROLS AND SECURITY IN ACCOUNTING INFORMATION SYSTEMS

CHAPTER 9
Introduction to Internal Control Systems

CHAPTER 10
Computer Controls for Accounting Information Systems

CHAPTER 11
Computer Crime and Ethics

CHAPTER 12
Auditing Computerized Accounting Information Systems

Part Three analyzes the topic of internal control within AISs, emphasizing computerized systems for handling accounting data. Internal control systems are stressed in this text because, in most organizations, accountants have a major responsibility for developing, implementing, and monitoring these systems. Effective internal control systems can reduce the risk of errors and irregularities going undetected in an AIS.

Chapter 9 introduces the subject of internal control by analyzing the components and control activities within organizations' internal control systems. We provide examples of control procedures throughout this chapter. In practice, organizations with computerized AISs may encounter difficulties with their internal control systems. Chapter 10 therefore examines the types of computer controls that are commonly used within AISs. In addition, the chapter discusses various control procedures that should be designed and implemented for e-business. When internal control systems fail, computer security is threatened and computer crime may result. Chapter 11 discusses the important and interesting topic of computer crime. Examples of real world cases of computer abuse are illustrated in this chapter. One useful way of both preventing and detecting fraudulent acts within the environment of computerized AISs is to perform audit procedures. Chapter 12 analyzes some of the important auditing activities associated with computerized AISs.

Chapter 9

Introduction to Internal Control Systems

INTRODUCTION

INTERNAL CONTROL SYSTEMS: DEFINITION AND COMPONENTS

Definition of Internal Control

Components of Internal Control

CONTROL PROCEDURES ANALYZED

Preventive Controls

Detective and Corrective Controls

Interrelationship of Preventive and Detective Controls

CONTROL ACTIVITIES WITHIN AN INTERNAL CONTROL SYSTEM

Good Audit Trail

Sound Personnel Policies and Practices

Separation of Duties

Physical Protection of Assets

Internal Reviews of Controls by Internal Audit Subsystem

Timely Performance Reports

COST-BENEFIT CONCEPT FOR DEVELOPING CONTROLS

Illustrations of Cost-Benefit Analyses

AIS AT WORK: PTO TREASURER CHARGED WITH THEFT OF FUNDS

SUMMARY

KEY TERMS YOU SHOULD KNOW

DISCUSSION QUESTIONS

PROBLEMS

INTERNET EXERCISES

CASE ANALYSES

Dagwood Discount Department Store

Alden, Inc.

Old New England Leather

Fairfax Recreation Center

Herron Company

REFERENCES, RECOMMENDED READINGS, AND WEB SITES

After reading this chapter, you will:

1. *Know* what an internal control system is and be familiar with the interrelated components of this system.

2. *Be familiar with* the roles played by COSO and COBIT in the internal control area.

3. *Understand* the difference between preventive controls and detective controls and why they are interrelated.

4. *Be aware of* some of the control activities that should be included in an organization's internal control system.

5. *Understand* the reason an organization might be willing to let customers shoplift some of its merchandise inventory.

Senior executives have long sought better ways to control the enterprises they run.

Committee of Sponsoring Organizations,
Executive Summary, *COSO Report,* 1993.

INTRODUCTION

Accounting information systems encompass an organization's financial resources. These resources (cash and merchandise inventory are examples) must be protected from activities such as loss, waste, or theft by the organization's employees. Protecting assets requires the development and implementation of an internal control system within the organization's AIS, as well as within other parts of the organizational system. In addition to protecting assets, an internal control system performs other functions, such as helping to ensure the reliability of the accounting data processed by an accounting information system and helping to promote operational efficiency in an organization.

This is the first of four chapters related to internal controls, which are controls established within an organization's system. The present chapter extensively examines internal control systems and their important role in accounting information systems. The components that should be included in companies' internal control systems are stressed.

INTERNAL CONTROL SYSTEMS: DEFINITION AND COMPONENTS

An internal control system consists of the various methods and measures designed into and implemented within an organizational system to achieve the following four objectives: (1) safeguarding assets, (2) checking the accuracy and reliability of accounting data, (3) promoting operational efficiency, and (4) encouraging adherence to prescribed managerial policies.

Definition of Internal Control

As an illustration of the importance of internal control systems and as a lead-in to the definition of internal control, it is useful to review an important act passed by the U.S. Congress and signed into law in December 1977, the **Foreign Corrupt Practices Act (FCPA).** This act grew out of a desire to prohibit bribes to foreign officials by publicly owned corporations. To accomplish this objective, the FCPA contained several provisions regarding internal control. One of these provisions—the requirement that publicly owned corporations implement effective internal control systems—is intended to reduce the risk of questionable or illegal foreign payments. The FCPA applies only to publicly owned corporations registered under Section 12 of the 1934 Securities and Exchange Act, which are essentially those business organizations listed on a national stock exchange or those business organizations having at least $1 million in assets and 500 or more shareholders. Specifically, with respect to their internal control systems, these organizations are required to design and implement control systems that provide reasonable assurances that assets are accounted for appropriately, that transactions are recorded in conformity with generally accepted accounting principles, that access to assets is properly controlled, and that periodic comparisons of existing assets to the accounting records are made.

The FCPA has made managers of publicly owned corporations more aware of the importance of controls within their systems. This major effect has resulted from a provision within the FCPA that makes these organizations' board members and managers personally liable should illegal payments be made to foreign officials. The FCPA has also led to the increased growth and importance of the internal audit function (discussed later) within many corporations' systems.

The requirement that corporations coming under the Foreign Corrupt Practices Act must implement effective internal control systems has generated enormous interest among accountants, auditors, and management regarding the design and evaluation of these systems. As a result, both the private and public sectors have made a number of studies, proposals, and recommendations on internal control. One of the most prominent of these studies examined the causes of fraudulent financial reporting and made recommendations to reduce its occurrence. This study was performed by the Treadway Commission (National Commission on Fraudulent Financial Reporting).

Among the Treadway Commission's recommendations was to have the organizations that sponsored the commission work together to develop a common definition for internal control and to provide guidance for judging the effectiveness of internal control as well as improving it. The committee established for this purpose was the **Committee of Sponsoring Organizations (COSO)** of the Treadway Commission.

The report issued by the COSO in 1992 defines internal control and describes its components, presents criteria against which internal control systems can be evaluated,[1] and provides guidance for public reporting on internal control while offering materials that auditors, managers, and others can use to evaluate an internal control system. The COSO report defines **internal control** as: a process, effected by an entity's board of directors, management, and other personnel, designed to provide reasonable assurance regarding the achievement of objectives in the following categories—effectiveness and efficiency of operations, reliability of financial reporting, and compliance with applicable laws and regulations.

According to the COSO report, a company's internal control system is a tool of, rather than a substitute for, management, and controls should be built into, rather than onto, operating activities. Although the report defines internal control as a *process,* it recommends the evaluation of the effectiveness of internal control as of a point in time, such as at the end of a particular month.

Other groups besides the Committee of Sponsoring Organizations have addressed the important issue of internal control. For example, the American Institute of Certified Public Accountants (AICPA) issued Statement on Auditing Standards (SAS) No. 55 in 1998, which stressed that management should establish an internal control structure that includes the following three components: the control environ-

---

[1] Committee of Sponsoring Organizations of the Treadway Commission (CSOTC), *Internal Control—Integrated Framework (COSO Report),* 1992.

ment, the accounting system, and the control procedures.[2] In 1995, the AICPA amended SAS No. 55 with SAS No. 78. SAS 78 replaced the definition of the internal control structure in SAS 55 with the definition of internal control given in the COSO report. In 2001, the AICPA issued SAS No. 94, which further amended Statement No. 55. SAS No. 94, "The Effect of Information Technology on the Auditor's Consideration of Internal Control" in a Financial Statement Audit, takes into account the pervasive effects of IT on an audit.

Another group that has extensively examined the internal control area is the Information Systems Audit and Control Foundation (ISACF). **Control Objectives for Business and Information Technology (COBIT),** the result of four years of intensive research by a team of international experts, was the largest project ever undertaken by the ISACF in terms of scope, time, and effort. COBIT adapted its definition of internal control based on the COSO report: the policies, procedures, practices, and organizational structures that are designed to provide reasonable assurance that business objectives will be achieved and that undesired events will be prevented or detected and corrected.[3] COBIT, as well as COSO and SASs 55/78/94, emphasizes that "people" at every level of a company are a very important part of the company's system of internal control. COBIT classifies people as one of the primary resources managed by various information technology (IT) processes. COBIT, COSO, and SASs 55/78/94 all agree that management is responsible for establishing, maintaining, and monitoring a company's internal control system.

To emphasize the important role of organizational managers in internal control systems, in January 1998 the Basle Committee on Banking Supervision published a framework for evaluating internal control systems in banking organizations. This committee consists of senior representatives of bank supervisory authorities and central banks from Belgium, Canada, France, Germany, Italy, Japan, Luxembourg, Netherlands, Sweden, Switzerland, United Kingdom, and the United States. The Basle Committee's report stressed that a strong internal control system can help to ensure that a banking organization's goals and objectives will be accomplished, that the bank will achieve its long-term profitability targets, and that the bank will maintain reliable financial and managerial reporting systems. For banking organizations to design and implement strong internal control systems as well as to effectively evaluate these systems, the committee specified a number of principles in the internal control area that directly involve banking organizations' managers. Examples of these principles are:

1. Senior management within a banking organization should have responsibility for establishing appropriate internal control policies and for monitoring the effectiveness of the internal control system.

2. Senior management (and the board of directors) are responsible for promoting high ethical and integrity standards, and for establishing a culture within a banking organization that emphasizes and demonstrates to all levels of personnel the importance of internal controls.

---

[2] These three components of the internal control structure are examined extensively in "Consideration of the Internal Control Structure in a Financial Statement Audit," *Statement on Auditing Standards No. 55* (New York: AICPA, April 1988).

[3] Information Systems Audit and Control Foundation (ISACF), *COBIT: Control Objectives for Information and Related Technology,* 1995.

3. Senior management should ensure that the risks affecting the achievement of a banking organization's strategies and objectives are continually being evaluated. To accomplish this, internal controls may need to be revised to adequately address any new or previously uncontrolled risks.

4. Control activities should be an integral part of a banking organization's daily operations. This can be accomplished by having senior management establish an appropriate control structure whereby control activities at every business level are defined.

Topics such as *risks* and *control activities* are examined later in the chapter.

One last group that is concerned about properly functioning internal control systems within companies is the *International Federation for Information Processing (IFIP)*. In November of 2001, for example, the IFIP sponsored a conference in Brussels, Belgium on the topic of "Integrity and Internal Control in Information Systems." The aim of this conference was to establish the basis for an ongoing dialogue between information technology security specialists and internal control specialists so that both groups could work together more effectively to assist in developing reliable business systems for companies (which necessitate well-designed and implemented internal control systems) in the future. One goal of achieving the above is to enable business managers of companies to have more confidence in the integrity of their information systems and the data generated from these systems.

Components of Internal Control

The COSO report states that an internal control system should consist of five interrelated components: (1) control environment, (2) risk assessment, (3) control activities, (4) information and communication, and (5) monitoring. COBIT and SAS 78 both agree with the COSO report regarding the inclusion of these five components within an internal control system.

Control Environment   The **control environment** establishes the tone of a company, influencing the control awareness of the company's employees. It is the foundation for all the other internal control components, providing discipline and structure. Factors included within the control environment are as follows:

1. The integrity, ethical values, and competence of an organization's employees.
2. Management's philosophy and operating style.
3. The way management assigns authority and responsibility as well as organizes and develops its people.
4. The attention and direction provided by the board of directors.

By establishing an effective control environment within which an organizational system functions, management attempts to promote operational efficiency and encourage adherence to its policies. It is important for managers, as well as owners, of companies to have positive attitudes about the importance of controls being designed and implemented within their organizational systems. Otherwise, the controls introduced into their systems will likely be ineffective.

Management's philosophy about personnel policies and practices comes under the control environment. Regarding personnel matters, an important control procedure that should be implemented by management is the use of training programs to teach new employees how to be efficient in performing their duties. In addition, the training programs should familiarize the employees with the specific operating policies of the company's management (for instance, the amount of authority and responsibility employees will be given in performing their job functions) and encourage them to adhere to those policies.

As another example, a control procedure that should be implemented within the control environment is to have regular reviews of a company's actual operations to determine if they comply with management's operating policies. Large enterprises (and certain medium-sized ones) often have separate internal audit subsystems, or departments, with internal auditors performing these reviews. The internal auditors spend considerable time evaluating whether previously designed and implemented internal controls are functioning properly. In small enterprises, where they typically cannot afford the cost of internal audit departments, the reviews of compliance with operating policies are commonly performed by the owners and managers.

Risk Assessment   When designing controls for a company, consideration must be given to the risk factor by a process called **risk assessment.** This assessment process recognizes that every organization faces risks to its success. These risks come from both external and internal sources of the organization. For control purposes, risks that appear to affect the accomplishment of a company's goals should be identified, analyzed, and acted upon.

To illustrate, in attempting to accomplish the goal of safeguarding a company's assets, control procedures should be established for each asset to provide reasonable assurance that one or more company employees do not misappropriate the asset. A general rule that should be followed when developing control procedures for assets is as follows: The more liquid an asset is, the greater the risk of its misappropriation. To compensate for this increased risk factor, stronger controls are required. The COSO report recommends the use of a *cost-benefit analysis* (discussed and illustrated later in this chapter) in assessing the risk associated with the decision on implementing a specific control procedure.

Control Activities   The policies and procedures that help ensure that management directives are carried out are the focus of **control activities.** Within a company's control activities, it is important to design and implement specific control procedures to help ensure that necessary actions are taken to address risks to the achievement of a company's objectives. This chapter provides several examples of control procedures. In addition, control activities that should be included in every company's internal control system will be discussed and illustrated later in the chapter.

Information and Communication   The term **information** refers to the accounting system, which includes the methods and records used to record, process, summarize, and report a company's transactions as well as maintain accountability for the company's assets, liabilities, and equity. The accounting system (and the control procedures established within this system) should focus on safeguarding assets and checking the accuracy and reliability of accounting data. It is management's responsibility to make sure that its company's accounting system is measuring, processing, and communicating financial data from business transactions to interested users of these data, such as potential investors and creditors. Through properly designed and implemented *control procedures* (also referred to as **accounting control procedures**), management will have more confidence that its company's assets are being safeguarded and that the accounting data processed by the accounting system are reliable.

Communication refers to providing a company's personnel with an understanding of their roles and responsibilities pertaining to internal control over financial reporting. It emphasizes the importance of personnel understanding how their activities within the financial reporting information system relate to the work of others. With open communication channels, it is hoped that any exceptions within the internal control system (e.g., the control procedure for the cash asset is not functioning properly) are reported to management and corrective action then initiated. Communication can be achieved through documents such as *policies and procedures manuals* (discussed later). Finally, communication can also be made orally and through memoranda from management.

Monitoring   The process that assesses the quality of internal control performance over time is called **monitoring.** It involves evaluating the design and operation of controls on a timely basis and initiating corrective action when specific controls are not functioning properly. A company's management should be responsible for ensuring that implemented controls continue to operate as intended. The use of timely performance reports to achieve the monitoring component of an internal control system is illustrated later in this chapter.

CONTROL PROCEDURES ANALYZED

The importance of control procedures was mentioned within the discussion of the *control activities* component of an internal control system. This section analyzes the subject of control procedures in considerable detail. A company's control procedures are often classified into three major types: *preventive controls, detective controls,* and *corrective controls.*

Preventive Controls

Certain control procedures within an organization's internal control system should be designed and implemented to *prevent* some potential problem from occurring when an activity is performed. These control procedures are called **preventive controls,** and they should become operative before an activity is performed. For example, a company's management may decide that, as one of its control procedures, the accountant responsible for recording cash receipts transactions should not have access to the cash itself. Employees who have no recording functions regarding cash receipts transactions would be responsible for such activities as counting cash receipts and making daily bank deposits for these receipts.

This control procedure, which is a preventive control, is designed to safeguard the company's cash asset, as well as to check the accuracy and reliability of the accounting data recorded in the company's records. By separating the duties associated with cash (that is, the recording of cash receipts transactions and the actual handling of cash), one employee's work activities serve as a check on the work activities of another employee. The amount of cash receipts recorded by the accountant, for instance, should equal the actual amount of cash counted and deposited in the bank by a different employee. Furthermore, if the employee handling cash attempts to steal some of the cash receipts, he or she would have a difficult time concealing this theft, since the employee would not have access to the accounting records to cover up the shortage of actual cash deposited. The importance of *separation of duties* within an internal control system is stressed later in this chapter.

Detective and Corrective Controls

An organization's internal control system needs additional control procedures that provide feedback to management regarding whether or not operational efficiency and adherence to prescribed managerial policies have been achieved. These control procedures are called **detective controls.**

As an example of a detective control procedure, a company's information processing subsystem should prepare timely responsibility accounting performance reports for management that disclose significant variations of actual production costs from standard production costs. As a result, the company's management obtains feedback regarding any inefficient manufacturing performance. Corrective action can then be initiated.

This corrective action should occur through the development of control procedures called **corrective controls.** A company's corrective control procedures are designed to remedy problems discovered through detective controls. Let's assume, based on the above detective control example, that performance reports continually disclose that the company's actual direct labor hours for production work significantly exceed the standard direct labor hours. A corrective control procedure that may be implemented is training programs that teach employees to perform their job functions more efficiently and effectively.

Corrective controls include procedures to identify the cause of a company's problem, correct any difficulties or errors arising out of the problem, and modify the company's processing system so that future occurrences of the problem will be eliminated or at least minimized. An example of this type of corrective control procedure is the modification of a company's system so that backup copies of important transactions and master files are maintained to enable the files to be restored in the event that the originals are damaged or destroyed. The important topic of *backup* is discussed in Chapter 10.

Interrelationship of Preventive and Detective Controls

Within a company's internal control system, the preventive control procedures and the detective control procedures should not be treated as mutually exclusive. Rather, these controls should be interrelated.

To illustrate this important interrelationship, assume that every Friday afternoon the Martin Beverage Company's sales departments (soft-drink sales department, snack-food sales department, and so on) within the marketing subsystem send their week's batch of sales invoices to the information processing subsystem. This subsystem performs the necessary work so that timely performance reports (such as sales reports by departments, by product lines, and by sales personnel) are prepared. A preventive control procedure established within the sales departments is to ascertain the total dollar sales from all the invoices before they are sent to the information processing subsystem. This control total of sales invoice amounts is called a **batch control total (BCT).**

The detective control procedure's implementation is as follows:

The information processing subsystem's computer is programmed to add the sales invoice amounts and print out the total after all the week's invoices have been processed. The BCT of sales invoice amounts reported in a computer printout is then compared with the sales departments' BCT of invoice amounts. Ideally, the two amounts should agree, proving that all the sales invoices sent to the information processing subsystem were actually processed. If the two batch control totals disagree, management is informed that something went wrong; for example, one or more sales invoices may have been lost "in transit" to the information processing subsystem. (This would result in the company never billing a customer for a credit sales transaction.)

Figure 9-1 illustrates the important interrelationship between the Martin Beverage Company's preventive and detective control procedures for the movement of sales invoices into the information processing subsystem.

The detective control procedure within the information processing subsystem would not be effective without the initial preventive control procedure within the sales departments. In other words, a computer printout disclosing the total amount of the sales invoices processed is not useful for control purposes unless there is a previously ascertained total (known by the sales departments) for comparison purposes. Furthermore, the preventive control established by the sales departments would have little, if any, usefulness without the existence of the detective control

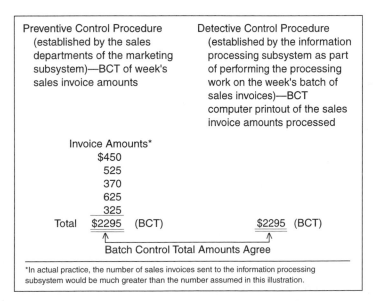

FIGURE 9–1 Martin Beverage Company's control procedures for sending sales invoices to the information processing subsystem.

within the company's information processing subsystem. What good is an initial BCT if there is no subsequent BCT with which to compare it?

CONTROL ACTIVITIES WITHIN AN INTERNAL CONTROL SYSTEM

Each organization's system is somewhat unique. As a result, there is no standardized package of control procedures that can be implemented by every company. Specific controls should be designed and implemented by an organization based on its own particular needs. However, certain control activities should be included in each company's internal control system. Those activities that we will look at here are: (1) a good audit trail, (2) sound personnel policies and practices, (3) separation of duties, (4) physical protection of assets, (5) internal reviews of controls by internal audit subsystem, and (6) timely performance reports. Within the framework of these activities, specific control procedures are designed and implemented for every company that contribute toward achieving the *objectives* of the company's internal control system. (Four objectives were listed at the beginning of this chapter.)

Good Audit Trail

The basic inputs to an organization's AIS are business transactions that are monetarily measured. An **audit trail** (initially discussed in Chapter 1) of these transactions should be maintained within the organization's AIS. A good audit trail enables, for example, an accounting department manager as well as auditors to follow the path of the data recorded in transactions from the initial source documents (for instance, a sales invoice) to the final disposition of the data on a report. In addition, under a good audit trail, data from transactions can be traced, if so desired, from their locations on reports (such as expenses on an income statement) back to the source documents. Both of these processes involve verifying the accuracy of recorded business transactions and are examples of work performed in *auditing* a company's transactions.

The audit trail enables groups such as management and auditors "to know what is happening" throughout all phases of accounting data processing. As a result, an accounting department manager should be able, for example, to detect an error or an irregularity that occurs in the processing of transactions. Without a good audit trail, it is more likely that errors and irregularities in processing accounting data will not be detected.

As part of establishing its audit trail, a company should develop a *policies and procedures manual.* Among the items included in this manual are:

- A chart of accounts describing the purpose of each general ledger account so that the debits and credits from accounting transactions are recorded in the correct accounts.

- A complete description of the types of source documents that will be used as the basis for recording accounting transactions and the correct procedures for preparing and approving the data to be included on these documents.

- A comprehensive description of the authority and responsibility assigned to individual employees for organizational functions such as making decisions on when to deny further credit sales to customers.

Sound Personnel Policies and Practices

An essential control activity that should be included within an organization's internal control system is sound personnel policies and practices, which should contribute toward competent employees. As mentioned earlier, personnel policies and practices and management's philosophy regarding them come under the *control environment* component of an internal control system. Sound personnel policies and practices relate directly to a previous statement in this chapter—COBIT, as well as COSO and SASs 55/78, emphasizes that "people" at every level of a company are a very important part of the company's system of internal control.

The risk associated with *human behavior* cannot be overlooked or overemphasized in organizations. Sound personnel practices are essential to control both business events and information processes. This is becoming increasingly important as companies empower employees in attempting to streamline their operations and cut costs. The quality of a company's employees directly affects the quality of the goods and services provided by the company. In general, competent and honest employees are more likely to help create value for the company.

Employees work continually with organizational assets—for example, handling cash, acquiring and issuing inventory, and using equipment. Without competent and honest employees functioning in an environment of fair and equitable personnel policies, inefficient use of the company's assets may occur. This will lead to operational inefficiency and a failure to accomplish organizational goals.

In general, little can be done to completely stop employees who are determined to embarrass, harm, or destroy an organization. For example, employees may band together (called *collusion*) to commit an irregularity such as embezzling cash receipts from customers. One of the biggest problems companies have in encouraging ethical behavior among employees is in setting the right example. Unfortunately, a number of organizations have too many "picky" rules that employees do not understand. To avoid this type of problem, organizations should continually review their rules and decide whether they are rational, defensible, and effective. Once rules are established that make a positive contribution to the productivity and effectiveness of a company, managers should be responsible for explaining the importance of the rules and leading by example.

It is important that personnel policies be established and followed by an organization. Examples of personnel policies are:

1. Specific procedures for hiring and retaining competent employees.
2. Training programs that prepare employees to perform their organizational functions efficiently.
3. Good supervision of the employees as they are working at their jobs on a daily basis.
4. Fair and equitable guidelines for employees' salary increases and promotions.
5. Rotation of certain key employees in different jobs so that these employees become familiar with various phases of their company's system.
6. The requirement that all employees take their earned vacations.
7. Insurance coverage on those employees who handle assets that are subject to theft.
8. Regular reviews of employees' performances to evaluate whether they are carrying out their functions efficiently and effectively, with corrective action initiated for those employees not performing up to company standards.

The requirement that all employees must take their earned vacations (personnel policy 6) is important for two reasons. First, if an employee is embezzling cash from his organization, this employee will probably not want to take a vacation. By requiring the person to go on vacation and having another employee perform his job functions while he is away, there is a strong likelihood that the other employee will detect the embezzlement.

Second, required vacations should be enforced to enable employees to leave their jobs temporarily and do other activities, such as playing tennis and reading novels. This might prevent the employees from getting into a rut. When the employees return to work following their vacations, they should be refreshed and ready to perform their job functions in an efficient and effective manner.

For employees who handle assets susceptible to theft, such as a company's cash and inventory of merchandise, it is also a good personnel policy (number 7) to obtain some type of insurance coverage on them. One approach used by many organizations to reduce the risk of loss caused by employee theft of assets is to obtain **fidelity bond coverage** from an insurance company on those employees having direct access to assets subject to misappropriation. The insurance company will investigate the backgrounds of all employees that an organization desires to have bonded. In issuing the fidelity bond, the insurance company assumes liability (up to a specified dollar amount) for the employees named in the bond. Should any of these employees later embezzle assets from the organization, the insurance company compensates the organization for the resulting loss.

Separation of Duties

The **separation of duties** control activity of an internal control system focuses on structuring work assignments among employees so that, as previously discussed, one employee's work activities serve as a check on those of another employee. In designing and implementing an effective internal control system into an organization, the responsibilities for the following three functions should be assigned to different employees: *authorizing* transactions, *recording* transactions, and maintaining *custody* of assets.

Authorizing involves decision making to approve transactions (e.g., a sales manager authorizing a credit sale to a customer). *Recording* includes functions such as preparing source documents, maintaining journals and ledgers, preparing reconciliations, and preparing performance reports. Finally, *custody of assets* can be either direct, such as handling cash or maintaining an inventory storeroom, or indirect, such as receiving customer checks through the mail or writing checks on a company's bank account. If two of these three functions are the responsibility of the same employee, problems can occur, as will be illustrated shortly.

The risk of undetected errors and irregularities is greatly reduced if the following duties are separated within a company's internal control system:

1. Separate the custody of assets from the recording associated with the assets.
2. Separate the authorizing of transactions from the custody of assets related to the authorization function.
3. Separate the authorizing of transactions from the recording associated with the authorization function.

To demonstrate the importance of separating duties, three real-world Cases-in-Point are provided below, with a brief analysis, to show what can happen when each of the above three separation relationships does not exist.

> ***Case-in-Point 9.1*** The former city treasurer of Fairfax, Virginia, was convicted of embezzling approximately $600,000 from the city treasury over a six-year period. She executed this embezzlement scheme as follows: When Fairfax residents used currency to pay their personal property and real estate taxes, the city treasurer would keep the currency. She would then record the tax collections within her property tax records. However, she would not report these collections to the city controller. To bring her records into agreement with those of the controller, she would eventually record an adjusting journal entry. Furthermore, when currency was received by the city treasurer from residents for such things as court fees and business license fees, this currency would be recorded on a cash register and deposited daily. The treasurer would steal portions of the currency and make up any discrepancy in the bank deposit by substituting miscellaneous checks she had received through the mail that would not be missed when they were not recorded.

Analysis The control weakness that enabled the city treasurer to successfully execute her fraudulent activity was that she had responsibility for both the *custody* of cash receipts and the *recording* of these receipts. Consequently, she was able to embezzle cash receipts and falsify the accounts to conceal her embezzlement activity.

> ***Case-in-Point 9.2*** The utilities director of Newport Beach, California, was convicted of embezzling $1.2 million from the city of Newport Beach over an 11-year period. The utilities director would initially forge invoices or easement documents that authorized payments, for example, to real or fictitious city property owners for the rights to put water lines through their land. Officials within the Finance Department would give him the checks for delivery to the property owners. The utilities director would then forge signatures, endorse the checks to himself, and deposit them in his own accounts.

Analysis The control weakness that enabled the utilities director to successfully execute his fraudulent activity was that he had physical *custody* of checks for the transactions he had previously *authorized*. This lack of separation of duties enabled the director to authorize fictitious transactions and subsequently divert the related payments to his own accounts.

> ***Case-in-Point 9.3*** The former payroll director of the Los Angeles Dodgers baseball team pleaded guilty to embezzling approximately $330,000 from the team. One way he performed the embezzlement was by crediting employees for hours not worked and then receiving kickbacks of around 50 percent of their extra pay. In addition, the payroll director added fictitious employees to the Dodgers payroll and then cashed the checks of these employees. The payroll director's fraudulent activity was discovered when he became ill and another employee took over his duties.

Analysis The control weakness that enabled the payroll director to successfully execute his fraudulent activity was that he was responsible for both *authorizing* the hiring of new employees and *recording* the hours worked by employees. The payroll director was not involved in preparing or handling the actual paychecks. However, this did not prevent his fraudulent activity, since the baseball team's treasurer (who did prepare and handle the actual paychecks) would simply mail paychecks to the addresses specified by the payroll director.

The *separation of duties concept* is important in IT environments. However, the way in which this concept is applied in these environments is often different. In modern information systems, for example, the computer can be programmed to perform one or more of the previously mentioned functions (i.e., authorizing transactions, recording transactions, and maintaining custody of assets). Thus, the computer replaces employees in performing the function (or functions). For example, the pumps at many gas stations today are designed so that customers can insert their credit cards to pay for their gas. Consequently, the computer performs both the custody of the "cash" asset and the recording function. The subject of separation of duties in IT environments is examined further in Chapter 10.

Physical Protection of Assets

A vital control activity that should be part of every organization's internal control system is the physical protection of its assets. By keeping a company's assets in a safe physical location, the risk of damage to the assets or theft by employees or outsiders (such as customers) is lessened. For example, a control procedure to physically protect inventory is to keep it in a storage area accessible only to employees with custodial responsibility for the inventory asset. This physical protection control should prevent an unauthorized person from walking into the storage area and stealing inventory items.

With regard to the functions surrounding the purchase of inventory from vendors, an important control procedure is to require that each shipment of inventory be delivered directly to the storage area, followed by the preparation of a *receiving report* source document. This report, as illustrated in Figure 9-2, provides documentation about each delivery, including the date received, vendor, shipper, and purchase order number. For every type of inventory item received, the receiving report shows the item number, the quantity received (based on a count), and a description. The report also includes space to identify the employee (or employees) who received (i.e., counted) and inspected the inventory items as well as space for remarks regarding the quality of the inventory items. By signing the receiving report, the inventory clerk (Katie Smith in Figure 9-2) formally establishes responsibility for the inventory items. Any authorized employees requesting some inventory items from the storage area (for instance, to replenish the shelves of the store) should be required to sign the inventory clerk's *issuance report,* which is another source document. The clerk is thereby relieved of further responsibility for these requisitioned inventory items.

An organization's important documents, such as the corporate charter, all major contracts with other companies, blank checks (see Case-in-Point 9.4), and registration statements required by the Securities and Exchange Commission, should be accessible only to authorized management personnel. For control purposes, many organizations keep important documents in fireproof safes on their own premises or in rented storage vaults at banks.

Case-in-Point 9.4 An unfortunate event took place a few years ago in Inglewood, California, because adequate control over important documents was lacking. A janitor employed by the city of Inglewood was convicted of stealing 34 blank checks while cleaning the city Finance Office. The janitor forged the names of city officials on these checks and cashed them for amounts ranging from $50,000 to $470,000.

Sarah's Sporting Goods Receiving Report		**No.** 7824
Vendor: Richards Supply Company		**Date Received:** July 10,2003
Shipped via: UPS		**Purchase Order** **Number:** 4362

Item Number	Quantity	Description
7434	100	Spalding basketballs
7677	120	Spalding footballs
8326	300	Spalding baseballs
8687	600	Penn tennis balls

Remarks:
Container with footballs received with water damage on outside, but footballs appear to be okay.

Received by: *Katie Smith*	**Inspected by:** *Katie Smith*	**Delivered to:** *Larry Plochask*

FIGURE 9–2 Example of receiving report (items in boldface are preprinted).

The susceptibility of cash to theft by employees as well as the risk of human error in handling cash (due to the large volume of cash receipts and disbursements transactions that many organizations have) makes it essential that an organization institute physical protection safeguards for its cash asset. In addition to acquiring fidelity bond coverage on those employees handling cash, the following two control procedures for cash should also be implemented: (1) the majority of cash disbursements for authorized expenditures should be made by check rather than in cash, and (2) the daily cash receipts (either received in the mail from credit customers or through cash sales) should be deposited intact at the bank.

Cash Disbursements by Check A good audit trail of cash disbursements is essential to avoid undetected errors and irregularities in the handling of cash. To this end, most organizations use prenumbered checks (to maintain accountability for both issued and unissued checks) for making authorized cash disbursements. With regard to cash disbursements to vendors for the acquisition of inventory, there are two basic systems for processing vendor invoices: *nonvoucher systems* and *voucher systems.*

Under a **nonvoucher system,** every approved invoice is posted to individual vendor records in the accounts payable file and is then stored in an open invoice file. When a cash disbursement check is written to pay an invoice, the invoice is removed from the open-invoice file, marked paid, and then stored in the paid-invoice file.

Under a **voucher system,** a document called a *disbursement voucher* is also prepared. It identifies the specific vendor, lists the outstanding invoices, specifies the

Sarah's Sporting Goods Disbursement Voucher				No. 76742	
Date Entered: July 20,2003				**Debit Distribution**	
Prepared by: $\mathcal{SM}$				**Account No.**	**Amount**
Vendor Number: 120				27-330	$750.00
				27-339	450.00
Remit to: Valley Supply Company 3617 Bridge Road Farmington, CT 06032				28-019	300.00
				29-321	425.00
Vendor Invoice			**Returns & Allowances**	**Purchase Discount**	**Net Remittance**
Number	**Date**	**Amount**			
4632	6/30/03	$1250.00	$150.00	$22.00	$1078.00
4636	7/2/03	675.00	0.00	13.50	661.50
Voucher Totals:		$1925.00	$150.00	$35.50	$1739.50

FIGURE 9–3 Example of disbursement voucher (items in boldface are preprinted).

general ledger accounts to be debited, and shows the net amount to be paid the vendor after deducting any returns and allowances as well as any purchase discount. Figure 9-3 illustrates a disbursement voucher.

As Figure 9-3 discloses, the disbursement voucher summarizes the information contained within a set of vendor invoices. When an invoice is received from a vendor for the purchase of inventory, it is compared with the information contained in copies of the *purchase order* and *receiving report* to determine the accuracy and validity of the invoice. The vendor invoice itself should also be checked for mathematical accuracy. When supplies or services are purchased, which do not normally involve purchase order and receiving report source documents, the invoice is sent to the appropriate supervisor for his approval.

The use of a voucher system with disbursement vouchers has several advantages over a nonvoucher system. Two of these advantages are (1) it reduces the number of cash disbursement checks that are written, since several invoices to the same vendor can be included on one disbursement voucher, and (2) the disbursement voucher is an internally generated document. Thus, each voucher can be prenumbered to simplify the tracking of all payables, thereby contributing to an effective audit trail over cash disbursements.

Making cash disbursements with prenumbered checks is an effective control procedure to reduce the risk of employees' misappropriation of cash. However, if a company has various small cash expenditures occurring during an accounting period, it is more efficient to pay cash for these expenditures than to follow the formal company procedure of using checks. For good operating efficiency, an organization should use a **petty cash fund** for its small, miscellaneous expenditures. To exercise control over this fund, one employee, called the *petty cash custodian,* should be given the responsibility for handling petty cash transactions. The petty cash money should be kept under the custodian's control in a locked box, and the custodian should be the only individual with access to the fund.

Cash Receipts Deposited Intact   The importance of having physical protection safeguards for an organization's cash disbursements activities also holds true for its cash receipts activities. As an effective control procedure, each day's accumulation of cash receipts should be "deposited intact" at a bank. In the typical retail organization, the total cash receipts for any specific working day will come from two major sources: checks arriving by mail from credit-sales customers and currency and checks received from retail cash sales.

Daily intact deposits of cash receipts means that company employees should use none of these cash inflows to make cash disbursements. Rather, every penny collected should go directly to the bank, and a separate checking account should be used for cash disbursements. The intact deposit of cash receipts enables the audit trail of cash inflows to be easily traced to the bank deposit slip and the monthly bank statement. On the other hand, if employees of a company are permitted to use some of the day's receipts for cash disbursements, the audit trail for cash can become quite confusing, thereby increasing the risk of undetected errors and irregularities.

Internal Reviews of Controls by Internal Audit Subsystem

Many organizations, especially the larger ones, have within their systems a separate subsystem called **internal audit.** Individuals working as internal auditors often have backgrounds in accounting; however, they may come from other disciplines, such as information technology. Internal auditors often become involved in *information systems auditing,* which is discussed in Chapter 12.

As a service function that should report directly to a company's top management or to the board of directors (in order to be independent of the other subsystems, as discussed later), the internal audit staff makes periodic reviews, called **operational audits,** of each department (or subsystem) within its organization. These audits focus on evaluating the efficiency and effectiveness of operations within a particular department. On completing an audit of a department and discovering any deficiencies, the internal auditors make recommendations to management for improving the department's operations. A company's internal auditors may also be asked to perform a *fraud investigation* if their management suspects fraud within the organization.

The internal auditors' important role in reviewing their organization's internal control system is indicated by the American Institute of Certified Public Accountants, as follows:

> *When an entity has an internal audit department, management may delegate to it some of its supervisory functions, especially with respect to the review of internal control. This particular internal audit function constitutes a separate element of internal control undertaken by specially assigned staff*

within the entity with the objective of determining whether other internal controls are well designed and properly operated.[4]

It is preferable to have the internal audit function established as a separate subsystem rather than having it under the accounting subsystem. As a result of this organizational design, it is hoped that the internal audit subsystem can be completely independent of all the other subsystems within a company and can therefore be objective when reviewing the various operations of each subsystem. On the other hand, if the internal audit function is assigned to the accounting subsystem, for example, complete objectivity is more difficult, if not impossible, to achieve because the internal auditors would be evaluating their own subsystem's operations.

In performing regular reviews of their company's internal control system, the internal auditors may find that certain controls are not operating properly. They should then make recommendations to management as to how the controls can be modified to make them function better. For example, through a *cost-benefit analysis* (discussed later), the internal auditors may find that the *cost* of operating a specific control procedure is greater than the *benefit* being obtained from this procedure. Consequently, the internal auditors should recommend to management ways the control procedure can be changed to reduce its cost, thereby making it *cost-effective*. A control is considered cost-effective when its anticipated benefit exceeds its anticipated cost.

To illustrate the various types of functions performed by internal auditors working in a real-world organization, Case-in-Point 9.5 describes the role of the internal audit department at a large insurance company in Connecticut.

Case-in-Point 9.5 Internal auditing within our company performs examinations and evaluations to determine whether:

- The system of internal control and the degree of compliance with related procedures are adequate to provide reasonable assurance that material errors and irregularities will be detected.
- Established policies, plans, procedures, laws, and regulations are being observed.
- Company assets are accounted for and satisfactory safeguards exist to prevent their loss.
- Resources are used economically and efficiently.
- Reports to management are factual and reliable.

In its framework for the evaluation of internal control systems, the Basle Committee on Banking Supervision emphasized the importance of the internal audit function in banking organizations, as follows:

The internal audit function is an important part of the ongoing monitoring of the system of internal controls because it provides an independent assessment of the adequacy of, and compliance with, the established controls. By reporting directly to the board of directors or their audit committee, and to senior management, the internal auditors provide unbiased information about line activities. Due to the important nature of this function, internal

---

[4] "Using the Work of an Internal Auditor," *Codification of Statements on Auditing Standards* (New York: American Institute of Certified Public Accountants, 1985), AU Section 8010.02.

audit must be staffed with competent, well-trained individuals who have a clear understanding of their roles and responsibilities. The frequency and extent of internal audit review and testing of the internal controls within a bank should be consistent with the nature, complexity, and risk of the organization's activities. In all cases, it is critical that the internal audit function is independent from the day-to-day functioning of the bank and that it has access to all activities conducted by the banking organization.[5]

Timely Performance Reports

Another control activity that should be part of each company's internal control system is timely performance reports, which contribute toward achieving the *monitoring* component of an internal control system. From the viewpoint of evaluating a company's internal control system, a **performance report** provides information to management on how efficiently and effectively its company's internal controls are functioning. Through correctly prepared performance reports, management obtains *feedback* on the success or failure of the previously implemented package of internal controls. Thus, preparing a performance report, as mentioned earlier, is a detective control procedure.

Figure 9-4 shows an example of a performance report for a publishing company. This report, prepared by the company's internal auditor, evaluates the company's control procedure for cash receipts. The "recommended change" indicated in Figure 9-4 is a corrective control procedure.

Accounting Control Procedure as Designed and Implemented

Each morning the mail is opened by two secretaries. For each piece of mail that contains a customer cash payment, the secretaries place the check in one pile and the payment source document included with the check in another pile.

Upon completing this process, the payment source documents are sent to Employee A, who uses these documents to record the day's cash receipts in the accounting records.

The actual checks are sent to Employee B, who totals them and prepares the daily bank deposit.

At the end of each day, a third employee, C, compares the total cash receipts recorded by Employee A to the total of the bank deposit to ascertain if these two amounts are equal.

Accounting Control Procedure as Actually Operating

Upon observing the operation of this control procedure, the only weakness noted was that whenever customers' checks did not include payment source documents with them, the secretaries sent the actual checks to employee A for recording. After recording the cash receipts, Employee A immediately sent the checks to Employee B for use in preparing the daily bank deposit.

Recommended Change

Employee A should not have access to the actual checks. It is recommended that whenever payment source documents are not included with checks, the secretaries make photocopies of the checks for Employee A's use in recording them in the accounting records. By implementing this additional procedure into the control that currently exists, Employee A does not actually handle the physical checks themselves.

FIGURE 9-4 Performance report to evaluate cash receipts control procedure.

---

[5] Basle Committee on Banking Supervision, *Framework for the Evaluation of Internal Control Systems,* January 1998, p. 1

The sooner managers are provided information concerning internal control problems, the quicker they can take action to correct these problems. Therefore, performance reports should be prepared on a *timely* basis so that very little time elapses between the occurrence of operational problems with certain controls and the feedback to management on these poorly functioning controls. Computers have been a tremendous aid to companies in enabling their organizational systems to provide timely performance reports to managers.

COST-BENEFIT CONCEPT FOR DEVELOPING CONTROLS

As previously discussed, a standardized package of control procedures for all companies does not exist. An optimal internal control package is developed for individual companies by applying the **cost-benefit concept.**

Under this concept, a cost-benefit analysis is performed on every control procedure being considered for implementation by comparing the expected cost of designing, implementing, and operating each control to the control's expected benefit. Only those controls whose benefits are expected to be greater than, or at least equal to, the expected costs should be implemented in a company's system.

Illustrations of Cost-Benefit Analyses

To illustrate a cost-benefit analysis, let's assume that Avon Variety Store sells products such as clothing, jewelry, and kitchen appliances. The company's managers are quite concerned about how much inventory customers have shoplifted during the last several months. They are therefore considering some additional control procedures that would reduce this shoplifting problem.

If no additional controls are implemented, the company's accountant estimates that the total annual loss to the company from shoplifting will be approximately $120,000. Two alternative control procedures being considered to solve the problem and thereby safeguard the company's inventory asset are:

1. Hire eight plain-clothed security guards to patrol every one of the retail store's aisles. Based on the annual salaries that would have to be paid to the security guards, this control would cost Avon Variety Store an estimated $240,000 a year.

2. Hire two plain-clothed security guards who would patrol the aisles and also install several cameras and mirrors throughout the company's premises to permit managers to observe any shoplifters. The estimated annual cost of this control would be $66,000.

Based on the managers' goal of reducing shoplifting, alternative 1 (hiring eight security guards) would appear to be the ideal control procedure to implement. Assuming that the guards are properly trained and perform their jobs in an effective manner, the shoplifting of inventory should be reduced to practically zero. Even if shoplifting were completely eliminated, however, alternative 1 should not be implemented, since the control's expected cost ($240,000 a year) is greater than the control's expected benefit ($120,000 a year—the approximate annual shoplifting loss that would be eliminated).

If alternative 2 (hiring two security guards plus installing cameras and mirrors) were implemented, Avon Variety Store's accountant estimates that the total annual loss from shoplifting could be reduced from $120,000 to $25,000. The net benefit is therefore $95,000 ($120,000 minus $25,000). Since the second alternative's expected benefit ($95,000 a year reduction of shoplifting) exceeds its expected cost ($66,000 a year), the company's managers should select alternative 2.

The point of this cost-benefit analysis example is that in some situations, the design and implementation of an *ideal control procedure* may be impractical. We are using the term **ideal control** to mean a control procedure that reduces to practically zero the risk of an undetected error (such as debiting the wrong account for the purchase of office supplies) or irregularity (such as shoplifting inventory items). If a specific control's expected cost exceeds its expected benefit, as was true with the alternative 1 control procedure discussed above, the effect of implementing that control will be to decrease operating efficiency for the entire organizational system.

From a cost-benefit viewpoint, therefore, managers are sometimes forced to design and implement control procedures for specific areas of their company that are less than ideal. These managers must learn to live with the fact that, for example, some irregularities may occur in their organizational system that will not be detected by the internal control system.

Another approach to cost-benefit analysis attempts to quantify the risk factor associated with a specific area of a company. (*Risk assessment,* as discussed earlier, is one of the interrelated components of an internal control system.) In general, the benefits of additional control procedures result from *risk of loss reductions.* A measure of loss should include both the *exposure* (that is, the amount of potential loss associated with a control problem) and the *risk* (that is, the probability that the control problem will occur). An example of a loss measure is **expected loss,** computed as follows:

$$\text{expected loss} = \text{risk} \times \text{exposure}$$

Based on estimates of risk and exposure, the expected loss from a potential control problem is determined. To ascertain the cost-effectiveness of a new control procedure associated with the potential control problem, the expected loss both with and without the new procedure is computed. On completing these calculations, the estimated benefit of the new control procedure is equal to the reduction in the estimated expected loss from implementing this procedure. The estimated benefit is then compared with the incremental cost of the new control procedure. Whenever the estimated benefit exceeds this incremental cost, the decision should be made to implement the newly designed control procedure.

To demonstrate this method of cost-benefit analysis, assume that a company's payroll system prepares 12,000 checks biweekly. Data errors sometimes occur that require reprocessing the entire payroll. The cost of the payroll reprocessing is projected to be $10,000. The company's management is considering the addition of a data validation control procedure that is estimated to reduce the risk of the data errors from 15 percent to 1 percent. This validation control procedure is expected to cost $600 per pay period. Should the data validation control procedure be implemented? Figure 9-5 illustrates the analysis to answer this question.

Figure 9-5 indicates that the reprocessing cost expected (or the expected loss) is estimated to be $1,500 without the validation control procedure and $100 with the validation control procedure. Thus, implementing this control procedure provides an estimated reprocessing cost reduction of $1,400. When this $1,400 estimated cost

	Without Control Procedure	With Control Procedure	Net Expected Difference
Cost of payroll reprocessing	$10,000	$10,000	
Risk of data errors	15%	1%	
Reprocessing cost expected ($10,000 x risk)	$ 1,500	$ 100	$1,400
Cost of validation control procedure (an incremental cost)	$ 0	$ 600	$ (600)
Net estimated benefit from validation control procedure			$ 800

FIGURE 9–5   Cost-benefit analysis of payroll validation control procedure.

reduction is compared to the $600 estimated incremental cost of implementing the control procedure, a decision should be made by the company's management to implement the procedure due to the net estimated benefit of $800.

It is important to point out that *nonmonetary* (or *qualitative*) items are often important in evaluating decision alternatives in a cost-benefit analysis. For example, when evaluating whether or not to implement a particular control procedure into a company's system, a qualitative item may be the effect on employee morale (a human factor) from implementing the control procedure. This item would be difficult, if not impossible, to quantify. Thus, because qualitative items often exist in a cost-benefit analysis decision-making situation, the actual decision to be made by a firm's management may require *subjectivity* beyond the cost-benefit analysis results.

AIS AT WORK
PTO Treasurer Charged with Theft of Funds

Many small businesses lack the internal control procedures that can help them prevent fraud and abuse. Frequently the problem is that smaller organizations do not employ enough personnel to be able to have appropriate separation of duties. This means that fraud, theft, or embezzlement can occur undetected for some time. This was likely the case when the treasurer of Ohio's Monroe Elementary School Parent Teacher Organization (PTO) was charged with theft of about $16,000 in funds used to provide teacher materials and other supplies for the school. The school raises the money through a bookstore and fund-raisers. For about a year, the treasurer kept the cash instead of depositing it in the organization's bank account.

The crime came to light slowly as unpaid creditors began contacting the school principal seeking payment for their bills. The treasurer assured the principal that the bills would be processed. However, several months later, the principal again received several past-due notices. When she contacted the bank, she found that the organization had only a few hundred dollars left in the account. The treasurer was then arrested and charged with a fourth-degree felony-theft count and can receive up to $5,000 in fines and a prison term. In a larger organization, control procedures such as having one person write and deposit checks and another individual reconcile the bank accounts would prevent such a fraud.

Source: Kiesewetter, Sue, "PTO Treasurer Expected to Surrender to Police," *Cincinnati Enquirer,* February 8, 2002, p. B1.

SUMMARY

An organization's internal control system has four objectives: (1) to safeguard assets, (2) to check the accuracy and reliability of accounting data, (3) to promote operational efficiency, and (4) to encourage adherence to prescribed managerial policies. It is management's ultimate responsibility to develop an internal control system within its company's organizational system. The control environment, risk assessment, control activities, information and communication, and monitoring are the five interrelated components that make up an internal control system.

Six control activities to include in each organization's internal control system are: (1) a good audit trail, (2) sound personnel policies and practices, (3) separation of duties, (4) physical protection of assets, (5) internal reviews of controls by internal audit subsystem, and (6) timely performance reports. These control activities are all important to the efficient and effective operation of an internal control system. Within the six activities, specific control procedures should be designed and implemented for each company based on its particular control needs.

If problems exist in a company's system, they may be caused by weaknesses within the internal control system. To develop an optimal internal control package for an organization, a cost-benefit analysis should be performed on each control procedure being considered for implementation. Only those controls whose expected benefits exceed, or at least equal, their expected costs should be implemented in the organization's system.

KEY TERMS YOU SHOULD KNOW

accounting control procedures

audit trail

batch control total (BCT)

Committee of Sponsoring Organizations (COSO)

communication

control activities

control environment

Control Objectives for Business and Information Technology (COBIT)

corrective controls

cost-benefit concept

detective controls

expected loss

fidelity bond coverage

Foreign Corrupt Practices Act (FCPA)

ideal control

information

internal audit

internal control

monitoring

nonvoucher system

operational audits

performance report

petty cash fund

preventive controls

risk assessment

separation of duties

voucher system

DISCUSSION QUESTIONS

9-1. What are COSO and COBIT? What role did COSO and COBIT play in the internal control area?

9-2. Briefly discuss the interrelated components that should exist within an internal control system. In your opinion, which component is the most important and why?

9-3. Why are accountants so concerned about their organization having an efficient and effective internal control system?

9-4. This chapter provided an example of a batch control total (BCT) for processing sales invoices. Try to think of other situations in which a BCT could be an effective control within an organization's accounting information system.

9-5. Discuss what you consider to be the major differences between preventive, detective, and corrective control procedures.

9-6. Comment on the following statement: "Because an internal audit subsystem does not directly contribute to an organization's revenue-earning functions, and, in fact, often interferes with the other subsystems' operating activities (e.g., by entering a subsystem's work area and taking the time to evaluate the operating efficiency of its specific control procedures), the organization would probably increase its overall profitability by completely eliminating the internal audit staff."

9-7. Why is an organization's accountant so concerned about a good audit trail through the accounting information system?

9-8. Why are competent employees important to an organization's internal control system?

9-9. How can separation of duties reduce the risk of undetected errors and irregularities regarding a company's asset resources?

9-10. Discuss some of the advantages to an organization from using a voucher system and prenumbered checks for its cash disbursement transactions. Are there any circumstances when prenumbered cash disbursement checks would not be efficient for an organization to use? Explain.

9-11. What role does cost-benefit analysis play in an organization's internal control system?

9-12. Why should timely performance reports be an important control activity within a company's internal control system?

9-13. Listed below are 12 internal control procedures or requirements for the expenditure cycle (purchasing, payroll, accounts payable, and cash disbursements) of a manufacturing enterprise.

Requirements

For each procedure or requirement, identify the error or misstatement that would be prevented or detected by its use.

a. Duties between the cash payments and cash receipts functions are segregated.

b. Signature plates are kept under lock and key.

c. The accounting department matches invoices to receiving reports or special authorizations before payment.

d. All checks are mailed by someone other than the person preparing the payment voucher.

e. The accounting department matches invoices to copies of purchase orders.

f. The blank stock of checks is kept under lock and key.

g. Imprest accounts are used for payroll.

h. Bank reconciliations are to be performed by someone other than the one who writes checks and handles cash.

i. A check protector is used.

j. Surprise counts of cash funds are conducted periodically.

k. Orders can be placed with approved vendors only.

l. All purchases must be made by the purchasing department.

9-14. The Mary Popkin Umbrella Manufacturing Company maintains an inventory of miscellaneous supplies (e.g., pens, pencils, paper, floppy disks, and envelopes) for use by its clerical workers. These supplies are stored on shelves at the back of the office facility, easily accessible to all company employees.

The company's accountant, Alan Most, is concerned about the poor internal control over the company's office supplies. He estimates that the monthly loss due to theft of supplies by company employees averages about $350. To reduce this monthly loss, Alan has recommended to management that a separate room be set aside to store these supplies, and that a company employee be given full-time responsibility for supervising the issuance of the supplies to those employees with a properly approved requisition. By implementing these controls, Alan believes that the loss of supplies from employee misappropriation can be reduced to practically zero.

If you were the Mary Popkin Umbrella Manufacturing Company manager responsible for either accepting or rejecting Alan Most's control recommendations, what would your decision be? Explain. Try to think of some additional control procedures that the company might implement to reduce the monthly loss from theft of office supplies by employees.

9-15. Ron Mitchell is currently working his first day as a ticket seller and cashier at the First Run Movie Theater. When a customer walks up to the ticket booth, Ron collects the required admission charge and issues the movie patron a ticket. To be admitted into the theater, the customer then presents his or her ticket to the theater manager, who is stationed at the entrance. The manager tears the ticket in half, keeping one half for himself and giving the other half to the customer.

While Ron was sitting in the ticket both waiting for additional customers, he had a "brilliant" idea for stealing some of the cash from ticket sales. He reasoned that if he merely pocketed some of the cash collections from the sale of tickets, no one would ever know. Because approximately 300 customers attend each performance, Ron believed that it would be difficult for the theater manager to keep a running count of the actual customers entering the theater. To further support his reasoning, Ron noticed that the manager often has lengthy conversations with patrons at the door and appears to make no attempt to count the actual number of people going into the movie house.

Do you think that Ron Mitchell will be able to steal cash receipts from the First Run Movie Theater with his method and not be caught? Explain why you think Ron's theft will not be detected or, if you believe that he will be caught, explain how his stealing activity will be discovered.

PROBLEMS

9-16. The Laura Plocharski Company manufactures various types of clothing products for women. To accumulate the costs of manufacturing these products, the company's accountants have established a computerized cost accounting system. Every Monday morning, the prior week's production cost data are batched together and processed. One of the outputs of this processing function is a production cost report for management that compares actual production costs to standard production costs, and computers variances from standard. Management focuses on the significant variances as the basis for analyzing production performance.

Errors sometimes occur in processing a week's production cost data. The cost of the reprocessing work on a week's production cost data is estimated to average about $12,000. The company's management is currently considering the addition of a data validation control procedure within its cost accounting system that is estimated to reduce the risk of the data errors from 16 percent to 2 percent. Management's data validation control procedure is projected to cost $800 per week.

Requirement

Using these data, perform a cost-benefit analysis of the data validation control procedure that the Laura Plocharski Company's management is considering for implementation in its cost accounting system. Based on this analysis, make a recommendation to management regarding the data validation control procedure.

9-17. The wing commander of a tactical fighter wing has requested the implementation of a formal information system to assist him in evaluating the quality of aircrew members. Although many factors are related to determining an individual's quality level, it has been recommended that one source of objective data is from the testing process administered by the Standardization/Evaluation Section in the fighter wing. Each flight crew member is tested periodically either by an instrument check or by a tactical/proficiency check to detect violations of standardized operating procedures or errors in judgment. The result of a test is either pass or fail, and discrepancies such as single-engine landing, dangerous pass, incorrect holding pattern, and so forth are noted where applicable. A general feeling exists in the Standardization/Evaluation Section that if these reports were prepared and distributed in a timely fashion, the wing commander could take swift corrective action to prevent a hazardous practice or critical weakness from occurring. Further analysis indicates that such a report can be prepared daily, five days a week throughout the year, at a cost of $14.10 per report. This time period for reporting is judged acceptable by the Standardization/Evaluation Section.

Although there are many benefits anticipated from implementing such a system in terms of preventing the loss of aircrew members' lives and the loss of aircraft property, as well as increasing the effectiveness of the fighter wing, the wing commander has requested that all new information systems be initially justified on purely economic grounds before other considerations are evaluated. As the management consultant assigned to this project, you have decided to take the approach that the proposed system will help reduce the rate of major accidents from 2 to 1.5 percent (as similar systems have done elsewhere to economically justify their implementation). From your investigation, you have gathered the following statistics concerning major accidents.

Cost of Major Accident	
Certain Costs	
Aircraft	$1,600,000
Accident investigation	6,000
Property damage (impact point)	2,000
Total	$1,608,000
Possible Costs (both crew members are lost)	
Invested training in crew members	
2 @ $25,000	$ 50,000
Survivors' benefits and mortuary costs	
2 @ $50,000	100,000
Total	$ 150,000
Probability of crew loss is .25	

Requirement

Can the proposed system be economically justified using the approach described in this problem? Explain.

INTERNET EXERCISES

9-18. Using your computer and the Internet, find a web site that has information about a real-world organization's experience with adopting the internal control concepts defined by COSO. Upon accessing the web site, write a summary of your findings and relate it to this chapter's subject matter. In addition, submit a printout of the web site information that you accessed.

9-19. Using your computer and the Internet, find a web site that examines the internal audit function. Upon accessing the web site, write a summary of your findings and relate it to this chapter's subject matter. In addition, submit a printout of the web site information that you accessed.

CASE ANALYSES

9-20. Dagwood Discount Department Store (Control Suggestions to Strengthen Payroll System)

As a recently hired internal auditor for the Dagwood Discount Department Store (which has approximately 500 employees on its payroll), you are currently reviewing the store's procedures for preparing and distributing the weekly payroll. These procedures are as follows.

Each Monday morning the managers of the various departments (e.g., the women's clothing department, the toy department, and the home appliances department) turn in their employees' time cards for the previous week to the accountant (Morris Manning). Morris then accumulates the total hours worked by each employee and submits this information to the store's computer center to process the weekly payroll. The computer center prepares a transaction tape of employees' hours worked and then processes this tape with the employees' payroll master tape file (containing such things as each employee's social security number, exemptions claimed, hourly wage rate, year-to-date gross wages, FICA taxes withheld, and union dues deduction). The computer prints out a payroll register indicating each employee's gross wages, deductions, and net pay for the payroll period.

The payroll register is then turned over to Morris, who, with help from the secretaries, places the correct amount of currency in each employee's pay envelope. The pay envelopes are provided to the department managers for distribution to their employees on Monday afternoon.

To date, you have been unsuccessful in persuading the store's management to use checks rather than currency for paying the employees. Most managers that you have talked with argue that the employees prefer to receive currency in their weekly pay envelopes so that they do not have to bother going to the bank to cash their checks.

Requirements

Assuming the Dagwood Discount Department Store's management refuses to change its current system of paying the employees with cash, suggest some control procedures that could strengthen the store's current payroll preparation and distribution system.

9-21. Alden, Inc. (Recommendations for Improving Internal Control)

You have been hired by the management of Alden, Inc. to review its control procedures for the purchase, receipt, storage, and issuance of raw materials. You have prepared the following comments, which describe Alden's procedures.

- Raw materials, which consist mainly of high-cost electronic components, are kept in a locked storeroom. Storeroom personnel include a supervisor and four clerks. All are well trained, competent, and adequately bonded. Raw materials are removed from the storeroom only upon written or oral authorization from one of the production foremen.

- There are no perpetual inventory records; hence, the storeroom clerks do not keep records of goods received or issued. To compensate for the lack of perpetual records, a physical inventory count is taken monthly by the storeroom clerks, who are well supervised. Appropriate procedures are followed in making the inventory count.

- After the physical count, the storeroom supervisor matches quantities counted against a predetermined recorder level. If the count for a given part is below the reorder level, the supervisor enters the part number on a materials requisition list and sends this list to the accounts payable clerk. The accounts payable clerk prepares a purchase order for a predetermined reorder quantity for each part and mails the purchase order to the vendor from whom the part was last purchased.

- When ordered materials arrive at Alden, they are received by the storeroom clerks. The clerks count the merchandise and see that the counts agree with the shipper's bill of lading. All vendors' bills of lading are initialed, dated, and filed in the storeroom to serve as receiving reports.

Requirements

Describe the internal control weaknesses and recommend improvements in Alden's procedures for the purchase, receipt, storage, and issuance of raw materials. Organize your answers as follows.

Weaknesses	Recommended Improvements

9-22. Old New England Leather (System Revision for Providing Control Information)

Old New England Leather is a large manufacturer and marketer of quality leather goods. The product line ranges from wallets to saddles. Because of the prevailing management philosophy at Old New England Leather, the company will accept orders for almost any leather product to be custom-made on demand. This is possible since the leather craftsmen employed by the company perform a job in its entirety (i.e., the company does not utilize production-line techniques). Each leather craftsman is responsible for the complete manufacturing of a given product. Currently, the company employs about 150 leather craftsmen and has been growing at an annual rate of 20 percent during each of the last three years. However, management does not anticipate this growth rate in the future, but instead sees a steady annual growth rate of 5 percent over each of the next 10 years.

Old New England Leather markets a proprietary line of leather goods worldwide. However, these stock products compose only 50 percent of the output from the craftsmen. The remaining products are produced to special order. When a custom order is received, the specifications for the order are posted along with an expected shipping date. Each craftsman is then eligible to bid on the order or a part of it. Once the bids are evaluated, the company's management determines which individual has agreed upon the date, and accepts the lowest bid for production. This custom part of the business has shown the greatest growth in recent years. During the last twelve months, there has been an average of 600 orders in process at any one time.

Along with growth, Old New England Leather's management has incurred many problems related to providing consistent, on-time delivery. It appears that the skilled craftsmen often fail to report on a timely basis when a job is complete. In addition, management has never had a satisfactory control for ensuring that orders are worked on in a priority sequence. Other problems, such as a craftsman over-committing himself in a given time period or simply losing an order, are also becoming serious.

The company owns a medium-size computer for processing payroll, inventory, accounts receivable, accounts payable, and so forth. This computer has capabilities for online processing with as many as twenty terminals. Currently, there are ten terminals in operation throughout the plant.

Requirements

Propose a system for controlling the production of orders that will benefit the craftsmen, management, and the company's customers.

9-23. Fairfax Recreation Center (Internal Control Recommendations to Improve System)

The Fairfax Recreation Center is a neighborhood fitness center equipped with an indoor swimming pool, exercise equipment, and a running track. The Center is open seven days a week, from 8:00 a.m. to 10:00 p.m. Stationed just inside the front doors is a turnstile. An employee oversees access through the turnstile. Before anyone can enter the facility, they must either present their membership card or pay a $6 daily fee.

When the employee at the turnstile collects cash for daily fees, he or she also has the visitor complete a waiver form. The employee then deposits the cash in a locked box and files the forms. At the end of each day the Recreation Center accountant collects the cash box, opens it, removes the cash, and counts it. The accountant then gives a receipt for the cash amount to the employee on turnstile duty. The accountant takes the cash to the bank each evening. The next morning, the accountant makes an entry in the cash receipts journal for the amount indicated on the bank deposit slip.

Susan Porcano, the Fairfax Recreation Center General Manager has some concerns about the internal controls over cash. However, she is concerned that the cost of additional controls may outweigh benefits. She decides to ask the organization's outside auditor to review the internal control procedures and to make suggestions for improvement.

Requirements

Assume that you are the outside auditor. Indicate weaknesses in the existing internal control system over cash admission fees and recommend one improvement for each of the weaknesses identified. Organize your answers as follows:

Weaknesses	Recommended Improvements

9-24. Herron Company (Risk Assessment and Recommending Control Procedures)

Herron Company, a regional retail clothing franchise of 17 stores, opened its doors in 1992. Since the founder Jack Merritt was an accountant, management has always insisted on a state-of-the art accounting system. Similarly, the company places value on internal controls.

Herron employs two internal auditors who monitor internal controls and also seek ways to improve operational effectiveness. As part of the monitoring process, the internal auditors take turns conducting periodic reviews of the accounting records. For instance, the company takes a physical inventory at all stores once each year and an internal auditor oversees the process.

Sue McKinley, the most senior internal auditor, just completed a review of the accounting records. She discovered several items that concerned her. These were:

1. At four of the stores, bank deposit slips did not match cash receipts.
2. One of the stores had an unusual number of bounced checks. It appeared that the same employee was responsible for approving each of the bounced checks.
3. In seven of the stores, the amount of petty cash on hand did not correspond to the amount in the petty cash account.
4. Physical inventory counts varied from inventory book amounts by more than 5 percent at two of the stores. In both cases, physical inventory was lower.
5. Two of the stores seem to have an unusually high amount of sales returns for cash.
6. In ten of the stores gross profit has dropped significantly from same time last year.

Requirements

For each of the six concerns Sue discovered:

1. Identify a risk that may have created the problem.
2. Recommend an internal control to prevent the problem in the future.

REFERENCES, RECOMMENDED READINGS, AND WEB SITES

References and Recommended Readings

American Institute of Certified Public Accountants, "Consideration of the Internal Control Structure in a Financial Statement Audit," in *Statement on Auditing Standards,* no. 55 (New York, 1988).

American Institute of Certified Public Accountants, "Using the Work of an Internal Auditor," in *Codification of Statements on Auditing Standards* (AU Section 8010.02), (New York, 1985).

Basle Committee on Banking Supervision, *Framework for the Evaluation of Internal Control Systems,* Bank for International Settlements in Basle, January 1998.

Casson, Peter, "Framework for the Evaluation of Internal Controls," *Financial Regulations Report* (February 1998), pp. 12-13.

Committee of Sponsoring Organizations of the Treadway Commission, "Accounting Groups Issue Report on Internal Control," *Management Accounting* (December 1992), p. 62.

Committee of Sponsoring Organizations of the Treadway Commission, *Internal Control—Integrated Framework,* New York: Exposure Draft, March 12, 1991.

Committee of Sponsoring Organizations of the Treadway Commission (CSOTC), *Internal Control—Integrated Framework (COSO Report),* New York: 1992.

Curtis, Mary, "Internal Control Issues for Data Warehousing," *IS Audit & Control Journal,* vol. IV (1997), pp. 40-45.

Foltz, Ronald, "Monitoring a Small Firm," *Journal of Accountancy* (June 1997), p. 54.

Greengard, Samuel, "Rethinking the Cost Benefit Equation," *Business Finance* (March 2000), pp. 41-44.

Hawkins, Kyleen W., and Bill Huckaby, "Using CSA to Implement COSO," *Internal Auditor* (June 1998), pp. 50-55.

Information Systems Audit and Control Foundation (ISACF), *COBIT: Control Objectives for Information and Related Technology* (1995).

Institute of Internal Auditors, "COSO Addendum Receives GAO Endorsement," *IIA Today* (July/August 1994), p. 1.

Luehlfing, Michael S., Cynthia M. Daily, Thomas J. Phillips, Jr., and L. Murphy Smith, "Defending the Security of the Accounting System" *The CPA Journal* (October 2000), pp. 62-65.

Moscove, Stephen A., "Enhancing Detective Controls Through Performance Reporting," *Journal of Cost Management* (March/April 1998), pp. 26-29.

Ridley, Jeffrey, and Erroll Yates, "Worth Repeating-Internal Audit: A Managerial Control," *Internal Auditor* (December 2001), pp. 37-43.

Root, Steven J., *Beyond COSO: International Control to Enhance Corporate Governance* (New York: John Wiley & Sons, May 1998).

Rose, Frederick, "Risk Guru," *Wall Street Journal* (January 20, 1998), p. A1.

Roth, Jim, "A Hard Look at Soft Controls," *Internal Auditor* (February 1998), pp. 30-33.

Ruchala, Linda V., "Managing and Controlling Specialized Assets," *Management Accounting* (October 1997), pp. 20-27.

Scarbrough, D. Paul, Dasaratha Rama, and K. Raghunandan, "Audit Committee Composition and Interaction with Internal Auditing: Canadian Evidence," *Accounting Horizons* (March 1998), pp. 51-62.

Tucker, George H., "IT and the Audit," *Journal of Accountancy* (September 2001), pp. 41-43.

Willis, Alan, and William Bradshaw, "Risky Business," *CA Magazine* (August 1998), p. 37.

Web Sites

The web site of COSO is www.coso.org.

To learn more about COBIT, visit the following web site: www.isaca.org/cobit.htm.

To learn more about internal controls and management practices, visit the following web site: www.cftc.gov/sym.html.

Chapter 10

Computer Controls for Accounting Information Systems

INTRODUCTION

GENERAL CONTROLS WITHIN IT ENVIRONMENTS

Personnel Controls

File Security Controls

Fault-Tolerant Systems, Backup, and Contingency Planning

Computer Facility Controls

Access to Computer Files

APPLICATION CONTROLS WITHIN IT ENVIRONMENTS

Input Controls

Processing Controls

Output Controls

DATABASE CONTROLS

CONTROLS IN THE INFORMATION AGE

Risks Unique to the Micro Environment

Controls for Microcomputers

Controls for Computer Network Systems

AIS AT WORK: OMEGA ENGINEERING

SUMMARY

KEY TERMS YOU SHOULD KNOW

DISCUSSION QUESTIONS

PROBLEMS

INTERNET EXERCISES

CASE ANALYSES

Ashley Company

Simmons Corporation

OBrien Corporation

MailMed Inc.

Choate and Choate

REFERENCES, RECOMMENDED READINGS, AND WEB SITES

After reading this chapter, you will:

1. *Be familiar with* the term "general computer control objectives" and *understand* how these objectives are achieved.

2. *Understand* the types of general controls that should be designed and implemented into accounting information systems.

3. *Know* what input controls are and *be familiar with* specific examples of input control procedures.

4. *Know* what processing controls are and *be familiar with* specific examples of processing control procedures.

5. *Know* what output controls are and *be familiar with* specific examples of output control procedures.

6. *Be familiar with* control procedures that should be designed and implemented for microcomputers, and computer network systems to reduce risk.

SAS no. 94 says an organization's IT use may affect any of the five internal control components – the control environment, risk assessment, control activities, information and communication and monitoring – as well as how businesses initiate, record, process and report transactions.

George H. Tucker, "IT and the Audit," *Journal of Accountancy*, September 2001, p. 41.

INTRODUCTION

Chapter 9 extensively discussed the importance of internal control procedures within AISs. This chapter continues the analysis of internal control systems by focusing on control procedures within organizations' *information technology (IT)* environments.

Computer controls are frequently classified into one of two major categories: (1) general controls or (2) application controls. **General controls** are designed and implemented to ensure that a company's control environment is stable and well managed to strengthen the effectiveness of application controls. **Application controls** are designed and implemented to prevent, detect, and correct errors and irregularities in transactions as they flow through the input, processing, and output stages of data processing work. Each of these categories of computer controls will be extensively discussed in this chapter.

The last topic of Chapter 10 focuses on controls in the information age. These include controls over microcomputers or PCs and networked systems. We discussed another important internal control area unique to the information age, control issues associated with e-business, in Chapter 2.

GENERAL CONTROLS WITHIN IT ENVIRONMENTS

An organization's management is responsible for directing and controlling operations and for establishing, communicating, and monitoring policies and procedures. Management characteristics are a significant factor in the internal environment of an organization. They help to establish the level of "control consciousness," which is the basis for the **control environment**—the framework in which an accounting system operates. Formal codes of conduct and ethics policies contribute to a disciplined control environment. All companies should adopt formal codes of conduct that include conduct related to IT resources. For example, a company may require all employees to periodically sign a formal code of conduct stipulating that computer resources are to be used only for appropriate business purposes and any acts of fraud or abuse will be prosecuted. In the process of designing and implementing a system of computer controls for a company's accounting system, the consistency, speed, and flexibility of a computer raise the following control concerns:

- The effects of errors may be magnified. As an example that illustrates the consistency of the computer, assume that a company's computer prepares sales invoices by taking the quantity input and multiplying this input by a price from the sales price master file. If, for instance, the computer program to perform the process is selecting incorrect sales prices, all sales invoices will likely be incorrect.

- The decreased manual involvement within the accounting system may lead to inadequate separation of duties.

- Audit trails may be reduced, eliminated, or exist only for a brief time in computer-readable form.

- Changes to accounting data and computer programs may be made by individuals lacking sufficient understanding of control procedures and accounting policies, or such changes may be made without adequate testing or without the consent of management.

- More individuals may have access to accounting data, which are a critical organizational resource. This situation is especially acute when online computer systems and computer networks are in use, since individuals can access data from various points where terminals and online microcomputers are located. As a result, knowledgeable but unauthorized persons may more easily gain access to important files.

- Accounting data stored in computer-based systems are oriented to the characteristics of magnetic or optical media. These characteristics differ significantly from the paper-oriented and therefore human-oriented media familiar to many accounting data users. First, the data are invisible. Although this characteristic does not in itself cause a serious problem, it is necessary for accounting data users to initiate specific steps to retrieve the data in readable form. Second, stored accounting data (except for read-only memory) are erasable. Consequently, valuable data, such as inventory and accounts receivable records, may be lost. Third, accounting data are stored in compressed form. For instance, a single magnetic disk can hold as much data as several file cabinets. Thus, damage to the single disk can result in the loss of a large quantity of valuable accounting data.

On the one hand, a computer's involvement in a company's accounting system often has a positive impact. On the other hand, this involvement does not necessarily mean that the accounting information generated by computers is correct. To increase the likelihood that processed accounting data are accurate and complete, the company must design and implement computer control procedures.

The major objectives of an organization's controls over its data processing environment are to provide reasonable assurance that (1) development of, and changes to, computer programs are authorized, tested, and approved before their usage, and (2) access to data files is restricted to authorized users and programs. These objectives are referred to as **general computer control objectives** because they affect many computerized accounting activities. To achieve the general computer control objectives, an organization should design and implement a cost-effective package of general controls. To examine the nature of these controls, we will look at five types of general controls within IT environments: (1) personnel controls; (2) file security controls; (3) fault-tolerant systems, backup, and contingency planning; (4) computer facility controls; and (5) access to computer files.

Personnel Controls

An AIS depends heavily on people for the initial creation of the system, the input of data into the system, the supervision of data processing during computer operations, the distribution of processed data to authorized recipients, and the use of approved controls to ensure that the aforementioned tasks are performed properly. General controls within IT environments that affect personnel include (1) separation of duties, (2) use of computer accounts, and (3) informal knowledge of employees.

Separation of Duties   Chapter 9 indicated that the separation of duties concept is important in IT environments. Within these environments, separation of duties should be designed and implemented in two ways: (1) *separate* accounting and information processing subsystems, or departments, from the other subsystems, or departments, and (2) *separate* the responsibilities within the IT environment.

Separate Accounting and Information Processing from Other Subsystems

An organization's accounting and information processing subsystems are support functions for the other organizational subsystems and should be independent, or separate, from the subsystems that *use* data (accumulated by the accounting function and processed by the information processing subsystem) and *perform* the various operational activities. To achieve this separation, the functional design indicated in Figure 10-1 should exist within organizations.

Separate Responsibilities within IT Environment

Highly integrated AISs often combine procedures that used to be performed by separate individuals. Consequently, an individual who has unlimited access to the computer, its programs, and live data could have the opportunity to execute a fraud and subsequently conceal the fraud. To reduce the risk of this happening, a company should design and implement effective *separation of duties* control procedures. Figure 10-2 describes several functions within a company's IT environment where it is essential to have the *authority* and *responsibility* for these functions clearly divided.

The design and implementation of effective separation-of-duties control procedures makes it difficult for any one employee to commit a successful fraudulent activity. However, detecting fraud is more difficult when two or more individuals *collude* to override separation-of-duties control procedures, as illustrated in Case-in-Point 10.1.

> *Case-in-Point 10.1*   Two women working for a credit card company colluded to steal funds. One woman was authorized to establish credit card accounts, while the other woman was authorized to write off unpaid accounts of less than $1,000. The woman who established

---

1. User subsystems initiate and authorize all systems changes and transactions.
2. Asset custody resides with designated operational subsystems.
3. Corrections for errors detected in processing data are entered on an error log, referred back to the specific user subsystem for correction, and subsequently followed up on by the *data control group* (discussed shortly).
4. Changes to existing systems as well as all new systems require a formal written authorization from the user subsystem.

FIGURE 10−1   Functional design to separate accounting and information processing subsystems from other subsystems.

1. *Systems Analysis Function.* It involves analyzing information and processing needs as well as designing or modifying application programs. The person performing systems analysis functions should not perform other related functions. For example, a programmer for a bank should not be allowed to use actual data to test her program for processing loan payments. If she were allowed to use actual data, she could conceivably erase her own car loan balance while conducting the test.

2. *Data Control Function.* This function is achieved through the use of a **data control group.** In addition to data control groups following up on user subsystem error corrections, as mentioned in point 3 of Figure 10-1, they also perform functions such as maintaining registers of computer access codes, helping in the acquisition of new accounting software or the enhancement of existing accounting software, coordinating security controls with specific computer personnel (such as the database administrator), reconciling input and output, and distributing output to authorized users. The data control group should be organizationally independent of computer operations. The data control function inhibits unauthorized access to the computer facility and contributes to more efficient data processing operations.

3. *Programming Function.* Program changes should require formal authorizations. A written description of these changes should be submitted to a supervising manager for approval. In addition, modifications to programs should be completely tested prior to their implementation.

4. *Computer Operations Function.* Computer operators should be rotated among jobs to avoid having any single operator always overseeing the running of the same application. Furthermore, they should not have access to program documentation or logic. Ideally, two operators should be in the computer room during the processing of data. A processing log should be maintained and periodically reviewed for evidence of irregularities. Without these control procedures, for example, a computer operator processing the payroll could alter the program to increase his salary.

5. *Transaction Authorization Function.* With each batch of input data, user subsystems should submit a signed form to verify that the input data have been authorized and that the proper batch control totals have been compiled. Data control group personnel should verify the signatures and batch control totals before submitting the input data for computer processing. These control procedures should, for example, prevent a payroll clerk from successfully submitting an unauthorized form to increase his pay rate.

6. *AIS Library Function.* The AIS librarian should maintain custody of files, databases, and computer programs in a separate storage area called the AIS library. As a means of separating the custody and operations functions, access to files, databases, and programs for usage purposes should be limited to authorized operators at scheduled times or with user authorization. The AIS librarian should maintain records of all usage. The librarian himself should not have computer access privileges. On a regular basis, the records should be reviewed by data control group personnel for evidence of unauthorized computer access.

FIGURE 10-2 Functions within IT environment where authority and responsibility should be divided.

credit card accounts simply created a new account for each of the women by using fictitious data. When the amounts outstanding in their accounts neared the $1,000 limit, the woman in collections wrote the accounts off. The woman authorized to set up credit card accounts would then create two new cards, and the process would be repeated. The women were caught when a jilted boyfriend of one of them sought revenge by calling the credit card company and disclosing the fraudulent scheme.

Use of Computer Accounts Most computer systems (e.g., network systems such as LANs or WANs) maintain a system of separate *computer accounts* that are assigned to users on either an individual or a group basis. Usually, each account is assigned a unique password. When the user logs onto the computer, the system checks the password against a master list of accounts. Only users with current passwords are permitted access to further computer resources. The account numbers assigned to users are also used for accumulating computer charges. This control procedure is important when computer resources are scarce or there is some fear that computer time may be used for unauthorized uses.

When a user is trying to gain access to the computer system from a remote terminal, a *callback procedure* may be used. After the user enters the password, the connection is broken. The computer uses an automatic dialback device to call back the authorized phone number for the terminal that has logged on. Failure to reconnect indicates that someone has attempted access from an unauthorized terminal.

A further use of computer accounts is to limit user access to particular computer files or programs. This protects certain files or programs from unauthorized use. In addition, it is possible to place resource limitations on account numbers, for example, limiting the user to so much connect time, so much disk space, and so much CPU time. This controls against such accidental errors as when a programmer accidentally throws the computer into an endless loop.

Informal Knowledge of Employees   An informal knowledge of employees and their activities can be an important clue in the detection of fraudulent activity, as demonstrated in Case-in-Point 10.2.

> *Case-in-Point 10.2*   The manager of a Midwestern company became suspicious when he found out that one of his employees took expensive vacations in Acapulco, Mexico every year. An investigation revealed that the employee had been embezzling thousands of dollars from the company.

File Security Controls

It is essential that an AIS safeguard its computer files (such as data stored on a magnetic disk) from both accidental and intentional errors. Figure 10-3 describes several reasons for these safeguards.

---

1. The computer files are not human-readable. Controls must be installed to ensure that these files *can* be read when necessary.
2. The typical computer file contains a vast amount of data. In general, it is not possible to reconstruct such files from the memories of employees.
3. The data contained on computer files are in a very compact format. The destruction of as little as one inch of recording medium means the loss of thousands of characters of data.
4. The data stored on computer files are permanent only to the extent that tiny bits have been recorded on the recording tracks. Power disruptions, power surges, and even accidentally dropping a disk pack, for example, may cause damage.
5. The data stored on computer files may be confidential. Information such as advertising plans, competitive bidding plans, payroll figures, and innovative software programs must be protected from unwarranted use.
6. The reconstruction of file data is costly no matter how extensive a company's recovery procedures. It is usually more cost-effective to protect against file abuse than to depend on backup procedures for file protection.
7. File information itself should be considered an asset of a company. As such, it deserves the same protection accorded other organizational assets.

FIGURE 10–3   Reasons for safeguarding computer files from both accidental and intentional errors.

1. *External file labels* identify the contents of a computer file and help to prevent an individual from, for example, accidentally writing over a disk file.
2. *Internal file labels* record the name of a file, the date the file was created, and other identifying data on the file medium that will be read and verified by the computer. Internal file labels include *header labels* and *trailer labels*. A header label is a file description recorded at the beginning of a file, whereas a trailer label indicates the end of a file and contains summary data regarding the contents of the file.
3. *Lock-out procedures* are utilized by database management systems to prevent two applications from updating the same record or data item at the same time.
4. *File protection rings* permit data to be written on a magnetic tape computer file. Upon removing the ring, the data on the tape are protected from accidental writeovers.
5. The *read-only file designation* is used to earmark data available for reading only. The data within a file cannot be altered by users, nor can new data be stored on the file.

FIGURE 10−4   Examples of file security control procedures.

The purpose of file security controls is to protect computer files from either accidental or intentional abuse. This requires control procedures to make sure that computer programs use the correct files for data processing. Control procedures are also needed for the purpose of creating backup copies of critical files in the event that original copies of a file are lost, stolen, damaged, or vandalized. Figure 10-4 provides examples of file security control procedures to verify that the correct file is being updated and to prevent accidental destruction of files. It should be noted that file security control procedure number 4 in Figure 10-4 concerns itself with *magnetic tape* as a storage medium for a computer file. Magnetic tape is a secondary storage device that can be used for storing computer file data. However, largely because of its slowness in handling data compared to other secondary storage devices (such as magnetic disks, floppy disks, CD-ROMs, and DVDs), magnetic tape is rarely used in industry today.

Fault-Tolerant Systems, Backup, and Contingency Planning

Many of the control procedures discussed in this chapter are designed and implemented with the objective of reducing financial risk. **Financial risk** is the chance that a company's financial statements are misstated. Misstatement might arise as a result of such things as carrying assets on the balance sheet that no longer exist, overstating income, or understating expenses. Another risk that control procedures seek to reduce is business risk. **Business risk** (originally defined in Chapter 2) refers to the likelihood that an adverse occurrence or unwanted event that could be injurious to an organization will occur. Fault-tolerant systems (discussed below), adequate backup of data stored in an AIS (also discussed below), and **contingency planning** (which, for our purposes, is defined as planning for events that could impede the data processing function) are examples of controls designed to mitigate or reduce business risk.

Many of us have had the unpleasant experience of inadequately backing up data stored in a computer or on a diskette. For companies, the loss of data can cause severe interruption of business and loss of income. Unforeseen circumstances do arise, and organizations as well as individuals need to guard against them. Backup is a specific activity that results from contingency planning.

Fault-Tolerant Systems   In the study of engineering, students learn about **fault-tolerant systems.** These are systems designed to tolerate faults or errors. Engineers recognize that errors do occur, and they plan for them. Fault-tolerant systems are often based on the concept of *redundancy.* For example, although an airplane can fly with only two engines, it has four engines so that if one or two of them fail, the plane will continue to fly.

Many organizations implement a high degree of fault tolerance in their computer systems because computer failures can corrupt data and completely disrupt operations. For example, computer networks can be made fault-tolerant by instituting duplicate communication paths and communications processors. Two major approaches to redundant central processing unit (CPU) *processing* are as follows:

1. Systems with **consensus-based protocols** contain an odd number of processors; if one processor disagrees with the others, it is thereafter ignored.

2. Some systems use a second **watchdog processor;** if something happens to the first processor, the watchdog processor then takes over the processing work.

Disks can be made fault-tolerant through a process called **disk mirroring** (also referred to as **disk shadowing**). This process involves writing all data in parallel to two disks. Should one disk fail, the application program being run can automatically continue by using the good disk. At the transaction level, a fault-tolerant system can be implemented using, for example, rollback processing. Under **rollback processing,** transactions are never written to disk until they are complete. Should there be a power failure or should another fault occur while a transaction is being written, the database program, at its first opportunity, automatically *rolls* itself back to its prefault state.

Backup   Backup is similar to redundancy in creating fault-tolerant systems. Suppose you have written an important research paper for a class and give that paper to the instructor for grading purposes. Keeping a copy of the paper for yourself is a good idea in case your instructor loses it or the school burns down. If you were writing the research paper on a computer, you would be wise to back up your hard disk on a diskette in case your hard disk becomes corrupted. You have thus created *redundancy* so that a fault or an error will not cause the system (or you!) to fail.

Because of the risk of losing data before, during, or after processing work, companies should establish backup procedures for their files. The backup and reconstruction procedure typically used under *batch processing* is called the **grandfather-parent-child** procedure, as illustrated in Figure 10-5 for processing transactions to update a company's general ledger.

Three generations of *reference data* (i.e., previously processed data stored on master files) are retained with the transaction data used during the general ledger updating process. If the most recent master file, the "child" copy, is destroyed, the data are reconstructed by rerunning the pertinent transaction data against the prior copy of the reference data (the "parent" master file). Should a problem occur during this reconstruction run, there is still one more set of backup data (the "grandfather" master file) to reconstruct the parent. The "parent" master file is then used to reconstruct the "child" master file.

Backup and reconstruction procedures are also used under *real-time processing.* This is illustrated in Figure 10-6 for processing transactions to update an organization's general ledger. During processing, the reference data (master file) are periodically

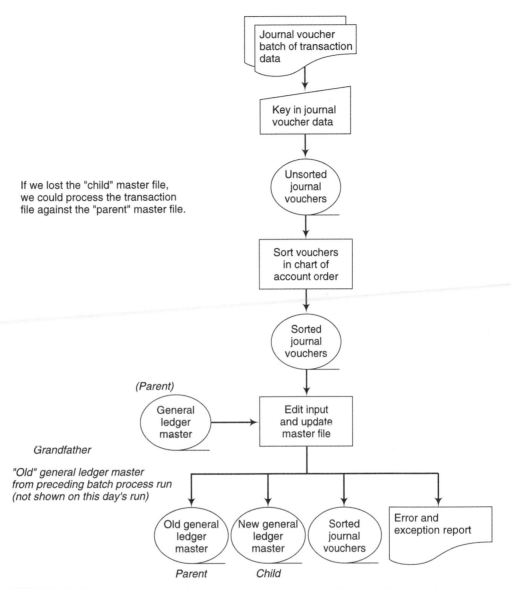

If we lost the "child" master file,
we could process the transaction
file against the "parent" master file.

(Parent)

Grandfather

*"Old" general ledger master
from preceding batch process run
(not shown on this day's run)*

FIGURE 10–5 Grandfather-parent-child procedure under batch processing.

copied on a backup medium such as magnetic tape. A copy of all transaction data is stored as a *transaction log* as these data are entered into the system. The backup copies are then stored at a remote site. Storing backup copies at a remote site allows data to be recovered in the event a disaster occurs that affects a company's data processing center. (Through a process called **electronic vaulting,** the data on backup tapes can be electronically transmitted to a remote site rather than physically delivering backup tapes to an off-site storage location.) Should the master file be destroyed or damaged, computer operations will *roll back* to the most recent backup copy of the master file. Recovery is then achieved by reprocessing the contents of the data transaction log against this master file backup copy.

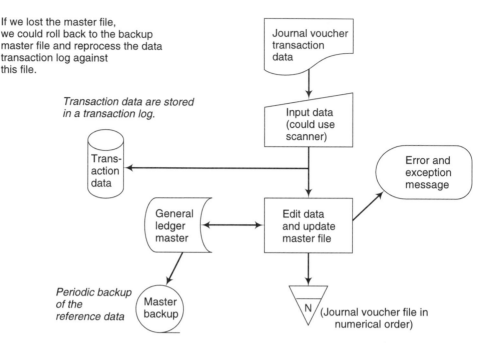

If we lost the master file, we could roll back to the backup master file and reprocess the data transaction log against this file.

Transaction data are stored in a transaction log.

Journal voucher transaction data

Input data (could use scanner)

Trans-action data

General ledger master

Edit data and update master file

Error and exception message

Periodic backup of the reference data

Master backup

N (Journal voucher file in numerical order)

FIGURE 10–6   Grandfather-parent-child procedure under real-time processing.

Redundancy in data processing is not limited to the backup of data files. Hardware and electrical power are also likely to be backed up or *redundant,* to use the terminology of fault-tolerant systems. As will be discussed later, a good disaster recovery plan includes backups for hardware. With regard to electrical power backup, surge protectors provide protection in the case of short, intermittent power shortages or failures. However, large data processing centers may require additional generators for backup power. As an example of a method to minimize system downtime should a power problem occur, an **uninterruptible power system (UPS)** can be employed. UPS is an auxiliary power supply that can smooth the flow of power to the computer, thereby preventing the loss of data due to momentary surges or dips in power. Should a complete power failure occur, the UPS provides a backup power supply to keep the computer system functioning.

Contingency Planning   Contingency planning includes the development of a formal **disaster recovery plan.** Such a plan is necessary because a variety of unforeseen disasters could render a data processing center inoperational. Examples of these disasters include natural events such as fires, floods, and earthquakes, as well as manmade catastrophes such as the terrorist attack of September 11, 2001 on the World Trade Center in New York City.

A company's complete disaster recovery plan will describe procedures to be followed in the case of an emergency, as well as the role of every member of the *disaster recovery team* (which is made up of specific company employees). Regarding this team, the company's management should appoint one person to be in charge of disaster recovery and one person to be second-in-command.

Part of the disaster recovery plan specifies backup sites to be used for alternate computer processing. These backup sites may be other locations owned by the company, such as another branch of the same bank. Alternatively, these sites may be owned by other organizations and contracted for short-term periods in the event of a disaster. It is a good idea for the various hardware locations for data processing to be some distance away from the original processing sites in case a disaster affects a regional location. An example would be companies located near the San Andreas Fault in California. Since a severe earthquake could destroy the data processing centers of those companies within the earthquake area, organizations within this area should have disaster recovery arrangements with organizations located outside any area likely to be affected by an earthquake.

Disaster recovery sites may be either hot sites or cold sites. A **hot site** is a location that includes a computer system configured similarly to the system used regularly by the company for its data processing activities. A location that includes everything contained in a hot site *plus* up-to-date backup data and software is called a **flying-start site.** (This type of site is capable of assuming full data processing operations within a matter of seconds or minutes; thus, the term *flying-start.*) A **cold site** is a location where power and environmentally controlled space are available to install processing equipment on short notice. If a disaster recovery plan designates a cold site, then separate arrangements are also necessary to obtain computer equipment matching the configuration of equipment lost in the disaster. In practice, the type of disaster recovery site used by a company should be determined based on a *cost-benefit analysis.*

Simply preparing a disaster recovery plan does not provide assurance that the plan will work when needed. It is important to periodically test the disaster recovery plan thoroughly by simulating a disaster. Testing may reveal weaknesses in the plan that might otherwise have gone undiscovered if this testing had not been performed. As an example of what could happen when testing of a disaster recovery plan is not undertaken, a major virus was introduced in the recent past that brought down many companies' computers that were networked internationally. A few of these companies' computer centers found that some of the disaster recovery plan data required for recovery, such as phone numbers to call in the event of emergency, were stored only within the very computer systems rendered inoperable by the virus! Copies of a disaster recovery plan will not be of much use if they are located only in computer systems that are destroyed by a disaster. For this reason, members of a company's disaster recovery team should each keep an up-to-date copy of the plan at their homes. Finally, in addition to periodic testing, a disaster recovery plan should be reviewed on a *continuous* basis and revised where necessary. In fact, to emphasize the importance of an organization's disaster recovery planning process being performed on a continuous basis, this process is an integral part of many companies' planning activities referred to as *business continuity planning.*

Computer Facility Controls

Like any other investment, the physical assets of the data processing center (such as the CPU, the peripheral devices, and the disk files of the computer library) deserve protection. Destruction of, or damage to, these assets represents both a real danger and an important area of computer systems control. Physical loss can happen in only one of two ways: through accident or intent. Thus, current effort in the area of physical security is devoted to **computer facility controls** that prevent both unintentional and intentional harm.

Locate the Data Processing Center in a Safe Place

Case-in-Point 10.3 illustrates the importance of locating a company's data processing center in a safe place.

Case-in-Point 10.3 Several years ago, a disgruntled taxpayer decided to teach the Internal Revenue Service a lesson. First, the taxpayer walked to the outside of the IRS building where his tax forms had been processed. The unhappy man then proceeded to shoot at the agency's central processing unit through an open window with his 12-gauge shotgun!

Although some might argue that the major lesson to be learned from this story is that taxes are too high, there is also the suggestion that the data processing center of the typical organization should not be placed in a location that has easy public access. Thus, for most business data processors, the ground-floor showroom, once the desired location for many computer operations, has given way to separate buildings and other sites away from passageways that are easily accessible to employees or the public. Locations guarded by personnel are obviously the most preferred, but any placement that has a limited number of secured entrances is desirable.

The location of the data processing center should also guard against natural disasters (e.g., a fire). Although it is impossible to protect a computer completely from such hazards, advanced planning can minimize exposure to them. For example, companies can increase their protection from fires by locating computer facilities away from boiler rooms, heating furnaces, or fuel storage areas. Similarly, locating computer facilities on high ground or the upper stories of office buildings provides protection from floods. Finally, locating computer facilities in single-story buildings or in heavily reinforced ones can control earthquake damage.

Limit Employee Access

Few people have reason to be *inside* the data processing center. Once the computer software has been fully developed, implementation can proceed smoothly through the computer operators' use of documentation manuals. Therefore, executives, data-entry personnel, and company programmers have little reason to enter a data processing center.

Facility controls discourage potential mischief-makers. One facility control is to require company personnel to wear *color-coded identification badges* with full-face pictures. Only people authorized to enter the data processing center would be assigned an identification badge of a particular color. Modern security badges, in addition to including full-face pictures, also incorporate magnetic, electric, or optical codes that can be read only by special badge-reading devices. With advanced identification (ID) techniques, it is possible to have each employee's entry into and exit from the data processing center automatically recorded in a computer log, which would be periodically reviewed by supervisory personnel.

Another facility control is to place a *guard* at the entrance to the data processing center; the door to the center is self-locking and can be "buzzed" open only by the control person, who permits only authorized personnel to enter. Finally, the issuance of keys to authorized personnel or the use of dial-lock combinations limits access to the data processing center. With regard to this last control, it is also a good idea to change locks or lock combinations often and to use keys that cannot easily be duplicated.

Buy Insurance

Although the purchase of insurance is the first activity that occurs to many persons when computer controls are discussed, it is actually the protection of last resort. The reason is that insurance does not actually protect the purchaser from loss; rather, it merely compensates for such losses when they occur.

Insurance policies for computer damages are usually limited in coverage and may not reimburse policyholders for such occurrences as civil disorder, acts of God, or employee larceny. Furthermore, compensation usually is restricted to the actual losses suffered by a company. As you may imagine, a fair estimate of what these actual losses entail is not an easy matter. Of special difficulty is placing dollar values on a company's computer equipment that has long since lost any real market value, yet performs vital data processing services for the company.

Access to Computer Files

An important type of general control involves access to computer files. Here, we are not referring to physical access but rather to "logical access" or usage, for example, via a remote terminal. Such logical access would permit a user to call for printouts of sensitive corporate data (e.g., sales projections or executive salaries) and permit access to a company's software. Thus, regulating who is permitted logical access to computer files is an important general control in terms of safeguarding sensitive organizational data and software.

Remote terminals may be placed anywhere in the country and hooked up to a company's computer by means of ordinary telephone lines. (Some computer facilities have normal telephone numbers for this purpose.) As a result, it is difficult to safeguard logical computer access with direct physical surveillance of terminals. Most data processing centers therefore use secret **password codes** to restrict access. Such codes vary in length and type of password information required, but all have the same intent: to limit logical access to the computer only to those individuals authorized to have it.

Passwords are not a foolproof safeguard because they can be lost, given away, or stolen. Certain precautions can improve their effectiveness (e.g., changing passwords on a frequent basis). The importance of frequent password changes is reflected in Case-in-Point 10.4.

> *Case-in-Point 10.4* Based on the need for tighter security over its computer files, the Hartford Insurance Company recently implemented a 60-day password change frequency for all logon IDs in all environments, replacing the 99-day frequency that had been in place for several years. Corporate Information Security personnel initially introduced this change in the mainframe environments. Upon completing the password change within the mainframe environments, it was then implemented for all mid-tier and LAN administrators.

Security can be increased significantly, for instance, if a user is required to have both an ID card (with information such as name, ID number, and picture) and a password before obtaining access to a computer system. However, even the most elaborate security system can be broken easily if the computer "thief" has obtained the important information necessary for computer access. This is illustrated in Case-in-Point 10.5.

> *Case-in-Point 10.5* Not too long ago, a hacker broke into Motorola Corporation's computer system by calling the help desk and telling the person at the desk telephone that he was an employee of Motorola working at home who had forgotten his ID card (which generated random passwords that change every few seconds). The help desk employee believed him and let him into the corporate network. On a positive note, the hacker did no permanent damage to the corporation's computer system.

A very effective ID approach for safeguarding logical computer access bases user recognition on **biometric identifications.** Under this approach, biometric identification devices *identify* distinctive user physical characteristics such as voice patterns, fingerprints, facial patterns and features, retina prints, body odor, signature dynamics, and keyboarding methods (i.e., the way a user types certain groups of characters). When an individual wants to access a company's computer system, her biometric identifications are matched against those accumulated within the computer. A match must occur in order for the individual to be given access to the computer system.

APPLICATION CONTROLS WITHIN IT ENVIRONMENTS

Whereas *general controls* focus on the framework within which accounting systems operate, *application controls* are concerned with preventing, detecting, and correcting errors and irregularities in transactions that are processed within an IT environment. The three major stages of data processing work are accumulating the *input data, processing* the data, and accumulating the processed data in some form of *output* (e.g., a performance report).

Various application control procedures for AISs are now discussed and illustrated based on these three stages. Thus, application controls over data input (called *input controls*) are examined first, application controls over the processing of data (called *processing controls*) are analyzed second, and application controls over data output (called *output controls*) are surveyed third. Figure 10-7 emphasizes the important point that a company's application controls consist of input, processing, and output controls.

Since every company's system is somewhat different, each company must consider the risk of errors and irregularities going undetected in processing its accounting data within an IT environment. The company must then design and implement its own cost-effective package of input, processing, and output application controls.

Input Controls

In many organizations, the stage of data processing having the most human involvement is the input stage. As a result, the *risk* of undetected errors and irregularities is typically higher in this data processing stage compared to the processing and output

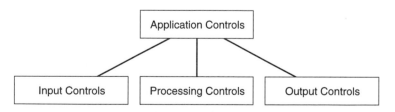

FIGURE 10-7   The composition of a company's application controls.

stages. In an attempt to reduce this risk factor, the strongest package of application controls is commonly found within the input stage of data processing.

Input controls attempt to ensure the validity, accuracy, and completeness of the data entered into an AIS. In data processing work, it is desirable to test input data for the attributes of validity, accuracy, and completeness as early as possible. There are at least five reasons for this test:

1. Data that are rejected at the time they are input can be more easily corrected, for example, by reference to a source document.

2. Data that have been transcribed accurately are not necessarily good data, merely data that have been copied correctly. Further data testing is useful.

3. It is not cost-effective to screen accounting data continuously throughout the processing cycles of an AIS. Past some point in the data processing work, all data are considered valid and error-free.

4. It is vital that an AIS not use inaccurate data in later data processing operations. This protects master files from inaccuracies and safeguards computer processing in subsequent stages of the data processing work.

5. An AIS cannot provide good information if it does not start with good data. The alternative is *GIGO-garbage in, garbage out.*

For discussion purposes, it is convenient to divide the topic of input application controls into three categories: (1) observation, recording, and transcription of data; (2) edit tests; and (3) additional input controls.

Observation, Recording, and Transcription of Data

In general, data enter an AIS through the recording of business transactions. An organization often finds it useful to install one or more observation control procedures to assist in collecting data that are recorded within an AIS.

One such observation control procedure is the introduction of a *feedback mechanism.* A common example of a feedback mechanism for collecting data would be the use of a confirmation slip in the preparation of a sales order. With such a mechanism, a salesperson might prepare a sales invoice and present the completed source document to the customer for approval. The customer confirms the order with a signature, thereby attesting to the accuracy and completeness of the data contained within the sales invoice.

The data observation process can also make use of *dual observation.* Under this control procedure, the accuracy of the data observation process is enhanced because more than one employee is involved in the process. In some organizations, the dual observation control procedure is *supervisory.* Here, the supervisor of the employee (or employees) involved in collecting data is required to confirm the accuracy of the data gathered by the employee.

Once accounting data have been collected, they must be recorded. Data collection and the subsequent recording of these data are areas in which a great deal of automation has taken place. For example, the use of *point-of-sale (POS) devices* (such as *bar code readers* that interpret the universal product code—UPC—commonly printed on store products and *smart cash registers* that are connected to offsite computers) to encode data has been found to lessen substantially the error rate in the recording process as well as to eliminate the expense involved in *transcribing the data* to machine-readable formats (*machine* refers to the computer).

In some instances, automated data collection and recording are not feasible, and an initial source document must be prepared manually. To encourage accuracy in the data collection and recording processes in these situations, several control procedures are possible. One example is to use *preprinted recording forms,* such as the inventory receipts form illustrated in Figure 10-8. In general, these forms ensure that all the data required for processing have been collected and also enhance accuracy in the recording process. For example, the exact number of spaces required for such field items as the inventory part number and the supplier account number is clear because a box has been provided for each numerical digit, thus guarding against the loss or addition of digits in these fields.

Performing **data transcription** refers to preparing data for computerized processing. In AISs, data should be organized on source documents in such a way as to facilitate the transcription process. Thus, well-designed, preprinted source-document forms are an important input control because they encourage adherence to the general principle of source-document/computer-input compatibility.

In an IT environment that employs either an online hard disk or diskettes in the data transcription process, the user typically sits at a workstation consisting of a keyboard and a display terminal screen. One important input control procedure is the use of *preformatted screens* to assist in the data transcription process. A preformatted screen is much the same as the preprinted recording form discussed earlier, except that it is shown on the display terminal screen instead of printed on paper. A special type of preformatted screen makes use of a *mask.* For input purposes, a mask is a set of blinking boxes on the screen with each box the size of a single input character. As the user inputs data, the boxes on the screen are replaced with the input characters.

Edit Tests Programs or subroutines within an IT environment that check the validity and accuracy of input data after the data have been entered and recorded on a machine-readable file are called **input validation routines** (or **edit programs**). The specific types of validity and accuracy checks that input validation routines per-

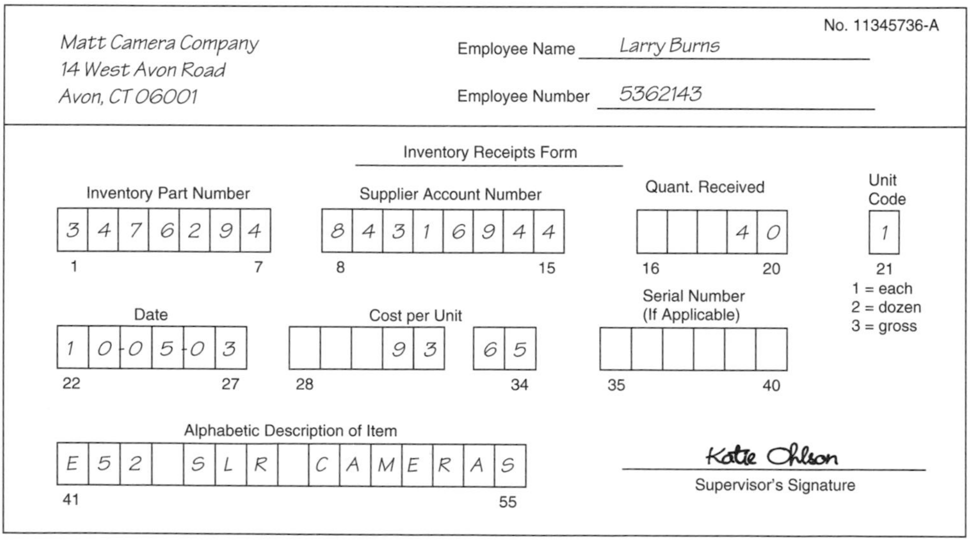

Matt Camera Company
14 West Avon Road
Avon, CT 06001

No. 11345736-A

Employee Name Larry Burns

Employee Number 5362143

Inventory Receipts Form

Inventory Part Number: 3 4 7 6 2 9 4 (1–7)

Supplier Account Number: 8 4 3 1 6 9 4 4 (8–15)

Quant. Received: 4 0 (16–20)

Unit Code: 1 (21)
1 = each
2 = dozen
3 = gross

Date: 1 0-0 5-0 3 (22–27)

Cost per Unit: 9 3 6 5 (28–34)

Serial Number (If Applicable): (35–40)

Alphabetic Description of Item: E 5 2 S L R C A M E R A S (41–55)

Katie Ohlson
Supervisor's Signature

FIGURE 10–8 A preprinted recording form for inventory receipts.

form are referred to as *edit tests* (or *edit checks*). **Edit tests** examine selected fields of input data and reject those transactions (or other types of data input) whose data fields do not meet the preestablished standards of data quality.

In real-time processing systems, edit tests are performed during the data-entry process. Under batch processing systems, as illustrated in Figure 10-9, edit tests are executed by a separate edit program before regular data processing. Examples of edit tests are listed in Figure 10-10.

Edit tests can also be coordinated in what is called a *redundant data check* to ensure data accuracy. The idea is to encode repetitious data on a file or transaction record, thereby enabling a later processing test to compare the two data items for compatibility. For example, a candy company could use both a numeric code designator and an alphabetic code designator to represent the same inventory item. The computer program performing the inventory processing would maintain a master list of numeric and alphabetic designators. If, in a transaction, the inventory code number 75642 (representing chocolate caramels) were encoded incorrectly with the alphabetic designator

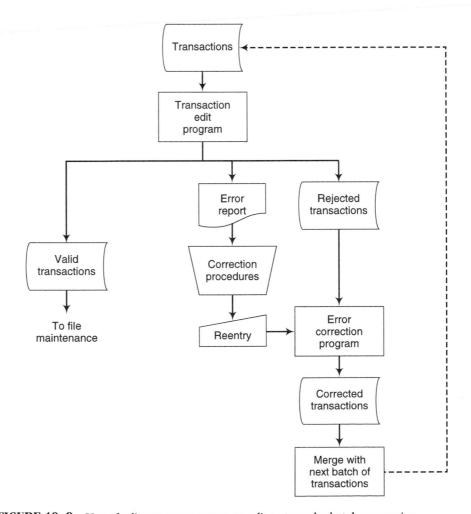

FIGURE 10-9   Use of edit program to execute edit tests under batch processing.

1. *Tests of numeric field content*, which make sure that such data fields as social security number, sales invoice number, and date contain only numbers.
2. *Tests of alphabetic field content*, which make sure such fields as customer name contain only alphabetic letters.
3. *Tests of alphanumeric field content*, which make sure that fields such as inventory parts descriptions contain letters and/or numbers, but no special characters.
4. *Tests for valid codes* (e.g., 1 = cash sale; 2 = credit sale).
5. *Tests of reasonableness* (e.g., total hours worked by an employee during a weekly pay period does not exceed 50).
6. *Tests of sign* (e.g., paycheck amounts always positive).
7. *Tests of completeness*, which check that there are no blanks in fields requiring data.
8. *Tests of sequence*, which make sure that successive input data are in some prescribed order (e.g., ascending, descending, chronological, or alphabetical).
9. *Tests of consistency* (e.g., that all transactions for the same sales office have the same office code number).

FIGURE 10–10   Examples of edit tests.

"VC" (standing for vanilla caramels), the transaction would be rejected because the two different designators for supposedly the same inventory item failed to match.

Additional Input Controls   It is possible for a data field to pass all of the edit tests previously described and still be invalid. To illustrate, a bank might use the incorrect account number 537627 (instead of the proper account number 537621) when processing a customer's transaction. When the incorrect account number is keyed into a remote terminal and submitted to edit tests, it will, for example, (1) pass a test of numeric field content ensuring that all digits were numeric, (2) pass a test of reasonableness ensuring that the account number itself fell within a valid range of values (e.g., account number greater than 100,000 and less than 800,000), (3) pass a test of sign (i.e., account number positive), and (4) pass a test of completeness (i.e., no blanks in fields).

Thus, it is apparent that additional control procedures are required for this error to be detected. One control procedure is to incorporate an *unfound-record test* into the data processing routine used to update the master file of bank records. With this approach, any transaction for which there is no corresponding master file record would be recognized as invalid and rejected from the transaction sequence (it would be returned for correction). But what if a master file record did exist for account 537627—the incorrect account number? This would indeed be unfortunate because our "unfound-record" control procedure would not detect the error, and, what is even worse, the legitimate master file record with account number 537627 would be updated with the transaction data generated by another customer.

Continuing with our bank example, an alternative to this unfound-record test is to expand the six-digit data field of customer bank account numbers to seven digits with *a check-digit control procedure*. Normally, the check digit is computed as a mathematical function of the other digits in a numeric field, and its sole purpose is to test the validity of the associated data. To illustrate, consider the original (correct) account number 537621. The sum of these six digits is $5 + 3 + 7 + 6 + 2 + 1 = 24$. One type of check digit would append the low-order digit of this sum (4) to the account number. The seven-digit value 5376214 would be used instead of the six-digit series 537621 to represent the account number. The computer program would duplicate this computational procedure at the time of data access, and therefore validate the accuracy of the data before the transaction data were used to update a master file record.

A check digit does not guarantee data validity. For example, the check-digit procedure described here would be unable to distinguish between the correct account number 5376214 and the transposed number 5736214 because the transposition of digits does not affect the sum. There are, however, check-digit techniques that do include "ordering of digits" in the construction of check-digit values. An example of one of these techniques is the **Modulus 11 technique.** Through this technique, the check digit is calculated by subtracting the sum of the digit products from the next highest multiple of **11.** An example to illustrate the calculation of a check digit under the Modulus 11 technique is provided in Figure 10-11.

Processing Controls

Processing controls focus on the manipulation of accounting data after they are input to the computer system. An important objective of processing controls is to contribute to a good audit trail. A clear audit trail is essential, for example, to enable individual transactions to be traced, to provide documentation for changes in general ledger account balances, to prepare financial reports, and to correct errors in

Let's assume that in preparing the Alan Company's biweekly payroll, two of the employees have the following payroll numbers: 3478 and 3748. To utilize the Modulus 11 technique for our check-digit control procedure, we determine the check-digit value for an employee's payroll number by applying an algorithm based on each employee's four digits. The calculation below shows under the Modulus 11 technique how we arrived at the check-digit value of 9 to append to the payroll number 3478 to come up with the employee's new payroll number using the Modulus 11 technique.

Four digits of employee number:	3	4	7	8
Weighting factors:	5	4	3	2
Digit products:	15	16	21	16
Sum of digit products:				68
Next higher multiple of 11 (11 × 7):				77
Check digit (difference of above two numbers):				9
Employee's new payroll number:				34789

Validation involves having the computer recompute the check digit, using the same algorithm by which this digit was predetermined. The computer then compares the result of the recomputation to the original keyed-in value. If a particular payroll transaction involves the correct employee number 34789 and this number was properly keyed into the system, the algorithm will generate a 9 as the check digit. Since the digit 9 is the same as the last digit on the employee payroll number, the computer accepts the number as correct. On the other hand, if the incorrect number 37489 is entered by mistake for the above payroll transaction (the digits 3748 represent the four digits of the other employee's payroll number before a check digit is added), the check digit generated by the algorithm will be 6, computed as follows: $(3 \times 5) + (7 \times 4) + (4 \times 3) + (8 \times 2) = 71$. The next highest multiple of 11 is 77: 77 minus 71 = 6. Since this check digit of 6 is not the same as the last digit on the entered number (which is a 9), the employee payroll number 37489 will be rejected by the computer as incorrect.

FIGURE 10-11   Illustration of Modulus 11 technique for calculating a check digit.

transactions. To achieve a good audit trail, processing procedures should require that a printed *transaction listing* be prepared during each file-updating run by batch processing systems and at the end of every day by online processing systems.

Furthermore, a unique and sequentially assigned transaction reference designator should be used to identify each transaction in a listing. These transaction reference designators should be posted to the general ledger account records and recorded on the specific source documents pertaining to the transactions. Figure 10-12 illustrates an audit trail for a computer-based system, showing how source documents can be easily located by tracing back from an activity (or proof) listing, which is discussed shortly under output controls.

Our remaining discussion of processing controls is divided into two parts: (1) those controls related to processing at the time of *data access* and (2) those controls that primarily involve *data manipulation* at a later phase in the processing activities.

Data-Access Controls   Suppose you were the data processing manager at a bank. The transactions each day consist of a large number of checks written by the bank's 100,000 customers. These checks are magnetically encoded pieces of paper of varying length and width. The account number and bank number are precoded magnetically on the checks, and the amount of each check itself is later encoded by one of the bank's clerical staff after the check has been presented to the bank for payment. The problem: how to make sure that all these checks are correctly processed by the computer.

Control Totals   One common processing control procedure that addresses the above problem is to batch the checks in separate bundles of, for example, 100, 150, or 200 checks and prepare a special *batch control document* to serve as a control on the contents of each bundle. The information on this document might include the bundle number, today's date, and the total dollar amount for the checks themselves. The total dollar amount represents the *batch control total*. When computer processing commences, the special information on the lead control record (i.e., the batch control document) is accessed first and the batch control total is stored in computer memory. As the checks are accessed individually, their amounts are also accumulated in computer memory. Once all the checks in the batch have been read, the accumulated total is compared with the batch control total. A match signals acceptable processing. A nonmatch signals an error, which may then be traced either to an error in the batch control total or to some difficulty in the processing itself (e.g., the inability of the MICR reader to understand the data on one or more checks).

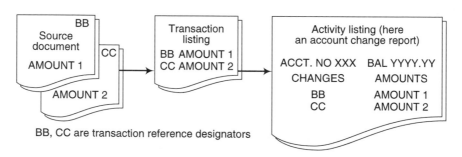

FIGURE 10–12   An audit trail for a computer-based system.

A control total such as the one discussed in this example involves a dollar amount and is therefore called a *financial control total.* Other examples of financial control totals include the sum of cash receipts in an accounts receivable application, the sum of cash disbursements in an accounts payable application, and the sum of net pay in a payroll application. AISs also use *nonfinancial control totals,* which compute nondollar sums, for example, the sum of the total number of hours worked by employees.

Control totals do not have to make sense to be useful. For example, when cash receipts from accounts receivable customers are being processed by a company's accountant, the sum of the customers' account numbers in a batch of transactions might be computed to form a *hash total.* This sum is meaningless except for control purposes (which is the idea behind the hash total). The computed hash total figure is only useful as a check against an "internal" tally of this same hash total by the computer at the time of data access.

Another type of control total often used by data processing facilities is the *record count.* With this control procedure, the number of transaction items is counted twice: once when preparing transactions in a batch and again when actually performing the data processing.

Data Manipulation Controls   Once data have been validated by earlier portions of data processing, they usually must be manipulated (i.e., processed) in some way by computer programs to produce useful output. One processing control procedure is to make sure that the computer programs are complete and thorough in their data manipulation. Ordinarily, this is accomplished by examining *software documentation.* System flowcharts, program flowcharts, data flow diagrams, and decision tables can also function as controls because they help systems analysts do a thorough job in planning data processing functions.

After computer programs have been coded, they are translated into machine language by an error-testing *compiler.* The compiler controls the possibility that a computer program contains programming language errors. A computer program can also be tested with specially designed *test data* that expose the program to all the exception conditions likely to occur during its actual use. The subject of test data is examined in Chapter 12.

Whereas test data are used to examine the processing capabilities of a single computer program, *system testing* is used to test the interaction of several computer programs in a job stream. In AISs, the output from one computer program is often the input to another. Thus, system testing is an important processing control for AISs because it tests not only the processing capabilities of individual programs, but also the linkages between these programs. Techniques for system testing are beyond the scope of this text and will therefore not be examined here.

Output Controls

Once data have been processed internally by a computer system, they are usually transferred to some form of output medium for storage or, in the case of printed output, prepared as a report. The objective of **output controls** is to ensure the output's validity, accuracy, and completeness. Two major types of output application controls within IT environments are (1) validating processing results and (2) regulating the distribution and use of printed output.

Validating Processing Results   As an example of validating processing results, the validity, accuracy, and completeness of computerized output in AISs can be established through the preparation of *activity (or proof) listings* that document processing activity. (A simplified activity listing was illustrated in Figure 10-12.) These listings provide complete, detailed information about all changes to master files and thus contribute to a good audit trail. Organizational employees use such activity listings to trace file changes back to the events or documents that triggered these changes and thereby verify current file information or printed information as valid, accurate, and complete output.

Regulating Distribution and Use of Printed Output   One of the more compelling aspects of output control deals with the subject of *forms control.* Perhaps the most interesting situations involve computerized check-writing applications in which MICR forms or perforated printer forms become the encoding media for preparing a company's checks. Usually, these forms are preprinted with the company's name, address, and bank account number. Control over the forms associated with check writing is obviously vital.

The most common type of control utilized with computer-generated check-writing procedures is the coordination of a preprinted check number on the printer form with a computer-generated number that is linked on the same form at print time. The numbers on these *prenumbered forms* advance sequentially and are prepared by the forms' supplier according to the specifications of an organization. The computer-generated numbers also run sequentially and are initialized by adding 1 to the check sequence number stored from the last processing run. The numbers on the prenumbered forms and the computer-generated numbers should match during normal processing. Discrepancies should be examined carefully and the causes fully resolved.

Cash-disbursement checks are not the only type of printer form using preprinted numbering as a control mechanism. Almost any type of printer form that can be burst (i.e., separated) should be prenumbered and therefore controlled. Other examples of forms that enjoy a special control advantage when prenumbered include reports containing sensitive corporate information and computer-generated lottery and athletic event tickets.

Another dimension of output control concerns *report distribution.* Computer reports often contain sensitive information, and it is important that such information be restricted. Thus, for example, a payroll register, indicating the earnings of each employee during a given pay period, is a type of report whose distribution should be restricted.

The most common approach to distributional control is through an *authorized distribution list.* For each output report, the computer facility keeps a list of authorized users and prepares only enough copies of the report to satisfy the number of users on this list. Where data processing activities are centralized, it is sometimes possible to have a representative from each user group physically visit the computer facility to pick up a copy of a sensitive report. In these instances, a notebook, or log, of pickups can be maintained and the pickup employee asked to sign the book. The employee's identification number is recorded for security purposes at the time the report is taken.

In situations where it is not possible to have representatives from user groups pick up reports, bonded employees can be authorized to deliver the reports to users. Subsequently, random checks on the distribution of these reports can be made by the bonded employees' supervisors to verify distribution.

After sensitive reports are no longer needed, it is important to destroy them properly. Most companies have *paper shredders* for this purpose. Shredding reports is more desirable than throwing them away because discarded reports can be retrieved from trash bins.

DATABASE CONTROLS

The general and application controls discussed in the previous two major sections of this chapter are also applicable to *database systems.* Listed below are several specific controls that are especially relevant to organizations that use database systems.

- Database management software that controls all accesses to data.
- Layered passwords that restrict user access to precisely designated data sets and files and even to individual data elements.
- Complete documentation, with particular emphasis on an updated and comprehensive data dictionary that is online.
- A database administrator who monitors and supervises operations within the database environment. For example, the administrator should have adequate authority regarding standardization of data elements and sets, assignment of passwords, and maintenance of change procedures with respect to data and the database management system.
- Sound security modules that are protected from unauthorized access.
- Authorization and approval of all significant in-house and manufacturer modifications to the database management software.
- Changes to data already within the database (due to errors) to be made only by authorized individuals using specially assigned passwords. Also, all changes should be recorded on *change logs* and be reviewed by user departments as well as internal auditors.

CONTROLS IN THE INFORMATION AGE

General and application control procedures are important to microcomputer environments (where, for example, *client/server computing* is quite popular) in the information age. Most risks associated with AISs (whether mainframe-based, micro-based, or a combination of both) usually result from one of three sources: errors, irregularities (or fraud), and general threats to security (such as a *computer virus*). This last major section of Chapter 10 first examines some of the *risks* that are unique to the microcomputer (or just *micro*) environment and looks at some control procedures for micros that will hopefully reduce these risks. Then, in continuing our analysis of risks unique to information age systems, we discuss control procedures to reduce *risks* associated with *computer network systems* and with *e-business firms.*

Risks Unique to the Micro Environment

To reduce the risks of errors, irregularities, and general threats to security within a company's micro environment for processing accounting data, cost-effective general and application control procedures of the type we have discussed in this chapter should be designed and implemented. As a result of the special *control risks* (discussed later) associated with microcomputers (also referred to as *personal computers*), several inexpensive hardware and software controls should also be used in a micro environment. The use of microcomputers presents special control risks over and above their mainframe counterparts in two basic areas:

- *Hardware.* Because microcomputers are portable, they can easily be stolen or destroyed. Restricting access to microcomputer equipment is difficult. It is simple to remove a hardware card from a unit or take a monitor home. The problem is compounded further with laptop computers, since many types of powerful laptops can now be hidden inside a briefcase. (The subject of laptop controls will be discussed shortly.)
- *Data and Software.* Data and software are easy to access, modify, copy, or destroy, and therefore are difficult to control. An individual with reasonable computer know-how and access to a micro can access all the data and software on the machine. As a result, there is a danger that an employee of a company using micros might access unauthorized records and manipulate the data, or that a disgruntled employee might decide to reformat a micro's hard disk, destroying all software and data the disk contained.

Controls for Microcomputers

Microcomputers are relatively inexpensive. Therefore, it would not be cost-effective for a company to go to elaborate lengths to protect this equipment. What are needed are *inexpensive,* yet effective, control procedures for micros. It should be noted, however, that because of the compact nature of laptop computers, laptop theft has become a big problem for both corporate entities and government, as illustrated in Case-in-Point 10-6.

Case-in-Point 10.6 In the recent past, one insurance company handled $1 billion in claims for stolen laptops in a single year. In a survey of major corporations and large government agencies conducted a few years ago by the Computer Security Institute and the FBI computer crime squad, 69 percent of the respondents acknowledged incidents of laptop theft. One hundred fifty organizations cited a total of $13,038,000 in financial losses. The average annual price tag of losses per organization was $86,920.

Development of control procedures for an organization's microcomputers begins by taking an *inventory* of all micros used throughout the organization. The various applications for which each micro is used should also be identified. This should be followed by classifying each microcomputer according to the types of *risks* and *exposures* associated with its applications. For example, a microcomputer system used to maintain payroll records and prepare weekly employee paychecks is exposed to much greater risk than a microcomputer system used by a secretary for word processing activities. Stronger control procedures would be required for the former system compared to the latter system.

The use of *locks* can protect most of a company's microcomputer systems. For example, *keyboard locks* are available that are built into the CPU and can only be activated with a key. It would be quite rare to find a situation where locks are not cost-effective. Managers should insist that employees lock their keyboards when they finish work. To discourage outright theft of micros, many companies bolt them in place or attach monitors to desks with strong adhesives. A control procedure for *laptops* is to lock them in cabinets before employees leave at night. Additional control procedures for laptops are as follows.

1. *Identify your laptop.* How much do you know about the laptop for which you have assumed responsibility? Many users will only be able to blurt out, "Oh, it's a PowerBook," or "Oh, it's a Dell." Which model? What configuration? Others who consider themselves "power-users" may know a great deal about the type of computer and its specific configuration but have not taken the time to look for any serial numbers or other unique identifiers of the lost or stolen laptop. Without these details, the law enforcement agencies, airlines, hotels, and so on, involved will have little chance of retrieving your company's stolen laptop property. Furthermore, any insurance claims against the theft of the laptop could be jeopardized. Keep a copy of all relevant information about your laptop for which you have accepted responsibility in a safe place. Leave it either in your desk at the office or at your home. Never tape the relevant information to the laptop or store the information electronically on the laptop's hard disk.

2. *Use nonbreakable cables to attach laptops to stationary furniture.* If you are, for example, going to keep your laptop in your hotel room, be sure to use a cable or other security device to attach the laptop to some stationary object, for example, a desk or some other piece of heavy furniture.

3. *Load antivirus software onto the hard disk.* Your laptop must be set up to automatically perform an antivirus scan whenever it is turned on as well as whenever a diskette is inserted. It is also advisable to have the antivirus scanning software check all changed or new files. It is imperative that the antivirus software be kept up to date. The number of viruses is increasing constantly. Unless the software is kept current with the latest update, you run the risk of losing data or at the very least impairing your productivity.

4. *Backup Laptop Information.* It's certainly not effective to keep your backups in the laptop case. While traveling, you should keep backup diskettes in your coat pocket or your briefcase instead. If you are able to back up to your company's internal network via modem, you should also do so. Make backups frequently. It is also important to test backups regularly to ensure data integrity.

With regard to laptop control procedure (4) above, Case-in-Point 10.7 discusses how to avoid laptop wipeout.

Case-in-Point 10.7 When Christopher Walters called DriveSavers Data Recovery in Novato, California, he was in a panic. A faulty disk had caused his laptop to die, and, with his arrangements for a 72-piece orchestra for country singer Barbara Mandrell locked in it, he was afraid his fledgling career as an arranger was about to go down the drain. With only three days left before show time, DriveSavers recovered 94 percent of his data. Walters reconstructed the rest and the show—and his career—went on.

Walters' predicament isn't unusual. As laptops become more sophisticated, people are using them as primary PCs and are saving large amounts of critical data on portable disk drives. But "laptops hardly ever get backed up," laments Scott Gaidano, president of DriveSavers. And because laptops are portable, "they get into more adventures," Gaidano adds. Among the many disasters he has seen: a laptop that had fallen into the Amazon, one that melted in a car fire, one that was run over by a bus, and four dumped in bathtubs. In each case, although the machine was trashed, the data were salvaged.

Protecting accounting data through software protection procedures for microcomputers can be *cost-effective*. Secret passwords that are periodically changed should be required for all authorized users of micros. Chips can contain algorithms, which *encrypt* data (*data encryption,* as a control technique, is discussed shortly) and prevent a hacker from tampering with the data; secret passwords, if tampered with, will cause a micro to shut down. Boards are available that will authenticate or identify micro users on the basis of a password program. If the correct password is entered, the board will release control to the operating system. On the other hand, if the correct password is not entered, the board shuts the microcomputer down. In addition, some boards will allow access for micro users but restrict them to a predetermined directory or file. When an employee is terminated, his or her password should be immediately removed from the system.

There are several common-sense microcomputer control procedures for protecting data that cost virtually nothing. For example, micro users should be required to *back up* (backups discussed above for laptops) all important data and program files and to store these backup files in a locked storage area. When dealing with sensitive file data (e.g., future plans for new product lines), the file can be copied from the hard disk to diskette. The diskette can then be secured behind locked doors, and the file on the hard disk can be erased. Finally, the doors to offices containing microcomputing equipment should be closed and locked when authorized personnel leave.

Controls for Computer Network Systems

In the early days of computer use in organizational systems, factors such as control, efficiency, and personnel considerations caused many companies to consolidate their systems into one large *centralized data processing system.* As companies became larger and more diversified, however, this centralization approach frequently was inconvenient. Data had to be brought to the computer center, entered into the system and processed, and finally returned to the user in the form of output.

When minicomputers were implemented into a company's data processing system, they were often placed in remote locations within the company and linked to a centralized computer to form a *distributed data processing (DDP) system.* The basic objective of each remote minicomputer was to meet the specific processing needs of the remote location and communicate summary results to the centralized (host) computer.

The popularity of microcomputers for business use has increased the trend toward DDP systems. The use of distributed data processing is very popular in today's business organizations. As a result, large volumes of data are regularly transmitted over long-distance telecommunications facilities. The on-site transmission of data using local area networks is also very popular. The routine use of information-age systems, such as DDP systems and client/server computing, increases the potential control problems for companies. These problems include unauthorized access to the computer system and its data through **electronic eavesdropping** (which allows computer users to observe transmissions intended for someone else), hardware or software malfunctions causing computer network system failures, and errors in data transmission.

The risk of unauthorized access to data through electronic eavesdropping is minimized by using **data encryption** (discussed in Chapter 2). It can be employed to prevent a company's competitors from electronically monitoring confidential data transmissions. Through an encryption technique, data are converted into a scrambled format prior to their transmission and converted back in a meaningful form once data transmission is finished. The encrypted data can be read only by a person with a matching decryption key. Data encryption is relatively inexpensive. Consequently, today many companies are, for example, encrypting all of their e-mail messages on LANs, WANs, and MANs.

To reduce the risk of computer network system failures, a company should design its network so that there is adequate capacity to handle periods of peak data processing volume. In addition, redundant components, such as modems, should be employed so that the system can switch to a backup unit in the event of hardware failure. Manual backup procedures should be instituted in the event that system failure is not avoided. Finally, a control procedure, such as a **checkpoint,** should be established to facilitate recovery from a system failure. Under a *checkpoint control procedure,* which is performed at periodic intervals during processing, a company's computer network system temporarily does not accept new transactions. Rather, it completes updating procedures for all partially processed transactions and then generates an exact copy of all data values and other information needed to restart the system. The checkpoint is recorded on a separate tape or disk file. This process may be executed several times per hour. Should a hardware failure occur at any time, the system could be restarted by reading in the last checkpoint and then reprocessing only those transactions that have occurred subsequent to that checkpoint.

Two control procedures that reduce the risk of errors in data transmission are routing verification procedures and message acknowledgment procedures. **Routing verification procedures** help to ensure that no transactions or messages are routed to the wrong computer network system address. They work in the following manner: any transaction or message transmitted over a network should have a *header label* that identifies its destination. Before sending the transaction or message, the system should verify that the transaction or message destination is valid and is authorized to receive data. Finally, when the transaction or message is received, the system should verify that the identity of the receiving destination is consistent with the transaction's or message's destination code.

Message acknowledgment procedures are useful in preventing the loss of part or all of a transaction or message on a computer network system. For example, if messages are given a *trailer label,* the receiving destination (or unit) can check each message for the trailer label's presence to verify that the complete message was received. Furthermore, if large messages or sets of transactions are being transmitted in a batch, each message or transaction segment can be numbered sequentially. The receiving destination can then check whether all parts of the messages or transactions were received and were in the correct sequence. The receiving unit will signal the sending unit regarding the outcome of this evaluation. Should the receiving unit detect a data transmission error, the data will be retransmitted once the sending unit has been signaled about this error.

A question frequently asked by a company's managers is: How *vulnerable* is our computer network system? (A *vulnerability* is a flaw in a computer system that can cause a security problem.) Through the design and implementation of cost-effective controls for computer network systems, it is hoped that vulnerabilities within these systems can be minimized.

AIS AT WORK
Omega Engineering

A fired employee intentionally launched a logic bomb that permanently caused irreparable damage to Omega Engineering's computer system by deleting all of the firm's software, inflicting $10 million in damages. Could it have been prevented? Maybe. Could the damages and computer downtime have been minimized through effective internal controls? Definitely. That's the assessment of control experts after the recent indictment of Timothy Lloyd, the former chief computer network program designer and network administrator at Omega Engineering in Bridgeport, New Jersey.

Omega is the classic situation of an inside hack attack, in this case a logic bomb that detonates at a specified time. "Logic bombs are the most difficult to defend against," said William Cook, a partner at Brinks, Hofer, Gilson & Lione, a Chicago-based law firm. "This is exactly what happened," said Al DiFrancesco, Omega's director of human resources. "Three weeks after Lloyd was fired, our employees came to work and could not boot their computers," he said.

Like many victimized businesses, Omega had thought it had implemented reliable control mechanisms into its information systems. "These control mechanisms did lead back to Lloyd and resulted in his indictment," DiFrancesco said. Moreover, Omega canceled all of Lloyd's access rights and privileges on the date of his termination.

So what went wrong? For starters, besides being Omega's chief computer network program designer, Lloyd was also the company's network administrator. Thus, he knew the ins and outs of the system and had all the supervisory privileges to make network additions, changes, and deletions. In the wake of the damage caused by the logic bomb, Omega has installed state-of-the-art internal control procedures, and the firm will no longer put all its eggs in one basket. It is making sure that duplicates of all database information, software code, and files are stored off-site.

Source: Adapted from Kim Girard, "Ex-Employee Nabbed in $10M Hack Attack," *Computerworld* (February 28, 1998), p. 6.

SUMMARY

This chapter has stressed control procedures within IT environments. The two major categories under which computer controls are commonly classified are general controls and application controls.

Controls over a company's data processing activities are extremely important. To provide a stable control environment within which AISs can function, various types of cost-effective general controls should be designed and implemented. The five types discussed in this chapter were (1) personnel controls, such as separation of duties; (2) file security controls to protect computer files from either accidental or intentional abuse; (3) fault-tolerant systems, backup, and contingency planning, which are all controls designed to mitigate or reduce business risk; (4) computer facility controls, such as locating the data processing center in a safe place; and (5) access to computer files, such as by using biometric identifications.

Application controls focus on the prevention, detection, and correction of errors and irregularities in accounting transactions processed within an IT environment. Three major types of application controls that should be designed and implemented for AISs were discussed: (1) input controls, such as edit tests and a check-digit control procedure; (2) processing controls, such as control totals and examination of software documentation; and (3) output controls, such as forms control.

Controls in the information age were examined in the last section of this chapter. Some of the unique risks and important controls associated with microcomputers were discussed. Regarding risks, the portable nature of micros (especially laptops) increases the risk of their being stolen or destroyed. In addition, it is difficult to control data and software in a micro environment because both are easy to access, modify, copy, or destroy. Controls for companies implementing computer network systems include data encryption, checkpoint, routing verification, and message acknowledgment.

KEY TERMS YOU SHOULD KNOW

application controls	fault-tolerant systems
backup	financial risk
biometric identifications	flying-start site
business risk	general computer control objectives
checkpoint	general controls
cold site	grandfather-parent-child procedure
computer facility controls	hot site
consensus-based protocols	input controls
contingency planning	input validation routines
control environment	message acknowledgment procedures
data transcription	Modulus 11 technique
disaster recovery plan	output controls
disk mirroring	password codes
disk shadowing	processing controls
edit programs	rollback processing
edit tests	routing verification procedures
electronic eavesdropping	uninterruptible power system (UPS)
electronic vaulting	watchdog processor

DISCUSSION QUESTIONS

10-1. Discuss what you consider to be the major difference, if any, between *general controls* and *application controls* for accounting systems.

10-2. Discuss the important control concerns associated with an organization's accounting system.

10-3. Discuss the importance of a company establishing a formal *disaster recovery plan.*

10-4. What is *backup,* and why is it important when operating an accounting system?

10-5. Discuss some of the unique control risks associated with the use of microcomputers as compared to using mainframes. List what you consider to be three of the most important control procedures that should be implemented for microcomputers. For each control procedure, give your reason for including this procedure as an important control.

10-6. Information-age systems have caused potential control problems for organizations that implement these systems. Indicate the potential problems as well as control procedures for dealing with these problems.

10-7. Jean & Joan Cosmetics has a complete line of beauty products for women and maintains a computerized inventory system. An eight-digit product number identifies inventory items, of which the first four digits classify the beauty product by major category (hair, face, skin, eyes, etc.) and the last four digits identify the product itself. Enumerate as many controls as you can that the company might use to ensure accuracy in this eight-digit number when updating its inventory-balance file.

10-8. The sales manager of an insurance office called a sales personnel meeting to discuss the problems he had been having with his salespeople filling out the insurance forms. "Ladies and gentlemen," he explained, "you all know how hard our Ms. Wiskovski works around here, and she is too busy with her other chores to correct your mistakes on our intake forms. So from now on, I will dock each person $5 for every mistake we catch on the form." Comment.

10-9. Explain how each of the following can be used to control the input, processing, or output of accounting data: (a) edit tests, (b) check digits, (c) passwords, (d) activity listings, and (e) control totals.

10-10. What is the difference between *logical* access to the computer and *physical* access to the computer? Why is the security of both important?

10-11. Discuss the following statement: "The separation of duties control is very difficult in computerized accounting information systems because computers often integrate functions when performing data processing tasks. Therefore, such a control is not advisable for those organizations using computers to perform their accounting functions."

10-12. Discuss the role of the *control total* in accounting information systems. Why are control totals insufficient to guard against data inaccuracies?

PROBLEMS

10-13. E. Wilson and Associates hired a consulting team from Meat, Hardwick, and Thistle to discuss application controls for the company's accounting data processing. In one of the workshops, the seminar leader stated, "We can classify all errors in processing accounting data as either accidental or intentional. Controls such as edit tests are primarily aimed at the former type of error whereas controls such as personnel controls are primarily aimed at the latter type of error." Comment.

10-14. Mark Goodwin, a computer programmer, had a grudge against his company. To get even, he coded a special routine in the mortgage loan program that erased a small, random number of accounts on the disk file every time the program was run. The company did not detect the routine until almost all of its records had been erased. Discuss what controls might have protected this company from its own programmer.

10-15. Jack Drucker, an accountant working for a medium-size company, set up several dummy companies and began directing the computer to write checks to them for fictitious merchandise. He was apprehended only when several of the company executives began to wonder how he could afford a ski vacation in the Alps every year. What might have prevented this fraudulent activity?

10-16. Identify one or more *control procedures* (either *general* or *application* controls, or both) that would guard against each of the following errors or problems.

    a. Leslie Thomas, a secretary at the university, indicated that she had worked 40 hours on her regular time card. The university paid her for 400 hours worked that week.

    b. The aging analysis indicated that the Grab and Run Electronics Company account was so far in arrears that the credit manager decided to cut off any further credit sales to the company until it cleared up its account. Yet, the following week, the manager noted that three new sales had been made to that company—all on credit.

    c. The Small Company employed Mr. Fineus Eyeshade to perform all its accounts receivable data processing. Mr. Eyeshade's 25 years with the company and his unassuming appearance helped him conceal the fact that he was embezzling cash collections from accounts receivable to cover his gambling losses at the racetrack.

    d. The Blue Mountain Utility Company was having difficulty with its customer payments. The payment amounts were entered directly onto a terminal, and the transaction file thus created was used to update the customer master file. Among the problems encountered with this system were the application of customer payments to the wrong accounts and the creation of multiple customer master file records for the same account.

    e. The Landsford brothers had lived in Center County all their lives. Ben worked for the local mill in the accounts payable department, and Tom owned the local hardware store. The sheriff couldn't believe that the brothers had created several dummy companies that sold fictitious merchandise to the mill. Ben had the mill pay for this merchandise in its usual fashion, and he wrote off the missing goods as "damaged inventory."

10-17. Identify one or more *control procedures* (either *general* or *application* controls, or both) that would guard against each of the following errors or problems.

    a. A bank deposit transaction was accidentally coded with a withdrawal code.

    b. The key-entry operator keyed in the purchase order number as a nine-digit number instead of an eight-digit number.

    c. The date of a customer payment was keyed 2001 instead of 2010.

    d. A company employee was issued a check in the amount of $-135.65 because he had not worked a certain week, but most of his payroll deductions were automatic each week.

    e. A patient filled out her medical insurance number as 123465 instead of 123456.

    f. An applicant for the company stock option plan filled out her employee number as 84-7634-21. The first two digits are a department code. There is no department 84.

    g. A high school student was able to log onto the telephone company's computer as soon as he learned what telephone number to call.

    h. The accounts receivable department sent 87 checks to the computer center for processing. No one realized that one check was dropped along the way and that the computer therefore processed only 86 checks.

10-18. To achieve effective *separation of duties* within a company's IT environment, the company's accounting and information processing subsystems should be separate from the departments that use data and perform operational activities. Discuss some of the ways this "separation of duties" is achieved.

10-19. Bristol Company has a high turnover rate among its employees. It maintains a very large computer system that supports approximately 225-networked PCs. The company maintains fairly extensive databases regarding its customers. These databases include customer profiles, past purchasing patterns, and prices charged.

    Recently, Bristol Company has been having major problems with competitors. It appears that one competitor seems to be very effective at taking away the company's customers. This competitor has visited most of Bristol Company's customers, and identical products have been offered to these customers at lower prices in every case.

Requirements

What do you feel is the possible security problem at Bristol Company? What can be done about this problem?

10-20. The Blatz Furniture Company uses an online data input system for processing its sales invoice data, salesperson data, inventory control, and purchase order data. Representative data for each of these applications are shown in Figure 10-13. Identify specific editing tests that might be used to ensure the accuracy and completeness of the information in each data set.

INTERNET EXERCISES

10-21. Using your computer and the Internet, find a web site that discusses the control of computer-based information systems. Upon accessing the web site, write a summary of your findings and relate it to this chapter's subject matter. In addition, submit a printout of the web site information that you accessed.

10-22. Using your computer and the Internet, find a web site that discusses contingency planning. Upon accessing the web site, write a summary of your findings and relate it to this chapter's subject matter. In addition, submit a printout of the web site information that you accessed.

Application	Field Name	Field Length	Example
Invoicing	Customer number	6	123456
	Customer name	23	Al's Department Store
	Salesperson number	3	477
	Invoice number	6	123456
	Item catalog number	10	9578572355
	Quantity sold	8	13
	Unit price	7	10.50
	Total price	12	136.50
Salesperson activity	Salesperson number	3	477
	Salesperson name	20	Kathryn Wilson
	Store department number	8	10314201
	Week's sales volume	12	1043.75
	Regular hours worked	5	39.75
	Overtime hours worked	4	0.75
Inventory control	Inventory item number	10	9578572355
	Item description	15	Desk lamp
	Unit cost	7	8.50
	Number of units dispersed this week	4	14
	Number of units added to inventory	4	20
Purchasing	Vendor catalog number	12	059689584996
	Item description	18	Desk pad
	Vendor number	10	8276110438
	Number of units ordered	7	45
	Price per unit	7	8.75
	Total cost of purchase	14	313.75

FIGURE 10-13 Data for the Blatz Furniture Company's applications.

CASE ANALYSES

10-23. Ashley Company (Computer Virus Problem in a Network)

Ashley Company has had a problem with some of its employees using the computer network to play games. In the past, the company has not been very strict about controlling the use of its network, because employees often have slack time during the off-season. Recently, however, a serious problem occurred. It appears that one of the game programs run on the network contained a virus. The virus "looks around" the network and checks to see if other computer programs in the network are infected with the virus. If not, the virus program will then infect them.

Part of this infection process involves making certain random changes to the other programs. These random changes are such that the infected program will produce unpredictable or invalid results at some specified date subsequent to the infection. For example, an accounting program might be modified so that it will scramble all the accounting databases exactly six months after its infection. The nature of the virus is particularly bad, because a program, once infected, has the ability to spread the infection to the other programs. Therefore, once a virus is introduced into the computer network, all programs in the network might be infected within a few weeks. To make things worse, the infection process may carry over to all of the company's backup copies as well. This is particularly true if the virus program lies dormant for a long period of time before producing its disastrous results.

On October 15 of the current year, Ashley Company went into a state of disaster. The virus had evidently invaded all major portions of the computer network. The network database manager looked with great horror to find that all the databases were completely scrambled. To make things worse, the virus had also scrambled all the backup copies. Inspection of the backup copies of databases revealed that they were completely worthless. As a result, the company was unable to perform its accounts receivable billing. Two months later Ashley Company was forced to file for a Chapter 11 bankruptcy.

Requirement

Discuss the means by which the problem at Ashley Company should have been prevented.

10-24. Simmons Corporation (Problems with Computer-based Information System)

Simmons Corporation is a multilocation retailing concern with stores and warehouses throughout the United States. The company is in the process of designing a new, integrated, computer-based information system. In conjunction with the design of the new system, the management of the company is reviewing the data processing security to determine what new control features should be incorporated. Two areas of specific concern are (1) confidentiality of company and customer records, and (2) safekeeping of computer equipment, files, and data processing center facilities.

The new information system will be employed to process all company records, which include sales, purchase, financial budget, customer, creditor, and personnel information. The stores and warehouses will be linked to the main computer at corporate headquarters by a system of remote terminals. This will permit data to be communicated directly to corporate headquarters or to any other location from each location within the terminal network.

At the current time, certain reports have restricted distribution because not all levels of management need to receive them or because they contain confidential information. The introduction of remote terminals in the new system may provide access to these restricted data by unauthorized personnel. Simmons's top management is concerned that confidential information may become accessible and be used improperly.

The company's top management is also concerned with potential physical threats to the system, such as sabotage, fire damage, water damage, or power failure. Should any of these events occur in the current system and cause a computer shutdown, adequate backup records are available so that the company could reconstruct necessary information at a reasonable cost on a timely basis. However, with the new system, a computer shutdown would severely limit company activities until the system could become operational again.

Requirements

1. Identify and briefly explain the problems Simmons Corporation could experience with respect to the confidentiality of information and records in the new system.
2. Recommend measures Simmons Corporation could incorporate into the new system that would ensure the confidentiality of information and records in this new system.
3. What safeguards can Simmons Corporation develop to provide physical security for its (a) computer equipment, (b) files, and (c) data processing center facilities?

10-25. OBrien Corporation (Recommendations for Correcting System Weaknesses)

OBrien Corporation is a medium-sized, privately owned industrial instrument manufacturer supplying precision equipment manufacturers in the Midwest. The corporation is ten years old and operates a centralized accounting information system. The administrative offices are located in a downtown building, while the production, shipping, and receiving departments are housed in a renovated warehouse a few blocks away. The shipping and receiving areas share one end of the warehouse. OBrien Corporation has grown rapidly. Sales have increased by 25 percent each year for the last three years, and the company is now shipping approximately $80,000 of its products each week. James Fox, OBrien's controller, purchased and installed a computer last year to process the payroll and inventory. Fox plans to fully integrate the accounting information system within the next five years.

The Marketing Department consists of four salespersons. Upon obtaining an order, usually over the telephone, a salesperson manually prepares a prenumbered, two-part sales order. One copy of the order is filed by date, and the second copy is sent to the Shipping Department. All sales are on credit, FOB destination. Because of the recent increase in sales, the four salespersons have not had time to check credit histories. As a result, 15 percent of credit sales are either late collections or uncollectible.

The Shipping Department receives the sales orders and packages the goods from the warehouse, noting any items that are out of stock. The terminal in the Shipping Department is used to update the perpetual inventory records of each item as it is removed from the shelf. The packages are placed near the loading dock door in alphabetical order by customer name. The sales order is signed by a shipping clerk indicating that the order is filled and ready to send. The sales order is forwarded to the Billing Department where a two-part sales invoice is prepared. The sales invoice is only prepared on receipt of the sales order from the Shipping Department so that the customer is billed just for the items that were sent, not for back orders. Billing sends the customer's copy of the invoice back to Shipping. The customer's copy of the invoice serves as a billing copy, and Shipping inserts it into a special envelope on the package to save postage. The carrier of the customer's choice is then contacted to pick up the goods. In the past, goods were shipped within two working days of the receipt of the customer's order; however, shipping dates now average six working days after receipt of the order. One reason is that there are two new shipping clerks who are still undergoing training. Because these two clerks have fallen behind in their work, the two clerks in the Receiving Department, who are experienced, have been assisting the shipping clerks.

The Receiving Department is located adjacent to the shipping dock, and merchandise is received daily from many different carriers. The Receiving Department clerks share the computer terminal with the Shipping Department. The date, vendor, and number of items received are entered on receipt to keep the perpetual inventory records current.

Hard copy of the changes in inventory (additions and shipments) is printed once a month. The receiving supervisor makes sure the additions are reasonable and forwards the printout to the shipping supervisor who is responsible for checking the reasonableness of the deductions from inventory (shipments). The inventory printout is stored in the Shipping Department by date. A complete inventory list is only printed once a year when the physical inventory is taken. The flowchart in Figure 10-14 presents the document flows employed by OBrien Corporation.

Requirements

OBrien Corporation's marketing, shipping, billing, and receiving information system has some weaknesses. For each weakness in the system:

1. Identify the weakness and describe the potential problem (s) caused by this weakness.

2. Recommend controls or changes in the system to correct the weakness.

Use the following format in preparing your answer.

Weaknesses and Potential Problem(s)	Recommendation(s) to Correct Weaknesses

10-26. MailMed Inc. (Control Weaknesses and a Disaster Recovery Plan)

MailMed Inc. (MMI), a pharmaceutical firm, provides discounted prescription drugs through direct mail. MMI has a small systems staff that designs and writes MMI's

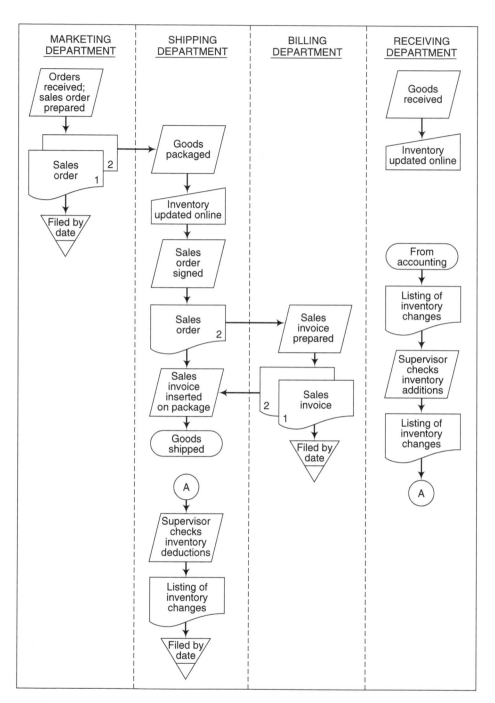

FIGURE 10-14   Flowchart for OBrien Corporation.

customized software. Until recently, MMI's transaction data were transmitted to an outside organization for processing on its hardware.

MMI has experienced significant sales growth as the cost of prescription drugs has increased and medical insurance companies have been tightening reimbursements in order to restrain premium cost increases. As a result of these increased sales, MMI has purchased its own computer hardware. The data processing center is installed on the ground floor of its two-story headquarters building. It is behind large, plate-glass windows so that the state-of-the-art data processing center can be displayed as a measure of the company's success and attract customer and investor attention. The computer area is equipped with halon gas fire suppression equipment and an uninterruptible power supply system.

MMI has hired a small computer operations staff to operate its data processing center. To handle MMI's current level of business, the operations staff is on a two-shift schedule, five days per week. MMI's systems and programming staff, now located in the same building, has access to the data processing center and can test new programs and program changes when the operations staff is not available. Because the systems and programming staff is small and the work demands have increased, systems and programming documentation is developed only when time is available. Periodically, but not on a scheduled basis, MMI backs up its programs and data files, storing them at an off-site location.

Unfortunately, due to several days of heavy rains, MMI's building recently experienced serious flooding that reached several feet into the first-floor level and affected not only the computer hardware but also the data and program files that were on-site.

Requirements

1. Describe at least four computer control weaknesses that existed at MailMed Inc. prior to the flood occurrence.

2. Describe at least five components that should be incorporated in a formal disaster recovery plan so that MailMed Inc. can become operational within 72 hours after a disaster affects its computer operations capability.

3. Identify at least three factors, other than the plan itself, that MailMed Inc.'s management should consider in formulating a formal disaster recovery plan.

10-27. Choate and Choate (Identifying Controls for a System)

Choate and Choate is an advertising agency that employs 625 salespersons, who travel and entertain extensively. Each month, salespersons are paid both salary and commissions. The nature of their jobs is such that expenses of several hundred dollars a day might be incurred. In the past, these expenses were included in each salesperson's monthly paycheck. Salespersons were required to submit their expense reports, with supporting receipts, by the 20th of each month. These reports would be reviewed and then sent to data entry in a batch. Suitable controls were incorporated on each batch during input, processing, and output. This system worked well from a company viewpoint, and the internal auditor was convinced that, while minor padding of expense accounts might occur, no major losses had been encountered.

As interest rates began to climb, the salespersons became unhappy. They pointed out that they were often forced to carry several thousand dollars for an entire month. If they were out of town around the 20th, they might not be reimbursed for their expenses for two months. They requested that Choate and Choate provide a service whereby a salesperson or his or her representative could submit receipts and expense reports to the accounting department and receive a check almost immediately.

The data processing manager said that this procedure could be done. A computer terminal would be set up in the accounting office, along with a small printer. The salesperson's name would be entered along with the required expense amount broken down into the standard categories. A computer program would process these data to the proper accounts and, if everything checked out suitably, print the check on presigned check blank stock in the printer.

Requirement

Identify important controls, and explain why they might be implemented into the advertising agency's system. These control procedures may be physical, they may relate to jobs and responsibilities, or they may be part of the computer program.

REFERENCES, RECOMMENDED READINGS, AND WEB SITES

References and Recommended Readings

Barrier, Michael, "Preparing For the Worst," *Internal Auditor* (December 2001), pp. 57–61.

Bigler, Mark, "Computer Forensics," *Internal Auditor* (January 2000), pp. S3–S5.

Cerullo, Virginia M., and Michael J. Cerullo, "Client/Server Systems: Security and Control," *Internal Auditor* (May 1999), pp. 56–59.

Dash, Julekha, "Crash!" *Software Magazine* (February 1997), pp. 48–51.

Davis, Beth, "In Certificates We Trust," *Information Week* (March 23, 1998), pp. 60–64.

Furchgott, Roy, "Avoiding Laptop Wipeout," *Business Week* (February 14, 2000), p. 146.

Honig, Susan A., "The Changing Landscape of Computerized Accounting Systems," *The CPA Journal* (May 1999), pp. 14–17, 20, 87.

Ivancevich, Susan H., and Gilbert W. Joseph, "Zacha Technology Corporation: Internal Control Assurance Service Reporting Issues in an e-Commerce Environment," *Issues in Accounting Education* (August 2001), pp. 473–483.

Jacobs, Joel, and Stanley Weiner, "The CPA's Role in Disaster Recovery," *The CPA Journal* (November 1997), pp. 20–58.

Kring, Richard, "Systems Control Strategies," *Internal Auditor* (April 1998), pp. 60–63.

Patrowicz, Lucie Juneau, "A River Runs Through IT," *CIO* (April 1, 1998), pp. 36–44.

Pushkin, Ann B., and Bonnie W. Morris, "Understanding Financial EDI," *Management Accounting* (November 1997), pp. 42–46.

Rodetis, Susan, "Can Your Business Survive the Unexpected?" *Journal of Accountancy* (February 1999), pp. 27–32.

Semer, Lance J., "Disaster Recovery Planning in Distributed Environments," *Internal Auditor* (December 1998), pp. 40–47.

Warigon, Slemo, "Data Warehouse Control and Security," *Internal Auditor* (February 1998), pp. 54–60.

Yasin, Rutrell, "Assessing and Reducing Security Risks," *Internetweek* (February 8, 1999), p. 12.

Web Sites

There are many web sites that discuss disaster recovery. The AICPA web site, for example, includes a listing of disaster recovery resources. Several journals on disaster recovery are available online. These include the *Disaster Recovery Journal* (www.drj.com), *Survive! Magazine* (www.survive.com), and *Contingency Planning & Management Magazine* (www.contingencyplanning.com).

Chapter 11

Computer Crime and Ethics

INTRODUCTION

COMPUTER CRIME: AN OVERVIEW

What Is Computer Crime?

Computer Crime Legislation

The Lack of Computer-Crime Statistics

The Growth of Computer Crime

The Importance of Computer Abuse

EXAMPLES OF COMPUTER-CRIME CASES

Compromising Valuable Information: The TRW Credit Data Case

Computer Hacking: The Kevin D. Mitnick Case

Computer Viruses: Robert T. Morris and the Internet Virus Case

THWARTING COMPUTER ABUSE

Enlist Top-Management Support

Increase Employee Awareness and Education

Protect Passwords

Implement Controls

Identify Computer Criminals

Recognize the Symptoms of Employee Fraud

Employ Forensic Accountants

COMPUTERS AND ETHICAL BEHAVIOR

Ethical Issues and Professional Associations

Meeting the Ethical Challenges

AIS AT WORK: FIRMS FIGHT BACK

SUMMARY

KEY TERMS YOU SHOULD KNOW

DISCUSSION QUESTIONS

PROBLEMS

INTERNET EXERCISES

CASE ANALYSES

The Equity Funding Case

Ashley Company

Mark Goodwin Resort

The Department of Taxation

Ajax Products

REFERENCES, RECOMMENDED READINGS, AND WEB SITES

After reading this chapter, you will:

1. *Understand* why it is difficult to define computer crime.

2. *Know* why there is an absence of good data on computer crime.

3. *Be able to provide reasons why* computer crime might be growing.

4. *Be familiar with* several known computer-crime cases and the proper controls for thwarting them.

5. *Be able to describe* a profile of computer criminals.

6. *Understand* the importance of ethical behavior within the environment of computerized AISs.

> *Every year companies are sustaining staggering losses at the hands of computer-related crooks, with as much as $250 billion a year lost by American corporations from theft of intellectual property alone...*

> Ara C. Trembly, "Cyber Crime Means Billions in Losses," *National Underwriter,* vol. 103, no. 26 (June 28, 1999), p. 19.

INTRODUCTION

The connection between AISs and computer crime is both straightforward and important. Managers, accountants, and investors all use computerized information to control valuable resources, help sell products, authenticate accounting transactions, and make investment decisions. But the effectiveness of these activities can be lost if the underlying information is wrong or seriously compromised. This is why computerized information is itself a valuable asset that must be protected. It is also why knowing about computer crime and its deterrents helps protect AISs.

This chapter describes computer crime, fraud, and other irregularities that have occurred in the past and that may also occur in the future. In the first section, we take a closer look at computer crime and review the available facts about it. In the second section, we examine three specific cases of computer abuse. The third section of this chapter identifies what organizations can do to protect themselves from computer abuse. For example, this section describes ways of recognizing employee computer frauds and what organizations can do to avoid them.

Finally, not all computer-related abuses are illegal—some are simply unethical. Because of the importance of ethical behavior within the environment of computerized AISs, the last section of our chapter discusses the topic of computers and ethical behavior.

COMPUTER CRIME: AN OVERVIEW

Articles in such prestigious publications as *Fortune, Business Week,* and the *Wall Street Journal* testify to the high level of public interest in computer abuse. In contrast, however, the number of in-depth surveys of computer abuse conducted to date has been surprisingly small. One reason for this is the relatively small proportion of computer crime that we believe is detected and the even smaller proportion that ultimately gets reported in sufficient detail to permit accurate classification and evaluation. The most informative reports of computer abuses are still found in computer trade journals, of which *Computerworld* continues to be an especially important source.

What is Computer Crime?

The term **computer crime** is a misnomer because *computers* do not commit crimes—*people do.* The terms *computer-assisted crime, computer abuse,* or *crime* *by computer* are probably better descriptors. Because of their common usage, however, we shall utilize all these terms interchangeably in this chapter.

No matter what name we use, it is difficult to define computer crime. Suppose, for example, we define computer crime as "using a computer to deceive for personal gain." With this definition, we could accuse the police chief who was caught altering his own driving record through an online computer terminal as having committed a computer crime. But it is often not this easy because the motive for other computer abuses have been "revenge" or "challenge," not "personal gain."

Figure 11-1 describes several additional cases that might qualify as computer crimes. But do they? In the first case, the primary objective was to disrupt a computer network—not personal gain. In the second case, "misrepresentation" would probably more accurately describe the problem. In the third case, a CRT screen and not a computer was damaged, and again, there was no personal gain. In the fourth case, the attempt to sell credit information might better be described as "solicitation" or "bribery." In the fifth case, no computer was used, so it is difficult to call this a computer crime. Finally, although the sixth case involved a computer and resulted in personal gain, the programmer's act could just as easily be called "embezzlement."

A strict definition of computer crime is important because it determines what law enforcement officials can and cannot prosecute as well as how statistics on such crimes are accumulated. For example, the largest computer crime on record, the Equity Funding Case, involved $200 million if only direct corporate losses are counted, but more than $2 billion if indirect losses to other companies and investors are counted. But was this a computer crime? Case 11-20 requires you to investigate this crime and answer this question for yourself.

Perhaps the "purest" form of computer abuse involves acts resulting in **denial of service.** Two examples of such abuse are (1) computer viruses (discussed later) that affect computer files, operating system activities, or software, and (2) computer programs that flood computer networks with excessive e-mail traffic. A third such example are **logic bombs** (i.e., computer programs that remain dormant until some specified circumstance or date triggers them). Once "detonated," a logic bomb program sabotages a system by destroying data, computer programs, or both.

---

1. A graduate student infected a computer network with a virus that eventually disrupted over 10,000 separate systems.
2. A company accused a computer-equipment vendor of fraudulently representing the capabilities of a computer system, charging that the full system was never delivered and that the software was inadequate.
3. In a fit of resentment, a keyboard operator shattered a CRT screen with her high-heeled shoe.
4. Some employees of a credit bureau sent notices to some of the individuals listed as bad risks in its files. For a fee, the employees would withhold the damaging information, thereby enhancing the credit worthiness of the applicants.
5. A computer dating service was sued because referrals for dates were few and inappropriate. The owner eventually admitted that no computer was used to match dates, even though the use of a computer was advertised.
6. A programmer changed a dividends-payment program to reduce the dividends of selected stockholders, and to issue a check to himself for the sum of the reductions—$56,000.

FIGURE 11-1 Some examples of computer abuse.

Case-in-Point 11.1   Donald Burleson was a disgruntled computer programmer who set off a logic bomb that erased 168,000 sales commission records at his former company. Consequently, company paychecks were held up for a month. He embedded the logic bomb in a legitimate program, which he designed to go off periodically to erase still more records. But a fellow programmer who was testing a new employee bonus system discovered the bomb before it could execute again. The company's computers were shut down for two days while the bomb was located and diffused.

Computer Crime Legislation

A strict definition of what constitutes computer crime must come from the law. Figure 11-2 lists some important federal legislation governing activities involving computers. Of these acts, the most important is probably the **Computer Fraud and Abuse Act of 1986** (the CFAA, which has been amended in 1994 and 1996). This act defines computer fraud as any illegal act for which knowledge of computer technology is essential for its perpetration, investigation, or prosecution. What follows is a list of fraudulent acts found in the CFAA, and one or more actual examples of each type of computer abuse.

Use or the Conspiracy to Use Computer Resources to Commit a Felony
Paul Sjiem-Fat used desktop publishing technology to perpetrate one of the first cases of computer forgery. Sjiem-Fat created bogus cashier's checks and used these checks to buy computer equipment, which he subsequently sold in the Caribbean. He was caught while trying to steal $20,000 from the Bank of Boston. The bank

---

Fair Credit Reporting Act of 1970. This act requires that an individual be informed why he or she is denied credit. The act also entitles the individual to challenge information maintained by the credit-rating company and to add information if desired. Seven years after this law was put into effect, the annual number of complaints filed under it exceeded 200,000.

Freedom of Information Act of 1970. This is a federal "sunshine law" guaranteeing individuals the right to see any information gathered about them by federal agencies.

Federal Privacy Act of 1974. This act goes further than the Freedom of Information Act of 1970 by requiring that individuals be able to correct federal information about themselves, by requiring that agency information not be used for alternate purposes without the individual's consent, and by making the collecting agency responsible for the accuracy and use of the information. Under this act, an individual may ask a federal judge to order the correction of errors if the federal agency does not do so.

Small Business Computer Security and Education Act of 1984. This act created an educational council that meets annually to advise the Small Business Administration on a variety of computer crime and security issues affecting small businesses.

Computer Fraud and Abuse Act of 1986. This act makes it a federal crime to intentionally access a computer for such purposes as (1) obtaining top-secret military information, personal financial or credit information; (2) committing a fraud; or (3) altering or destroying federal information.

Computer Security Act of 1987. This act requires more than 550 federal agencies to develop computer security plans for each computer system that processes sensitive information. The plans are reviewed by the National Institute of Standards and Technology (NIST).

FIGURE 11−2   Federal legislation affecting the use of computers.

called in the Secret Service, which raided his apartment and found nine bogus checks totaling almost $150,000. Sjiem-Fat was prosecuted and sent to prison.

Unauthorized Theft, Use, Access, Modification, Copying, or Destruction of Software or Data.

The PC manager at a King Soopers supermarket in Colorado was called repeatedly to correct computer errors that were thought to be responsible for a large number of sales voids and other accounting errors. In 1998, the company discovered that this manager was in fact the cause of these problems. Over the course of five or more years, officials estimate that he and two head clerks used a number of simple methods to steal more than $2 million from the company—for example, by voiding sales transactions and pocketing the customers' cash payments.

Theft of Money by Altering Computer Records or the Theft of Computer Time

To commit an inventory fraud, several employees at an East Coast railroad entered data into their company's computer system to show that more than 200 railroad cars were scrapped or destroyed. These employees then removed the cars from the railroad system, repainted them, and sold them.

Computer programmers can use the **salami technique** to steal small amounts of money from many accounts over a period of time. In one instance, the frustrated chief accountant for a California produce grower systematically increased each of the company's production costs by a fraction of a percent, which he subsequently raised over time. Because all business expenses were rising during the same period, no single account or expense called attention to the fraud, and the accountant was able to enter these small amounts into the accounts of dummy customers, which he then pocketed. He was eventually caught when an alert bank teller brought to her manager's attention a check that the accountant tried to cash because she did not recognize the payee's name on it.

Theft, Vandalism, or Destruction of Computer Hardware

A disgruntled tax payer became enraged with his tax bill. He was arrested for shooting at an IRS computer through an open window of the building.

Intent to Illegally Obtain Information or Tangible Property Through the Use of Computers

To execute a disbursement fraud, one man used a desktop publishing package to prepare fictitious bills for office supplies that he then mailed to companies across the country. He kept the dollar amount on each bill low enough (less than $300) because many companies do not bother with formal purchase orders or approvals for small amounts. An amazingly large percentage of the companies paid the bills without question.

Data diddling means changing data before, during, or after they are entered into the computer system. The change can delete, alter, or add important system data. In one instance, a clerk for a Denver brokerage altered a transaction to record 1,700 shares of Loren Industries stock worth about $2,500 as shares in Long Island Lighting worth more than $25,000. In a second case, a ring of travel agents in California received prison sentences for compromising an American Airlines reservations system and stealing $1.3 million worth of frequent-flier tickets.

Trafficking in Passwords or Other Login Information for Accessing a Computer

Two former software developers of Interactive Connection (now known as Screaming Media) were arrested for breaking into Interactive's computer system on the night before Thanksgiving in 1998. They allegedly stayed on the system for about four hours and copied proprietary files and software.

Extortion that Uses a Computer System as a Target   The disgruntled employee of a European company removed all of the company's tape files from the computer room. He then drove to an off-site storage location and demanded half a million dollars for their return. He was arrested while trying to exchange the data files for the ransom money.

Using a computer, fraud perpetrators are able to steal more, in much less time, with much less effort, and leave little or no evidence. Consequently, computer fraud is typically much more difficult to detect than other types of fraud. **Economic espionage,** which is the theft of information and intellectual property, increased by 323 percent during one five-year period. At any point in time, the FBI is investigating approximately 800 separate incidents of economic espionage.

> ***Case-in-Point 11.2***   One case of industrial espionage involved Reuters Analytics, whose employees were accused of breaking into the computers of their competitor, Bloomberg, and stealing lines of programming code. These lines were supposedly used in software that provides financial institutions with the capability to analyze historical data on the stock market.

The federal government has not passed more legislation governing computer abuse in part because every state now also has at least one computer crime law. Most of the laws have provisions that (1) define computer terms (many of which vary from state to state), (2) define some acts as misdemeanors (minor crimes), and (3) declare other acts as felonies (major crimes). These laws also require willful intent for convictions. Thus, words like *maliciously, intentionally,* or *recklessly* often appear in the wording of the computer-crime laws, and willful intent must be established for successful prosecutions. The National Center for Computer Crime Data (NCCCD), a collector of computer-crime statistics, reports that 77 percent of computer cases brought to state courts end in guilty pleas and that another 8 percent of the defendants are found guilty at trials.

The Lack of Computer-Crime Statistics

Nobody really knows how much is lost each year as the result of computer abuse: good statistics on computer crime are mostly unavailable. One explanation for this is the fact that a large proportion of computer abuse takes place in private companies, where it is handled as an internal matter. Unfortunately, no law now requires organizations to report computer abuse, and most managers prefer to avoid official investigations and therefore adverse publicity. But "non-reporting" is not limited to the private sector. When an agency of the U.S. federal government performed a "test attack" on 38,000 of its own computers, fully 65 percent of them were successful, only 4 percent were detected, and only about 1 percent was reported.

Despite the lack of reporting, we have ample reason to believe that computer crime is pervasive. A 1997 survey of Fortune 1000 companies, for example, found that all of the respondents had been "hacked" (penetrated) at least once that year, and that many of them had suffered more than 30 events. But surveys of computer abuse can be ambiguous, making it difficult to interpret the results. For example, when several thousand employees at one federal agency were asked to enumerate all the computer crimes that had been detected during the last year, there was only one positive reply. When the survey was redistributed to these same employees and they were asked about deceptions in data that would eventually be processed by a computer, there were thousands of responses.

The most important reason we know so little about computer abuse is because we believe most of it is not discovered. Recently, for example, the FBI estimated that only 1 percent of all computer crime is detected. Other estimates of computer-crime detection are between 5 and 20 percent. We mostly catch computer criminals through luck, chance, or accident. This is why experts believe that what computer crime we do detect is just the tip of the iceberg.

The Growth of Computer Crime

Despite our lack of statistics, we believe computer crime is growing. One reason is the exponential growth in computer resources—for example, microcomputers, computer networks, and the Internet. As more people become knowledgeable about how to use computers, more people also learn how to compromise computer systems. For example, there are now millions of microcomputer users in the world, but many of them are not aware of, or conscientious about, computer security. Then, too, some users are dishonest and now have a new tool with which to commit frauds. Lastly many Internet pages now give step-by-step instructions on how to perpetrate computer crimes. For example, an Internet search found more than 17,000 matches for "denial of service," a rapidly growing form of computer abuse, and there are now thousands of web pages that detail how to break into routers and disable web servers.

> *Case-in-Point 11.3* Dan Farmer, who wrote SATAN (a network security testing tool), tested 2,200 high-profile web sites at governmental institutions, banks, newspapers, and so forth. Only three of these web sites detected his probes and contacted him to find out what he was trying to do. His conclusion: two out of every three web sites have serious vulnerabilities and most of the control procedures at these sites are ineffective.

A final reason why we believe computer crime is growing comes from comparing annual computer expenditures with annual spending on computer controls. Figure 11-3 suggests that spending on computer equipment over the last few years has grown at an accelerated rate, while spending on computer controls has at best grown linearly. The exact figures for these spending categories are not important. It is the widening gap between them, which represents an increasing vulnerability to computer abuse, that is important. This gap suggests that the potential for computer abuse is increasing, and therefore leads us to believe that computer crime is growing whether or not we detect it.

The Importance of Computer Abuse

The absence of good computer-crime statistics does not detract from the importance of computer abuse to accountants. One reason for this is because AISs help control an organization's financial resources and thus are favored targets of computer abusers. As noted previously, AISs are also prized targets for disgruntled employees seeking to compromise computer systems for reasons other than financial gain—for

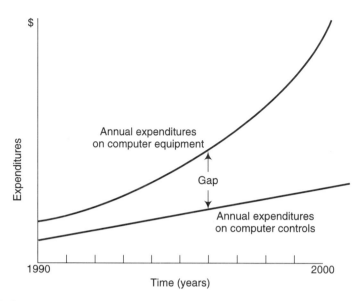

FIGURE 11–3   The gap between annual expenditures on computer equipment and computer controls is widening, thereby increasing exposure to computer abuse. (Source: NCCCD.)

example, revenge. Yet a third reason computer crime is important is because accounting professionals are responsible for designing, implementing, and monitoring the control procedures for AISs.

Computer abuse is also important because of the large proportion of firms that suffer computer-related losses. A 1998 study by the Computer Security Institute (CSI), for example, found that about two thirds of all U.S. organizations suffer at least one serious computer abuse each year. The figure over time (rather than for any given year) probably exceeds 90 percent for all U.S. organizations.

The impact on the firms that suffer computer abuse varies widely. Losses from one-time hits can be as little as a few thousand dollars. But most computer abuse is systematic, with the perpetrator(s) stealing for years. The average loss in the 1998 CSI study was approximately $57,000. Experts also note that when organizations do discover computer abuse, the subsequent investigative audit costs can exceed the actual monetary losses. As a result, the financial impact ranges from "substantial" to "catastrophic."

> ***Case-in-Point 11.4***   In a parallel universe, the master accountant for the great warlord was teaching his new apprentice about computer crime. "It seems to me," said the apprentice, "that computer crime is really just old wine in new bottles."
>
> "In a way, you are right," replied the master accountant. "But they are pretty big bottles."

EXAMPLES OF COMPUTER-CRIME CASES

Computer crime is perhaps best understood by studying selected cases that have occurred in the past. As one reads the fascinating accounts of different computer crimes, a pattern begins to emerge. One type of crime depends mostly on the falsification of input data, while another depends on unauthorized access to computerized files. This section of the chapter examines three specific cases of computer abuse, each of which provides important lessons on a different type of computer crime.

Compromising Valuable Information: The TRW Credit Data Case

A major class of computer crime involves illegal access to, or misuse of, the information stored in an AIS, and is thus **valuable-information computer crime.** In the **TRW Credit Data case,** the valuable information involved was computerized credit data. TRW is one of several large, credit-rating companies in the United States. When the fraud was discovered, the company was collecting and disseminating credit information on approximately 50 million individuals. Clients of TRW included banks, retail stores, and such credit-conscious concerns as Diner's Club, American Express, MasterCard, Visa, Sears, Roebuck and Co., and several leasing establishments.

TRW advised its clients of bad credit risks on the basis of the information it maintained in its databases. Clearly, however, this information could be changed. The fraud began when six company employees, including a key TRW clerk in the consumer relations department, realized this fact and began selling good credit to individuals with bad credit ratings. The names and addresses of the bad credit risks were already on file. It merely remained to contact these individuals and inform them of a newfound method of altering their records. Accordingly, individuals with bad credit ratings were approached and offered a clean bill of health in return for a "management fee."

Those people who decided to buy good credit ratings paid TRW employees "under the table," and the clerk in the consumer relations department then inserted into TRW's credit files whatever false information was required to reverse the individual's bad credit rating. In some cases, this required deleting unfavorable information that was already stored in the individual's credit record. In others, it required adding favorable information. Fees for such services varied from a few hundred dollars to $1,500 per individual. Ironically, the TRW clerk who ultimately input the false information to the computer system received only $50 for each altered record. However, the losses resulting from these activities were not so inconsequential. Independent estimates have placed this figure at close to $1 million.

The principal victims of the fraud were TRW's clients, who acted on credit information that ultimately turned out to be inaccurate. Exactly how many file records were altered is difficult to say. Lawyers for the prosecution documented 16 known cases of altered file records, but had reason to believe the number exceeded 100 cases. Paradoxically, the prosecution had difficulty acquiring testimonies because the buyers of good credit standing as well as the TRW sellers were technically in violation of the law by conspiring to falsify credit-rating information.

Analysis   In most cases of valuable information computer crime, the information is contained in a company's computer programs or databases because such items (1) are proprietary, (2) may give a firm a competitive advantage in its industry, and/or (3) are usually worth more than a company's hardware in terms of development and replacement costs. Thus, several cases of corporate computer espionage involving the theft, or attempted theft, of key computer programs or data have been reported in the literature on computer crime.

The TRW case involves two key issues: (1) the propriety of the input information used in updating a specific AIS, and (2) the protection afforded both consumer and user in the accuracy and use of credit information that is gathered by a private company. With regard to the first point, it is clear that the fraud was successful only because the perpetrators were able to enter false information into the computer system. This observation points to the importance of control procedures (e.g., authorization and validation of credit changes) to safeguard the accuracy and completeness of file information. In fact, as is true of so many cases of computer crime, the six TRW employees involved in the fraud were caught only by chance: an individual approached with an offer to buy a good credit rating for $600 became angry and called the FBI. Later, the TRW clerk in the consumer relations department decided to turn state's evidence.

The second point involving the protection of the consumer and user of credit information encompasses a much larger issue. In 1970, Congress passed the Fair Credit Reporting Act, which requires that an individual be told why he or she is denied credit. The consumer also has the right to contest the information maintaned by the credit-rating company, although there is clearly a vast difference between the right to *challenge,* versus the right to *change,* credit information.

TRW has reported that, directly after the Fair Credit Reporting Act went into effect, consumer inquiries increased a hundred fold and that at the time the fraud was detected, approximately 200,000 consumers annually were complaining about their credit ratings. The fact that, by TRW's own admission, fully one third of these inquiries resulted in a file change or update is unsettling. Moreover, it is not known how much more information collected by TRW is still inaccurate but simply not challenged—for example, because an individual is not aware of an inaccuracy, or because the consumer does not know his or her rights under the law.

Computer Hacking: The Kevin D. Mitnick Case

This is the story of **Kevin D. Mitnick,** who, at the time of his arrest in February 1995 at the age of 31, had become the FBI's most wanted **computer hacker** (i.e., a person who breaks into the computer files of others for fun or personal gain). Mitnick grew up in southern California, where, as part of a gang of high school hackers, he learned how to tap phone lines and copy computer access codes. At age 17, he was caught stealing technical computer manuals from Pacific Bell and software from a computer firm but was given a probationary sentence because of his age. A year later, Mitnick broke into a computer used by the North American Air Defense Command and stole $1 million worth of software from Digital Equipment Corporation. This time he was sentenced to one year in jail.

After his jail time, Mitnick seemed to reform. His license plate even read "X Hacker." But in June 1992, the California Department of Motor Vehicles caught Mitnick impersonating a state official, probably to obtain classified information that would enable him to create false identification for himself. To avoid arrest, Mitnick disappeared.

Mitnick was a compulsive hacker who continued his bad habits. In 1995, he broke into the personal files of Tsutomu Shimomura, a researcher at the San Diego Supercomputer Center. Shimomura realized that a hacker was active on the network and reported the break-in to the FBI. Together, Shimomura and the FBI tracked Mitnick to an apartment in Raleigh, North Carolina. At 2 AM on February 15, 1995, FBI agents raided Mitnick's apartment and arrested him. Among other things, FBI agents discovered that Mitnick had logged onto the Internet and stolen 20,000 credit card numbers worth more than $1 million.

Analysis Hacking is a widespread problem. This is due, in part, to the fact that many computer applications now run on local and wide area networks, where computer files becomes accessible to unauthorized users. Then, too, the Internet enables users to log onto computers from remote sites, again increasing vulnerability to hacking.

It is not clear whether Mitnick stole the credit card numbers for personal gain or merely for the challenge of doing it. This "challenge" motive is one reason why hacking is not universally condemned. For example, a close friend of Mitnick's argued, "If you think you can beat the system, you have to beat it." This person also said, "Stealing implies taking something and leaving nothing. If he's just copying something, he's not stealing."[1] But hackers often do steal.

> ***Case-in-Point 11.5*** In 1995, Citibank Corporation discovered that it had been the victim of a massive fraud. Over the course of two years, an obscure Russian programmer named Volodya Levin had used his personal computer and a Sprint telephone link to transfer over $10 million of bank funds to personal accounts in over half a dozen countries around the world.

Hacking is also a favorite technique for compromising telephone systems. One activity is stealing the computer codes of private branch exchange (PBX) telephone systems, which hackers then use to make free long-distance calls or sell to others for the same purpose. A related abuse is stealing cellular phone identification numbers and using them to make free long-distance calls. A third activity is **shoulder surfing,** which involves stealing calling card numbers at public phones such as airport phones and that costs consumers $450 million annually.

Computer hacking is common in universities, where students often view the activity as a harmless game of "beating the system." Recently, for example, a group of student hackers called the "Legion of Doom" stole data from the BellSouth Telephone Company and disrupted its 911 emergency phone system just to see if they could do it. Educational institutions view hacking as a particularly perplexing problem because the need for tight system security conflicts with the objective of providing easy and simple computer access to bona fide users.

Although better state and federal laws may help discourage computer hacking, the most effective deterrents are likely to be preventive rather than punitive. One helpful tactic is user education—i.e., making potential hackers aware of the ethics of computer usage and the inconvenience, lost time, and costs incurred by victim organizations. Another safeguard is to require user passwords, which limit computer access to bona fide users. But passwords are not foolproof mechanisms because, at present, computers cannot distinguish between authorized employees using their own passwords and unauthorized users entering compromised passwords. Thus, until bio-safeguards such as retina or fingerprint scanners become widely available, protecting passwords is paramount. We will review some methods for this in the next section of the chapter.

Many hackers brag that they can compromise any type of file information once they have successfully logged into a computer system. One way they achieve this is to

---

[1] *San Francisco Chronicle,* February 17, 1995, p. 17.

elevate their system status to that of a "privileged user" or "network manager," a security level that gains the hackers access to password files, system control data, and other high-security information. These activities are thwarted by using system programming routines that test for, and deny, such bootstrapping and that also immediately communicate such attempts to computer supervisors as possible security violations.

Case-in-Point 11.6 When hackers invaded NDA, a consulting firm in Woburn, Massachusetts, they installed a program that enabled them to record users' passwords and access the network freely. The invaders copied files containing ID codes for cellular phones, gathered sensitive information on NDA's business customers, and then launched similar attacks on those companies.

Computer Viruses: Robert T. Morris and the Internet Virus Case

A **computer virus** is a program that disrupts normal data processing and is usually able to replicate itself onto other files, computer systems, or networks. The Internet makes it easy for virus programs to spread from one system to another. **Robert Tappan Morris** exploited these characteristics to create one of the world's most famous computer viruses. His father worked as a computer security expert for the National Security Agency, and Morris himself was a well-mannered, respected, 23-year-old graduate student at Cornell University, with several hobbies besides programming computers.

What made Morris special was his secret interest in virus programs. On November 2, 1988, Morris used his university Internet link to send an e-mail program containing a worm program to an MIT computer. The program Morris wrote exploited a little-known feature of Unix operating systems that allows users to encrypt computer programs in e-mail messages. But once this e-mail was received, it began executing—specifically, by finding the names of online users and sending itself to their computers, thus replicating itself repeatedly.

At his trial, Morris stated, "I wanted to see if I could write a program that would spread as widely as possible on the Internet." He succeeded. Within a few hours of sending his initial e-mail, the program was out of control. In a panic, Morris called friends at other universities, asking for advice and requesting them to warn others. By then, however, it was too late. The virus had replicated itself so often that the Internet computers affected were overloaded with extra files and thus could not receive the e-mail warnings.

Analysts estimate that the virus Morris created disrupted about 6,200 Internet computers, including several operated by NASA, the Defense Advanced Research Project Agency (DARPA), and the U.S. Air Force. Most of these organizations' systems had to be shut down while system administrators spent days ferreting out the virus, deleting the many copies of it, and rebuilding files and programs from backups.

Morris was quickly arrested. When he was arraigned in July 1989, he became the first person to be indicted under the Computer Fraud and Abuse Act of 1986. A grand jury convicted Morris in January of 1990. Estimates of the damages resulting from his virus program run as high as $100 million. In view of these damages, many observers feel that the subsequent sentence given to Robert T. Morris—a $10,000 fine, a probationary three-year jail term, and 400 hours of community service—was not enough. (Morris might also have been disciplined by Cornell University, but he left voluntarily before that could happen.)

Analysis Computer virus infections are the number one type of computer abuse (Figure 11-4). Some computer viruses are relatively benign—for example, a "playful virus" that merely displays a message on screen. Most, however, are more destructive, such as viruses that destroy complete disk files. By 1997, McAffee Associates, an antivirus software developer, had identified more than 11,000 different computer viruses. A recent survey of 300 private and public computer sites conducted by the International Computer Security Association, in Carlisle, Pennsylvania, found viruses in more than 3 percent of the survey sites.

Most computer viruses reside on floppy diskettes or hard disks, where they hide until finding an opportunity to execute. There are several variations of these viruses. **Boot-sector viruses** hide in the boot sectors of a disk, where the operating system accesses them every time it accesses the disk itself. **Worm programs** do not actually destroy data but merely replicate themselves repeatedly until the user runs out of internal memory or disk space. **Trojan horse programs** reside in legitimate copies of computer programs, for example, spreadsheet programs. Logic bomb programs are similar to Trojan horse programs, except that they remain dormant until the computer system encounters a specific condition, such as a particular day of the year or a particular Social Security number in a file. (Trojan horse and logic bomb programs are termed "programs" rather than "viruses" because they sometimes contain code to defraud users rather than viruses that destroy computer resources.)

The Internet is a perfect environment for computer viruses because so many people use it for e-mail, conducting research, and downloading files or software. For example, a virus might be stored in a java **applet** (i.e., a small program that is stored in a web page and designed to run by web browser software). Friendly applets animate web pages, allow users to play games, or perform processing tasks. But unfriendly applets contain viruses that can infect other computers and cause damage.

The case of Robert T. Morris illustrates the vulnerability of computer networks to virus infections. Once a programmer has lodged a computer virus program on the

Virus infection	83%
Abusive use of internet	69%
Laptop theft	58%
Unauthorized inside user	40%
Telecommunications fraud	27%
Information theft	21%
Network break-in	20%
Sabotage	14%
Financial fraud	12%
Telecom eavesdropping	11%
Active wiretap	4%

FIGURE 11-4 The most common types of computer crimes. (Source: CSI, 1997.)

file server of a computer network, the program can affect thousands of other computers or disks before it can be detected and eradicated. Estimating the business costs of recovering from a virus infection is difficult. The costs can be small—for example, limited to the inconveniences of reformatting a hard disk and reloading a few software programs. On the other hand, the business costs to recover from virus infections can be large. According to one survey of U.S. corporations, virus infections now cost businesses nearly $2 billion a year.

Two major ways to thwart computer viruses are through (1) antivirus software and (2) antivirus control procedures. **Antivirus software** are computer programs that can scan computer inputs for virus-like coding, identify active viruses that are already lodged in computer systems, cleanse computer systems already infected, or perform some combination of these activities. Recent versions of Microsoft's Windows operating system incorporate software of this type. Generally speaking, however, antivirus programs provide less than complete protection because misguided individuals continuously write new, more powerful viruses that can avoid current detection schemes. Even worse, some antivirus programs have themselves contained virus routines.

For many microcomputer users, antivirus control procedures are often better safeguards. These include (1) buying shrink-wrapped software from reputable sources, (2) avoiding illegal software copying, (3) not downloading suspicious Internet files, (4) deleting e-mail messages from unknown sources before opening them, and (5) maintaining complete backup files in the event you must rebuild your system from scratch. Additional safeguards include loading operating systems only from your own disks, being wary of public-domain software available on Internet bulletin boards, and being suspicious of unusual activity of your computer system—for example, spontaneous disk writing that you did not initiate.

In organizational settings, effective control procedures against computer viruses include educating users about viruses and encouraging computer users to follow the virus prevention and detection techniques just discussed. Additional control procedures include (1) adopting policies that discourage the free exchange of computer disks or externally acquired computer programs, (2) requiring computer passwords to limit unauthorized access to computing resources, (3) using antivirus filters on local and wide-area networks, and (4) developing and testing a **disaster recovery plan** that enables a business to replace its critical computer systems in a timely fashion.

THWARTING COMPUTER ABUSE

What can organizations do to protect themselves against computer abuse? Experts note that, for all their intricacy and mystique, we can protect computer systems from abuses just as well as we can manual systems, and sometimes better. For example, computers can be programmed to automatically search for anomalies and to print exception conditions on control reports. These computerized monitoring systems are often superior to manual surveillance methods because they are automatic and can screen 100 percent, instead of merely a sample, of the target population data. The New York Stock Exchange now uses an Integrated Computer-Assisted Surveillance System (ICASS) to search for insider trading activities. This section of the chapter discusses several methods for thwarting computer abuses.

Enlist Top-Management Support

Because many top managers are not fully aware of the dangers of computer abuse, it is not surprising that many of them are unconcerned about this type of abuse. What is surprising is how many technically competent IT managers also fail to rank "computer security" among the top 20 management issues in their companies. Computer safeguards are only effective if management takes computer crime seriously and chooses to implement and enforce control procedures to stop, or at least minimize, computer abuse. Thus, most computer systems experts point to the critical importance of top-management support as a primary computer-crime safeguard. This awareness then filters down through the management ranks with practical safeguards built into each employee's general training and thinking.

Increase Employee Awareness and Education

Ultimately, controlling computer crime means controlling people. This is because people commit computer crimes, not computers. But which people? The idea that computer crimes are "outside jobs" is a myth. With the exception of hackers, most computer abusers are the employees of the same companies at which the crimes take place. Many retail firms have clear prosecution policies regarding shoplifting. In contrast, prosecution policies associated with other types of employee fraud are notable for their absence in most organizations. Yet, the evidence suggests that prosecuting computer abuses may be one of the most effective restraints on computer crime.

In fairness, employees cannot be expected to automatically understand the problems or ramifications of computer crime. Thus, another dimension of preventing computer abuse is employee education. Informing employees of the significance of computer abuse, the amount it costs, and the work disruption it creates helps employees understand why computer abuse is a serious matter. Studies suggest that "informal discussions," "periodic departmental memos," and "formal guidelines" are among the most popular educational tools for informing employees about computer abuse. In a KPMG Peat Marwick study, the most favored approach was to establish corporate codes of conduct.

Protect Passwords

Beyond protecting computer systems from unauthorized access, passwords help organizations limit classes of users to specific computer resources or files (e.g., deny university students access to administrative records), allocate computer time or printing activities, and trace specific computer inputs to particular users. Such uses make clear how important it is to protect such passwords from unauthorized use or abuse. But how can organizations protect passwords?

One safeguard is educating users to protect their own passwords—for example, by not lending them to others or taping them to their monitors or desktops. To steal passwords, computer criminals often use simulation programs that try all the words in a standard dictionary as potential passwords. To control for this abuse, passwords should be nonsense words (e.g., words with embedded capitals or random numbers) rather than recognizable words. Another control is to require employees to change their passwords periodically. A third control is to install password-checking software in file servers that test passwords for such requirements.

Hackers often use a tactic called **social engineering** to gain access to passwords (i.e., posing as bona fide employees and convincing network administrators to give them passwords over the phone). While it is advisable to distribute new passwords through external channels rather than through computer systems themselves, the practice of giving passwords to unknown employees over the phone compromises standard security procedures, and therefore should not be allowed.

Two additional password safeguards are lock-out systems and dialback systems. **Lock-out systems** disconnect telephone users after a set number of unsuccessful login attempts, thereby thwarting microcomputer users from using dictionary programs. Similarly, **dialback systems** first disconnect all login users but reconnect legitimate users after checking their passwords against lists of bona fide user codes. Dialback systems may be even more effective than lock-out systems because only authorized users at already recognized stations are reconnected.

Implement Controls

Computer-crime studies mostly reach the same conclusion: the number of organizations without proper computer security is high by almost any standard. Is it any wonder, then, that most computer abuse succeeds because of the absence of controls rather than the failure of controls? In other words, computer abuse flourishes mostly because there is nothing to stop it and there are no control procedures to expose it to managerial scrutiny.

There are many reasons why businesses do not implement control procedures to deter computer crime. One is the all-too-common belief of those managers who have not suffered a computer crime that they have nothing to fear. Then, too, those businesses that do not have a specific computer security officer have no one to articulate this concern or to argue for specific control procedures. Finally, at least some businesses do not feel that security measures are cost-effective—until they incur a problem!

The solution to the computer-security problems of most organizations is straightforward: design and implement controls. This means that organizations should install control procedures to deter computer crime, managers should enforce them, and both internal and external auditors should test them. Experts also suggest that employee awareness of computer controls and the certainty of prosecution may also act as deterrents to computer crime.

In the United States, a disproportionate amount of computer fraud and security break-ins occur during the end-of-the-year holiday season. Reasons for this include. (1) extended employee vacations and therefore fewer people to "mind the store," (2) students are out of school and therefore have more free time on their hands, and (3) counterculture hackers get lonely at year-end and increase their attacks on computer systems. Thus, it is especially important to make sure that effective control procedures are in place during the holidays.

Identify Computer Criminals

To prevent given types of crimes, criminologists often look for common character traits that can be used to screen potential culprits. What are the characteristics of the individuals who abuse computers, and what can be done to create a composite profile that organizations can use to evaluate job applicants?

Nontechnical Backgrounds   Most computer abuse is performed by a company's own employees—not external hackers. How technically competent are such employees? Figure 11-5 identifies the job occupations of computer abusers from a survey performed by Hoffer and Straub. Although this figure suggests that some computer abuse is committed by those with strong technical backgrounds, this study found that almost as much computer abuse is performed by clerical personnel, data-entry clerks, and similar individuals with limited technical skills. A similar study by the U.S. Sentencing Commission (USSC) found that most of the 174 computer criminals convicted under the Computer Crime and Abuse Act of 1986 were corporate insiders with only "pedestrian levels" of computer expertise. There is good reason for this. It is usually easier and safer to alter data before they enter a computer than midway through automated processing cycles. Then too, input data can often be changed anonymously, whereas most computerized data cannot. These facts explain why many computer criminals are not even computer literate, and also why computer security must extend beyond IT personnel.

Morals and Criminal Backgrounds   The USSC study also found that most of the convicted defendants had no prior criminal backgrounds. In addition, most computer criminals tend to view themselves as relatively honest. They argue, for example, that "beating the system" is not the same as stealing from another person or that they are merely using a computer to take what other employees take from a filing cabinet. Furthermore, many perpetrators think of themselves as long-term borrowers rather than thieves, and several have exercised great care to avoid harming individuals when they committed their computer abuses. These ideas are as misguided as they are common.

Education, Gender, and Age   Computer abusers tend to be bright, motivated, talented, and qualified individuals with good intellects and superior educational backgrounds—the very qualifications that impress hiring managers in the first place. If there are any common characteristics of the computer abusers that we have caught to date, it is the fact most are males under thirty years of age. In a study performed by the National Center for Computer Crime data, for example, more than 70 percent of computer crime defendants were such men. However, because we believe that most computer abuse is not detected or prosecuted (when it is detected), we do not know how representative these findings are about the "general population" of computer abusers.

Programmers and Systems Analysts	27%
Clerical, Data Entry, and Machine Operators	23%
Managers and Top Executives	15%
Other System Users	14%
Students	12%
Consultants	3%
Other Information Processing Staff	3%
All others	3%
Total	100%

FIGURE 11-5   Occupations of computer abuse offenders.

Recognize the Symptoms of Employee Fraud

The clues that signal some computer abuses can be subtle and ambiguous, but many more are relatively self-evident. For example, the study conducted by KPMG Peat Marwick concluded that nearly half the employee fraud would have been detected more quickly if obvious telltale symptoms had not been ignored. Although recognizing the symptoms of computer abuse will not thwart computer abuse, knowing the telltale signs may help detect it and minimize damage. Consider, for example, Case-in-Point 11.7:

> **Case-in-Point 11.7** The Elgin Corporation was a manufacturing company that had created its own health care plan for its employees. The plan was self-insured for medical claims under $50,000, which it handled internally, but plan administrators forwarded claims for larger amounts to an independent insurance company. The managers of Elgin Corporation believed that the company had excellent control procedures for its system, which included both internal and external audits. Yet, over a period of four years, the manager of the medical claims department was able to embezzle more than $12 million from the company!

Although the "Elgin" name is fictitious, the events described above are not. How can such events be avoided? Here are five typical symptoms of computer abuse that actually occurred at the Elgin Corporation.

Accounting Irregularities To embezzle funds successfully, employees commonly alter, forge, or destroy input documents, or perform suspicious accounting adjustments. An unusually high number of such irregularities are cause for concern. At the Elgin Corporation, no one noticed that payments to 22 of the physicians submitting claims to the company were sent to the same two addresses or that these payments totaled over $12 million in four years.

Internal Control Weaknesses Control procedures are often absent, weak, or ignored in computer-abuse cases. At the Elgin Corporation, the medical claims manager had not taken a vacation for years, those employees submitting claims were never sent confirmation notices of the medical payments made in their behalf, and the physicians receiving these payments were never first investigated or approved.

Unreasonable Anomalies Perhaps the most important clue to computer abuse is the presence of many odd or unusual anomalies that somehow go unchallenged. Examined critically, such anomalies are unreasonable and require observers to suspend common sense. At the Elgin Corporation, for example, why were 100 percent of the medical payments to those 22 physicians all paid from the self-insured portion of the company program? Why were checks to those 22 physicians always endorsed by hand and deposited in the same two checking accounts? And why did some of the medical claims include hysterectomies for male employees?

Lifestyle Changes Employees who miraculously solve pressing financial problems or suddenly begin living extravagant lifestyles are sometimes merely broadcasting fraud. At the Elgin Corporation, why did the medical claims manager announce that she had inherited a lot of money but never took a vacation? And why did she treat her employees to lunches in chauffeured limousines?

Behavioral Changes   Employees who experience guilt or remorse from their crimes, or who fear discovery, often express these feelings in unusual behavior. At the Elgin Corporation, employees joked that the medical claims manager had recently developed a "Jekyll and Hyde personality," including intense mood swings that were unusual even for her.

Employ Forensic Accountants

Forensic accountants concern themselves with the prevention and detection of fraud and white-collar crime. When an organization suspects an ongoing computer abuse, it often turns to one or more forensic accountants to investigate problems and make recommendations. Many such individuals are professional accountants who have passed the two-day certified fraud examiner (CFE) examination administered by the **Association of Certified Fraud Examiners**—an international professional organization committed to detecting, deterring, and preventing fraud and white-collar crime.

Forensic accountants have the prerequisite technical and legal experience to research a given concern, follow leads, establish audit trails of questionable transactions, document their findings, organize evidence for external review and law enforcement bodies, and (if necessary) testify in court. Forensic accounting is one of the fastest-growing areas of accounting, and there are now more than 15,000 CFEs working in organizations such as law firms and CPA firms.

COMPUTERS AND ETHICAL BEHAVIOR

Computerized AISs often raise ethical issues that we did not have to face under manual AISs. An example is the practice of unauthorized software copying. Thus, thwarting computer abuse is sometimes more dependent on ethical behavior than observing legal restrictions. **Ethics** is a set of moral principles or values. Therefore, ethical behavior involves making choices and judgments that are morally proper and then acting accordingly. Ethics can govern organizations as well as individuals. In the context of an organization, an underlying ethical principle is that each individual in the organization has responsibility for the welfare of others within the organization, as well as for the organization itself. For example, the managers of a company should make decisions that are fair to the employees as well as gainful to the company.

Ethical Issues and Professional Associations

Ethical concerns often become important when computer abuse is not performed for financial gain. In cases involving hacking, for example, "ignorance of proper conduct" or "misguided playfulness" may be the problem. To some, the challenge of defrauding a computer system and avoiding detection is irresistible because success brings recognition, notoriety, and even heroism. In these cases, ethical issues are overlooked and the costs of recovering from the abuse are ignored. The acceptability of these motives comes down to issues of morality. But "morality" in corporate cultures is typically a relative value. In one case, for example, a man named Fred

Darm stole a computer program from a rival firm through his computer terminal. At his trial, the defense argued that it was common practice for programmers of rival firms to "snoop" in each other's data files to obtain competitive information. Thus, when he was apprehended for his offense, Darm was not only surprised, he was quite offended!

Such professional accounting associations as the Institute of Management Accountants (IMA), the American Institute of Certified Public Accountants (AICPA), the Institute of Internal Auditors (IIA), and the Information Systems Audit and Control Association (ISACA)—formerly the EDP Auditor's Association—have had codes of ethics or codes of professional conduct in force for a number of years. These professional accounting association codes are self-imposed and self-enforced rules of conduct. One of the most important goals of a code of ethics or conduct is to aid professionals in selecting among alternatives that are not clear-cut. Included within professional association codes are rules pertaining to subjects such as independence, technical competence, and proper practices during audits and consulting engagements involving information systems. The certification programs of these associations increase awareness of the codes of ethics and are essential in developing professionalism.

In recent years, professional accounting associations at both the national and state level have established ethics committees to assist practitioners in the self-regulation process. These ethics committees provide their members with continuing education courses, advice on ethical issues, investigations of possible ethics violations, and instructional booklets covering a variety of ethics case studies. Some of the ethics committees provide their members with a "hot line" to advise them on the ethical and moral dilemmas experienced in the workplace. These committees also encourage the instruction of ethics in accounting curricula at colleges and universities.

Professional computer associations, such as the Association of Information Technology Professionals (AITP), formerly the Data Processing Management Association (DPMA), and the Association for Computing Machinery (ACM), have developed codes of ethics, ethics committees, and certification programs. The codes of these professional computer associations examine such issues as obligations to their professional associations, clients, and society. Next, we present a few examples of ethical issues in computer usage.

Honesty   Organizations expect their employees to perform their own work, to refrain from accessing unauthorized information, and to provide authentic results of program outputs. Conversely, submitting false or outdated computerized information may not be illegal but is almost certainly classified as "dishonest."

Protecting Computer Systems   Computer users can deny others access to system resources without damaging the system itself. Examples include tying up network access ports with multiple logins, sending voluminous (but useless) e-mails and computer files to others, and complaining to system administrators about fictitious hardware or software failures. The extreme of such behavior, of course, is introducing computer viruses into networks. It is also unethical to give unauthorized users access to private computer systems or to allow such individuals to view the information available from such systems.

Protecting Confidential Information   Computerizing sensitive information sometimes also makes this information available to those without an immediate right to see it—for example, when the financial data on a mortgage loan application or the results of diagnostic medical tests are stored in the files of local area networks. Organizations may not be legally bound to protect this information, although most professionals would argue that employees are morally bound to do so.

Social Responsibility Individuals should act responsibly, especially where public safety is at stake. Sometimes, however, social responsibility conflicts with other organizational goals. For example, suppose a programmer discovers a possible error in a software program that controls a missile guidance system. His boss tells him to ignore it—the design team is already over budget and this is only a possible error.

Rights of Privacy Computers can be used to monitor the activities of others. But do organizations have the right to do so if they violate individual privacy? For example, do organizations have the right to read the personal e-mail of their employees? For that matter, do employees have the right to use their business e-mail accounts for personal correspondence?

Acceptable Use The availability of computer hardware and software in workplaces does not automatically convey unrestricted uses of them. At universities, for example, ethical conduct forbids downloading microcomputer software for personal applications or using free mainframe time for personal gain.

Meeting the Ethical Challenges

Because a significant amount of business activity and data communications now takes place on the Internet, it is not surprising that an increasing amount of computer abuse also happens within the Internet's environment. Examples include thieves supplying fake credit card numbers to buy everything from investment securities to Internet access time itself, copying web pages without permission, denying legitimate users Internet access, and posing as someone else for any number of illicit purposes.

How we respond to the above ethical issues is determined not so much by laws or organizational rules as by our own sense of "right" and "wrong." Ethical standards of behavior are a function of many things, including social expectations, culture, societal norms, and even the times in which we live. More than anything else, however, ethical behavior requires personal discipline and a commitment to "do the right thing."

How can organizations encourage ethical behavior? Some argue that morals are only learned at an early age and in the home—they cannot be taught to adults who think otherwise. However, others suggest that it helps to (1) inform employees that ethics are important, (2) formally expose employees to relevant cases that teach them how to act responsibly in specific situations, (3) teach by example, that is, by managers acting responsibly, and (4) use job promotions and other benefits to reward those employees who act responsibly. Informing employees that ethics are important (point 1 above) is emphasized in Case-in-Point 11.8, which summarizes the computing code of ethics at the University of Northern Colorado.

Case-in-Point 11.8 The ethical principles that apply to everyday community life also apply to computing. At the University of Northern Colorado, every member has two basic rights: privacy and a fair share of resources. It is unethical for any other person to violate these rights. This code of ethics lays down general guidelines for the use of computing and information resources. Failure to observe the code may lead to disciplinary action.

Encouraging employees to join professional accounting and computer associations with ethical codes is important. (These associations and their ethical codes were examined in the previous section.) To provide more specific and detailed examples from a professional association's ethical code, the **Codes of Conduct and Good Practice for Certified Computer Professionals** are presented in Figure 11-6.

---

2. Code of conduct

2.1: Disclosure: Subject to the confidential relationships between oneself and one's employer or client, one is expected not to transmit information which one acquires during the practice of one's profession in any situation which may harm or seriously affect a third party.

2.2: Social responsibility: One is expected to combat ignorance about information processing technology in those public areas where one's application can be expected to have an adverse social impact.

2.3: Conclusions and opinions: One is expected to state a conclusion on a subject in one's field only when it can be demonstrated that it has been founded on adequate knowledge. One will state a qualified opinion when expressing a view in an area within one's professional competence but not supported by relevant facts.

2.4: Identification: One shall properly qualify oneself when expressing an opinion outside of one's professional competence in the event that such an opinion could be identified by a third party as expert testimony, or if by inference, the opinion can be expected to be used improperly.

2.5: Integrity: One will not knowingly lay claims to competence one does not demonstrably possess.

2.6: Conflict of interest: One shall act with strict impartiality when purporting to give independent advice. In the event that the advice given is currently or potentially influential to one's personal benefit; full and detailed disclosure of all relevant interests will be made at the time the advice is provided. One will not denigrate the honesty or competence of a fellow professional or a competitor, with intent to gain an unfair advantage.

2.7: Accountability: The degree of professional accountability for results will be dependent on the position held and the type of work performed.

2.8: Protection of privacy: One shall have special regard for the potential effects of computer-based systems on the right of privacy of individuals, whether this is within one's own organization, among customers or suppliers, or in relation to the general public.

Because of the privileged capability of computer professionals to gain access to computerized files, especially strong strictures will be applied to those who use their positions of trust to obtain information from computerized files for their personal gain.

Where it is possible that decisions can be made within a computer-based system which could adversely affect the personal security, work, or career of an individual, the system design shall specifically provide for decision review by a responsible executive, who will thus remain accountable and identifiable for that decision.

3. Code of good practice

3.1: Education: One has a special responsibility to keep oneself fully aware of developments in information processing technology relevant to one's current professional occupation. One will contribute to the interchange of technical and professional information by encouraging and participating in education activities directed both to fellow professionals and to the public at large. One will do all in one's power to further public understanding of computer systems. One will contribute to the growth of knowledge in the field to the extent that one's expertise, time, and position allow.

3.2: Personal conduct: Insofar as one's personal and professional activities interact with the public, one is expected to apply the same high standards of behavior in one's personal life as are demanded in one's professional activities.

3.3: Competence: One shall at all times exercise technical and professional competence at least to the level one claims. One shall not deliberately withhold information in one's possession unless disclosure of that information could harm or seriously affect another party, or unless one is bound by a proper, clearly defined confidential relationship. One shall not deliberately destroy or diminish the value or effectiveness of a computer-based system through acts of commission or omission.

3.4: Statements: One shall not make false or exaggerated statements as to the state of affairs existing or expected regarding any aspect of information technology or the use of computers.

In communicating with laypersons, one shall use general language whenever possible and shall not use technical terms or expressions unless there exist no adequate equivalents in the general language.

3.5: Discretion: One shall exercise maximum discretion in disclosing, or permitting to be disclosed, or using to one's own advantage, any information relating to the affairs of one's present or previous employers or clients.

3.6: Conflict of interest: One shall not hold, assume, or consciously accept a position in which one's interests conflict or are likely to conflict with one's current duties unless that interest has been disclosed in advance to all parties involved.

3.7: Violations: One is expected to report violations of the Code, testify in ethical proceedings where one has expert or firsthand knowledge, and serve on panels to judge complaints of violations of ethical conduct.

FIGURE 11-6 Selections from the "Codes of Conduct and Good Practice for Certified Computer Professionals," published by the Institute for Certification of Computer Professionals (ICCP).

Case-in-Point 11.9   In a parallel universe, the master accountant had finished the lesson on computer crime, but the apprentice had one more question. "I can see why it is important to safeguard computer systems from many forms of computer abuse. But is this necessary when most people are honest?"

   The master accountant replied sadly, "I used to think that 95 percent of the people are 100 percent honest. I now think that 100 percent of the people are 95 percent honest."

AIS AT WORK
Firms Fight Back

Charles Schwab and Co. is a San Francisco discount brokerage firm that handles more than $400 billion in assets in 4 million active customer accounts worldwide. But unlike many businesses that hesitate to report computer-crime incidents, Charles Schwab actively works with law enforcement agencies to report and prosecute computer abuse.

Says Ed Ehrgott, the company's director of internal audit, "We have a fraud unit that consists of about twenty IT security people who constantly assess and monitor network traffic operations both internally and externally, checking on traffic usage and audit trails. In the event the worst happens and we get hit, we're ready with a trail of evidence to turn over to the proper authorities."

Not all companies are willing to work that hard to limit their vulnerability, experts say. Notes John Davis, the director of the National Computer Security Center at the National Security Agency in Baltimore, "Risk is what companies must live with when they only allocate limited monies and resources for network security. And corporations that do that have to hope they can live with the threat."

Like many of her fellow managers, Christine Snyder, a vice president at a major public accounting firm in Baltimore, thinks that "company insiders" are the biggest security threat. Consequently, her staff works hard to enforce security policies and educate managers and end users. For example, the staff issues handouts and updates on company policies and informs employees about the penalties they can incur for breaking the rules, including dismissal. "As far as I'm concerned, there are no lasting technical solutions to social problems," Snyder says.

Being specific about the threats that face an organization is the best way to get the attention of managers who can approve spending on security, according to users at a recent security conference. One security manager compiled a long list of potential network vulnerabilities with an itemized list of each network component. "I was able to show my CIO that even a simple network outage would require two or three network administrators at least two hours to fix and cost us about $10,000," said the manager, who works for a West Coast manufacturing company with 30,000 users. "A severe network security breach—one that made us lose data and suffer an outage of one to three days—could run into the millions. That made the extra $75,000 I was asking for look like a pretty good investment. I got the money."

Source: Laura DiDio, "Computer Crime Costs on the Rise," *Computerworld,* vol. 32, no. 16 (April 20, 1998), p. 55.

SUMMARY

We know very little about computer crime. For a variety of reasons, few cases are reported, and we suspect that many more cases go undetected. What is worse, we now catch most computer abusers by accident. From our limited information, we can make three tentative conclusions about computer abuse: (1) it is difficult to define exactly what is, and what is not, computer crime, (2) by almost any definition, computer crime is growing, and (3) computer crime is likely to be expensive for those organizations that suffer from it. AISs are vulnerable to computer abuse because they directly or indirectly control the valuable assets of organizations. This chapter discussed several specific cases of real-world computer abuse. The subjects of these cases included (1) compromising valuable information (TRW case), (2) computer hacking (Kevin Mitnick case), and (3) inserting computer viruses (Robert Morris case).

Organizations can protect themselves against computer abuse in a variety of ways. Among the methods discussed in this chapter are (1) obtain the support of top management, (2) educate users about computer abuse, (3) protect passwords, (4) design and implement control procedures, and (5) recognize the symptoms of computer abuse. Organizations can also help themselves by knowing which employers are most likely to become computer abusers and by employing forensic accountants to investigate suspected problems.

Computer abuse also depends on unethical behavior. This means distinguishing between right and wrong rather than interpreting legal rights. Examples of ethical behavior include protecting confidential information, being socially responsible, respecting rights of privacy, avoiding conflicts of interest, and understanding unacceptable uses of computer hardware and software. Organizations can encourage ethical behavior by educating employees about it, rewarding it, and stimulating employees to join professional associations with ethical codes of conduct.

KEY TERMS YOU SHOULD KNOW

antivirus software	economic espionage
applet	ethics
Association of Certified Fraud Examiners	forensic accountants
boot-sector virus	lock-out systems
Codes of Conduct and Good Practice for Certified Computer Professionals	logic bomb program
	Mitnick, Kevin D.
computer crime	Morris, Robert Tappan
Computer Fraud and Abuse Act of 1986	salami technique
computer hacker	shoulder surfing
computer virus	social engineering
data diddling	trojan horse programs
denial of service	TRW Credit Data case
dialback systems	valuable-information computer crime
disaster recovery plan	worm program

DISCUSSION QUESTIONS

11-1. Why is a definition of computer crime elusive? Would you be willing to call computer crime a white-collar crime? Why or why not? Also, the known cases of computer crime have been described as just "the tip of the iceberg." Would you consider this description accurate? Why or why not?

11-2. Most computer crime is not reported. Give as many reasons as you can why much of this crime is purposely downplayed. Do you consider these reasons valid? Discuss several arguments favorable to the reporting of all computer crime.

11-3. Why have most computer experts suggested that computer abuse is growing despite the fact that so little is known about it?

11-4. The TRW Credit Data case involves two issues: (1) the propriety of computer-based information and (2) the protection afforded the consumer in the use of credit information. Identify each of these issues more fully and explain your own position on these matters. Do you feel, for example, that a company has the right to collect, store, and disseminate information about your purchasing activities without your permission?

11-5. What enabled the employees at TRW to get away with their crime? What controls might have prevented the crime from occurring? The TRW case has been identified as an unusual case because the information stored on the company's computer files, rather than any liquid assets, was the major target of the perpetrators. From your reading of this chapter plus your outside readings, discuss other cases that appear to fall into this category of computer crime.

11-6. What is hacking? Why do people hack? Do you think that the growth of microcomputer usage has contributed to hacking? What can be done to prevent hacking?

11-7. What is a computer virus? Is it really a biological entity? Is it an infection? Is it contagious? Explain each of your answers in detail.

11-8. Discuss the motivations for computer crime. Is all computer crime ultimately for financial gain? Explain.

11-9. What are the lessons to be learned from computer crime, if any? From what you have read in this chapter, would you say that there is such a thing as a "secure" computer system? Discuss.

11-10. How can educating employees help stop computer crime? Is the support of top management important, or can employees be educated about computer abuse without this support? Explain your answer.

11-11. How "technical" are computer criminals? For example, do most of them know how to program computers? If a person who is computer-illiterate commits a fraud using a computer (for example, by altering input data), is it fair to call that act a computer crime? Do computer abusers have morals? How can a company avoid hiring computer abusers?

11-12. Discuss computer crime and the Internet. For example, what computer crimes, if any, are committed on the Internet? How important are these crimes? What assets are involved? What can be done to safeguard these assets?

11-13. How would you define "ethics"? What types of ethical issues are involved in computerized accounting information systems? How can organizations encourage their employees to act ethically?

11-14. The Rivera Regional Bank uses a computerized data processing system to maintain both its checking accounts and its savings accounts. During the last three years, several customers have complained that their balances have been in error. Randy Allen, the information systems bank manager, has always treated these customers very courteously and has personally seen to it that the problems have been rectified quickly, sometimes by putting in extra hours after normal quitting time to make the necessary changes. This extra effort has been so helpful to the bank that this year, the bank's top management has made plans to award Mr. Allen with the Employee-of-the-Year Award. Mr. Allen has never taken a vacation. Comment.

PROBLEMS

11-15. (Library Research) Newspapers and such journals as Datamation and Computerworld are prime sources of computer-crime articles. Find a description of a computer crime not already discussed in this chapter and prepare an analysis of the crime.

11-16. Recall that the salami technique means using a computer to skim a small amount of money from hundreds or thousands of accounts, and then diverting the proceeds for personal gain. Suppose that a computer programmer uses this technique to skim a penny from each customer's account at a small bank. Over the course of three months, he takes $200,000 and is never caught. Assuming that this hacker took only one penny per month from each customer, how many accounts did the bank have? If the bank had 100,000 accounts and the hacker stole one penny from each account's interest (which was computed daily), how much could the hacker steal in three months?

11-17. What control procedures would you recommend to prevent each of the following activities?

a. A clerk at the Paul Yelverton Company faxes a fictitious sales invoice to a company that purchases a large quantity of goods from it. The clerk plans to intercept that particular payment check and pocket the money.

b. The bookkeeper at a construction company has each of the three owners sign a paycheck for her. Each check is drawn from a separate account of the company.

c. A clerk in the human relations department creates a fictitious employee in the personnel computer file. When this employee's payroll check is received for distribution, the clerk takes and cashes it.

d. A clerk in the accounts receivable department steals $250 in cash from a customer payment, then prepares a computer credit memo that reduces the customer's account balance by the same amount.

e. A purchasing agent prepares an invoice for goods received from a fictitious supplier. She sends a check for the goods to this supplier, in care of her mother's post-office box.

f. A hacker manages to break into a company's computer system by guessing the password of his friend—Champ, the name of the friend's dog.

g. An accounts receivable clerk manages to embezzle more than $1 million from the company by diligently lapping the accounts every day for three consecutive years.

h. A computer virus on the company's local area network is traced to an individual who accidentally introduced it when he loaded a computer game onto his microcomputer.

i. A clerk at a medical lab recognizes the name of an acquaintance as one of those whose lab tests are "positive" for an infectious disease. She mentions it to a mutual friend, and before long, the entire town knows about it.

INTERNET EXERCISES

11-18. Use some of the web sites listed at the end of this chapter to expand your knowledge of forensic accountants. What do these individuals do? What information do they gather? Who employs them?

11-19. Investigate the Computer Emergency Response Team (CERT) center web site at www.cert.org. What statistics on computer crime are available at this site? Provide information from this web site for the most current year and report your findings.

CASE ANALYSES

11-20. The Equity Funding Case (Library Research)

No one knows what was the first computer crime, but certainly one of the earliest and largest crimes on record is the Equity Funding Case. This crime involved $200 million in losses if only direct corporate losses are counted, but more than $2 billion if indirect losses to other companies and investors are also counted. Besides the magnitude of the losses involved, this case is also noteworthy because it required collusion among several employees, sophisticated programming efforts, and extensive falsified documentation to conceal irregularities. By the time it was discovered in 1973, nearly two-thirds of the company's computer insurance policies—more than 64,000 of them—were found to be phonies! But was this a computer crime?

Requirements

Research the Equity Funding Case and write a report that describes the facts of this case in detail. (Hint: this case is old, so your best sources of information will probably *not* be the Internet.) In your report, describe each of the following items:

1. How was the crime discovered? Was this an accident or purposeful event?
2. What were the inflated earnings phase, the insurance phase, and the foreign phase of this crime? Indicate whether or not you think these phases were "computer crimes."
3. What was the role of the auditors in this problem? Were the initial auditors diligent? If so, how? If not, why not?
4. Overall, was this a computer crime? State your reasons for calling it, or not calling it, a computer crime.

11-21. Ashley Company (Diskless PC System and Security Threats)

To address the need for tighter data controls and lower support costs, the Ashley Company has adopted a new diskless PC system. It is little more than a mutilated personal computer described as a "gutless wonder." The basic concept behind the diskless PC is simple: A LAN server-based file system of high-powered diskless workstations is spread throughout a company and connected with a central repository or mainframe. The network improves control by limiting user access to company data previously stored on desktop hard disks. Since the user can destroy or delete only the information currently on the screen, an organization's financial data are protected from user-instigated catastrophes. The diskless computer also saves money in user support costs by distributing applications and upgrades automatically, and by offering online help.

Requirements

1. What threats in the information processing and storage system do the diskless PC minimize?
2. Do the security advantages of the new system outweight potential limitations? Discuss.

11-22. Mark Goodwin Resort (Valuable-Information Computer Abuse)

The Mark Goodwin Resort is an elegant summer resort located in a remote mountain setting. Guests visiting the resort can fish, hike, go horseback riding, swim in one of three hotel pools, or simply sit in one of the many lounge chairs located around the property and enjoy the spectacular scenery. There are also three dining rooms, card rooms, nightly movies, and live weekend entertainment.

The resort uses a computerized system to make room reservations and bill customers. Following standard policy for the industry, the resort also offers authorized travel agents a 10 percent commission on room bookings. Each week, the resort prints an exception report of bookings made by unrecognized travel agents. However, the managers usually pay the commissions anyway, partly because they don't want to anger the travel agencies and partly because the computer file that maintains the list of authorized agents is not kept up to date.

Although management has not discovered it, several employees now exploit these facts to their own advantage. As often as possible, they call the resort from outside phones, pose as travel agents, book rooms for friends and relatives, and collect the commissions. The incentive is obvious: rooms costing as little as $100 per day result in payments of $10 per day to the "travel agencies" that book them. The scam has been going on for years, and several guests now book their rooms exclusively through these employees, finding these people particularly courteous and helpful.

Requirements

1. Would you say this is a "computer crime?" Why or why not?
2. What controls would you recommend that would enable the resort's managers to thwart such abuse?
3. How does the matter of "accountability" (tracing transactions to specific agencies) affect the problem?

11-23. The Department of Taxation (Data Confidentiality)

The Department of Taxation of one state is developing a new computer system for processing state income tax returns of individuals and corporations. The new system features direct data input and inquiry capabilities. Identification of taxpayers is provided by using the Social Security numbers of individuals and federal identification numbers for corporations. The new system should be fully implemented in time for the next tax season. The new system will serve three primary purposes:

- Data will be input into the system directly from tax returns through CRT terminals located at the central headquarters of the Department of Taxation.
- The returns will be processed using the main computer facilities at central headquarters. The processing includes (1) verifying mathematical accuracy; (2) auditing the reasonableness of deductions, tax due, and so forth, through the use of edit routines; these routines also include a comparison of the current year's data with prior years' data; (3) identifying returns that should be considered for audit by revenue agents of the department; and (4) issuing refund checks to taxpayers.

- Inquiry service will be provided to taxpayers on request through the assistance of Tax Department personnel at five regional offices. A total of 50 CRT terminals will be placed at the regional offices.

A taxpayer will be able to determine the status of his or her return or to get information from the last three years' returns by calling or visiting one of the department's regional offices. The state commissioner of taxation is concerned about data security during input and processing over and above protection against natural hazards such as fires or floods. This includes protection against the loss or damage of data during data input or processing, and the improper input or processing of data. In addition, the tax commissioner and the state attorney general have discussed the general problem of data confidentiality that may arise from the nature and operation of the new system. Both individuals want to have all potential problems identified before the system is fully developed and implemented so that the proper controls can be incorporated into the new system.

Requirements

1. Describe the potential confidentiality problems that could arise in each of the following three areas of processing and recommend the corrective action(s) to solve the problems: (a) data input, (b) processing of returns, (c) data inquiry.

2. The State Tax Commission wants to incorporate controls to provide data security against the loss, damage, or improper input or use of data during data input and processing. Identify the potential problems (outside of natural hazards such as fires or floods) for which the Department of Taxation should develop controls, and recommend possible control procedures for each problem identified.

(CMA Adapted)

11-24. Ajax Products (The Ethics of a Security Breach)

Greg Schwartz, an internal auditor for Ajax Products Company, is pursuing a graduate degree on a part-time basis. Greg and another graduate student, Linda Stephens, have been given an assignment to produce a database for an accounting information systems class. Greg's company has a site license for a relational database management system on a local area network (LAN). Linda is a full-time student with no access to the needed database management system.

Greg invites Linda to work at his office after hours to complete the project. He greets her at the security desk, cosigns her identification card, and leads her to his office. Linda has studied data communications and is eager to gain some experience. Greg describes to Linda how to access the database management systems on the LAN. He first enters his user-ID and password to gain access to the LAN, and then he lets Linda enter the commands to start the database management system. Linda misunderstands Greg's instructions and mistakenly types a transposed set of characters. The computer responds with the message, "Access Code?" Greg comments that he's never had to do that before and leans over and types his password.

The computer screen flickers, then a colorful display of the company's logo appears above the words "Welcome to Ajax Company's Executive Information System." Instinctively, Linda presses the enter key and the computer screen presents a menu listing of ten files and programs available, including such entries as "Budgets," "Plans," and "Benefits." Greg comments that he's unfamiliar with that menu and asks Linda if she remembers what she typed when she signed on. "Whatever you told me to type," she replies. Curious, Greg selects "Benefits" and, after a moment, a list of the top company officers appears on the screen along with a summary of their salary and benefits packages, plus an entry for the projected bonus for the current year. Greg is somewhat shocked to see substantial bonuses. By quickly paging down, he discovers that the total in the bonus category for 12 executives is in the high six figures.

Because Ajax is a privately held company, none of the data would be released to the public. What is shocking and disturbing to Greg is that the company recently announced a workforce reduction plan that will reduce the workforce by 6 percent in the coming weeks. Greg says to Linda, "This is the company that parades its Code of Ethics in public, with the CEO constantly talking of honesty, integrity, and fairness."

Greg recovers his poise in a moment and remarks, "I don't think this is the system we want." He types "BYE" and exits the executive information system. Once back at the LAN system prompt, he types the commands he had described to Linda and gets access to the LAN version of the database management system they needed. They work for several hours to develop the database. Greg and Linda then save the file, sign off the system, and go home.

Later that night, Greg muses about what he had seen and the fact that Linda, an outsider to the firm, had also seen the information. If he reports the breach in the computer security system, it will be suspected that he has seen confidential information. If he doesn't report the breach, someone else may get access to the sensitive data and take advantage of the information. Greg also knows that the LAN operating system audit log will show that he gained access to the executive information system. He is responsible for reviewing the log and reporting unauthorized accesses and access attempts. He is also uncertain as to whether his access to the executive information system is actually a security breach. Internal audit has routinely been given access to all applications and data due to its job function. He also knows at least two long-term employees whose jobs will be terminated due to the workforce reduction.

Greg also wonders how the Institute of Internal Auditors' Code of Ethics applies in this case. He recalls that, in Standard of Conduct II, the Code suggests that internal auditors should be loyal to their employer. However, internal auditors should avoid actions that violate the law. In addition, as it says in Standard of Conduct VIII, he knows that the internal auditor should refrain from disclosing information for personal benefit or in a way that will damage the employer.

Requirements

1. Has Linda or Greg done anything illegal? Why or why not?
2. What are the ethical issues involved in this case?
3. What do you recommend that Greg Schwartz do?

REFERENCES, RECOMMENDED READINGS, AND WEB SITES

References and Recommended Readings

Barthel, Matt, "Rent-a-Hackers Fight Online Bank Robbers," *American Banker,* vol. 58, no. 190 (October 4, 1993), pp. 16–17.

Beets, S. Douglas, "Personal Morals and Professional Ethics: A Review and an Empirical Examination of Public Accounting," *Business and Professional Ethics Journal* (Summer 1991), pp. 70–76.

Belts, Mitch, "Recovering from Hacker Invasion," *Computerworld,* vol. 27, no. 4 (January 25, 1993), pp. 45ff.

Bloombecker, Jay J., "Are You Vulnerable to Cybercrime?" *USA Today* (February 20, 1995), p. 3B.

Breidenbach, Susan, "Outlaws on the Loose," *Network World* vol. 15, no. 7 (February 16, 1998), p. 1, 35.

Caryl, Christian, "Russia's Hackers: Reach Out and Rob Someone," *U.S. News and World Report,* vol. 22, no. 1 (April 21, 1997), p. 58.

Charney, S., and K. Alexander, "Computer Crime" *Emory Law Journal,* vol. 45 (1996), pp. 931–957.

"Clinton Proposes $91M Cyber-Security Initiative," *Bristol Press,* January 8, 2000, p. A6.

Cobb, Stephen, and David Brussin, "Hackers in White Hats," *Byte* (June 1998), p. 112.

Coderre, David G., "Full Service Fraud," *Internal Auditor* (April 1998), pp. 77–78.

Coffee, Peter, "What You Don't Know Will Hurt You," *PC Week* (February 8, 1999), p. 43.

Conley, John M., and Robert M. Bryan, "A Survey of Computer Crime Legislation in the United States," *Information & Communications Technology Law,* vol. 8, no. 1 (March, 1999), pp. 35–57.

Corbin, Terry, "Detecting White Collar Crime," *Management Accounting* (November 1998), pp. 64–65.

Cottrell, David M., and W. Steve Albrecht, "Recognizing the Symptoms of Employee Fraud," *Healthcare Financial Management* (May 1994), pp. 19–25.

Daly, James, "Virus Vagaries Foil Feds," *Computerworld,* vol. 27, no. 28 (July 12, 1993), pp. 1, 15.

DeDio, Laura, "Special FBI Unit Targets Online Fraud, Gambling," *Computerworld,* vol. 32, no. 17 (April 27, 1998), p. 47.

Doney, Lloyd D., "The Growing Threat of Computer Crime in Small Businesses," *Business Horizons* (May 15, 1998), p. 81.

Farell, David W., and Nevella N. Clevenger, "Ethics Training for Accountants: Necessity or Nicety?" *New Accountant,* vol. 10, no. 3 (November/December 1994), pp. 22–25.

Field, Tom, "Sweat about the Threat," *CIO* (December 1, 1998), pp. 35–43.

Frank, Craig, "How to Face Down Fraud," *Security Management* (September 1998), p. 73.

Furnell, S. M., and M. J. Warren, "Computer Hacking and Cyber Terrorism," *Computers and Security* (1999), pp. 28–34.

Gentile, Olivia F., "Fraud Grows with the Economy," *Hartford Courant* (January 16, 2000), pp. B1–B2.

Haines, Jason D. "New Crimes, New Tools—Old Crimes, New Tools" *Journal of Financial Crime* vol. 9, no. 1 (September 2001), pp. 6–7.

Highland, Harold Joseph, "A History of Computer Viruses—The Famous Trio," *Computers & Security,* vol. 16, no. 5 (August 1997), pp. 416–430.

Hiltebeitel, Kenneth M., and Scott K. Jones, "An Assessment of Ethics Instruction in Accounting Education," *Journal of Business Ethics* (January 1992), p. 37.

Hoffer, Jeffrey A., and Detmar W. Straub, Jr., "The 9 To 5 Underground: Are You Policing Computer Crimes?" *Sloan Management Review,* vol. 30, no. 4, (Summer, 1989), pp. 35–44.

Horowitz, Alan S., and Michael Cohn, "Ensuring the Integrity of Your Data," *Beyond Computing* (May 1998), pp. 27–30.

Macodrum, Donald, Hedieh Nasheri, and Timothy O'Hearn, "Spies In Suits: New Crimes of the Information Age from the United States and Canadian Perspectives" *Information & Communications Technology Law,* vol. 10, no. 2 (June 2001), pp. 139–166.

McCollum, Tim, "Computer Crime" (includes related articles on security software, backup systems, and security policies), *Nation's Business,* vol. 85, no. 11 (November 1997), pp. 18-26.

Meall, Lesley, "Foiling the Fraudsters," *Accountancy,* vol. 110, no. 1191 (November 1992), pp. 56-57.

Moukheiber, Zina, "Cybercops," *Forbes* (March 10, 1997), pp. 170-172.

Mungo, Paul, *Approaching Zero: The Extraordinary Underworld of Hackers, Phreakers, Virus Writers, and Keyboard Criminals* (New York: Random House, 1992).

Nash, Kim S., "PC Manager at Center of $20M Grocery Scam: Inside Job Spotlights Critical Security Threat," *Computerworld,* vol. 32, no. 13 (March 30, 1998), p. 1.

Pasternak, Douglas, and Bruce B. Auster, "Terrorism at the Touch of a Keyboard," *U.S. News & World Report* (July 13, 1998), p. 37.

Pearsall, Kathy, "No News May Be Good News for Victims of IT Crimes," *Computing Canada,* vol. 24, No. 13 (April 6, 1998), p. 11.

Scarponi, Diane, "Hacker Steals Credit Card Numbers From CT Retailer," *Bristol Press* (January 11, 2000), pp. A1-A2.

Scheier, Robert L., "Lock the Damned Door!" *Computerworld,* vol. 31, no. 6 (February 10, 1997), pp. 66-68.

Sibley, Kathleen, "It's Virus Season 12 Months a Year," *Computing Canada* (February 23, 1998), pp. 21-22.

Stamps, David, "The IS Eye on Insider Trading," *Datamation* (April 15, 1995), pp. 35-43.

Teach, Edward, "Look Who's Hacking Now," *CFO,* vol. 14, no 2 (February 1998), pp. 38-50.

Trembly, Ara C., "Cyber Crime Means Billions in Losses" *National Underwriter,* vol. 103, no. 26 (June 28, 1999), p. 19.

Vistica, Gregory L., and Evan Thomas, "The Secret Hacker Wars," *Newsweek* (June 1, 1998), pp. 60-61.

Web Sites

A good index to computer-crime information sources and worldwide legislation may be found at www.npru.gov.au/cit/crime&sec.htm.

The web site of the Computer Emergency Response Team (CERT) center at Carnegie Mellon University is www.cert.org. This site contains a form for reporting computer crime incidents, and tips for recovering from such an incident and for surveying, improving, and testing computer security.

The web site for the Computer Security Institute (CSI) is www.gosci.com. It contains links to firewall product resource.

A web site devoted to international computer and Internet security resources may be found at: www.virtuallibrarian.com/legal/org.html.

Chapter 12

Auditing Computerized Accounting Information Systems

INTRODUCTION

THE AUDIT FUNCTION

Internal versus External Auditing

Information Systems Auditing

Evaluating the Effectiveness of Information Systems
 Controls

AUDITING THROUGH THE COMPUTER

Testing Computer Programs

Validating Computer Programs

Review of Systems Software

Continuous Auditing

AUDITING WITH THE COMPUTER

General-Use Software

Generalized Audit Software

Automated Workpaper Software

AUDITING IN THE INFORMATION AGE

Auditing Electronic Spreadsheets

Third Party Assurance

Information Systems Reliability Assurance

AIS AT WORK: HACKER PRACTICES

SUMMARY

KEY TERMS YOU SHOULD KNOW

DISCUSSION QUESTIONS

PROBLEMS

INTERNET EXERCISES

CASE ANALYSES

Stephanie Rose Company

Wang Plumbing Wholesalers

Tiffany Martin, CPA

Goldstein's

**REFERENCES, RECOMMENDED READINGS,
AND WEB SITES**

After reading this chapter, you will:

1. *Know* how external auditing differs from internal auditing.

2. *Understand* the information systems audit process and the nature of careers in information systems auditing.

3. *Know* how to determine the effectiveness of internal controls over specific information systems.

4. *Understand* what it means to audit "through," "around," and "with" the computer.

5. *Be familiar with* techniques used to audit computerized information systems.

6. *Understand* how auditors of all types use computers to do their jobs.

7. *Appreciate* how electronics spreadsheet technologies impact the audit process.

8. *Be familiar with* third-party and systems reliability assurance services.

While there are risks inherent to information systems, these risks impact different systems in different ways. The risk of non-availability even for an hour can be serious for a billing system at a busy retail store.

S.A. Sayana, "The IS Audit Process," *Information Systems Control Journal*, vol. 1, 2002, p. 21.

INTRODUCTION

Chapters 9 and 10 stressed the importance of control procedures in the efficient operation of an AIS. To esnsure that these controls are functioning properly and that additional controls are not needed, business organizations perform examinations or audits of their accounting systems. Auditing is usually taught in one or more separate courses within the typical accounting curriculum, and a single chapter of a book is not sufficient to cover the spectrum of topics involved in a complete audit of an organization. Thus, this chapter will be merely introductory and limited to areas of immediate consequence to AISs.

To narrow the discussion still further, we have chosen to focus primarily on the audit of computerized AISs because this area is central to our textbook. This discussion is likely to complement, rather than repeat, the coverage within an auditing course. An accountant who specializes in auditing computerized AISs is referred to as either an *information systems auditor* or an *electronic data processing (EDP)* auditor. This chapter describes the work that such a person does.

The chapter begins with some introductory comments about the nature of auditing, including a discussion that emphasizes the distinction between internal and external auditing. We then describe the relationship between an information systems audit and a financial audit. Next, the chapter discusses how to evaluate the effectiveness of internal controls. These comments provide a context for the more detailed material concerning methodologies for auditing *through* the computer and *with* the computer. The chapter ends with several topics related to auditing in the information age. These include an examination of the impact of spreadsheet technologies on auditing, and discussion of third party and systems reliability assurance services.

THE AUDIT FUNCTION

To audit is to examine and to assure. The nature of auditing differs according to the subject under examination. We can differentiate auditing in other ways as well. This section discusses internal, external, and information systems auditing.

Internal versus External Auditing

Conventionally, we distinguish between two types of audits: an internal audit and an external audit. In an **internal audit** a company's own accounting employees perform the audit, whereas accountants working for an independent CPA firm conduct the external audit. Generally, internal auditing positions are staff positions reporting to top management. Whereas an audit might be internal to a company, it is invariably *external* to the corporate department or division being audited. Thus, the auditing function preserves its objectivity and professionalism.

The internal audit is concerned primarily with employee adherence to company policies and procedures, for example, the use of an official form when preparing payroll vouchers or completing purchase orders. It is also relatively broad in scope, including such activities as auditing for fraud and ensuring that employees are not copying software programs illegally. Internal auditors can provide assurance to a company's top management about the efficiency and effectiveness of almost any aspect of its organization.

In contrast to the broad perspective of internal auditors, the chief purpose of the **external audit** is the **attest function.** This entails giving an opinion on the fairness of financial statements. This fairness evaluation is conducted in the context of generally accepted accounting principles (GAAP) and requires application of generalized auditing standards. In the past few years, the external auditor's role has expanded with respect to auditing for *fraud.* Statement on Auditing Standards (SAS) No. 82, Consideration of Fraud in a Financial Statement Audit, requires auditors working for public accounting firms to plan and conduct an audit that provides reasonable assurance about whether an organization's financial statements are free of erroneous or fraudulent material misstatements. However, cost constraints and the need to audit efficiently prevent auditors from providing absolute assurance that a particular organization is free from fraud. A favorable audit opinion really means that the auditors found support for the amounts presented on financial statements.

Today there are specialized auditors called **fraud auditors.** (Fraud auditors are also referred to as *forensic accountants.*) These auditors specialize in investigating fraud, and they often work closely with internal auditors and attorneys. Many fraud auditors are employed in the fraud investigation units of the FBI, large public accounting firms, the IRS, insurance organizations, and other types of large corporations.

As mentioned in Chapter 1, external auditors are expanding the services they offer to include a variety of *assurance services.* Many of these services involve IT in some way. However, the attest function remains the external auditor's primary responsibility. Although the primary goals of external and internal audits differ, they are complementary within the context of an AIS. For example, the controls that internal auditors examine within a company's IT environment are in part designed to increase the accuracy of the external financial reports of interest to the external auditors. Similarly, the use of an acceptable method of inventory valuation such as FIFO or LIFO, as required by the external auditors, is likely to be an important corporate policy falling under the domain of the internal auditors.

Despite the difference in purpose between internal audits and external audits, internal auditors and external auditors perform a number of similar functions in the area of auditing computerized AISs. Therefore, most of the discussion that follows regarding the audit of computerized AISs is applicable to both internal and external auditors. Thus, we use the term *auditor* broadly to encompass both types of auditors. It should be pointed out, however, that even though internal and external auditors perform a number of similar functions, this is not to say that much audit work is duplicated. Rather, the opposite is true, owing to the large degree of cooperation and interaction that often exists between a company's internal auditors and a public accounting firm's external auditors. Internal auditors commonly undertake audits that are reviewed and relied upon by the external auditors as they audit an organization's financial statements.

Information Systems Auditing

Information systems auditing involves evaluating the computer's role in achieving audit and control objectives. Traditional objectives are also present in information systems auditing. These include attest objectives such as the safeguarding of assets and data integrity, and management objectives such as operational effectiveness.

The Information Systems Audit Process   As illustrated in Figure 12-1, the information systems audit function encompasses all the components of a computer-based AIS: people, procedures, hardware, data communications, software, and databases. These components are a system of interacting elements that auditors examine to accomplish the purposes of their audits described above.

External auditors examine an organization's computer-based AIS primarily to evaluate how the organization's control procedures over computer processing might affect the financial statements (attest objectives). The controls in place will directly influence the scope of the audit. For instance, if computer controls are weak or nonexistent, auditors will need to do more **substantive testing.** Substantive tests are detailed tests of transactions and account balances. An example of substantive testing is the confirmation of accounts receivable with customers. If the control procedures over a company's computerized financial accounting system are strong, the auditors may limit the scope of their audit by examining fewer transactions underlying accounts receivable account balances. For our example, this would mean contacting fewer customers to confirm accounts receivable than would be the case if little or no reliance could be placed on the computer-based controls.

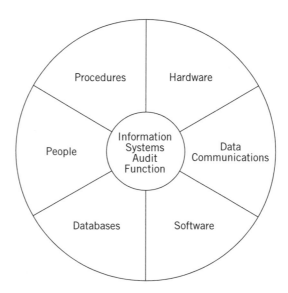

FIGURE 12–1   The six components of a computer-based AIS examined in an information systems audit.

Figure 12-2 shows a flowchart of the steps that generally take place in information systems auditing. These steps are similar to those performed in any financial audit. What is different is that the auditor's examination in this case concerns a *computer-based* AIS. In Figure 12-2, the process begins with a preliminary evaluation of the system. The auditor will first decide if computer processing of accounting data is significant or complex enough to warrant an examination of the computer-based information system itself. Sometimes, if the system is neither large nor complex, the audit might proceed as it would in a manual data processing environment. Most often, computer-based processing warrants a preliminary review by the information systems auditor to make a quick assessment of the control environment.

Typically, an auditor will find enough computer-based controls in place to warrant further examination. In this situation, an auditor will want to make a more detailed analysis of both *general* and *application controls.* (These controls were discussed in Chapter 10.) After examining these controls in some detail, *compliance testing* will be performed to ensure that the controls are in place and working as prescribed. This may entail using some **computer-assisted audit technique (CAATs)** to audit *through* the computer. Finally, the auditor will need to substantively test some account balances. As explained earlier, the results of the previous analysis and testing affect the scope of this testing. Auditors often make use of CAATs at this stage in auditing *with* the computer. Auditing *through* and *with* the computer are discussed later in this chapter.

Careers in Information Systems Auditing   As organizations increasingly make use of computer-based AISs and as these systems become more technologically complex, the demand for information systems auditors is growing. Information systems

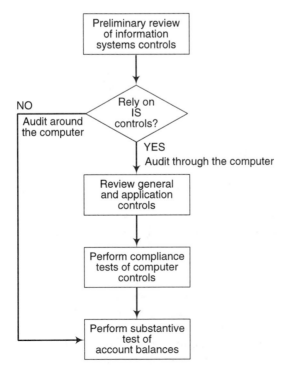

FIGURE 12-2   Flowchart of information systems audit process. Auditing *through* and *around* the computer are discussed later in the chapter.

auditing requires a variety of skills. Some information systems auditors have college degrees in computer science or information systems, while others have accounting degrees with perhaps some general audit experience. The ideal background includes a combination of accounting and information systems or computer science skills.

As discussed in Chapter 1, information systems auditors may choose to obtain professional certification as **Certified Information System Auditors (CISAs).** Applicants achieve this certification by successfully completing an examination given by the Information Systems Audit and Control Association and by meeting specific experience requirements. The CISA examination tests knowledge of (1) the IS audit process; (2), management, planning, and organization of IS; (3) technical infrastructure and operational practices; (4) protection of information assets; (5) disaster recovery and business continuity, business application system development, acquisition, implementation, and maintenance; and (6) business process evaluation and risk management. Much of the subject matter is technical (e.g., business application development methodologies) and more closely oriented toward information systems than accounting.

Information systems auditors may be employed as either internal or external auditors. In both cases, these auditors focus on evaluating control procedures rather than substantive testing. Evaluating controls over information systems hardware and various AIS applications requires a high level of expertise. As an example, an information systems auditor evaluating controls that limit access to certain information needs to be familiar with the way a particular application organizes its access security. Compared with external auditors, internal auditors can more easily specialize in knowledge about their particular organization's hardware, operating system platform, and application programs.

An external auditor is likely to audit many different client organizations' information systems. The external auditor may, however, choose to specialize in a particular operating system platform, security software package, microcomputer network system, or certain minicomputer or mainframe computer systems. To effectively perform information systems auditing, both specialized skills and a broad-based set of technical knowledge are needed. The external information systems auditor may or may not be part of the regular financial audit team. In some cases, the financial audit team only calls on external information systems auditors when a special risk assessment appears warranted.

Evaluating the Effectiveness of Information Systems Controls

The more confidence that auditors have (as a result of strong controls) that data are input and processed accurately in a computer-based system, the less substantive testing they perform. On the other hand, a computer-based system with weak controls over data input and processing will call for more detailed testing of financial transactions.

Risk Assessment   An external auditor's main objective in reviewing information systems control procedures is to evaluate the *risks* (associated with any control weaknesses) to the integrity of accounting data presented in financial reports. Control strengths and weaknesses will affect the scope of the audit. A secondary objective of the external auditor's review is to make recommendations to managers about improving these controls. This secondary objective is also an objective of internal auditors.

Under a **risk-based audit approach** to evaluating a company's internal control procedures, the following four steps provide a logical framework for performing the risk-based audit of the company's AIS:

1. Determine the threats (i.e., errors and irregularities) facing the AIS.

2. Identify the control procedures that should be in place to minimize each of these threats and thereby prevent or detect the errors and irregularities.

3. Evaluate the control procedures within the AIS. The process of reviewing system documentation and interviewing appropriate personnel to determine whether the necessary control procedures are in place is called a **systems review.** In addition, **tests of controls** are conducted to determine whether these control procedures are satisfactorily followed. The tests include such activities as observing system operations; inspecting documents, records, and reports; checking samples of system inputs and outputs; and tracing transactions through the system.

4. Evaluate weaknesses (i.e., errors and irregularities not covered by control procedures) within the AIS to ascertain their effect on the nature, timing, or extent of auditing procedures. This step focuses on the *control risks* and whether a company's control system as a whole adequately addresses the risks. If a control deficiency is identified, the auditor should determine whether there are **compensating controls,** or procedures, that compensate for the deficiency. Control weaknesses in one area of an AIS may be acceptable if these weaknesses are compensated for by control strengths in other areas of the AIS.

The risk-based audit approach provides auditors with a good understanding of the errors and irregularities that can occur in a company's AIS environment and the related risks and exposures. This understanding provides a sound basis for the auditors' development of recommendations to the company's management on how its AIS control system should be improved.

The desirability of an internal control procedure is a function of its ability to *reduce business risk.* In fact, it is the business risk itself that is important, not the internal control system. For example, natural disasters, such as floods or earthquakes, pose a *risk* to an organization's ability to continue its business without interruption. A *disaster recovery or business continuity plan* is an internal control procedure designed to reduce this risk. Focusing on business risk ensures implementing only those controls that are absolutely necessary and also cost-effective. One method by which an auditor can evaluate the desirability of IT-related controls for a particular aspect of business risk is through an **information systems risk assessment.** (Chapter 9 introduced the subject of risk assessment.) This risk assessment requires auditors and managers to answer each of the following questions:

- *What assets* or *information* does the company have that unauthorized individuals would want?
- *What is* the *value* of these identified assets or information?
- *How* can unauthorized individuals obtain valuable assets or information?
- *What* are the *chances* (i.e., *probabilities*) of unauthorized individuals obtaining valuable assets or information?

The answer to the first question requires a detailed analysis of a company's tangible and intangible assets. The second question may be more difficult to tackle.

Although asset values for a company's tangible assets are typically available, it is particularly hard to place a value on an organization's information. Information includes data files, mailing lists, proprietary company documents, and many other data and information items. The third and fourth questions are related. It is necessary to figure out *how* unauthorized individuals can take assets in order to calculate the probability that they will do so. The *how* is also important because it will guide an auditor in deciding which control procedures provide the best protection.

Figure 12-3 shows how an auditor might answer the above questions regarding one specific transaction, customer payments on account. Based on the analysis in this figure, a business would be willing to spend about $1,000 each month on controls such as supervision, forced job rotation, and customer confirmation of accounts receivable balances to mitigate the described risk.

In addition to the questions posed previously, auditors must also consider risk with respect to errors or accidents. Not only are assets vulnerable as a result of intentional fraud, but they are also affected by unintentional events. As an example, incorrect data input can lead to misrepresentation on financial statements in the form of incorrect asset valuations. An information systems risk assessment should take into account the risks associated with errors or accidents as well as fraud.

The loss of company secrets, unauthorized manipulation of company files, and interrupted computer access are all business risks in an IT environment. As mentioned earlier, it is much easier to value a tangible asset, such as cash, than to place a value on information. It is also often a guessing game to estimate the probability of losses. Nevertheless, an information systems risk assessment is an important part of an audit and of the design of an internal control system. For those areas where estimated costs of protection are less than anticipated losses, the auditor recommends implementing control procedures. For those areas in which the costs of protection are greater than anticipated losses, the auditor may recommend against installing the specific controls.

Guidance in Designing and Evaluating IT Controls   Two guides are available to information systems auditors for designing and evaluating internal controls related to IT. The Institute of Internal Auditors first issued the **Systems Auditability and Control (SAC) report** in 1977. Advances in IT led to revisions in 1991 and 1994. This report identifies important information technologies and the specific risks related to these technologies. It also recommends controls to mitigate risks and sug-

---

ASSET AT RISK—Cash

AMOUNT AT RISK—Average monthly payments on account, $1,000,000

RISK—Lapping of accounts receivable (embezzling customer payments and misapplying subsequent payments to cover up)

PROBABILITY OF RISK—

- Amount exposed to successful lapping estimated as 1% of average monthly payments on account
- Chances of risk occurrence estimated as 10%

MAXIMUM AMOUNT TO BE SPENT ON CONTROLS =
($1,000,000 x 1%) x 10% = $1,000/month

FIGURE 12-3   Sample risk assessment to determine the amount that can be effectively spent to control a specific risk.

gests audit procedures to validate the existence and effectiveness of these controls. The SAC report consists of a set of reference volumes that identify risk, controls, and audit techniques for a variety of areas, such as telecommunications, end-user systems, and emerging technologies. The 1994 SAC report added object technology, document management, and multimedia technologies sections. Both internal and external auditors rely on the SAC report for guidance on controls over IT and in auditing computer-based applications.

Chapter 9 pointed out that the Information Systems Audit and Control Foundation developed the **Control Objectives of Business and Information Technology (COBIT)** framework. This framework provides auditors with guidance in assessing and controlling for business risk associated with IT environments. COBIT consists of control objectives and a set of audit guidelines for evaluating the effectiveness of controls. Using the framework, management and auditors can design a cost-effective control system for IT resources and processes. The COBIT framework takes the approach that IT resources provide information to business processes. Auditors need to define, implement, and monitor controls to ensure that an organization's information requirements are met. Interestingly, COBIT has adopted both the Committee of Sponsoring Organizations (COSO) definition of internal control (see Chapter 9) and the SAC report's definition of IT control objectives. Both COBIT and SAC define control objectives as: a statement of the desired result or purpose to be achieved by implementing control procedures in a particular IT activity.[1] Case-in-Point 12.1 describes a government agency's adoption of COBIT.

> ***Case-in-Point 12.1*** In 2001, the Office of Inspector General (OIG), adopted COBIT in a number of ways. The organization included the framework in its Policy and Procedures Manual. They also used COBIT as a tool for planning their audits and to help them in assessing the amount of training their staff would need to perform planned audit work. In determining opportunities to deliver training, OIG created a database of courses that could provide a skill set supporting the domains and control objectives within COBIT.[2]

As part of the process of performing an **IT audit** (also called an *information systems audit*), auditors should determine that the following *control objectives* (which are based on the definition of IT control objectives in the SAC report) are met:

1. Security provisions protect computer, equipment, programs, communications, and data from unauthorized access, modification, or destruction.

2. Program development and acquisition are performed in accordance with management's general and specific authorization.

3. Program modifications have the authorization and approval of management.

4. Processing of transactions, files, reports, and other computer records is accurate and complete.

5. Source data that are inaccurate or improperly authorized are identified and handled according to prescribed managerial policies.

6. Computer data files are accurate, complete, and confidential.

---

[1] Information Systems Audit and Control Foundation research Board, *Control Objectives of Information Technology Framework*, April 1996, p. 11.
[2] Source: www.isaca.org (March 23, 2002).

AUDITING THROUGH THE COMPUTER

When computers were first used for accounting data processing functions, the typical auditor knew very little about automated data processing. The basic auditing approach, therefore, was to follow the *audit trail* up to the point at which accounting data entered the computer and to pick these data up again when they reappeared in processed form as computer output. This is called **auditing around the computer.** It assumes that the presence of accurate output verifies proper processing operations. This type of auditing pays little or no attention to the control procedures within the IT environment. Although auditing around the computer is straightforward and requires little training in computers, it is not generally an effective approach to auditing a computerized environment. This is because it tests normal transactions but ignores the exceptions. (It is the exceptions, however, that are of interest to the auditor.) In a high technology, complex computerized information systems environment, it is all but impossible to manually perform the same computerized computations or processing and compare results with computer-generated output.

When **auditing through the computer,** an auditor follows the *audit trail* through the internal computer operations phase of automated data processing. Unlike auditing around the computer, through-the-computer auditing attempts to verify that the processing controls involved in the AIS programs are functioning properly. Through-the-computer auditing also attempts to verify that the accounting data processed are accurate. Because this type of auditing tests the existence and functioning of control procedures, it normally occurs during the compliance phase of the flowchart shown in Figure 12-2.

Auditing through the computer usually assumes that the CPU and other equipment are functioning properly. This leaves the auditor the principal task of verifying processing and control logic as opposed to computer accuracy. The four primary approaches to through-the-computer auditing with the aid of *computer-assisted audit techniques* are: (1) use of test data, integrated test facility, and parallel simulation to *test programs,* (2) use of audit techniques to *validate computer programs,* (3) use of logs and specialized control software to *review systems software,* and (4) use of embedded audit modules to achieve *continuous auditing.* Each of these approaches is now discussed.

Testing Computer Programs

In testing computer programs, the objective is to ensure that the programs accomplish their goals and that the data are input and processed accurately. Three of the most commonly used techniques that auditors employ to test computer programs are (1) test data, (2) integrated test facility, and (3) parallel simulation.

Test Data   It is the auditor's responsibility to develop a set of transactions that tests, as completely as possible, the range of exception situations that might occur under normal processing conditions. Conventionally, these transactions are called **test data.** Possible exception situations for a payroll application, for example, include out-of-sequence payroll checks, duplicate time cards, negative hours worked, invalid employee numbers, invalid dates, invalid pay rates, invalid deduction codes, and use of alphabetic data in numeric codes. In sophisticated AISs, it is common to find that an initial set of transaction data will serve as the input to more than one processing routine. This makes the development of suitable test data challenging because the set of exceptions must be expanded to include the possibilities involved for all programs using the same input data. The point is that the auditor should build as many different exception situations as possible into the test data to provide a thorough audit test. An alternative to the auditor developing a set of test data is to use software programs called *test data generators*.

Once an auditor has assembled appropriate sample data (usually transactions of some type), these data are arranged into test sequence in preparation for computerized data processing. To complete the audit test, an auditor will compare the results obtained from processing test data with a predetermined set of answers on an audit work sheet. If processing results and worksheet results do not agree, further investigation is necessary. Discrepancies found in an audit test are *not always* attributable to deficient data processing or the lack of good controls. The use of nonstandard procedures, the introduction of spurious data, the possibility of machine malfunction, or the presence of other random irregularities are also possible causes of unanticipated results.

Test data are effective for checking that program edit test controls are in place and working. As an example, consider an online order entry application where edit tests exist to ensure that a customer account number is entered in its entirety, and to prevent the entry of alphabetic characters as part of that account number. An auditor could test these controls with, for instance, two test data entries. In the first test, the auditor would try entering an incomplete customer account number. Either a warning sound or an error message printed on the screen should result if the completeness control is working. In the second test, entering alphabetic characters in the customer account field will test the numeric field type control. A sample set of program edit tests and test data appears in Figure 12-4. (Chapter 10 provided several examples of these edit tests; see Figure 10-10.)

Integrated Test Facility   Although a test data technique works well in validating the *input controls* (discussed in Chapter 10) associated with data processing, it is not so effective in evaluating integrated online systems or complex programming logic. In these situations, it may be better to use a more comprehensive test technique such as an **integrated test facility (ITF).** The purpose of an ITF is to audit an AIS in an operational setting. This involves: (1) establishing a fictitious entity such

Program Edit Test	Required by Program	Test Data
Completeness	6 characters required	12345
Numeric Field	Numeric characters only	123C45
Sign	Positive numbers only	−123456
Reasonableness	Hours worked should not exceed 80 per week	110
Valid Code	Accept only I (invoice), P (payment), M (memo)	C
Range	Accept only dates between 01/01/01 and 12/31/02	09/07/99

FIGURE 12–4   Program edit tests and test data.

as a department, branch, customer, or employee; (2) entering transactions for that entity; and (3) observing how these transactions are processed. For example, an auditor might create a number of fictitious credit customers and place appropriate accounts receivable master records on the company's accounts receivable computer files. From the standpoint of the auditor, of course, the information contained on these records is for test purposes only. To most of the employees of the company, however, these records represent bona fide customers entitled to purchase company merchandise inventory or services on credit.

To use the ITF, an auditor will introduce *artificial transactions* into the data processing stream of the AIS and have the company routinely handle the business involved. In a truly integrated test facility, this may mean actually shipping merchandise (not ordered by anyone) to designated addresses or billing customers for services not rendered. Because of the amount of work involved, however, it may be necessary to intercept the ordered merchandise at the shipping department and reverse the billing transactions at the managerial level.

The auditor's role is to examine the results of the transaction processing and to find out how well the AIS performs the tasks required of it. The auditor does this by examining printouts based on the computer file records and data processing runs used in processing the transactions, and by then comparing the information on these printouts with anticipated results. Discrepancies between actual results and anticipated results form the basis for further inquiry.

The major advantage of an ITF is that it enables the auditor to examine both the manual steps and the computerized steps that a company uses to process business transactions. The major drawback of the ITF is that it introduces artificial transactions into the data processing stream. For the sake of accuracy in the company's financial statements, these transactions must be reversed.

Parallel Simulation   With **parallel simulation,** the auditor uses *live* input data, rather than test data, in a program actually written or controlled by the auditor. The auditor's program *simulates* all or some of the operations of the real program that is actually in use. For this method to be effective, an auditor must thoroughly understand the audited organization's computer system and know how to predict the results. The latter is necessary to intelligently compare the results of processing data using the test programs with those results from using the real programs.

As you might imagine, it can be very time-consuming and thus cost-prohibitive for an auditor to write computer programs entirely replicating those of the client. For this reason, parallel simulation usually involves replicating only certain critical functions of a program. For example, a program written to replicate the payroll-processing program might just calculate net pay for employees rather than making all the payroll distributions that exist in the entire payroll program. An alternative to writing a new program is for the auditor to obtain a copy of company processing programs following their implementation and then maintain control over those programs. Running live data through these programs periodically, and comparing results with those from the company program versions currently in use, would protect against any unauthorized changes. This approach can only work, however, when an auditor has a relatively long-standing relationship with the company being audited.

Parallel simulation eliminates the need to prepare a set of test data. It also avoids the possibility of co-mingling test data with company data, a situation that could result when using an ITF. To employ parallel simulation, however, an auditor must, as mentioned previously, have a complete understanding of the company's computer system. In addition, the auditor must have enough technical knowledge to write computer programs.

Validating Computer Programs

A clever programmer can thwart the use of test data by substituting a legitimate, but unused, program for a dishonest one when an auditor asks for the processing routine(s) required for the audit. Therefore, an auditor must validate any program with which he or she is presented. Although there is no 100 percent foolproof way of validating a computer program, several procedures may be used to assist in this task, including (1) tests of program change control, (2) program comparison, and (3) surprise audits and surprise use of programs.

Tests of Program Change Control The process by which a newly developed program or program modification is put into actual use should be subject to **program change control.** It is a set of internal control procedures developed to ensure against unauthorized program changes. Sound program change control requires documentation of every request for application program changes. It also requires computer programmers to develop and implement changes in a separate test environment rather than a live processing environment. Depending on the size of an organization, the change control process might be one of many duties performed by one individual. Alternatively, responsibility might be assigned to more than one individual. The basic procedures in program change control include testing program changes and obtaining proper authorizations as programs move from a testing stage to actual production (live) use. The auditor's responsibility is to ensure that a company's management establishes and executes proper authorization procedures and that the company's employees observe these procedures.

A test of program change control begins with an inspection of the documentation maintained by the information processing subsystem. It is not unusual for an organization to have on hand a flowchart of its change control process. The organization should also have special forms that authorize a change to an existing program or development of new programs. Included on these *program authorization forms* should be the name of the individual responsible for the work and the signature of the supervisor responsible for approving the final programs. Similarly, there should be forms that show the work has been completed and a signature authorizing the use of the program(s) for present data processing. These authorizing signatures affix responsibility for the data processing routines and ensure accountability when problems arise. We call this a **responsibility system of computer program development and maintenance.** Figure 12-5 describes the processes in this system that an auditor should validate.

The chief purpose of a responsibility system at the computer center is not to affix blame in the event of program failures but to ensure accountability and adequate supervisory controls in the critical area of data processing. Tighter control over both the development of new programs and changes to existing programs is likely to result in better computer software, since individuals tend to do better when they are responsible for a given piece of work.

Program Comparison A **trojan horse computer program** is a program with a hidden, intentional error created by a programmer for private gain. Usually, a Trojan

---

- Programmers document all program changes on the proper change-request forms.
- Users and accountants properly cost all program change requests and the planning committee reviews high-cost projects.
- Both computer development committee personnel and users sign the outline specification form, thereby establishing authorization for the programming work.
- Program changes match those in the programs in the production load library (where currently used programs are stored).
- Documentation matches the production version of a computer program.
- Information systems personnel properly carry out librarian functions, especially a review of the paperwork involved with the documentation of program change requests.

FIGURE 12–5   Each of the above processes is checked by an auditor in reviewing a responsibility system of computer program development and maintenance.

horse program is difficult to detect because the typical commercial accounting computer program contains thousands of instructions; the very few unauthorized instructions that might cause difficulties in the computer program may be hidden anywhere in the programming code.

To guard against unauthorized program tampering, especially at the machine-language level, it is possible to perform certain control total tests of program authenticity. The most common is a *test of length*. To perform this test, an auditor obtains the latest version of an accounting computer program to be verified and determines the number of bytes of computer memory required to store the program in machine language when it resides in the computer. The auditor compares this length count with a security table of length counts of all valid accounting programs. If the accounting program's length count fails to match its control total, the program is then further scrutinized.

Another way to ensure consistency between the authorized version of an accounting computer program and the program version currently in use is to compare the code directly on a line-by-line basis using a *comparison program*. Comparison programs are special computer programs that use source language accounting programs as data input. A comparison program will detect any changes a programmer might have made, even if the programmer has been clever enough to ensure that the program length for the two versions is the same. Auditors must evaluate the tradeoff between efficiency and effectiveness in choosing whether to use control totals, perform detailed program comparison, or rely on general controls over program changes to prevent unauthorized tampering of computer programs.

Surprise Audits and Surprise Use of Programs   The **surprise audit approach** involves examining accounting application programs unexpectedly. The auditor will appear unannounced during scheduled processing runs and request duplicate copies of the computer programs just after they have been run. Usually, the auditor copies these programs and then compares the "in-use" programs with previously acquired "authorized" versions, using either a control-total approach or program comparison software.

With the **surprise use approach,** an auditor visits the computer center unannounced and requests that previously obtained authorized accounting computer programs be used for the required data processing. If the information systems manager denies this request, the auditor carefully documents and investigates the reasons for the denial. If the manager honors the request, the auditor then performs the specific accounting tasks required using the previously obtained authorized programs. The auditor should carefully scrutinize unusual conditions that occur during the processing runs.

Review of Systems Software

Systems software controls include (1) operating system software, (2) utility programs that do basic "housekeeping" chores such as sorting and copying, (3) program library software that controls and monitors storage of programs, and (4) access control software that controls logical access to programs and data files.

When auditing through the computer, auditors will want to review the systems software documentation. In addition, auditors will request management to provide certain output or runs from the software. For instance, the auditor, in reviewing how passwords within the system are set, will request the information systems manager to provide a listing of all *parameters* or password characteristics designated in the system. Figure 12-6 lists some of the characteristics of passwords that the auditor will examine.

Auditors may choose to use software tools to review systems software. A number of tools are available, ranging from user-written programs to commercial packages such as *CA-Examine*. There are also general analysis types of software tools, such as

Parameter	Definition	Sample Setting	Risk
Minimum password length	Minimum number of characters required	6 digits	Short passwords are more easily guessed
Required password change	Require users to change passwords at specific intervals	60 days	Compromised passwords can be used forever
Minimum interval before password change	Minimum number of days before user can change password	1 day	If a user believes someone has learned the password, how much time must pass before it can be changed?
Maximum number of repeating characters allowed	Specifies how many characters may be repeated within the password	2 characters	Passwords such as "AAAAAA" are easily guessed
Alphabetic characters	Passwords may not consist of only numbers	Alpha	Protects against use of birthdates or other easily guessed numbers
Dictionary entries	Passwords cannot be dictionary words	ROOTTOOT	Hackers use standard dictionaries to find passwords
Assignment	Only bona fide users are given passwords	Employee	Passwords ensure accountability in addition to providing access

FIGURE 12–6   Examples of parameters that might be set to control passwords.

SAS, SPSS, and *FOCUS.* These software tools can query operating system files to analyze the system parameters.

Systems software usually generates automatic reports that are important for monitoring a company's computer system. In auditing the company's system, an auditor will want to inspect these reports, which include logs and incident reports. The company's management uses *logs* for accounting purposes and for scheduling the use of computer resources efficiently. Auditors will make use of these logs to evaluate system security. Unusual occurrences, such as programs run at odd times or programs run with greater frequency than usual, are noted and subsequently investigated. Management may manually maintain *incident reports,* or systems software may automatically generate these reports. The reports list events encountered by the system that are unusual or interrupt operations. Incidents typically recorded are security violations (such as unauthorized access attempts), hardware failures, and software failures.

Continuous Auditing

Some audit tools can be installed within an information system itself to achieve **continuous auditing.** It is particularly effective when most of an application's data are in electronic form. Some tools available for continuous auditing include (1) embedded audit modules or audit hooks, (2) exception reporting, (3) transaction tagging, (4) snapshot technique, and (5) continuous and intermittent simulation. These tools allow auditing to occur even when an auditor is not present. With *embedded audit modules,* application subroutines capture data for audit purposes. These data usually are related to a high-risk area. For example, an application program for payroll would include a code that causes transactions meeting prespecified criteria to be written to a special log called a *systems control audit review file (SCARF).* Transactions that might be recorded in a SCARF file include those affecting inactive accounts, deviating from company policy, or involving write-downs of asset values. For payroll applications, these transactions could reflect situations where, for instance, employees worked more than a predetermined number of hours. Another example might be the recording of related transactions occurring in a particular sequence, as described in Case-in-Point 12.2.

> *Case-in-Point 12.2*   At State Farm Life Insurance, the information system makes a record of every transaction requiring a name and address change. This file is very large, and auditors do not review it in its entirety. However, the system records each incidence where a policyholder surrenders a life insurance policy for its cash value. The system updates a review file each time a transaction appears on both files within a specified period of time. This review file is a type of audit hook, which is an audit routine that flags suspicious transactions. Since at State Farm, a fictitious policyholder could remove cash by surrendering an insurance policy, auditors will want to look closely at suspicious transactions such as those described above.

The practice of *exception reporting* is also a form of continuous auditing. If the information system includes mechanisms to reject certain transactions that fall outside predefined specifications (such as an unusually large vendor check), then the ongoing reporting of exception transactions allows the system to continually monitor itself.

Using *transaction tagging,* one can tag certain transactions with a special identifier so that they can be recorded as they pass through the information system. For example, a specific number of employees have tags attached to their transaction records so that an auditor can verify the processing logic in the payroll system. Tagging in this instance could also check to see that controls within the system are operating. Suppose that a control procedure requires rejection of payroll transactions if the number of hours worked during a pay period is unreasonable (according to some predefined criteria). Auditors can review tagged transactions to make sure that this control procedure is functioning properly.

Through the *snapshot technique,* the way transactions are processed is examined. Selected transactions are marked with a special code that triggers the snapshot process. Audit modules in the computer program record these transactions and their master file records both before and after processing activities. Snapshot data are recorded in a special file and reviewed by the auditor to verify that all processing steps have been properly performed.

Continuous and intermittent simulation (CIS) embeds an audit module in a database management system (DBMS). The CIS module examines all transactions that update the DBMS, employing criteria similar to those of SCARF. If a transaction has special audit significance, the audit module independently processes the data (in a manner similar to *parallel simulation*), records the results, and compares them with those results obtained by the DBMS. If any discrepancies exist, the details of these discrepancies are written onto an audit log for subsequent investigation. If serious discrepancies are discovered, the CIS may prevent the DBMS from executing the update process.

AUDITING WITH THE COMPUTER

Auditors can use *computer-assisted audit techniques (CAATs)* to help them in various other auditing tasks in addition to *auditing through the computer.* In an automated AIS, **auditing with the computer** is virtually mandatory because data are stored on computer media and manual access is impossible. However, there are many reasons for auditing with the computer beyond the need to access computerized accounting data.

One of the most important reasons for auditing with the computer is that computer-based AISs are rapidly increasing in sophistication. Soon, the *only* effective way to audit such systems will be with a computer. CAATs also save time. Imagine footing and cross-footing large spreadsheets or schedules without using a computer. Or picture selecting sample accounts receivable data for confirmation *manually.*

A variety of software is available to auditors in auditing with the computer. Examples include *general-use software* such as word processing programs, spreadsheet software, and database management systems. Other software is more specifically oriented toward auditor tasks. Included here is *generalized audit software (GAS)* and *automated workpaper software.*

General-Use Software

Auditors have come to rely on **general-use software** as productivity tools that can improve their work. For instance, word processing programs improve effectiveness when writing reports because built-in spell checks can significantly reduce spelling errors. An example of improvement in efficiency involves the mail-merge feature found in general-use software. An auditor can write a customer confirmation letter with a word processing program and merge it with an address file so that each letter appears to have been individually prepared.

Spreadsheet software allows both accountants and auditors to make complex calculations automatically. It also allows the user to change one number and update all related numbers at the click of a mouse. One of the most common uses of electronic spreadsheets by accountants and auditors is for making mathematical calculations, such as interest and depreciation. Spreadsheet software can also be used to perform analytical procedures, such as computing ratios. Different presentation formats for data contained in spreadsheets contribute to the usefulness of these data for management decision-making and other managerial functions.

Accountants and auditors can use a *database management system (DBMS)* to perform some of the same functions as spreadsheet software. For instance, DBMSs can sort data and make certain mathematical computations. However, they are distinguished from spreadsheet software by their ability to manipulate *large* sets of data in fairly simple ways. As a general rule, accountants and auditors use spreadsheet software to make complex calculations with relatively small sets of data, whereas they will use DBMSs for simpler calculations or manipulations, such as sorting, on large data sets.

A DBMS controls almost all organizational accounting systems. The auditor can select subsets of a client company's data for manipulation purposes. This can be done either on the client's computer system, or, after the data are downloaded, on the auditor's computer. A valuable tool for retrieving and manipulating data is **Structured Query Language (SQL),** a popular data manipulation language. Auditors can use SQL to retrieve a client's data and display these data in a variety of formats for audit purposes. As an example, an auditor may use the SELECT command to retrieve inventory items meeting certain criteria, such as minimum dollar amount. Other data manipulation capabilities of SQL include (1) selecting records matching specified criteria, (2) deleting records from a file based on established criteria, (3) generating customized reports based on all or a subset of data, and (4) rearranging file records in sequential order.

Generalized Audit Software

Generalized audit software (GAS) packages (or programs) enable auditors to review computer files without continually rewriting processing programs. Large CPA firms have developed some of these packages in-house; many other programs are available from various software suppliers. GAS packages are available to run on microcomputers, minicomputers, or mainframes. GAS programs are capable of the basic data manipulation tasks that spreadsheet or DBMS software might also perform. These include mathematical computations, cross footing, categorizing, summarizing, merging files, sorting records, statistical sampling, and printing reports. The advantage GAS packages have over other software is that these programs are specifically tailored to auditor tasks. Auditors can use GAS programs in a variety of ways in specific application areas, such as accounts receivable, inventory, and accounts payable. Figure 12-7 shows some of the ways auditors might use GAS to audit inventory applications. Case-in-Point 12.3 illustrates how an auditor, by using GAS, was able to obtain evidence to have a former tax collector arrested for embezzlement.

- Merge last year's inventory file with this year's and list those items with unit costs greater than a certain dollar amount and which have increased by more than a specified percentage.

- List inventory quantities on hand in excess of units sold during a specified period and list those inventory items with a last sales date prior to a specified date to identify possible obsolete inventory items.

- Select a sample of inventory tag numbers and print the sample selection.

- Scan the sequence of inventory tag numbers and print any missing or duplicate numbers.

- Select a random sample of inventory items for price testing on a dollar-value basis, and list all items with an extended value in excess of a specified amount.

- Perform a net-realizable-value test on year-end inventory quantities, and list any items where inventory cost exceeds net realizable value.

FIGURE 12–7 Various ways to use generalized audit software packages to audit inventory.

Case-in-Point 12.3 In a small New England town, a new tax collector was elected, defeating the incumbent. The new tax collector requested an audit of the city's tax collection records. Using GAS, the auditors accessed the tax collection records for the past four years, sorted them by collection date, summed the amount of taxes collected monthly, and prepared a four-year summary report of monthly tax collections. The analysis revealed that tax collections during January and July, the two busiest months, had declined by 58 percent and 72 percent, respectively. The auditors used the GAS to compare the tax collection records, one by one, with the city's property records. The ensuing report identified several discrepancies, including one case where the former tax collector used another taxpayer's payment to cover her own delinquent tax bills. The former tax collector was arrested and charged with embezzlement.

Two popular GAS packages used by auditors are *Audit Command Language (ACL)* and *Interactive Data Extraction and Analysis (IDEA)*. These programs allow auditors to examine a company's data in a variety of formats. They include commands such as STRATIFY, EXTRACT, and JOIN. Each of these commands provides an auditor with a different view of the data. For example, the STRATIFY command lets an auditor group data into categories. This is useful, for example, in sorting inventories into various classes based on their cost. Stratification lets an auditor concentrate on high-dollar-value inventory items. As another example, stratification is helpful in auditing accounts receivable. Auditors will want to verify balances of customers owing large dollar amounts in greater proportion than small accounts receivable balances owed by customers. Most GAS packages allow auditors to *extract* data according to some specification. This capability is an invaluable audit tool. Auditors can extract data to detect a variety of exception conditions, such as duplicate invoice numbers, inventory items that have not been sold in more than one year, and customers with negative accounts receivable balances. By *joining* files, auditors can compare data. For example, combining the employee file with the vendor file may show that an employee has perpetrated a fraud by creating a fictitious vendor. Case-in-Point 12.4 shows how one company used ACL effectively.

Case-in-Point 12.4 Sara Lee used ACL to create an audit toolbox by capturing commands and converting them into batch routines. The purpose was to provide some standardized tools and routines for auditors to use in auditing Sara Lee's computerized systems. Use of the toolbox led to more significant audit findings. As an example, Sara Lee's auditors found unusual situations by matching vendor and employee addresses. Another example was the discovery of duplicate payments to certain vendors.

Automated Workpaper Software

Automated workpaper software is similar to general ledger software because it can also generate trial balances. The difference is that automated workpaper software handles accounts for many organizations in a flexible manner. The functions of automated workpaper software vary with specific programs. Some of the features of this software are (1) generated trial balances, (2) adjusting entries, (3) consolidations, and (4) analytical procedures. Using automated workpaper software, an auditor can produce an unadjusted trial balance, make adjusting journal entries, and automatically generate an adjusted trial balance. The advantage of using automated workpaper software is that it automates footing, cross footing, and reconciliation to schedules. Auditors can use this software to prepare consolidated trial balances and financial statements (that combine accounts of multiple companies). Automated workpaper software can also help auditors create common-size income statements and balance sheets. (These financial statements show account balances as percentages.) In addition, automated workpaper software can easily calculate financial statement ratios and measurements, such as the *current ratio,* the *working capital,* the *inventory turnover rate,* and the *price-earnings ratio.*

AUDITING IN THE INFORMATION AGE

While auditing today has the same basic objectives as in past years, there is no question that advances in technology have greatly affected the audit process. Many technologies in the information age require special audit procedures. One of these technologies that is particularly important is *electronic spreadsheets.* This chapter describes auditing spreadsheets in some detail. The section also discusses two other important topics related to auditing in today's advanced technological environment: third party assurance services and systems reliability assurance.

Auditing Electronic Spreadsheets

The extensive computational and formatting capabilities of today's spreadsheets enable users to create professional outputs. But good-looking reports can mask a host of input errors, formula mistakes, and other problems. Experts estimate that as many as one in every three spreadsheets have a major error in them. Thus, it is important for accountants to know how to build and validate spreadsheets, and also how to audit the applications built by others. This section of the chapter examines the subject of spreadsheet auditing in detail.

Building Auditing Modules in Spreadsheets One way to audit spreadsheets is to embed **auditing modules** in them, in effect, making them self-auditing. These modules contain separate computations that help ensure that a spreadsheet model works properly and that its outputs are accurate. Because spreadsheet applications vary widely, these auditing modules must be customized on a case-by-case basis. To illustrate, however, consider the (Excel) payroll spreadsheet in Figure 12-8, which computes the regular and overtime earnings for the employees of a construction company. (The overtime pay rate is 1.5 times the regular pay rate.) Most such spreadsheets would only include the first few lines shown in Figure 12-8, plus perhaps the "Total" line in row 14. But this spreadsheet includes several additional rows, an auditing module, that can help an accountant audit the application and ascertain its validity and accuracy.

The figure in the "Counts" row uses Excel's CountIf function to count the number of positive values in columns B, C, and D of the spreadsheet. An auditor can compare the largest of these numbers to the total number of employees known to work for the company. If we assume that this company has upper limits for the pay rate ($13), regular hours (40), and overtime hours (10), an auditor can also compare the values in the "Maximums" row against these upper limits to determine if any entries are too large.

Microsoft Excel - Excel Example.xls						

File Edit View Insert Format Tools Data Window Help

TimesNew Roman 10 B U $ %

14 =

	A	B	C	D	E	F	G
1	**Choi Construction Company**						
2	**Payroll for Week Ending: 3/15/XX**						
3							
4		**Payrate**	**Regular Hours**	**Overtime Hours**	**Regular Pay**	**Overtime Pay**	**Total**
5	Adams	8.90	40	3	356.00	40.05	396.05
6	Baker	12.55	35	0	502.00	0.00	502.00
7	Carlton	9.60	40	2	384.00	38.80	422.80
8	Daniels	10.20	35	0	408.00	0.00	408.00
9	Englert	9.60	40	5	384.00	72.00	456.00
10	Franklin	11.55	40	0	462.00	0.00	462.00
11	Griffin	10.80	35	0	432.00	0.00	432.00
12	Hartford	9.90	40	10	396.00	148.50	544.50
13							
14	Totals:		305	20	$3,324.00	$ 299.35	$3,623.35
15							
16	Totals:						
17	Counts:	8	8	4			
18	Maiximums:	12.55	40.00	10.00			
19	Sum: Reg + O'time						$3,623.35
20	Max Regular Pay:				$4,016.00		
21	Max Overtime Pay:					$ 753.00	

FIGURE 12-8 This simple spreadsheet to compute regular and overtime payments contains several errors.

Now let us look at the remaining rows of this spreadsheet. First, note that the grand total of $3,623.35 in cell G14 is a column total. But we can also compute this value as the sum of the regular pay and overtime pay shown in cells E14 and F14. This is the figure in cell G19, and of course should match the value in cell G14.

Finally, we can use the counts in row 17 and the maximum values in row 18 to compute upper limits for the regular and overtime pay totals in row 14. In particular, the regular pay total cannot exceed the following product:

(Count for   (Maximum   (Maximum
Regular Pay) * Pay Rate) * Regular Hours) = 8 * 12.55 * 40 = $4,016.00

We can create a similar computation for the maximum overtime pay total. The auditor can compare these values to the actual totals showing in cells E14 and F14.

Auditing Spreadsheet Data and Formulas   It is possible for a spreadsheet application to pass all the auditing tests discussed above and still be incorrect. This can happen, for example, if a user inputs a particular data value incorrectly or makes a mistake when creating a formula. In such cases, the embedded auditing modules may not signal any errors, but the results will nonetheless be wrong.

In addition to using embedded audit modules in spreadsheets, therefore, it may be desirable to examine the data and formulas in spreadsheet models using additonal methods, again to ensure their accuracy and completeness. Although there are sophisticated computer programs now available for such tasks, we can employ several useful tools that are immediately available with current spreadsheet software to accomplish such tasks. To illustrate, we will again use the spreadsheet example in Figure 12-8.

Display Formulas   One procedure for auditing existing spreadsheet computations is to create, and then inspect, the formulas that were used to create the outputs. With Excel, for example, we can view such formulas using the following steps:

1. Copy the existing spreadsheet to a separate worksheet.
2. Using the new worksheet, select the following options from Excel's main menu: Tools/Options/View/tab/Formulas checkbox.

Figure 12-9 shows the formulas for the cells in Columns E and F of Figure 12-8. Here, we see two common errors. First, in Column E, we observe that only the formula for cell E6 is correct. All the formulas for the other cells in this column are incorrect because they multiply each pay rate by "40." This is an error because the value for Regular Hours is not always 40. This type of error commonly occurs when a user enters a formula correctly, and then fails to copy that formula into similar row or column cells.

Column F contains a different kind of error. Here, we observe the constant "38.8" embedded in cell F9, instead of a formula. This is an error because this cell should contain a formula similar to the other cells in this column, not a constant. Auditors can use similar inspections to find similar constants in cell ranges that should only contain formulas (a common error), or formulas where they should see constants.

Use Data Validation Rules   A **data validation rule** is a customized edit test that you can create and that enables a spreadsheet to reject entries that violate it. To illustrate, assume that the Choi Construction Company has the following rules:

	E	F	G
4	**Regular Pay**	**Overtime Pay**	**Total**
5	=B5*C5	=B5*1.5*D5	=E5+F5
6	=B6*40	=B6*1.5*D6	=E6+F6
7	=B7*40	38.8	=E7+F7
8	=B8*40	=B8*1.5*D8	=E8+F8
9	=B9*40	=B9*1.5*D9	=E9+F9
10	=B10*40	=B10*1.5*D10	=E10+F10
11	=B11*40	=B11*1.5*D11	=E11+F11
12	=B12*40	=B12*1.5*D12	=E12+F12
13			
14			
15	=AVERAGE(E5:E12)	=AVERAGE(F5:F12)	
16	=SUM(E5:E12)	=SUM(F5:F12)	=SUM(G5:G12)
17			
18			

FIGURE 12–9   A partial listing of the formulas used to create the spreadsheet in Figure 12-8.

(1) all pay rates must fall between $6.75 and $13.00, (2) regular hours worked must be at least 0 and no more than 40, and (3) overtime hours worked must be at least 0 and no more than 10. Using Excel, you can create the validation rule (Figure 12-10) using the following steps:

1. Highlight the pay rate values in Column B (i.e., the data range B5:B12).
2. Select the choices Data/Validation from the main menu.
3. Select "Decimal" from the choices in the "Allow" box.

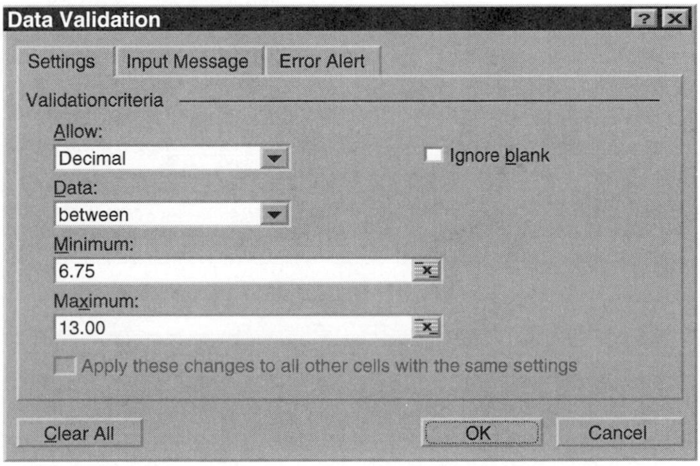

FIGURE 12–10   Excel's Data Validation dialog box. This example illustrates data validation rule for column B of Figure 10.A.

4. Select "Between" from the choices in the "Data" box.

5. Enter the value "6.75" in the "Minimum" box.

6. Enter the value "13.00" in the "Maximum" box.

Highlighting the data range *before* creating the data validation rule tells Excel to apply this rule to all values in the range.

Excel's Audit Toolbar   Imagine that you create separate data validation rules for columns B, C, and D of the current spreadsheet. These validation rules will block users from making *further* data entry errors, but *will not* identify errors that already exist in the affected cell ranges. However, we can use Excel's auditing tools for this purpose as follows:

1. Make sure that you have created data validation rules for all cells you wish to audit.

2. From the main menu, select Tools/Auditing/Show Auditing Toolbar.

3. Click on the "Circle Invalid Data" icon in this toolbar (the second icon from the right). This causes *Excel* to circle all those data entries that violate the data validation rules that you created for them.

Figure 12-11 illustrates the results of such work for a spreadsheet similar to Figure 12-8 (but that contains more errors for illustration). Again, correcting these errors does not guarantee that the spreadsheet is accurate (there could still be formula errors, for example), but it helps.

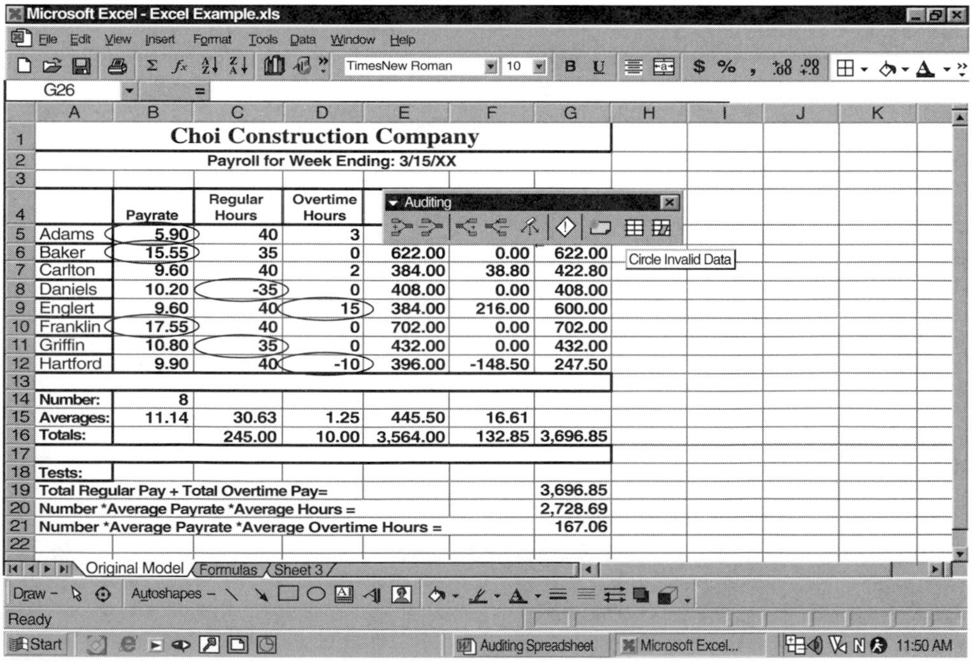

FIGURE 12–11   The results when you click on the "Circle Invalid Data" icon in Excel's audit toolbar.

We can also use Excel's audit toolbar to display precedence and dependence relationships. For example, if you first click on cell G14 (containing the value $3, 623.35) and then click on the "Trace Precedents" icon in the audit toolbar, Excel will display a heavy, dark blue line in cells G6 through G13, signifying that all the cells in this column affect cell G14. If you click on the "Trace Precedents" icon again, the heavy line will remain, but the new lines and dots in the data range E5:F12, as well as the arrows in column G, will appear. These items indicate that the values in cells E5 and F5 determined the value in cell G5, the values in cells E6 and F6 determined the value in cell G6, and so forth.

The ability to graphically depict precedence relationships is useful for debugging purposes, for example, to correct a formula known to contain an error. But you can also use this capability to *find* mistakes. For example, if you click on cell E6 and then click on the Trace Precedents icon in Excel's audit toolbar, you will see a thin line in cells B6 through E6. The absence of a dot in cell C6 alerts you to an error because Regular pay *should* be the product of the Pay Rate times Regular Hours.

You can also use Excel's audit toolbar to show *dependence relationships* (i.e., cells that depend on a given value). For example, if you select cell C18 and then click again on the "Trace Dependents" icon in the audit toolbar, Excel will draw an arrow to cell E20. This arrow indicates that cell E20 contains a formula that references cell C18. When auditing a spreadsheet, this feature is useful for examining "strange" spreadsheet values that seemingly have no useful purpose. For example, selecting such a value and then examining its dependent values can help an auditor understand how it is used.

Specialized Spreadsheet Audit Software   Finally, there are a number of software products on the market today that can help you audit important worksheets. An example is *Spreadsheet Professional*. These tools can examine spreadsheets and look for such common errors as (1) sum functions that do not appear to add all the elements in a data range, (2) numeric values that are never referenced by other cells, (3) mathematical functions that reference blank cells or labels, or (4) calculations containing constants (such as the preceding example). For more information on these packages, see the spreadsheet-auditing references at the end of this chapter.

Third-Party Assurance

Auditing electronic commerce is a specialized field, partly because of the skill level involved, and partly because many of the safeguards inherent in non e-commerce systems do not exist. One problem is the lack of hard-copy documents with which to verify the existence of accounts, purchases, or payments, a characteristic of electronic communications. Similarly, the arrival of an electronic transaction on a company computer does not guarantee its validity or authenticity, only that something was transmitted. As an increasing number of companies publish their financial statements online, auditors will need to attest to this type of format. An audit report or digital signature can provide those viewing online financial information with the same assurances as found in a traditional audit report.

The importance of the Internet and electronic commerce impacts auditors' work in other ways. In recent years auditors have shifted away from audits of transactions to audits of business risk issues. Because Internet systems and web sites are a source of risk for many companies, specialized audits of these systems, particularly in terms of security and privacy, are becoming commonplace. In fact, the risks introduced by a business' Internet presence have created a market for **third-party assurance services.**

Independent third parties may provide business users and individual consumers with some level of comfort over their Internet transactions. The comfort level varies with the type of assurance services offered. In some cases, third-party assurance is limited to data privacy. The *TRUSTe* assurance seal is an example of this type of limited assurance. *TRUSTe* is a nonprofit organization that issues a privacy seal. Some professional service firms, such as Ernst and Young LLP, incorporate the *TRUSTe* seal into their information systems audit services.

Other assurance services offer different kinds of protection. Consumers and business partners are not just concerned about privacy and security of data transmissions. They also worry about an Internet business' policies, its ability to deliver goods and services in a timely fashion, and its billing procedures. The Better Business Bureau's *BBBOnline* seeks to verify the business policies of Internet businesses. *CPA Web Trust,* offered by the AICPA, is a third-party assurance seal that promises data privacy and security, in addition to reliable business practices and integrity in processing transactions. *Better Web,* offered by PricewaterhouseCoopers, provides customers engaged in online transactions with assurance regarding a business' sales terms, privacy, security, and handling of complaints.

Information Systems Reliability Assurance

Auditors must take risks associated with information systems into account with respect to their possible impact on financial statements. In addition, many businesses seek assurance as to the *reliability* of their information systems. Recently, the AICPA introduced **SysTrust,** an assurance service that evaluates the reliability of information systems with respect to their availability, security, integrity, and maintainability. CPAs offering *SysTrust* services to their clients may evaluate all or some of these reliability characteristics. For instance, a company may have concerns about the security of its information systems. A CPA would evaluate that client's system in terms of its controls over unauthorized access. As increasing numbers of parties rely on organizations' information systems, assurance over the reliability of those systems is likely to grow in importance.

AIS AT WORK
Hacker Practices

Ernst & Young LLP's national Security and Technology Solutions group offers a range of security and assurance services, including penetration testing. *Penetration testing* involves trying to "hack" into a client's computer system—for a fee. Ernst & Young's practice is not unique; many large professional service organizations offer penetration studies to clients. These services allow clients to learn what and where weaknesses exist in their information systems security.

The Internet has increased exposure to security breaches dramatically. Although businesses spend billions of dollars on Internet security, vulnerabilities persist. The Internet isn't the only problem; internal computer networks and intranets pose security threats too.

Penetration testing practices employ accountants and information systems specialists, as well as a variety of other skilled individuals with a love of computers. The job is to try to break into the client's system, much as a hacker would do. The difference, of course, is that the penetration tester doesn't take anything, but rather writes a report detailing the control weaknesses that allowed the access. Hackers for hire use many of the same tools that the bad guys do, including *war dialers*. War dialers are available on the Internet (for free), and hackers use them to continuously dial phone numbers until they connect with a computer. Consultants conducting penetration studies also surf the Internet for hacker bulletin boards where they pick up tips about new tools for penetrating systems. These consultants are usually skilled, too, at *social engineering*—getting people to ignore controls. A talented social engineer can convince an individual to divulge user Ids and passwords. Hacking for hire may sound glamorous, particularly if you enjoy using computers, but it can be tedious and involve poring through detailed documents. One certainty is that given continuing increases in Internet traffic, this business is likely to continue to grow.

SUMMARY

Although both the internal and external auditors are concerned with computerized systems, there are important differences in the goals of each type of auditor. Both internal and external auditors may engage in information systems auditing. This type of auditing complements the financial audit, since it provides a basis for determining the appropriate scope of the financial audit based on an assessment of control procedures surrounding the information processing function. Information systems auditors differ from financial auditors in their areas of expertise and technical knowledge. Knowledge of both accounting and information systems makes for the best auditors since these two areas are so closely related.

An auditor may also be asked to evaluate the effectiveness of control procedures either already installed within a company's AIS or contemplated for the system when design changes are about to be made. A useful device for this evaluation process is an information systems risk assessment. Using a risk assessment approach, auditors ensure that the costs of control procedures do not outweigh their value.

Auditors today have some special tools available to them in designing and evaluating internal controls in IT environments. Three approaches to auditing a computerized AIS are (1) auditing *around* the computer, (2) auditing *through* the computer, and (3) auditing *with* the computer. Today, auditing *around* the computer is the least viable investigative approach; the auditor must audit *through* the computer to do a thorough job. Auditing through the computer involves both testing and validating computer programs, as well as a review of systems software. The use of *embedded audit modules* is one of the tools discussed in this chapter to audit through the computer continuously. When auditing *with* the computer, the computer becomes a tool to assist in the various audit processes. Many different software packages are available to help auditors in their work. These include general-use software such as spreadsheet and database packages, as well as generalized audit software developed specifically to do audit-related functions. Auditors also make wide use of automated workpaper software to perform functions such as generating trial balances and recording adjusting journal entries to accounts.

The information age poses new challenges for auditors. Advancing technologies, such as electronic spreadsheets, do not impact audit objectives but certainly influence the audit process. This chapter showed how to audit electronic spreadsheets, using features available in popular spreadsheet software.

The information age offers opportunities for auditors too. For instance, advanced information technologies have created the need for new assurance services such as *CPA Web-Trust* and *SysTrust.*

KEY TERMS YOU SHOULD KNOW

attest function

auditing around the computer

auditing modules

auditing through the computer

auditing with the computer

automated workpaper software

Certified Information Systems Auditor (CISA)

compensating controls

computer-assisted audit techniques (CAATs)

continuous auditing

Control Objectives for Information and Related Technology (COBIT)

CPA WebTrust

data validation rule

external audit

fraud auditors

general-use software

generalized audit software (GAS)

information systems auditing

information systems risk assessment

integrated test facility (ITF)

internal audit

IT audit

parallel simulation

program change control

responsibility system of computer program development and maintenance

risk-based audit approach

spreadsheet audit software

Structured Query Language (SQL)

substantive testing

surprise audit approach

surprise use approach

Systems Auditability and Control (SAC)

SysTrust

systems review

test data

tests of controls

third-party assurance services

trojan horse computer program

DISCUSSION QUESTIONS

12-1. Distinguish between the roles of an internal auditor and an external auditor. Cite at least two examples of auditing procedures that might reasonably be expected of an internal auditor but not an external auditor. Which type of auditor would you rather be? Why?

12-2. How does information systems auditing differ from financial auditing? Make a list of the skills you think are important for financial auditors and for information systems auditors. Do you think all auditors should have all the skills on both lists? Why or why not?

12-3. Explain the difference between auditing around the computer, through the computer, and with the computer. Do you think it is possible to conduct a thorough audit by auditing around the computer? Is it ever efficient to audit *without* a computer?

12-4. Through-the-computer auditing has several advantages over around-the-computer auditing, but it also has some disadvantages. What are some of these disadvantages? For each disadvantage discussed, suggest a method for eliminating the disadvantage or at least lessening it, without abandoning the through-the-computer audit approach.

12-5. The Pan Pacific Computer Company purchases independent computer components, which it then uses to manufacture custom-made computer hardware. Because it deals with a number of vendors, it has computerized the accounting procedures for its accounts payables. Describe how an auditor might use through-the-computer techniques such as test data, integrated test facility, parallel simulation, or validation of computer programs, to accomplish audit objectives relative to accounts payable.

12-6. How does an auditor evaluate the control procedures of an automated AIS? How is the element of uncertainty handled in the audit examination?

12-7. Jose Rodriguez was the only internal auditor of a medium-sized communications firm. The company used a computer for most of its accounting applications, and recently several new software packages had been implemented to handle the increased volume of the company's business. To evaluate the packages' control capabilities, Jose performed a cost-benefit analysis and found that many of the control procedures were potentially useful but not clearly cost-effective. The problem, therefore, was what to say in his report to management. After pondering this question for some time, he decided to recommend almost all the controls based on the idea that a company was "better to be safe than sorry." Comment.

12-8. Describe the differences between general-use software and generalized audit software. How might you use spreadsheet software, database software, and word processing software in conducting an audit of fixed assets?

12-9. One advance in technology that seems likely to significantly impact auditing is *image processing*. Auditors have traditionally relied on a paper audit trail in performing their work. The absence of this paper trail provides both control advantages and disadvantages. Explain how you think certain audit tasks might be changed or performed differently as a result of this image processing technology.

12-10. According to the AICPA *SysTrust* service, there are four components of information systems reliability. These are availability, security, integrity, and maintainability. Discuss these components.

PROBLEMS

12-11. The Espy Company recently had an outside consulting firm perform an audit of its information systems department. One of the consultants identified some business risks and their probability of occurrence. Estimates of the potential losses and estimated control costs are given in Figure 12-12.

   a. Using the Figure 12-12 information, develop a risk assessment for the Espy Company.

   b. If you were the manager responsible for the Espy Company's information processing system, which controls would you implement and why?

12-12. Bogle Billboards is an outdoor advertising company that maintains several hundred billboards and side-of-building advertising displays in and around Center City. The company's accounting operations are computerized, and one of its computer files is called BOARD1. This file describes all of its poster billboards. The data fields in the typical

Hazard	Probability That Loss Will Occur	Low Estimate	High Estimate	Estimated Control Costs
		Losses		
Equipment failure	.08	$ 50,000	$150,000	$2,000
Software failure	.10	4,000	18,000	1,400
Vandalism	.65	1,000	15,000	8,000
Embezzlement	.05	3,000	9,000	1,000
Brownout	.40	850	2,000	250
Power surge	.40	850	2,000	300
Flood	.15	250,000	500,000	2,500
Fire	.10	150,000	300,000	4,000

FIGURE 12-12 A risk analysis for the Espy Company.

Field	Type	Size (in characters)
Billboard number (used as record key)	Numeric	4
Location (description)	Alphabetic	50
Direction board faces (e.g., NW)	Alphabetic	2
Illumination ("no" or code for type of lighting)	Alphabetic	2
Zone of town (commercial, residential)	Numeric	1
Exposure value (how many people drive by it per day)	Numeric	4
Date last scraped	Numeric	6
Data available	Numeric	6
Presently reserved for future? (Y or N)	Alphabetic	1

FIGURE 12-13 A computer record for Bogle Billboards.

computer record for this file are listed in Figure 12-13, along with character information. The file is arranged in ascending sequence by billboard number.

Outdoor advertising is Bogle Billboards' primary business, so information concerning its billboards is very important in determining the net worth of the company. Describe what an auditor might do to audit the BOARD1 file in order to verify the information contained within this file. Be as thorough as possible.

12-13. The Li Corporation is the publisher of *Computerweek* magazine, a popular trade publication for microcomputer users. The company maintains subscriber information on a computer file. A typical computer record is illustrated in Figure 12-14. Numbers in the record format represent the number of characters in each field of the record.

From time to time, the Li Corporation prepares copies of this file, which it sells to other companies interested in soliciting business from *Computerweek* readers. Thus, the file is itself an asset to the Li Corporation. As an auditor, describe what tests you would perform to verify the information on this file. Be as thorough as possible.

Last Name	First Name(s)	Street Address and City	State	Zip Code	Date Subscrip- tion Expires	Type Code (1 = Bus- iness, 2 = Personal)	Number of Re- newals	Blank
Subscriber Name								
30		30	2	5	6	1	1	40

FIGURE 12-14 The record layout of the subscriber file of the Li Corporation.

INTERNET EXERCISES

12-14. Information systems auditors sometimes use tools or information they can download from the Internet. These tools or information may include software, audit guides, or computer security advisories. Locate some examples from the Internet of audit tools, audit guides, or computer security advisories that you would find useful in conducting an audit of a client's computer system.

12-15. Many accounting firms have expanded their practices to offer audit services related to a client's IT. Visit the home pages of three accounting firms offering these types of services and document any information you can find about each organization's practice in this area.

12-16. Search the Internet to identify the use of each of the following third party assurance seals: *CPA WebTrust, BBB Online, BetterWeb,* and *TRUSTe.*

CASE ANALYSES

12-17. Stephanie Rose Company (Use of Computer Audit Software)

The internal audit department of Stephanie Rose Company is considering the purchase of computer software that will aid the auditing process. Stephanie Rose's financial and manufacturing control systems are completely automated on a large mainframe computer. Joyce Jones, the director of internal auditing, believes that Stephanie Rose Company should acquire computer audit software to assist in the financial and procedural audits that her department conducts. Jones is considering the following types of software packages:

- A generalized audit software package that assists in basic audit work, such as the retrieval of live data from large computer files. The internal audit department would review these data using conventional audit investigation techniques. More specifically, the department could perform criteria selection, sampling, basic computations for quantitative analysis, record handling, graphical analysis, and the printing of output.

- An integrated test facility (ITF) package that uses, monitors, and controls dummy test data as these data are processed by existing computer programs. The ITF package also checks the computer programs and the existence and adequacy of program data-entry and processing controls.

- A parallel simulation package that uses actual data to conduct the same tests using another computer program, which is a computer logic program developed by the auditor. The package can also be used to seek answers to difficult audit problems (involving many comparisons) within statistically acceptable confidence limits.

Requirements

1. Without regard to any specific computer audit software, identify the general advantages of using computer audit software to assist with audits.

2. Describe the audit purpose facilitated and the procedural steps to be followed by the internal auditor in using the following:

   a. Generalized audit software package
   b. Integrated test facility package
   c. Parallel simulation package

(CMA Adapted)

12-18.   Wang Plumbing Wholesalers (Audit and Control in a Microcomputer Environment)

In response to a management directive, you have completed a study of control procedures over the accounts receivable function of Wang Plumbing Wholesalers, a plumbing wholesaler that your company plans to acquire. Wang's financial statements show sales of $4,000,000 and accounts receivable of $650,000. Sixty percent of Wang's sales are to plumbing contractors, and 40 percent are to small independent hardware stores. A four-tiered pricing system is used, with customer price determined by previous purchases volume. Results of your study of the controls over accounts receivable are presented below.

- After determining product availability, sales personnel write up the customer order using prenumbered sales invoices. Prices to be charged are determined by reference to an approved price list and to an annual customer sales volume report. Credit is automatically granted to previous customers, while first-time customers must receive credit approval from the sales manager. Ninety percent of sales are credit sales.
- A four-part sales invoice is used for all sales. One copy authorizes shipment or customer pickup, and a second copy goes to the customer. A third copy is used to compile sales data. The fourth copy goes to accounts receivable for those sales on credit. This fourth copy is destroyed at the time of the sale for cash sales.
- Accounts receivable data, including all subsidiary accounts receivable ledgers, are maintained on a microcomputer using an off-the-shelf software package. There is an automatic interface between the general ledger and the accounts receivable data. The fourth copy of sales invoices for credit sales is sent directly to the computer operator at the same time as the sales manager collects cash register receipts and prepares the daily bank deposit.
- Customer statements are prepared each month, immediately following the last posting of the month. A receptionist picks up customer statements from the computer operator, prepares the mailing, and sends the statements to the post office by courier. Before the mailing, the sales manager reviews each statement to ensure that unusually large balances are investigated.
- Payments on accounts receivable are separated from remittance advices in the mailroom, with remittance advices sent to the computer operator for posting and payments forwarded to the cashier for preparation of a bank deposit. Credits to accounts receivable arising from merchandise returned originate with the sales manager, who authorizes and prepares a two-part credit memorandum. One copy goes to the customer, and another copy goes to accounts receivable. No other means of reducing accounts receivable are authorized.

Requirements

1. Identify at least four control strengths and four control weaknesses in Wang Plumbing Wholesalers' system.
2. What are some audit steps suggested by the study results that might be performed to complete the audit of accounts receivable account balances?
3. Describe some of the advantages and disadvantages inherent in auditing a microcomputer-based AIS.

(CIA Adapted)

12-19. Tiffany Martin, CPA (Information Systems Audit Skills)

Tiffany Martin is an audit manager in a medium-size public accounting firm. Tiffany graduated from college seven years ago with a degree in accounting. She obtained her CPA certification soon after she joined the firm where she currently works. Tiffany is a financial auditor; she has had little training in auditing computerized information systems.

The current engagement Tiffany is working on includes a complex information processing system. The financial accounting transactions are processed on an AS/400 minicomputer. The Management Information Systems (MIS) department employs 25 personnel, including programmers, systems analysts, a database administrator, computer operators, technical support personnel, and a director. Tiffany has not spoken with anyone in the department because she is fearful that her lack of technical knowledge relative to MIS will cause some concern with the client.

Because Tiffany does not understand the complexities of the computer processing environment, she is unable to determine what risks might result from the computerized system's operations. She is particularly worried about unauthorized changes to programs and data that would affect the reliability of the financial statements.

Tiffany has spoken to Dick Stanton, the partner who has responsibility for this audit client, about her concerns. Dick has suggested that Tiffany conduct more substantive testing than she would undertake in a less complex processing environment. This additional testing will hopefully ensure that there are no errors or fraud associated with the computer processing of the financial statements.

Requirements

1. Do you think that Dick Stanton's suggested approach is the most efficient way to control risks associated with complex computer environments?
2. How should Tiffany respond to Dick's suggestion?
3. What can a public accounting firm, such as the one in which Tiffany works, do to ensure that audits of computerized accounting information systems are conducted efficiently and effectively?
4. Should Tiffany be allowed to conduct this audit given her limited level of skills? How might she acquire new skills?

12-20. Goldstein's (Internal Control Evaluation)

Management at Goldstein's, a large retail company with over 125 stores, has become concerned about the increasing number of customer complaints. Customers reported that electronic scanners are not charging proper prices in the stores in the Southeast region. While there has been some decline in profitability in the southeast, the company has not experienced unusual fluctuations in profitability. Although the company has strong central management, each region controls its own prices and, within limits, an individual store manager can change prices in a store to compete locally.

The internal audit department has just completed an audit of the southeast region. The following are excerpts from the auditors' notes:

- Each store operates in a client/server computing environment. All prices are maintained in the regional database. The database is downloaded daily to each store to run the computer checkout system. Because the database is administered in a client/server environment, there is no need to reconcile the downloaded database with the master database. Furthermore, there is no need to use control totals or other similar totals because the company does not operate in a batch mode.
- All price changes are approved by the buyer responsible for procuring the goods.
- Buyers are evaluated on the profitability of items that they purchase.
- Each buyer has access to the database for price changes. Access to the overall database is limited by passwords. However, a buyer will often delegate access to an assistant to perform the mechanical duties of keypunching in the data and updating the database.
- Each buyer has the responsibility to develop promotional campaigns and advertising for each store in the region. However, within limits, a local store manager can place an ad for some special closeouts.
- Each store manager has the ability to change the price table on the store's price database. However, those changes are not uploaded and thus cannot affect other stores.
- To maintain the integrity of the price database, the full database is downloaded from the regional database each morning before the start of business.
- Closeout items are specially marked and are required to be entered at the cash register rather than scanned in. To expedite customer service, the cashier enters only the price of the product, not its number. The price entered does not affect the selling price recorded in the store's database.
- The stores have been complaining about inventory shrinkage on certain products. In other words, the stores do not have inventory on hand when the perpetual inventory indicates goods are present.
- The price table database is reconciled with the authorized price list kept by each buyer on a quarterly basis. The reconciliation is performed by an assistant to the merchandising manager, who is separate from the buyers making changes to the database.
- The company prepares daily reports of sales per store and per department within each store.
- Before any new product can be input into the price database, its product number and purchase approval must first be entered. Approval is required from the merchandise manager, and data are input by an assistant separate from the buyer. The merchandise manager has a separate password to access the database.
- Any new product entry must conform to the company's existing product numbering scheme. An edit check is run to determine that the product number is valid.

Requirements

1. Given the description of the company's system and the audit findings, identify five control strengths and five control weaknesses.
2. For each weakness identified, state the potential impact of the weakness on the company.

(CIA Adapted)

REFERENCES, RECOMMENDED READINGS, AND WEB SITES

References and Recommended Readings

Aerts, Luc, "A Framework for Managing Operational Risk," *Internal Auditor* (August 2001), pp. 53-59.

Attaway, Morris C., "What Every Auditor Needs to Know About E-Commerce," *Internal Auditor* (March 2000), pp. 56-60.

Austin, Gary R., "Moving into the Next Millennium: Systems Auditing Capability Development for Internal Auditing," *Internal Auditing* (September-October 1998), pp. 21-26.

Balkaran, Lal, "Curbing Corruption," *Internal Auditor* (February 2002), pp. 40-47.

Campbell, Diane Sears, "Focus on Cyber-Fraud," *Internal Auditor* (February 2002), pp. 28-33.

Chan, H.C., C. Ying, and C.B. Peh, "Strategies and Visualization Tools for Enhancing User Auditing of Spreadsheet Models" *Information and Software Technology*, vol. 42, no. 15 (December 1, 2000), pp. 1037-1043.

Cohen, Morgan, "Auditing Spreadsheets," *Accountancy Ireland*, vol. 29, no. 1 (February, 1997), pp. 12-13.

Helms, G. L., and J. Mancino, "The Electronic Auditor," *Journal of Accountancy* (April 1998), pp. 45-48.

Higgins, H. N., "SQL Language for Accounting Auditors," *Information Systems Audit and Control Journal*, vol. 5 (1997), pp. 22-24.

Hormann, F. "Getting the OOPS! Out of Spreadsheets," *Journal of Accountancy* (October 1999), pp. 79-83.

Jenne, Stanley E., "Microcomputers Present a New Internal Control Challenge," *National Public Accountant* (June 1998), p. 34.

Lanza, R. B., "Take My Manual Audit, Please," *Journal of Accountancy* (June 1998), pp. 33-36.

Marks, Norman, "The New Age of Internal Auditing," *Internal Auditor* (December 2001), pp. 44-49.

Pae, Suil, and Seung-Weon Yoo, "Strategic Interaction in Auditing: An Analysis of Auditors' Legal Liability, Internal Control System Quality, and Audit Effort," *The Accounting Review* (July 2001), pp. 333-356.

Panko, R. R., "What Should We Do about Spreadsheets?" *Information Systems Audit and Control Journal*, vol. 3 (1998), pp. 29-32.

Panko, R. R. "Applying Code Inspection to Spreadsheet Testing" *Journal of Management Information Systems*, vol. 16, no. 2 (Fall, 1999), pp. 159-176.

Pyzik, K. P., "Building a Better Toolbox," *Internal Auditor* (April 1997), pp. 32-35.

Raghunandan, K., William J. Read, and Dasaratha V. Rama, "Audit Committee Composition, Gray Directors, and Interaction with Internal Auditing," *Accounting Horizons* (June 2001), pp. 105-118.

Richards, Dave, "Consultant Auditing: Charting a Course," *Internal Auditor* (December 2001), pp. 30-35.

Roesch, L., and L. J. Henry, "Client/Server Systems," *Internal Auditor* (August 1997), pp. 40-43.

Shields, Greg, "Non-stop Auditing," *CA Magazine* (September 1998), pp. 39-40.

Teach, E., "Look Who's Hacking Now," *CFO* (February 1998), pp. 38-50.

Thompson, Courtenay, "Fraud Findings," *Internal Auditor* (October 2001), pp. 69-71.

Wilks, T. J. "Predecisional Distortion of Evidence as a Consequence of Real-Time Audit Review," *The Accounting Review* (January 2002), pp. 51-71.

Web Sites

The web site for *Audit Command Language (ACL)* is www.acl.com. The vendor for IDEA software is at www.cica.ca.

The Information Systems Audit and Control Association's homepage is located at www.isaca.org.

The homepage for the Institute of Internal Auditors is www.rutgers.edu/accounting/raw/iia.

More information about COBIT can be found at www.isaca.org/cobit.htm.

There is a wealth of information about auditing and assurance services available through the American Institute of Certified Public Accountants. Its homepage is www.aicpa.org.

PART FOUR

DEVELOPING EFFECTIVE ACCOUNTING INFORMATION SYSTEMS

CHAPTER 13
Systems Study: Planning and Analysis

CHAPTER 14
Systems Study: Systems Design and Selection

CHAPTER 15
Systems Study: Impementation, Follow-up, and Maintenance

The purpose of systems studies—the subject of Part Four of the text—is to analyze, design, develop, and implement effective information systems. Thus, this part of the book integrates many of the subjects discussed in the previous chapters—for example, information technology, database concepts, and internal control procedures. Companies perform such studies for a variety of reasons, but one important reason is a lack of good accounting data for management decision making. Consequently, accountants often participate in systems studies to help their organizations overcome inadequate information flows or increase the ability to audit their systems.

Chapter 13 discusses the first two steps in a systems study: planning and analysis. These first two steps enable an organization to investigate a current system, analyze its strengths and weaknesses, and decide how to proceed. Typically, the analysis work leads to the design of changes—either by modifying the existing system or by creating or acquiring a new one. The desired result is a system that retains system strengths and eliminates (or at least reduces) system weaknesses.

Chapter 14 examines how an organization designs and evaluates system changes. For example, a company's top managers should not automatically assume that a proposed system is necessarily a good one. Rather, these managers should evaluate the feasibility of any suggested system and should proceed only if the system justifies itself. Chapter 14 describes this feasibility analysis in some detail and outlines how system professionals design, prototype, and possibly outsource the design, development, or modification of a new system.

Once design changes have been planned, finalized, and completed, these changes must be implemented. This is the subject of Chapter 15. Thus, this chapter discusses the work involved in installing and maintaining a new or improved system, as well as the task of analyzing its effectiveness.

Chapter 13

Systems Study: Planning and Analysis

INTRODUCTION

THE SYSTEM DEVELOPMENT LIFE CYCLE: AN INTRODUCTION

The Four Stages in the Systems Development Life Cycle

Systems Studies and Accounting

SYSTEMS PLANNING AND THE INITIAL INVESTIGATION

Planning for Success

The Preliminary Investigation

SYSTEMS ANALYSIS

Understanding Organizational Goals

Systems Survey Work

Data Analysis

The Final Systems Analysis Report

AIS AT WORK: MAKING THE RIGHT CHOICE WHEN HIRING A CONSULTANT

SUMMARY

KEY TERMS YOU SHOULD KNOW

DISCUSSION QUESTIONS

PROBLEMS

INTERNET EXERCISES

CASE ANALYSES

Wright Company

Rose Publishing Company

American Cross

Analyzing Critical Success Factors

PriceRight Electronics

Perform Your Own Preliminary Investigation

REFERENCES, RECOMMENDED READINGS, AND WEB SITES

After reading this chapter, you will:

1. *Understand* the roles of an organization's analysis team and steering committee in a systems study.

2. *Be able to describe* a preliminary investigation and explain why it is important.

3. *Understand* why system analysts must understand the strategic and operational goals of a company.

4. *Become familiar with* some of the methods used to survey an existing system and some of the techniques used to analyze the gathered survey data.

5. *Appreciate* the importance of analyzing a company's internal control procedures when accumulating systems survey information.

6. *Become familiar with* the deliverables in systems analysis work, especially the systems analysis report.

To overcome suspicion and skepticism, consultants are increasingly working side by side with managers to analyze operations, draft recommendations, and implement changes. The days when the outside SWAT team worked in isolation, only to draft a report and leave, are over.

John A. Byrne, "The Craze for Consultants," *Business Week* (July 25, 1994), pp. 60-66.

INTRODUCTION

There are many reasons why an organization might want to study, and perhaps revise or modify, one or more of its major accounting systems. One common cause is a breakdown or inefficiency in a current system—the symptoms of which may include delays in communicating financial information to specific managers or an absence of feedback information necessary for effective managerial decision making. Another reason is the need to combine two formerly separate accounting systems into one—as, for example, when two banks merge. Finally, the power of the Internet has many firms scrambling to develop a marketing presence on the web, as well as to create the software and hardware infrastructure required to support Internet commerce. All these possibilities lead to the same requirement—the need to perform a *systems study.*

It is convenient to think of a systems study as a set of four phases—planning, analysis, design, and implementation and follow-up—which together compose the system development life cycle of an information system. This chapter discusses the first two of these phases, the planning and analysis phases. The remaining phases are covered in Chapters 14 and 15. After studying these three chapters, you should have a good understanding of why an organization performs a systems study, how an organization performs a systems study, what deliverables are typically created in each phase of a systems study, and how organizations implement new or improved systems once they have been designed and developed.

Finally, we note that classic descriptions of the systems development life cycle are sometimes likened to a waterfall, with each phase cascading into the next and with no turning back. Today, such a **waterfall model** is rarely followed. Thus, although the steps outlined here follow a logical progression, we note that organizations often perform a mix of analysis, design, implementation, and maintenance tasks in sequences that diverge from the one presented here, often with good results.

THE SYSTEM DEVELOPMENT LIFE CYCLE: AN INTRODUCTION

As you might imagine, studying a large AIS is itself a large and difficult task. A **systems study** (also called *systems development work*) is a formal investigation of an existing information system. This means examining an existing information system or environment, and in most cases, developing new and innovative solutions for it. The pages that follow discuss the various stages of a systems study in general, and the planning, investigation, and analysis tasks of such a study in particular.

Who actually performs a systems study? This varies from company to company as well as from study to study. Many large organizations have in-house professionals to perform this work. In contrast, smaller organizations with limited technical expertise as well as larger organizations with other priorities for their internal experts are more likely to hire a team of outside consultants for this work. Our discussion in this and the following two chapters assumes that most of the work is performed by a generic "study team" of experts, which may or may not be outside consultants.

The Four Stages in the Systems Development Life Cycle

Traditionally, we can identify four major steps or phases of a systems study:

1. **Plan and Investigate.** This step involves performing a preliminary investigation of the existing system, organizing a systems study team, and developing strategic plans for the remainder of the study.
2. **Analysis.** This step involves analyzing the company's current system in order to identify the information needs, strengths, and weaknesses of the existing system.
3. **Design.** In this step, an organization designs changes that eliminate (or minimize) the current system's weak points while preserve its strengths.
4. **Implement, Follow-up, and Maintain.** This phase includes acquiring resources for the new system as well as training new or existing employees to use it. Companies conduct follow-up studies to determine whether the new system is successful and, of course, to identify any new problems with it. Finally, businesses must maintain the system, meaning correct minor flaws and update the system as required.

These four phases together constitute the **system development life cycle (SDLC)** of a business information system. Figure 13-1 illustrates that this life cycle spans the time during which a company's system is operating normally and is subsequently revised as a result of some problem (or problems). Each time a newly revised system takes over the company's daily operating activities, a new life cycle begins.

The dashed arrows in Figure 13-1 emphasize that follow-up studies of a system should be a continuous process. Thus, an organization should reevaluate a system periodically (e.g., annually) to confirm that it is still operating efficiently and effectively,

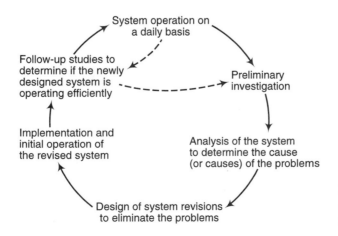

FIGURE 13-1 System development life cycle of a business information system.

and that no further revisions are necessary. However, if the follow-up studies indicate that previous problems have recurred or new ones have developed, an organization should take the dashed-arrow route from the follow-up studies to the recognition of systems problems and begin a new systems study.

> ***Case-in-Point 13.1***   Hydro Agri North America, a fertilizer maker in Tampa, Forida, is one of many firms that has installed SAP AG R/3–a popular enterprise resource planning (ERP) system. The firm originally implemented the system in 1998 but put the project on hold in January 1999 to focus on Y2K work. In response to user requests and its own follow-up studies, the firm is now hard at work revising the system and "making it better." Improvements include one module that enables the company to better track inventory transfers between warehouses and another one that handles rebates owed to customers.

It is important to remember that, although we discuss each of the four major phases of a systems study as separate entities in this and the next two chapters, there is usually much overlap between them in practice. For example, although a study team attempts to isolate specific systems weaknesses in a company (the analysis phase), its members may simultaneously consider possible design changes to eliminate them. Therefore, the subsequent discussion of a systems study will use the same approach. That is, while analyzing a specific systems study step, we include comments that may also apply to one or more other steps in the systems study.

Systems Studies and Accounting

Accounting information systems are a prime target for systems studies—for example, because they may not currently support electronic commerce, cannot use EDI (electronic data interchange), or do not integrate data efficiently in data warehouses. But in general, a systems study means more than just replacing or modifying existing information systems. Typically, altering an information system also affects work flows, data gathering and recording tasks, employee responsibilities, and even the way an organization rewards its managers. Thus, one important reason why organizations perform systems studies is because such studies are part of the greater task of reengineering one or more of its core systems.

It is easy to dismiss the complexities of system studies as jobs for system analysts—certainly not accountants. If you think this way, think again. In this information age, for example, a systems analysis of your job is highly likely. Thus, an understanding of why organizations perform systems studies and how AISs operate will enable you to better explain how you fit into your organization and why your work is both valuable and productive.

Forward-thinking companies are constantly seeking ways to improve their products or services. In fact, the search for better ways to serve customers or better deliver products is another reason why systems studies are conducted in the first place. Thus, such studies are the perfect opportunity for accountants to express their ideas for improving their AISs. For bright, talented people, a systems study is also an opportunity to contribute to a successful project in a meaningful way and, coincidentally, get noticed.

Finally, accountants are often asked to serve on systems study teams for the simple reason that so many of the information systems under study are themselves either AISs or systems that strongly impact AISs. Accounting expertise is therefore required to ensure that any changes will continue to safeguard the integrity and completeness of accounting data, and that any new system will also include the internal control procedures required by law or good business practices. Thus, you may need to know about systems studies for the simple reason that you may soon be serving on a team that conducts one!

SYSTEMS PLANNING AND THE INITIAL INVESTIGATION

The first phase of a systems study involves systems planning and an initial investigation. Case-in-Point 13.2 illustrates how good systems planning is used in the restaurant industry.

> ***Case-in-Point 13.2***   Systems technology is key to the continuing success of many restaurant chains. One example is Wendy's International, which uses a database of sales transactions to help it track order fulfillment times, speed customer services, and reduce labor costs. Similarly, Papa John's Pizza uses a proprietary Internet application to guarantee local callers pizza delivery in 30 minutes. The Cheesecake Factory now has a data warehouse that helps it analyze customer preferences and better forecast its supply needs. The Cracker Barrel now uses the Internet and a satellite system to video conference, update training programs, and distribute new menus to retail outlets. And finally, Burger King's new POS system helps it forecast demand patterns, schedule its workforce, and plan its payroll needs. Common to all these applications is the need for careful systems planning and analysis before building such systems.

To illustrate systems study work in more concrete terms, imagine a medium-size manufacturing company called BSM, Inc., which sells its products to both wholesale distributors and retail consumers. To date, the company has sold most of its products through its dedicated sales force and phone line order takers. But both foreign and domestic competition has increased in the last few years, and top management believes that a stronger Internet presence would enable the company to reach new customers as well as improve both sales and profits. The company already has a web site, but it is mostly informational. Thus, these top executives think that BSM should develop an improved web site that supports direct sales. Is this a good idea, and, if so, what kind of system or systems should the firm develop? This is the starting point of the planning and analysis phase of a system study for BSM.

Planning for Success

There is an old joke that says "anyone can make a mistake; to really mess things up you need a computer." The saying applies with admirable precision and remarkable consistency to the design and development of new accounting systems. In large organizations, system redesigns or new development work typically involve millions of dollars, making mistakes very costly. In smaller organizations, major errors can be catastrophic, leading a firm to bankruptcy. What else can happen when organizations do not plan carefully? Here are some examples:[1]

---

[1] Ian A. Gilhooley, "A Methodology for Productive Systems Development," *Journal of Information Systems Management* (Winter 1986), p. 36.

- Systems are developed that do not meet users' needs, causing employee frustration, resistance, and even sabotage.
- Systems are developed that are not flexible enough to meet the business needs for which they were designed, and are ultimately scrapped.
- Project expenditures significantly overrun what once seemed like very adequate budgets.
- The time required to complete the new system vastly exceeds the development schedule—often by years.
- Systems are developed very carefully, but solve the wrong problems. (This is called a "Type III error.")
- Systems are developed without top management approval or support, dooming them (and the lower-level managers who paid for them) to failure.
- Systems are developed that are difficult and costly to maintain.

Studies of unsuccessful information system projects suggest that the mistakes made at the outset of a systems study are the most common reason why information systems projects ultimately fail. Thus, the purpose of systems planning and an initial investigation is to avoid critical missteps that lead to disaster. "Planning for success" means beginning a systems study with a carefully focused investigation that follows three major study guidelines: (1) approach specific organizational problems from a broad point of view, (2) utilize an interdisciplinary study team to evaluate an organization's information systems, and (3) make sure that the company's study team works closely with a steering committee in all phases of the work.

Broad Viewpoint in a Systems Study   When performing a systems study, the participants should use a **systems approach,** that is, a broad point of view. This will clearly identify the goals top management really desires (as compared to any superficial or minor objectives that might be mentioned) and find the "real problems" of the current AIS (as compared to the symptoms of these problems). Similarly, the participants must recognize that any changes they make to an important information system are likely to have major impacts on other organizational divisions, and perhaps also on relationships with employees, customers, or suppliers.

Case-in-Point 13.3   In one small town, repeated traffic studies failed to solve the vehicular gridlock on the roads near the new entrance to the state freeway. No matter how the lights were reset, the end result was the same—a traffic nightmare. The town fathers and a broad point of view finally identified the real problem—the fact that several large manufacturing plants in the vicinity all had the same 8-to-5 work schedule for their employees. The traffic problem was solved when the plant managers agreed to stagger their employees' working hours.

Like changes in traffic patterns, the changes made to one aspect of a company's information system are likely to affect many other parts of the system. Unless the study team realizes this fact and takes into consideration what effect a specific recommendation will have on the total system, their systems work may be unproductive. At BSM, for example, the study team quickly realizes that any direct sales web site will also impact the company's accounts receivable system, inventory system, and marketing systems, thus considerably expanding the scope of the project.

The Interdisciplinary Study Team   Using an interdisciplinary study team follows from the need for a broad viewpoint when performing a systems study. Because most accounting and computer professionals are specialists, it is unlikely that any one or two people will have the broad background and experience necessary to understand and change a large AIS. For this reason, the recommended approach is to form (or hire) a team of specialists—a "study team"—to perform the system's study work.

The exact composition of a study team depends on the type of information system under review and will necessarily differ from study to study. Most teams include a mix of individuals with expertise in computer technology as well as employees with direct application experience with the system under review. Thus, for AIS studies, typical team participants include (1) an IT specialist who is familiar with system study techniques and procedures, (2) a middle-level manager possessing direct experience with the system under study, (3) an operational supervisor familiar with how the system currently functions (including all its "quirks"), (4) an accountant who understands the financial dimensions of the system, and (5) an auditor who can help the team understand and design cost-effective internal controls as well as ensure that any new modules or systems are "auditable." This is almost exactly the composition of the study team at BSM, except that the company controller, who has both computer and accounting expertise, will assume roles (1) and (4).

Large organizations with sufficient staff can create such study teams entirely from their own employee ranks. Smaller organizations, as well as those larger organizations desiring outside help or wishing to outsource the task, may choose instead to hire a consulting team of outside experts to perform the systems study. Finally, for the smallest businesses (e.g., revising the AIS for a small law office), a team of experts would normally be unnecessary; a knowledgeable accountant from a consulting firm should be able to handle this study job alone.

The Steering Committee   It is important that the study team communicate closely and meaningfully with the company's top managers. To provide this interface, the company's top management should also appoint a **steering committee** to work with the study team as it performs its tasks. Ideally, the committee will include top management personnel—for example, the controller, the vice president of finance, the top-level information systems manager (information systems vice president or chief information officer), other functional vice presidents, and perhaps one or more staff auditors. The rationale for such involvement is straightforward: *top management commitment is critical to the ultimate success of a new or revised system.*

The presence of a steering committee serves several purposes. First, simply having such a committee requires top management to focus on the information systems study and development, and demonstrates executive commitment to it. Second, the presence of a steering committee ensures that top management will be informed of the progress of the systems study efforts and will therefore better understand any changes to the system. Finally, a steering committee helps ensure that the newly designed system is one that the company wants and needs, not just the system that the study team thinks the company wants and needs. For these reasons, it is important that the steering committee members participate in all phases of the systems study work.

The Preliminary Investigation

The first task of a systems study team is to perform a **preliminary investigation** of the information system in question and to advise the steering committee of its findings. One important part of this work is to investigate current needs or problems and, where appropriate, separate symptoms from causes. Rarely are the real problems of an AIS obvious at the outset, although usually the symptoms of these problems are readily apparent.

> ***Case-in-Point 13.4*** The owner of a new, 10-story apartment building was soon swamped with complaints that the lone elevator for the complex was too slow. One consulting firm hired to study the problem suggested that the new owner build a second elevator tower, at a cost of $100,000. A second consulting firm recommended that the owner build two towers at opposite ends of the building, at a cost exceeding $200,000. The owner's problems were finally solved by a third consultant, who correctly realized that the real problem was that tenants had nothing to do while they waited for the elevator, not the speed of the elevator itself. The problem was solved by installing large mirrors opposite the elevator doors on each floor of the building. Total cost: less than $5,000.

In its deliberations, the study team may also consider alternatives to the current system, attempt to estimate the costs and benefits of its proposed solutions, or make recommendations for desired alternatives. In this phase of the project, the study team enjoys wide latitude in what it can choose to examine, and it is usually encouraged to "think outside the box" (i.e., to consider vastly different and innovative approaches to address current problems).

The duration of a preliminary investigation is comparatively brief—typically, a matter of a few weeks. The "deliverable" from this phase of the systems study is a preliminary investigation report that describes the problems or objectives the study team identified, the solutions or alternatives it investigated, and the further course(s) of action it recommends. The study team submits this report to the company steering committee, which (perhaps through additional consultation with top management) makes a final determination. The three major choices are (1) disband the study team and do nothing (a common result when the team finds that there is no real problem), (2) perform further preliminary investigations, or (3) proceed to the formal systems analysis stage of the systems study.

At BSM, the study team's findings are indeed eye-opening. Although the company has no direct web-sales experience, for example, it learns that Internet marketing is helping similar firms increase sales revenues by anywhere from 20 to 100 percent, as well as sell products to new customers in both domestic and foreign markets. The study team is less sure about the costs of developing a web-based system, but the steering committee is sufficiently impressed to proceed to the formal systems analysis phase of the study.

SYSTEMS ANALYSIS

The basic purpose of the **systems analysis** phase of a system study is to study a system in depth. Thus, if the steering committee approves, the study team will familiarize itself with the company's current operating system, identify specific inputs and outputs, identify system strengths and weaknesses, and eventually make recommendations for further work. Figure 13-2 shows the logical procedures that the team should follow.

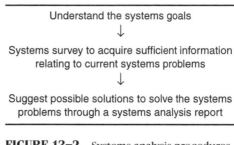

FIGURE 13-2   Systems analysis procedures.

In performing its work, the study team should strive to avoid **analysis paralysis** (i.e., overanalyzing a company's system). Instead, the team should try to achieve three major objectives: (1) identify and understand the goals of top managers, middle managers, and operational managers as they relate to the system under study, (2) perform a systems survey, and (3) prepare one or more reports that describe its findings.

Understanding Organizational Goals

For the study team to do an adequate job—for example, determine the real problems within a company's information system—its members must first understand the system's goals. Of special importance is determining which goals are not being achieved under the present system and why this happens. For discussion purposes, we will examine a company's information systems goals at three levels: (1) general systems goals, (2) top management systems goals, and (3) operating management systems goals.

General Systems Goals   The principles of good systems design encompass systems goals of a general nature that should contribute to the operation of an efficient and effective business information system. These include:

1. **Cost awareness.** When designing a system, the benefits associated with a specific system component should equal or (better) exceed the component's costs (including the design and implementation of internal control procedures).

2. **Relevant output.** The information provided by a system should be accurate, be communicated to management on a timely basis, and be useful for management's decision-making functions.

3. **Simplified structure.** An information system's data processing and reporting capabilities should be straightforward, so that employees can use these capabilities when needed—for example, enable managers to generate their own customized reports.

4. **Flexible structure.** A system should be able to accommodate the changing information needs of management and should include emergency procedures that will permit processing to continue when minor breakdowns occur. Similarly, there should be a formal disaster recovery plan, as discussed in Chapter 10. Finally, "flexible structure" also means that the system can easily be modified as new requirements become known.

These systems goals are general, meaning that they apply to most organization's information systems, and that each usually contributes positively to an efficient and effective information system. Thus, it is important that the study team determine whether the current information system helps to achieve them. For example, if an AIS has excessive costs associated with using traditional paper documents (e.g., purchase orders, receiving reports, and vendor invoices), this will violate goal number 1 (cost awareness), and the study team might recommend that the company use an image processing system instead.

Critical Success Factors   Some experts argue that the strategic success of an information system is determined not by satisfying a large number of general objectives, but by achieving a smaller number of **critical success factors (CSFs).** Figure 13-3 provides some examples of such critical success factors and implies that they necessarily differ from organization to organization and perhaps from system to system.

Using a CSF approach in a systems study enables a study team to narrow the broad scope of its study, focus on a small set of goals, and ask specific questions about how the current system does or does not achieve these goals. There are two weaknesses of this method: (1) it is biased toward the perceptions of top management, and (2) it is difficult to analyze the responses to open-ended questions and managerial opinions about a system.

Top Management Systems Goals   AISs typically play key roles in satisfying top management goals. For example, AISs usually provide top managers with long-range budget planning data so they can make effective strategic decisions regarding future product-line sales or similar business activities. Similarly, periodic performance reports provide top management with vital control information about corporate operations— for example, how sales of new product lines are doing. Finally, top management needs to know about the short-range operating performance of its organization's subsystems—for example, summary information about individual department operating results and how these results compare with budgetary projections.

Although the decision-making functions of a company's top management affect the entire organization, it is often difficult to provide the information these managers need. For example, some of the information required for long-range planning and controlling functions often depends on the external environment (e.g., interest rates, competitor activities, and consumer confidence). Nonetheless, it is essential for a

Organization	Objectives	Critical Success Factors (CSFs)
Automobile Manufacturer	Profits Earnings/share Return on investment Market share	Excellent customer support Efficient communications with dealers Cost control Effective EDI with suppliers JIT inventory control
Health Maintenance Organization	Meet federal and state government regulations Satisfy member needs Control costs	Good communications with federal, state, and regional health care providers Excellent membership support Timely inputs, outputs, and payments Continued monitoring and updating of standard cost allowances

FIGURE 13-3   Examples of critical success factors for the information systems of two organizations.

study team to identify the information needs and goals of top management and then determine whether the company's current information system satisfies those needs. Generally speaking, a poor information system is often ineffective simply because it fails to contribute to top management goals. Consider the following Case-in-Point:

> ***Case-in-Point 13.5*** The legislature of one state created an interdisciplinary study team to evaluate the effectiveness of an ongoing, experimental, million-dollar health-and-welfare program that had been installed in selected high schools. After months of research and finding no discernable benefits, the study team recommended against funding the program any further. The legislators thanked the team members for their hard work, disbanded the committee, trashed the report, and suppressed the results. The team had made a fatal error: the real purpose of that study had been to find reasons to support a politically popular project.

Operating Management Systems Goals   Compared to top management, the information needs of operating managers (i.e., managers working within specific organizational subsystems) are normally easier to determine. This is because the decision-making functions of operating managers typically relate to well-defined and narrower organizational areas. In addition, the majority of operating managers' decisions are for the current business year (in contrast to top management's long-range decision-making functions). Much of the information required for operating mangers' decisions is generated internally as a byproduct of processing a company's accounting data.

When analyzing the systems goals of operating managers and determining whether their information needs are being satisfied, the study team may find, for example, that the company's accountants overemphasize the importance of monetary data. As a result, the company's AIS fails to meet these managers' goals associated with obtaining relevant information to aid their decision-making functions. (Note: An accountant's preoccupation with reporting monetary data is often cited as a major criticism of AISs.) Because many subsystem managers are likely to make decisions based on nonmonetary data (e.g., standard versus actual units produced per shift, standard versus actual quantities of raw materials per unit of product manufactured, and so on), accountants perform a disservice by overemphasizing monetary data in reports to these managers.

> ***Case-in-Point 13.6*** Grupo Financeiro Bital is a Mexican bank with almost 1,200 branches, 3 million customers, and $9 billion in assets. To work effectively, branch managers need access to information about customer accounts at other branches. At one point in time, such managers could ask Bital's massive databases for information, but the output was sometimes a 500-page report instead of the specific information a manager required. A redesign of this information system resulted in a corporate Intranet (i.e., an internal Internet that stores data on web servers). The new Intranet enables branch managers to access exactly the data they need, as well as top managers to view performance measures of the individual branches.

Systems Survey Work

The objective of a **systems survey** is to enable the study team to obtain a more complete understanding of the company's current operational information system and its environment. Of special importance is identifying the strengths and weaknesses of the current system. The overall objective is to retain the system's strengths while eliminating the system's weaknesses, especially those weaknesses causing problems in the current system. These weaknesses will likely relate to specific goals that the current system does not now accomplish.

Understanding the Human Element and Potential Behavioral Problems

Because the appearance of a study team on the work scene usually signals impending changes within an organization, employees are often resistant to help. Unless the study team deals directly with this problem at the beginning, there is a good chance that employees will oppose the changes that the team recommends in a revised system. In short, therefore, a systems study must gain the full cooperation and support of those employees who are crucial to the effectiveness of a new system. The best-designed system "on paper" is likely to cause behavioral problems when implemented if the system does not have wide user support. Figure 13-4 provides several guidelines that a study team can follow to minimize such problems.

One technique that system analysts can employ to gain user confidence in a revised system is **joint application development (JAD).** With this technique, the analysts hold meetings on a regular basis with the system's users, and the users work as consultants in developing the revised system. This fosters positive employee attitudes toward the newly designed system because the users become stakeholders in its success.

Data Gathering   A systems survey requires the study team to gather data about the existing system. There are several ways of doing this, including (1) reviewing existing documentation, (2) observing the current system in operation, (3) using questionnaires to determine user and perhaps customer satisfaction, (4) reviewing internal control procedures, and (5) conducting interviews with individual system participants.

Review Existing Documentation   A review of the existing documentation in a systems survey is an important step in understanding how the present system operates. One general documentation category is descriptive data about the organization—for example, organization charts, manuals of company policies and procedures, charts of accounts, and job descriptions of both managerial and operational employees. Another general category is technical documentation—for example, system flowcharts, entity relationship diagrams, data flow diagrams, and user training manuals.

Observe the Current System in Operation   In an IT environment, the study team focuses on computer operations and attempts to answer such questions as:

- Does the system operate as described in the system documentation?
- Are job functions performed in a manner consistent with job descriptions?
- Does the system deliver information to users in a timely manner?
- What is the general atmosphere or morale of workers as they perform tasks related to the information system?
- Is the computerized system often down?
- Are employees consistently busy, or is the workload mostly cyclical?

The study team can answer some of these questions by observation alone, while it may need to address some of the others after it collects survey data.

Guidelines	Discussion
1. System output meets user needs.	It is very important that the form, content, and volume of system output be designed to satisfy the needs of the users.
2. Lines of communication always open.	Managers and all other users should be completely informed of any system changes as soon as possible. They should be made aware of what changes are being made and why. In addition, they should be shown how the revised system will benefit them. As a result, the employees will hopefully identify with the company's efforts to improve the system. This open communication approach helps in preventing the spread of damaging and inaccurate misunderstandings and rumors.
3. Management support needed.	In addition to providing resources for the system, management can motivate others to assist and cooperate with systems development.
4. Preserve a *safe* atmosphere.	Everyone affected by systems development should have an attitude of cooperation and trust. When employees become hostile, it is very difficult to change their attitudes and thereby have a successful system implementation.
5. Alleviate employee fears.	To the extent possible, assurances should be provided to employees that no major job losses or responsibility shifts will take place. Relocation, normal attrition, and early retirement should contribute toward some of an anticipated workforce reduction. If employee terminations are still necessary, severance pay and outplacement services should be provided.
6. Request user participation.	Those who will use the system (as well as those affected by the system) should participate in its development by making suggestions, providing data, and helping make decisions. Participation enhances one's ego, is challenging, and is intrinsically satisfying. Users who participate in systems development should be more knowledgeable, better trained, and more dedicated in using the system.
7. Provide sincere feedback.	To avoid misconceptions, users should be told which of their suggestions are being used in the system and how, which suggestions are not being used and why, and which suggestions will be implemented at a later date.
8. Need for users to understand the system.	Effective use (as well as support) of a system will not occur if users do not understand or are confused about the system. Often, people with a working knowledge of computers will underestimate the need for user training.
9. Humanize the system.	System acceptance is unlikely if people feel the computer is controlling them or has seized their positions.
10. Delineate new challenges and opportunities.	Developers of systems should stress important and challenging tasks that can be performed with the revised system. It should also be stressed to employees that the system should provide greater job satisfaction as well as increased opportunities for advancement.
11. Reconsider performance evaluation.	The standards and criteria for evaluating users' performance should be reexamined to ensure that they are adequate based on changes designed and implemented into the revised system.
12. Test the system's integrity.	To minimize initial negative impressions of the revised system, it should be properly tested prior to implementation.
13. Avoid emotionalism.	Typically, logic doesn't win out when it vies with emotion. Issues of an emotional nature related to system changes should be sidestepped, allowed to cool, or handled in a nonconfrontational manner.
14. Introduce the system in the proper context.	Users are highly concerned about how system changes will affect them personally. Appropriate explanations should be provided that address their concerns, rather than the concerns of managers or systems developers.
15. Control the expectations of users.	A revised system is marketed too well if users have unrealistic expectations of its performance capabilities. Being realistic is important when describing the virtues of the system.
16. Keep the system simple.	If possible, avoid complex systems that cause drastic changes. Make the system changes as simple as possible by adapting to existing organizational procedures.

FIGURE 13-4 Guidelines to deal with behavioral problems.

Use Questionnaires To gather data about a large system, study teams often use questionnaires, which can be directed at any group of employees (e.g., clerical personnel or top management). Because questionnaires can protect the confidentiality of respondents, they are often an excellent means of gathering data needed about sensitive issues (e.g., the level of dissatisfaction with the current system).

In systems studies, *open-ended questionnaires* allow respondents to answer in a free flow of ideas, whereas *closed-ended questionnaires* such as those on multiple choice tests have predetermined answeres (Figure 13-5). Open-ended questions are useful because respondents are not limited to any preconceived responses and thus give a study team the most opportunity to learn about an existing system. The problem with open-ended questions is that the answers are usually difficult to categorize and summarize. Closed-ended questions are easier to ask as well as analyze statistically, and thus are more efficient when surveying large employee populations.

Review Internal Control Procedures Earlier chapters of this text emphasized the importance of effective internal control procedures within an organization. Because weaknesses in these procedures can cause major organizational problems, the study team will normally spend considerable time reviewing the company's internal control system. The team may also use a standardized **internal control questionnaire** to help it identify the strengths and weaknesses of a company's internal control procedures. For the high-risk areas identified by the questionnaire, the study team should determine what negative effects may result from the absence of particular control procedures. After further investigation, the study team may conclude that major improvements could be made in the company's information system by implementing previously nonexistent control procedures.

Conduct Interviews Face-to-face interviews may be superior to questionnaires for gathering system information in greater depth because they allow members of the study team to speak directly and candidly with system participants. For example, when an interviewer sees that a respondent displays discomfort or becomes vague when answering a specific question during an interview, he or she can then ask additional questions to uncover more detail. Good interviewing skills—for example, the

---

Example of an Open-ended Question on a Systems Survey Questionnaire:

Please explain why you are either satisfied or dissatisfied with the current general ledger system?

Example of a Closed-ended Question on a Systems Survey Questionnaire:

Please indicate your level of satisfaction with the current general ledger system by checking the appropriate response below:

_____ Very satisfied
_____ Somewhat satisfied
_____ Neither satisfied nor dissatisfied
_____ Somewhat dissatisfied
_____ Very dissatisfied

FIGURE 13-5 Sample questions on a systems survey questionnaire.

ability to listen carefully and ask probing questions—are critical to this task. Although interviews typically take more time than questionnaires, they can also be very revealing!

> **Case-in-Point 13.7** When the managers of one federal agency were asked about the usefulness of a particular report, most managers indicated in a questionnaire that it was highly desirable. In-depth interviews revealed that, in fact, no manager used the report, but many had answered positively because they thought other managers needed it. The system designers eliminated the report in the revised system, and no one missed it.

Data Analysis

Once the study team completes its survey work, it must analyze the results. Often, this means nothing more than creating summary statistics, but it can also involve hypothesis testing or developing system flowcharts, data flow diagrams, or document flowcharts. Document flowcharts can be particularly valuable here because they provide a logical picture of the current flow of information, starting with key source documents and ending with performance reports for specific organizational areas (see Chapter 3). For example, a key problem in a current system may be inadequate data communications to those managers making decisions. By understanding the types of report data required by these managers, the study team can analyze their document flowcharts and determine if the current system satisfies their information needs.

An analysis of employee productivity illustrates some of the tools for performing data analysis. For example, **work measurement techniques** evaluate the efficiency of employees in jobs that are repetitive in nature (e.g., inputting data into a computer terminal or working on an assembly line at a production plant). One (older) work-measurement technique uses **throughput** (i.e., the amount of productive work that can be performed within a specific period of time with respect to a particular task). Here, the study team uses the average results from many individuals working together during a typical work shift to evaluate overall employee performance, thus ignoring the differences in individual employee capabilities.

A newer, alternative approach is **work distribution analysis,** which focuses on a particular job. Rather than examining the efficiency of the worker, therefore, the technique analyzes the work—that is, the job function. Here, the study team analyzes the amount of time spent on each particular task in the job description. Based on the work distribution analysis and considering future system revisions, the study team can determine whether any changes are necessary in the specific tasks so that the job function can be performed effectively within the revised system.

The Final Systems Analysis Report

Systems analysis work necessarily takes longer than a preliminary investigation, typically months of work. Where required, therefore, the study team will provide interim reports to the steering committee about its progress. The most important deliverable from the analysis portion of the systems study, however, is the **final systems analysis report,** which signals the end of the analysis phase of the system study. Like other reports, the study team submits this report to the steering committee, which then considers the report's findings and debates the recommendations it contains. Some of the discussions may take place in a formal meeting in which the study team presents its analyses and steering committee members have an opportunity to ask questions.

As representatives of top management, the steering committee has, within limits, the prerogative to do whatever it wants. One possible decision is to abandon the project. A second possibility is to ask for additional analyses and a set of revised recommendations. Finally, the steering committee may vote to proceed to the systems design phase of the project (discussed in Chapter 14). The main point to understand here is that no further project work commences until the steering committee formally approves the findings of the study team and gives the project a "go-ahead."

At BSM, the analysis for a new, web-based marketing system suggests that such a system holds much promise. Because this will be a new system, there was no current one to investigate. (BSM's small, current web site is maintained by its Internet service provider.) But the study team recognizes that a new system will require the company to acquire additional personnel to create and maintain a web site, and may enable the company to eliminate some of its current phone-line order takers. Again, the crucial question is: "Is the proposed system cost effective?" The steering committe decides to find out by designing a prototype system and estimating potential costs and benefits. We'll look at this analysis in Chapter 14.

AIS AT WORK
Making the Right Choice When Hiring a Consultant

Both large and small companies hire outside consultants to perform systems studies. Here are tips from consulting experts themselves for hiring one.

- You don't always need a consultant. Sometimes a board of directors or other outsiders can provide the needed perspective and expertise to initiate change.

- If you're looking for help in management consultancy (which advises senior management), several sources say the Certified Management Consultant designation given through the Institute of Management Consultants should be a required credential. Consultants must put in at least three to five years of practical experience, have client references, take a course, and meet other requirements to obtain the certification. However, David Lord, editor of *Consultant News* at Kennedy Publications, notes that, although holding out for a consultant with such a designation might be ideal, only 2,000 of the 80,000 management consultants in the country have it. Many of the biggest and most prestigious management consulting firms ignore it.

- In areas such as communications—for example, writing, speaking, and other hands-on activities—look for people with a track record in this area. Not everyone who has worked in a discipline may have the skills to teach it. The ideal person is someone with both experience in the discipline and experience teaching it.

- Consultants often have confidentiality agreements with clients, but it's a good idea to talk to former clients if you can. Thus, get a list of former clients and, if possible, recommendations from them. Speaking to peers at competitive consulting firms is also desirable.

- Calls to references are critical. If a consulting company's own references do not provide ringing endorsements, what does this say about the company's dissatisfied clients?

- "One size does not fit all," warns Arthur Layton, president of the Fairfield, Connecticut county chapter of the Institute of Management Consultants and a management consultant on employee relocation issues. Some consultants tend to use the same approach for everyone. "Every organization is different; every organization requires unique solutions," he says.

- "Prospective consultants should be able to discuss with you the process they will use to obtain results," Layton emphasizes. "Ideally, that process should be participatory—gathering advice from all of the necessary people involved—if proposed solutions are to work."

Source: Modified from the "Business Weekly" of *The Hartford Courant,* February 7, 1994, p. 15.

SUMMARY

There are many reasons why an organization might want to modify or replace one or more of its information systems, and the idea that accountants need not concern themselves in such matters is particularly inaccurate. The first major part of a systems study is the planning and initial investigation phase. During this phase, a company's management recognizes that there are problems with one of its current information systems and begins the strategic planning for a new or revised system. Typically, this includes creating an interdisciplinary study team to perform a preliminary investigation of the current system and to make recommendations to management's steering committee.

To do a good job, modern organizations should utilize a systems approach when considering changes to their information systems. Under this approach, a study team examines an organization's information systems problems with a broad point of view, considers the positive and negative effects that might occur as a result of a specific change recommendation, and performs its work with an eye toward separating symptoms from causes.

The second phase of a systems study is systems analysis. One task in this phase of the study is to identify three types of organizational goals: (1) general systems goals, (2) top management systems goals, and (3) operating management systems goals. System problems are often caused by a failure to achieve specific goals.

Another systems analysis task is to perform a system survey. This is a detailed investigation of the current system in order to identify system strengths and weaknesses. During its survey work, the study team may review documentation related to the existing system, observe the system in operation, and study its current internal control procedures. The team may also use questionnaires, interviews, and flowcharts of various types to help it understand and document the system. Finally, because employees often resist outside investigations and the changes such investigations often signal, the study team should be aware of potential behavioral problems—for example, fear of job losses—and be prepared to deal with them.

After completing its analysis work, the study team should be able to make recommendations about how to proceed—for example, suggest changes that eliminate the system's weak points while preserving its strengths. But before beginning any intensive systems design work, the team must communicate its finding to the organization's steering committee through a final systems analysis report. If this committee reacts positively, the team can then proceed to the design phase of the systems study.

KEY TERMS YOU SHOULD KNOW

analysis paralysis	systems approach
critical success factors (CSFs)	systems planning
internal control questionnaire	systems study
final systems analysis report	systems survey
joint application development (JAD)	throughput
preliminary investigation	waterfall model
steering committee	work distribution analysis
system development life cycle (SDLC)	work measurement techniques
systems analysis	

DISCUSSION QUESTIONS

13-1. The Rodriguez McRooter Company has been in business 50 years without completing a single "life cycle" of its information system. Is this situation good or bad? Explain.

13-2. Discuss the major differences, if any, between the planning phase, analysis phase, and design phase of a systems study.

13-3. What is a steering committee? Discuss its role in a systems study performed by a consulting firm.

13-4. Why perform a preliminary investigation of a company's information system? Why not simply start the formal analysis and save time?

13-5. Consider the following quote: "For consultants to determine the real problems that currently exist in their client company's information system, they must first understand the goals of the client's system." Do you agree or disagree with this statement? Discuss.

13-6. A systems study team should understand three levels of corporate goals: general systems goals, top management systems goals, and operating management systems goals. If you had to select one of these categories of systems goals as the most important to the effective operation of an organization's information system, which one would you choose? Explain the reasons for your choice.

13-7. An organization's AIS should be able to communicate relevant decision-making information to both top management and operating management. For which of these two managerial groups are such communication tasks normally easier? Why?

13-8. In systems studies, why isn't it always desirable to completely eliminate an organization's current information system and replace this system with a new one?

13-9. What is the major objective of a systems survey?

13-10. In this day and age, do you think it is feasible for a systems analyst to use a work measurement technique such as "throughput" to evaluate the operating efficiency of a company's top management personnel? Explain.

13-11. In its systems study work, a study team normally pays considerable attention to the "human element" because of the potential for behavioral problems. Discuss a number of guidelines that a study team should follow to prevent (or at least minimize) behavioral problems in a systems study.

PROBLEMS

13-12. Classify each of the following as a "problem" or a "symptom" at Mason Manufacturing, Inc. Assume that the company has made no changes in its policies.

(a) decreasing gross revenues

(b) decreasing profits

(c) increasing employee turnover

(d) increasing labor rates

(e) increasing labor costs

(f) increasing customer returns

(g) increasing interest rates

(h) decreasing employee productivity

(i) increasing inventory shrinkage

(j) increasing costs for raw materials

(k) increasing executive travel expenses

13-13. The Chris Hall Company manufactures and distributes low-priced bottled wines to retailers. You are hired as a management consultant to help this company solve some of its systems problems. Describe the types of decision-making information that probably would be needed by the company's (a) supervisor of the production plant, (b) top management, and (c) marketing manager.

13-14. You have recently graduated from college, passed the CPA examination, and accepted a management consultant position in the management advisory services department of Koote, Katch, and Kramer, a major public accounting firm. On your first systems study job, your supervisor tells you to use a "systems approach" in performing your investigative work on the client company's information system. Discuss in detail what the supervisor means when she uses this term. Do you think that this approach will increase or decrease your opportunities for creative thinking when performing the systems study? Explain.

13-15. Assume that you are one of the partners of a major consulting firm and are responsible for hiring an additional consultant to work in your firm. You believe that this new employee's educational specialty (e.g., marketing) is not too important because the consulting firm already has professional employees with a wide variety of educational backgrounds. You believe, however, that the new employee should have other qualifications. List the four most important traits that you would want this newly hired consultant to possess. (Note: Trait 1 should be the most important employee characteristic, trait 2 the second most important characteristic, etc.) For each of these listed traits, indicate why you think the specific trait is important.

13-16. At lunch yesterday, Don Wilson was telling his friend Manny Koral about the valuable changes that were introduced into this company's system five months ago by the Zebra Consulting Firm. Don indicated that, as a result of these systems changes, his company's net operating income has increased threefold. Manny was so impressed with Don's comments that when he returned to his office after lunch, he immediately called the Zebra Consulting Firm. Manny indicated to the firm's chief consultant that he had heard about the successful consulting work in Don Wilson's company and that he would therefore like to have the same changes incorporated into his company's system. Do you agree with Manny's reasoning? Explain.

13-17. Identify several advantages and disadvantages of using "yes/no-type" questions to analyze a company's internal control procedures. For each item you list, indicate your reasons for including it as either an advantage or a disadvantage.

13-18. At the annual awards banquet of the Society for Consenting Consultants, the guest speaker was Arnold A. Arnstein. Mr. Arnstein has been a practicing management consultant for the past 40 years. In concluding his three-hour speech, Arnstein made the following comments. "In today's sophisticated business world, you must let your client know from the beginning who is the boss—which is obviously you! Don't waste your time listening to suggestions from the client company's employees. It will only delay the completion of the consulting job. After all, if the client's employees were that bright in the first place, the company would not have requested your services. Should the company's management initially dislike your systems change recommendations, don't worry. As soon as your systems revisions are implemented, management will love you for making such valuable contributions to its organization's operating efficiency. Good luck and just remember—the business world could not survive without us consultants!"

As a novice management consultant attending the awards banquet, how would you react to Arnstein's closing observations? Explain.

13-19. Stevenson Apparel is a manufacturer of fashion apparel that has just opened its first large retail store for selling in-season clothes at regular prices. The company's competitive strategy depends on a comprehensive point-of-sale (POS) system supporting on-line, up-to-the-minute sales totals, day-to-day tracking of stock information, and quick checkout of customer purchases. Because cashiers were already familiar with electronic cash registers, management decided that only minimal training was required.

Cashiers enter four-digit stock tracking numbers (STNs) into one of the POS terminals that retrieves price and description data, computes the tax and total amount due, accepts the type of payment, and controls the cash drawer. A unique STN identifies each of the 9,500 pieces of merchandise. The central microcomputer server maintains stock information.

In the first month of operation, new cashiers were awkward using the new system. They eventually became proficient users but were frustrated with the slow printing of sales tickets and the unpredictable action of their cash drawers. Each checkout stand has a telephone that cashiers use to call for approval of credit-card transactions. Customers became impatient when credit approvals delayed the checkout process or when the microcomputer was down, thus stopping all sales, including cash sales.

Identify four problems with the system and describe how you would remedy each of them.

INTERNET EXERCISES

13-20. Using your browser, find a web site that discusses management consultants and their role in the business world. Write a summary of your findings and relate it to this chapter's subject matter. In addition, submit a printout of the web site information that you accessed.

13-21. Using your web browser, search the Internet for web pages that discuss "critical success factors" (CSFs). List at least five sites that you find. Are CSFs uniquely used within the context of systems studies, or are they used to describe other facets of business? Based on your findings, would you say that critical success factors are consistent across organizations in the same types of businesses? Are they necessarily the same for different types of businesses?

CASE ANALYSES

13-22. Wright Company (Analyzing System Reports)

Wright Company employs a computer-based data processing system for maintaining all company records. The current system was developed in stages over the past five years and has been fully operational for the last 24 months.

When the system was being designed, all department heads were asked to specify the types of information and reports they would need for planning and controlling operations. The systems department attempted to meet the specifications of each department head. Company management specified that certain other reports be prepared for department heads. During the five years of systems development and operation, there have been several changes in the department head positions due to attrition and promotions. The new department heads often made requests for additional reports according to their specifications. The systems department complied with all of these requests. Reports were discontinued only on request by a department head, and then only if it was not a standard report required by top management. As a result, few reports were discontinued. Consequently, the information processing subsystem was generating a large quantity of reports each reporting period.

Company management became concerned about the quantity of report information that was being produced by the system. The internal audit department was asked to evaluate the effectiveness of the reports generated by the system. The audit staff determined early in the study that more information was being generated by the information processing subsystem than could be used effectively. They noted the following reactions to this information overload:

1. Many department heads would not act on certain reports during periods of peak activity. The department heads would let these reports accumulate with the hope of catching up during subsequent lulls.

2. Some department heads had so many reports they did not act at all on the information, or they made incorrect decisions because of misuse of the information.

3. Frequently, actions required by the nature of the report data were not taken until the department heads were reminded by others who needed the decisions. These department heads did not appear to have developed a priority system for acting on the information produced by the information processing subsystem.

4. Department heads often would develop the information they needed from alternative, independent sources, rather than use the reports generated by the information processing subsystem. This was often easier than trying to search among the reports for the needed data.

Requirements

1. Indicate whether each of the foregoing four reactions contributes positively or negatively to the Wright Company's operating effectiveness. Explain your answer for every one of the four reactions.

2. For each reaction that you indicated as negative, recommend alternative procedures the Wright Company could employ to eliminate this negative contribution to operating effectiveness.

(CMA Adapted)

13-23. Rose Publishing Company (Revising Data Collection and Processing Procedures)

Rose Publishing Company devotes the bulk of its work to the development of high school and college texts. The printing division has several production departments and employs 400 people, of which 95 percent are hourly production workers. Production workers may work on several projects in one day. They are paid weekly based on total hours worked.

A manual time card system is used to collect data on time worked. Each employee punches in and out when entering or leaving the plant. The timekeeping department audits the time cards daily and prepares input sheets for the computerized functions of the payroll system.

Currently, a daily report of the previous day's clockcard information by department is sent to each departmental supervisor in the printing division for verification and approval. Any changes are made directly on the report, signed by the supervisor, and returned to the timekeeping department. The altered report serves as the input authorization for changes to the system. Because of the volume and frequency of reports, this report-changing procedure is the most expensive process in the system.

Timekeeping submits the corrected hourly data to general accounting and cost accounting for further processing. General accounting maintains the payroll system that determines weekly payroll; prepares weekly checks; summarizes data for monthly, quarterly, and annual reports; and generates W-2 forms. A weekly and monthly payroll distribution report prepared by the cost accounting department shows the labor costs by department.

Competition in college textbook publishing has increased steadily in the last three years. Although Rose has maintained its sales volume, profits have declined. Direct labor cost is believed to be the basic cause of this decline in profits, but insufficient detail on labor utilization is available to pinpoint the suspected inefficiencies. Chuck Hutchins, a systems consultant, was engaged to analyze the current system and to make recommendations for improving data collection and processing procedures. Excerpts from the report that Hutchins prepared are reproduced in Figure 13-6.

...An integrated Time and Attendance Labor Cost (TALC) system should be developed. Features of this system would include direct data entry; labor cost distribution by project as well as department; online access to time and attendance data for verification, correction, and update; and creation and maintenance of individual employee work history files for long-term analysis.

...The TALC system should incorporate uniquely encoded employee badges that would be used to electronically record entry to and exit from the plant directly into the data system.

...Labor cost records should be maintained at the employee level, showing the time worked in the department by project. Thus, labor cost can be fully analyzed. Responsibility for correct and timely entry must reside with the departmental supervisors and must be verified by project managers on a daily basis because projects involve several departments.

...Online terminals should be available in each department for direct data entry. Access to the system will be limited to authorized users through a coded entry (password) system. Departmental supervisors will be allowed to inspect, correct, verify, and update only time and attendance information for employees in their respective departments. Project managers may access information recorded for their projects only and exceptions to such data must be certified outside the system and entered by the affected supervisor.

...Appropriate data should be maintained at the employee level to allow verification of employee personnel files and individual work history by department and project. Access to employee master file data should be limited to the personnel department. Work-history data will be made available for analysis only at the project or departmental level, and only to departmental supervisors and project managers for whom an employee works.

FIGURE 13-6   Excerpts from Hutchins' report.

Requirements

1. Compared with the traditional clockcard system, what are the advantages and disadvantages of the recommended system of electronically recording the entry to and exit from the plant?
2. Identify the items to be included in the individual employee's master file.
3. The TALC system allows the employee's departmental supervisor and the personnel department to examine the data contained in an individual employee's master file data. (a) Discuss the extent of the information each should be allowed to examine. (b) Describe the safeguards that may be installed to prevent unauthorized access to the data.
4. The recommended system allows both the departmental supervisors and the project managers to obtain current labor distribution data on a limited basis. The limitations mentioned can lead to a conflict between a departmental supervisor and project manager. (a) Discuss the reasons for the specified limitations. (b) Recommend a solution for the possible conflict that could arise if a departmental supervisor and a project manager do not agree.

13-24. American Cross (Analyzing Expansion Options)

American Cross, a not-for-profit organization, is considering expanding both personnel and office space. The organization currently owns two buildings. Building A is used exclusively for operations, and Building B is used exclusively to lease to other companies or individuals on a yearly basis. The lease periods are staggered throughout the year. The occupancy rate for Building B ranges from 80 percent to 90 percent. Lease fees are currently $10.50 per square foot. Both buildings are over 30 years old, with no loans outstanding.

Construction of office and retail space is increasing in the area, with a corresponding decrease in lease rates. Contractors are anticipating a strengthening of building codes and restrictions for the area within the next six months. As a result, construction prices are expected to increase 10 percent to 12 percent more than the cost of living increases in the next two years. Revenues and expenses reported for the last two years and the project amounts for the current year are:

Description	2003 Projected	2002	2001
Revenue from Operations	13,855,000	13,253,000	12,622,000
Revenue from Leases	416,000	384,000	432,000
Expenses	12,534,000	12,649,000	11,987,000
Excess of Revenues over Expenses	1,737,000	988,000	1,067,000

Management is considering several options for expansion. The first option is to sell both buildings and buy or lease a bigger building at a different location. The second option is to tear down both buildings and construct a new building on the original site. A third option is to move the organization into Building B, tear down Building A, and construct a new building. Because of the physical location of the two buildings, this last option would work only if Building A was the building torn down. Because of the age of the buildings, management is not considering expanding the current buildings. Management has asked the internal auditing department to review the options, list the risks associated with each option, and identify any additional information needed.

Requirements

1. Identify the major risks associated with management's decision to expand. The risks must be specific to the situation.
2. Identify additional risks associated with each of the three options. The risk must be specific to the situation.
3. List additional items of nonfinancial information needed in order for management to choose among the options.
4. Assume that management has decided to enter into a contract to construct a new building on another site. Until the new building is completed, the employees will remain in the old facilities. Management intends to sell the old buildings. To plan for the implementation of this alternative, management has prepared financial projections for the next five years (income statement and statement of cash flows). List four areas affecting costs and revenues where management will need to make assumptions in order to prepare these financial projections.

13-25. Analyzing Critical Success Factors (CSFs)

There are many factors that *can* contribute to the success of a new or revised system. In the planning phase, some positive items are:

1. Perform a preliminary investigation.
2. Give end users what they want.
3. Use state-of-the-art analytical techniques.
4. Include an auditor as part of the study team.
5. Insist that the company CEO be part of the steering committee.
6. Focus on outcomes, not inputs.
7. Understand, and design for, top management goals.
8. Use a systems approach.
9. Understand the human element and anticipate potential behavioral problems.
10. Use joint application development techniques (JAD).

Requirement

Create a table with ten rows. In the first column, list each of the items above. In the second column, explain how the item can contribute to a successful project. In the third column, list a possible exception to this factor. Here's an example:

Factor	Contribution	Exception
Perform a preliminary investigation	It is important to determine exactly what the problem is, and to separate symptoms from problems.	A microcomputer user requiring word processing software would probably not require such a step.

13-26. PriceRight Electronics (Identifying System Strengths and Weaknesses)

PriceRight Electronics Inc. (PEI) is a wholesale discount supplier of a wide variety of electronic instruments and parts to regional retailers. PEI commenced operations a year ago, and its records processing has been on a manual basis except for its stand-alone, automated inventory and accounts receivable systems. The driving force of PEI's business is its deep-discount, short-term (three-day) delivery reputation, which allows retailers to order materials several times during the month and therefore minimize in-store inventories. PEI's management has decided to continue automating its operations, but because of cash-flow considerations, realizes that this must be accomplished on a step-by-step basis.

The managers decide that the next function to be automated should be sales order processing to enhance quick response to customer needs. PEI's implementation team selects and then implements an off-the-shelf software package, which it modifies to fit PEI's current mode of operations. In response to increasing numbers of slow-paying and delinquent accounts, the implementation team also installs a computerized database of customer credit standings to permit automatic credit limit checks when customers place orders. Figure 13-7 is a document flowchart that shows the new systems modules, which are as follows:

Marketing: Customers place sales orders by telephone, fax, or mail, which PEI marketing personnel enter into the sales order system. The orders are automatically compared to the customer database for determination of credit limits. If credit limits are met, the system generates multiple copies of the sales order.

Credit: On a daily basis, the credit manager reviews new customer applications for creditworthiness, establishes credit limits, and enters them into the customer database. The credit manager also reviews a month-end accounts receivable aging report to identify slow-paying or delinquent accounts for potential revisions to or discontinuances of credit. In addition, the credit manager issues credit memos for merchandise returns based on requests from customers and forwards copies of these credit memos to Accounting for appropriate accounts receivable handling.

Warehousing: Warehouse personnel update the inventory master file for purchases and disbursements, confirm availability of materials to fill sales orders, and establish back orders for sales orders that cannot be completed from stock on hand. Warehouse personnel assemble and forward materials with corresponding sales orders to Shipping and Receiving. They also update the inventory master file for merchandise returns that are received by Shipping and Receiving.

Shipping and Receiving: Personnel in Shipping and Receiving accept materials and sales orders from Warehousing, pack and ship the order with a copy of the sales order as a packing slip, and forward a copy of the sales order to Billing. These employees also unpack, sort, inspect, and forward to Warehousing the merchandise returns the company receives from customers.

Accounting: Accounting personnel enter billing prices on all sales orders approximately five days after the orders are shipped. To spread the work effort throughout the month, customers are categorized into 30-day billing cycles. There are six billing cycles for which invoices are rendered during the month. Monthly statements, prepared by Billing, are sent to customers during the billing cycle period. Outstanding carry-forward balances reported by Accounts Receivable and credit memos prepared based on credit requests received from the credit manager are included on the monthly statement. Billing also prepares sales and credit memo journals for each cycle. Copies of invoices and credit memos are forwarded

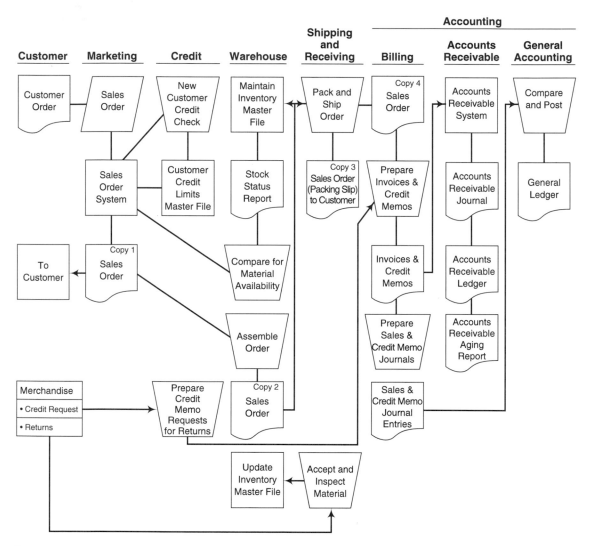

FIGURE 13-7 Systems modules of sales order processing for PriceRight Electronics.

to Accounts Receivable for entry into the accounts receivable system by customer account. An aging report is prepared at the end of each billing cycle and forwarded to the credit manager.

The accounts receivable journal, reflecting total charges and credits processed through the accounts receivable system for each cycle, is forwarded to the General Accounting staff. General Accounting compares this information to the sales and credit memo journals and posts the changes to the general ledger.

Requirements

1. Analyze the flowchart in Figure 13-7, identifying several strengths of the system and explaining why they are strengths.

2. Identify and explain several internal control weaknesses of the system. Recommend solutions to the identified weaknesses, using the following format.

Weakness	Reason for Weakness	Solution to Weakness

(CMA Adapted)

13-27. Perform Your Own Preliminary Investigation (Performing the First Phase of a System Study)

With the help of your instructor, identify a particular information system that is not working very well and perform a preliminary investigation of it. In your work, be sure to talk to (1) at least one external "customer" who is affected by the system, (2) one employee who uses the system on a daily basis, and (3) one person who manages this type of employee. For example, at a university, you might study the student parking information system. The "customers" are those car owners who purchase parking permits (e.g., students, faculty, and university staff members), data input clerks are the employees who use the system daily, and the parking manager is the person who supervises these employees. Ask each such person what he or she feels are the problems of the system, and what they think should be done to address these problems.

Requirement

Prepare a preliminary investigation report that describes your system and outlines the following items: (1) the problems that each person experiences with the system, (2) the actions that each person thinks might solve the problems, and (3) your opinion of which difficulties are the "real problems" and which are just symptoms of these problems. Also include some recommendations. Should the present system be replaced, or are just minor modifications required?

REFERENCES, RECOMMENDED READINGS, AND WEB SITES

References and Recommended Readings

Anastas, Mike, "The Changing World of Management Accounting and Financial Management," *Management Accounting* (October 1997), pp. 48-51.

Ansel, Daryl and Chris Dyer, "A Framework for Restaurant Information Technology," *Cornell Hotel and Restaurant Administration Quarterly* vol. 40, no. 3 (June, 1999), pp. 74-84.

Anthes, Gary H., "Planning Spells Results at MCI," *Computerworld* (January 27, 1992), p. 31.

Bagranoff, Nancy A., "Select Your Next System with High-Tech Tools," *Strategic Finance* (May 1999), pp. 75-79.

Bruttig, Dana, "What Automated Expense Reporting Management Can Do for You," *Management Accounting* (February 1998), pp. 38-43.

Byrne, J. A., "The Craze for Consultants," *Business Week* (July 25, 1994), pp. 60-66.

Casher, Jonathan D., and Robert H. Metzger, "Leverage Your Vendor Relationships and Enhance Your Bottom Line," *Management Accounting* (March 1998), pp. 51-54.

Cottrell, D.M., K.D. Stocks, and M.R. Swain, "Continuous Improvement at Clorox," *Internal Auditor* (February 1995), pp. 38–44.

Denna, Eric L., Lee Tom Perry, and Sean Jasperson, "Reengineering and REAL Process Modeling," in *Business Process Change: Reengineering Concepts, Methods, and Technologies,* Varun Grover and Bill Kettinger, Eds. (Harrisburg, PA: Idea Group Publishing, 1995).

Dykman, Charlene A., and Ruth Robbins, "Organizational Success Through Effective Systems Analysis," *Journal of Systems Management* (July 1991), pp. 6–8.

Hunton, James E., "Setting Up a Paperless Office," *Journal of Accountancy* (November 1994), pp. 77–85.

McPartlin, John P., "$11M System Development Failure: Arizona Begins the Postmortem," *Information Week* (September 6, 1993), p. 13.

Messmer, Max, "Developing Your Technology Skills," *Management Accounting* (January 1998), p. 10.

Messmer, Max, "Pay Per Project," *Management Accounting* (June 1998), pp. 36–41.

Ratliff, R.L., and S.M. Beckstead, "How World-Class Management is Changing Internal Auditing," *Internal Auditor* (December 1994), pp. 38–44.

Walker, Kenton B., and Eric L. Denna, "A New Accounting System is Emerging," *Management Accounting* (July 1997), pp. 22–30.

Web Sites

A discussion of accounting, business, and technology headlines is located at www.accountingnet.com.

Information about consultants is available at the following web site: www.fsforum.com/consult/.

Information on activity-based performance measurement and work measurement can be found at www.pbviews.com/magazine/articles/activity_based.html, www.acsco.com/workmeas.htm, and www.ideafinder.com/history/inventors/taylor.htm.

Information on critical success factors (CSFs) can be found at www.knowledgeuk.com/critical_success_factors.htm, cor-ex.com/CXPerspectives/cxp2a.htm, www.itmweb.com/essay016.htm, and www.utsystem.edu/OIR/success.htm.

Information on joint application development (JAD) can be found at www.franz.org/bb12.htm, www.carolla.com/wp-jad.htm, www.ul.ie/~cscw/shug/cs4417/tbb12.htm, and www.creativedata.com/research/jad.htm.

Chapter 14

Systems Study: System Design and Selection

INTRODUCTION

THE FEASIBILITY EVALUATION

The Five Components of a Feasibility Evaluation

An Example

Concluding Comments on the Feasibility Evaluation

DETAILED SYSTEMS DESIGN

Designing System Outputs

Process Design

Designing System Inputs

Prototyping

The System Specifications Report

SELECTING A FINAL SYSTEM

Selection Criteria

Making a Final Decision

AIS AT WORK: SONY CORPORATION USES A CASE TOOL

SUMMARY

KEY TERMS YOU SHOULD KNOW

DISCUSSION QUESTIONS

PROBLEMS

INTERNET EXERCISES

CASE ANALYSES

The Hometown Clippers

Milok Company

Kenbart Company

Quadrant Controls Company

Stephen Kerr Cosmetics

REFERENCES, RECOMMENDED READINGS, AND WEB SITES

After reading this chapter, you will:

1. *Know* what a feasibility evaluation is and why it is an important part of systems design work.

2. *Become familiar with* some of the benefits and costs that are likely to occur when a company converts or creates an information system.

3. *Understand* some of the tools and techniques used in systems design work.

4. *Know* what a systems specifications report is and the kinds of information it contains.

5. *Understand* some of the key factors that a company's design team and steering committee should consider when comparing vendor proposals.

6. *Know* what prototyping is and understand how it is used to help design an information system.

7. *Become familiar with* some evaluation criteria and selection techniques for choosing computer vendors.

Every company I know has an elaborate process for studying capital allocation, but not more than one or two among hundreds look three years later at whether that capital investment produced the promised results. In fact, most of them don't even ask the question "What results do we expect?"

Peter Drucker, "Drucker: IT Hasn't Done Job"
(an interview), *Computerworld,* vol. 33, no. 17
(April 1999), p. 51.

INTRODUCTION

Recall from Chapter 13 that the final output in the analysis phase of a systems study is a report containing recommendations about how to proceed. If the steering committee approves, the organization can move forward to the design phase of the systems study. This chapter describes some of the design tools and techniques that an organization can use to prepare a detailed system specifications report. In addition, this chapter reviews some of the key factors that an organization should consider when evaluating computer vendor proposals.

Who actually performs the systems design work? Like the analysis phase of a systems study, this varies from project to project and from company to company. One possibility is to ask the original study team that conducted the analysis phase to perform this work. Another possibility is to create a new team—for example, one that includes more IT professionals and fewer outside managers. Yet a third possibility is to hire (or retain) outside consultants for this task. For the purposes of discussion, this chapter assumes that a generic "design team" performs the design work.

THE FEASIBILITY EVALUATION

After obtaining a positive response from the steering committee, the design team must perform a detailed investigation of different potential systems. Figure 14-1 shows that this work involves five major procedures or activities. The first of these is a **feasibility evaluation** in which the design team determines the practicality of alternative proposals. Only after this step is completed can the design team tackle the other steps.

The Five Components of a Feasibility Evaluation

For each system alternative, the design team must examine five feasibility areas: (1) technical feasibility, (2) operational feasibility, (3) schedule feasibility, (4) legal feasibility, and (5) economic feasibility. Because the accountants on a design team are normally responsible for performing the economic feasibility evaluation work, the following discussions emphasize the economic feasibility portion of these activities.

Technical Feasibility　The **technical feasibility** of any proposed system attempts to answer the question, "What technical resources are required by a particu-

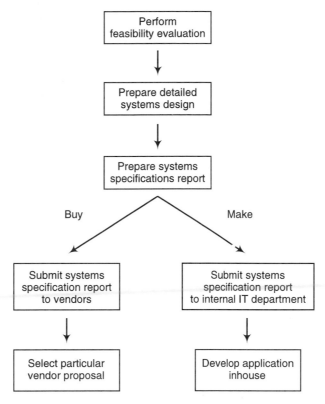

FIGURE 14-1 Steps in the systems design phase of a systems study.

lar system?" Hardware and software are two obvious components of this question. For example, a proposed system that can interface with critical existing software is more desirable than one requiring the organization to buy new software. Figure 14-2 provides further examples of such technical considerations. Computer experts typically work on this phase of the feasibility evaluation because a thorough understanding of information technology is essential.

In addition to developing a preliminary hardware configuration for a proposed system, the design team must also determine whether current employees possess the technical skills to use it. (This evaluation overlaps the operational feasibility investigation described next.) If a specific computerized system is too sophisticated for a company's employees, it is unlikely that using it in subsequent daily operations will be successful.

Operational Feasibility The **operational feasibility** of a proposed system examines its compatibility with the current operating environment (i.e., answers the question, "How consistent will the tasks and procedures of the new system be with the those of the old system?"). Thus, the design team must analyze the capabilities of current employees to perform the specific functions required by each proposed system, and determine to what extent employees will require specialized training.

Operational-feasibility analysis is mostly a human relations study because it is strongly oriented toward "people problems." For this reason, human-relations specialists

Design Considerations	Design Alternatives
Communications channel configuration	Point to point, multidrop, or line sharing
Communications channels	Telephone lines, coaxial cable, fiber optics, microwave, or satellite
Comunications network	Centralized, decentralized, distributed, or local area
Computer programs	Independent vendor or in-house
Data storage media	Tape, floppy disk, hard disk, CD Rom, DVD, or hard copy
Data storage	Files, database, data warehouse, or data mart
File organization and access	Direct access or sequential files
Input media	Terminal, OCR, MICR, POS, EDI, web, or voice
Operations	In-house or outsourcing
Output frequency	Instantaneous, hourly, daily, weekly, or monthly
Output medium	CRT, hard copy, voice, or turnaround document
Output scheduling	Predetermined times or on demand
Printed output	Preprinted forms or system-generated forms
Processor	Micro, mini, or mainframe
Transaction processing	Batch or online
Update frequency	Instantaneous, hourly, daily, weekly, or monthly

FIGURE 14-2 Examples of system design alternatives.

participate heavily in it. As noted in Chapter 13, employees commonly have negative attitudes toward changes that will affect their organizational duties, while positive employee motivation is an essential prerequisite to successful systems revisions. Ideally, if managers encourage employees to suggest changes and keep them well informed about how the new system will affect their job functions, an organization can limit employee resistance.

> **Case-in-Point 14.1** After a three-week operational period of a new computerized inventory system, the top managers at one company were amazed to find that there were more processing errors in the new system than there had been in the old, manual one. The problem persisted for months. Finally, the company hired a team of outside management consultants, which quickly found the difficulty: the new system was so automated that employees had very little to do but punch buttons. These employees were sabotaging the system out of boredom!

Schedule Feasibility Schedule feasibility involves the design team's estimating how long it will take a new or revised system to become operational and communicating this information to the steering committee. For example, if a design team projects that it will take sixteen months for a particular system design to become fully functional, the steering committee may reject the proposal in favor of a simpler alternative that the company can implement in a shorter time frame.

Legal Feasibility Legal feasibility is largely concerned with whether there will be any conflict between a newly proposed system and the organization's legal obligations. For example, a revised system should comply with all applicable federal and state statutes about financial reporting requirements, as well as the company's contractual obligations.

Case-in-Point 14.2   Nevada is one of five states in the United States that does not have a state income tax. You would think, therefore, that any payroll system a Nevada company chose to implement would not need a module to withhold state income taxes from employee paychecks. But Reno, Nevada, is only ten miles from the California border, California does have a state income tax, many Reno employees live there, and California residents must pay state income taxes even if they work in Nevada. Thus, Reno, Nevada, corporations must have state withholding modules in their payroll systems for such employees!

Economic Feasibility   Through **economic feasibility** evaluation, the design team attempts to assess the cost-effectiveness of a proposed system (i.e., to determine whether the anticipated benefits of the system exceed its projected costs). To assess the cost-effectiveness of any proposed system, the design team's accountants should perform a cost-benefit analysis. The next section provides an example.

An Example

To illustrate an economic feasibility study in greater detail, let us return to BSM, the manufacturing company discussed in Chapter 13, and its interest in creating one or more web-based sales systems. The study team has analyzed the operating environment and decides to examine three courses of action. One possibility is to develop a new, web-based system for only its retail customers. A second possibility is to develop a web-based system for its retail customers and a separate, extranet system for its distributors. A third possibility is to develop a single system that serves both types of buyers. The objective of the design phase of a systems study is to examine such proposals in depth and determine the design specifications for the preferred system(s).

Figure 14-3 reflects the cost-benefit analysis performed by the design team's accountants for BSM's first proposal—the one to develop a web system for just the

Projected Cash Benefits and Costs for BSM Retail Customer Web Project					
Years					
	1	2	3	4	5
Cash Benefits					
1. Reduced clerical costs	$ 150,000	$ 200,000	$ 200,000	$ 200,000	$ 200,000
2. Enhanced sales	500,000	1,000,000	1,250,000	1,500,000	2,000,000
3. Better customer service	100,000	200,000	300,000	400,000	500,000
4. Miscellaneous benefits	200,000	200,000	200,000	200,000	200,000
Total Benefits	950,000	1,600,000	1,950,000	2,300,000	2,900,000
Cash Costs					
1. Initial computer hardware and software	500,000	100,000	–	–	–
2. Additional IT staff (salares + benefits)	600,000	700,000	800,000	900,000	1,000,000
3. Operation Costs	250,000	250,000	250,000	250,000	250,000
4. Miscellaneous Costs	300,000	500,000	400,000	400,000	400,000
Total Costs	1,650,000	1,550,000	1,450,000	1,550,000	1,650,000
Excess of annual cash benefits over annual cash costs	(700,000)	50,000	500,000	750,000	1,250,000

FIGURE 14–3   The projected cash benefits and costs for an Internet ordering system.

company's retail customers. The proposed system has an estimated five-year useful life and must be integrated with the company's current receivables data processing system. The following paragraphs describe some estimates for this system. The team would have to perform a similar analysis for the other two alternatives before selecting a preferred system.

Before examining the specific cash benefits and cash costs in Figure 14-3, a few general comments are necessary. First, we note that the benefits from any proposed system are usually difficult to identify, hard to quantify, complex in scope, and for these reasons, involve a large degree of subjectivity. The analysis that follows is therefore a simplified example. Second, in actual practice, the design team will usually convert the projected cash benefits and cash costs from a cost-benefit analysis to present values using capital budgeting techniques. For simplicity, we will ignore such calculations here. Third, because the design team has not discussed the details of this proposal with internal IT specialists or outside computer vendors (which occurs later in systems design work), the costs in Figure 14-3 are only estimates—not "hard dollar" figures.

Finally, before preparing a detailed design for a computerized information system, it is critical that the design team examines the overall feasibility of the proposed system, not just the economic feasibility of the project. For example, if the firm cannot implement a specific system in a reasonable amount of time, it makes little sense to go ahead with the project, even if the other dimensions of the system are favorable. The projected benefits of BSM's system are as follows.

Reduced Clerical Costs   The first benefit listed in Figure 14-3 is the savings from reduced clerical costs. The proposed Internet system allows customers to create their own orders, so by default the system will automatically capture sales data in machine-readable format. This in turn will allow the company to reduce the clerical staff now required to take phone and fax orders, key data into BSM's order-entry system, and perform similar clerical duties. The design team estimates that these advantages will allow the company to reduce its clerical staff by four positions. The team also thinks that this reduction can be accomplished through natural employee attrition or, if necessary, reassignment, so it does not include any offsetting employee-termination costs.

Enhanced Sales   The proposed web-based retail system will essentially be an online catalogue, complete with pictures, technical descriptions, and prices of individual products. Thus, the design team expects the new system to enhance sales considerably because customers from around the world will now be able to place orders 24 hours a day, 7 days a week. The team is especially optimistic about sales to foreign customers because BSM currently has no international marketing representatives and thus has limited itself to the domestic market. BSM's sales are now about $10 million per year. In light of the above considerations, the enhanced sales estimates in Figure 14-3, which start at 5 percent of sales and grow to 20 percent, seem conservative.

Better Customer Service   Surveys consistently indicate that "providing better customer service" is the most important reason why companies now invest in information technology. This certainly applies to the proposed system, which will enable BSM's retail customers to order products whenever and wherever they like. The new system will also enable the company to process orders faster because no data transcription is required and the customer's purchase information can be sent directly to the company's order fulfillment department. The end result is to reduce the amount of time that a customer waits to receive his or her purchase. Finally, the new system will also enable customers to ask about the status of an order—for example, whether or not it has been shipped. Although it is difficult to quantify these consumer benefits, the design team feels that the dollar equivalents ranging between $100,000 and $500,000 in Figure 14-3 are reasonable estimates.

Miscellaneous Benefits   The design team feels that BSM will enjoy many miscellaneous benefits from the proposed system. One advantage is the ability to match or beat BSM's competition, which may also be developing web systems—a fact that explains why the design team was sworn to secrecy when it began its work. A second benefit is an enhanced ability to estimate customer demand for its products, leading to better plans for manufacturing processes and perhaps the ability to reduce investments in raw materials inventories and work in process. A third benefit is a projected reduction in accounts receivable balances, which happens when a retail customer prepays for merchandise by credit card rather than waiting for a bill. This also results in a concomitant reduction in allowances for bad debt. A fourth benefit is a current, computerized list of BSM retail customer names, addresses, and e-mail addresses, which the company can use in future marketing efforts. Like the other benefits discussed previously, the design team finds it difficult to translate these advantages into dollar terms, but the $200,000 figure— just 2 percent of sales—seems justifiable.

Figure 14-3 summarizes the anticipated dollar benefits for each of the first five years of the project. Note that the anticipated benefits increase from year to year, reflecting the expectation that they will grow as customers gain familiarity and confidence with the new ordering system. But the bottom portion of Figure 14-3 indicates that the proposed system comes at a price. Thus, the design team must also estimate what the system is likely to cost. Figure 14-3 lists four projected cost categories as follows:

Initial Computer Hardware and Software   The design team finds that the cost of Internet servers, routers, modems, and similar hardware has dropped considerably in the last few years, making it much cheaper to install a web system these days. The team thus estimates initial hardware and software costs of $500,000 for the first year and an additional $100,000 in equipment (to handle a projected increase in processing requirements) the second year. The team also learns that the company can outsource this part of the system to a third-party vendor, who will provide all the required hardware, backup, and maintenance support for a contractual fee. The team decides to explore this avenue as a separate possibility (not discussed here).

Additional IT Staff   The design team estimates that BSM will need to hire five new IT employees at various technical levels to design and develop its web pages, install and maintain the new hardware, develop at least some of the software, and program the new system to interface with the existing manufacturing system, integrated accounting system, and Oracle customer database. Because so many other organizations have similar web-development projects in progress, the design team learns that IT professionals are currently in high demand, often command premium salaries, and may require special employee benefits and signing bonuses. The data in Figure 14-3 reflect these facts.

Operation Costs The proposed system will incur ongoing costs of operation, including hardware and software maintenance, on-site repairs and enhancements, office supplies, backup resources, electrical power, insurance, and disaster-recovery standby costs. Another important ongoing expenditure is the cost of maintaining the web site itself—for example, keeping displayed products, prices, descriptions, and links to other web sites current. Finally, although the design team assumes that the company will purchase its computer equipment outright, it also decides to inform the steering committee that BSM can lease the equipment instead for (typical) lease terms of three to five years. This option will reduce the costs of initial computer hardware and software outlays, but increase operating costs.

Miscellaneous Costs This is a catchall category. One component is the short-term costs of preparing the company's premises for new computer equipment, as well as the additional costs of site preparation for the new employees. Training costs are often high for new information systems but are likely to be small here because the company assumes its new IT employees will already possess the technical expertise required to develop and run the system. Similarly, the normally high costs of computer conversion and testing will not be significant here because the proposed Internet system will interface with, rather than replace, the company's other accounting and production systems. The design team concludes that incremental costs of between $300,000 and $500,000 are reasonable for all these items.

The bottom line in Figure 14-3 computes the excess of projected benefits over projected costs for each of the first five years of the proposed system. The figures suggest that the initial costs of the project will be high and exceed immediate benefits, but that benefits are likely to more than offset the costs in future years. Based on these numbers, the project looks promising. However, although the neatly organized figures in Figure 14-3 can create a reality of their own, the data in this analysis are just estimates, not certainties, of future operations.

Concluding Comments on the Feasibility Evaluation

The economics of BSM's proposed web-based retail system look promising. It is also important to remember that a project must be not only economically feasible, but also technically feasible, operationally feasible, schedule feasible, and legally feasible. If one or more of these areas is not feasible for a specific system proposal, or top management has negative reactions to it, the proposal will not be accepted.

The design team will complete feasibility evaluations for each system proposal, which explains why the design phase of a system study can take months of work. When the team completes these tasks, it submits a **final feasibility report** to the steering committee. This report summarizes the team's feasibility work and makes recommendations about how to proceed. If none of the design team's system proposals is totally feasible, the steering committee may ask the design team to rework its figures or may request alternative proposals that are more suitable for the company. Alternatively, if several proposals appear to be totally feasible, the steering committee must select a finalist, thereby enabling the design team to proceed with a detailed systems design. Finally, where projects are not totally feasible or managerially acceptable, a steering committee should face facts and reach a "no-go" decision. After all, it is better to lose some money now abandoning an infeasible system than a lot of money later developing an unsuccessful one.

DETAILED SYSTEMS DESIGN

Once the steering committee approves the feasibility of a general system plan (project), the design team can begin work on a **detailed systems design.** This involves specifying the outputs, processing procedures, and inputs for the new system. Just as construction blueprints create the detailed plans for building a house, the detailed design of a new system becomes the specifications for creating or acquiring a new information system. Figure 14-4 provides examples of the detailed requirements that the design team must create, and these requirements in turn explain specifically what the proposed system must produce.

From an accounting standpoint, one of the most important elements in a new system is its control requirements. In this matter, the design team should have a "real-time" mentality when designing control procedures for a system. In other words, rather than adding controls after a system has been developed and installed, the team should design cost-effective general and application control procedures into the system as integrated components. The Committee of Sponsoring Organizations (COSO) of the Treadway Commission—a voluntary organization dedicated to "improving the quality of financial reporting"—emphasizes the importance of this view:

> *Whenever management considers changes to its company's operations or activities, the concept that it's better to "build-in" rather than "build-on" controls, and to do it right the first time, should be the fundamental guiding premise.*[1]

Requirements	Discussion
Processes	Descriptions of the various processes to be performed in the revised system, stressing what is to be done and by whom.
Data elements	Descriptions of the required data elements, including their name, size, format, source, and importance.
Data structure	Preliminary data structure that indicates how the data elements will be organized into logical records.
Inputs	Copies of system inputs and descriptions of their contents, sources, and who is responsible for them.
Outputs	Copies of system outputs and descriptions of their purpose, frequency, and distribution.
Documentation	Descriptions of how the revised system and each subsystem will operate.
Constraints	Descriptions of constraints such as staffing limitations and regulatory requirements.
Controls	Controls to reduce the risk of undetected errors and irregularities in the input, processing, and output stages of data processing work.
Reorganizations	Necessary changes such as increasing staff levels, adding new job functions, and terminating certain existing positions.

FIGURE 14-4 Examples of detailed requirements for a system proposal.

---

[1] Summarized from Committee of Sponsoring Organizations of the Treadway Commission (CSOTC), Internal Control-Integrated Framework (COSO Report), New York: 1992.

Designing System Outputs

At this point in the design process, the design team can focus on developing the input, processing, and output requirements of a new system. When performing these tasks, it is perhaps curious that the design team first focuses on the outputs—not the inputs or processing requirements—of the new system. The reason for this is straightforward: the most important objective of an AIS is to satisfy users' needs. Thus, the design team prepares output specifications first, and lets these requirements in turn dictate the inputs and processing tasks required to produce them.

The design team will use the data gathered from the prior systems analysis work to help it decide what kinds of outputs are needed, as well as the formats that these outputs should have. Although it is possible for the design team to merely copy the outputs of an older system, this would make little sense—the new system would be just like the old one. Instead, the team will attempt to create better outputs—that is, design outputs that will better satisfy their users' information needs than did the old system.

Outputs may be classified according to which functional area uses them (e.g., marketing, human resources, accounting, or manufacturing) as well as how frequently they must be produced (e.g., daily or weekly). Where a specific report is not needed on a regular basis, the system should be able to provide it when requested (a **demand report**) or triggered when a certain condition is met (an **exception report**). For example, an accounts receivable report on a specific customer's payment history might be issued on demand, or generated automatically when a customer owes more than a specified amount. Although many organizations still rely heavily on hard-copy (printed) reports, systems designers should also consider the possibility of creating soft-copy (screen) reports as an alternative, which use less paper and of course, do not require a printer for viewing. This consideration will be especially important to BSM, whose proposed system will rely heavily on web page displays.

Once the design team has determined the number and types of outputs the new system must generate, it can design the formats for the outputs themselves. Although many accounting reports use tabular formats, some reports can be improved by displaying numerical data in graphs and charts (Figure 14-5).

Process Design

Until now, the system designers have focused on *what the system must provide* rather than *how the system can provide it.* After designing the outputs, their next step is to identify the processing procedures required to produce them. This involves deciding which application programs are necessary and what data processing tasks each program should perform.

Over the years, systems designers have created a large number of tools for modeling computer processes. Among them are the system flowcharts, data flow diagrams, program flowcharts, process maps, and decision tables discussed in Chapter 3. Another popular tool is the entity-relationship (E-R) diagram discussed in Chapter 8. Common to all these design methodologies is the idea of **structured, top-down design,** in which system designers begin at the highest level of abstraction and then "drill down" to lower, more detailed levels until the system is completely specified.

A good example of this top-down methodology is a **structure chart.** Figure 14-6 illustrates an example—a high-level chart for a sales transaction processing application

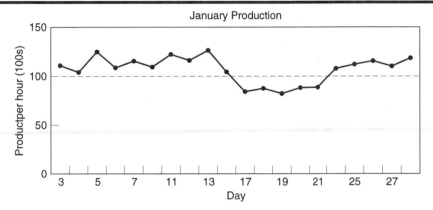

Day:	3	4	5	6	7	10	11	12	13	14	17	18	19	20	21	24	25	26	27	28
Shift 1:	23	34	23	23	22	32	45	46	23	32	34	25	35	34	20	35	24	25	45	35
Shift 2:	35	33	34	21	43	28	32	34	53	43	34	36	32	21	34	23	33	35	44	32
Shift 3:	34	32	21	23	31	36	24	24	21	35	25	43	34	34	23	44	31	24	32	35
Total:	92	99	78	96	96	101	104	97	110	93	94	101	89	77	102	88	84	84	121	102
Units Produced: (thousands)	102	103	98	73	111	105	124	121	123	115	78	82	83	78	68	111	99	97	134	121
Prod/hour	111	104	126	109	116	109	123	116	127	105	84	87	82	88	88	109	113	115	111	119

ABC Corporation, Monthly Production Report January, 20xx, Hours in Each Shift

FIGURE 14–5   Which format makes it easier to determine whether production is "under control" (production/hour at least 100 units)?

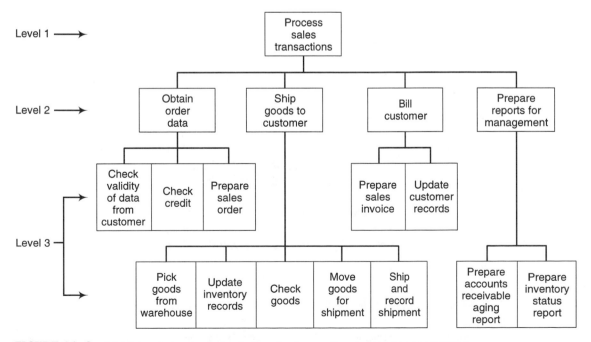

FIGURE 14–6   A high-level structure chart of a sales transaction processing application.

that uses a hierarchy of three levels. Each successive level provides more detail about the activity above it. In Figure 14-6, for example, Level 2 discloses the four activities (obtain order data, ship goods to customer, etc.) that are involved in processing sales transactions. Level 3 activities provide more detailed processing information about the activities at the second level. Even though Figure 14-6 does not show it, the system designers can decompose the activities at the third level into even more detail at a fourth level, fifth level, and so forth. For example, the "prepare sales invoice" activity at Level 3 can be broken down into several detailed steps (or activities), such as "access sales order and shipping data" and "enter heading of sales invoice." This decomposition process continues until the designers have completely specified the processing requirements of the entire system.

At present, **object-oriented design methods** are gaining in popularity because (1) they employ the *Unified Modeling Language (UML)* to represent business systems, and (2) they are especially adapted to designing the event-driven systems (in which user mouse clicks and similar events trigger programming code) that are common to Windows applications. The idea behind object-oriented design is to create reusable processing modules (i.e., "objects") that serve as independent building blocks in the task of creating complete application systems. Typically, this means that each object's data are hidden from other modules, manipulated entirely internally, and output in a prespecified format. This allows designers to treat each object as a "black box" and encourages them to focus on what each object does rather than how it does it. Because each module performs its processing tasks independently of other modules, this approach also increases the flexibility of the application's processing structure and facilitates software maintenance when programs must later be modified.

To draw these various diagrams and charts, systems designers commonly use the **computer-aided software engineering (CASE) tools** discussed in Chapter 3. These are software packages that typically run on microcomputers and that enable their users to develop and revise system designs in much the same way that word processors help writers develop and revise text documents. Advanced CASE tools can help users create successive levels of detail using any one of many methodologies (e.g., data flow diagrams or E-R diagrams), create and maintain data dictionaries, and even generate computer code from a finished design. The "AIS at Work" feature at the end of this chapter describes the successful use of a CASE tool at Sony Corporation.

Designing System Inputs

Once the design team has specified the outputs and processing procedures for a new project, its members can think about what data the system must collect to satisfy these output and processing requirements. Thus, the team must identify and describe each data element in the systems design (e.g., "alphabetic", "maximum number of characters," and "default value") as well as specify the way data items must be coded. This is no easy task, because there are usually a large number of data items in even a small business application. Chapters 7 and 8 discuss the subject of data modeling in greater detail.

> *Case-in-Point 14.3* A new POS (point-of-sale) system implemented by Brewers Retail, a $2 billion Canadian beer distributor and retailer, allowed company managers to all but eliminate manual price lists, inspect up-to-the-minute data on sales, and better forecast labor needs and delivery requirements. The company estimates that this system has saved tens of thousands of dollars in annual labor costs.

FIGURE 14-7 An input screen created in Visual Basic, an event-driven programming language for designing Windows applications.

After the design team identifies and describes the input data, it can determine the source of each data element. For example, customer information such as name, address, and telephone numbers may be gathered directly from web screens, while the current date can be accessed from the computer system itself. Wherever possible, the design team will attempt to capture data in computer-readable formats, inasmuch as this avoids costly, time-consuming data transcription as well as the errors such transcription typically introduces into the job stream.

Finally, system designers try to create systems that streamline data entry tasks because this facilitates the process and helps users avoid errors. Examples include substituting system default values, screen menus, and mouse clicks for system commands or other inputs that must otherwise be entered manually. Additional examples include using dialogue boxes for special user inputs (Figure 14-7) and employing message boxes that help explain why a particular input value is unacceptable (Figure 14-8).

Case-in-Point 14.4 In the United States, some gambling casinos now issue magnetic-striped cards to their customers, who use them as internal credit cards for playing slot machinies. These cards also allow managers to gather data on player activities—information that they can subsequently use to make better decisions regarding extending credit limits or providing complimentary meals and hotel rooms.

Prototyping

Prototyping means developing a simplified model, or prototype, of a proposed information system. Thus, the prototype is a scaled-down, experimental version of a

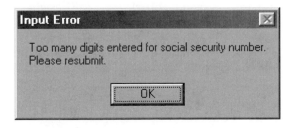

FIGURE 14-8 An AIS might display this error message if the user made a mistake entering a Social Security number in the dialogue box of Figure 14-7.

nonexistent information system that a design team can develop cheaply and quickly for user-evaluation purposes. The prototype model does not run, but presents users with the "look and feel" of a completed system. By allowing users to experiment with the prototype, the designers can learn what users like and dislike in the mockup, and then modify the system's design in response to this feedback. Thus, prototyping is an iterative process of trial-use-and-modification that continues until users are satisfied.

> **Case-in-Point 14.5** UNUM Life Insurance is one of the nation's largest disability insurance carriers. The company realized that the various systems it had developed in the 1970s and 1980s only automated its manual processes and were not integrated very well. UNUM wanted to utilize new technologies, such as image processing, to link its many systems with each other and also with its users. Top management, however, had a difficult time getting middle managers to visualize how image processing could help. These middle managers mostly thought this was just a method to replace filing cabinets. After observing a prototype, the middle managers caught on to the positive outcomes associated with image processing, realized its business potential, and endorsed the project.

Prototyping can be viewed as a series of four steps:

Step 1: Identify Information System Requirements We reviewed the tasks of identifying system requirements in Chapter 13. However, because the design team needs only fundamental system requirements to build the initial prototype, the process can be less formal and time-consuming than when performing traditional systems analysis. (The team can develop the detailed requirements of the system later after users have had time to interact with the prototype and provide feedback.)

Step 2: Develop the Initial Prototype In this step, the designers create an initial base model—for example, using fourth-generation programming languages or CASE tools. In this phase, the goals are "rapid development" and "low cost." Thus, the designers give little consideration to such matters as internal controls or data storage requirements, but instead emphasize such system characteristics as "simplicity," "flexibility," and "ease of use." These characteristics enable users to interact with tentative versions of data-entry display screens, menus, and source documents. The users also need to be able to respond to system prompts, make inquiries of the information system, judge response times of the system, and issue commands.

Step 3: Test and Revise After finishing the initial prototype, the designers first demonstrate the model to users and then give it to them to experiment. At the outset, users must be told that the prototype is incomplete and requires subsequent modifications based on their feedback. Thus, the designers ask users to record their likes and dislikes about the system and recommend changes. Using this feedback, the design team modifies the prototype as necessary and then resubmits the revised model to system users for reevaluation. This iterative process of modification-and-reevaluation continues until the users are satisfied—commonly, through four to six iterations.

Step 4: Obtain User Signoff of the Approved Prototype At the end of Step 3, users formally approve the final version of the prototype, which commits them to the current design and establishes a contractual obligation about what the system will, and will not, do or provide. Approximately half of these approved prototypes become fully functional systems. The remaining, throwaway prototypes are not developed—typically because the modifications required to make them functional are too costly or in other ways not practical. But this does not mean that the prototyping exercise has been a failure. To the contrary, it signals an impractical system and thus saves an organization a great deal of time and money!

Figure 14-9 summarizes the advantages and disadvantages of prototyping. In general, the procedure is useful when one or more of the following conditions exist:

1. End users do not understand their informational needs very well.
2. System requirements are hard to define.
3. The new system is mission-critical or needed quickly.
4. Past interactions have resulted in misunderstandings between end users and designers.
5. The risks associated with developing and implementing the wrong system are high.

Prototyping is not always the best systems design approach. For example, both managers and IT professionals can distrust it—the managers, if they perceive prototyping as "too experimental" and the IT professionals, if they harbor fears that the results lead to poor design solutions. Then, too, a design team can be misled if it relies

---

Advantages of Prototyping

1. Prototyping requires intensive involvement by the system users. Therefore, it typically results in a better definition of these users' needs and requirements than does the traditional systems development approach.
2. A very short time period (e.g., a week) is normally required to develop and start experimenting with a prototype. This short time period allows system users to immediately evaluate proposed system changes. In contrast, it may take a year or longer before system users can evaluate proposed system changes when the traditional systems development approach is used.
3. Since system users experiment with each version of the prototype through an iterative process, errors are hopefully detected and eliminated early in the developmental process. As a result, the information system ultimately implemented should be more reliable and less costly to develop than when the traditional systems development approach is employed.

Disadvantages of Prototyping

1. Prototyping can only be successful if the system users are willing to devote significant time in experimenting with the prototype and provide the system developers with change suggestions. The users may not be able or willing to spend the amount of time required under the prototyping approach.
2. The iterative process of prototyping causes the prototype to be experimented with quite extensively. Because of this, the system developers are frequently tempted to minimize the testing and documentation process of the ultimately approved information system. Inadequate testing can make the approved system error-prone, and inadequate documentation can make this system difficult to maintain.
3. Prototyping may cause behavioral problems with system users. These problems include dissatisfaction by users if system developers are unable to meet all user demands for improvements as well as dissatisfaction and impatience by users when they have to go through too many iterations of the prototype.

FIGURE 14-9 Advantages and disadvantages of prototyping.

on a small portion of the user population for developing its models and thus satisfies the informational needs of nonrepresentative employees. (For this reason, prototyping is not normally appropriate for designing large or complex information systems that serve many users with significantly different informational needs). Finally, prototyping is not recommended for developing traditional AIS applications such as accounts receivable, accounts payable, payroll, or inventory management, where the inputs, processing, and outputs are already well known and clearly defined.

The System Specifications Report

After the design team completes its work of specifying the inputs, outputs, and processing requirements of the new system, the members will summarize their findings in a (typically large) **systems specification report.** Figure 14-10 provides some representative information in such a report. The design team then submits this report to the steering committee for review, comment, and approval.

The Make or Buy Decision The project is now at a critical juncture. If the steering committee approves the detailed design work, it now faces a **make-or-**

---

1. *Historical background information about the company's operating activities.* Included here would be facts about the types of products manufactured and sold by the company, the financial condition of the company, the company's current data processing methods, the peak volume of data processing activities, and the types of equipment currently being used in the company's data processing system.

2. *Detailed information about the problems in the company's current data processing system.* By understanding the present systems problems, the computer vendors should have a better idea of what type of specific computer application will eliminate the company's system weaknesses. The design team may also include information about how soon they would like to receive the vendors' recommendations and the approximate date that the final decision will be made by their client regarding which computerized system will be purchased (or leased).

3. *Detailed descriptions of the systems design proposals.* For every design proposal, information should be included about such things as the data input and output of specific computer processing runs, the types of master files needed and the approximate volume of each file, the frequency of updating each master file, the format of each output report, the approximate length of each output report, the types of information included in each report and how often the various reports will be prepared, the organizational managers to whom every report will be distributed, and the company's available space for computer facilities.

4. *Indication of what the vendors should include in their proposals to the company.* This section of the systems specifications report, in effect, tells the vendors how detailed they should make their proposals. The company might request information regarding the speed and size of the central processing unit needed, the type of microcomputers needed for the company's local area network, the type and quantity of input and output devices as well as the capabilities of these devices, the availability of prewritten software packages for specific processing activities, the training sessions offered by the vendors on the operating details of the new system, the help provided by the vendors in implementing and testing the new system, the maintenance services available from the vendors, and the vendors' provisions for backup data processing facilities.

5. *Time schedule for implementing the new system.* This final section of the report will request the computer vendors to estimate the number of weeks, months, or years that will be necessary to implement their recommended computer systems within the company.

FIGURE 14-10 Systems specifications report information.

buy decision. In large organizations, one possibility is to use internal IT staff to develop the project inhouse. This choice offers the tightest control over project development, the best security over sensitive data, the benefits of a custom product that has been tailor-made for the exact requirements of the application, the luxury of replacing the old system piecemeal as modules become available, and a vote of confidence for the organization's IT staff. But this choice also utilizes valuable employee time and can divert the organization's resources from its main objectives—for example, manufacturing products.

Another possibility is to outsource the project's development to a contractor. This choice is useful when an organization lacks internal expertise to do the work or simply wishes to avoid the headaches of internal project development. But internal IT staffers have a name for this choice—"outhouse programming."

Finally, the steering committee can choose to purchase prewritten software (commonly called **canned software**) and perhaps modify it to suit the firm's needs. If the organization requires both hardware and software, the committee may also choose to shop for a complete, "ready-to-go" **turnkey system.** The steering committee can ask the computer vendors to submit bid proposals for such a complete system, or alternatively, can ask each vendor to provide separate bids for hardware and software.

Back to BSM   At BSM, the study team works hard developing mockups of the web pages that will allow customers to order company products online. The team also surveys key customers to obtain their reactions. Most are favorable, although one still prefers "speaking to a person" to "buying items from impersonal computers." The team also develops detailed modification plans for the company's billing, receivables, and order-fulfillment departments (i.e., the systems most affected by the proposed web-sales system). The study team summarizes all this work in a systems specification report and submits it to the steering committee.

> *Case-in-Point 14.6*   In a parallel universe, the master programmer for the great warlord was asked which was harder to design: an operating system or an accounting application. Without hesitation, the programmer replied "an accounting system."
>
> "Why is this true?" asked the inquirer. "Surely an operating system is a much more complicated piece of software."
>
> The master programmer replied "Yes, but an operating system must worry only about itself because all the application programs that run under it must comply with its rules. Accounting systems must worry about humans."

SELECTING A FINAL SYSTEM

Because internal project management and systems development are beyond the scope of this text, we shall assume here that the steering committee opts to acquire most of its system resources from outside vendors. If the committee takes this course of action, the systems specifications report helps them create a **request for proposal (RFP),** which outlines the specific requirements of the desired system. Thus, upon finalizing the systems specifications, the committee (with the help of the design team and perhaps outside consultants) will decide which vendors should receive an RFP, and send each one a copy. Typically, the RFP also contains a deadline for bidding, the length of which depends on the complexity of the project—for example, just a few weeks for hardware, and longer periods of time for systems requiring custom development tasks.

After the deadline has passed, an evaluation committee supervised by the steering committee will review vendor submissions and schedule separate meetings with those vendors who provide viable system proposals. The participants at each meeting include representatives from the vendor, representatives from the steering committee, and representatives from the design team. The vendor's role is to present its proposal and to answer questions from the other participants. The evaluation committee's role is to listen to the vendor proposals, provide input to the steering committee about the pros and cons of each one, and perhaps make a recommendation for a preferred provider.

Selection Criteria

The steering committee's responsibility is the simplest: to make a final selection. In this regard, the committee is not restricted in its choices. It can accept one bid totally, negotiate with one vendor for specific resources, or spread its purchases among two or more providers. Here are some key factors that a steering committee should consider when evaluating vendor proposals:

The Performance Capability of Each Proposed System It is imperative that a vendor system be capable of processing the organization's data within the time frames desired by management. Otherwise, delays in providing needed outputs will occur once the computer system is operational. There are many measures of performance, including speed, response time, number of users supported, and system testing. One way to examine the operating efficiency of a particular system is to use a **benchmark test.** With this approach, the vendor's system performs a data processing task that the new system must perform (e.g., payroll processing), and representatives of the organization then examine the outputs for accuracy, consistency, and efficiency.

> *Case-in-Point 14.7* The IT manager of a large resort complex was impressed by one vendor's claims that its payroll package was "vastly superior" to the one she was currently using. This manager was particularly unhappy with the time it currently took to process payroll checks—approximately four hours. The results of a benchmark test using duplicate time cards and the new payroll system were startling: it took the new vendor's system the better part of an entire weekend to process the same number of checks! The manager kept her old system.

The Costs and Benefits of Each Proposed System The accountants on the design team will analyze the costs of every vendor's proposed system in relation to the system's anticipated performance benefits (i.e., will perform a cost-benefit analysis for each proposed system). In this effort, the accountants should also investigate the differences between purchasing and leasing each vendor's system. If the steering committee elects to purchase a system, the accountants should then advise the committee on a realistic depreciation schedule for the new system.

The Maintainability of Each Proposed System *Maintainability* refers to the ease with which a proposed computer system can be modified. For example, this flexibility enables a firm to alter a portion of a payroll system to reflect new federal tax laws. Because the costs of maintaining a large information system are typically five times as much as the costs of initially acquiring or developing a system, the evaluators should place considerable emphasis on this dimension. (We shall return to this point in Chapter 15.)

The Compatibility of Each Proposed System with Existing Systems *Compatibility* refers to the ability to implement and interface the new system with existing computer hardware, software, and operating procedures. In some instances, this comes down to hardware issues. For example, it may not be possible to run specific software modules of the new system on some of the company's older local area network servers, which will consequently have to be upgraded. But compatibility issues can also involve the operating system, existing application software, or operational concerns as well—for example, the requirement that employees learn a whole new set of procedures for inputting data.

Vendor Support *Vendor support* includes such things as (1) training classes that familiarize employees with the operating characteristics of the new system, (2) help in implementing and testing the new system, (3) assistance in maintaining the new system through a maintenance contract, and (4) backup systems for temporarily processing company data if required. The availability of "business-hours-only" versus "round-the-clock" support is another consideration. Most vendors charge extra for enhanced services.

Making a Final Decision

Because this book is about accounting information systems, our focus here will be on acquiring accounting software. Selecting an accounting system is a major responsibility that requires careful planning. After all, a software package that fails to meet the needs of a company or its accounting staff can throw an organization into turmoil, losing it time and money.

> *Case-in-Point 14.8* When deregulation hit the California utility industry in 1998, customers were permitted to choose their energy suppliers and Pacific Gas & Electric (PG&E) had to keep track of fast-changing prices and multiple suppliers of energy. Thus, beginning in 1996, PG&E spent millions of dollars on an IBM system that would handle customer billing and many other tasks. Although massive, the new system couldn't handle the additional burden quickly enough. As a result, PG&E scrapped the fancy IBM system and went back to the drawing board. Today, PG&E has a new four-year project under way. However, the company is also keeping its 30-year-old, first-generation computer system, which it is upgrading and replacing only gradually. Ironically, the new system won't include the latest in point-and-click features for the utility's 1,000 customer-service representatives. Rather, the company will keep old-fashioned keyboard strokes and menus—1970s-era technology that is reliable and surprisingly swift.

For smaller businesses, one factor that makes selecting microcomputer-based accounting packages so difficult is the large number of vendors that offer them. A further complication is that many vendors offer multiple versions of their products, each of which typically has somewhat different features. For example, at the present time, Solomon IV comes in two editions: (1) a Select Edition (with a starting price of $3,500) that the developer targets to smaller firms (20 to 100 employees and annual revenues of $2 to $20 million), and (2) a Premier Edition (with a starting price of $200,000) that it targets to midsized businesses (100 to 1,000 employees and revenues of $10 to $250 million). Similarly, an accounting software package might include the standardized chart of accounts desired by a company but lack the custom-design sales invoicing capabilities it needs.

To make a selection, experts recommend that an evaluation committee concentrate on the more complex and demanding requirements first—for example, complicated order-entry tasks or the software's ability to access a specific type of database. This is because these specialized needs can help the committee eliminate those contender packages that cannot perform the required tasks.

Point-Scoring Analysis   Another approach for evaluating those accounting packages that meet most of a company's major requirements is a **point-scoring analysis** such as the one illustrated in Figure 14-11. (This analysis can also be used to evaluate hardware as well.) To illustrate, assume that in the process of selecting an accounts payable system, an organization finds three independent vendors whose packages appear to satisfy current needs. Figure 14-11 shows the results of the analysis. (Because the cost to purchase or lease each vendor's accounts payable software package is about the same, "cost" is not an issue in this selection process.)

When performing a point-scoring analysis, the evaluation committee first assigns potential points to each of the evaluation criteria based on its relative importance. In Figure 14-11, for example, the committee feels that "adequate controls" (10 possible points) is more important than whether other users are satisfied with the software (8 possible points). After developing these selection criteria, the evaluation committee proceeds to rate each vendor or package, awarding points as it deems fit. The highest point total determines the winner. Thus, in Figure 14-11, the evaluation indicates that Vendor B's accounts payable software package has the highest total score (106 points) and the committee should therefore acquire this vendor's system.

Although point-scoring analyses can provide an objective means of selecting a final system, many experts believe that evaluating accounting software is more art

Software Evaluation Criteria	Possible Points	Vendor A	Vendor B	Vendor C
Does the software meet all mandatory specifications?	10	7	9	6
Will program modifications, if any, be minimal to meet company needs?	10	8	9	7
Does the software contain adequate controls?	10	9	9	8
Is the performance (speed, accuracy, reliability, etc.) adequate?	10	7	8	6
Are other users satisfied with the software?	8	6	7	5
Is the software well documented?	10	8	8	7
Is the software compatible with existing company software?	10	7	9	8
Is the software user-friendly?	10	7	8	6
Can the software be demonstrated and test-driven?	9	8	8	7
Does the software have an adequate warranty?	8	6	7	6
Is the software flexible and easily maintained?	8	5	7	5
Is online inquiry of files and records possible?	10	8	9	7
Will the vendor keep the software up to date?	10	8	8	7
Totals	123	94	106	85

FIGURE 14–11   A point-scoring analysis for evaluating three independent vendors' accounts payable software packages.

than science. There are no absolute rules in the selection process, only guidelines for matching user needs with software capabilities. Thus, even for a small business, the evaluators must consider such issues as the company's data processing needs, its in-house computer skills, vendor reputations, software costs, and so forth. Additional pointers on selecting accounting software can be found at the web sites listed for this task at the end of the chapter.

Selecting a Finalist   After each vendor presents its proposal to the organization, the steering committee must select the best one. Although a vendor's reputation is relative, a buyer can obtain clues by checking with the Better Business Bureau and speaking with some of the vendor's other clients. It is also possible that, say, because of the cost factor, none of the computer vendors' proposals is satisfactory. (At the time the design team performed their economic feasibility study, the results were favorable, but the subsequent detailed design specifications result in actual costs that are considerably higher than anticipated.) At this point, the organization's steering committee can (1) request the design team to obtain additional systems proposals from other vendors, (2) abandon the project, or (3) outsource needed data processing services.

The Final Decision for BSM   At BSM, the evaluation committee finds that all aspects of the proposal to develop a web-based sales system are feasible, as are the other two proposals. However, the steering committee decides to commit to only the first system, reasoning that this system is the smallest and most manageable, and also has the largest sales potential. Top management is delighted, as the benefits of the new system seem so compelling. But there is much work to do before the project becomes operational, and this is the focus of Chapter 15.

AIS AT WORK
Sony Corporation Uses a Case Tool

Selling goods to a manufacturer that employs a just-in-time (JIT) inventory system requires immediate and reliable information from a company's information system—just ask Sony Corporation of America. The need for more timely information is partially a result of a shift in business strategies at Sony. Over the past decade Sony has increased market penetration by supplying electronic parts to computer manufacturers. However, the information system at Sony was built for the consumer market. It was simply not prepared to handle this shift in information needs.

The problem with the old system was readily apparent—not getting current information from Sony's factories. As a result, the company was not able to provide good delivery information to its customers. And that caused a big problem, because if Sony wasn't responsive to its customers' needs, someone else would be, and Sony would lose them.

To speed program development, system designers at Sony are using a computer-aided software engineering (CASE) tool from Texas Instruments that links their local workstations to a mainframe and uses artificial intelligence to develop program code. To use the CASE tool, a designer enters statements that describe the corporate data to use and the relationships between the files that will store the data. The tool checks the data relationships to ensure that they are consistent and, after correcting any inconsistencies, produces code that describes the relationships. The tool then stores this information in a global encyclopedia of corporate information. This process continues until the system has a model of how the company operates. The CASE tool allows this model to be updated and altered as relationships change.

Sony enjoys several advantages in using CASE technology. One benefit is the fact that it requires developers to learn a certain amount of application knowledge, thus forcing designers to become more effective in translating business problems into systems solutions. The tool is also boosting programmer productivity: recent smaller development projects at Sony have seen sixfold increases in programming productivity. CASE tools also require significant planning long before any source code is written. But such planning minimizes wasted programming time and helps overcome the possibility of a "runaway system."

Source: David Gabel, "A Yen for Just-in-Time Decisions Aids Sony's Drive for Coprocessing," *Computerworld* (April 10, 1995), p. SR/5.

SUMMARY

This chapter continues the discussions started in Chapter 13 by examining the design phase of a systems study. The first step in this phase is to examine five feasibility areas for any proposed system: (1) technical feasibility, (2) operational feasibility, (3) schedule feasibility, (4) legal feasibility, and (5) economic feasibility. The accountants on the design team will focus principally on the economic feasibility area—in particular, by performing a cost-benefit analysis for each preliminary design proposal. However, the evaluation committee will give any proposed system further consideration only if all five feasibility areas are positive.

The second major step is to prepare detailed system designs for those systems passing the preliminary feasibility evaluation. For each proposal, the design team begins by designing system outputs (i.e., the types and contents of reports and computer screens). These outputs then dictate what inputs and data processing the system must perform to produce them. Here, the design team is likely to use a wide range of tools, such as CASE tools and prototyping, to make its design tasks easier, faster, and more complete.

The next step in systems design work is to prepare a system specifications report. This report contains detailed information about the desired system and includes background information about the organization, detailed descriptions of the current data processing system and its problems, and complete specifications of the desired outputs, processing requirements, and inputs. If the development work for a system is to be outsourced, the systems specification report serves to guide vendors about what to include in their proposals.

After vendors have responded to the organization's request for proposal (RFP), the organization must choose a final system. Potential selection criteria include system performance capabilities, relative costs and benefits, system maintainability, system compatibility with related processing systems, and vendor support. Once the steering committee chooses a finalist, it remains to implement the chosen system and make sure it works as planned.

KEY TERMS YOU SHOULD KNOW

benchmark test	detailed systems design
canned software	economic feasibility
computer-aided software engineering (CASE) tools	exception report
demand report	feasibility evaluation
	final feasibility report

legal feasibility	schedule feasibility
make-or-buy decision	structure chart
object-oriented design methods	structured, top-down design
operational feasibility	systems specification report
point-scoring analysis	technical feasibility
prototyping	turnkey system
request for proposal (RFP)	

DISCUSSION QUESTIONS

14-1. Why does the design phase of a systems study follow the analysis phase?

14-2. What is the purpose of a systems feasibility evaluation? Should this activity precede or follow the preparation of a systems specifications report for computer vendor evaluation? Explain.

14-3. As part of their systems design work, a design team should examine five feasibility areas. Discuss the reasons for evaluating each of these feasibility areas.

14-4. Discuss some of the annual cash benefits and annual cash costs that a company might have when converting from a manual data processing system to a computerized system.

14-5. Discuss some of the annual cash benefits and annual cash costs that a company might have when it creates an online ordering system on the World Wide Web.

14-6. Why does the detailed systems design work begin with the design of system outputs rather than inputs or processing tasks?

14-7. What is prototyping? Under what circumstances should prototyping be used? Under what circumstances should it not be used?

14-8. Why do design teams use special design tools such as structure charts?

14-9. Neil Cronin, a management consultant for the International Consulting Organization, has just completed a feasibility evaluation for converting his client company's current system to an online, web-based system. The results of his technical, operational, legal, and schedule feasibility evaluations are all positive. However, the economic feasibility evaluation outcome is negative. In your opinion, what course of action should Neil recommend?

14-10. What is the purpose of a systems specifications report? In what ways, if any, do the data included in this report differ from the data accumulated by the design team during their feasibility evaluation work?

14-11. The data contained within a systems specifications report include "detailed information about the problem (or problems) in a company's current data processing system." Why is it necessary to include this type of information in the systems specifications report?

14-12. Discuss some of the relevant factors that a company should consider when comparing system proposals from various computer vendors. For each factor, indicate why it is important to the decision-making process of selecting a specific vendor's computer system.

PROBLEMS

14-13. Jay Beck, employed by the AAZ Consulting Firm, was asked by his friend Hank Henley (the general manager and majority stockholder of the Pacific Worldwinds, a professional football team) to design an online, real-time computer system for "the more efficient operation of the football franchise." Jay was quite confused because he could not think of any possible uses for an online, real-time system within the operational activities of a football team (or any other type of atheletic team). Assume that you are also employed at the AAZ Consulting Firm. Provide several suggestions to Jay concerning specific areas of athletic teams' (football teams, baseball teams, etc.) information systems where an online, real-time computer configuration might be beneficial to managerial decision making.

14-14. Sandown Power and Light Company (SP&L Co.) is an electric utility in the southwest United States. The demand for electricity is seasonal because of heavy air conditioning usage during the summer months. Currently, customers receive monthly bills for the amount of electricity they consumed during the previous month. The rates charged by SP&L Co. for the consumption of electricity are the same for all volume levels.

SP&L Co.'s assistant to the financial vice president has suggested that the company adopt an equal monthly billing system. Under this plan, the company will estimate a customer's total annual electrical needs for the coming year from past experience and bill the customer on the first of each month for one-twelfth this estimated amount. At the end of the billing year, SP&L will send a bill to the customer for the amount of electricity consumed in excess of the annual estimate or a check for the under usage. Thus, customers will receive a bill for the same amount each month and then either an additional bill or a reimbursement, depending on the customer's actual usage of electricity, at the end of the twelfth month. SP&L Co.'s rate structure for electricity consumption will not change with the new billing system.

The billing cycle would begin in November and end with October. The annual settlement would occur at the end of October.

1. Discuss the advantages and disadvantages of an equal monthly billing system for Sandown Power and Light Company. Include in your discussion the effect(s) of this billing system on SP&L's cash flow, accounts receivable balances, and profitability.

2. If you were a residential customer of SP&L Co. and had been offered a choice between the new equal monthly billing system and the current billing system, what would be the important factors that you would consider before reaching a decision as to which system to select?

14-15. The managers at BJW, Inc., have decided to purchase a $100,000 integrated accounting system that they project will reduce annual expenses by $40,000. Assume that the entire system has a five-year life with no salvage value and straight-line depreciation.

1. What is the system's payback period, ignoring taxes?

2. Assume a 50 percent income tax rate. What is the system's payback period now?

INTERNET EXERCISES

14-16. The term "feasibility analysis" means different things to different people. Use an Internet search engine to search for web sites containing this term. List at least three different meanings of this term and their sources. Did you find any web sites that were consistent with the concept discussed in this chapter?

14-17. Using your computer and the Internet, find a web site that discusses the use of CASE tools. Upon accessing the web site, write a summary of your findings and relate it to this chapter's subject matter. In addition, submit a printout of the web site information that you accessed.

14-18. Visit the web site of the Committee on Sponsoring Organizations (COSO) of the Tread-way commission at www.coso.org. What is the history of this organization (i.e., when was it founded and for what purpose)? Who is James Treadway? Select one of the publication reports or articles appearing on this web site and prepare your own report, summarizing its contents.

CASE ANALYSES

14-19. The Hometown Clippers (Designing Controls for the Ballpark)

Brent Gordon is the owner of a minor league baseball team that has now completed 60 games of its 140-game schedule. Brent is currently worried about two major problems: (1) low attendance at home games and (2) the strong possibility that many of his cashiers working at the ticket windows are pocketing portions of each game's cash receipts. To help solve these problems, Brent has hired an outside consultant, Cathy Bennett.

Cathy learns from the baseball team's traveling secretary that the business managers have tried many promotional activities in an effort to draw fans to home games. Most of these promotions, however, were financial disasters. For example, at one of last week's games, the franchise gave every paying customer a baseball autographed by the team. Even though a large crowd came to the ball park for this promotional event, the cost per baseball (approximately $4.50) exceeded the average ticket price paid by each customer (approximately $4.25) attending that night's game. Similarly, regarding the problem with the cashiers, the only suggestion that has been made by the baseball team's management is to fire all the cashiers and hire a completely new crew.

Assuming that you are Cathy Bennett, what are some possible suggestions that you could offer to solve the baseball team's two systems problems?

14-20. Milok Company (Integrating Microcomputers with a Mainframe)

Vincent Maloy, Director of Special Projects and Analysis for Milok Company, is responsible for preparing corporate financial analyses and projections monthly and for reviewing and presenting to upper management the financial impacts of proposed strategies. Data for these financial analyses and projections are obtained from reports developed by Milok's Systems Department and generated from its mainframe computer. Additional data are obtained through terminals via a data inquiry system. Reports and charts for presentations are then prepared by hand and typed. Maloy has tried to have final presentations generated by the computer but has not always been successful.

The Systems Department has developed a package utilizing a terminal emulator to link a microcomputer to the mainframe computer. This allows the microcomputer to become part of the current data inquiry system and enables data to be downloaded to the microcomputer's disk. The data are in a format that allows printing or further manipulation and analyses using commercial software packages (e.g., spreadsheet analysis). The Special Projects and Analysis Department has been chosen to be the first users of this new computer terminal system.

Maloy questioned whether the new system could do more for his department than implementing the program modification requests that he had submitted to the Systems Department. He also believed that his people would have to become programmers.

Lisa Brandt, a supervisor in Maloy's department, has decided to prepare a briefing for Maloy on the benefits of integrating microcomputers with the mainframe computer. She has used the terminal inquiry system extensively and has learned to use spreadsheet software to prepare special analyses, sometimes with multiple alternatives. She also tried the new package while it was being tested.

Requirements

1. Identify five enhancements to current information and reporting that Milok Company should be able to realize by integrating microcomputers with the company's mainframe computer.

2. Explain how the utilization of computer resources would be altered as a result of integrating microcomputers with the company's mainframe computer.

3. Discuss what security of the data is gained or lost by integrating microcomputers with the company's mainframe computer.

(CMA Adapted)

14-21. Kenbart Company (Redesigning Computerized Profit Plan Report)

The managers at Kenbart Company have decided that increased emphasis must be placed on profit planning and comparing "results" to "plans." A new computerized profit planning system has been implemented to help in this objective.

The company employs contribution margin reporting for internal reporting purposes and applies the concept of flexible budgeting for estimating variable costs. Kenbart's executive management uses the following terms when reviewing and analyzing actual results and the profit plan.

- Original Plan—Profit plan approved and adopted by management for the year
- Revised Plan—Original plan modified as a consequence of action taken during the year (usually quarterly) by executive management
- Flexed Revised Plan—The most current plan (i.e., either original plan or revised plan, if one has been prepared) adjusted for changes in volume and variable expense rates
- YTD Actual Results—The actual results of operations for the year
- Current Outlook—The summation of the actual year-to-date results of operations plus the flexed revised plan for the remaining months of the year

Executive management meets monthly to review the actual results compared with the profit plan. Any assumptions or major changes in the profit plan usually are incorporated on a quarterly basis once the first quarter is completed.

An outline of the basic Profit Plan Report, which was designed by the information processing subsystem, is reproduced in Figure 14-12. This report is prepared at the end of each month. In addition, this report is generated whenever executive management

Kenbart Company Profit Plan Report
Month, Year-to-Date

	Month				Year-to-Date			
			Over/(Under)				Over/(Under)	
	Actual	Plan	$	%	Actual	Plan	$	%
Sales								
Variable manufacturing costs								
Raw materials								
Direct labor								
Variable overhead								
Total variable manufacturing costs								
Manufacturing margin								
Variable selling expenses								
Contribution margin								
Fixed costs								
Manufacturing								
Sales								
General administration								
Income before taxes								
Income taxes								
Net Income								

FIGURE 14-12   Basic Profit Plan Report outline.

initiates a change or modification in its plans. Consequently, many different versions of the firm's profit plan exist, which makes analysis difficult and confusing.

Several members of executive management have voiced disapproval of the Profit Plan Report because the "Plan" column is not well defined and varies in meaning from one report to another. Furthermore, the report does not include a current-outlook column. Therefore, the accounting subsystem has been asked to work with the information processing subsystem in modifying the report so that users can better understand the information being conveyed and the reference points for comparison of results.

Requirements

1. What advantages are there to Kenbart Company from having its profit plan system computerized?

2. Redesign the layout of the Profit Plan Report so that it will be more useful to Kenbart's executive management in its task of reviewing results and planning operations. Explain the reason for each modification you make in the report.

3. What types of data would Kenbart Company be required to capture in its computer-based files to generate the plans and results that executive management reviews and analyzes?

14-22. Quadrant Controls Company (Recommending Control Procedures for Internal Control Risks)

Quadrant Controls Company designs, develops, and manufactures automated machinery for the apparel industry. The design and development of this machinery requires a considerable variety of fabrication materials in small quantities. For the past three years, the volume of activity in the Purchasing Department has risen dramatically. Management is concerned that a disproportionate increase in operating costs can be traced to this increased volume of activity. Lisa Lockwood, the Purchasing Department manager, has been asked by Bill May, vice president of manufacturing, to review the causes for the increased costs and offer some recommendations for reducing them. Lockwood's analysis reveals the following:

- The average cost of processing a purchase requisition, purchase order, receiving report, purchase invoice, or payment is $22 per order.
- Forty percent of all purchase orders issued by Quadrant Controls Company are for less than $50, with an average value of $28 each.
- The lag time in processing all of the purchasing-related paperwork results in a significant loss of cash discounts.

Lockwood's systems design recommendations to reduce costs include the following:
- Issue a company credit card to each departmental person who is authorized to purchase materials and supplies. The person would be responsible for ordering materials and supplies up to a maximum dollar amount of $50 per order and for confirming monthly charges. These changes would replace the usual purchase order system for materials and supplies. The company would automatically pay the monthly bill upon receipt unless told otherwise by the person responsible for the purchase.
- Take advantage of cash discounts on all other purchase orders because of lower volume and faster processing.

Based on the total estimated annual volume of 50,000 orders, Lisa Lockwood feels that the yearly cost savings from reduced paperwork will be $440,000 if 40 percent of the purchase orders are eliminated. After reviewing Lisa's recommendations, Bill May is pleased with the possibility of saving $440,000 in costs; however, he is concerned that the company would be exposed to greater internal control risks.

Requirements

1. Identify at least four internal control risks of implementing Lisa Lockwood's recommendations at Quadrant Controls Company.
2. For each risk identified in Question 1, recommend a control procedure to strengthen the overall internal control system at Quadrant Controls Company.

14-23. Stephen Kerr Cosmetics (Point Scoring Analysis)

Kerr Cosmetics distributes cosmetic products to large retailers across the country. The firm was started in 1975 by its first president, Stephen Kerr, who still serves as chairman of the board. Over the years, the company has grown in size and complexity. As the company has prospered, Richard Mason, the controller, has acquired and installed new accounting software to accommodate the increasing demands on the firm's accounting systems.

This year, Richard has convinced Stephen that it is time to upgrade their payroll system, which is now 7 years old. The company hires an outside consultant, who examines their situation and concludes that either one of two systems can meet their requirements. Richard therefore asks two of his most competent employees, Fritz Grupe and Meg Chrisman, to help him perform a point-scoring analysis and make a final choice.

The three individuals meet as a study team and agree upon five qualities for rating the two vendors: (1) need for further modifications, (2) ease of use, (3) strength of internal controls, (4) flexibility for updating and internet options, and (5) vendor support. To help them rate the two vendors on these five criteria, the committee invites representatives from each vendor to visit the company and make a presentation. Fritz makes arrangements for the presentation team from Vendor A to present on a Friday morning, and a similar team from Vendor B to visit that same afternoon. Unfortunately, an emergency makes it impossible for Richard to attend either presentation. Meg and Fritz attend both sessions, but come away with very different impressions of the competing software. The table below provides some relevant data.

Requirements

1. To start their analysis, Meg and Fritz decide to use their own ratings to perform separate point scoring analyses. For this part, use equal weightings of 0.2 for each category. Perform similar analyses using a spreadsheet. Which vendor does each person prefer?

2. Both Meg and Fritz decide that using equal weight for each category doesn't make sense. After some discussion, they agree to the alternate, "compromise weightings" shown here. They again perform their analyses. Which vendor does each person prefer now?

3. Fritz and Meg show their results to Richard, who suggests that they use their "compromise weights" but use combined averages for their "grades" for each vendor. They perform yet a third analysis. Which vendor receives the highest total now?

4. What do these exercises suggest about point scoring analyses? Does this method still seem "objective" to you? Why or why not?

	Equal Weights	Compromise Weights	Fritz's Ratings		Meg's Ratings	
			Vendor A	Vendor B	Vendor A	Vendor B
Required Modifications	0.2	0.2	3	2	3	3
Ease of Use	0.2	0.3	8	3	4	6
Internal Controls	0.2	0.1	3	4	2	4
Flexibility	0.2	0.1	4	5	3	7
Vendor Support	0.2	0.3	7	5	3	9

REFERENCES, RECOMMENDED READINGS, AND WEB SITES

References and Recommended Readings
Bartholomew, Doug, and Frank Hayes, "Utility's Bright Idea," *Information Week* (March 13, 1995), p. 28.

Booth, Stephen A., "Leading the Charge," *World Traveller* (January 1998), pp. 82–85, 120.

Bouwens, Jan, and Margaret A. Abernathy, "The Consequences of Customization on Management Accounting System Design" *Accounting, Organizations and Society,* vol. 25, No. 3 (April, 2000), p. 221.

Clague, Martin C., "Riding the New Wave of Computing," *Internal Auditor* (February 1995), pp. 18–20.

Collins, J. Carlton, "How to Select the Right Accounting Software," *Journal of Accountancy,* vol. 188, no. 3 (September 1999), pp. 31–38.

Drucker, Peter "Drucker: IT Hasn't Done Job" (an interview), *Computerworld,* vol. 33, no. 17 (April 1999), p. 51.

Eva, Malcolm, "Requirements Acquisition for Rapid Applications Development" *Information & Management,* vol. 39, no. 2 (December 2001), pp. 101–107.

Gawiser, Sheldon R., "Who's in Charge: CIO or CFO?" *Management Accounting* (October 1994), pp. 41–44.

Grannan, Philip P., "Electronic Commerce Today: Financial EDI Solutions for Tomorrow," *Management Accounting* (November 1997), pp. 38–41.

Hume, Stan, Tom DeVane, and Jill Smith Slater, "Transforming an Organization Through Prototyping: A Case Study" *Information Systems Management,* vol. 16, no. 4 (Fall, 1999), pp. 49–59.

Kaplan, Ronald E., "Automation of an Accounting Firm—A Case History," *CPA Journal* (December 1987), pp. 123–129.

Moynihan, Tony, "Coping With Requirements-Uncertainty: The Theories-of-Action of Experienced IS/Software Project Managers," *The Journal of Systems and Software,* vol. 53, no. 2 (August 31, 2000), pp. 99–109.

Roxas, Maria L., Lucia E. Peek, and George S. Peek, "Developing Multi-Objective Projects in the Accounting Curriculum: Sexual Harassment, Teamwork, Technology and Communication," *Issues in Accounting Education* (May 1998), pp. 383–393.

Seilheimer, Steven D., "Information Management During Systems Development: A Model for Improvement in Productivity" *International Journal of Information Management,* vol. 20, no. 4 (August 2000), pp. 287–295.

Web Sites

There are several web sites that help users select the right accounting software. One, entitled "Twenty Secrets of Software Selection," can be found at: www.ctsguides.com.small-business.asp. Another is a three-part article published by the Journal of Accountancy Online entitled "How to Select the Right Accounting Software," which may be found at www.aicpa.org/pubs/jofa/specialf.htm. Sections include "A Process for Evaluating the Best Packages for Your Organization," "How the Underlying Database Influences Price and Effectiveness," and "Handling the Web and International Commerce." There is also a special sidebar entitled "How to Contact the Vendors."

The computer vendors' guide can be found at the following web site: guide.sbanetweb.com/.

A bibliography of recent papers on prototyping can be found at: www.indiana.edu/viing/articles/prototyping/bib.html.

Information on the systems design research group is available by going to: info.1boro.ac.uk/departments/el/research/sys/index.html.

The home page for the Committee on Sponsoring Organizations (COSO) of the Treadway commission may be found at www.coso.org.

Chapter 15

Systems Study: Implementation, Follow-up, and Maintenance

INTRODUCTION

SYSTEMS IMPLEMENTATION

Implementation Activities

Program Evaluation and Review Technique (PERT)

Gantt Charts

Project Management Software

SYSTEMS FOLLOW-UP AND MAINTENANCE

Post-Implementation Review

System Maintenance

OUTSOURCING

Advantages of Outsourcing

Disadvantages of Outsourcing

AIS AT WORK: BLUE CROSS ABANDONS A RUNAWAY PROJECT

SUMMARY

KEY TERMS YOU SHOULD KNOW

DISCUSSION QUESTIONS

PROBLEMS

INTERNET EXERCISES

CASE ANALYSES

Intercontinental Airways

Audio Visual Corporation

Plocharski Company

Newton Industries Inc.

Family Health Care, Limited

Marshall Associates

REFERENCES, RECOMMENDED READINGS, AND WEB SITES

After reading this chapter, you will:

1. *Be familiar with* the activities required to implement a large information system.

2. *Understand* the difference between "direct conversion" and "parallel conversion" when installing a new system.

3. *Understand* how PERT network diagrams and Gantt charts help organizations implement new information systems.

4. *Be familiar with* systems follow-up and maintenance work.

5. *Understand* why organizations choose to outsource some of their IT tasks.

It's clear that corporate executives view business process outsourcing as a strategic tool that can help them to run their businesses more competitively, efficiently, and cost effectively.

Richard D. Dole of KPMG, in Kathy Williams, ed.,"Is Outsourcing Valuable?" *Management Accounting* (October 1997), p. 16.

INTRODUCTION

This chapter continues the systems studies described in Chapters 13 and 14. After an organization selects a specific system from a vendor (or develops its own), it must implement that system into its normal business activities. This chapter describes this implementation process in detail. But even when the implementation work is finished, a system study is not complete: the organization must also perform follow-up work to determine if the system is functioning as planned. The minor modifications and changes that organizations make in response to this follow-up work are called "maintenance," and this chapter examines these activities as well.

The individuals who implement a new AIS necessarily vary from project to project. For small systems, one possibility is for an outside consultant to do most of the work. In larger projects, a team of internal employees or outside consultants may be in charge. For discussion purposes, this chapter assumes that a generic "implementation team" headed by a "project leader" performs these tasks.

As an alternate to installing one or more information systems in-house, an organization can contract with one or more outside vendors to perform selected data processing tasks—for example, prepare payrolls or run web servers. This outsourcing alternative is useful, for example, to medical facilities whose primary focus is health care rather than computer processing, or to small businesses that lack the expertise, personnel, or interest in running a system for itself. The final part of this chapter discusses outsourcing in greater detail.

SYSTEMS IMPLEMENTATION

Systems implementation is often called the "action phase" of a systems study because the recommended changes from the prior analysis, design, and development work are now put into operation. But systems implementation can also be a stressful time. As the time draws near for installing a new system, end users and clerical personnel become nervous about their jobs, middle managers wonder whether the new system will deliver the benefits as promised, and top managers become impatient when installations run longer than anticipated or go over budget. Even if an organization has done a perfect job of analyzing, designing, and developing a new system, the entire project can fail if its implementation is poor. Here are some examples of what can go wrong:

- The new system is not fully developed or tested, but is installed anyway.
- The organization fails to budget sufficient time, money, and related resources to the installation tasks of the project.
- Complete system and application documentation is lacking, causing confusion and misunderstandings.
- Users are forced to use the new system without adequate training.
- The implementation team fails to test the new system, which turns out to have major "bugs" in it.
- After the initial installation is completed, the organization fails to evaluate the system's performance, especially against the original objectives.
- The organization fails to allocate sufficient resources for system maintenance. Over time, the new system deteriorates and becomes ineffective.

Case-in-Point 15.1   In 1999, the State of Nevada finally installed its proprietary Genesis system to handle the Department of Motor Vehicles (DMV) registration tasks. But the system was implemented without adequate system testing or user training. As a result, DMV employees were unfamiliar with the new procedures required to perform what used to be simple tasks and began to spend hours with Nevada residents wishing to register their vehicles. Long lines formed in front of DMV counters, waits of up to eight hours became common, and complaints about the system became so bitter that the governor had to reassign additional personnel to DMV offices.

Implementation Activities

What are the tasks required in a systems implementation project? In this section, we illustrate them using the BSM project discussed in Chapters 13 and 14—a web-based, order-entry system for retail customers. Here, we assume that BSM will purchase and install its own hardware and operating system software, and hire its own IT staff to create and maintain its web system. These activities are listed in Figure 15-1. The following discussions describe the implementation activities of Figure 15-1 in greater detail.

Activity A: Prepare the Physical Site   An organization must have physical space for any new hardware and personnel. If it can allocate existing space, the work required to prepare the physical site may not be too time-consuming or difficult. If it involves major construction or structural modifications, however, the incremental costs in time and money can be much larger. Similarly, the time required to complete these tasks necessarily varies, but (for BSM) it certainly includes the time required to order and receive hardware and software, string cabling through buildings and walls, arrange for Internet access, supply regular and backup power, and so forth. Similar concerns apply to the office space required for new employees.

Activity B: Determine the Functional Changes   Whenever a company makes major changes to a major accounting system, it must also consider the effects of such changes on its reporting structure and personnel relationships. Otherwise, problems with the new information system are inevitable. These problems often deal with personnel and their organizational assignments before and after a new system becomes operational.

Activity	Estimated Time (in weeks)	Predecessor Activities	Description of Activity
A	17	None	Prepare the physical site location for the delivery of the computer system.
B	14	None	Determine the necessary functional changes in the system.
C	2	B	Select and assign personnel.
D	6	C	Train personnel.
E	1	A	Acquire and install new computer equipment.
F	7	B	Establish controls.
G	6	E, F	Convert data files to computer storage media.
H	6	E, F	Acquire computer software.
I	5	H	Test computer software.
J	26	D, G, I	Test new system's operational capabilities by parallel conversion and eliminate old system.

FIGURE 15-1   Systems implementation activities.

At BSM, the new web system will enable customers to create their own orders online, thus permitting the company to reduce its order-taking staff by an estimated four positions. But BSM's new system will also require the services of several new IT personnel and will also affect the company's work flow. For example, the new system will route new orders directly to the shipping department rather than through the accounting department. Some accounting personnel will therefore have to be retrained to handle the new order flow as well as the new procedures for handling canceled orders, returns, misshipments, and so forth.

Case-in-Point 15.2   Blue Cross and Blue Shield chose to have its own technical staff develop a new $200 million computerized system for handling all aspects of its business operations. But these staffers did not understand the company's business requirements, and the system failed to work properly once it was implemented. Problems included sending hundreds of checks to a nonexistent town, making $60 million in overpayments, and other snafus that lost the company 35,000 clients. When the system's problems were analyzed, one major observation was that its implementation did not include a restructuring of the organization. When this restructuring was finally performed, one outcome was eliminating three layers of management personnel.

Activity C: Select and Assign Personnel   Because the design team has developed detailed specifications for the new system, the organization should also have a firm idea at this point about the job descriptions of system users. But because implementation projects also spur false rumors among employees about the changes involved, organizational morale can deteriorate. To deal with this problem, members of the implementation team and steering committee should communicate openly with affected workers about how the new system will impact them. Organizations should give those employees whose jobs are either eliminated or materially altered an opportunity to apply for the new jobs and obtain retraining, if necessary. Similarly, terminated employees should receive ample notice to enable them to apply for other jobs before their employment ends. Some companies even set up internal outplacement offices for displaced employees or create early retirement plans for qualified employees.

Where highly technical job functions must be performed in a company's new system, it may be impossible to fill vacancies with current employees. This is the situation for BSM, which must hire several new technically qualified employees from outside the company to develop and run its new web system. Computer vendors can often help locate personnel with the specialized knowledge needed to perform computer-related job functions.

Activity D: Train Personnel   Both the implementation team and computer vendors can help train company employees to work with the new system, while seminars can acquaint other employees with the new system's advantages and capabilities. They should give specific procedural training to those employees whose job functions are altered as a result of the system revisions. This training can take place either in a classroom (where training approaches such as case studies and videotaped presentations may be used) or on the job.

The newly hired IT employees may also require training, even though they already possess a general knowledge of web development and Internet programming. For example, these employees may require orientation classes about their new company, instruction that familiarizes them with the other systems with which the new system will interface, or even programming classes that teach new skills in specific computer languages or applications. Vendors often provide such technical training for free, or at reduced costs, to corporate users as incentives to use their products (see Internet Exercise 15-21). If the computer equipment or software is not yet installed on the company's premises, the vendor (or an independent training company) may be able to provide training at its own facilities.

Activity E: Acquire and Install Computer Equipment   After preparing the physical site location for the new computer system (activity A), the company must acquire computer equipment such as microcomputers, web servers, routers, modems, and printers from outside vendors (Figure 15-2). Although a vendor may have the major responsibility for installing computer equipment, internal employees and IT staffers may also participate in this task. At BSM, for example, the internal IT staff will have to decide where to place particular devices and perhaps coordinate the physical connections among the various computer and communications devices it has acquired from its equipment vendors and Internet provider.

Activity F: Establish Internal Controls   In addition to determining the functional changes for the new system (activity B), an organization must install control procedures that safeguard its assets, ensure the accuracy and reliability of accounting data, promote operating efficiency, and encourage employee compliance with prescribed managerial policies. Examples of general controls include personnel controls, file security controls, and computer facility controls. Examples of application controls include edit tests that check input data for accuracy and completeness, control totals for processing data, and forms controls for sensitive outputs such as vendor or payroll checks. As noted in Chapter 14, all of these controls should be *built into a system* rather than added later.

Controls that ensure continuity of service are particularly important to BSM because the success of its web-based order-entry system relies on round-the-clock operation. Thus, IT staffers will need to develop backup procedures, disaster recovery plans, and obtain one or more uninterruptible power supplies (UPSs). Similarly, BSM

FIGURE 15-2 This web server from Hewlett Packard (HP) includes current Pentium processor chips, up to 12 SCSI disk drives (for storing web pages), and up to 1 gigabyte of RAM memory.

will depend heavily on application controls because untrained customers, rather than knowledgeable staff members, will input data to the system. Two additional problems that BSM must consider are (1) automaing the process of verifying credit card numbers while a customer is online, and (2) deciding how to disallow web sales to uncreditworthy customers.

Activity G: Convert Data Files When converting to a new system, an organization may have to convert its data files to newer, more-useful formats. For small companies converting from manual to computerized systems, for example, the data stored in ledgers, journals, and similar manual media must be input to newly created databases. But even where data files are already computerized, organizations may need to modify record formats, form layouts, and similar inputs and outputs to accommodate new information requirements.

This concern may be particularly important for BSM and its web-based order-entry system. For example, this company may want to let online customers know if a particular product is immediately available for purchase or, alternately, is on back order. BSM already has a competent inventory database that contains a balance-on-hand field for each of its retail items. But it may now want to expand the record format of its inventory records to include an "on-order" field that totals the number of units of the product in unfulfilled customer orders. The new system can then compute the difference between the balances in these two fields to determine whether a new order for this product must wait for shipment.

Activity H: Acquire Computer Software The implementation team must also install the software that was acquired or developed for the project. The software from independent vendors is often called **canned software,** which sometimes comes bundled (i.e., combined) with hardware in complete **turnkey systems.** Integrated, turnkey accounting systems are especially appealing to small businesses such as dry-cleaning establishments or travel agencies because they enable their owners to avoid the technical tasks of finding and matching hardware and software components for themselves. However, many large companies now also use commercially available software, leaving only the largest organizations with unique processing requirements to develop their own accounting software.

Case-in-Point 15.3 A recent survey by Deloitte & Touche concluded that a large majority of CIOs (chief information officers) plan to replace their current accounting systems with commercial packages rather than develop them inhouse. This explains why Pacific Gas & Electric Company signed a $750,000 contract to acquire Dun & Bradstreet's General Ledger software to replace its proprietary general ledger system. It also explains why Lockheed Aeromod Center, an aircraft maintenance services company, signed a contract for $1 million to obtain this same General Ledger system and related professional services from that company. Finally, approximately 90 percent of Dow Chemical's software systems are canned packages that the company acquired from independent vendors and modified to match its specific business needs.

BSM will need software for its Internet system, especially programming modules that will allow its new order-entry system to interface with its existing accounting systems and customer databases. For example, every order that a customer places online creates a sales transaction for BSM's accounts receivable system, an inventory transaction for the warehouse, and a shipping transaction for the shipping department. The company will therefore need to decide how to generate these items and develop software for them. (At first, some companies simply have their web systems print manual orders, which they can then process through normal channels. But this makes little sense in today's era of automation, and BSM in particular wants a modern, streamlined system.)

In general, the process of acquiring (and possibly making modifications to) computer programs from an independent vendor takes considerably less time than developing the programs inhouse. Thus, we shall assume here that BSM can develop and install the basic software interfaces in a short amount of time (i.e., six weeks for activity H in Figure 15-1). But, as in most projects, the work of developing better interfaces, creating new enhancements, and "tweaking" the system will probably be ongoing tasks that may take years.

Activity I: Test Computer Software   Software testing is closely related to the previous activity of acquiring computer software. Programs must be tested regardless of where they came from or who wrote them in order to ensure day-to-day processing accuracy and completeness. Three methods for testing computer software are (1) unit testing, (2) process testing, and (3) acceptance testing. With **unit testing,** the individual programs of a system are each tested as separate components. An advantage of unit testing is the ability to test modules independently, as their developers finish them. A disadvantage is that the tests must necessarily examine programs in isolation, and therefore do not test the compatibility of the programs with one another (called **system testing**).

With **process testing,** the objective is to determine whether a complete set of computer programs operate as they should. Thus, the implementation team first develops hypothetical test transactions (and, where necessary, hypothetical file records) in order to create all processing scenarios and conceivable errors. For every test transaction, the correct system response must be known in advance to evaluate the test results. The team then has the system process the test transactions to see if it deals with them properly and detects and handles the errors.

With **acceptance testing,** the new system's users, rather than the implementation team, develops test transactions and acceptance criteria for the new system. Rather than using hypothetical transactions and hypothetical file records, however, acceptance testing normally uses real transactions and real file records. After processing a selection of transactions with the new system, the users will review the results and decide if the program is "acceptable."

Activity J: Conversion The implementation team has now completed all prior activities, and the new system is ready to take over operations. Three changeover possibilities are (1) direct conversion, (2) parallel conversion, or (3) modular conversion. With **direct conversion,** the organization immediately discontinues using the old system and the new system "sinks or swims." Most microcomputer users install new software in this manner.

Direct conversion is relatively inexpensive and may be useful under the following circumstances: (1) the old system has so many weaknesses that parallel conversion (discussed below) serves no useful purpose, (2) the new system is really a modification of an old one with only minor revisions, (3) the new system differs drastically from the old one, thereby making comparisons between the two systems meaningless, or (4) the new system adds new functionality and there really isn't any "replacement." However, "direct conversion" is a dangerous process whose risks increase with the importance of the system to the overall mission of the organization.

Case-in-Point 15.4 The Bank of America hired a software vendor to replace the 20-year-old batch processing system it was using to manage institutional trust accounts worth billions of dollars. After two years of development, the bank immediately switched over to the new software system (consisting of 2.5 million lines of code), despite warnings that the new system had not been adequately tested. During the ten months the new system was in operation, the bank lost 100 institutional accounts, which in turn contained $4 billion in assets. Within a year, the bank's top systems and trust executives had resigned, the bank took a $60 million writeoff to cover the expenses related to the software system, and the new system was scrapped.

Rather than immediately replace an old but working system with a new but untested one, many companies take a more-gradual approach and employ **parallel conversion.** Using this method, an organization operates both the old system and the new system simultaneously (or "in parallel") for a certain period of time. The implementation team then compares the outputs from each system, reconciles any differences, and corrects any remaining errors before fully adopting the new system. The time necessary for parallel conversion depends on the number of processing discrepancies and the time required to correct errors. In addition to testing for processing discrepancies under the parallel conversion method, the implementation team should also test the new system's controls (established in activity F) to make sure they are functioning as planned.

Perhaps the biggest advantage of parallel conversion is an organization's ability to operate normally during the transition period, with minimal disruptions to normal business work. This is important for companies such as banks, utility companies, and resort casinos where daily operations are critical and major disruptions are intolerable. The biggest disadvantage of parallel conversion is its cost. For example, when processing accounting transactions, each transaction must be processed by both the old and new systems throughout the conversion period. The resources required to handle this dual workload place a drain on an organization—for example, overtime costs.

Finally, with **modular conversion** (or **pilot conversion**), the implementation team divides the users involved in a specific data processing task (such as processing inventory transactions) into smaller units or modules. The team then installs the new data processing system "piecemeal," module by module. For example, if a company has five separate divisions that each purchase and sell inventory, the team can treat each division as a separate module. The team then implements the new inventory system for only one of the five divisions (sometimes called the **beta site**). After satisfactorily testing the computerized inventory system's operation in this division, and perhaps making modifications, the team then implements the system for the second division. Successful results now allow for implementation in the third division, and so on.

The major advantage of modular conversion is the ability to isolate any specific problems that are discovered in a new system to only one module, which can therefore be corrected before implementing the system further. A drawback of modular conversion is the long time period normally required to complete the entire implementation process.

Program Evaluation and Review Technique (PERT)

The preceding section made clear that there are many tasks involved in implementing a new accounting system. Moreover, an organization cannot perform these tasks randomly, but rather must complete them in a logical sequence (i.e., by performing some tasks before others). A good analogy is to building a house, which requires completing the foundation, subfloors, and load-bearing walls before putting on the roof. Alternately, if an organization does not plan its systems implementation in an orderly fashion, the project's coordination is almost sure to suffer and its completion may be prolonged unreasonably.

PERT (Program Evaluation and Review Technique) is a technique for scheduling and monitoring the activities involved in large projects—for example, building a bridge or moving corporate offices from one location to another. PERT is therefore also useful for planning and controlling the activities involved in implementing a new information system in an organization. To begin, the project leader first prepares a list of systems implementation activities, identifies the prerequisite activities that must be completed before others can start, and estimates the amount of time required to complete each activity. The tasks outlined above and summarized in Figure 15-1 provide an example.

Using the data in Figure 15-1, the project leader can then sequence the activities in a PERT network diagram, such as the one illustrated in Figure 15-3. The lines with arrows in this diagram conventionally flow from left to right and represent the activities required to implement the system. The circles (called *nodes*) in the diagram represent project milestones—i.e., the starting points or completions of specific activities—and therefore do not require any time. In Figure 15-3, node 1 represents the beginning of the implementation project, and node 8 represents its completion. Because neither activity A nor activity B requires any predecessor activities (refer back to Figure 15-1), both activities can begin simultaneously at node 1. This means that, assuming there is adequate staffing, team members will work in parallel on both tasks A and B. Similarly, once the team completes Activity B (with an estimated completion time of 14 weeks—at node 2), activities C and F can begin. The project leader continues to draw the PERT chart in this manner.

Top managers may not be interested in PERT analyses, but they are usually very concerned about the time required to finish the entire project. The project leader can estimate this completion time by examining the various paths in the PERT network. To illustrate the logic for this, note that in Figure 15-3, both routes B-F and A-E must be completed to reach node 5. So what is the earliest time the activities beginning from node 5 can start? Because path B-F takes 21 weeks (= 14 weeks + 7 weeks) while path A-E takes 18 weeks (= 17 weeks + 1 week), the answer is "21 weeks." Why is the an-

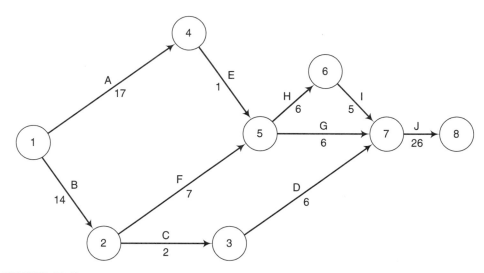

FIGURE 15–3 PERT network diagram for a systems implementation project.

swer "21 weeks" and not "17 weeks?" The reason is because the team must complete all predecessor activities before the next activities can begin. In other words, the earliest start time for a node is equal to the longest path from node 1 to this milestone.

To estimate the completion time for the entire project, the project leader must find the longest path from node 1 (the start of the project) to node 8 in our example. Because PERT diagrams in actual practice are so large (often covering entire walls!), project leaders normally use a computer to identify the longest paths through such networks. The diagram in Figure 15-3 is relatively small, so we can determine the answer by enumerating all the possibilities:

A—E—H—I—J	= 55 weeks (17 + 1 + 6 + 5 + 26)
A—E—G—J	= 50 weeks (17 + 1 + 6 + 26)
B—F—H—I—J	= 58 weeks (14 + 7 + 6 + 5 + 26)
B—F—G—J	= 53 weeks (14 + 7 + 6 + 26)
B—C—D—J	= 48 weeks (14 + 2 + 6 + 26)

The project leader now knows that the earliest the implementation team can complete the entire project is 58 weeks, and reports this to the steering committee. Because the most time-consuming path is B-F-H-I-J, the project leader also knows that delays in any activity on this path will also delay the entire project. For this reason, this longest-path is called the **critical path,** and the project leader will closely monitor the work on each critical-path activity to avoid setbacks.

A related question is "how much extra time is there for each noncritical activity?" The term **slack time** describes this—i.e., the amount of delay time that can occur in each noncritical activity and still not delay the entire project. Obviously, the greater the slack time for an activity, the less closely that activity has to be monitored, and vice versa. Because delays in critical-path activities will automatically delay the entire project, the slack times for all critical-path activities are always zero.

To determine the slack time of an activity, compute the activity's earliest and latest possible completion times. The difference between these two estimates is that activity's slack time. To illustrate, let's look at activity G. From Figure 15-3, we can tell that the earliest possible completion time for activity G is "27 weeks" (= B + F + G = 14 + 7 + 6). To determine the latest possible completion time for activity G, take the project's total estimated implementation time (= 58 weeks) and subtract the time required to complete all the activities following it. In Figure 15-3, the latest possible time for completing activity G is "32 weeks," which we determine as follows: 58 weeks (the estimated completion time for the entire project) minus the 26 weeks for completing activity J (the only activity performed after activity G). The slack time for activity G is therefore "5 weeks" (= 32 weeks - 27 weeks). Again, the usefulness of slack time computations is to enable the project leader to determine which activities are critical, which are "near-critical," and which can sustain larger time delays.

As a project moves forward, it is only natural that the completion times of some activities will not coincide precisely with the values in the original PERT diagram. This is because the diagram numbers are only *estimates,* not certainties, of activity completion times. In the course of events, some activities will finish sooner than these estimates, while unforeseen delays on others are inevitable. Knowing the slack time for each activity helps a project leader keep large-scale implementations on track. In particular, as long as the delay for a particular activity does not exceed that activity's slack time, the project leader knows that the implementation team can still complete the entire project "on time" (i.e., in 58 weeks for the project in Figure 15-3). Alternately, if a problem causes a delay that exceeds the activity's slack time, then that activity becomes critical, requiring the project leader to compute a new critical path and reevaluate everything.

As the implementation team performs specific activities, it also provides feedback reports to the steering committee that compare actual implementation times with planned times. These reports enable both parties to focus on delays in completing specific activities and to estimate what effect these delays may have on the entire installation project. If, for example, a specific critical activity is behind schedule, the project leader may allocate additional human resources to speed its completion. Alternately, if another activity is ahead of schedule, the project leader may reduce the resources assigned to it and use them elsewhere. Where a project leader can make time-cost tradeoffs in a project, the analysis is known as PERT/Cost.

Gantt Charts

Another tool that an organization can use in planning and controlling a systems implementation project is a **Gantt chart** (Figure 15-4). Gantt charts are useful for both scheduling and tracking the activities of systems implementation projects because actual progress can be indicated directly on the Gantt chart and contrasted with the planned progress.

Gantt charts are straightforward, easy to understand, and can be used with PERT to compare estimated completion times against actual ones. A disadvantage of Gantt charts is that they do not indicate the relationships among the project activities, as do PERT charts. Rather, a Gantt chart treats each activity as if it were independent of the others, which of course is not really the case. For this reason, Gantt charts are better suited for systems implementation projects that are not highly complex and have relatively few interrelationships among implementation activities. Also, in most projects, there is the "human element:"

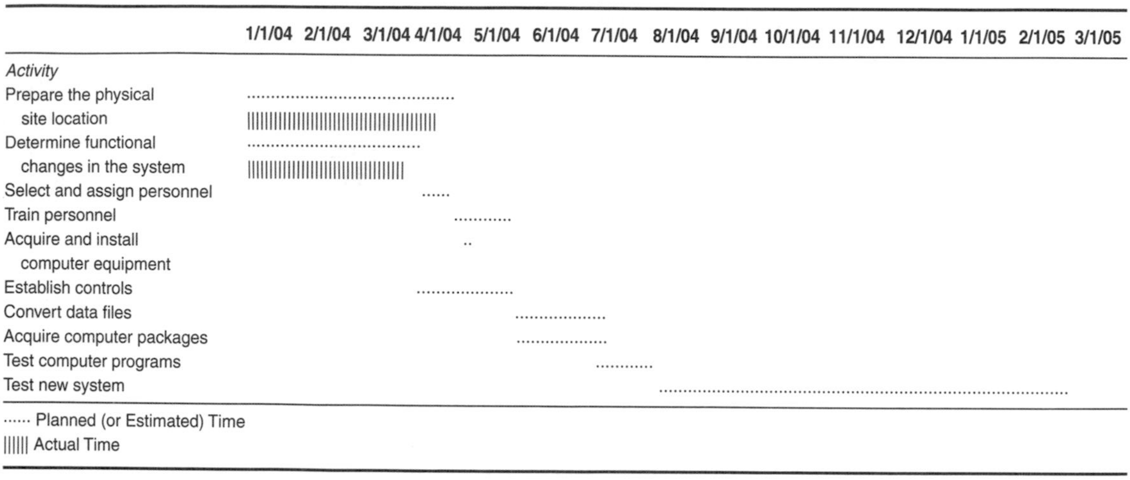

Activity	1/1/04	2/1/04	3/1/04	4/1/04	5/1/04	6/1/04	7/1/04	8/1/04	9/1/04	10/1/04	11/1/04	12/1/04	1/1/05	2/1/05	3/1/05
Prepare the physical site location	······	······	··												
	‖‖‖‖‖‖	‖‖‖‖‖	‖‖‖												
Determine functional changes in the system	······	······	··												
	‖‖‖‖‖	‖‖‖‖‖													
Select and assign personnel					······										
Train personnel					······										
Acquire and install computer equipment					··										
Establish controls				······											
Convert data files						······									
Acquire computer packages						······									
Test computer programs							······								
Test new system								··········	······	······	······	······	······	······	······

······ Planned (or Estimated) Time
‖‖‖‖‖ Actual Time

FIGURE 15–4 Gantt chart for systems implementation activities.

Case-in-Point 15.5 In her first job as a project leader, a 22-year-old IT professional was placed in charge of two 50-year-old male programmers and what she estimated with a Gantt chart was a three-month systems project. After meeting with the programmers, she was delighted to learn that they were "80-percent done." She updated her chart accordingly and reported this fact to her supervisor. Nine months later, the project was still "80-percent completed." It was only after several beers on a Friday night she learned that these programmers had been "yanking her chain" for all those months and had only now agreed to finish the project. The following Monday, the project was done, and the project leader learned the importance of "verifying deliverables" when using Gantt charts.

Project Management Software

As noted above, PERT diagrams can become complex, making the calculations required to compute and recompute critical paths and slack times difficult. **Project management software** that runs on microcomputers can perform these tasks easily and quickly, thus enabling a project leader to plan and control implementation tasks and helping a team install a new system on time and within budget. Examples of project management packages include *Harvard Total Project Manager, Superproject, Microsoft Project,* and *Time Line.*

Project management software requires users to break down complex projects into smaller, simpler activities and to estimate the time, cost, and other resources required for each of them. The project leader then enters these estimates into the computer running the project software, along with the precedence relationships associated with the various activities. The software can then schedule tasks, identify critical and noncritical activities, compute slack times, and so forth. Project management software also allows the project leader to perform **what-if analyses**—for example, to experiment with different systems implementation work schedules or determine how delays in specific activities are likely to affect other project tasks.

Case-in-Point 15.6 Thomas Brothers Maps, Inc., uses project management software to schedule the more than 250 projects it undertakes every year. This software indicates when additional employees are needed and determines when each job will be completed based on personnel assignments. The project management software also provides relevant data, such as payroll information, to the company.

SYSTEMS FOLLOW-UP AND MAINTENANCE

Regardless of which conversion method is employed, the new system will eventually become the sole system in operation. This brings us to the final, **follow-up and maintenance phase** of our systems development life cycle. The purpose of this phase is to monitor the new system and make sure that it continues to satisfy the three levels of organizational goals discussed in Chapter 13: (1) general systems goals, (2) top management systems goals, and (3) operating management systems goals. When these goals are not adequately satisfied, problems normally occur and the system requires further modifications to address them.

Post-Implementation Review

After the new system has been in operation for a period of time (one year, for example), the implementation team should reevaluate the new system's effectiveness by gathering data in the following areas:

- Talking with top management personnel and operating management personnel about their satisfaction with the new system.
- Talking with end users to ascertain their satisfaction.
- Evaluating the control procedures of the system to verify whether they are functioning properly.
- Observing employee work performance to determine whether they are able to perform their job functions efficiently and effectively.
- Evaluating whether computer processing functions, including data capture and preparation, are performed efficiently and effectively.
- Determining whether output schedules for both internal and external reports are met with the new computer system.

At the conclusion of the initial follow-up study, the project leader prepares a report called a **post-implementation review report** for the steering committee that summarizes the implementation team's findings. As Figure 13-1 of Chapter 13 illustrated, follow-up studies can lead in one of two directions. If the implementation team is satisfied that the new system is working satisfactorily, no further revisions are required. If follow-up studies reveal that problems still exist in the new system, however, the team will communicate these findings to the steering committee and perhaps recommend further systems studies. Upon receiving approval from the steering committee, the organization will then perform the systems study steps again with the objective of making revisions to the system.

A post-implementation review is also beneficial to the implementation team. At this point in the systems development life cycle, the team members are now in a position to evaluate their own work, learn from the mistakes they made or successfully avoided, and become more skilled "systems people" in future engagements.

System Maintenance

In practice, implementation teams do not normally perform follow-up studies of their company's new information system. Instead, the team turns over control of the system to the company's IT subsystem, which now shoulders the responsibility for maintaining it. In effect, therefore, **system maintenance** continues the tasks created by the initial follow-up study, except that experts from the company's IT subsystem now perform the modifications exclusively. When, for example, users complain about errors or anomalies in the new system, it becomes the IT subsystem's responsibility to respond to these needs, estimate the cost of fixing them, and (often) perform the necessary modifications. The IT departments of even medium-size companies typically have forms for such requests, policies for prioritizing maintenance tasks, and formulas for allocating maintenance costs among the various user departments.

It is common for business systems to require continuous revisions. For example, because of increased competition or new governmental regulations, the information needs of top management personnel may change, requiring further revisions to the new system. In fact, studies show that, over the life of a typical information system, organizations spend only about 20 to 30 percent of the total system costs developing and implementing it. They spend the remaining 70 to 80 percent maintaining it (Figure 15-5)—for example, on further modifications or software updates. In other words, "maintenance" may not be the most glamorous part of a systems development life cycle, but it is almost always the most expensive part. For this reason, smart systems teams try to develop or acquire **flexible systems**—that is, systems that are easily modified—because such systems save businesses money in the long run (even if they cost more in the short run).

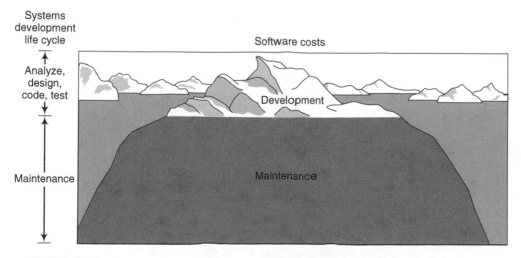

FIGURE 15–5 In the systems development life cycle, the costs of analysis, design, development, and implementation are often just the tip of the iceberg: software maintenance costs are the most expensive part.

Case-in-Point 15.7   Approximately 70 percent of Hartford Insurance Group's personnel resources are devoted to maintaining its existing information systems, including over 34,000 computer program modules containing 24 million lines of COBOL code. These maintenance tasks have become increasingly difficult over time because prior modifications to accommodate changes in insurance regulations and business strategies have complicated the code and made it more difficult to revise.

OUTSOURCING

With **outsourcing,** a company hires an outside organization to handle all or part of its data processing tasks. Examples of major outsourcing organizations are Electronic Data Systems, IBM, ADP Digital Equipment, and Computer Sciences Corporation. The degree to which a company outsources its data processing work can range from routine assistance with a single application such as payroll to running the entire IT department.

Outsourcing contracts are typically signed for five to ten years. Annual costs depend on the amount of data processing work to be performed and range from "thousands" to "millions" of dollars. When a large company decides to outsource its IT functions, it is not uncommon for the vendor to purchase all of its clients' hardware and software, and hire almost all of that company's IT employees. The outsourcing organization then operates and manages the client company's entire information systems, either on the client's site or by migrating the client's systems to its own computers.

Case-in-Point 15.8   A large producer of natural gas signed a $750 million contract with Electronic Data Systems (EDS) to operate and manage the company's information systems. EDS purchased the producer's computers, software, and transmission network, and hired all 550 of the company's information systems staff at comparable wages and benefits. The corporation pays EDS a fixed monthly fee plus additional fees based on processing volume. During the ten-year life of the contract, the managers estimated that outsourcing will save the company $200 million.

Advantages of Outsourcing

Why do organizations outsource their IT functions? Among the advantages are (1) an attractive business solution, (2) effective use of assets, (3) lower costs, (4) avoids seasonal fluctuations, and (5) facilitates downsizing.

Attractive Business Solution   For some companies, outsourcing is an attractive business solution rather than simply an information systems solution. Case-in-Point 15.9 illustrates this advantage for Eastman Kodak.

Case-in-Point 15.9   The top managers at Eastman Kodak believe that their company should focus on what it does best—selling film and cameras—and thus transferred most of its data processing operations to three outsourcing organizations. Thus, the company sold its mainframes to IBM to perform its data procesing functions, outsourced its telecommunications functions to Digital Equipment, and transferred its microcomputer operations to Businessland. The results have been dramatic. Capital expenditures for computers have fallen 90 percent, operating expenses have declined between 10 percent and 20 percent, and the company projects annual savings of about $130 million over the ten-year life of its contracts.

Effective Use of Assets Many companies have millions of dollars invested in information systems technology. Because technology is continually changing, the information systems function can be a major drain on cash as organizations invest millions to keep up with advancing technologies. To relieve this cash drain, a number of companies are trying outsourcing, with the hope that the cash made available from outsourcing can be used more effectively.

Lower Costs The cost-effectiveness of outsourcing comes in part from the cost savings that outsourcing companies achieve with economies of scale. These economies include buying computer hardware at wholesale prices, standardizing user applications, spreading development and maintenance costs among several clients, and operating at higher, more-efficient activity volumes. An example is a web-server company ("web farm") that maintains web pages for clients and can thus operate the same hardware and software for several clients almost as cheaply as it can for a single client. Furthermore, outsourcing fees can all be written off for income tax purposes in the year incurred, thus reducing federal and state income taxes.

Avoid Seasonal Fluctuations Like ice cream sales and ski resort operations, many corporate businesses are seasonal. When a company's sales are seasonal, so are some of its data processing operations. Outsourcing enables such businesses to stabilize their processing costs—especially the hiring and termination costs of fluctuating personnel requirements—by paying outsourcing organizations fixed monthly fees plus additional fees based on the volume of items processed.

Facilitate Downsizing Downsizing may leave a company with an IT staff and related resources that are much larger than it now needs. In such cases, outsourcing may be a viable alternative for those organizations that now have more-limited processing requirements.

> *Case-in-Point 15.10* General Dynamics was compelled to downsize drastically in the early 1990s due to reduced spending in the defense industry. But even after cutting a thousand IT jobs, the company's information systems department was still too large–a bitter pill for a company whose information systems function was rated number one in the aerospace industry in both 1989 and 1990. Thus, management decided to outsource its information systems operations by signing a ten-year contract with Computer Sciences Corporation (CSC). General Dynamics sold all of its data processing centers to CSC for $200 million and relocated the 2,600 employees working in them to CSC.

Disadvantages of Outsourcing

Although the advantages of outsourcing are compelling, outsourcing is not always the best alternative for every organization. Here are some disadvantages.

Inflexibility The typical outsourcing contract requires a company to commit to services for an extended time period, with a ten-year contract being the most common. Should the contracting company become dissatisfied with the services it receives during this period of time, however, it is usually difficult to break the agreement. And even if the outsourcing contract contains a termination clause, the company may still be locked into outsourcing itself—for example, because it has already sold its data processing centers and terminated its IT staff.

Loss of Control   When an outsourcing vendor performs a significant portion of an organization's data processing, that organization loses control of its information systems data and processing. For example, the contracting company can no longer control its data, data errors, or other processing irregularities that occur from the outsourcer's processing work. This is an especially important problem if the data are sensitive or vulnerable to abuse.

Reduced Competitive Advantage   A company's information systems should continue to evolve, thereby adding value to the company and contributing to its long-term goals. However, when a company uses an outsourcing organization to process its data over extended periods of time, that company can lose a basic understanding of its own information system needs or how its information systems provide it with competitive advantages.

AIS AT WORK
Blue Cross Abandons a Runaway Project

Blue Cross and Blue Shield of Massachusetts hoped that its new "System 21" would usher in a new era. However, after six years and $120 million, the project was behind schedule and significantly over budget. Blue Cross managers therefore canceled the project and turned its computer operations over to Electronic Data Systems, an outsourcing organization.

Although information system failures of this magnitude are rare, they happen more often than one would expect. According to a KPMG Peat Marwick survey, 35 percent of all major information system projects become a "runaway"—that is, a project that is millions of dollars over budget and months or years behind schedule.

One major reason for the systems study problems at Blue Cross was the company's failure to properly supervise the information system project. Blue Cross hired an independent vendor to develop the software but failed to appoint someone to coordinate and manage the project. In addition, top management did not establish a firm set of priorities that stated which features of the information system were essential and which applications should be developed first.

When the independent vendor presented the claims-processing software to Blue Cross, the vendor thought the software was a finished product. However, the managers and users at Blue Cross had other ideas. They were not happy with the software and requested numerous changes, delaying the entire project and resulting in ever-increasing cost overruns. By the time System 21 was implemented, Blue Cross had fallen way behind its competitors in its ability to process an ever-swelling load of paperwork. As a result, between 1985 and 1991, Blue Cross lost a million subscribers and came close to bankruptcy. It also had a poorly integrated system, including nine different claims processing systems running on hardware dating back to the early 1970s.

The lesson that Blue Cross learned with System 21 was a painful one. It had to abandon a system it had spent six years developing and seek an outside vendor to bail it out. Fortunately, although the information system died, the patient survived.

Source: Geoffery Smith, "The Computer System That Nearly Hospitalized an Insurer," *Business Week* (June 15, 1992), p. 133.

SUMMARY

Systems implementation, follow-up, and maintenance are the final parts of a system study. Systems implementation encompasses the many tasks involved in installing and testing a new system. One such task is to prepare the physical site for new computer hardware and personnel. At the same time, the implementation team must determine what functional changes are necessary. After completing this activity, the organization can select, assign, and train personnel—work that is particularly important because the human element is usually so crucial to the success of a new system. The remaining implementation activities include acquiring and installing computer hardware and software, establishing internal controls, converting data files, testing computer programs, and finally, placing the new system in operation.

In large projects, organizations often use PERT (program evaluation and review technique) to organize, plan, and control the activities in this phase of the project. A PERT diagram depicts the logical sequence of conversion activities and also includes time estimates for performing each of them. Thus, the network diagram indicates how to implement the new system in an orderly manner. The project leader should closely monitor the activities on the longest path through the PERT network—that is, the "critical path"—because delays in these activities delay the completion of the entire implementation portion of the project.

After a new system has been functioning for a period of time, an organization should perform follow-up work to determine whether the system is working as planned. If the revised system has failed to solve previous systems problems or possibly caused new problems, the system requires further changes. If the new system works satisfactorily, an organization typically gives responsibility for the ensuing maintenance work to professionals within its IT subsystem. Although "maintenance" appears at the tail end of a systems project, it is almost always the most expensive part of it.

The last part of this chapter discussed outsourcing—i.e., hiring outside vendors to perform all or part of an organization's data processing functions. Many firms prefer such a solution—for example, because IT is not their primary business, data processing costs may be lower, or because it enables them to avoid seasonal fluctuations in personnel requirements. But such an approach also comes at the cost of flexibility, a loss of control over processing, and perhaps even reduced competitive advantage.

KEY TERMS YOU SHOULD KNOW

acceptance testing	modular conversion
beta site	outsourcing
canned software	parallel conversion
critical path (PERT)	PERT (Program Evaluation and Review Technique)
direct conversion	
flexible systems	pilot conversion
follow-up and maintenance phase	post-implementation review report
Gantt chart	process testing

project management software   systems implementation
slack time (PERT)   turnkey system
system maintenance   unit testing
system testing   what-if analysis (PERT)

DISCUSSION QUESTIONS

15-1. An important implementation activity that must be performed when converting to a new AIS is "determining the necessary functional changes in the system." Describe some of the functional changes that would likely be necessary when converting a manual system to a computerized one. (Note: Because you are not provided with detailed information about an actual systems change, your discussion will have to be in general terms. Feel free, however, to make any reasonable assumptions about an imaginary company that is currently undergoing functional changes.)

15-2. When a company acquires a computerized data processing system for the first time, what are some of the incremental costs the company normally incurs?

15-3. When implementing a new computer system, two activities required are (1) establish controls and (2) convert data files. What is the rationale for performing activity 1 before activity 2?

15-4. Three methods for implementing a new system in an organization are direct conversion, parallel conversion, and modular conversion. Discuss the advantages and disadvantages of using each of these three systems implementation methods.

15-5. Cook Consultants is currently in the process of completing the systems implementation activities for converting Samuel Company's old system to a new one. Because of unexpected delays in performing specific implementation activities, Jerry Hazen, the project manager, is concerned about finishing the project on time. The one remaining activity is testing the new computer system and subsequently eliminating the old one. Jerry's assistant, May Fong, suggests that they can still meet their completion deadline if they use "direct conversion" rather than "parallel conversion." Assuming that you are the CIO of the company, how would you react to May Fong's suggestion? Discuss.

15-6. What is a PERT chart? What is a Gantt chart? Discuss the advantages and disadvantages of using PERT network diagrams versus Gantt charts for planning and controlling the activities involved in implementing an information system.

15-7. Al Choy recently graduated from college and is working as a management consultant for Diamond Consulting Firm. Al's first major consulting assignment involves a systems study to convert the Bogie Company's manual accounts receivable system to a computerized one. Upon performing the analysis and design phases of the systems work, Al and his consulting team were ready to implement the newly designed system. Markus Williams, the chief consultant supervising Bogie Company's systems work, assigns Al the job of preparing a PERT network diagram for the systems implementation activities. Because Al is unfamiliar with PERT networks, he has asked Percy Sneed (who has been with Diamond Consulting Firm for five years) to advise him regarding the preparation of a PERT network diagram.

Assuming that you are Percy Sneed, first explain to Al Choy the advantages, if any, of using a PERT network diagram in performing systems implementation work. Second, describe the procedures that a company should use to prepare a PERT network diagram for implementing the necessary changes into Bogie Company's system.

15-8. What is the purpose of follow-up in a systems study? Describe some of the specific activities that the management implementation team would perform in their follow-up work.

15-9. Discuss what effects downsizing might have on the design and implementation of a new computerized data processing system into an organization.

15-10. Discuss the two major ways that a company's software can be acquired. Which of these ways for acquiring software do you recommend? Explain your reasoning.

15-11. What factors cause a company to perform systems maintenance on a properly functioning AIS? Given that it comes last in the life cycle of an information system, why is "systems maintenance" often considered the most important part? Do you agree with this assessment? Why or why not?

15-12. What is outsourcing? Why do firms outsource their IT functions?

15-13. Discuss some advantages and disadvantages of outsourcing. Do you think that outsourcing might be a viable option for each of the following organizations: (1) hospital, (2) university, (3) manufacturing company, (4) state government agency, (5) dry-cleaner chain?

PROBLEMS

15-14. The Monarch Company is currently implementing a new computer system. Bob See, the president, is concerned about this project because many of the implementation activities are taking more time to complete than was originally estimated by the implementation team. To hasten the implementation process, Bob asks the implementation team to postpone establishing controls until after the new computer system becomes operative. As one of the implementation team members, how do you think you would react to this request? Explain.

15-15. Tommy Solton has just finished implementing a new AIS for a client, the Archy Bald Company. At a cocktail party the other night, Tommy bragged to one of his friends about how efficient he had been in performing the systems study work. Tommy's comments were as follows:

"The company's president, Archy B. Bald, was very frustrated with the slowness of reports coming from his organization's manual data processing system. About three days before I was contacted by Bald, I read an advertisement in a trade journal about IBM's new system. Therefore, as soon as I arrived at Archy Bald Company to discuss my potential systems job, I immediately showed this advertisement to Mr. Bald. He was so excited that he immediately hired me to supervise the implementation of the new system. The next day I contacted the IBM people and a short time thereafter the new computer system was delivered and implemented within the company. Before the company's employees knew what had happened, their old, outdated system had been replaced by this superior system. Bald was so pleased with my speed in implementing the new system that he paid me an extra $1,000 over the fee I charged his company. I deserved this extra money, of course, because Bald's new accounting information system should function so efficiently that he will never need to call me back for further work."

What are your reactions to Tommy Solton's comments?

15-16. Jordan Finance Company opened four personal loan offices in neighboring cities on January 3, 2000. The company makes small cash loans to borrowers, who repay them in monthly installments over a period not exceeding two years. Ralph Jordan, the president of the company, uses one of the branch offices as a central office and visits the other offices periodically for supervision and internal auditing purposes.

Mr. Jordan is concerned about the honesty of his employees. In December, he visits your management consulting firm and states, "I want to hire you to install a system that foils my employees from embezzling cash." He also says, "Until I went into business for myself, I worked for a nationwide loan company with 500 offices. I'm familiar with that company's system of accounting and internal control. I want to describe that system to you so you can install it for me because it will absolutely prevent fraud."

Requirements

1. How would you advise Mr. Jordan about his request that you install the large company's system of accounting and internal control in his firm? Discuss.

2. How would you respond to the suggestion that the new system would prevent fraud? Discuss.

15-17. Because its current minicomputer was no longer adequate, the Whitson Company has just ordered a new one to run its financial information systems. But this means that the company must test, and perhaps modify, all the current financial system programs before they can be run on the new computer. In addition, Whitson has several new applications that it wants to implement, and these have been identified and ranked according to priority.

Sally Rose, the company's CIO, is responsible for implementing the new computer system. Rose lists the specific activities that have to be completed and determines the estimated time to complete each activity. In addition, she prepares a PERT network diagram to aid in the coordination of the activities. Figure 15-6A is an activity list, and Figure 15-6B is a PERT network diagram.

Activity	Description of Activity	Expected Time Required to Complete (in weeks)
AB	Wait for delivery of computer from manufacturer.	8
BC	Install computer.	2
CH	General test of computer.	2
AD	Complete an evaluation of workforce requirements.	2
DE	Hire additional programmers and operators.	2
AG	Design modifications to existing applications.	3
GH	Program modifications to existing applications.	4
HI	Test modified applications on new computer.	2
IJ	Revise existing applications as needed.	2
JN	Revise and update documentation for existing applications as modified.	2
JK	Run existing applications in parallel on new and old computers.	2
KP	Implement existing applications as modified on the new computer.	1
AE	Design new applications.	8
GE	Design interface between existing and new applications.	3
EF	Program new applications.	6
FI	Test new applications on new computer.	2
IL	Revise new applications as needed.	3
LM	Conduct second test of new applications on new computer.	2
MN	Prepare documentation for the new applications.	3
NP	Implement new applications on the new computer.	2

FIGURE 15–6A Activities of Whitson Company for installing a new computer system.

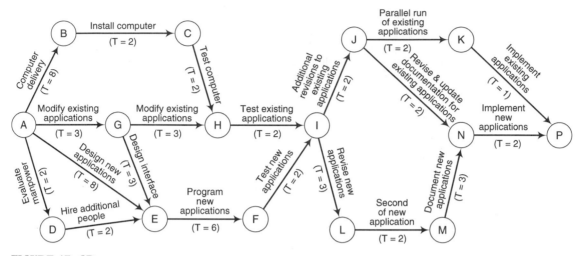

FIGURE 15–6B PERT network diagram for Whitson Company.

Requirements

1. Determine the number of weeks that will be required to fully implement the Whitson Company's financial information system (i.e., both existing and new applications) on its new computer and identify the activities that are critical in completing the project.

2. Project leaders often use the term "slack time" in conjunction with network analysis.

   a. Explain what is meant by slack time.

   b. Identify an activity that has slack time and indicate the amount of slack time available for that activity.

3. Whitson Company's top management would like to reduce the time necessary to begin operation of the entire system.

   a. Which activity times should Sally Rose attempt to reduce first in order to implement the system sooner? Explain your answer.

   b. Discuss how Sally Rose might proceed to reduce the time of these activities.

15-18. Crespi Construction Company uses PERT and critical-path analysis in scheduling its projects. Figure 15-7 presents a list of activities and a PERT network diagram that were prepared by Crespi for the Cherry Hill Apartment project prior to starting work on the project. The Cherry Hill Apartment project is now in progress. An interim progress report indicates that the city water and sewage lines, rough plumbing, and wiring are all one-half complete, and the exterior siding and painting have not yet begun.

Crespi will also soon begin work on a building for Echelon Savings Bank. Work on the building was started by another construction firm that has now gone out of business. Crespi has agreed to complete the project. Figure 15-8 shows Crespi's schedule of activities and related expected completion times for the Echelon Savings Bank project.

Requirements

1. Explain what a "critical path" is for a project.

2. Refer to the list of activities and the PERT network diagram that were prepared for the Cherry Hill Apartment project.

   a. Identify the critical path by letters and determine the expected completion time in weeks for the project.

Activity	Description of Activity	Estimated Time Required (in weeks)
A	Site selection and land purchase	6
B	Survey	1
C	Excavation	3
D	Foundation	4
E	City water and sewer lines	8
F	Rough plumbing	8
G	Framing and roofing	6
H	Wiring	4
I	Interior walls	3
J	Plumbing fixtures	3
K	Exterior siding and painting	9
L	Landscaping	2

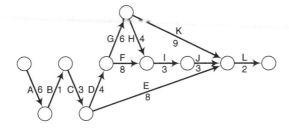

FIGURE 15-7 List of activities and PERT network diagram for the Cherry Hill Apartment project.

b. Identify an activity that has slack time for this project and indicate the amount of slack time available for that activity.

3. Refer to Crespi's schedule of activities and related expected completion times (Figure 15-8) for the work to be completed on the Echelon Savings Bank project.

a. Draw a PERT diagram for this project.

b. Identify the critical path by letters and determine the expected time in weeks for the project.

c. Explain the effect on the critical path and expected time for the project if Crespi were not required to apply and obtain the waiver to add new materials.

Activity	Description of Activity	Predecessor Activity	Estimate Time Required (in weeks)
A	Obtain on-site work permit.	—	1
B	Repair damage done by vandals.	A	4
C	Inspect construction materials left on site.	A	1
D	Order and receive additional construction materials.	C	2
E	Apply for waiver to add new materials.	C	1
F	Obtain waiver to add new materials.	E	1
G	Perform electrical work.	B,D,F	4
H	Complete interior partitions.	G	2

FIGURE 15-8 Schedule of activities and related expected completion times for the Echelon Savings Bank project.

INTERNET EXERCISES

15-19. Using your computer and the Internet, find a web site that contains information about "outsourcing." After accessing the web site, write a summary of your findings and relate it to this chapter's subject matter. In addition, submit a printout of the web site information that you accessed.

15-20. Using your computer and the Internet, find a web site that describes the training courses that a computer vendor such as IBM or Oracle provides to its customers. Does the vendor offer discounts for customers, students, or others? After accessing the web site, write a summary of your findings and relate it to this chapter's subject matter. In addition, submit a printout of the web site information that you accessed.

15-21. Several software developers now offer classes that train users on their software. Four examples are Sun Microsystems, Oracle, Cisco Systems, and Executrain. Select one of these companies and find their training web site. What courses do they offer? When do they offer them? Where do they offer them? Are all classes the same length of time? Select a particular class that interests you and determine when and where you could take it. How much does it cost to enroll in such a class? Were you surprised at this cost?

CASE ANALYSES

15.22 Intercontinental Airways (A Conversion Problem)

Intercontinental Airways (IA) currently flies routes from the United States to several countries in Western Europe. With the opening of Eastern Europe to greater travel and trade, IA decides to revise its "SeatEm" reservation system to not only accommodate additional travel on its existing routes, but also to allow for anticipated route additions to Eastern Europe and Asia. The system enhancements also provide for the addition of new travel agents and for handling a greater number of overall transactions.

The enhancements were placed online in May and were in operation for three months before IA's reservations personnel uncovered a problem. Passenger travel was lower than expected during the peak vacation months of June through August because several categories of discounted fares were prematurely closed out by the new system. As a result, travel agents ticketed passengers on other airlines, and IA lost several million dollars of potential revenue. The company's chief information officer believes IA would have discovered the problem before the software enhancements were brought online if the company had performed more rigorous testing.

Requirements

1. Describe several steps that Intercontinental Airways could have taken to prevent this problem during (a) software design, and (b) software implementation.

2. Describe several steps that IA could have taken during daily operations to provide early detection of this problem.

(CMA Adapted)

15-23. Audio Visual Corporation (Problems Associated with a Revised Computerized System)

Audio Visual Corporation manufactures and sells visual display equipment. The company is headquartered near Boston. The majority of sales are made through seven geographical sales offices located in Los Angeles, Seattle, Minneapolis, Cleveland, Dallas, Boston, and Atlanta. Each sales office has a warehouse located nearby to carry an inventory of a new equipment and replacement parts. The remainder of the sales are made through manufacturers' representatives.

Audio Visual's manufacturing operations are conducted in a single plant that is highly departmentalized. In addition to the assembly department, several departments are responsible for various components used in the visual display equipment. The plant also has maintenance, engineering, scheduling, and cost accounting departments.

Early in 1999, management decided that its management information system needed upgrading. As a result, the company ordered an advanced computer in 1999, and it was installed in July 2000. The main processing equipment is still located at corporate headquarters, and each of the seven sales offices is connected with the main processing unit by remote terminals.

The integration of the new computer into Audio Visual Corporation's information system was carried out by the MIS staff. The MIS manager and the four systems analysts who had the major responsibility for the integration were hired by the company in the spring of 2000. The MIS department's other employees—programmers, machine operators, and data-entry operators—have been with the company for several years.

During its early years, Audio Visual had a centralized decision-making organization. Top management formulated all plans and directed all operations. As the company expanded, some of the decision making was decentralized, although the information processing was still highly centralized. Departments had to coordinate their plans with the corporate office, but they had more freedom in developing their sales programs. However, as the company expanded, information problems developed. As a consequence, the MIS department was given the responsibility to improve the company's information processing system when the new equipment was installed.

The MIS analysts reviewed the information system in existence before the acquisition of the new computer and identified weaknesses. They then redesigned old applications and designed new applications in developing the new system to overcome the weaknesses. During the 18 months since the acquisition of the new computer equipment, the following applications have been redesigned or developed and are now operational: payroll, production, scheduling, financial statement preparation, customer billing, raw material usage in production, and finished goods inventory by warehouse. The operating departments of Audio Visual affected by the systems changes were rarely consulted or contacted until the system was operational and the new reports were distributed to the operating departments.

The president of Audio Visual is very pleased with the work of the MIS department. During a recent conversation with an individual who was interested in Audio Visual's new system, the president stated, "The MIS people are doing a good job, and I have full confidence in their work. I touch base with the MIS people frequently, and they have encountered no difficulties in doing their work. We paid a lot of money for the new equipment and the MIS people certainly cost enough, but the combination of the new equipment and new MIS staff should solve all of our problems."

Recently, two additional conversations regarding the computer and information system have taken place. One was between Jerry Adams, plant manager, and Bill Taylor, the MIS manager; the other was between Adams and Terry Williams, the new personnel manager.

Taylor-Adams Conversation

ADAMS: Bill, you're trying to run my plant for me. I'm supposed to be the manager, yet you keep interfering. I wish you would mind your own business.

TAYLOR: You've got a job to do but so does my department. As we analyzed the information needed for production scheduling and by top management, we saw where improvements could be made in the work flow. Now that the system is operational, you can't reroute work and change procedures because that would destroy the value of the information we're processing. And while I'm on that subject, it's getting to the point where we can't trust the information we're getting from production. The mark sense cards we receive from production contain a lot of errors.

ADAMS: I'm responsible for the efficient operation of production. Quite frankly, I think I'm the best judge of production efficiency. The system you installed has reduced my workforce and increased the workload of the remaining employees, but I don't see that this has improved anything. In fact, it might explain the high error rate in the cards.

TAYLOR: This new computer costs a lot of money and I'm trying to be sure that the company gets its money's worth.

Adams-Williams Conversation

ADAMS: My best production assistant, the one I'm grooming to be a supervisor when the next opening occurs, came to me today and said he was thinking of quitting. When I asked him why, he said he didn't enjoy the work anymore. He's not the only one who is unhappy. The supervisors and department heads no longer have a voice in establishing production schedules. This new computer system has taken away the contribution we used to make to company planning and direction. We seem to be going way back to the days when top management made all the decisions. I have more production problems now than I used to. I think it boils down to a lack of interest on the part of my management team. I know the problem is within my area, but I thought you might be able to help me.

WILLIAMS: I have no recommendations for you now, but I've had similar complaints from purchasing and shipping. I think we should get your concerns on the agenda for our next plant management meeting.

Requirements

1. The development of, and transition to, the new computer-based system seem to have created problems among the personnel of Audio Visual Corporation. Identify and briefly discuss the apparent causes of these problems.

2. How could the company have avoided these problems? What steps can a company take to avoid such problems in the future?

(CMA Adapted)

15-24. Plocharski Company (Automation: Yes or No?)

The production and inventory managers of Plocharski Company, a fast-growing manufacturer of outdoor clothing, recognize that they need a better system for tracking orders and maintaining raw materials inventory. The manual job order and inventory cards currently in use were adequate when the firm was smaller. However, now many orders are not completed by their promised dates, partially finished batches often wait several weeks for backordered raw materials, and substantial amounts of raw materials are often left over after production runs. These excess materials cannot be used and are eventually written off.

Job order and raw materials inventory cards are only updated once a week, and the updating process takes a week. When customers inquire about their orders, production-expediting clerks estimate the percentage of completion and a shipping date. But these estimates are almost always wrong. Customers like the manufacturer's clothing, but many of them are beginning to hint that they will be reluctant to place further orders because the manufacturer can't seem to provide reliable delivery dates.

Plocharski's operating managers have unsuccessfully tried to convince the president and vice president of the need to improve the timeliness of information flow between inventory and production. But the president and vice president steadfastly believe that the key factor in their success is the creative design of the company's product lines, not its information systems. The executives believe that customers will wait for the clothing because consumers want to buy their products. As proof, the president notes that last year, other manufacturers began imitating the company's clothing designs. Furthermore, the president expresses concern that automating inventory and production control would cost too much and the conversion process would cause too much trouble.

Requirements

The production and inventory managers of Plocharski Company have asked you to help them make a last attempt to convince the president and vice president that a new information system is essential to the continued success of the firm.

1. Identify five problems associated with the existing system.
2. Identify the relevant information that should be gathered to support the decision of whether or not to automate.
3. Recommend an effective approach for developing and implementing a new system for inventory and production control. Be specific in explaining your approach.

15-25. Newton Industries Inc. (Implementing an ABC System)

Newton Industries Inc. manufactures water filters, air filters, and filtering systems for both consumer and industrial use. The company had $500 million in sales in 2002 but an operating loss of over $1 million. Thomas Bainbridge, controller, is convinced that this dilemma is due to the current product mix. Marketing has been emphasizing the industrial filtering systems because Newton's accounting system indicates that this is the most profitable product line. However, Bainbridge believes that the company's cost accounting system does not generate adequate cost information and that, consequently, the company cannot make optimal product mix decisions.

Newton currently uses a standard costing system and applies overhead to its products on the basis of direct labor hours.

After attending a seminar recently on activity-based costing (ABC), Bainbridge is convinced that Newton should implement ABC. Also, a consultant recently retained by Newton has recommended that ABC would provide a better understanding of the company's costs, as well as reveal hidden profits and losses.

After persuading Judith Kerrigan, chief executive officer, to convert to ABC, Bainbridge's financial team and a systems study team design a new ABC system. On completion of the systems design work, Bainbridge released the following memorandum to all operating managers:

To: All Operating Managers
From: Thomas Bainbridge
Date: June 5, 2003
Subject: New Cost System

Please be advised that executive management has decided to implement an activity-based costing (ABC) system. Our analysis shows that such a system will provide much better information about our costs, and help us make some difficult, but necessary, decisions.

We have purchased a software package that will help us implement the new system. The systems design has already been completed. You can expect the new software to be installed on our minicomputer within the next month. All managers are expected to become familiar with the basics of ABC and with this new software by September 1. Effective October 1, we will begin implementing ABC as a parallel run.

Enclosed is a listing of local firms that conduct seminars on ABC and on the new software package. Please attend these seminars as you see necessary. (Charge expenses of the seminars to your department's education and training budget.)

I will hold a meeting to answer any questions on Wednesday, July 12 at 8:00 A.M. in my office.

Requirements

1. Managing organizational change is essential to the successful implementation of any new system. Identify and discuss at least three techniques that Thomas Bainbridge could use to prevent or overcome possible resistance to change to the new activity-based costing system.

2. Besides possible resistance to change, discuss at least three likely motivational effects that Thomas Bainbridge's directive will have on Newton Industries Inc.'s operating managers.

3. Identify and explain at least three weaknesses of Thomas Bainbridge's memorandum as a communication device.

15-26. Family Health Care, Limited (Systems Implementation using PERT)[2]

Family Health Care, Limited (FHCL) is a private, nonprofit family health clinic that was established in 1994 to provide health care services to a high-density, low-income

---

[2] Contributed by Professor Stephen Kerr, University of Nevada, and used with permission.

community. The response to the clinic has been positive and demand for its services has grown rapidly. The clinic's treasurer is Sara Stanton, who handles all of the accounting functions herself, including FHLC's banking, financial reporting, and budgeting. At present, most of the clinic's accounting functions are performed manually except payroll (which is outsourced).

Before joining FHCL, Sara was the administrator at a larger clinic, which used a computerized medical accounting and patient management system. With FHCL growing so fast, Sara feels that the clinic needs a computerized system to keep up with the higher volume of paperwork and to better handle information requests. Thus, she decides on her own to purchase the same $30,000 software package that she used in her last job for the current clinic. The package includes a file server, four work stations, two printers, and medical software capable of billing, payroll, inventory control, and generating the required financial statements.

The equipment is scheduled to arrive next month. Although Sara had not been involved in the purchase or installation of her previous employer's system, she feels that the job will be straightforward and that the package will fully meet the needs of FHCL. The board members are surprised to learn of this purchase, but all of them are doctors who know very little about computerized accounting packages. The clerical staff members who will use the system regularly are not so sure. All of them realize that the new system could change their jobs in many ways.

The chairman of the board, Dr. Brooks, wants to keep transition disruptions to a minimum, and expresses his concerns. Sara assures him that there will be a smooth transition from the old, manual system to the new, computerized one. She even

Step	Prerequisite	Time (hours)	Description
A	—	5	Inspect the equipment and fill in the warranty cards.
B	—	3	Redesign the present chart of accounts to fit the new system.
C	A	6	Thread the wiring through the ceiling tiles to the work stations.
D	A	4	Place the terminals at the work stations and install the software (1 hour each work station).
E	I, D	3	Conduct an orientation session for the staff on the new procedures and software using the new computer equipment.
F	I, D	4	Load the opening account balances into the new system.
G	C, E	2	Adjust the work stations for use of the new system.
H	F	3	Test the new system and the wiring by printing some key reports.
I	B	5	Determine the opening account balances for the new system from the closing account balances under the manual accounting system.
Total		35	

Notes:
• In order to avoid disruption, four staff members who will be working on the new system will come in on Saturday to help Sara install the system. They all have personal computers at home and are comfortable working on the installation.
• The above schedule will require a total of seven hours per person to finish the installation. Invitations have been extended to the board of directors to observe a demonstration of the new system at 5:00 P.M. on Saturday.

FIGURE 15–9 System implementation plan for Family Health Care, Limited.

provides him with a list of system implementation activities, with time durations in hours (Figure 15-9). She also believes that (with some help), she can install the entire system in a single weekend. To Dr Brooks, the plan appears to be complete, but he does not know how to evaluate it.

Requirements

1. Drawing on your knowledge from Chapters 13 and 14, comment on the systems analysis and design work described above. Can you suggest some alternate approaches that the clinic might have used?

2. Create a PERT chart from the information provided in Figure 15-9, and compute the critical path through the network. (Hint: the last two activities are G and H.) Comment on Sara's predictions for completing the required installation activities over a single weekend.

3. Compute the slack time for activities A and B. What do these time durations mean?

4. When Sara begins installation, she finds that it takes her 9 hours to determine the opening and closing account balances in activity I instead of 5 hours. Assuming all other activity durations go as planned, will this delay the installation of the entire project? If so, by how much? If not, why not?

15.27 Marshall Associates (A Review of the System Development Life Cycle)

Marshall Associates is a sports gear manufacturer that plans to install a new computer system to integrate its marketing, accounting, and customer information systems. At a recent meeting, Marshall's managers discussed how to proceed with this project as well as asked questions about the project's economic feasibility. They also discussed the roles of management and users in developing this project. Marshall's managers identified the four phases of the systems life cycle as (1) systems analysis, (2) systems design, (3) systems acquisition, and (4) systems implementation.

Requirements

1. Describe the role of management in the development and design of a new information system.

2. Describe the role of users in the development of a new system.

3. Describe at least three benefits of installing a new computer system at Marshall Associates.

4. Identify at least three distinct and mutually exlusive types of documentation that a company would use in each of these four life cycle phases—a total of 12 elements in all.

(CMA Adapted)

REFERENCES, RECOMMENDED READINGS, AND WEB SITES

References and Recommended Readings

Appleby, Chuck, "Power Failure: Five Years into a Client-Server Conversion, Pacific Gas & Electric Backs Up and Starts Over," *Information Week* (February 21, 1994), pp. 12–15.

Appleby, Chuck, John P. McPartlin, and Linda Wilson, "The Human Face of Outsourcing," *Information Week* (January 17, 1994), pp. 30–34.

Berson, Wayne, "How to Build an Outsourcing Niche," *Journal of Accountancy,* vol. 192, no. 5 (November 2001), pp. 47–53.

Black, George, "Simplify End-User Computing: Outsource It," *Datamation* (September 15, 1995), pp. 67–69.

Castellano, Joseph, Donald Klein, and Harper Roehm, "Minicompanies: The Next Generation of Employee Empowerment," *Management Accounting* (March 1998), pp. 22–30.

Chapman, Christy, "SEC Chief Accountant Expresses Concern over Independence and Outsourcing," *Internal Auditor* (February 1996), p. 8.

Harper, Pamela "How to Keep Your Organizational Reality From Sabotaging Your Outsource Strategy," *The Secured Lender,* vol. 58, no. 1 (Jan/Feb 2002), pp. 64–67.

Larson, Linda Lee, "Third-Party Software," *Internal Auditor* (April 1995), pp. 44–47.

Lee, Louise, "Rent-a-Techs: Hiring Outside Firms to Run Computers Isn't Always a Bargain," *Wall Street Journal* (May 18, 1995), pp. A1, A15.

McCarthy, Chris, "Using Technology as a Competitive Tool," *Management Accounting* (January 1998), pp. 28–33.

McCausland, Richard, "Ralph Kubek: Process Makes Perfect" *Accounting Technology,* vol. 16, no. 9 (October 2000), p. 82.

Morgan, Mark, "Staying Competitive in Applications Software," *Management Accounting* (May 1998), pp. 20–26.

Rigdon, Joan E., "Frequent Glitches in New Software Bug Users," *Wall Street Journal* (January 18, 1995), pp. B1, B5.

Switser, Jim, "Trends in Human Resources Outsourcing," *Management Accounting* (November 1997), pp. 22–27.

Tate, John, "Systems Implementation: Some Practical Guidance," *Management Accounting* vol. 77, no. 10 (November 1999), pp. 37–39.

Williams, Kathy, "Is Outsourcing Valuable?" *Management Accounting* (October 1997), p. 16.

Williams, Kathy, and James Hart, "Open Systems: Traversing the Accounting Software Field," *Management Accounting* (June 1998), pp. 54–57.

Web Sites

A discussion of downsizing's disadvantages can be found at (1) www.govexec.com/dailyfed/0497/042497b3.htm and (2) www.henrygeorge.org/intdown.htm.

Information on outsourcing publications is available at www.outsourcing-mgmt.com.

Information on project management software is available at www.wst.com.

A list of current project management books is available at www.projectmanagementbooks.com.

A list of PERT software sellers may be found at: www.nnh.com/ev/links.html.

Glossary

Acceptance testing a method of testing computer software whereby the new system's users develop test transactions (normally using real transactions and real file records) and acceptance criteria for the new system.

Accounting information system the information subsystem within an organization that accumulates and processes information (both financial and nonfinancial) from the entity's various subsystems and communicates this information to the organization's users.

Advanced planning and scheduling systems (APS) systems that work to synchronize the flow of materials within the supply chain.

Alphanumeric codes codes that use numbers and letters.

Antivirus software computer programs such as Norton Antivirus or MacAffee that end users typically install in their microcomputers to guard against computer viruses.

Application controls a major category of computer controls that are designed and implemented to prevent, detect, and correct errors and irregularities in transactions as they flow through the input, processing, and output stages of data processing work.

Application service provider (ASP) source through which companies can rent rather than buy software.

Application software computer software that performs specific tasks such as accounting tasks, spreadsheet tasks, marketing tasks, or word-processing tasks.

Assurance services services provided, for example, by accountants of public accounting firms to their clients in areas such as risk assessment, information systems reliability, the Internet, and electronic commerce.

Audit trail enables information users within a company's system to follow the flow of data through the system.

Auditing around the computer audit approach whereby an auditor follows a company's audit trail up to the point at which accounting data enter the computer and then picks these data up again when they reappear in processed form as computer output; this audit approach pays little or no attention to the control procedures within the IT environment.

Auditing modules an approach to auditing spreadsheets whereby modules are embedded in the spreadsheets, thus making the spreadsheets self-auditing.

Auditing through the computer audit approach whereby an auditor follows a company's audit trail through the internal computer operations phase of automated data processing; this audit approach attempts to verify that the processing controls involved in the AIS programs are functioning properly.

Auditing with the computer audit approach whereby the auditor uses the computer to aid in performing various auditing procedures (e.g., selecting a sample of accounts receivable data for confirmation).

Automated workpaper software software that aids an auditor in performing such accounting functions as generating trial balances, recording adjusting journal entries, and preparing income statements and balance sheets.

Balanced scorecard an approach to performance measurement that uses measures in four categories (financial performance, customer knowledge, internal business processes, and learning and growth) to evaluate and promote certain activities and behaviors.

Bar code reader a device that interprets the familiar bar code stripes printed on merchandise packages, shipping labels, and similar documents, and inputs the data into a computer.

Benchmark test an approach for examining the operating efficiency of a particular system whereby a computer vendor's system performs a data processing task that a company's new system must perform and company representatives then examine the processing outputs for accuracy, consistency, and efficiency.

Block code a sequential code in which specific blocks of numbers are reserved for particular uses—for example, block codes are often used in developing a chart of accounts.

Bluetooth a wireless data transmission standard ("protocol") created by a consortium of mobile phone, digital camera, portable computer, and chip manufacturers to allow dissimilar equipment to communicate with one another.

Budget a financial projection for the future that aids managerial planning.

Business entity a separate unit of accountability, such as a partnership or a corporation.

Business intelligence (BI) tools data analysis software that helps managers obtain the most information from their customer relationship management systems.

Business process reengineering (BPR) techniques used by organizations to redesign their business processes from scratch.

Business processes the focus of operational accounting, which reflects a collection of activities or flow of work in an organization that creates value (e.g., the revenue process).

Business risk the likelihood that an adverse occurrence or unwanted event that could be injurious to an organization will occur.

Byte eight bits of computer memory or disk storage which a computer combines to represent exactly one character of text data.

Cache memory high-speed computer memory that acts as a buffer between the internal (RAM) memory of a computer and its microprocessor unit.

Canned software software acquired from independent vendors.

Cardinalities a notation reflecting the nature of relationships among entities as one-to-one, one-to-many, none-to-one, none-to-many, or many-to-many.

CASE tools computer aided software engineering tools that automate documentation tasks such as drawing or modifying flowcharts, generating graphics and screen designs, and developing report formats.

Cash receipts forecast a numerical analysis that is used to predict future cash receipts and their dates.

Cash requirements forecast a numerical analysis that is used to predict future cash payments and their dates.

CD-ROM an acronym for "compact disk-read only memory." CD-ROM disks can store approximately 640 megabytes of data.

Central processing unit (CPU) the component of a computer that performs that processing tasks of the system. The processor part of the CPU is typically a single silicon chip that can manipulate data—e.g., perform mathematical functions such as addition as well as logic operations such as comparing text or number values.

Checkpoint a computer network system control designed to facilitate recovery from a system failure.

Child record the lower-level record of two adjacent records in a hierarchical data structure.

Client/server computing an alternate to mainframe computing in which processing tasks are shared between a centralized host computer called the "server" and a smaller microcomputer called the "client."

Cold site a disaster recovery location where power and environmentally controlled space are available to install computer processing equipment on short notice.

Collaborative business partnerships situations in which organizations work with other businesses, even their competitors, to increase their power to meet customer demands.

Committee of Sponsoring Organizations (COSO) committee established by the Treadway Commission to develop a common definition for internal control and to provide guidance for judging the effectiveness of internal control as well as improving it.

Compiler a computer program that translates computer programming instructions written in a high-level language such as Visual Basic into the (binary) machine language that a computer can understand and execute.

Computer-assisted audit techniques (CAATs) used by auditors when auditing through the computer; CAATs can aid in the performance of compliance testing to ensure that a company's controls are in place and working as prescribed.

Computer Fraud and Abuse Act of 1986 this act defines computer fraud as any illegal act for which knowledge of computer technology is essential for its perpetration, investigation, or prosecution.

Computer record a set of data fields about one file entity—for example, one employee, one inventory item, or one sales transaction.

Computer terminal a keyboard and display screen that allows users to input data into, or display data from, a computer. Unlike microcomputers, a "dumb" computer terminal cannot process very much data or run independent computer applications.

Computer virus a program that disrupts normal data processing and is usually able to replicate itself onto other files, computer systems, or networks; examples of these viruses are boot-sector viruses, worm programs, trojan horse programs, and logic bomb programs.

Concurrency controls prevents two or more users of a database to access the same record from the same file at the same time.

Context diagram high-level data flow diagram that provides an overall picture of an application or system.

Contingency planning the process of planning for events that could impede a company's data processing function.

Continuous auditing requires the use of tools (such as embedded audit modules) that allow auditing to occur even when an auditor is not present; it is particularly effective when most of an application's (e.g., a payroll application) data are in electronic form.

Control activities component of internal control whereby specific control procedures are designed and implemented to help ensure that necessary actions are taken to address risks to the achievement of a company's objectives.

Control environment component of internal control that establishes the tone of a company, influencing the control awareness of the company's employees.

Control Objectives for Information and Related Technology (COBIT) project undertaken by the Information Systems Audit and Control Foundation to develop a definition of internal control.

Corrective controls control procedures within a company's internal control system that are designed to remedy problems discovered through detective controls.

Cost of capital the cost of obtaining financial resources.

Cost-benefit concept employed, for example, in the process of developing an optimal package of internal control procedures within a company's internal control system; a cost-benefit analysis is performed on each control procedure being considered for implementation.

Critical path within a PERT network diagram, the longest path through the network; each activity on the critical path has zero slack.

Customer relationship management (CRM) systems employed to gather, maintain, and use data about a company's customers with the objective of improving customer satisfaction and company profitability.

Data raw facts about events that have no organization or meaning.

Data definition language (DDL) part of a DBMS that enables its users to define the record structure of any particular database table.

Data dictionary describes the data fields in each database record of a database system.

Data diddling involves changing data before, during, or after they are entered into a computer system.

Data communications protocol the settings that create a communications standard for a specific data communications application. Examples of such settings include the transmission speed, parity bit, duplex setting, or synchronous-versus asynchronous transmission type.

Data compression techniques mathematical algorithms that enable a computer to reduce the final size of a computer file.

Data encryption a computer network system control designed to prevent a company's competitors from electronically monitoring confidential data transmissions.

Data flow diagram primarily used in the systems development process to document the flow of data through an AIS.

Data hierarchy   storing data electronically in the following ascending order: bit→character→data field→record→table→database.

Data mining   a set of data analysis and statistical tools that enables companies to detect relationships, patterns, or trends among stored data within a database.

Data modeling   term used to describe the process of designing databases.

Data transcription   the task of converting manually-prepared source documents such as credit-card application forms to computer-readable file records. Where possible, AIS developers try to avoid data transcription because it is costly, labor-intensive, time-consuming, and likely to introduce errors into the data.

Data validation rule   a customized edit test that can be created which enables a spreadsheet to reject entries that violate the validation rule.

Data warehouse   a large collection of historical data that organizations use to integrate their functions, thus allowing managers (and to some extent external parties) to obtain the information needed for planning, decision making, and control.

Database   a large collection of related data that are typically stored in computerized, linked files and manipulated by specialized software packages called database management systems.

Database administrator   the person responsible for supervising the design, development, and installation of a large database system; this person is also responsible for maintaining, securing, and revising the data within the database system.

Database management system (DBMS)   a separate software system that enables users to create database records, delete records, access specific information, query records for viewing or analysis, alter database information, and reorganize records as needed.

Database schema   reflects the totality of the information in a database and the relationships of its tables (i.e., records).

Database structure   the particular method used to organize the individual records in a database.

Decision table   a matrix of conditions and processing tasks for a computer program that indicates the appropriate action to take for each possibility.

Denial of service attack   an attack on an online company (such as eBay) when hackers "flood" the company's web site with bogus traffic.

Detailed systems design   the systems design work that involves specifying the outputs, processing procedures, and inputs for a new system.

Detective controls   control procedures within a company's internal control system that provide feedback to management regarding whether or not operational efficiency and adherence to prescribed managerial policies have been achieved.

Dialback system   a password safeguard that initially disconnects all login users but reconnects users after checking their passwords against lists of bona-fide user codes.

Digital signature   used, for example, to authenticate documents (such as purchase orders) by including a portion of a document's message in an encrypted format (which reflects the digital signature).

Digital time stamping the process of attaching time stamps to business transactions to authenticate the time and possibly the place of individual transactions.

Digital video disk (DVD) an optically-read disk similar in size and shape to a CD but that is capable of storing as much as 17 gigabytes of data.

Direct conversion method of systems implementation in which a company's old system is immediately dropped and the new system takes over the complete processing of the company's transaction.

Disaster recovery plan part of contingency planning that describes the procedures to be followed if a company's data processing center becomes disabled.

Document flowchart traces the physical flow of documents through an organization.

Domain address an Internet address, also referred to as a universal resource locator (URL).

Dot-matrix printer an impact printer that uses a print head of tiny wires, arranged in a grid—for example, 5 wires in each of 7 rows—to create our familiar letters and other printing characters. Many cash registers still use dot-matrix printers today.

Economic espionage involves the theft of information and intellectual property.

Economic feasibility the feasibility area of a feasibility evaluation that analyzes the cost-effectiveness of a proposed system.

Electronic commerce conducting business (often over the Internet) with computers and data communications.

Electronic conferencing enables accountants and others to use computers and phone lines to communicate with clients, etc., through the use of high-end groupware communications packages.

Electronic Data Gathering and Retrieval (EDGAR) database contains the financial report filings of U.S. publicly held companies.

Electronic Data Interchange (EDI) a communications technique that allows organizations to transmit standard business documents over high-speed data communications channels.

Electronic funds transfer (EFT) a cash management technique whereby the transfer of funds is electronic or computer-to-computer.

Electronic mail creating a message on your microcomputer and then sending it electronically to someone else using the recipient's e-mail address.

End-user computing refers to the ability of noncomputer employees to create computer applications of their own.

Enterprise resource planning (ERP) systems software (e.g., *Oracle*) that provides for integration among all of an organization's major business processes through the use of a central database; ERP II systems are extended with e-business and other front-office capabilities.

Enterprise-wide database a large repository of organizational data that comes from, and is available to, a wide range of a company's employees.

Entity-relationship (E-R) diagram graphical documentation technique used by database designers to depict database elements and their direct relationships.

Event-driven programming language a computer programming language such as Visual Basic that enables a computer to respond to specific events—for example, clicking on a menu choice.

Events-based accounting system (EBAS) system in which companies record data about activities simply because these activities occur, not because a particular information system requires these data.

Expected loss a measure of loss used in cost-benefit analyses for assessing control procedures that considers both risk and exposure factors (expected loss = risk × exposure).

Extended application interfaces (EAI) software application interfaces that allow different software applications to share information among them.

External audit performed by accountants working for an independent CPA firm; the external audit function focuses on giving an opinion on the fairness of a company's financial statements.

Extranets enable selected outside users to access organizations' intranets.

Fault-tolerant systems systems designed to tolerate faults or errors that are often based on the concept of redundancy.

Feasibility evaluation the first major procedure in systems design work whereby the design team determines the practicality of alternative proposals.

File server a computer whose principal task is to store and output the contents of computer files. For example, most Internet applications use file servers to store and output web page files.

Final systems analysis report report presented to a company's steering committee by the systems study team at the conclusion of systems analysis work.

Financial accounting the component of an AIS whose major objective is to provide relevant information to individuals and groups outside an organization's boundaries.

Financial planning models information systems that aid financial managers in selecting an optimum strategy for acquiring and investing financial resources.

Financial risk the chance that a company's financial statements are misstated.

Financial statements primary output of a financial accounting system; for example, income statement, balance sheet, and cash flow statement.

Financing process the process by which a company acquires and uses financial resources such as cash, other liquid assets, and investments.

Flexible systems refers to systems that are easily modified.

Flying-start site a disaster recovery location that includes everything contained in a hot site plus up-to-date backup data and software.

Followup and maintenance phase of a systems study that involves monitoring a company's new system to make sure it continues to meet the company's goals.

Foreign Corrupt Practices Act (FCPA) act passed by the U.S. Congress in December 1977 to prohibit bribes to foreign officials by publicly owned corporations.

Foreign keys data fields within some accounting records that enable these records to reference one or more records in other tables.

Forensic accountants (also called **fraud auditors**) individuals who concern themselves with the prevention and detection of fraud and white-collar crime.

Gantt chart a tool for planning and controlling a systems implementation project.

General controls a major category of computer controls that are designed and implemented to ensure that a company's control environment is stable and well managed in order to strengthen the effectiveness of application computer controls.

General ledger collection of detailed monetary information about a company's various assets, liabilities, owners' equity, revenues, and expenses.

General-use software the software used by auditors as productivity tools for improving their work; for example, the use of a word processing program by an auditor when writing an audit report.

Generalized audit software (GAS) computer packages (or programs) that enable auditors to review computer files without continually rewriting processing programs.

Gigabyte a unit of disk storage approximately equal to one billion bytes.

Graphical user interface (GUI) one of more visual computer screens that enable an end user to communicate with a computer—typically by selecting items from menus or clicking on choices using a computer mouse. Computer programs that did not use GUIs typically were command-driven systems that required users to memorize and type in system commands and instructions.

Group code results from combining two or more subcodes; for example, use of group codes in creating product codes for sales catalogs.

Hacker a person who breaks into the computer files of others for fun or personal gain.

Hot site a disaster recovery location that includes a computer system configured similarly to the system currently in use by a company for its data processing activities.

Human resource management activity of an organization that includes the personnel function and the payroll function.

Ideal control a control procedure within a company's internal control system that reduces to practically zero the risk of an undetected error or irregularity.

Image processing storing, manipulating, or outputting the graphical information that usually first appear on hard-copy documents such as contracts, architectural plans, machinery schematics, or real-estate photos.

Information overload too much information being provided to users.

Information system a set of interrelated subsystems that work together to collect, process, store, transform, and distribute information for planning, decision making, and control.

Information systems auditing process that involves evaluating the computer's role in achieving audit and control objectives.

Information systems auditors auditors who concern themselves with analyzing the risks associated with computerized information systems.

Information systems risk assessment method used by an auditor to evaluate the desirability of IT-related controls for a particular aspect of business risk.

Information technology   the hardware and software used in computerized information systems.

Ink-jet printer   a printer that uses very small nozzles to spray ink onto blank pages and create printed outputs. An advantage of ink-jet printers over dot-matrix printers is their ability to print in color. But ink-jet printers are slower and more costly, per-page, then laser printers.

Input controls   computer application controls that attempt to ensure the validity, accuracy, and completeness of the data entered into a company's AIS; for example, edit tests.

Input-processing-output cycle   the three steps that a computer uses to process computer records—i.e., inputting a record, processing the information it contains, and outputting the results. A classic example is creating payroll checks from time-card data.

Integrated services digital network (ISDN) line   high speed data transmission lines, typically using fiber optics, that end users can rent from phone companies and that support transmission rates up to 1.5 million bits per second (Mbps).

Integrated test facility (ITF)   used by auditors to test a company's computer programs; ITF technique (for auditing an AIS in an operational setting) is effective in evaluating integrated online systems or complex programming logic.

Internal control   as defined by the COSO, a process, effected by an entity's board of directors, management, and other personnel, designed to provide reasonable assurance regarding the achievement of objectives in the following categories— effectiveness and efficiency of operations, reliability of financial reporting, and compliance with applicable laws and regulations.

Internet   a global collection of tens of thousands of interconnected business, government, military, and education networks that communicate with each other.

Internet connectivity   software that permits small businesses to create web sites and engage in electronic commerce.

Internet service provider   examples are America Online, AT&T, and Sprint, which each maintains its own Internet computers.

Intranets   networks using the same software as the Internet, but which are internal (for communications purposes) to the companies that created them.

I/O-bound computer   a computer whose input speeds and/or output speeds are slower than its computational speed.

Job costing system   a system of costing that keeps track of the specific costs for raw materials, labor, and overhead associated with each product or group of products.

Joint application development (JAD)   technique used by system analysts to gain user confidence in a revised system; analysts hold meetings with the system's users and the users work as consultants in developing the revised system.

Just-in-time inventory system   an inventory system whose objective is to minimize inventories at all levels of production.

K (kilobytes)   exactly 1,024 bytes of computer storage.

Knowledge workers   employees of companies (such as accountants) who produce and use information and knowledge.

Laser printer   a type of printer that uses a laser to sensitive portions of a rotating drum. These sensitized portions attract small graphite particles called toner that can then be transferred to a blank piece of paper and permanently "fixed" to the page with heat.

Legacy system   a business's older, customized computer system that typically runs on a mainframe computer and that is often too large and expensive to replace.

Legal feasibility   the area of a feasibility evaluation that analyzes whether there will by any conflict between a newly proposed system and a company's legal obligations.

Local area network (LAN)   a collection of microcomputers, printers, file servers, and similar electronic components that are physically located near one another—for example, in the same building—and connected together for communication purposes.

Lock-box system   a tool used by a company to reduce the float period during which checks clear the bank.

Lock-out systems   a password safeguard that disconnects telephone users after a set number of unsuccessful login attempts.

Logic bombs   computer programs that remain dormant until some specified circumstance or date triggers them.

Magnetic (hard) disk   a secondary storage device that enables a computer to store billions of bytes of information. Unlike primary (RAM) memory, whose information is lost when its computer loses power, magnetic disk memory is permanent.

Magnetic ink character recognition (MICR)   the technology used primarily by banks to encode magnetically readable symbols at the bottom of checks or similar financial documents. Because the magnetic flux of the ink used in these symbols loses strength over time, MICR is not widely used elsewhere.

Mag-strip card   a credit card, hotel "key," employee badge, or similarly-sized plastic card with a magnetic stripe on one side that has been encoded with information about the user and/or account.

Managerial accounting   the component of an AIS whose principal objective is to provide relevant information to a company's managers to aid their planning, control, and decision-making functions.

Manufacturing resource planning (MRP II) system   a more complex version of the material requirements planning system that not only coordinates the purchase and use of raw material inventories in production, but also integrates with the purchasing and revenue processes.

Mark-sense media   documents such as academic test forms, surveys, and similar papers that users complete with simple pencils or pens but that can be read and evaluated by computerized input devices.

Material requirements planning (MRP I) system   a system that monitors the acquisition and use of raw materials needed by production processes.

Megabyte   a unit of computer storage approximately equal to one million bytes.

Message acknowledgment procedures   a control for computer network systems that is useful in preventing the loss of part or all of a company's transactions or messages on a computer network system.

Microprocessor   the portion of a CPU that performs arithmetic and logic tasks of a computer, and that also interprets and executes computer instructions.

Mnemonic code   a code that helps the user remember what it represents (e.g., *M* to represent medium-size shirts.)

Modem (modulator/demodulator)   a device for converting the digital data that a computer uses into sound pitches that can be transmitted over phone lines.

Modular conversion   a method of systems implementation whereby the users involved in specific data processing tasks are divided into smaller units or modules; the data processing system is then installed module by module.

Multimedia databases   object-oriented databases that include graphics, audio information, and animation.

Network structure   used with AIS databases to link related records together and adequately capture the records' relationships.

Normalization   the process of examining and arranging file data in a way that helps avoid problems when these files are used or modified later; data can be in first, second, or third normal form.

Not-for-profit organizations   organizational entities that lack a profit goal and thus exist primarily to provide services for the protection and betterment of society; for example, public schools, museums, churches, and public governmental agencies.

Numeric codes   codes that use numbers only.

Object-oriented database (OODB)   a database that contains both the text data of traditional databases and information about the set of actions that can be taken on these data fields.

Object-oriented design methods   approach to systems design work that involves creating reusable processing modules that serve as independent building blocks in the task of creating complete application systems.

Object-oriented programming (OOP) languages   computer programming languages that have strict rules (particularly "inheritance" and "encapsulation") that govern the properties, attributes, and operations of language objects (such as variables and form controls). OOP also includes the developer's ability to create new objects with these characteristics that can be used by other procedures and programs.

Online analytical processing (OLAP)   allows database users to extract multidimensional information from one or more database tables for the purpose of making complex decisions.

Operating system (OS)   a set of software programs that helps a computer run itself as well as the application programs designed to run under it. Examples include Windows 2000, Windows XP, and Unix.

Operational audit   an audit performed by a company's internal audit staff that focuses on evaluating the efficiency and effectiveness of operations within a particular department.

Operational feasibility   the area of a feasibility evaluation that examines a proposed system's compatibility with the current operating environment.

Optical character recognition (OCR)   an older technique that enables computer input devices to interpret machine-printed (and to a limited extent, hand-written) data using optical technology.

Output controls computer application controls that are designed to assure the validity, accuracy, and completeness of the output from a company's computer systems; for example, regulating the distribution and use of printed output.

Outsourcing process whereby a company hires an outside organization to handle all or part of its data processing tasks.

Parallel conversion method of systems implementation where both the old and new system of a company operates simultaneously for a period of time; the old system is dropped once the company is satisfied with the functioning of the new system.

Parallel simulation technique used by auditors to test a company's computer programs; the auditor uses live input data, rather than test data, in a program (which simulates all or some of the operations of the real program that is actually in use) written or controlled by the auditor.

Parent record the higher-level record of two adjacent records in a hierarchical data structure.

Password codes general computer controls designed to limit logical access to a company's computers only to those individuals authorized to have this access.

Peripheral equipment devices such as keyboards, display monitors, and printers, that typically physically surround a computer processor.

Personal data assistant (PDA) device a computerized device that includes such functions as calculator, address book, memo storage, daily planner, and perhaps even provides wireless Internet access.

PERT (Program Evaluation and Review Technique) a technique for scheduling and monitoring the activities in large systems implementation projects.

Petty cash fund used for a company's small, miscellaneous expenditures.

Physical data flow diagram first level of detail of a data flow diagram.

Pivot tables a feature which enables a database user to create two-dimensional statistical summaries of database information.

Pixels (picture elements) the tiny dots that a monitor uses to create a complete screen image. For example, a monitor might have a pixel resolution of 1024 x 768, meaning the ability to display 1,024 pixels across the screen by 768 pixels down the screen.

Point-of-sale (POS) device an input device such as a bar code reader that enables a user to input data directly into a computer from a checkout stand in a supermarket or merchandise store and avoid manual keystrokes.

Point-scoring analysis approach used to evaluate accounting software packages (as well as hardware) of vendors that meet most of a company's major requirements.

Portal a web site that allows outsiders with authorized access to view a company's internal information systems (i.e., its ERP).

Post-implementation review report a report that is prepared at the conclusion of the followup study of systems development work that summarizes the implementation team's evaluation of the new system's operating efficiency and effectiveness.

Preliminary investigation   the first task performed by a systems study team whereby the team, for example, investigates current needs or problems in a company's present system and reports its findings to the steering committee.

Preventive controls   control procedures that are designed and implemented within a company's internal control system to *prevent* some potential problem from occurring when an activity is performed.

Primary memory   the internal random-access memory or RAM that a computer uses to temporarily store computer programs and immediate data.

Process costing system   a system that uses averages to calculate the costs associated with goods in process and finished goods produced.

Process map   a special type of flowchart used to better understand and communicate a company's current business processes.

Process measures   nonmonetary measures often used by not-for-profit organizations to measure performance output.

Process testing   a method for testing computer software whose objective is to determine whether a complete set of computer programs operates as they should.

Processing controls   computer application controls that focus on the manipulation of accounting data after they are input to a company's computer system— for example, data-access controls.

Professional service organizations   business establishments that provide a special service to customers—for example, accounting firms, law firms, and consulting firms.

Program change control   a set of internal control procedures developed to ensure against unauthorized program changes.

Program flowchart   graphical documentation that outlines the processing logic for each part of a computer program and also indicates the sequence of processing steps.

Programming language   a language such as Java or Visual Basic that enables a programmer to create instructions (called "code") that a computer can understand.

Project management software   software that runs on microcomputers and that can aid in planning and controlling the tasks involved in a systems implementation project.

Prototyping   approach to systems design work that involves developing a simplified model, or prototype, of a proposed information system that is then experimented with by the system's users.

Proxy server   a computer and related software that creates a transparent gateway to and from the Internet which can be used to control web access.

Production process   process that begins with a request for raw materials and ends with the transfer of finished goods to warehouses.

Queries   allow database users to create subschemas of interest to them.

REA model   an approach to data modeling that focuses on resources (R), events (E), and agents (A).

Record structure   the specific data fields in each record of a database table; this structure is fixed in many accounting applications.

Relational database structure enables database users to identify relationships either at the time the data are initially created or at a future time as new informational requirements are ascertained.

Relationship table an approach to represent relationships between two database tables when you have many-to-many relationships between database entities.

Remote job entry (RJE) system a computer system such as a bank system that accepts data from local input terminals (such as teller terminals) but which processes this data at remote sites. Similar examples include ATM machines and travel agency systems.

Request for proposal (RFP) report sent to computer vendors in systems design work that outlines the specific requirements of a company's desired system.

Responsibility accounting system an accounting-type reporting structure whereby each subsystem within a company is accountable only for those items over which its employees have control.

Risk assessment component of internal control that considers the risk factor when designing controls for a company.

Risk-based audit approach used by auditors to evaluate a company's internal control procedures.

Routing verification procedures a control for computer network systems that helps to ensure that no transactions or messages of a company are routed to the wrong computer network system address.

Salami technique a computer crime whereby computer programmers steal small amounts of money from many accounts over a period of time.

Schedule feasibility the area of a feasibility evaluation that involves estimating the time frame for a new or revised system to become operational.

Secondary record keys data fields that are typically not unique among records but that can also be used to search records for specific information.

Segment reports reports that are concerned with the reporting of disaggregated information.

Separation of duties activity of an internal control system that focuses on structuring work assignments among employees so that one employee's work activities serve as a check on those work activities of another employee.

Sequence code a sequential set of numbers used to identify, for example, missing customer accounts, employee payroll checks, and customer sales invoices.

Sibling records two adjacent records on the same level in a hierarchical data structure.

Slack time in a systems implementation project, the amount of delay that can occur in implementing each noncritical activity without delaying the entire project.

Software computer programs and operating systems that are loaded into the CPU of a computer and then executed (run). Computer software also includes the instructions, training manuals, and similar non-hardware items.

Source document a manually prepared document that becomes the source of subsequent computer records and processing activities. Examples of source documents include time cards in payroll systems, employee application forms, doctor medical diagnoses, insurance claim forms, and personal bank checks.

Special journals   typically used to record accounting transactions occurring frequently within a company (i.e. credit sales).

Spoofing   masquerading as an authorized Internet user.

Steering committee   committee made up of a company's top management personnel and possibly one or more staff auditors that works with the systems study team throughout all phases of the systems development activities.

Structure chart   graphical documentation that is developed in a hierarchy in which each successive level within the chart provides more detail about the activity above it.

Structured programming   techniques used to develop large computer programs in a hierarchical fashion.

Structured query language (SQL)   a popular data manipulation language for retrieving and manipulating data; auditors can use SQL to retrieve a client's data and display these data in a variety of formats for audit purposes.

Structured, top-down design   a tool for modeling computer processes in systems design work in which the designers begin at the highest level of abstraction and then "drill down" to lower, more detailed levels until the system is completely specified.

Supply chain management (SCM)   applications that enable an ERP system, or an extension of the system, to interface with a company's suppliers and customers.

Surprise audit approach   used by an auditor to examine a company's accounting application programs unexpectedly.

Surprise use approach   an auditor visits a company's computer center unannounced and requests that previously obtained authorized accounting computer programs be used for the required data processing work.

System   an entity consisting of interacting parts or components that attempts to achieve one or more goals.

System development life cycle (SDLC)   involves the following four phases of a systems study: planning the systems study, analyzing current system, designing changes in current system, and implementing the newly-designed system and performing follow-up studies.

System flowchart   graphical documentation that depicts the logical flows of data and processing steps in an AIS.

Systems analysis   phase of a systems study whereby the study team thoroughly familiarizes itself with a company's current operating system by focusing on strengths and weaknesses within this system and eventually making recommendations for further systems study work.

Systems approach   using a broad point of view in performing a systems study.

Systems implementation   the phase of a systems study whereby the recommended changes from the prior analysis, design, and development work are now put into operation.

Systems review   process used by auditors to review a company's system documentation and interview appropriate personnel to ascertain whether the necessary control procedures are in place.

Systems study   a formal investigation of a company's existing information system (also called *systems development work*).

Systems survey   part of systems analysis work in which the study team obtains a more complete understanding of a company's current operational information system and its environment.

SysTrust   an assurance service introduced by the AICPA that evaluates the reliability of information systems with respect to their availability, security, integrity, and maintainability.

Technical feasibility   the area of a feasibility evaluation that analyzes the technical resources required by a particular system.

Test data technique   used by an auditor to test a company's computer programs; the auditor develops a set of transactions that tests, as completely as possible, the range of exception situations that might occur under normal processing conditions.

Third-party billing   used by health care organizations whereby they bill insurance companies or government agencies rather than directly billing their customers for services received.

Trojan horse computer program   a destructive or deceptive computer program hidden inside an accepted program.

Turnaround document   a hard-copy document such as a bank check or confirmation slip that a business creates, sends to a second party for completion or approval, and then receives back for further processing. For convenience, most turnaround documents are computer readable.

Turnkey systems   computer systems acquired from independent vendors that include both software and hardware.

Unit testing   a method for testing computer software whereby the individual programs of a system are each tested as separate components.

Utility programs   computer programs that are typically included with computer operating systems, but which perform specific end-user tasks. Examples include programs that format disks, transfer file data from one medium to another, or test e-mails for viruses.

Validation Rule   a versatile data entry control found in many DMSSs, which provides the user with the ability to create his or her own validation tests.

Valuable-information computer crime   a computer crime that involves illegal access to the valuable information stored in an AIS.

Value-added networks (VANs)   proprietary networks that large IT organizations design and maintain for their customers in order to implement EDI or intranet applications.

Value-added resellers   special type of systems consultants that are licensed to sell particular software programs and provide consulting services to companies.

Vertical markets   markets or industries that are distinct in terms of the services they provide or the goods they produce.

View controls   security feature within a database system that limits each user's access to information on a need-to-know basis.

Virus   a computer program that rogue programmers embed in other programs, e-mails, or computer files, and that (when executed) typically perform such destructive acts as erasing files, disrupting e-mails, or interfering with operating system functions.

Voice recognition system   computer hardware and software that enables a computer to hear and interpret the audio signals of end-user speech. An alternate term is "speech recognition system."

Web browser   a software package (such as Microsoft's Internet Explorer) that enables one to view the graphics files within the World Wide Web of the Internet.

Wide area network (WAN)   computer networks spanning regional, national, or global geographic areas.

Work measurement techniques   used to evaluate the efficiency of employees in jobs that are repetitive in nature; examples of these techniques are *throughput* and *work distribution analysis*.

World Wide Web   the graphics portion of the Internet.

XBRL   a specialized software language for the financial reporting industry.

Index

acceptance testing, 453
Access Certificates for Electronics Services project (ACES), 45
access control lists, 45–46
accounting, separation from other subsystems, 284
accounting control procedures, 255
accounting cycle, 10
  financial, 98–100
accounting information
  collecting, 106–109
  reporting. *See* reports
accounting information systems (AISs), 4–9
  careers in, 17–21
  role in organizations, 6–9
accounting software. *See* integrated accounting software programs; software
accounting transactions, 109
accounts
  charts of, 99–100
  computer, internal control and, 285–286
accuracy of database processing, 209
activity-based costing systems, 12–13, 149
activity listings, 302
addresses, Internet, 31–32
advanced planning and scheduling systems (APS), 174
agents in REA model, 199
aging reports, 114
alphanumeric codes, 101
Amazon.com, 41, 44, 211, 237
American Institute of Certified Public Accountants (AICPA)
  CPA Web Trust of, 376
  internal control defined by, 251–252
  Special Committee on Assurance Services of, 15
  Special Committee on Financial reporting of, 11
  SysTrust of, 376
American University, 178
analysis step in system development life cycle, 391, 396–404
antivirus software, 332
applets, 331
application controls, 282, 294–303
  input, 294–299
  output, 301–303
  processing, 299–301

application interfaces of ERP systems, 176
application service providers (ASPs), 169
approved customer listing reports, 114
artificial transactions in integrated test facilities, 362
assets
  custody of, separation of duties and, 260, 261
  fixed, 139, 140
  physical protection of, 262–265
  retired, report on, 140
Association of Certified Fraud Examiners, 337
assurance in auditing, 15–16
assurance services, 353
attest function, 353
attributes of entities, 203–204
auditing, 14–17, 351–377. *See also* Statements on Auditing Standards (SASs)
  around the computer, 360
  through computers. *See* auditing through the computer
  with computers. *See* auditing with the computer
  electronic spreadsheets and, 370–375
  evaluating effectiveness of controls and, 356–359
  external, 352–354
  information systems, 354–356
  internal, 265–267, 352–354
  third-party assurance and, 375–376
auditing around the computer, 360
auditing modules, building, 370–372
auditing through the computer, 360–367
  continuous, 366–367
  systems software review and, 365–366
  testing computer programs and, 360–363
  validating computer programs and, 363–365
auditing with the computer, 367–370
  automated workpaper software for, 370
  generalized audit software for, 368–370
  general-use software for, 367–368
auditors, information systems, 19–20
audit trails, 10–11
  auditing through the computer and, 360
  internal control and, 258
authentication, 45
authorized distribution lists, 302

authorizing, separation of duties and, 260, 261
automated workpaper software, 370
Automatic Data Processing (ADP), 137

back-end CASE tools, 77–78
back-office functions, 172
backup, 288–290
    for databases, 210
bad debt reports, 114
balanced scorecard approach, 13
bank statements, 147
bar code readers, 295
batch control documents, 300
batch control totals (BCTs), 257, 300
batch processing, backup for, 288–290
Belvedere Co., 170
benchmark tests, 434
best-of-breed (BOB) approach, 176
best practices, 177
beta sites, 455
billable hours, 150–151
bills of lading, 119
biometric identifications, 294
block codes, 102
Bloomberg, 324
Blue Cross and Blue Shield, 450, 463–464
Boise Cascade Office Products (BCOP), 121
boot-sector viruses, 331
Brewers Retail, 428
budgeting, 13–14
business cases, 182
business continuity planning, 291, 357
business entities, 5
business events, 109
    in REA model, 198–199
business intelligence (BI) tools, 174
business processes, 9, 109–121, 133–148
    ERP and, 177–179
    financing, 144–148
    integration of, 177
    production, 140–144
    purchasing, 114–121
    resource management, 134–140
    sales, 109–114
    in vertical markets, 148–154
business process reengineering (BPR), 18, 154–157
    ERP systems and, 177–179
    failures of, reasons for, 155–156
    principles for, 155

business risk, 287, 357
business-to-business (B2B) e-commerce, 41–42

callback procedures, 286
canned software, 433, 452
capital, cost of, 147
capital expenditures, 139
cardinalities, 201–202
careers
    in accounting information systems, 17–21
    in information systems auditing, 355–356
cash
    deposited intact, 265
    disbursement by check, 263–265
    physical protection of, 263
cash budgets, 147
cash receipts forecasts, 114
cash registers, smart, 295
cash requirements forecasts, 119, 121
central databases in ERP systems, 175–176
centralized data processing systems, 306
certificate authority, 48–49
Certified Information Systems Auditors (CISAs), 19–20, 356
Certified Information Technology Professionals (CITPs), 17–18
change logs, 303
change management, 179, 181
Charles Schwab and Co., 341
charts of accounts, 99–100
check-digit control procedures, 298–299
checkpoints, 307
check registers, 119, 136–317
checks, 119, 147
    prenumbered, for cash disbursements, 264
child records, 204
Chiropractors Assistant, 154
Citibank Corporation, 329
Codes of Conduct and Good Practice for Certified Compute Professionals, 340
coding systems, 100–104
    codes for, 102
    design considerations in, 102–104
    purposes of, 101–102
    types of, 100–101
cold sites, 291
collaborative business partnerships, 175
Committee of Sponsoring Organizations (COSO), 251, 252

communication, internal control and, 255
CompanyStore, 179
comparison programs, 363–364
compatibility of systems, 435
compensating controls, 357
compilers, 301
completeness of database processing, 209
compliance testing, 355
computer accounts, internal control and, 285–286
computer-aided software engineering (CASE) tools, 77–78, 428
computer-assisted audit techniques (CAATs), 355, 360
computer-based information systems, 6
computer controls, 281–309
  application. *See* application controls
  for computer network systems, 306–308
  for databases, 303
  general. *See* general controls
  for microcomputers, 304–306
  for risks unique to micro environment, 304
computer crime, 319–337
  defined, 320–322
  examples of, 326–332
  growth of, 325
  identifying criminals and, 334–335
  implementing controls to prevent, 334
  importance of, 325–326
  lack of statistics on, 324–325
  legislation on, 322–324
  protecting against, 332–337
  valuable-information, 327–328
computer facility controls, 291–293
computer files
  access to, 293–294
  data file conversion in system implementation and, 452
  file security controls and, 286–287
Computer Fraud and Abuse Act (CFAA) of 1986, 322
computer hackers, 328–330
computer networks, controls for, 306–308
computer programs. *See* integrated accounting software programs; software
computer records. *See* records
computers
  acceptable use of, 339
  auditing around, 360
  auditing through. *See* auditing through the computer
  auditing with. *See* auditing with the computer
  controls for microcomputers and, 304–306

equipment purchase and installation in system implementation, 451
  protecting computer systems and, 338
  software for. *See* integrated accounting software programs; software
Computer Security Act of 1987, 322
computer viruses, 35, 330–332
concurrency controls, databases and, 209–210
confidential information, protecting, 338–339
consensus-based protocols, 288
consultants
  for ERP implementation, 180
  hiring, 404–405
context data flow diagrams, 68–69
contingency planning, 287, 290–291
continuous and intermittent stimulation (CIS), 367
continuous auditing, 366–367
control. *See* application controls; computer controls; general controls; internal control
control activities, 254
control environment, 253–254, 282
control objectives, information systems auditing and, 359
Control Objectives for Information and Related Technology (COBIT), 252, 359
conversion in system implementation, 454–455
conversion process. *See* production process
corrective controls, 256
cost accounting, 12–13
cost accounting subsystem, 140–142
cost-benefit analysis, 266, 268–270, 434
cost-benefit concept, 268
cost of capital, 147
CPA Vision Project, 20–21
CPA WebTrust, 15, 376
credit memoranda, 113
crime. *See* computer crime
critical path, 456
critical success factors (CSFs), 398
custody of assets, separation of duties and, 260, 261
customer billing statements, 114
customer relationship management (CRM), 113, 174

data, 6
  extracting from databases, 230–235
  scrubbing, 237
  validation of, 228–229
data-access controls, 300–301

data analysis, 403

database administrators, 206

database management systems (DBMSs), 194, 223–225

databases, 193–212, 219–238

    administration of, 206

    backup and security and, 210

    concurrency and, 209–210

    controls for, 303

    database management systems and, 223–225

    data definition languages and, 225–226

    data hierarchy in, 196

    data integrity and, 209

    data validation and, 228–229

    data warehouses, 8, 236–238

    defined, 194–195

    documentation and, 207–208

    enterprise-wide, 237

    extracting data from, 230–235

    importance to AISs, 195–196

    indexing, 234

    linking tables and, 226–228

    multimedia, 235–236

    normalization and, 220–223

    object-oriented, 235–236

    processing accuracy and completeness and, 209

    programming, 234

    REA model for creating. *See* REA model

    record keys for, 197–198

    record structures for, 196–197

    sorting, 234

database schemas, 230

database structure, 204–206, 207

database transactions, 209

data conversion for ERP implementation, 180

data definition languages (DDLs), 225–226

data dictionaries, 207–208

data diddling, 323

data encryption, 47–48, 307

data encryption standard (DES), 47

data file conversion in system implementation, 452

data flow diagrams (DFDs), 67–73

    context, 68–69

    guidelines for drawing, 72–73

    level 0, 71

    level 1, 71

    logical, 70–72

    physical, 69

    symbols used in, 67–7368

data hierarchy, 196

data integrity, 209

data manipulation controls, 301

data marts, 238

data mining, 234–235

data modeling, 198. *See also* REA model

data processing centers

    limiting employee access to, 292

    location of, 292

data redundancy, 221

data risks, 304

data transcription as input control, 295

data validation rules, 372–374

data warehouses, 7, 236–238

Dean Witter and Company, 210

debit memoranda, 113

decision tables, 75–76

decomposing data flow diagrams, 69, 71–72

deduction reports, 137

default value, 229

deletion anomalies, 221–222

demand reports, 426

denial of service attacks, 47, 321

deposit of cash receipts, 265

deposit slips, 147

depreciation registers, 140

design step in system development life cycle, 391

detailed systems design, 425–433

    input design in, 428–429

    output design in, 426, 427

    process design in, 426–428

    prototyping in, 429–432

    systems specifications report and, 432–433

detective controls, 256–258

    interrelationship with preventive controls, 256–258

dialback systems, 334

digital certificates, 48–49

digital signatures, 48–49

digital signature standard (DEE), 48

digital time stamping, 49

Digital Time Stamping Service, 49

direct conversion, 454

direct relationships among entities, 200

disaster recovery plans, 290–291, 332, 357

disaster recovery teams, 290

discrepancy reports, 119

disk mirroring, 288

disk shadowing, 288

distributed data processing (DDP) systems, 306

distribution lists, 302

documentation, 56–82. *See also* reports
    controls for, 80
    for databases, 207–208
    data flow diagrams for. *See* data flow diagrams
      (DFDs)
    decision tables for, 75–76
    end-user computing and, 78–81
    flowcharts for. *See* flowcharts
    importance of, 57–59, 79
    process maps for, 73–74
    software tools for, 77–78
    systems surveys and, 400
document flowcharts, 60–64
    guidelines for drawing, 63–64
domain addresses, 31
Dow Chemical Company, 238
DriveSavers, 305
dual observation as input control, 295
Du Pont Corporation, 78

Eastman Kodak, 462
e-commerce. *See* electronic commerce (EC)
economic espionage, 324
economic events, 109
    in REA model, 198
Eddie Bauer, 234–235
EdgarScan, 36
edit programs, 296–298
edit tests (checks), as input controls, 296–298
electronic commerce (EC), 15, 30, 38–44
    accounting software package Internet connectivity
      and, 167–168
    business-to-business, 41–42
    Electronic Data Interchange and, 42–44
    e-payments and, 40–41
    retail sales and, 39–40
electronic conferencing, 35–36
Electronic Data Interchange (EDI), 42–44
electronic eavesdropping, 307
electronic funds transfer (EFT), 145
Electronic Gathering and Retrieval (EDGAR) database,
    36
electronic mail, 34–35
electronic payments (e-payments), 40–41
electronic procurement, 41
electronic spreadsheet auditing, 370–375
    building auditing modules for, 370–372
    data and formulas and, 372–374
    specialized software for, 375

electronic vaulting, 289
e-mail, 34–35
employee listings, 136
employees
    computer crime committed by, 335
    computer crime prevention and, 333
    informal knowledge of, in internal control, 286
    recognizing symptoms of fraud committed by,
      336–337
    in system implementation, 450–451
    systems surveys and, 400
encryption keys, 47
end-user computing, documentation and, 78–81
enterprise resource planning (ERP) systems, 166, 167,
    170–184
    architecture of, 175–176
    business processes and, 177–179
    configurations of, 175
    extended, 172–175
    functionality of, 170–184171–175
    implementing, 179–181
    risks and benefits of, 181–182
    traditional functions of, 171–172
enterprise-wide databases, 237
enterprise-wide information systems, 8
entities, 5, 199
    attributes of, 203–204
    entity-relationship diagrams and, 202–203
    relationships among, 200–202
entity-relationship (E-R) diagrams, 202–203
Ernst & Young, 376–377
ERP II systems, 172
ethics, 337–341
    meeting ethical challenges and, 339–341
    professional associations and, 337–339
events
    business, 109, 198–199
    economic, 109, 198
e-wallets, 40–41
Excel for graphical documentation, 78
exception reports, 105, 366, 426
expected loss, 269
expenditures, capital and revenue, 139
extended application interfaces (EAI), 176
eXtensible Business Reporting Language (XBRL),
    36–38
eXtensible Markup Language (XML), 37
external audits, 351–354
extranets, 32

Fair Credit Reporting Act of 1970, 322
Fairfax, Virginia, 261
Farmer's Insurance, 73–74
fault-tolerant systems, 288
feasibility evaluation, 418–424
  components of, 418–421
  example of, 421–424
Federal Privacy Act of 1974, 322
feedback mechanisms as input controls, 295
fidelity bond coverage, 260
file security controls, 286–287
final feasibility reports, 424
final systems analysis reports, 403–404
financial accounting, 9–11
financial accounting cycle, 98–100
financial control totals, 301
financial planning models, 147
financial risk, 287
financial statements, 100
financing process, 144–148
  inputs to, 147
  objectives of, 145–147
  outputs of, 147–148
firewalls, 45–46
first normal form (1NF), 221–222
fixed asset change forms, 140
fixed asset management process, 137–139
  inputs to, 139–140
  outputs of, 140
fixed asset registers, 140
fixed asset requests, 139
flexible systems, 460
flowcharts, 59–67
  document, 60–64
  program, 74–75
  system, 64–67
flying-start sites, 291
follow-up and maintenance step in system development
    life cycle, 391, 459–461
  post-implementation review in, 459–460
  system maintenance in, 460–461
follow-up with ERP, 180
Foreign Corrupt Practices Act (FCPA), 250–251
foreign keys, 197, 205
forensic accountants, 337, 353
forms control, 302–303
FoxMeyer Drug Company, 58
fraud auditors, 353
Freedom of Information Act of 1970, 322

front-end CASE tools, 77
front-office functions, 172
functional changes in system implementation, 449–450

Gantt charts, 457–458
general computer control objectives, 283
general controls, 282–294
  of access to computer files, 293–294
  backup, 288–290
  computer facility, 291–293
  contingency planning, 287, 290–291
  fault-tolerant systems, 288
  file security, 286–287
  personnel, 284–286
General Dynamics, 462
General Electric (GE), 32
generalized audit software (GAS), 368–370
general journal, 99
general ledgers, 99
General Motors, 143
general-use software for auditing, 367–368
"going live" with ERP, 180
grandfather-parent-child procedure, 288–290
graphical documentation, software tools for, 77–78
group codes, 102
groupware, 35
Grupo Financiero Bital, 399

hackers, 19, 328–330
hardware risks, 304
Harley-Davidson, 115–116
Hartford Insurance Company, 293, 461
header labels, 307
health care industry, 152–154
Hershey, 181
hierarchical structures, 204
Holiday Inn Corporation, 148
Home Depot, 176
home pages, 34
honesty, professional associations and, 338
hot sites, 291
Hughes Supply, 80–81
human resource management process, 134–137
  inputs to, 134
  outputs of, 136–137
Hydro Agri North America, 392
hyperlinks, 34
hypertext, 234
hypertext markup language (HTML), 33
hypertext transfer protocol (HTTP), 34

ideal control, 269

identification badges for data processing centers, 292

identity fraud, 40

implementation step in system development life cycle, 391, 448–459. *See also* systems implementation

indexing databases, 234

Indian Motorcycle Company, 183

indirect relationships among entities, 200

information, 6. *See also* accounting information; reports
  confidential, protecting, 338–339
  internal control and, 254–255

information age, 5

information overload, 11, 105

information processing subsystem, 6–8
  separation from other subsystems, 284

information systems, 5–6. *See also* accounting information systems (AISs)
  computer-based, 6
  enterprise-wide, 8

Information Systems Audit and Control Association (ISACA), 19

information systems auditing, 354–356
  audit process and, 354–355
  careers in, 355–356
  control objectives and, 359

information systems auditors, 19–20

information systems risk assessment, 356–539

information technology, 4–5

Inglewood, California, 262

input controls, 294–299
  check-digit procedures, 298–299
  edit tests, 296–298
  observation, recording, and transcription of data, 295–296
  unfound-record test, 298

input design, 428–429

input masks, 228–229

input validation routines, 296–298

insertion anomalies, 221

Institute of Internal Auditors, Systems Auditability and Control report of, 358–359

insurance for computer damages, 292–293

integrated accounting software programs, 166–170
  selecting, 167–169
  specialized, 169–170

integrated business processes, 177

integrated test facilities (ITFs), 361–362

integrity of data, 209

interdisciplinary study teams, 395

internal audits, 265–267, 352–354

internal control, 249–271
  audit trail for, 258
  components of, 253–255
  cost-benefit concept for developing controls and, 268–270
  defined, 250–253
  detective controls and, 256–258
  internal audit subsystem and, 265–267
  performance reports for, 267–268
  personnel policies and procedures for, 259–260
  physical protection of assets for, 262–265
  preventive controls and, 255–258
  separation of duties for, 260–262
  in system implementation, 451–452

internal control questionnaires, systems surveys and, 402

International Federation for Information Processing (IFIP), 253

Internet, 5, 31–38. *See also* electronic commerce (EC)
  addresses and software and, 31–32
  connectivity of accounting software packages and, 167–168
  databases and, 195–196
  electronic conferencing and, 35–36
  e-mail and, 34–35
  financial reporting on, 36–38
  groupware and, 35
  intranets and extranets and, 32
  portals and, 176
  privacy on, 44
  security on, 45–50
  web sites for fake companies hosted by Securities and Exchange Commission and, 49–50
  World Wide Web and, 33–34

Internet addresses, 31–32

Internet protocol (IP) addresses, 31–32

Internet service providers (ISPs), 31

interviews, systems surveys and, 402–403

intranets, 32

inventories of microcomputers, 304–305

inventory control, 116, 133

inventory reconciliation reports, 144

inventory status reports, 144

inventory systems
  just-in-time, 142–143
  make-to-stock, 142

invoices, 140

issuance reports, 262

IT auditing. *See* information systems auditing

James River Corporation, 32
job costing, 142
job streams, 67
joint application development (JAD), 400
journals, 99
just-in-time (JIT) inventory system, 142–143

keyboard locks, 305
knowledge sharing, 36
KnowledgeSpace, 36
knowledge workers, 5
KPMG Peat Marwick, 59
Kroger, 113

lean manufacturing, 144, 174
ledgers, 99–100
legal feasibility, 420–421
level 0 data flow diagrams, 71
level 1 data flow diagrams, 71
linking tables, 226–228
lock-box systems, 145
lock-out systems, 334
locks for microcomputers, 305
logical data flow diagrams, 70–72
logic bombs, 321–322
Los Angeles Dodgers, 261
loss, expected, 269
LoveLetter worm, 35

macro program flowcharts, 75
maintainability of systems, 434–435
make-or-buy decisions, 432–433
make-to-order inventory systems, 142–143
make-to-stock inventory systems, 142
management, top
 computer crime prevention and, 333
 systems goals of, 398–399
management information systems (MISs), 8
management reports, 113
managerial accounting, 12–14. *See also* budgeting; cost
 accounting
manufacturing resource planning (MRP II), 144
 ERP systems for, 171
manufacturing status reports, 144
masks for data transcription, 296
material requirements planning (MRP I), 143–144
 ERP systems for, 171
materials price lists, 144
MCI, 393

Mervyn's Department Store, 204
message acknowledgement procedures, 307
microcomputers. *See* computers
Microsoft Excel for graphical documentation, 78
Microsoft Word for graphical documentation, 78
Mitnick, Kevin D., 328–330
mnemonic codes, 102
Mobil Oil Corporation, 74
modular conversion, 454–455
Modulus 11 technique, 299
monitoring, internal control and, 255
Monroe, Ohio Elementary School Parent Teacher
 Organization, 270–271
Morris, Robert Tappan, 330–332
Morton Salt, 208
Motorola Corporation, 293
multimedia databases, 235–236

NDA, 330
Nevada, State of, 421, 449
Newport Beach, California, 261
none-to-many relationships among entities, 201
nonfinancial control totals, 301
nonmonetary items in cost-benefit analysis, 270
nonvoucher systems for cash disbursements, 263
Nordstrom, 174
normalization, 220–223
not-for-profit organizations, 151–152
numeric codes, 101

object-oriented databases (OODBs), 235–236
object-oriented design methods, 428
object-oriented software, 59
observation, systems surveys and, 400
Omega Engineering, 308
one-to-one relationships among entities, 201
online analytical processing (OLAP), 232–233
operating management, systems goals of, 399
operational audits, 265
operational feasibility, 419–420
organizational goals in systems analysis, 397–399
output controls, 301–303
 forms control, 302–303
 validating processing results and, 302
output design, 426, 427
outsourcing, 461–463
 advantages of, 461–462
 disadvantages of, 462–463

Pacific Gas & Electric (PG&E), 435
packing slips, 119, 120
paper shredders, 303
parallel conversion, 454
parallel simulation, 362–363
parent records, 204
Partner Relationship Management (PRM) software, 175
partnerships, collaborative, 175
password codes, 293
passwords, protecting, computer crime prevention and, 333–334
Paypal, 40
payroll deduction authorizations, 134
payroll processing, 134
payroll summaries, 137
Penetration testing, 376
performance measurement, 13
performance reports, 267–268
periodic usage reports, 144
personnel action forms, 134
personnel controls, 284–285
personnel function, 134
personnel policies and procedures, 259–260
petty cash custodians, 265
petty cash funds, 265
physical data flow diagrams, 69
physical protection of assets, 262–263
physical site preparation in system implementation, 449
pilot conversion, 454–455
pivot tables, 233
plan and investigate step in system development life cycle, 391, 393–396
point-of-sale (POS) data, 149
point-of-sale (POS) devices, 295
point-scoring analysis, 436–437
policies and procedures manuals, internal control and, 258
portals, 176
post-implementation review reports, 459–460
Pratt and Whitney, 42–43
preformatted screens for data transcription, 296
preliminary investigation in systems studies, 395–396
prenumbered forms, 302
preprinted recording forms, 296
preventive controls, 255–258
interrelationship with detective controls, 256–258
primary key, 197, 203–204
privacy
of databases, 195
rights of, 339

privacy policies for Internet, 44
process costing center, 142
process design, 426–428
processing controls, 299–301
data-access, 300–301
data manipulation, 301
process maps, 73–74
process testing, 453
production cost reports, 144
production process, 140–144
cost accounting subsystem for, 140–142
inputs to, 143–144
just-in-time inventory systems and, 142–143
objectives of, 144
outputs of, 144
professional associations, ethical issues and, 337–339
professional service organizations, 149–151
program change control, tests of, 363
Program Evaluation and Review Technique (PERT), 455–457
program flowcharts, 74–75
programming databases, 234
project management software, 458–459
project teams for ERP implementation, 180
proof listings, 302
prototyping, 429–432
Provident Central Credit Union, 237–238
proxy servers, 46–47
public key encryption, 48
purchase invoices, 118
purchase orders, 106, 107
purchase requisitions, 118, 119
purchasing process, 114–121
events in, 117
inputs to, 116, 118–119, 120
objectives of, 115–116
outputs of, 119, 121

qualitative items in cost-benefit analysis, 270
queries, 230–231
questionnaires, systems surveys and, 402
Quick Checkout, 40–41

rapid application development (RAD), 78
ratio analyses, 148
real-time processing, backup, 288–289
REA model, 198–206
attributes of entities and, 203–204
business and economic events and, 198–199

REA model *(continued)*
  entities and, 199
  entity-relationship diagrams and, 202–203
  record creation and, 204–205, 207
  relationships among entities and, 200–202
receiving reports, 139, 262
record counts, 301
recording transactions, separation of duties and, 260, 261
record keys, 197–198
records, 196–197
  in hierarchical data structures, 204
  in relational data structures, 204–206
record structures
  in databases, 196–197
  data definition languages to define, 225–226
redundancy in data processing, 288, 290
redundant data checks, 297
reengineering of business processes. *See* business
      process reengineering (BPR)
reference data, 288–290
relational database structure, 204–206
relationship tables, 205–206
reliability, *SysTrust* and, 376
remittance advices, 113, 147
Reno, Nevada, 421
repair and maintenance forms, 140
report distribution, 302
reports, 104–109
  aging, 114
  approved customer listing, 114
  on assets retired, 140
  bad debt, 114
  demand, 426
  design considerations for, 105–106
  exception, 105, 366, 426
  final systems analysis, 403–404
  management, 113
  performance, 267–268
  post-implementation review, 459–460
  sales analysis, 114
  systems specifications, 432–433
  tax, 137
requests for proposal (RFPs), 433–437
resource management process, 134–140
resources in REA model, 199
responsibility accounting systems, 13
responsibility system of computer program development
      and maintenance, 363
retailing. *See also* electronic commerce (EC)
  information technology in, 156–157

retired assets, report on, 140
Reuters Analytics, 324
revenue expenditures, 139
risk
  business, 287, 357
  financial, 287
risk assessment, 254, 269
  information systems, 356–359
risk-based audit approach, 357
rollback processing, 288, 289
routing verification procedures, 307

salami technique, 323
sales analysis reports, 114
sales invoices, 106–107, 108, 113
sales orders, 113
sales process, 109–114
  events in, 110–112
  inputs to, 112–113
  objectives of AIS for, 109–110
  outputs of, 113–114
sandwich rule, 67
Sara Lee, 369–370
SATAN, 325
schedule feasibility, 420
scrubbing data, 237
Sears, Roebuck and Co., 137, 139
secondary record keys, 197
second normal form (2NF), 222–223
secret key cryptography, 48
Securities and Exchange Commission (SEC), fake
      company web sites hosted by, 49–50
security
  for databases, 210
  Internet, 45–50
segment reporting, 11
separation of duties, 260–262
  in IT environment, 284–285
sequence codes, 102
shipping notices, 113, 119
shoulder surfing, 329
sibling records, 204
simulation, parallel, 362–363
slack time, 456
Small Business Computer Security and Education Act of
      1984, 322
smart cash registers, 295
snapshot technique, 367
social engineering, 334, 377
social responsibility, 339

software, 7–8. *See also* integrated accounting software programs
   acquisition of, in system implementation, 452–453
   antivirus, 332
   canned, 433, 452
   ERP. *See* enterprise resource planning (ERP) systems
   for ERP implementation, 180
   for graphical documentation, 77–78
   systems, review of, 365–366
   validating, 363–365
software risks, 304
software testing, 360–363
   in system implementation, 453
Sony Corporation, 437–438
sorting databases, 234
source documents, 98, 106–109
special journals, 99
spoofing, 16
State Farm Life Insurance, 366
Statements on Auditing Standards (SASs)
   No. 55, 251–252, 252
   No. 78, 252
   No. 94, 252
steering committees, 395
structure charts, 426, 428
structured programming, 74
Structured Query Language (SQL), 231–232, 368
structured, top-down design, 426
subschemas, 230
subsidiary ledgers, 99
substantive testing, 354
subsystems, 5–6
supply chain management (SCM), 172–174
supply chains, 42, 115
surprise audit approach, 364–365
surprise use approach, 364–365
system development life cycle (SDLC), 390–392
   stages in, 391–392
system flowcharts, 64–67
   guidelines for drawing, 67
system maintenance, 460–461
systems, defined, 5
systems analysis, 396–404
   data analysis and, 403
   final systems analysis report and, 403–404
   organizational goals and, 397–399
   systems survey and, 399–403
systems approach, 394
Systems Auditability and Control (SAC) report, 358–359

systems consultants, 18–19
systems control audit file review (SCARF), 366
systems development work. *See* systems studies
systems implementation, 391, 448–459
   activities in, 449–455
   Gantt charts and, 457–458
   PERT in, 455–457
   project management software and, 458–459
systems reviews, 357
systems software, review of, 365–366
systems specifications reports, 432–433
systems studies, 14, 389–406, 417–438, 447–464
   accounting and, 392–393
   detailed systems design and. *See* detailed systems design
   feasibility evaluation in, 418–424
   final system selection and, 433–437
   system development life cycle and, 390–392
systems surveys, 399–403
system testing, 391, 453
SysTrust, 16, 376

tables
   databases and, 196
   linking, 226–228
   pivot, 233
tags, XML, 37
taxation, 17
tax reports, 137
technical feasibility, 418–419
test data, 360–361
testing software, 360–363
   in system implementation, 453
tests of controls, 357
third normal forms (3NF), 223
third-party assurance services, 375–376
third-party billing, 153–154
Thomas Brother Maps, Inc., 458–459
three-way matches, 118
throughput, 403
Timberjack, 174
time and billing AISs, 149
time sheets, 134
time stamping, digital, 49
top management
   computer crime prevention and, 333
   systems goals of, 398–399
trading communities, 177
trailer labels, 307

training
for ERP implementation, 181
in system implementation, 451
transaction listings, 300
transaction logs, 289
transactions
accounting, 109
artificial, in integrated test facilities, 362
database, 209
recording, separation of duties and, 260, 261
transaction tagging, 366–367
Treadway Commission, 251
tree structures, 204
trial balances, 100
Trojan horse computer programs, 331, 363–364
TRW Credit Data case, 327–328
tuples, 196–197
turnkey systems, 433, 452

unfound-record tests, 298
uninterruptible power systems (UPSs), 290
unit testing, 453
universal resource locators (URLs), 31
University of Northern Colorado, 339
UNUM Life Insurance, 430

Vail Reports, 178
validation of data, 228–229
Validation Rules, 229

valuable-information computer crime, 327–328
value-added networks (VANs), 43–44
value-added resellers (VARs), 18–19, 169
vendor support, 435
vertical markets, 148–154
examples of industries in, 149–154
specialized accounting information needs in, 148–149
view controls, 210
viruses, 35, 330–332
Visa, 210
voucher systems for cash disbursements, 263–264
vulnerability in computer systems, 308

Walgreen's, 195
Wal-Mart Stores, Inc., 39
watchdog processors, 288
waterfall model, 390
web browsers, 33
web sites for fake companies hosted by Securities and
Exchange Commission, 49–50
what-if analysis, 458–459
Woerner Turf, 108
Word for graphical documentation, 78
work distribution analysis, 403
work measurement techniques, 403
work orders, 140
World Wide Web, 33–34
worm programs, 331